City Politics

City Politics has received praise for the clarity of its writing, careful research, and distinctive theme—that urban politics in the United States has evolved as a dynamic interaction between governmental power, private actors, and a politics of identity.

The book's enduring appeal lies in its persuasive explanation, careful attention to historical detail, and accessible and elegant way of teaching the complexity and breadth of urban and regional politics which unfold at the intersection of spatial, cultural, economic, and policy dynamics. This 11th edition has been thoroughly updated while retaining the popular structure of past editions.

Key updates include:

- Individual chapters introducing students to pressing urban issues such as race and racism, gentrification, sustainability and the environment, urban crises, shrinking cities, immigration, and suburbanization, political polarization, and the COVID-19 pandemic's impact on cities
- The most recent census data integrated throughout to provide current figures for analysis, discussion, and a more nuanced understanding of current trends
- The effects of the events of 2020 on cities—namely the Coronavirus pandemic; the murder of George Floyd and its aftermath, the growth of the Black Lives Matter Movement; and the U.S. presidential election in November
- The new and present challenges of the climate crisis and its growing significance for cities.

Taught on its own, or supplemented with the optional reader *American Urban Politics in a Global Age* for more advanced readers, *City Politics* remains the definitive text on urban politics—and how they have evolved in the United States over time. This is a comprehensive resource for a new generation of undergraduate and graduate students, as well as established researchers in the discipline.

This book is accompanied by Support Material online: www.routledge.com/9781032006352

Annika Marlen Hinze is an Associate Professor of Political Science and the Director of Urban Studies at Fordham University, New York City, USA. Her research and teaching focus on urban politics, identity politics, the politics of immigration, qualitative methods, urban economic development, poverty, and minority politics in the United States, Canada, Germany, and Turkey.

Dennis R. Judd is Professor Emeritus of the Department of Political Science in the College of Liberal Arts and Sciences at the University of Illinois, Chicago, USA. For many years he has been a leading contributor to the literature on urban political economy, urban economic development, national urban policy, and urban revitalization. Over the last four decades, he has brought his urban politics research together in his pioneering textbook, *City Politics*, and he has published pioneering research on urban tourism.

Eleventh Edition

City Politics

Cities and Suburbs in 21st Century America

Annika Marlen Hinze and
Dennis R. Judd

Routledge
Taylor & Francis Group

LONDON AND NEW YORK

Cover image: © Getty Images

Eleventh edition published 2023
by Routledge
4 Park Square, Milton Park, Abingdon, Oxon OX14 4RN

and by Routledge
605 Third Avenue, New York, NY 10158

Routledge is an imprint of the Taylor & Francis Group, an informa business

First edition published by Pearson Education, Inc. 2015, 2012, 2010

Tenth edition published by Routledge 2019

British Library Cataloguing-in-Publication Data
A catalogue record for this book is available from the British Library

Library of Congress Cataloging-in-Publication Data
Names: Hinze, Annika Marlen, author. | Judd, Dennis R., author.
Title: City politics : cities and suburbs in 21st century America / Annika M. Hinze
    and Dennis R. Judd.
Description: Eleventh edition. | Abingdon, Oxon ; New York, NY : Routledge,
    2023. | Includes bibliographical references and index.
Identifiers: LCCN 2021061010 (print) | LCCN 2021061011 (ebook) | ISBN
    9781032006413 (hardback) | ISBN 9781032006352 (paperback) | ISBN
    9781003175315 (ebook)
Subjects: LCSH: Municipal government–United States. | Urban policy–United
    States. | United States–Economic policy. | Sociology, Urban–United States.
Classification: LCC JS331 .J78 2023 (print) | LCC JS331 (ebook) | DDC
    320.8/50973–dc23
LC record available at https://lccn.loc.gov/2021061010
LC ebook record available at https://lccn.loc.gov/2021061011

ISBN: 978-1-032-00641-3 (hbk)
ISBN: 978-1-032-00635-2 (pbk)
ISBN: 978-1-003-17531-5 (ebk)

DOI: 10.4324/9781003175315

Typeset in Sabon
by KnowledgeWorks Global Ltd.

Access the Support Material: www.routledge.com/9781032006352

To my Mama, Sabine Meinhardt-Hinze (1946–2021), an admirer of books, expert of prose, art, history, and tree and bush fauna, and source of the most contagious laughter, who loved Central Park during every season. I miss her every day.

BRIEF CONTENTS

PART III   THE FRACTURED METROPOLIS

CONTENTS

PART II   THE URBAN CRISIS OF THE TWENTIETH CENTURY

PART III   THE FRACTURED METROPOLIS

PREFACE

The first edition of *City Politics* was published in 1979, and since that time, the book has undergone changes as profound as the subject matter with which it deals. To keep it current and relevant, we have always taken care to describe the significant new developments both in the "real world" and in the literature of the field; in this eleventh edition, for example, we include material on the recent debates over race and immigration policy, voting rights, the continued fiscal problems that cities face, and the urban impacts of inequality. In making these changes, we have included enough citations so that students will be able to conduct further research of their own.

Over the years, *City Politics* has been used in college courses at all levels, from community colleges to graduate courses in research universities. *City Politics* has reached across disciplines, too; it has found its way into courses in urban politics, urban sociology, urban planning, urban geography, and urban history. We have relied upon three elements to make it relevant to such a broad audience: A strong and original thematic structure with a blending of the vast secondary literature with primary sources and recent scholarly materials, new data, and our own original research. To make the complex scholarship of the field as accessible and interesting as possible, we build the book around an admittedly sweeping narrative. As far as possible, each chapter picks the story up where the previous one left off so that the reader can come to appreciate that urban politics in America is constantly evolving; in a sense, past and present are always intermingled.

Three threads compose the narrative structure of the book. From the nation's founding, a devotion to the present, the private marketplace, and a tradition of democratic governance (albeit imperfect and often contested) have acted as the twin pillars of American culture. All through the nation's history, cities have been forced to strike a balance between the goal of achieving local economic prosperity and the task of negotiating among the many contending groups making up the local polity. An enduring tension between these two goals is the mainspring that drives urban politics in America, and it is also at the center of the narrative that ties the chapters of this book together.

The governmental fragmentation of urban regions provides a third dynamic element that has been evolving for more than a century. A complete account of

American urban politics must focus upon the internal dynamics of individual cities *and* also upon the relationships among the governmental units making up urban regions. The suburbs are an essential part of that story. Today, America's urban regions are fragmented into a patchwork of separate municipalities and other governmental units. With the rise of the suburbs in the first half of the twentieth century and of privatized gated communities in recent decades, this fragmentation has become even more complicated. In several chapters of this edition of *City Politics*, we trace the many consequences that flow from this way of organizing political authority in the modern metropolis.

We divide the book into three parts. Part I is composed of four chapters that trace the history of urban America in the first long century from the nation's founding in 1789 through the Great Depression of the 1930s. This "long century" spans a period of time in which the cities of the expanding nation competed fiercely for a place in the nation's rapidly evolving economic system. At the same time, cities were constantly trying to cope with the social tensions and disruptions caused by wave after wave of immigration and a constant movement from farm to city. These tensions played out in a struggle between an upper- and middle-class electorate and working-class newcomers. They have also always been characterized by racial struggles, as African Americans and people of color have pushed back against the ethnic and racial democracy forced upon them by the white founders. The New Deal of the 1930s brought the immigrants and the cities they lived within into the orbit of national politics for the first time in the nation's history, with consequences that reverberated for decades.

In Part II, we trace the arc of twentieth-century urban politics. Over a period of only a few decades, the old industrial cities went into a steep decline, the suburbs prospered, and a regional shift redistributed population away from the industrial belt to other parts of the country. For a long time, urbanization had been driven by the development of an industrial economy centered in a few great cities. But the decline of industrial jobs and the rise of a service economy profoundly restructured the nation's politics and settlement patterns; as a result, by the mid-twentieth century, the older central cities were plunged into a social and economic crisis of unprecedented proportions. In the years after World War II, millions of southern Blacks poured into northern cities, a process that ushered in a protracted period of open and institutionally backed race-based violence against Black Americans in the Northern industrial cities. This period of social unrest and racial animosity fundamentally reshaped the politics of the nation and of its urban regions. Affluent whites fled the cities, carving out suburban enclaves in an attempt to escape the problems of the metropolis, while federal, state (and often local) institutions of government, along with the private sector, deliberately excluded Black Americans from this avenue to social upward mobility. The imperative of governance—the need to find ways of brokering among the contending racial, ethnic, and other interests making up the urban polity—became crucially important, but this book also illustrates its many failures—as well as the consequences.

Part III of the book focuses on the urban politics produced by the deindustrialization and globalization processes of the 1980s and beyond. The emergence of a globalized economy is one of its defining features. Older central cities and entire urban regions that had slipped into decline began to reverse their fortunes by becoming major players in the post-industrial economy. At the same time, the fragmentation within metropolitan regions has taken on a new dimension because cities fiercely compete for a share of metropolitan economic growth. Today, central cities and their urban regions are more prosperous, but at the same time, more fragmented than ever, and one consequence is that social and economic inequalities are being reproduced on the urban landscape in a patchwork pattern that separates urban residents.

These developments can best be appreciated by putting them into historical context. As in the past, urban politics continues to revolve around the two imperatives of economic growth and the task of governance. As in the nation's first century, cities are engaged in a fierce competition for new investment. The great tide of immigration that took off in the nineteenth century shaped the politics of cities for well more than a century. The intense period of immigration that began in the 1970s has yet to run its course, and it, too, will reverberate through all levels of the American political system for a long time to come. Any account of urban politics in the present era will be greatly enriched if we recognize that we are a nation of immigrants and always have been. The several new features incorporated into this eleventh edition include:

- A more systematic discussion of institutionalized racism and its legacy in so many realms of urban (and suburban) life
- A comprehensive discussion of the bitter debates over immigration policy
- An expanded discussion of the controversies over voting rights
- A new chapter on the challenges of climate change
- An in-depth look at the impact of the COVID-19 pandemic on cities and governance
- A comprehensive discussion of the impact of political polarization and a resulting inconsistency in federal policy on cities
- Incorporation throughout the text of recent data from the U.S. Census Bureau

Attentive readers may also notice that Black (in reference to African Americans and people of African origin) is now capitalized throughout the book, whereas white is not. In the United States, this has been a growing movement. We chose to capitalize Black because it refers to a collective identity of a people intentionally robbed of any ties to their countries of ancestry. In that sense, the term refers to a common history, struggle, and strength of Black people in the Americas, and its usage is more akin to other capitalized references to ethnicity and/or origin, such as African American, Asian, Hispanic, and Native American. Capitalizing white, on the other hand, carries references to white supremacy. In addition, white Americans do not share a history of struggle and discrimination or cultural commonalities. In capitalizing Black, we follow the lead of many prominent news and academic organizations across the United States, such as the Associated Press, *The New York Times*, *The Washington Post*, and the APSA style manual.

Annika Marlen Hinze would like to thank Gregory Holyk, Andrew Becker, and Sarah Lockhart for their intellectual input and companionship while working on this book. There is nothing better than running one's thoughts by the brilliant minds of smart confidantes, who will push back, question, and critique.

Dennis R. Judd would like to thank Sam Bassett and Anahit Tadevosyan for their valuable research assistance and intellectual companionship.

We also wish to thank Emily Ross, our editor at Routledge, for helping to keep the book on track.

Annika Marlen Hinze
Dennis R. Judd

CHAPTER 1

City Politics in America: An Introduction

Three Themes

The political dynamics of America's cities and urban regions have remained remarkably similar over time. From the nation's founding to the present, a devotion to the private marketplace and a tradition of latent democratic governance (doubtlessly an imperfect one) have been the pivotal values defining American culture. Finding a balance between these two imperatives has never been easy; indeed, the tension between the two is the mainspring that energizes nearly all important political struggles that occur at the local level. The *politics of growth* becomes obvious when conflicts break out over public expenditures for such things as airport construction, convention centers, and sports stadiums. Projects like these are invariably promoted with the claim that they will bring prosperity to everyone in the urban community, but such representations do not lay to rest important concerns about whether these are the best or the most effective uses of public resources. The fact that there is conflict at all lays bare a second imperative: the *politics of governance*. Public officials and policymakers must find ways to arbitrate among the many contending groups and interests that demand a voice in local government. The complex social, ethnic, and racial divisions that exist within America's cities have always made governance a difficult challenge. A third dynamic has evolved in step with the rise of the modern metropolis over the past century: the *politics of metropolitan fragmentation*. During that period, America's urban regions have become increasingly fragmented into a patchwork of separate urban and suburban municipalities. One of the consequences of the extreme fragmentation of political authority within metropolitan regions is that it helps perpetuate residential segregation and makes it nearly impossible to devise regional solutions to important policy issues such as urban sprawl.

The growth imperative is so deeply embedded in the politics of American cities that, at times, it seems to overwhelm all other issues. Urban residents have a huge stake in the continued vitality of the place where they live; it is where

DOI: 10.4324/9781003175315-1

they have invested their energies and capital; it is the source of their incomes, jobs, and their sense of personal identity and community. Because of the deep attachments that many people form for their local community, its continued vitality is always a high priority. Throughout American history, "place loyalty" has driven civic leaders to devote substantial public authority and resources to the goal of promoting local economic growth and prosperity. In the nineteenth century, for instance, cities fought hard to secure connections to the emerging national railroad system by providing huge subsidies to railroad corporations. Today, the details are different but the logic is the same: Since the 1970s, cities have competed fiercely for a share of the growing market in tourism and entertainment, the "industry without a smokestack." In 2017, American cities were trying to outbid one another for Amazon's second headquarters (the first ones are located in Seattle). The [out]bidding process demonstrates the absurd lengths cities are willing to go to attract international corporations: Famously, the city of Tucson attempted to gift Amazon a 21-foot saguaro cactus along with its bid. Amazon refused to accept the gift and donated it to the Arizona-Sonora Desert Museum instead. To attract private industry, cities have spent huge amounts of public money for such things as convention centers, sports stadiums, cultural institutions, and entertainment districts. They also tend to offer huge tax breaks and favorable transit connections to corporations to sweeten the deal. These kinds of activities, all devoted to the goal of promoting local economic growth, are so central to what cities do that it would be impossible to understand urban politics without taking them into account.

One factor in the inter-urban competition for growth and investment that has definitely changed today is the detachment of business leaders from the local environment through the forces of globalization. While throughout the first half of the twentieth century, businesses were firmly rooted in the local context, and business leaders saw the health of the downtown business district as a vital factor in their economic success, corporations in a global world no longer have these local attachments. The borderless flows of capital, goods, and services (though not of people) have made it easy for transnational corporations to uproot themselves and choose the most fiscally and economically convenient location for their business headquarters. This means that inter-urban competition has not only grown much fiercer but it has also moved from a national to a global scale. This development has led local leaders and policymakers to more actively bargain for business investment, not only by creating greater incentives for businesses (by offering tax breaks or clearing favorable parcels of land through the use of eminent domain) but also by actively inviting private actors to partake in the urban development process, introducing more "public-private partnerships" as ways to implement major projects. Of course, private actors will not invest in development projects out of the goodness of their hearts. Instead, they look out for profits to be made, and they may decide to abandon projects that do not meet their expectations. Some scholars have also complained that the focus of state and local governments on attracting private actors and aestheticizing the urban environment takes away attention from the needs of poorer segments of the urban population.[1]

The imperative of governance arises from the social, racial, and ethnic differences that have always characterized American society. America is a nation of immigrants, and for most of the nation's history, anxiety about the newcomers has been a mainstay of local and, for that matter, national politics. Attempts to curb immigration can be traced back to the 1830s when the Irish began coming to American shores in large numbers. Episodes of anti-immigrant reaction have flared up from time to time ever since, especially during times of economic stress. The United States has a long history of being an ethnic and racial democracy, where people of color were not only disenfranchised but enslaved to build the colonial economy. Serious steps toward a more inclusive democracy have been implemented practically only throughout the past century—often including fallbacks and stagnation. It is embarrassing that even today, historically disadvantaged groups do not enjoy the same privileges as white people, from wealth accumulation to personal safety. Therefore, ethnic and racial conflicts have been such a constant feature of American politics that they have long shaped national electoral and partisan alignments. At the metropolitan level, bitter divisions have often pitted central cities against suburbs and one suburb against the next.

The extreme fragmentation of America's metropolitan areas has its origins in the process of suburbanization that began unfolding in the late nineteenth century. For a long time, the term "urban" referred to the great cities of the industrial era, their diverse mix of ethnic groups and social classes, and their commanding national presence as centers of technology and economic production. The second "urban" century was very different. Increasingly, the cities of the industrial era became surrounded by rings of independent political jurisdictions—what came to be called suburbs. Beginning as early as the 1920s, the great industrial cities went into a long slide even while the suburbs around them prospered. Much of this can be traced back to systemic racism, where state institutions closed the doors to social upward mobility (in terms of jobs, homeownership, and equity) to people of color. Ultimately, an urban geography emerged that was composed of a multitude of separate jurisdictions ranging from white, segregated suburbs to hypersegregated cities inhabited mostly by people of color. Recently, the central cities have begun to attract affluent (and especially younger) residents, and the suburbs have become more representative of American society as a whole. Even so, a complicated mosaic of governments and even privatized gated communities continue to be important features in the daily life of urban residents: Where people live greatly influences with whom they come into contact with, their tax burdens and level of municipal services, and even their political outlook. Within metropolitan areas, there is not one urban community but many.

The three strands that compose city politics in America—the imperative of economic growth, the challenge of governance, and the rise of the fragmented metropolis—can be woven into a narrative that allows us to understand the forces that have shaped American urban politics, both in the past and in our own time. Reading a letter to the editor of the local newspaper protesting a city's tax subsidy for a new stadium (a clash of values typical of the politics of growth); walking down a busy city street among people of every color and national background (which serves as a reminder of the diversity of interests and needs governance must address); entering a suburban gated community (and thus falling under the purview of a privatized governing association, still another of the many governing units that make up the metropolis): All of these experiences remind us that there are consistent patterns and recurring issues that shape the political dynamics of urban politics in America.

The Politics of Growth

Local communities cannot be preserved without a measure of economic vitality, and this is why growth and prosperity have always been among the most important priorities for urban residents and their civic leaders. Founded originally as centers of trade and commerce, the nation's cities and towns came into being as places where people could make money and find personal opportunities. From the very beginning, European settlement in North America involved schemes of town promotion. The first colony, Jamestown, founded in 1607, was the risky venture of a group of English entrepreneurs who organized themselves into a joint-stock company. Shares sold in London for about $62 in gold. If the colony was successful, investors hoped to make a profit, and of course, the colonists themselves had gambled their very lives on the success of the experiment. Likewise, three centuries later, when a flood of people began spilling beyond the eastern seaboard into the frontier of the new nation, they founded towns and cities as a way of making a personal bet on the future prospects of a particular place. The communities that grew up prospered if they succeeded in becoming the trading hub for a region and an export platform for agricultural and finished goods moving into the national economic system. For this reason, the nineteenth-century movement across the continent placed towns at the leading edge of territorial expansion:

> America was settled as a long, thin line of urban places, scattering outward and westward from the Atlantic seaboard. The popular imagination has it that farmers came first and villages later. The historian's truth is that villages and towns came first, pulling farmers along to settle the land around and between urban settlements.[2]

Each town was its own capitalist system in miniature, held together by the activities of entrepreneurs in search of profit and personal advancement. The restless pursuit of new opportunities encouraged the formation of what urban historian Sam Bass Warner has called a national "culture of privatism," which stressed individual efforts and aspirations over collective or public purposes: "[The] local politics of American cities have depended for their actors, and for a good deal of their subject matter, on the changing focus of men's private economic activities."[3] The leading philosophy of the day promoted the idea that by pursuing their own individual interests, people were also contributing to the welfare of the community.

On the frontier, the founders of cities and the entrepreneurs who made their money in them recognized that in order to ensure their mutual success, they would have to take steps to promote their city and region. Local boosters promoted their city's real or imagined advantages—a harbor or strategic location on a river, for example, or proximity to rich farming and mining areas. They also boasted about the local culture: music societies, libraries, and universities. And they went further than boasting; they used the powers of city government to promote local growth. Municipalities were corporations that could be used to help finance a variety of local undertakings, from subscriptions in railroad stock to improvements in harbors and docks. There was broad support for such undertakings because citizens shared the perception that local economic vitality was absolutely necessary to advance the well-being of the urban community and everyone in it.

Today, support for measures to promote the local economy continues to be bound up with people's attachments to place and community. Without jobs and incomes, people simply cannot stay in the place that gives life to family, neighborhood, and local identity. The environmental and social effects of the oil spill in the Gulf of Mexico in the spring and summer of 2010 illustrate this point. As the disaster unfolded, it seemed certain that thousands of jobs would be lost in a long arc stretching from southern Louisiana to the Florida coast. At the time, tourism was expected to drop by half on Florida's Gulf Coast, costing the state at least 200,000 jobs.[4] In Louisiana, fishing, shellfish, and other industries seemed to be on the verge of being wiped out. When people talked about the disaster to news reporters, they spoke not only of the loss of livelihood but also, with great emotion, about its effect on family values and community traditions—about the loss of a "way of life."

No matter how calamitous, the oil spill was not likely to make coastal communities disappear overnight, no matter how hard it may have been to recover (fortunately, the long-term consequences of the spill were not as severe as many feared). People identify with the community within which they live, and they are often reluctant to move even in the face of genuine hardship. The resilience of community was illustrated in the 1970s and 1980s when massive losses of businesses and jobs hit the industrial heartland of the Midwest and Northeast. The rapid deindustrialization of a vast region threatened the existence of entire communities. The Pittsburgh, Pennsylvania, region experienced a 44 percent loss in manufacturing jobs from 1979 to 1988, three-quarters of them related to steel. Unemployment levels reached as high as 20 percent, not only in Pittsburgh but also in Detroit and several other cities of the industrial belt.[5] Some people fled for more prosperous areas of the Sunbelt, but a great many of them elected to stay. Rather than giving up, in city after city public leaders took measures to rebuild their economies; indeed, in most places, the cause of local renewal took on the character of a permanent crusade. After the 2008 economic crisis, Detroit was essentially declared dead. In 2013, Detroit declared bankruptcy, becoming the largest American city to take this step.[6] Public buses drastically cut down service to only serve the most essential routes; trash collections were skipped, and the grid of streetlights was cut to only about 60% of its capacity.[7] There was even talk of consolidating the city, condensing its neighborhoods into a smaller grid, in order to cut down costs. By 2017, it looked like the city was starting to bounce back from the brink of death. In 2010, the mortgage lending company Quicken Loans moved its offices to downtown Detroit, where real estate was cheaper than ever before.[8] Artists have transformed abandoned buildings, young Millennials are flooding some of the city's downtown neighborhoods. It is clear, however, that the Creative Class alone won't save Detroit. It is also the resilience of those residents of Detroit, who stayed behind when others left, through disinvestment and bankruptcy, that staved off the end of the city.

Communities of the storm- and flood-stricken Gulf Coast reacted in a similar way. People resisted leaving; instead, they put their efforts into regenerating their local economies and strengthening their communities because they were not willing to abandon the traditions and cultures that brought meaning to their lives.

It might seem that the intimate connection between material well-being and community identity would leave little room for disagreement over the premise that cities must do everything they can do all the time to promote local prosperity. But this commitment does not always translate into support for every politician and developer's bright idea or ambitious proposal. Disputes break out because policies to promote growth cannot benefit everyone equally; they are not always sensible or plausible; and there are always winners and losers. For renters and low-income residents, the gentrification of their neighborhood may bring higher rents and home values that ultimately force them to move. Growth in the downtown corporate and financial sectors may create some high-paying jobs for educated professionals but exclude many other city residents with low-paying jobs or on the unemployment rolls. A downtown that encroaches on nearby neighborhoods may benefit the businesses located in the new office towers but may also compromise the quality of life for nearby residents. People who do not care about sports may resent helping to pay for a new football stadium. Different perspectives such as these explain why there is frequent disagreement about how to promote growth, even though everyone believes that local prosperity is a good thing.

The use of eminent domain by local governments illustrates the kinds of disputes that can divide communities. All across the nation, cities have aggressively used their power to take private property for "higher uses" to make way for big-box stores, malls, condominium projects, sports stadiums, and a great many other initiatives. For most of the nation's history, local governments have possessed the authority to take property without the owners' consent if it serves a legitimate public purpose.[9] Public officials have liberally interpreted this power as a useful tool for economic development, but homeowners and small businesses who find their property condemned so that it can be sold to a big developer look at it with a skeptical eye. On December 20, 2000, a group of homeowners led by Susette Kelo filed a suit challenging a decision by the city of New London, Connecticut, to cede its eminent domain authority to a private corporation that wanted to raze their homes. The Pfizer Corporation had expressed interest in expanding its office campus into a waterfront footprint in New London, which was largely occupied by single family homes. Things came to a head on June 23, 2005, when the U.S. Supreme Court upheld lower court rulings in favor of the development corporation, arguing that private development was in the "public interest," as it could serve as a way to attract revenue and economic development. The Court's decision ignited a firestorm of protest that swept the nation. In response to the public furor, by the fall of 2006, state legislatures in 30 states had enacted legislation to restrict the use of the eminent domain, and hundreds of towns and cities had done likewise. In the fall elections of 2006, voters in 12 states passed referendums prohibiting the taking of property for private development if it did not serve a clear public purpose.[10] In a twist of irony, after the City of New London had bought up all private properties and cleared the footprint, the Pfizer Corporation lost interest in the development and moved out of its adjacent office complex to nearby Groton, CT, taking 1,400 jobs with it.[11]

The lesson from the *Kelo v. New London* case is that despite the fact that almost everyone embraces the goal of local economic growth, sometimes the policies to promote it clash with other values, such as individual property rights, the health of a neighborhood, or a preference for less governmental intrusion. Everyone may seem to share the same interest in promoting the well-being of the urban community but they frequently disagree over how to make that happen.

The Politics of Governance

International migration is transforming societies around the globe, and the United States is no exception. More immigrants came to the United States in the 1990s than in any previous decade in the nation's history, and the flow has continued into the twenty-first century. The social and political effects of large-scale population movements are often on display in big global cities such as Miami, New York, Chicago, and San Francisco, and in many smaller places as well. For this reason, in the global era, as in the past, city politics often pivots around issues of racial and ethnic identity and feelings of community solidarity, at least as much as around issues of economic development.

Until the mid-nineteenth century, when colonial-era values still prevailed, men of wealth and high social standing made most of the decisions for the urban community. In the cities, "leadership fell to those who exercised economic leadership. All leadership, political, social, economic, tended to collect in the same set of hands."[12] Business owners, professionals, and aristocrats ran municipal affairs without challenge. The members of this social and political elite shared a mistrust of what Thomas Jefferson called "mobocracy," a word he used to signify his opposition to rule by popular majority. Governance was remarkably informal. Local notables served on committees formed to build public wharves, organize town watches, and build and maintain public streets, and even the most essential services, such as crime control and fire prevention, generally relied on the voluntary efforts of citizens. Such a casual governmental structure fit the pace of life and the social intimacy of small communities.

By the industrial era of the 1850s, cities were growing at breakneck speed, and they were also becoming socially stratified and ethnically complex. Waves of immigrants were crowding into densely packed neighborhoods. They came from an astonishing variety of national cultures, from England, Ireland, Germany, the Scandinavian countries, and later from Italy and a broad swath of eastern European countries. From time to time, ethnic tensions rose to a fever pitch and tipped over into violence time and again. In the industrial cities, the colonial-era style of politics could not survive the change, and in time, a new generation of urban leaders came onto the scene. They came from the immigrant precincts and entered politics by mobilizing the vote of the urban electorate. Their rise to power set off decades of conflict between wealthy and middle-class elites and the immigrants and their leaders, a story we tell in Chapters 3 and 4.

In the twentieth century, large movements of people continued to flood into the cities, but the ethnic and racial composition of these urban migrations changed dramatically. The immigrant flood tide ended in the early 1920s, when Congress, during a wave of anti-immigrant xenophobia, enacted legislation that nearly brought foreign immigration to a halt. By then, however, a massive internal population movement was already picking up speed. In the first three decades of the twentieth century and again in the years following World War II, millions of African Americans left the South for jobs and opportunities in the industrial cities. They were joined by successive waves of destitute whites fleeing the unemployment and poverty of Appalachia and other depressed areas and by Mexicans crossing the border to escape violence and poverty in their own country. These streams of migration were, of course, met with racist and xenophobic reactions in northern cities, leading to political and social tensions. One consequence of the increasing diversity of the cities, along with the 1954 Supreme Court decisions to desegregate public schools in *Brown v. Board of Education of Topeka, Kansas*, was that millions of white families left their inner-city neighborhoods and fled to the suburbs. The federal policy initially helped close off the suburbs to people of color until the civil rights legislation of the 1960s slowly paved the way for the suburbs to diversify. But the damage was already done: A social and racial chasm had started to separate cities from suburbs, and echoes of that period continue to reverberate to this day.

A vivid example of the continuing racial divide was on display in New Orleans in the late summer of 2005. When the storm surge from Hurricane Katrina breached the dikes surrounding New Orleans on August 29, 2005, 80 percent of the city was flooded and nearly 100,000 people were left to deal with the consequences. Wrenching images of human suffering filled television news programs: 25,000 people trying to live under impossible conditions in the Superdome, 20,000 more in the Convention Center, residents fleeing across bridges and overpasses and desperately waving from rooftops. More than 1.5 million people were displaced, 60,000 homes were destroyed, and 1,300 people died.[13] African American neighborhoods located in the lowest and least desirable parts of the city bore the brunt of the destruction. The racial segregation that made this possible is a legacy of New Orleans' past, and despite the civil rights advances that protect the rights of minorities to live where they choose to, it is a pattern that has not disappeared—in New Orleans or anywhere else.

In the meantime, bitter conflicts have, once again, broken out over immigration. The massive flows of immigrants in recent decades have made cities culturally and socially dynamic places, but they have also meant that ethnic identity has continued to fuel conflict in national and city politics. During the 2016 and the 2020 presidential election campaigns, immigration was a major topic. After former President Trump was inaugurated in 2017, he made anti-immigration policy a key cornerstone of his political agenda. The new president quickly passed two executive orders and one proclamation banning citizens of certain, mostly Muslim-majority countries from entering the United States, spent a massive amount of federal emergency funds to build a wall on the U.S.-Mexico border, and realized his threat to crackdown on undocumented immigrants with raids conducted by Immigration and Customs Enforcement (ICE) in the nation's major cities. In reaction, many states and municipalities attempted to take on a protective position regarding immigrants. The sanctuary city movement, which existed long before the Trump administration entered office, has resulted in major tensions between the Trump administration and urban governments, as laid out in later chapters. The Biden administration, which was inaugurated in January 2021, has attempted to reverse much of Trump's anti-immigrant agenda but immigration remains a contentious subject throughout the country.

The racial and ethnic complexity of metropolitan areas guarantees that the art of arbitrating among the contending groups making up the local political system will be hard to master. In the multiethnic metropolis of the global era, effective governance takes on real urgency. Governmental authority springs from the obligation of public institutions to make decisions that are binding upon all members of society. To retain the legitimacy to govern in a democratic system, the government must seem sufficiently responsive to a large enough proportion of the electorate, and at the same time, there must be opportunities for the politically disempowered to seek redress. The ethnic and racial complexity of cities makes this a daunting challenge.

The Fragmented Metropolis

Any account of city politics over the twentieth century must be located, in some part, within an often-rehearsed narrative that traces the decline of the central cities and rise of the suburbs, a period brought to a halt only recently by the unexpected revival of core cities. The process of suburbanization created the modern American metropolis, which is made up of a multitude of political jurisdictions, large and small, wealthy, middle class, and poor. For decades, the basic urban pattern involved an extreme racial segregation. More recently, the geography of the American metropolis can be more accurately described as a mosaic, with ethnic and racial groups scattered across the urban landscape. Despite the significant changes, however, suburban jurisdictions still differ sharply from one another, and the gap between the richest and the poorest is as great as ever. The fracturing of politics creates a dynamic in which central cities and suburbs compete with one another across many dimensions.

Today's metropolitan regions are typically fragmented into hundreds of governmental jurisdictions. By 2017, there were 90,075 governments in the United States. In addition to the federal government and the governments of the 50 states, there were 38,779 local governments: 3,031 county and 35,748 sub-county governments, including 19,495 municipalities and 16,253 townships. The remainder, comprising over one-half of the total, is composed of special-purpose local governments, including 12,754 school districts and 38,542 special districts,[14] each of them established at some point in time to take on particular tasks, such as the running of toll bridges or the building of sewer systems, or the financing of new suburban developments. In addition, special authorities by the hundreds have been created to finance and manage such things as convention centers, sports stadiums, entertainment districts, and waterfront developments. Every year more are added to the list.[15]

The consequences of metropolitan fragmentation are too numerous to describe fully. Perhaps the most basic is that people tend to identify themselves with a local place rather than as regional citizens. Except when their team wins the Super Bowl or the World Series, most people have no connection to anything as abstract as a metropolitan community. This tendency is encouraged by the fact that political fragmentation and the local identity that comes with it serves some practical ends and is especially advantageous for affluent suburban residents. Within all metropolitan regions, a vigorous competition takes place among jurisdictions for people and businesses capable of helping the local tax base. The winners in this metropolitan sweepstakes see the public revenues go up, which allows them to finance a higher level of services and more public amenities even if tax rates go down. This system of incentives prompts every local government to adopt policies that benefit their own citizens at the expense of neighboring communities. Cities fight hard to outbid one another for big-box stores, retailers, and malls. They typically retain consultants to help them negotiate deals with developers, which may include a combination of eminent domain for land acquisition, land improvements and public services, tax abatements, and even direct payments. If successful, these efforts bring in tax revenues that support schools, police and fire departments, and other services and amenities, and they leave less for everyone else.

Another reason urban residents tend to identify with their local community (the "home team") is that by keeping the government close to home, they are able to make critical decisions about taxes, services, land use, and other important public policies. Historically, residents of suburbs have been especially concerned about maintaining the "character" of their communities, and frequently this concern has been expressed as a desire to exclude people based on race, ethnicity, and social class. In the history of urban America, strategies of exclusion have been aimed at a remarkable array of different groups. In the twentieth century, the desire to maintain racial segregation prompted suburban jurisdictions to enact policies meant to protect their communities from change. More recently, privatized, gated communities have become important means for accomplishing the same goal. These residential developments, which are often defended by gates, walls, and other physical barriers, are governed by homeowners associations that assess fees for maintenance, services, and amenities; in this way, the residents are able to separate themselves from surrounding neighborhoods and even from the municipalities that surround them. Affluent homeowners manage to achieve a remarkable degree of separation from the less well-off, and by doing so, they have changed the contours of local politics almost as much as the suburbs did a generation ago.

The proliferation of condominium developments and gated communities has had a paradoxical effect. On the one hand, they have made it possible for people to live in extreme isolation from one another even when they are close by. On the other hand, they have facilitated a patchwork pattern of urban residence that breaks down the large-scale pattern of racial and ethnic segregation that once divided inner-city "slum" from affluent suburb. It is difficult, however, to tell if these spatial patterns make all that much difference to anyone except middle-class and affluent urban residents. A prominent urban scholar, Peter Marcuse, has proposed that a retreat into geographic isolation and fortification erodes a shared sense of community and citizenship.[16] This is, perhaps, the inevitable consequence of the fragmented metropolis, no matter what geographic form it may take.

The Challenge of the Global Era

A combination of immigration, domestic policy, xenophobia, racism, enclave policy, socio-economic polarization, and localism have created the fragmented and multiethnic metropolis of the twenty-first century. Spatial fragmentation interacts with racial and ethnic diversity in complex ways. In cities closely connected to the global economy, symbols of corporate power, personal wealth, and luxury consumption stand in stark contrast to neighborhoods exhibiting high rates of poverty, violence, and physical dereliction. Frequently, shocking levels of inequality are visible on the same block, a fact driven home when office workers walk by homeless people or stop to eat at an expensive restaurant staffed by minimum-wage employees. Highly paid professionals working in the global economy drive up the price of downtown real estate to stratospheric levels and lead the gentrification of nearby neighborhoods, leaving run-down areas behind. Gentrification and renewal have helped revive the fortunes of central cities but these processes have also had the effect of fragmenting the urban landscape.

Likewise, metropolitan areas are fractured by a geography that reflects the inequalities and demographic processes of the twenty-first century. Political fragmentation facilitates a pattern of segregation that sorts people out according to racial and ethnic identity and social class differences. A historical analysis would suggest that there is nothing new about this. All through the twentieth century, the white middle class escaped the cities by moving to the suburbs. Now, however, the city–suburban divide inherited from the past is breaking up into a much more complicated metropolitan pattern. Ethnic and racial groups are widely distributed throughout metropolitan areas. The 2016 census revealed that the country's most diverse counties were not the urban cores or "inner cities," but, in fact, the counties just outside those centers.[17] Many more suburbs than before are ethnically diverse. The 2016 census found that higher-density suburbs and lower-density suburbs in large metros had the comparatively highest percentage decline of the average share of the largest ethnic or racial group—2.2% and 2.7%, respectively.[18] This means that, increasingly, the suburbs directly surrounding large metros are diversifying. The trend has continued into 2021. The problem is that ethnic and racial diversity of this sort does not add up to a more coherent metropolitan community. Achieving effective governance in such a circumstance remains one of the unfinished challenges of this century.

Endnotes

1 Jamie Peck, Nik Theodore, and Neil Brenner, "Neoliberal Urbanism: Models, Moments, Mutations," *SAIS Review* 29, no. 1 (2009): 49–66.

2 Lawrence J. R. Herson and John M. Bolland, *The Urban Web: Politics, Policy, and Theory* (Chicago, IL: Nelson-Hall, 1990), p. 43.

3 Sam Bass Warner Jr., *The Private City: Philadelphia in Three Periods of Its Growth* (Philadelphia, PA: University of Pennsylvania Press, 1968), p. 4.

4 Douglas Hanks, "Oil Spill Disaster Could Cost Florida 200,000 Jobs," *Miami Herald* (June 9, 2010), www.miamiherald.com/2010/06/09/167269/oil-disaster.

5 Dennis Judd and Michael Parkinson, "Urban Leadership and Regeneration," in *Leadership and Urban Regeneration: Cities in North America and Europe*, ed. Dennis Judd and Michael Parkinson (Thousand Oaks, CA: Sage Publications, 1989), pp. 13–30.

6   Reif Larsen, "Detroit: The Most Exciting City in America?" *The New York Times* (November 20, 2017). Accessed online: https://www.nytimes.com/2017/11/20/travel/detroit-michigan-downtown.html?_r=0.

7   Ibid.

8   Ibid.

9   For history and full discussion, see Wikipedia, http://en.wikipedia.org/wiki/Eminent_domain.

10 See Institute of Justice, www.ij.org/private_property/connecticut/index; William Yardley, "Anger Drives Property Rights Measures," *The New York Times* (October 8, 2006), www.nytimes.com.

11 McGeehan, Patrick, "Pfizer to Leave City That Won Land-Use Case," *The New York Times* (November 12, 2009). Accessed online: http://www.nytimes.com/2009/11/13/nyregion/13pfizer.html.

12 Herson and Bolland, *The Urban Web,* p. 46.

13 Louise Comfort, "Cities at Risk: Hurricane Katrina and the Drowning of New Orleans," *Urban Affairs Review* 41, no. 4, (March 2006): 501–506.

14 United States Census Bureau, "Table 2: Local Governments by State and Type," *2017 Census of Governments—Organization,* https://www.census.gov/data/tables/2017/econ/gus/2017-governments.html.

15 Nancy Burns, *The Formation of American Local Governments: Private Values in Public Institutions* (New York: Oxford University Press, 1994).

16 Peter Marcuse, "The 'War on Terrorism' and Life in Cities After September 11, 2001," in *Cities, War, and Terrorism: Towards an Urban Geopolitics,* ed. Stephen Graham (New York: Blackwell, 2005), pp. 274–275.

17 Jed Kolko, "40 Years from Now, the U.S. Could Look Like Las Vegas. Demographically at Least." *FiveThirtyEight* (June 22, 2017). Accessed online: https://fivethirtyeight.com/features/40-years-from-now-the-u-s-could-look-like-las-vegas/.

18 Ibid.

PART I

The Origins of American Urban Politics: The First Century

CHAPTER 2

The Enduring Legacy

National Development and the Cities

When the U.S. Constitution was ratified in 1789, the cities of the new nation were perched on the edge of a ragged coastline of a vast, mostly unexplored continent. Only five of these cities—Boston, New York, Philadelphia, Baltimore, and Charleston—had reached a population of 10,000 people. In the decades to follow, the social and economic development of the nation depended as much on the growth of its cities as on the expansion into the continental interior. A little more than a century later, 40 percent of Americans lived in towns and cities, and the nation's economy had become more industrial than agricultural. The symbols and the reality of the industrial age—belching smokestacks, wave after wave of foreign immigrants, social disorder, and racial and ethnic strife— all were concentrated in the cities. Although most Americans were recently descended from immigrants themselves, many of them soon developed a fear and distrust of cities and the people who lived within them. The antiurban attitudes formed in this turbulent century became a defining feature of American culture that has endured right up to the present day.

The industrial economy required a constantly growing supply of cheap and plentiful labor. A flood of foreign immigration began to surge into the country in the 1840s, and it did not ebb until Congress passed legislation to curb it, in 1921 and 1924. Most of the immigrants settled in crowded urban neighborhoods close to the factories. Social and cultural differences divided the newcomers from the people who had arrived earlier, and sometimes the tensions escalated into violence. The new immigrants—many of them poor and often illiterate, some merely unfamiliar with the language and customs of their new country, and most of them unaccustomed to city life—struggled to cope with miserable conditions in overcrowded tenements. Those who had come to America at an earlier time generally viewed those who came later as culturally and morally inferior. The mixture of runaway urban growth, the industrial revolution, and the successive waves of immigration guaranteed that the nineteenth-century urban experience would be tumultuous.

This history is relevant because the same dynamics still energize urban politics today. Through all of the nineteenth century and in the first years of the

DOI: 10.4324/9781003175315-3

twentieth century, waves of foreign immigration provoked anxiety and conflict, and often this became expressed in a rejection of the city and of the distinctive and diverse urban culture it nurtured.[1] Similarly, massive demographic shifts created political and social backlash over the last half-century or more. In the years after World War II, at the same time that millions of southern Blacks poured into the cities of the North, millions of white families fled to the suburbs. One consequence of these historic movements was that those living in the suburbs came to think of the cities they had left behind almost as "dangerous" and "scary." So much so, in fact, that newly formed suburban communities became rapidly incorporated, so they could pass their own zoning ordinances to "defend" themselves from those urban residents (recent immigrants and people of color) who sought to join them in the suburbs.

More recently, a new, growing wave of foreign immigration has set off xenophobic reactions and fueled political conflict in both national and local politics. In some states and cities, the anxiety about the newcomers has been expressed in legislation intended to make it impossible to rent housing or provide jobs to undocumented immigrants and to reduce social spending and require English-only instruction in the schools. Understanding that these kinds of conflicts have a long history in (urban) America helps to put today's political controversies into a useful context.

OUTTAKE

City Building Has Always Required Public Efforts

In the nineteenth century, the intense competition among cities ignited a "struggle for primacy and power" in which "like imperial states, cities carved out extensive dependencies, extended their influence over the economic and political life of the hinterland, and fought with contending places over strategic trade routes." In the American West, local boosters sometimes faced a daunting challenge in promoting their towns because many of them were, in fact, hard, isolated places in which to live. Promoters bragged about any positive feature, and just as frequently they invented fanciful tales because they had a lot at stake: "Questioning a place's promise affected not just those doing the questioning but also all who had put

stock, mental and material, in the place." Everyone living in a place, from town councils to realtors and chambers of commerce, was vigilant in discouraging any negative information from leaking out. Instead, local boosters made the smallest places seem like centers of high culture and the most desolate deserts sound like fertile land waiting for the plow.

But town promoters did not rely upon marketing alone. After midcentury, when a national railroad network began to emerge, it became clear that in order to prosper or even survive, cities would have to find a way to connect to it. To do so, civic boosters aggressively employed the power and resources of local government. To induce railroad companies to make connections to their city, they raised private subscriptions to buy railroad stock, paid for local stations and offloading facilities, gave away free land, and sometimes offered direct cash subsidies. The railroads raised much of their capital for building new rail lines by striking good bargains with cities and ultimately secured more public subsidies from cities than from state governments or from Congress. The competition for rail connections became so frenzied that railroad companies were building new lines just to obtain subsidies from local governments. When a lot of these lines failed to generate enough freight and passengers to make them pay, hundreds of rail companies went belly up, leaving towns and cities with big debts but nothing to show for them and no way to pay.

There are striking parallels with the intense inter-urban competition that goes on today. In recent decades, huge public resources have again been devoted to the cause of boosting local economic vitality. As in the nineteenth century, civic boosters are fired with the conviction that their own prospects and the fate of their cities hangs in the balance. Since the 1970s, cities have engaged in a virtual arms race to revitalize waterfronts and build stadiums, convention centers, malls, and entertainment centers. Cities compete to host events like auto races, music festivals, and special museum exhibits. All of this activity is inspired by the idea that cities must replace the smokestacks of an earlier era with an economy revolving based on services as well as tourism, entertainment, and culture.

People who support such efforts make the argument that public expenditures benefit everyone because they form the basis of a healthy local economy. Obviously not everyone agrees. Heated debates regularly erupt over questions about what should be built, who should pay for it, and who really cashes in. Many people have a nagging suspicion that taxpayers foot the bill while well-connected developers and the business elite reap the rewards. When the controversies of the 1870s are compared to those of today, one can get a feeling of déjà vu all over again.

Sources: The two quotations are from Richard C. Wade, *The Urban Frontier: Pioneer Life in Early Pittsburgh, Cincinnati, Lexington, Louisville, and St. Louis* (Chicago: University of Chicago Press, 1959), 103; David M. Wrobel, *Promised Lands: Promotion, Memory, and the Creation of the American West* (Lawrence: University Press of Kansas, 2002), p. 71.

A Century of Urban Growth

In the industrial age, cities grew at a frantic pace that had no historical precedent. In 1800, London was the only city in the world to approach a population of 1 million people, and Paris, with a population of 547,000, ranked second among the cities of continental Europe.[2] At the time, just over 60,000 people lived in New York, which made it more than one-third larger than the second, Philadelphia, with its 41,000 people, and more than twice the size of the next in line, Baltimore. Astonishingly, only 100 years later, 11 cities had topped the million-person mark, including London at 6,586,000, Paris at 2,714,000,[3] New York at 3,437,000, and Chicago at 1,698,575. Over the span of the same century, the percentage of the population living in towns[4] and cities in England and Wales increased from 25 to 77. Never before had cities grown so big or so fast, and never before had such a high proportion of the population lived in cities. The urban historian Eric Lampard has noted that "the period c. A.D. 1750–1850 [is] one of the crucial disjunctions in the history of human society. Whatever constraints had hitherto checked or moderated the growth and redistribution of population were suddenly relaxed."[5] Commenting on the growth of cities in 1895, the *Atlantic Monthly* pointed out, "The great fact in ... social development ... at the close of the nineteenth century is the tendency all over the world to concentrate in great cities. This tendency is seen everywhere."[6]

The American experience paralleled these developments. In most of the decades between the first national census of 1790 to the census of 1920, the urban population (defined by the Census Bureau as people living in cities and towns of 2,500 or more) grew more than twice as fast as the U.S. population as a whole. The only significant exception to this trend showed up between 1810 and 1820, when homesteaders and farmers streamed across the Appalachian Mountains to settle the Old Northwest (now western Pennsylvania, Ohio, and Indiana). Soon, however, even the expanding frontier could not absorb enough people to keep up with the rate of growth in the cities. Urban change on this scale was an entirely new and often shocking experience. As late as 1840, a full half-century after the nation's founding, only one American in ten was officially classified in the census as "urban." In the two decades leading up to the Civil War, however, cities began growing at an astonishing rate. Immigrants began pouring into the industrial cities in search of jobs in the factories, and a steady migration from farm to city picked up speed for the same reason. As late as 1840, only 11 percent of the American population lived in cities and towns, but by 1860, the Census Bureau officially classified 20 percent of the American population as urban, and this proportion doubled to almost 40 percent by century's end (see Figure 2.1). Twenty years later, the national census revealed that more than half of all Americans—51 percent—lived in cities or towns. In much less than a century, the United States had gone from a mostly rural country to one that was rapidly becoming more urban.

Because they were important centers of finance and trade, right from the beginning the cities perched on the eastern seaboard benefited from national development even when it was occurring on the distant frontier. New York maintained its supremacy as a financial and commercial hub, and its status as the nation's premier city was ensured in 1825, the year the Erie Canal was completed. The canal linked the city directly to the Great Lakes, which placed it at the end of a giant funnel that gathered the resources of a vast hinterland into New York harbor, where they could be placed into a worldwide trading system. After the Civil War, New York consolidated its position when it became a great manufacturing city. Jostling throngs of immigrants passed through the port of New York, and many of them decided to go no further. From just 369,000 people in 1840, the city's population exploded to over 3.4 million by 1900—a shocking 10-fold increase in only 60 years! By 1920, when its

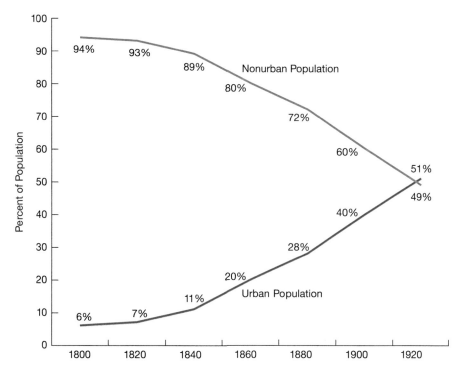

FIGURE 2.1 The Proportion Urban in the United States, 1790–1920

Sources: U.S. Department of Commerce, Bureau of the Census, *Historical Statistics of the United States, Colonial Times to 1970,* pt. 1, Bicentennial ed. (Washington, D.C.: U.S. Government Printing Office, 1975), p. 8; U.S. Department of Commerce, Bureau of the Census, *1970 Census of Population,* vol. 1, *Characteristics of the Population,* pt. 1 (Washington, DC: U.S. Government Printing Office, 1973), p. 42.

population reached 5.6 million, New York had firmly consolidated its position as a leading global center of finance, trade, and manufacturing.

Yet, despite its incredible growth, New York's share of the nation's urban population fell steadily throughout the century. This is because thousands of new towns and cities sprang up as the nation expanded westward, and these places often grew much faster even than New York—although, it must be emphasized, none of them were destined to challenge its supremacy. In 1800, 18 percent of the nation's urban population lived in New York City, but by the century's end, this proportion had fallen to 7 percent.[7] New York City remained the largest by far, but over time other cities assumed prominent places in an increasingly integrated national and international urban network. The data in Table 2.1 help tell this story. New York grew from a city of 137,388 in 1820 to a multimillion-person metropolis a century later, but over the same period other cities were also bursting at the seams. Philadelphia had a population of 64,000 in 1820, topped 565,000 by 1860, and grew to a city of more than 1.8 million by 1920. Boston increased its population from 43,000 in 1820 to nearly 178,000 in 1860 and to almost 750,000 by

TABLE 2.1 Population and Rate of Growth in Five Large Cities, 1820–1920[a]

	New York City[b]	Percentage Increase	Chicago	Percentage Increase	Philadelphia	Percentage Increase	St. Louis	Percentage Increase	Boston	Percentage Increase	Percentage Increase in U.S. Population
1820	137,388		—		63,802		4,598		43,298		
1830	220,471	60	—		80,462	26	5,847	27	61,392	42	33
1840	369,305	67	4,470		93,665	16	16,469	182	93,383	52	33
1850	660,803	79	29,963	570	121,376	30	77,860	373	136,881	47	36
1860	1,183,148	79	112,172	274	565,529	366	160,773	107	177,840	30	36
1870	1,546,293	31	298,977	167	674,022	19	310,864	93	250,526	41	27
1880	2,061,191	33	503,185	68	847,170	26	350,522	13	362,839	45	26
1890	2,507,474	22	1,099,850	119	1,046,964	24	451,770	29	448,477	24	26
1900	3,437,202	37	1,698,575	54	1,293,697	24	575,000	27	560,892	25	21
1910	4,766,883	39	2,185,283	29	1,549,008	20	687,029	20	670,585	20	21
1920	5,620,048	18	2,701,705	24	1,823,779	18	772,897	13	748,060	12	15

Note: [a] These five cities were ranked as the five largest in the 1910 census. [b] Using the consolidated borough boundaries of 1898.

Sources: Glen E. Holt, personal files; U.S. Department of Commerce, Bureau of the Census, *The Growth of Metropolitan Districts in the United States: 1900–1940,* by Warren S. Thompson (Washington, DC: U.S. Government Printing Office, 1947); Blake McKelvey, *American Urbanization: A Comparative History* (Glenview, IL: Scott Foresman, 1973), pp. 24, 37, 73.

1920. Meanwhile, a great many places, large and small, experienced a similar transformation.

Cities in the continental interior grew at almost unbelievable rates, often morphing from small frontier towns to busy urban centers in only a few years. St. Louis, the old French settlement where Lewis and Clark outfitted their expedition in 1805, exploded from a town of only 16,000 people in 1840 to a city 10 times that size by 1860 and reached 772,000 by 1920. But Chicago's growth was perhaps most startling of all. In the 20 years from 1840 to 1860, it was transformed from a swampy frontier village of 4,500 to a city of more than 112,000. And the people just kept on coming. Chicago quickly left St. Louis in the dust, and by 1920 its population had soared to 2.7 million people, putting it second only to New York.

Places such as St. Louis and New Orleans (on the Mississippi River), Chicago (at the foot of Lake Michigan), and Cincinnati (on the Ohio River) had begun as major trading centers, transferring goods through the Great Lakes or the inland river system to the eastern seaboard cities or directly to Europe. After the Civil War, they quickly emerged as leading industrial centers. Smaller cities and towns prospered by finding a specialized niche in this emerging urban hierarchy. At the top of the pyramid, the largest cities became industrial powerhouses and asserted commanding reach over vast hinterlands. Second-tier cities developed more specialized economies and generally served as transfer points to the larger urban centers. The bottom of the hierarchy was composed of the multitude of small towns that shipped agricultural and extractive resources gathered from mines, forests, and farms to feed the warehouses and factories located in the big urban centers, which then placed the raw materials into international commerce or used them to produce manufactured goods.

Inter-Urban Rivalries

Individual cities did not prosper by relying upon happenstance and chance. Town promotion became a way of life for local boosters, who competed for the settlers and investors who swept across the continent. The fortunes of cities were only partially determined by locational advantages—what might be called "place luck." Transportation connections—turnpikes, canals, and, later, railroads—were also crucial in determining a city's destiny. Links to the national transportation network could instantly secure a city's future by expanding its reach into the hinterland surrounding it and by tying it into national and international trade networks. Because such connections were so important to a city's prospects, promoters freely used the fiscal resources and powers of local governments to secure them. In the early century, canal building reached a fever pitch, but within a few years the railroads provided better links to other cities and to broader markets. Cities scrambled to offer subsidies to railroad corporations in the form of free land and terminal facilities and stock purchases. The logic was simple: Rising real estate values were expected to provide more than enough additional revenues to pay off the debts. These hopes did not always pan out, but any city that failed to make an effort to secure good rail links would surely die on the vine.

The battle for rail connections was fought with white-hot intensity. Before the railroads, it was possible to transport corn by wagon only 125 miles, and wheat only 250 miles, before the cost made them unmarketable.[8] Beyond that distance, agricultural land was almost worthless for anything except subsistence farming because there was no way of getting crops to market. The cost and inconvenience of hauling goods on horse-drawn wooden wagons guaranteed that settlements without access to water transportation would never amount to much. In the first decade of the nineteenth century, a ton of goods could be shipped all the way from Europe for the same amount it cost to haul it 9 miles over roads.[9] Inland cities without waterfronts could not conceivably compete with port and river cities as centers of trade. All that changed with the coming of the railroads. The emerging rail network opened up huge areas of farmland to commercial agriculture, which not only allowed the countryside to fill in but also resulted in soaring land values and population growth for the cities able to secure a connection. Local promoters were anxious to shape patterns of trade and economic development in their favor because they were keenly aware that they were involved in a competition in which some cities would prosper, but others would die on the vine.

The building of the Erie Canal demonstrated how cities might gain a measure of control over their own destinies. In 1817, the New York State legislature authorized money for the construction of a 364-mile waterway to connect the Hudson River to Lake Erie. When the canal opened in 1825, it became possible to ship huge volumes of agricultural and extractive goods from the continental interior through the Great Lakes to Buffalo, down the canal, and on to the port at New York, where they could be distributed along the eastern seaboard, used in factories, or shipped to Europe. Many producers and shippers abandoned the long, circuitous, and hazardous journey down the Ohio, Missouri, and Mississippi rivers to the port at New Orleans. New York's direct connection to the heartland via the canal quickly vaulted it past other eastern seaboard cities in population and volume of trade. By 1860, 62 percent of the nation's foreign trade passed through New York's harbor.[10]

The lesson was not lost on city boosters elsewhere. Civic leaders lobbied their state capitals for financial assistance to build canals. Pennsylvania, Maryland, Virginia, North Carolina, and South Carolina financed expensive canal projects designed to cut through the Appalachians. More than 3,000 miles of canals were dug between 1824 and 1840, most of them operated by state governments.[11] About 30 percent of the costs were raised through private sources, but public financing was essential for such ambitious undertakings.[12]

Canal building was so expensive, the engineering so complicated, and the natural barriers often so formidable that most cities could not hope to build them unless state legislatures helped out. Natural topographic barriers left many places out of the competition altogether. But the railroad era ignited an interurban competition that almost any city might join. Until the railroads, water was the singularly critical ingredient determining a city's fate; canals were just a means of trying to make up for what nature had not endowed. In the first decades of the nineteenth century, for the river towns such as St. Louis, Pittsburgh, Cincinnati, and New Orleans, the steamboat had been "an enchanter's wand transforming an almost raw countryside of scattered farms and towns into a settled region of cultivated landscapes and burgeoning cities."[13] In the 1850s, the enchanter's wand was passed to the railroads. The rail lines became rivers of commerce, capable of carrying huge volumes at amazing speeds over long distances. The railroads guaranteed that America's frontier would eventually vanish and a network of cities, towns, and villages would spread over the continent.

In 1840, only 2,800 miles of track had been laid, most of it in the urban East. No connection reached even as far west as Pittsburgh. The early steam locomotives were hazardous and unreliable contraptions, blowing up with a regularity that provoked opposition to their use in urban areas. Lacking the capital to take on bigger projects, railway companies built short lines. Because each company devised its own gauge (width between the rails), at the end of each line goods had to be unloaded from one company's cars and put onto cars that fit the next company's rails. Even with these limitations, however, the early rail system was vastly superior to the only alternative: horse-drawn wooden wagons.

Rail lines were built at astonishing speed, and by the 1880s the adoption of standard gauge sizes made the system much more efficient. In 1857, the newly consolidated Pennsylvania Railroad first connected Pittsburgh to Chicago. Three years later, 11 trunk lines ended in Chicago and 20 branch and feeder lines passed through it, making the city the nation's largest rail center terminus. By 1869 and with much fanfare, the symbolic Golden Spike was pounded in at Promontory Point, Utah. It completed the first cross-continental route by joining the Union Pacific line originating on the East Coast to the Central Pacific line starting in San Francisco. Within a few years, the outline of the modern rail system was almost complete, a spider's web with strands reaching into every section of the country. In just the half-century between 1850 and 1900, the network expanded from 9,021 miles of track to 258,784 miles.[14]

More miles of track were laid more quickly than in any other nation in the world. This explosive growth could be traced to the massive public subsidies pumped into railroad building. Until the 1890s, most private corporations lacked the ability to raise the capital that would later become routine for them. Subsidies from governments at all levels helped make the railroads "America's first big business."[15] In the Pacific Railways Acts of 1862 and 1864, the federal government gave huge swaths of land to the railroad corporations, which they could use for rail construction and raising capital. But some involvement by the states was critical because the federal government considered transportation to be mostly a state responsibility. Treasury Secretary Albert Gallatin's 1808 plan for a federal system of turnpike and harbor improvements had failed to gain congressional approval because of regional rivalries.[16] Following President Andrew Jackson's veto of a federal turnpike bill in 1830, transportation became viewed more as a state than a federal responsibility.

The states responded by feverishly subsidizing canal and railroad construction, but their eagerness to assume risk was also tempered by experience. The Panic of 1837 bankrupted scores of canal companies and some of the early steam railroad lines, which caused private investors and the states alike to lose their investments. Taxpayers and politicians were up in arms, and "revulsion against internal improvements" swept the country.[17] In the 1840s, many states wrote prohibitions against loaning money or buying stock in private corporations. Facing new restrictions at the state level, railroad promoters shifted their efforts to cities, which raced to outbid one another for railroad stock.

The anarchic competition for rail connections imposed many costs, including overbuilding and redundancies that resulted in bond defaults and bankruptcies. Up to 1861, 25–30 percent of all direct investment in railroad building was supplied by state and local governments. The cities were the biggest spenders; they contributed an estimated $300 million in direct subsidies; the states spent $229 million and the federal government $65 million.[18] In addition, the federal government and the states offered generous land grants, which the railroad companies quickly converted to cash by selling the land to settlers. In the post–Civil War period, the railroads accumulated so much property that they sent agents to the Scandinavian countries, Germany, and the United Kingdom to recruit immigrants to buy and settle it. This kind of recruitment was deliberately discriminatory, as railroad companies targeted white northern and western European immigrants. As one observer aptly noted: "When railroad promoters dreamed of settlers for their lines, they dreamed only in white."[19] In fact, settling the railroads became an explicitly racialized project for the American railroad companies—based on racist hierarchies and agrarian myths of European whiteness. Partly because the railroad companies recruited heavily there (and also because of hardships in their homeland), one-sixth of all Swedish citizens left for the United States in the last half of the nineteenth century, many of them settling in a broad swath of territory paralleling rail routes from the Great Lakes through the Dakotas and Montana. In their approach, railroad companies went well beyond merely the business of railroad building, but essentially an explicitly racialized approach to colonizing the heartland:

> Almost without exception, they [the railroad companies] targeted Northern Europeans because they had been experiencing economic and political dislocations. Railroads considered them hard workers, of the Protestant faith, and racially white. By choosing to advertise to these groups, railroads actively shaped the racial and ethnic makeup of the towns along their lines.[20]

Railroad owners became adept at playing cities against one another in an attempt to secure lucrative subsidies. By the 1850s, cities along the eastern seaboard were floating bond issues so they could invest in railroad stock, clear rights-of-way, and build terminal facilities—actions intended to ensure rail connections. The competition quickly spread west. In the 1860s, the business leaders of Kansas City, Kansas, sold bond issues to private investors, gave the proceeds to a railroad company, and persuaded Congress to approve a federal land grant to the company. As a result of its success in this venture, Kansas City prospered while its nearby rival Leavenworth stagnated (today, Leavenworth is known mainly for its federal prison).[21] Denver's board of trade raised $280,000 to finance a 100-mile spur line to obtain access to the intercontinental track that ran through Cheyenne, Wyoming.[22] Some of Denver's businesses had already moved to Cheyenne in the expectation that its position astride the intercontinental line would make it the premier city of the Rocky Mountain West. Their ambitions were frustrated when rail lines from all directions began to converge on Denver, thus securing its status as the dominant city of the Rocky Mountain region. The results of this long-ago battle are still obvious: Today, Cheyenne's image is tied mostly to its annual rodeo, the Cheyenne Frontier Days.

No city benefited from railroad building as dramatically as did Chicago, whose phenomenal growth was founded on its access to agricultural and extractive products gathered from a vast region. Corn and grain, cattle and hogs, and iron ore and coal poured into Chicago through the Great Lakes and over the rails. The city became a center for steelmaking; the manufacture of agricultural implements, tools, and machines; slaughtering and meatpacking; and trade. By the mid-1870s, Chicago eclipsed St. Louis as the Midwest's premier city, a feat accomplished partly through the success of its local business community in securing rail links. Chicago built its first railroad in 1852 and then helped finance feeder lines into the city. The city also invested in grain elevators, warehouses, switching yards, and stockyards. By contrast, for too long St. Louis's business community held fast to the faith that the Mississippi River steamboats would continue to be the key to the city's prosperity. By the time St. Louis began seeking rail connections, Chicago's lead was overwhelming. Although Chicago also enjoyed a considerable advantage because it was located on the Great Lakes and was right next door to the most fertile farming regions of the Midwest, its aggressive leadership reinforced its favorable location.

For many years, the question of whether cities should go into debt to secure rail connections was beyond public dispute. Urban voters enthusiastically supported the issuance of city bonds to finance railroad subsidy schemes. As long as everyone's attention was riveted on external threats to the local economy, nearly everyone supported the idea that everything possible should be done to attract rail connections. Local promoters were encouraged to think that virtually any scheme that benefited them personally was also in the public's interest: "Developmental policy was almost wholly a product of consensus-building among groups of merchant elites to support particular canal, turnpike, rail and other projects in response to merchant elites in nearby communities."[23] From 1866 to 1873, the legislatures of 29 states granted over 800 authorizations for aid by local governments to railroad projects.[24] A study of governmental aid to railroads in New York found that no community ever voted against subscribing to railroad stock.[25] The votes were usually so lopsided as to be a foregone conclusion.[26]

The fight for rail connections improved the fortunes of many a city, but the overheated competition brought disaster to some. Railroad promoters played one town against another in search of better subsidies. The inter-urban competition grew often so fierce that many cities bid up the subsidies beyond what was economically rational. City governments incurred huge debts on a hope and a promise. In New York State, 50 towns bypassed by a major rail line joined in a $5.7 million stock subscription to the New York and Oswego Railroad. Zigzagging across the state to link the towns, the company went bankrupt shortly after completing the line in 1873 because the areas it served had too few people and products to sustain a viable business. Most of the investments made by the towns were wiped out, with taxpayers left holding the bag.[27]

Promoters exaggerated the positive effects expected of public subsidies, predicting rapid town growth, rising real estate values, and overflowing municipal treasuries. Profits on railroad stocks, they often promised, would eliminate the need for local taxes altogether. For most cities, however, "the direct effect on government finances was on the whole unfavorable."[28] Too many cities bought stock that went bust, or the new lines brought far less prosperity than promised. Cities that had heavily invested in speculative railroad ventures regularly found themselves dragged into fiscal crisis. Some cities defaulted on their debts in the 1860s, but it was merely a harbinger of things to come. The three-year depression that began in 1873 was precipitated, more than anything else, by the overbuilding of railroads and the overvaluing of railroad stock and local real estate. Hundreds of towns and cities were forced into default. In 1873, an astounding $100 million to $150 million of municipal debt was involved in railroad bond defaults—one-fifth of all the municipal debt in the nation.[29]

Municipal defaults on railroad bonds and revelations of political corruption associated with railroad building affected politics at all levels. Citizens rebelled against paying back eastern financiers for bonds that had become worthless. In some cases, the lines had not even been built. When federal marshals came to towns to collect the debts, they were sometimes run off by shotgun-wielding mobs. Cries of debt repudiation filled the air, and some cities and states won court battles to forgive their debts.[30] From 1864 to 1888, the most common type of case before the U.S. Supreme Court involved railroad bonds.[31] Many states adopted restrictions on local debt and limited the aid that could be given to private corporations.[32] Financial and political abuses by railroad barons fueled a populist rebellion against big business that shook the national political system.[33]

Industrialization and Community

At the time of the nation's founding and for several decades after, the politics of American cities were controlled primarily by an aristocratic and merchant elite. Such a system could not survive the urban growth and the economic and technological changes wrought by industrialization. In only a few years, cities changed from relatively compact communities held together by personal relationships and shared community norms to sprawling industrial cities characterized by social stratification and segregation, constant population change, and social and political conflict. By degrees, the governing class inherited from an earlier era lost its grip on local political systems. Increasingly, urban politics became a battleground revolving around social class and ethnic identity.

Before the emergence of the industrial city, trading cities sprang up along navigable waterways and harbors. The economy of the merchant cities was intimately tied to trade and commerce: The importation and distribution of European goods; the regulation of docks and farmers' markets; the financing and insuring of ships and goods; the printing of accounting ledgers, handbills, and newspapers. Educated aristocrats, importers, bankers, wholesalers, and shopkeepers were numbered among a city's most prominent citizens. A notch down in the social order were the craft workers, artisans, and individual entrepreneurs—shoemakers, hatters, bakers, carpenters, blacksmiths, potters, butchers, wheelwrights, saddle and harness makers, and shipwrights. At the bottom were sailors, domestic workers, servants, and the unskilled workers who moved goods from docks to warehouses. At the time of the Revolution, about three out of four white persons in Pennsylvania, Maryland, and Virginia had come to America as indentured servants, and until they paid their debts they were not free to join the paid labor force.[34] The racialized caste system of American society further contributed to social differences. The Southern economy, which was, until the industrial period, entirely based on the institutionalized enslavement of Africans forcefully removed from their countries of origin, remained politically distinct and relatively less urbanized than the North far into the twenty-first century.[35] In general, however, the United States was, from the very beginning a society in which social upward mobility was severely constrained by racial and ethnic discrimination.

The lifeblood of the mercantile cities (called the "city of merchants" by historians) flowed along the waterfront. Wharves and docks, warehouses, clerks' offices, banks, newspapers and printing establishments, taverns and breweries, and private homes all clustered close to the riverfront or harbor. This compact "walking city" was bounded by the distance the inhabitants could walk within an hour or two. Typically, the area of urban settlement spread about 2 miles from the center, but most people lived in densely packed neighborhoods stretching only a few blocks from the water. The small size of the merchant cities moderated the effects of inequality by fostering "a sense of community identification similar to that of traditional societies."[36] Most goods were produced in small shops by skilled artisans who employed one or two apprentices, and these often lived on the premises. Workers clustered together in shanties or back alleys within a short distance of the comfortable homes of wealthy merchants.

In his study of colonial Philadelphia, the historian Sam Bass Warner found that people of different occupations lived apart, but it was a proximate segregation: "It was the unity of everyday life, from tavern, to street, to workplace, to housing which held the town together in the eighteenth century."[37] Class conflict was moderated by this intimate geography. The merchant class was expected to run the city's affairs, and it did. With few exceptions, wealthy aristocrats and merchants presided over the public affairs of the city.[38] Consistent with their view that the scope of local government ought to be limited, they spent little on public services. In 1810, for instance, New York City spent only $1 per capita on all governmental functions put together.[39]

Casual and consensual governance of this sort began to disappear by the second half of the nineteenth century. In 1850, not much more than 10 percent of all workers in America were engaged in manufacturing, and they produced less than 20 percent of the nation's economic output. Only two decades later, however, industrial production exceeded the commercial and agricultural sectors in value added to the economy, and by the turn of the century, manufacturing accounted for more economic value than both sectors combined.[40] Industrialization moved economic production from small shops and homes into factories. Before the Civil War, manufacturing establishments rarely employed more than 50 workers, and even in large cities they ranged between 8 and 20 workers. In 1832, for example, the average-sized manufacturing establishment in Boston employed 8.5 workers.[41] But in the years following the Civil War, manufacturing firms grew quickly in size. In agricultural implements and machinery, the number of employees per establishment increased from 7.5 in 1860 to 79 in 1910. In malt liquor breweries, the number of workers increased from 5 to 39, and in iron and steel establishments, from 54 to 426.[42]

The transformation of small businesses into big corporations spawned a class of industrial magnates who flaunted their wealth by building mansions and estates, throwing lavish parties, and constructing monuments to themselves.[43] Capital became increasingly concentrated in large firms. Limited-risk corporations,[44] which were relatively rare before the Civil War, produced 60 percent of value in manufacturing by the turn of the century.[45] (Such corporations raise capital by selling stocks to investors, who risk their investment but not their personal assets if the company fails.) Twelve firms were valued at over $10 million in 1896, but by 1903, 50 firms were valued at more than $50 million.[46] Several giant corporations formed between 1896 and 1905, including U.S. Steel, International Harvester, General Electric, and American Telephone and Telegraph, became models of the modern corporate form of the twentieth century.

As the workplace became increasingly impersonal, hierarchical, and rigid, relationships between employers and workers became distant and even hostile.

As machine-tooled, standardized parts replaced handcrafted goods, the number of unskilled workers multiplied. Standardized production had begun as early as 1798, when Eli Whitney designed a musket with interchangeable parts. Over time, standardized components made it possible to make a variety of goods rapidly and cheaply. Such products as clocks, sewing machines, and farm machinery, which had once been assembled by craft workers, were now made in big factories. The huge military orders placed during the Civil War prompted the mass production of shoes and clothing. Factory methods of production required specialized, repetitive work and a rigid distinction between management and workers and work became regimented and closely monitored.

Class differences sharply separated urban neighborhoods. While immigrant working-class tenement housing crowded close to the downtown business districts or in bottomlands near the docks and factories, middle-class neighborhoods tended to be located further away from the teeming crowd. The wealthy claimed exclusive areas, often located on hills, where the air was fresher and the residents commanded pleasing views (almost everywhere, "the heights" came to signify high social standing). Wealthy people began to spend their weekends and holidays on bucolic suburban estates.

A series of transportation improvements allowed people to commute farther from their place of work. When the omnibuses were introduced to the streets of New York City in 1828, they represented a minor revolution in urban transportation. The way people commuted to work had changed little for hundreds of years. The wealthy owned or rented carriages; everyone else walked or, rarely, rode a horse. The omnibus made it possible for larger numbers of people to ride, in effect, in an enlarged version of the carriage. From the 1830s until the Civil War, dozens of omnibuses careened down the streets of the industrial cities. Basically, an enlarged version of the long-distance stagecoach, the omnibus was pulled by a team of two to four horses and typically carried up to a dozen people. Omnibuses were crowded and uncomfortable, cold in the winter, hot in the summer, and slow, barely moving faster than a person could walk. The coaches swayed and lurched over cobblestones and rutted unpaved streets.[47] A newspaper of the time complained that "during certain periods of the day or evening and always during inclement weather, passengers are packed in these vehicles, without regard to comfort or even decency."[48]

Despite the discomforts, commuters who could afford the fares—merchants, traders, lawyers, artisans, managers, junior partners—crowded into these crude conveyances. The advantages were many. The omnibus ran on a fixed schedule and route, and it picked up and dropped off passengers at frequent intervals. The fixed fare, typically a nickel, was a small fraction of the cost of renting a hackney coach. The omnibus was thus more convenient and less expensive than any alternative mode of traveling except walking. By encouraging in some urban residents the "riding habit,"[49] the omnibus marked the beginning of the end of the walking city. Almost immediately, the American city began fragmenting into distinct neighborhoods and enclaves.

Steam railroad lines, which made their first appearance in Boston in the 1830s, made it possible for a select few commuters to live at some distance away, but there were a few drawbacks. Steam engines were suited for constant speed rather than for frequent stops and starts, they were expensive to build and operate, and they were fearfully loud and prone to blowing up. They did not, therefore, compete with omnibuses on crowded urban streets but instead facilitated a commute by a privileged few to smaller towns and villages some miles away from the urban center. The 40- to 75-cent fares were out of reach for all but the wealthy (the average laborer made about $1 a day; sometimes skilled workers made as much as $2 a day).[50] Even so, by 1848, one-fifth of Boston's businessmen commuted daily by rail.[51]

In the 1850s, horse-drawn streetcars replaced omnibuses on main thoroughfares. Because they were pulled on rails rather than over potholed streets, the horsecars carried twice as many passengers and traveled almost twice as fast as an omnibus. Horsecars were cheaper, too, and their affordable cost "contributed to the development of the world's first integrated transportation systems."[52] In the larger cities, the lines radiated from the center like spokes on a wheel. Because horsecars could travel 6–8 miles in an hour, middle-class residential settlements began to spread that far and more from the city center. (The rule of thumb, then as now, was that most people were willing to commute up to an hour, but not much more.) In addition, the horsecar lines sometimes extended well beyond built-up areas, serving hospitals, parks, cemeteries, and independent villages.[53] Wherever they reached, land speculators and builders bought up property in the expectation that development would follow and real estate values would rise.

In 1888, Frank Julian Sprague revolutionized urban transit when he installed the first electric streetcar system in Richmond, Virginia.[54] The motive force driving the electric streetcar came from a wheeled carriage that moved atop an overhead cable. This device trolled along the wires, pulling the car as it went. The "troller" gave the trolley car its name.[55] Trolley cars had so many advantages over horsecars that despite the expense of installing overhead wires, traction companies and cities rushed to install them. In 1890, 60 percent of the nation's streetcars were still pulled by horses, but 12 years later the figure was less than 1 percent.[56] Trolleys traveled almost twice as fast as horsecars. Areas 6–8 miles from the city center could now be reached in half an hour, making it possible for people to live 10 miles or more from work. And electric streetcars were infinitely cleaner than the horsecars they replaced. City residents had always complained about "an atmosphere heavy with the odors of death and decay and animal filth and steaming nastiness."[57] The trolley removed thousands of horses, together with their daily tons of manure, from the streets.

The horse-drawn streetcars and the electric trolleys (and a few decades later, the automobile) facilitated, each in its turn, an increasing segregation of settlement and land use. Until the 1870s, crowded financial and retailing districts were located close by and even mixed in with warehouses and factories.[58] In the last third of the nineteenth century, however, well-defined downtown shopping and financial districts sprang up. Middle-class people developed a new shopping habit. They rode the streetcars downtown to buy goods in the new generation of chain and department stores, which were able to grow larger because more people could get to them. The first chain retail company, the Great Atlantic and Pacific Tea Company, was organized in 1864, and A&P stores soon expanded to other cities. Frank W. Woolworth opened his five-and-dime store in Lancaster, Pennsylvania, in 1879, and by the 1880s Woolworth's became a familiar marquee in downtown areas.[59] The middle-class habit of shopping in downtown stores for major purchases persisted right up until the end of the 1950s, by which time the streetcar system had been dismantled in most cities.[60]

The development of social and ethnic segregation among neighborhoods, cities, and suburbs eroded the sense (if it had ever existed beyond sentimental memories) that everyone lived cooperatively in a mutually beneficial urban community. If the term "community" once evoked images of a diverse assortment of people rubbing shoulders in their daily lives, it gradually came to refer to the patterns of interaction among people living within homogeneous neighborhoods. The poor were increasingly pushed to inhabit distinct enclaves, as did the middle class and the wealthy. In addition, racial and ethnic segregation was always part and parcel of the colonization of the Americas in general and the United States in particular. The erasure of American native culture, Chinese and Asian exclusion acts, and the slave trade and subsequent development of a racialized caste society in the United States bear witness to this. Race- and ethnicity-based segregation became drastically more visible in American cities at the turn of the twentieth century, with a dramatic increase in urban diversity.

The Immigrant Tide

The industrial economy depended on a constantly expanding pool of cheap labor. Millions of foreign immigrants were pushed out of their homelands by war, civil unrest, and hardship and pulled to American shores by actual opportunity and the myth of the American Dream. They worked on the railroads, in meatpacking, in steelmaking, in coal and lead mining, and in factories of every kind. Simultaneously, an unprecedented migration from farm to city was set in motion. Between 1830 and 1896, developments in farm machinery cut in half the average time and labor required to produce agricultural crops. In the four decades after the Civic War, the time required to harvest wheat was cut by 95 percent and labor costs for farming fell by one-fifth.[61] The new machinery drove up the capital investment required to start and run a farm and it required fewer hands than before. The millions of farm laborers and young people who could no longer find work streamed into the industrial cities in search of jobs and opportunity.

In the century between 1820 and 1919, 33.5 million foreign immigrants came to America. The Irish and then the Germans set off the first big surge. A famine that swept Ireland in the mid-1840s pushed desperate families to make the wrenching decision to leave their homeland (forever after, an unrequited yearning has been the most common theme running through Irish music). Irish peasants subsisted primarily on potatoes and vegetables grown on tiny rocky plots of ground and in strips of soil along the roads, the only usable land not claimed by their English landlords. When a potato blight swept through Europe in the 1840s, its effects were more devastating in Ireland than elsewhere. Between 1845 and the mid-1850s, up to one-fourth of Ireland's peasants starved to death. Many of the survivors streamed into Liverpool and bought or bartered passage on ships heading for America.

In the same decade, years of civil war pushed a flood of German immigrants to America. The data displayed in Table 2.2 reveal that all through the 1840s and 1850s the Irish and Germans kept coming. In this period, these two groups accounted for made up more than 70 percent of all new arrivals. Immigrants from the American "motherland," England, made up less than 14 percent of the flow, with an assortment of different nationalities making up the rest. America would never be the same.

After the depression of 1873–1876 the numbers of immigrants surged to levels never before experienced in the nation's history. In the decade of the 1970s, 2.7 million foreign immigrants came to America, and this number doubled to 5.2 million in the 1880s. The depression of 1893–1896 slowed the flow for a brief time, but the number of arrivals in the first decade of the twentieth century soared to the highest level in American history, to over 8 million people, with an additional 6.5 million pouring in between 1910 and 1920. These astonishing numbers were driven by people coming from countries not much represented in the American population up to that point. Irish and Germans kept coming, but by the 1880s they accounted for just 40 percent of the immigrant flow, and after the turn of the century their numbers plummeted to 8 percent of the total. Immigration from the United Kingdom continued to fall decade by decade. Italians, Greeks, immigrants from several eastern European nations (Bohemians, Czechs, Slavs, Lithuanians, Poles), and Jews made up the difference. In the 1890s, Jews from Russia and Austria–Hungary, together with Catholics from Italy, accounted for 42 percent of arrivals, and their numbers swelled to more than 60 percent in each of the two decades from 1900 to 1920. Between 1900 and 1920, 14.5 million immigrants entered the country.[62] These numbers would surely have increased still more if Congress had not enacted restrictive immigration laws in 1921 and 1924.

Wherever they were headed, the Statue of Liberty gave them their first view of America, making it the most enduring symbol of America's immigrant history. Sixty percent of all European immigrants between 1820 and 1919 passed through New York harbor. Between the turn of the century and World War I, two-thirds of all the immigrants entering the United States were processed through New York's Ellis Island (which was closed in 1954). Almost three-fourths of the new arrivals, 24 million in all, settled in the cities. By 1870,

TABLE 2.2 Decennial Immigration to the United States, 1820–1919

	1820–1829	1830–1839	1840–1849	1850–1859	1860–1869	1870–1879	1880–1889	1890–1899	1900–1909	1910–1919
Total in Millions	0.1	0.5	1.4	2.7	2.1	2.7	5.2	3.7	8.2	6.3
Percentage of Total from										
Ireland	40.20	31.70	46.00	36.90	24.40	15.40	12.80	11.00	4.20	2.60
Germany	4.5	23.2	27	34.8	35.2	27.4	27.5	15.7	4	2.7
United Kingdom	19.5	13.8	15.3	13.5	14.9	21.1	15.5	8.9	5.7	5.8
Scandinavia	0.2	0.4	0.9	0.9	5.5	7.6	12.7	10.5	5.9	3.8
Canada	1.8	2.2	2.4	2.2	4.9	11.8	9.4	0.1	1.5	11.2
Russia					0.2	1.3	3.5	12.2	18.3	17.4
Austria–Hungary					0.2	2.2	6	14.5	24.4	18.2
Italy				0.5	1.7	5.1	16.3	23.5	19.4	

Source: From N. Carpenter, "Immigrants and Their Children," *U.S. Bureau of the Census Monograph*, no. 7 (Washington, D.C.: U.S. Government Printing Office, 1927), pp. 324–325.

remarkably, more than half the population of at least 20 American cities were foreign-born or children of parents who had immigrated. In some cities the proportion reached much higher levels. As shown by the data in Table 2.3, by 1870, first- and second-generation immigrants accounted for at least 72 percent of the populations of eight cities of more than 500,000 people. Eighty percent

TABLE 2.3 Proportion of Immigrant Population in Cities of 500,000 or More, 1870 and 1910

		Percentage Foreign-Born	Percentage Foreign-Born or Native-Born with at Least One Foreign Parent[a]
New York	1870	44	80
	1910	40	79
Chicago	1870	48	87
	1910	36	78
Philadelphia	1870	28	51
	1910	25	57
St. Louis	1870	36	65
	1910	18	54
Boston	1870	35	63
	1910	36	74
Cleveland	1870	42	75
	1910	35	75
Baltimore	1870	21	38
	1910	14	38
Pittsburgh	1870	32	58
	1910	26	62
Mean for all eight cities (each counted equally)	1870	40	72
	1910	32	72

Note: [a] Native-born with foreign parents is unavailable in the 1870 census. The figures for 1870 are estimated by adding 80 percent to the number of foreign-born. In all cases, this should yield a safely conservative estimate.

Sources: U.S. Department of the Interior, Superintendent of Census, The Ninth Census (June 1, 1870), vol. 1, Population and Social Statistics (Washington, DC: U.S. Government Printing Office, 1872), p. 386; U.S. Department of Commerce, Bureau of the Census, Thirteenth Census of the United States Taken in the Year 1910, vol. 1, Population 1910 (Washington, DC: U.S. Government Printing Office, 1913), p. 178.

of New York City's population was made up of first- and second-generation immigrants, and in Chicago an astounding 87 percent of the population was composed of the foreign-born and their American-born children.

And they kept on coming. Despite a huge and continuing migration from rural areas to the cities in the latter years of the nineteenth century, by 1910 the proportion of first- and second-generation immigrants in most cities was about the same as it had been 40 years before. In 1920, more than 80 percent of the Italians, Irish, Russian, and Polish newcomers were urban, as were 75 percent of the immigrants from the United Kingdom.[63] By the census of 1920, just before Congress passed restrictive legislation, 58 percent of the population of American cities of more than 100,000 people was first- or second-generation immigrant.[64]

Although clustered disproportionately in a few northeastern and midwestern industrial centers, immigrants spread out to all the cities that could offer industrial jobs. Large numbers also fanned out to the growing cities of the continental interior, went on to mining camps, or joined railroad construction gangs. About one-third of the arriving Germans settled outside towns and cities altogether. A smaller proportion of Scandinavians moved to cities than any other nationality group because many of them were enticed by agents sent to the Scandinavian countries by railroad corporations, which were trying to implement their racialized settlement policies by trying to find white, Protestant, Northern European buyers for some of the millions of acres of land the companies had secured through government land grants. Enough Scandinavians settled in rural areas in Wisconsin, Minnesota, the Dakotas, and throughout the Midwest that only 55 percent were classified as urban in the census of 1920.

As soon as they arrived, immigrants encountered hostility and sometimes violence. A special enmity was reserved for the Irish because they were raggedly poor and Catholic. Many Irish workers could barely read or claim a skilled occupation. Most of them took menial, temporary, low-paying jobs—moving goods on the waterfront, building streets and roads, and working in slaughterhouses and packinghouses. Because of their poverty, their religion, and their peasant origins, they became etched in the public mind as dangerous, alcoholic, criminal, and dirty. Anti-Catholic and anti-Irish riots broke out on a regular basis. Irish churches, taverns, and neighborhoods were attacked by mobs whipped up by a rhetoric that spoke of "an invasion of venomous reptiles …, long-haired, wild-eyed, bad-smelling, atheistic, reckless foreign wretches."[65] Protestant Yankees were in a position to hire, promote, and fire. Even as late as the 1920s, want ads in Boston frequently added "Protestant" as a qualification for employment.[66] The Irish clustered on the lowest rungs of the social and economic ladder well into the twentieth century.

The Germans encountered far less antipathy because many were wealthy or from middle-class backgrounds. Unlike the Irish, they were escaping war and political turmoil, not poverty and starvation. They brought with them music and literary societies and a commitment to formal education. Although the Germans nominally faced a greater language barrier than did the Irish, the widely used Gaelic and the Irish brogue sounded just as foreign to American ears as did the German language.

The opportunities available to the different ethnic groups varied in relationship to the level of animosity directed toward them. In late-nineteenth-century Boston, "a pecking order favored some groups over others."[67] The Irish and Italians competed for the lowest wages and lowest-skill jobs. Only the few Blacks who lived in cities occupied a lower social position. German and recent British immigrants were generally able to enter middle-class occupations right away, and those who possessed an exceptional education or a special skill might achieve success very quickly. Russian and eastern European Jews, who came in the 1890s and later, placed emphasis on formal education and business. Although anti-Semitism kept them out of corporations and larger business enterprises, they succeeded in carving out a distinct economic niche as job brokers, middlemen, and shopkeepers.

Most of the immigrants crowded into densely packed tenement housing in neighborhoods near the waterfront and factories. In the 1840s and 1850s, real estate speculators and landlords shoehorned them into deteriorated houses, attics and basements, and unused warehouses and factories. Housing was so scarce and rents so high that a lot of property-owning families made money by renting extra space in their own living quarters.[68] Narrow three- and four-story buildings divided into tiny spaces sprang up in alleyways and on back lots. On vacant lots and behind and between buildings, immigrants crowded into sheds and shanties.

The first tenement districts began to spread in New York City as early as the 1850s and made their appearance in other cities soon after. As middle-class families left the city center, it became cost-efficient to raze older structures and replace them with buildings designed to crowd as many people as possible into the available space. The tenement—the name given to any low-cost multiple-family rental building—became a universal symbol of the American urban working-class neighborhood, and by the twentieth century, multistory buildings of any kind came to represent city living. At the same time, the freestanding house evolved into a cultural expression of suburban living. The most notorious tenement structure was the dumbbell—so named because two 28-inch-wide air shafts provided the only light and air to the interior rooms. Based on an award-winning 1879 design, the dumbbell maximized economic return at the expense of ventilation and sanitation. Tenants on the upper floors would pitch their garbage down the shafts, where it was left to rot. On each floor, tenants shared one or two public toilets and a sink, and these were always located next to ventilation shafts, with their foul and fetid air. By 1893, 70 percent of the population of New York City lived in tenements, most of them dumbbells.[69]

Despite the problems caused by overcrowding, the concentration of the immigrant groups into densely packed enclaves was crucially important in easing their assimilation into urban life. Within these densely packed wards, a variety of religious and social institutions sprang up to nurture ethnic traditions and a sense of solidarity and shared identity. The immigrant neighborhoods also facilitated the rise of a style of politics based on ethnic solidarity that began to bring immigrants in the American political system. By the 1880s, urban party machines began to emerge based on the relationship forged between ethnic voters and a new breed of politicians skilled at mobilizing their followers. In Chapter 3, we describe this historic development.

Beyond the tide of immigrants flooding American cities, the Great Migration also strongly impacted the demographics of urban America: Between 1910 and 1970, approximately 6 million African Americans migrated from the rural South to the Northern cities. This was in part due to the developments mentioned earlier in this chapter: the mechanization of agricultural labor, along with a decline in work opportunities, as well as the luring promise of factory jobs in the North. For African Americans, beyond these economic motivations, there were important social factors to consider: People of color had very little opportunity for upward mobility in the deeply segregated Jim Crow South. However, contrary to the common narrative that Black rural-urban migrants were mostly uneducated agricultural workers, early South-to-North migrants typically had higher levels of educational attainment than their peers who chose to remain in the South, and not all of them came from exclusively rural settings: Quite to the contrary, early Black migrants from the South were a relatively socially diverse group, and a significant proportion came from Southern cities.[70] In addition, the myth that Southern Black migrants found "sanctuary" in the North has been decisively debunked: In the Northern cities, they faced discrimination akin to what they had experienced in the South, but without the strong family structures and supportive communities they had been able to rely on in the South. As the numbers of migrants swelled, social infrastructures in northern cities slowly improved with a growing number of NAACP chapters, African American churches and newspapers, and a changing racial balance in the Northern cities.[71] Interestingly, Black Southern migrants often fared better socio-economically than their Northern-born peers. This has been attributed to certain destabilizing social conditions in the North, such as a growing residential segregation, and, along with deindustrialization and urban decline after World War II, declining employment opportunities. In combination, this led to growing un- and under-employment of urban Black populations, who were often concentrated in cities due to residential segregation and increasing white flight to the suburbs.[72] On the other hand, the long-term consequences of the Great Migration were not predominantly negative, as is often insinuated. The swelling Black urban population also led to increased political representation with the election of Black mayors, a growing Black business elite, and a thriving cultural scene.[73] Of course, Black urban populations thrived in spite of the deeply institutionalized structures of racism in the North, but thrive they did nevertheless, and their contributions to American urban culture are central.

The Capacity to Govern

As the industrial cities grew, the capacity of local governments to respond to the needs of their residents came into question. For many urban dwellers, in the latter half of the nineteenth century the conditions of life ranged from squalid to barely tolerable. Epidemics periodically swept through, sometimes killing several hundred people in a summer. Streets turned to seas of mud in winter and to dust bowls in summer, and in every season they were littered with refuse and piles of steaming horse manure. A Swedish novelist commented that Chicago in 1850 (when it still had only 30,000 people) was "one of the most miserable and ugly cities," where people had come "to trade, to make money, and not to live."[74]

The residents of the cities complained about the conditions of daily life, but no one was sure what municipal governments should do about the situation. In the American political tradition, there was an abiding suspicion of government; most people seemed more concerned about its potential dangers than about the ways in which it might be put to positive use. This suspicion was reinforced by a deeply rooted culture of privatism—the idea that progress comes through individual rather than through collective endeavors. Although urban leaders were able to persuade their fellow citizens that local government should support schemes promoting the local economy, it was much more difficult to talk them into taxing themselves to support the services that might improve the local quality of life.

Even in the large cities full-time, paid, uniformed police forces were rare until the mid-nineteenth century. The law was generally enforced by part-time or volunteer night watches and constables. Volunteer fire gangs answered the fire alarm. Individual property owners swept the streets and collected refuse. Even as population growth made city life increasingly unpleasant, city residents were reluctant to acknowledge that municipal government might do better than the community's own efforts. Against this background, it is a puzzling fact that municipal governments vastly increased their responsibilities in the latter half of the nineteenth century. In New York City, for instance, per capita city expenditures increased from $6.53 in 1850 to $27.3 in 1900.[75] During this half-century, cities spent more money and employed more people than either the state governments or the national government. When governmental spending was cataloged for the first time in the federal census of governments in 1902, local governments accounted for half of all governmental expenditures in the United States.[76]

Despite a national culture that preferred minimal government, over the course of a century municipal responsibilities vastly increased. Three major reasons can be offered to explain this unexpected outcome. First, new services were provided in cases when urban residents of all classes felt threatened by imminent catastrophe or crisis. Second, local boosters assumed the lead in organizing public services when the absence or inadequacy of these services threatened the economic vitality of the city. And third, by the late nineteenth century, a growing middle class became intolerant of urban conditions that had previously been considered unpleasant but normal or inevitable.

In the colonial period and for many years after, urban services were minimal. Essential as they were to the basic health of urban citizens, for instance, water systems were chronically inadequate. In the early nineteenth century, most city residents got their water from wells, and these were often contaminated by waste. As a result, outbreaks of contagious diseases occurred with disturbing regularity. In the summer of 1793, 10 percent of Philadelphia's population died from yellow fever.[77] The city's economy came to a standstill, and a third of the population and virtually all wealthy families fled for the summer months. Outbreaks of yellow fever or cholera occurred in Philadelphia, Baltimore, and New Haven (Connecticut) in 1793; in New York City, Baltimore, and Norfolk (Virginia) in 1795; and in Newburyport (Massachusetts), Boston, and Charleston (South Carolina) the next year.[78] Nearly a dozen cities were hit in 1797; three-fourths of Philadelphia's population fled and 4,000 people died (which amounted to about 7 percent of the population).[79]

Such catastrophes prompted cities to invest in waterworks and drain swamps and to regulate the keeping of animals and the dumping of refuse. Philadelphia was goaded by its epidemics to construct the first municipal waterworks in the nation's history. Begun in 1799 and operational in some parts of the city by 1801, it piped water from the upper Schuylkill River. Over time, Philadelphia's system was constantly improved by the merchant elites who ran the Watering Committee. By the 1840s, however, these elites began to withdraw from political activities, partly because competition for political office from a new generation of public leaders had become more intense. Without their guiding hand on the committee, the water supply system became less and less adequate.[80] Only with great reluctance did the city government assume the responsibilities of an increasingly inept Watering Committee.

Despite the manifest need, municipal services tended to lag behind need because they were generally provided only in response to a crisis: "municipal authorities, loath to increase taxes, usually shouldered new responsibilities only at the prod of grim necessity."[81] Devastating outbreaks of yellow fever, typhoid, and cholera periodically made their rounds, especially in the cities such as New Orleans and Memphis that lagged furthest behind in providing uncontaminated water supplies. Several urban water systems were built in the 1850s, and by the Civil War 70 towns were served by waterworks. For the most part these were privately owned and operated by the 80 private companies that had sprung up for this purpose.[82] The systems were partial and primitive. Except in the wealthy neighborhoods where water was piped into homes, most people had to fetch the water from street hydrants and hand pumps. As late as 1860, only about one-tenth of Boston's residents had access to a bathtub, and only 5 percent of the homes had indoor water closets.[83]

Urban water supplies were generally polluted by human and animal waste. In most cities, sewage was collected in huge community cesspools, which had to be dug out frequently. Even when sewer pipes carried waste away from the city, the main result was merely to send the polluted water downstream. Serious typhoid epidemics broke out in the cities along the Merrimac River in Massachusetts in the 1880s because residents were drinking water that carried the sewage of cities located upstream. Because of Boston's habit of dumping wastes directly into its harbor, by 1877 Boston Harbor had become "one vast cesspool."[84] Until the 1920s, crowded residential districts were dotted with outdoor privies, and water, bearing a burden of horse manure and other refuse, flowed in open gutters along the streets. The sources of contamination were so numerous that only those cities that piped their water from watersheds far away from urban settlement were able to avoid a contaminated water supply.

Ultimately, the water supply problem could be solved only through the development of adequate technology. Even Philadelphia's relatively sophisticated system delivered its water with only the heaviest silt filtered out.[85] Pumps frequently failed; in the winter, pipes froze. People found dirt, insects, and even small fish gushing from the taps. During the first decade of the twentieth century, when modern filtration techniques were developed, death rates in New York, Boston, Philadelphia, and New Orleans fell by one-fifth.[86]

Epidemics prompted cities to build sewers to carry the waste away from heavily populated neighborhoods. In 1823, Boston began installing the nation's first sanitary sewers. Other large cities followed suit, but slowly. By 1857, New York City, which by then had a population of nearly a million people, had a system of sewers under only one-fourth of its streets, and most of these were storm water rather than sanitary sewers.[87] Taxpayers resisted the high cost of laying underground pipes and installing costly pumps. Although most of the big cities had constructed sewers by the 1870s, these were usually paid for by the property owners who subscribed, leaving vast areas—always the neighborhoods inhabited by the poor—without service.

A perceived crisis of a different sort forced cities to begin financing and organizing professional police forces. As cities grew in size and complexity, rising levels of violence, crime, and disorder threatened to disrupt the lives of every urban resident. The unceasing influx of immigrants provoked ethnic conflict, pushed up crime rates, and broke apart the bonds of community. In the 1830s and 1840s, rioting directed against Irish immigrants and free Blacks broke out regularly in Philadelphia. In frontier cities, the connection between rapid population growth and social instability was painfully obvious. A constant stream of river men, wagon drivers, and traders moved into and out of bustling cities like San Francisco, St. Louis, and New Orleans. Saloons proliferated; gambling and prostitution flourished. During the gold rush years of the 1850s, violent crime became such a fact of everyday life in San Francisco that merchants funded vigilante committees to keep order. Before long, however, the vigilantes organized their own crime rings and became almost as dangerous as the criminals they were supposed to catch.[88]

In 1845, Boston became the first city in the United States to provide uniforms for its officers. The same year, when its population numbered more than 400,000, New York finally replaced its rag-tag army of part-time police with a full-time force. Even then, though, the police continued to go about their jobs in street clothes, completely untrained and without supervision.[89] Eight years later, the city's police finally received uniforms and some modest training. Until the late 1830s, Philadelphia relied on a mix of part-time posses, militia, and night watches, and none of them wore uniforms.[90]

New York's police forces were in constant turmoil for many years. There was resistance to the idea of creating a professional police force because the two political parties that contended for power in the city regarded the police as an important source of patronage jobs. Following the 1857 mayoral election, the new mayor fired everyone on the force and installed officers who were loyal to him. The former officers refused to quit their jobs, and so for several months the city was patrolled by two competing police forces. In June of that year, a full-scale riot broke out between the two groups.[91] Similar confusion repeated itself in 1868, when the newly elected Democratic governor removed all of the city's police commissioners because they were Republicans. The commissioners refused to vacate their offices. Finally, the state legislature resolved the dispute by assuming the authority to appoint them.

Episodes like this illustrate why it took so long for the cities to build modern, fully professionalized police forces. Many people feared that, as a quasi-military organization, the police might be used by one political faction against another. This fear was well founded. Police departments were deeply affected by ethnic and racial prejudices and also by political loyalties. Such problems persist right up to the present day. A presidential commission investigating the urban riots of the 1960s found that police conduct was the most common provocation causing the rioting.[92] In the nineteenth century and still today, police officers are granted a great deal of discretion, and often enough they do not apply the law dispassionately.

The Black Lives Matter Protests of the pandemic summer of 2020, which followed the gruesome murder of George Floyd by Minneapolis police officer Derek Chauvin—one of many Black people killed by police without justifiable cause, sparked a renewed debate on police violence and alternative ways of policing communities. As can be seen in Table 2.4, in the years between 2015 and 2020, the number of Black Americans killed by police varies between 258 in 2015 and 224 in 2017—a horrifying toll, and more than half the number of white people, which is quite astonishing given the fact that African Americans only make up 13.4 percent of the U.S. population, compared to whites, who represent 76.3 percent of Americans. Put differently, when accounting for the percentage they make up among the total U.S. population, Black Americans

TABLE 2.4 Victims of Police Shootings by Race/Ethnicity

Year	Black	White	Hispanic	Total
Percentage of Total U.S. Population	13.4	76.3	18.5	100
2015	258 (26 percent)	503 (50.7 percent)	172 (17.3 percent)	993 (100 percent)
2016	237 (24.7 percent)	466 (48.5 percent)	162 (16.9 percent)	960 (100 percent)
2017	224 (22.7 percent)	460 (47.7 percent)	181 (18.4 percent)	986 (100 percent)
2018	232 (23.4 percent)	461 (46.6 percent)	167 (16.9 percent)	990 (100 percent)
2019	251 (25.1 percent)	424 (42.4 percent)	168 (16.8 percent)	999 (100 percent)
2020	243 (23.8 percent)	458 (44.8 percent)	171 (16.7 percent)	1021 (100 percent)

Sources: *United States Census Bureau*: Quick Facts: Population Estimates, July 1, 2019. Accessed online: https://www.census.gov/quickfacts/fact/table/US/PST045219; *The Washington Post*: "Fatal Force: 953 People Have Been Shot and Killed by Police in the Past Year" (May 29, 2021). Accessed online: https://www.washingtonpost.com/graphics/investigations/police-shootings-database/.

are getting shot by police at more than twice the rate (36 per one million) of white Americans (15 per one million).[93]

In the wake of this renewed debate on policing across the United States, calls for "defunding" police departments have gained traction in many places. This can mean different things, and, in the vast majority of cases, it does not mean taking all the money away from police. For instance, activists have criticized overtime policing and money spent on military-grade equipment for local police officers as unnecessary and overtly aggressive. Instead, they have argued that that money should be reallocated to mental health programs, housing, and education, in order to bring about long-term, systemic changes in poverty, social upward mobility, and health outcomes.[94] The New York City Police Department's budget, for example, hovers around $6 billion per fiscal year, which amounts to around 6 percent of the City's total budget.[95] As in proposals from other activist groups across the country, these cuts are intended to cut overtime and surveillance technology and cap the number of uniformed officers.[96] In addition, the cuts target abusive officers, who should be fired more regularly, proposes cuts to modified duty, and deducting settlement payouts from the operating budget itself.[97] The proposal further suggests a freeze on new hires, canceling the cadet training programs, and reducing the number of uniformed officers by 5 percent.[98] Finally, it proposes the removal of uniformed officers from schools, public transit, and homeless and mental health programs.[99] Other proposals in cities across the country address policing tactics, such as no-knock warrants, or military-style raids, among other things, as well as proposing less aggressive approaches to policing protests.[100] The present-day debate on policing is ongoing, and it remains to be seen what it will actually accomplish. Policing, just like any other public service, must serve to support and protect communities and earn their trust. When public service turns against its own communities, it is failing its intended mission. While not all proposals to defund or disband police departments may provide realistic alternatives, many of them do. A police force that uses military-grade equipment against its own citizens seems out of touch with democratic norms. The disproportionate use of force by police against people of color has been shamefully ignored for decades. While a conversation is a good start, it is time to fundamentally rethink the meaning of policing in American communities and the country as a whole.

In the early industrial cities, political leaders held ambitious aspirations for their cities and for themselves. Chronic problems such as crime, poor sanitation, and impassable streets not only diminished the quality of life for urban residents but these problems also threatened local economic vitality. Faced with this reality, civic elites and business leaders preferred to support public services rather than allow their city to slip into decline.

Once provided, urban services became institutionalized; they quickly seemed normal and routine; there could be no going back to a time when they were not available. This was especially true for services such as water systems and fire departments that required the construction of permanent infrastructure and investment in expensive equipment. In this way, the responsibilities of city governments grew inexorably, step by step. In the early nineteenth century, when confronted with a problem, the cities' aristocratic and merchant class would typically organize a committee to decide what to do. Over time, such informal arrangements gave way to services provided by full-time paid employees. Again, the evolution of Philadelphia's waterworks is instructive. At first, the Watering Committee raised money through private donations and individual subscriptions to the water service. Prominent merchants led the committee until 1837.[101] But over the next few decades, the system expanded until it provided water to all citizens, and it became necessary to impose taxes to support it.

Milwaukee's volunteer fire department gave way to paid professionals in the 1850s when new steam pumps proved too complicated for volunteers to maintain and operate.[102] In the same decade, public works employees began to maintain the streets when it became too difficult to find volunteers for the task. Trained employees were hired to run the sewer system when the city council provided funds to expand it to cover most of the city. When the Milwaukee city council required vaccinations for smallpox, local health services became too complex for volunteers. In this way, the day-to-day administration of municipal services was gradually put in the hands of paid employees. "Politics became a full-time business and professionals moved in to make careers of public office."[103]

In the last third of the nineteenth century, a growing middle class began to demand improved water and sewer systems,[104] and by the 1890s popular pressure was mobilized to demand better services of all kinds. From the 1850s to the 1870s, assistance to railroads had been the largest single cause of municipal debt. In striking contrast, during the last 30 years of the century, the cities went into debt mainly to finance the expansion of new services and to build infrastructure.[105] Because of rising standards of public health, new technologies, even when very expensive, were quickly adopted. The construction of integrated sewerage systems provides an instructive example. Systems of separate sanitary and storm sewers were not completed in most cities until very late in the nineteenth century. Laying sewer pipe was a huge public works project for any city. Nevertheless, the number of miles of sewer pipe increased fourfold from 1890 to 1909.[106]

By the turn of the century, American cities, in general, provided more and better services than did their European counterparts, with more miles of sewer and water mains, more miles of paved streets, more street lamps, better mass transportation, and more fire departments with better equipment.[107] Urban residents in the United States used more than twice as much water per capita as did their counterparts in England and many times more than city dwellers in Germany,[108] probably because flush toilets and bathtubs were far more widespread in American cities.[109] The cities also vastly expanded public health efforts. Using the new science of bacteriology, health inspectors examined children in schools, checked buildings for ventilation and faulty plumbing, and inspected food and milk.[110] Such public health measures, when combined with the completion of integrated sewer systems and installation of new water filtration technology, dramatically reduced typhoid mortality rates.[111] Overall death rates fell sharply in the big cities, by 20 percent or more in New York, Chicago, Cleveland, Buffalo, and other cities in the 1890s,[112] and just as sharply again after the turn of the twentieth century.[113]

The late nineteenth century was the golden age for American city building. The massive investment in physical infrastructure placed city governments at the cutting edge of technology, resulting in such engineering marvels as the Brooklyn Bridge and New York's Croton aqueduct system, with its thousands of miles of pipes and reservoirs. The Parks Movement and the City Beautiful Movement, both supported by urban elites and the middle class, swept the nation, resulting in urban amenities such as parks, ponds, formal gardens, bandstands, ball fields, broad tree-lined avenues, and ornate public buildings. Urban residents came to expect a level of municipal services that would have been inconceivable in an earlier time. The squalor of the nineteenth-century industrial city began to yield to the relative safety, cleanliness, and health of the twentieth-century metropolis.

Municipal services have continued to evolve over the past century. Cities today provide a remarkable array of services. They build and maintain a public infrastructure—roads, bridges, sewer lines, sewage treatment plants, water mains, parks, zoos, hospitals, and sometimes even universities. They provide police and fire protection. They collect garbage (or pay someone who does). They run public health services that inspect restaurants, vaccinate children, and test for the HIV (AIDS) virus. Through city zoning ordinances, they influence the location of homes, factories, office buildings, restaurants, and parking lots. Through local building codes, they regulate such matters as plumbing, wiring, building materials, the height of structures, and architectural styles. Cities poison rats and sometimes try to scare away pigeons. These public undertakings, and many more, are essential to the safety and well-being of people living in urban environments. Without them, urban life would quickly become not only dangerous but intolerable.

The Limited Powers of Cities

The ability of American cities to adapt to changing circumstances is a remarkable story, all the more so because they were mostly left on their own to devise solutions to the problems that faced them. The national government was distant and indifferent: Only in the twentieth century would the federal government establish any relationship to the cities. State legislatures were alternately hostile and indifferent. For the most part, the legislatures—made up as they were by part-time politicians who met for a few weeks or months every other year— paid little attention. More than anything else, rural legislators wanted to keep urban politicians and the constituencies that supported them from intruding into their domain. The independence of cities led Alexis de Tocqueville, in his classic work *Democracy in America* (1835), to emphasize that local governments in the United States were sovereign. He compared them to independent nations: "Municipal independence is … a natural consequence of the principle of the sovereignty of the people in the United States: all the American republics recognize it more or less."[114] But his assessment was not quite accurate. The autonomy of cities owed more to an attitude of indifference to how they governed themselves than to their legal status. Although state legislatures clearly possessed the legal authority to control the cities within their boundaries in almost every detail, they exercised that right only sometimes, although when they did they could be unpredictable and capricious. Cities might seem to be independent, but this was true only because state legislatures generally lacked the time and interest to notice what they were up to.

Advocates for the right of cities to govern themselves without outside interference pleaded their cause in articles, books, and court rulings.[115] Mostly it was to no avail; the courts consistently upheld the powers of the states to define the powers and obligations of local governments. In 1819, in the *Dartmouth College* case, the U.S. Supreme Court held that cities were created by the states and their charters could therefore be amended or rescinded at will. (By contrast, private corporations were protected from interference by the constitutional provision against "impairing the obligation of contract."[116]) A second definitive case was handed down in 1868, when the chief justice of the Iowa Supreme Court, John F. Dillon, declared that states could rightfully exert total control over their cities, with no restrictions whatsoever:

> Municipal corporations owe their origin to, and derive their powers and rights wholly from, the legislature. It breathes into them the breath of life without which they cannot exist. As it creates so it may destroy …. Unless there is some constitutional limitation on the right, the legislature might, by a single act, if we can suppose it capable of so great a folly and so great a wrong, sweep from existence all of the municipal corporations of the state, and the corporations could not prevent it …. They are, so to phrase it, the mere tenants at will of the legislature.[117]

Judge Dillon was motivated by the fact that cities had been active in providing subsidies to railroads, and he reasoned that if they could help private corporations so directly, they could regulate them as well. Dillon's missionary zeal was also fired by a conviction that dangerous riffraff governed the cities: "men the best fitted by their intelligence, business experience, capacity and moral character, for local governors and counselors are not always, it is feared—it might be added, are not generally—chosen."[118] His solution was that state governments and courts, like stern parents, should closely supervise their cities and strictly limit their privileges. In 1872, Dillon published his *Treatise on the Law of Municipal Corporations*. Originally 800 pages long, by the time the fifth edition was published in 1911, it had grown to five thick volumes.[119] By then, Dillon's work had become the bible on municipal law. By 1924, William Munro, the author of a leading textbook, *The Government of American Cities*, wrote that Dillon's rule was "so well recognized that it is not nowadays open to question."[120]

Motivated by a similar distrust of cities—or, rather, of immigrant voters—state legislators took steps to ensure that no matter how fast and big cities might grow, their representatives to the statehouse would never be able to gain a majority of seats in state legislatures. Most rural legislators would probably have agreed with the delegate to the New York State constitutional convention of 1894 who said, "the average citizen in the rural district is superior in intelligence, superior in morality, superior in self-government to the average citizen of the great cities."[121] This attitude reflected a long-standing animosity to cities and everything urban. Decades earlier, Maine's constitutional convention of 1819 had established a ceiling on the number of representatives who could serve towns in the state legislature. In 1845, the Louisiana legislature limited New Orleans to 12.5 percent of the state's senators and 10 percent of the state's assemblymen. (The population of New Orleans accounted for 20 percent of the state's total.[122]) By the end of the century, every state had ensured that no matter how large its cities became, representatives from rural legislative districts would continue to hold a commanding voting majority in state legislatures.

By then, more people lived in the cities of some states than outside them. If their influence in state legislatures had grown in step with their populations, cities would have been able to secure state financial support for the expansion of city services. In fact, however, cities received practically no help at all. If urban voters had managed to exert more influence in state politics and in state governments, they also could have asserted a political voice in national affairs. Rural elites firmly controlled the state party caucuses that nominated governors, members of Congress, senators, and presidents, and therefore ethnic minorities and other urban voters had no effective means of influencing governmental policies at the state or national levels. The underrepresentation of the cities resulted in indifference to their problems in state legislatures, governors' offices, Congress, and the White House. Traffic congestion, slum housing, orphaned children, contagious diseases, poverty—none of these problems interested rural and small-town legislators or the members of Congress and presidents beholden to state party leaders who answered to rural constituents.

Underrepresentation of cities throughout the federal system exerted profound and long-lasting consequences, for it allowed governmental leaders at all levels to wash their hands of the devastating effects of industrialization and urbanization. In the late nineteenth century, powerful populist movements pushed for the recognition of the right of labor unions to organize. In the first 20 years of the twentieth century, reformers lobbied state legislatures to adopt universal health insurance, workers' compensation, and relief programs for widows, children, and the elderly. A groundswell of opposition to child labor swept the country; nevertheless, the federal government did not adopt child labor legislation until 1916; even then it was struck down by the Supreme Court two years later.[123] These and other reforms that would have benefited cities and their residents were delayed until the New Deal of the 1930s. Many other policies, such as federal aid to education, health care for the aged and poor (Medicare and Medicaid), federal aid to the cities, and a variety of social programs, would surely have been adopted long before the 1960s if the cities had been represented in state and national politics in proportion to their share of the national population.

The federal courts finally moved against legislative malapportionment in the 1960s, more than 40 years after the 1920 census showed that a majority of Americans lived in urban places. In *Baker v. Carr* (1962), a group of Knoxville residents challenged the fact that the Tennessee legislature had not been reapportioned since 1901.[124] Their lawyers argued that citizens living in urban areas were being deprived of "equal protection of the law," as guaranteed by the

Fourteenth Amendment to the U.S. Constitution. The important court decision that decided this case, as well as others, came on June 15, 1964, when the U.S. Supreme Court, in *Reynolds v. Sims,* ruled that state legislative apportionments must follow a "one man, one vote" principle.[125] Within a few years, for the first time in the nation's history, state legislative and congressional districts were apportioned to give city residents equal representation.

By the time the courts imposed the one-man, one-vote remedy, it was too late to be much of much consequence. By the 1960s the older industrial cities were rapidly losing population, and the suburbs and the Sunbelt were booming. This demographic transformation brought about a historical shift in the balance of national power. If cities had gained equal representation in state legislatures and in Congress decades earlier, urban voters might have been able to secure from the federal government as well as from many states funding for such local priorities as mass transit, public housing, urban revitalization, and public health programs. But the American political system had been biased against the urban electorate for a reason: The people who lived in the cities of America had long been regarded as "strangers in the land."[126] In light of such deeply rooted attitudes, the fact that American cities responded to their problems as well as they did must be regarded as a remarkable success.

Endnotes

1   Robert A. Beauregard, *Voices of Decline: The Postwar Fate of U.S. Cities* (New York: Blackwell, 1993).

2   London proper had 957,000, but the greater London area had 1,117,000 people.

3   Brian R. Mitchell, *European Historical Statistics, 1750–1970* (New York: Columbia University Press, 1975), p. 76.

4   Defined as settlements with a population of at least 5,000.

5   Eric Lampard, "Historical Aspects of Urbanization," in *The Study of Urbanization,* ed. Philip M. Hauser and Leo F. Schnore (New York: Wiley, 1965), p. 523.

6   "The Inevitability of City Growth," reprinted from *Atlantic Monthly,* April 1985, in *City Life, 1865–1900: Views of Urban America,* ed. Ann Cook, Marilyn Gittell, and Herb Mack (New York: Praeger, 1973), p. 17.

7   Eric H. Monkkonen, *America Becomes Urban: The Development of U.S. Cities and Towns, 1780–1980* (Berkeley: University of California Press, 1988), p. 78.

8   D. Philip Locklin, *Economics of Transportation,* 7th ed. (Homewood, IL: Irwin, 1972).

9   Allan R. Pred, *The Spatial Dynamics of Urban–Industrial Growth, 1800–1914* (Cambridge, MA: MIT Press, 1966), p. 103.

10   David M. Gordon, "Class Struggle and the Stages of American Urban Development," in *The Rise of the Sunbelt Cities,* ed. David C. Perry and Alfred J. Watkins (Beverly Hills, CA: Sage, 1977), p. 64.

11   George Rogers Taylor, *The Transportation Revolution, 1815–1860* (New York: Holt, Rinehart & Winston, 1951), p. 52.

12 Carter Goodrich, *Government Promotion of American Canals and Railroads, 1800–1890* (New York: Columbia University Press, 1960), pp. 266–267.

13 Richard C. Wade, *The Urban Frontier: Pioneer Life in Early Pittsburgh, Cincinnati, Lexington, Louisville, and St. Louis* (Chicago: University of Chicago Press, 1959), p. 70.

14 U.S. Department of Commerce, *Historical Statistics of the United States, Colonial Times to 1970*, pt. 2 (Washington, D.C.: U.S. Government Printing Office, 1975), pp. 728, 731.

15 Alfred D. Chandler, *The Railroads: The Nation's First Big Business* (New York: Harcourt Brace Jovanovich, 1965).

16 Paul Kantor, *The Dependent City Revisited: The Political Economy of Urban Development and Social Policy* (Boulder, CO: Westview, 1995), p. 24.

17 Carter Goodrich, "The Revulsion against Internal Improvements," *Journal of Economic History* 10, no. 2 (November 1950): 145–169.

18 David Chalmers, *Neither Socialism nor Monopoly* (Philadelphia: Lippincott, 1976), p. 4.

19 Jason E. Pierce, *Making the White Man's West. Whiteness and the Creation of the American West* (Boulder, CO: The University Press of Colorado, 2016), p. 152.

20 Ibid., pp. 154–155.

21 Blake McKelvey, *American Urbanization: A Comparative History* (Glenview, IL: Scott Foresman, 1973), pp. 25–26.

22 Ibid.

23 Paul Kantor with Stephen David, *The Dependent City: The Changing Political Economy of Urban America* (Glenview, IL: Scott Foresman, 1987), pp. 499–500.

24 Goodrich, *Government Promotion*, p. 241. Goodrich estimates that until 1860, local governments provided 29 percent of total public subsidies (p. 268). The proportion of local contributions increased significantly after the Civil War. In his study of New York from 1826 to 1875, Harry Pierce concludes that three-quarters of the subsidy came from local governments and one-quarter from the state. See Harry H. Pierce, *The Railroads of New York: A Study of Government Aid, 1826–1875* (Cambridge, MA: Harvard University Press, 1953).

25 Pierce, *The Railroads of New York*.

26 In 1849, for example, the voters of Cleveland approved a $100,000 subscription to stock in the Cleveland and Pittsburgh Railroad by a vote of 1,157 to 27. Despite the enthusiasm of the voters, the stock never paid any dividends and eventually sold at far below par. Charles C. Williamson, *The Finances of Cleveland* (New York: Columbia University Press, 1907), pp. 218–220.

27 Goodrich, *Government Promotion*, p. 42.

28 Ibid., p. 272. One study gave the following figures for New York: "Only 52 of the 297 municipalities that bought stock in a railroad disposed of their securities at par or better, 162 held stock with no market value" (Pierce, *The Railroads of New York*), p. 273.

29 A.M. Hillhouse, *Municipal Bonds: A Century of Experience* (Upper Saddle River, NJ: Prentice Hall, 1936), p. 39.

30 Goodrich, *Government Promotion*, pp. 268–271. Repudiation goes beyond the default, which is simply a failure to pay the debt on time. Repudiation declares an unwillingness to ever repay the debt.

31 Alberta M. Sbragia, *Debt Wish: Entrepreneurial Cities, U.S. Federalism and Economic Development* (Pittsburgh, PA: University of Pittsburgh Press, 1996), p. 91.

32 Goodrich, "Revulsion against Internal Improvements"; see also Sbragia, *Debt Wish*, Chapter 5.

33 Lawrence Goodwyn, *The Populist Movement* (New York: Oxford University Press, 1978).

34 Philip Foner, *History of the Labor Movement in the United States* (New York: International, 1975), pp. 13–18.

35 Richard Lloyd, "Urbanization and the Southern United States," *Annual Review of Sociology* 38 (2012): 483–506.

36 Howard P. Chudacoff, *The Evolution of American Urban Society* (Upper Saddle River, NJ: Prentice Hall, 1975), p. 26.

37 Sam Bass Warner Jr., *The Private City: Philadelphia in Three Periods of Its Growth* (Philadelphia, PA: University of Pennsylvania Press, 1968), p. 21.

38 Kantor, *The Dependent City*, p. 22.

39 Ibid., p. 33.

40 Pred, *The Spatial Dynamics*, p. 16.

41 Ibid., p. 170.

42 Ibid., pp. 68–69.

43 The skyscraper boom on Fifth Avenue between 1900 and 1915 was largely fueled by the desire of rich individuals to outdo one another in pretentious architecture. See Seymour I. Toll, *Zoned American* (New York: Grossman, 1969), Chapter 2.

44 Chartered by the states, limited-risk corporations allowed the selling of shares to investors whose liability in case of corporate failure was limited to their direct investment. In partnerships, the partners were liable for all debts incurred by the company, and these could easily exceed the partners' own assets. The corporate form of business organization thus made it easier to raise capital, for investors risked less than in other forms of business investment.

45 U.S. Department of the Interior, Census Office, *Census Reports of 1900*, vol. 7, *Manufacturers*, pt. 1: "United States by Industries" (Washington, D.C.: U.S. Government Printing Office, 1902), pp. 503–509.

46 William Miller, "American Historians and the Business Elite," *Journal of Economic History* 9, no. 2, (1949): 184–208.

47 Kenneth Jackson, *Crabgrass Frontier: The Suburbanization of the United States* (New York: Oxford University Press, 1985), p. 35.

48 George Rogers Taylor, "Building an Intra-Urban Transportation System," in *The Urbanization of America: An Historical Anthology*, ed. Allen M. Wakstein (Boston, MA: Houghton Mifflin, 1970), p. 137.

49 Glen E. Holt, "The Changing Perception of Urban Pathology: An Essay on the Development of Mass Transit in the United States," in *Cities in American History*, ed. Kenneth T. Jackson and Stanley K. Schultz (New York: Knopf, 1972), p. 327.

50 Taylor, "Building an Intra-Urban Transportation System," p. 139.

51 C.G. Kennedy, "Commuter Services in the Boston Area, 1835–1860," *Business History Review* 26, no. 2, (1962): 277–287.

52 Jackson, *Crabgrass Frontier*, p. 41.

53 David Ward, *Cities and Immigrants: A Geography of Change in Nineteenth-Century America* (New York: Oxford University Press, 1971), p. 4.

54 Jackson, *Crabgrass Frontier*, p. 108.

55 Ibid.

56 Gary A. Tobin, "Suburbanization and the Development of Motor Transportation: Transportation and Technology and the Suburbanization Process," in *The Changing Face of the Suburbs,* ed. Barry Schwartz (Chicago, IL: University of Chicago Press, 1975), p. 99.

57 "The Smell of Cincinnati," *Enquirer* (Richmond, VA), November 15, 1874, in *City Life,* ed. Cook, Gittell, and Mack, p. 143.

58 Ward, *Cities and Immigrants,* Chapter 3.

59 Blake McKelvey, *The Urbanization of America, 1860–1915* (New Brunswick, NJ: Rutgers University Press, 1963), p. 54.

60 For an excellent history of America's downtowns, see Robert M. Fogelson, *Downtown: Its Rise and Fall, 1880–1950* (New Haven, CT: Yale University Press, 2001).

61 Samuel P. Hays, *The Response to Industrialism, 1885–1914* (Chicago, IL: University of Chicago Press, 1957), p. 14.

62 Thomas Monroe Pitkin, *Keepers of the Gate: A History of Ellis Island* (New York: New York University Press, 1975), p. ix.

63 Ward, *Cities and Immigrants,* p. 56.

64 Ibid., p. 52.

65 John Higham, *Strangers in the Land: Patterns of American Nativism, 1860–1925* (New Brunswick, NJ: Rutgers University Press, 1955), pp. 54–55.

66 Stephen Thernstrom, *The Other Bostonians: Poverty and Progress in the American Metropolis, 1880–1970* (Cambridge, MA: Harvard University Press, 1973), p. 160.

67 Ibid.

68 Charles N. Glaab and A. Theodore Brown, *A History of Urban America* (New York: Macmillan, 1967), p. 160.

69 Gwendolyn Wright, *Building the American Dream: A Social History of Housing in America* (Cambridge, MA: MIT Press, 1983), p. 123. Dumbbell waiters are rope-pulley devices used to move small items up and down a shaft in multistory buildings.

70 Stewart E. Tolnay, "The African American 'Great Migration' and Beyond," *Annual Review of Sociology* 29 (2003): pp. 209–232.

71 Ibid.

72 Ibid., p. 222.

73 Ibid., p. 223.

74 Glaab and Brown, *A History of Urban America,* p. 86.

75 Ibid., p. 180.

76 Terrence J. MacDonald and Sally K. Ward, eds., *The Politics of Urban Fiscal Policy* (Beverly Hills, CA: Sage, 1984), p. 14.

77 Nelson M. Blake, *Water for the Cities: A History of the Urban Water Supply Problem in the United States* (Syracuse, NY: Syracuse University Press, 1956), p. 6.

78 Ibid., pp. 102–103.

79 Ibid., p. 6.

80 Warner, *The Private City,* pp. 107–109.

81 Arthur N. Schlesinger, "A Panoramic View: The City in American Life," in *The City in American Life,* ed. Paul Kramer and Fredrick L. Holborn (New York: Capricorn Books, 1970), p. 23.

82 McKelvey, *The Urbanization of America,* p. 13.

83 Edgar W. Martin, *The Standard of Living in 1860* (Chicago, IL: University of Chicago Press, 1942), pp. 44–47, 89–112.

84 McKelvey, *The Urbanization of America,* p. 90.

85 Ibid., p. 13.

86 Ibid., p. 90.

87 McKelvey, *American Urbanization,* p. 44.

88 Fred M. Wirt, *Power in the City* (Berkeley: University of California Press, 1974), p. 110.

89 James F. Richardson, "To Control the City: The New York Police in Historical Perspective," in *Cities in American History,* ed. Kenneth T. Jackson and Stanley K. Schultz (New York: Knopf, 1972), pp. 272–289.

90 Warner, *The Private City,* Chapter 7.

91 Richardson, "To Control the City," p. 278.

92 *Report of the National Advisory Commission on Civil Disorders* (New York: Bantam Books, 1968).

93 *The Washington Post,* "Fatal Force: 953 people have been shot and killed by police in the past year" (May 29, 2021). Accessed online: https://www.washingtonpost.com/graphics/investigations/police-shootings-database/

94 Dionne Searcey, "What Would Efforts to Defund or Disband Police Departments Really Mean?" *The New York Times* (December 10, 2020). Accessed online: https://www.nytimes.com/2020/06/08/us/what-does-defund-police-mean.html

95 Ella Koeze and Denise Lu, "The N.Y.P.D. Spends $6 Billion a Year. Proposals to Defund It Want to Cut $1 Billion," *The New York Times* (June 20, 2020). Accessed online: https://www.nytimes.com/interactive/2020/06/20/nyregion/defund-police-nypd-budget.html

96 Ibid.

97 Ibid.

98 Ibid.

99 Ibid.

100 Dionne Searcey, "What Would Efforts to Defund or Disband Police Departments Really Mean?" *The New York Times* (December 10, 2020). Accessed online: https://www.nytimes.com/2020/06/08/us/what-does-defund-police-mean.html

101 Warner, *The Private City.*

102 Bayrd Still, *Milwaukee: The History of a City* (Madison: State Historical Society of Wisconsin, 1984), Chapter 10.

103 Warner, *The Private City,* p. 86.

104 Sbragia, *Debt Wish,* p. 76.

105 Ibid.

106 Ibid.

107 Jon Teaford, *The Unheralded Triumph: City Government in America, 1870–1900* (Baltimore, MD: Johns Hopkins University Press, 1984), Chapter 8.

108 Ibid., p. 222.

109 Ibid., p. 221.

110 Ibid., p. 247.

111 Stanley K. Schultz, *Constructing Urban Culture: American Cities and City Planning, 1800–1920* (Philadelphia, PA: Temple University Press, 1989), p. 174.

112 Ibid., p. 246.

113 McKelvey, *The Urbanization of America,* p. 90.

114 Alexis de Tocqueville, *Democracy in America,* vol. 1 (New York: Shocken Books, 1961), p. 60.

115 For citations, see Gerald Frug, "The City as a Legal Concept," *Harvard Law Review* 93, no. 6 (April 1980): 1113–1117.

116 See *Dartmouth College v. Woodward,* 4 Wheat. 518 (1819).

117 *City of Clinton v. Cedar Rapids and Missouri River Railroad Co.,* 24 Iowa 455–475 (1868).

118 Schultz, *Constructing Urban Culture,* p. 73.

119 Ibid., p. 69.

120 William Munro, *The Government of the American Cities,* 3rd ed. (New York: Macmillan, 1924), p. 53.

121 Mark I. Gelfand, *A Nation of Cities: The Federal Government and Urban America, 1933–1965* (New York: Oxford University Press, 1975), p. 11.

122 Ibid.

123 *Hammer v. Dagenhart et al.,* 247 U.S. 251 (1918).

124 *Baker v. Carr,* 369 U.S. 189 (1962).

125 *Reynolds v. Sims,* 377 U.S. 533 (1964). "One man, one vote" was the term used in the Court's decision.

126 Higham, *Strangers in the Land.*

CHAPTER 3

Party Machines and the Immigrants

Machines and Machine-Style Politics

The image of the rotund, cigar-smoking machine politician handing out buckets of coal to poor widows and cutting deals in smoke-filled rooms in the back of taverns holds a sacred place in the lore of American politics. What continues to make it fascinating is its colorful, larger-than-life aspect: The politician who is passionate, free-wheeling, and generous to his loyal constituents, but also self-serving, venal, and corrupt. The television series *The Sopranos* or Francis Ford Coppola's film *The Godfather* may come to mind because they serve as reminders that machine politicians and the Mafia shared a general style. The occasions when machine politicians crossed the line into thuggish violence are generally exceptions, but not enough for comfort. Recall, for example, *The Untouchables* television series and movie, based on the heyday of the Chicago machine of the 1920s and 1930s, when politicians, judges, and police officers were bought off by Al Capone and speakeasy owners, and FBI agent Elliott Ness arrived on the scene to take on not only Capone but an entire system of criminal and political corruption. There have been instances when information fed by machine members to criminal gangs has been used to kill informants and even cases when investigative reporters have been killed.[1] But lurid episodes such as this give an inaccurate impression of how most machines operated. The day-to-day business of maintaining a machine was ordinary and prosaic.

The impressions from the era of machine politics are still very much alive, but they are misleading in key respects. It is true that the machines thrived on corruption, some spectacularly so. But it is also true that machine politicians provided a path by which ethnic voters could gain a measure of access to a political system that had excluded them. Looked at in this way, the machines were, in effect, mechanisms that facilitated the assimilation of immigrants into American culture. Over time, the machines declined, and they pretty much disappeared by the second half of the twentieth century. Even so, they helped shape the contemporary American city, and their legacy still lives on.

DOI: 10.4324/9781003175315-4

Some degree of machine-style politics—a style that relies on material incentives to nurture loyalty—is present in every political system. Silver-haired, country-club "suits" who help their favored developers obtain zoning variances for a suburban mall are acting as much like machine politicians as a ward boss who provides assistance to a constituent dealing with a rat inspector who wants to close down a restaurant or apartment building. In politics, material incentives come in many forms: A patronage job, a government contract, a zoning variance, a fixed parking ticket, an expedited business license, and more. In all political systems, claims to lofty ideals are often little more than fig leaves covering naked self-interest. For this reason, something more than a style of politics based around material rewards is necessary if we are to accurately employ the term "machine."[2] Specifically, the urban machines were organizations held together by a combination of ethnic identity and partisan loyalty. They were also, to varying degrees, hierarchical and disciplined, often controlled by a single leader, a "boss," or a tightly organized clique that shared power. They were democratic in the sense that they expended great energy to mobilize voters, but they also preserved a high degree of independence from outside influences through an internal system of command, coordination, and control.

Machines prospered for a time because of the social and political circumstances of the industrial age, which nurtured tightly knit ethnic communities sharply divided from the rest of society. Many of America's big industrial cities were once governed by party machines. Between 1870 and 1945, 17 of the nation's 30 cities with populations of more than half a million people were governed through boss rule and a disciplined, hierarchical party organization at some point.[3] In most of these cities, a factional machine-style politics operated for some time before the actual machines emerged. With only rare exceptions, the classic machines flowered in the last years of the nineteenth century and the first two or three decades of the twentieth century, after which those that still remained went into to decline. Boss rule peaked sometime in the 1920s. In 1932, the year Democratic candidate Franklin D. Roosevelt won the presidency, 10 of America's 30 biggest cities were ruled by machine bosses. Today, the machine is pretty much extinct. The death of Chicago boss Richard J. Daley in 1976 marked the end of the era of the classic party machines, which relied on patronage and the distribution of material incentives to keep their organizations intact.[4]

Despite the demise of these storied organizations, any serious discussion of American urban politics must take them into account because the political struggles of that time still reverberate at all levels of the political system. Early in the twentieth century, the machines became the object of a sustained campaign to clean up politics and reduce the influence of immigrant voters. The reforms adopted to end machine rule undeniably reduced corruption, but they also changed the rules of the game to the disadvantage of people at the lower end of the social spectrum. Even today, conflicts regularly break out involving the question of whether it should be easy or hard for people to register to vote. Battles over the rules that govern participation in the political system are bitterly fought because political outcomes reflect the composition of the electorate and the mix of interest groups that try to exert influence. These skirmishes go back more than a century, and they continue to the present day because so much is at stake.

OUTTAKE

Machines Had Two Sides

The careers of two machine politicians, James and Tom Pendergast of Kansas City, Missouri, illustrate both the positive and the negative sides of machine politics.

In 1876, James Pendergast, an Irishman with a short, thick neck and massive arms and shoulders, moved to Kansas City. Just 20 years old and with only a few dollars in his pocket, he rented a room in the West Bottoms ward, an industrial section on the floodplain of the Missouri River. The residents of West Bottoms worked in the meat packinghouses, machine shops, railroad yards, factories, and warehouses of the area. Blacks, Irish, Germans, and rural migrants lived in crowded four- and five-story tenements and tiny shanties. Overlooking this squalid area of dirt streets and open sewers was Quality Hill, where the wealthy elite lived. Pendergast held jobs in the packinghouses and in an iron foundry until 1881, when he used racetrack winnings to buy a hotel and a saloon.

He named the saloon Climax, the name of the lucky long-shot horse that gave him his start. The Climax Saloon became a social center of the First Ward, which put Pendergast in a position to meet the people of the ward. His generosity made him many friends. On payday, he cashed payroll checks and settled credit agreements; he posted bonds for men who had been arrested for gambling. His business flourished: "Men learned that he had an interest in humanity outside of business and that he could be trusted, and they returned the favor by patronizing his saloon and giving him their confidence." In this way, Pendergast's politics and his everyday life became one and the same. He soon found himself being promoted for an alderman's seat, which he won in 1892.

The same year, Pendergast opened another saloon in the Second Ward, located in the city's North End. In that saloon he employed 22 men to run gambling tables, and in his West Bottoms ward he continued to employ a large gambling staff. Gambling was run on a large scale in Kansas City. Opening his own operations in the North End enabled Pendergast to forge close relationships with the politicians of that ward, and he soon became as influential in the Second Ward as he was in the First. He was able to secure police protection for gambling and liquor operations by paying off police officers and manipulating the choice of a police chief in 1895.

Pendergast could have run for mayor, but he preferred to exert his influence behind the scenes. By 1900 he was so powerful that he was able to select his preferred candidate for City Hall personally. In return, the grateful mayor gave Pendergast control over hundreds of patronage jobs and appointed Pendergast's brother, Tom, to the position of superintendent of streets. More than 200 men were employed by the streets department, which placed orders for gravel and cement with suppliers and contractors loyal to the machine. James Pendergast also gained control over positions in the fire department and was named the city's deputy license inspector, an important job because saloons and other business establishments needed licenses to operate. As the final step in consolidating his political authority, by 1902 he had personally selected 123 of the 173 patrolmen on the police force. Although he never ran for mayor, he was Kansas City's most powerful politician.

Like all the urban machines, Pendergast's organization was sustained by a web of mutually beneficial relationships. Machine bosses distributed material rewards and expected loyalty in return. Some of them made this implicit bargain explicit, but the most effective ones never had to. A politician could get a lot of mileage out of only a modest amount of help; the word spread. James Pendergast expressed the principle in this way: "I've been called a boss. All there is to it is having friends, doing things for people, and then later on they'll do things for you." The First Ward voters reliably elected him by at least a 3-to-1 margin and without discernible fraud. It never occurred to him that he would need to steal an election.

Jim Pendergast's style contrasted starkly with his brother Tom's.

Tom, who inherited the Kansas City Democratic organization after James died, resorted to a mixture of fraud and coercion to maintain discipline and win elections. In the summer of 1914, Tom Pendergast's organization "used money, repeat voters, and toughs to produce North Side majorities" to gain approval of a proposed railway franchise. Machine workers distributed liquor and money in Black and Italian neighborhoods. They "paid men to vote under assumed names; and election judges who questioned some of those dragged off the streets and out of flop houses to vote were intimidated and abused, both verbally and physically." On election day in 1934, four persons were killed by thugs. Two years later, an attempted assassination and massive fraud at polling places led to an investigation that eventually resulted in 259 convictions for election fraud and criminal behavior.

Jim Pendergast succeeded in politics because he went out of his way to ascertain the needs of his constituents. By building a powerful political organization, he was able to provide them with jobs and other prized benefits. When his brother Tom took over, corruption and intimidation became the order of the day because he had not nurtured any real connection to his electoral constituency. The story of the two Pendergasts highlights a question often asked about the classic party machines: Were they vehicles for democracy or were they inherently flawed by the concentration of power they facilitated?

Source: Lyle W. Dorsett, *The Pendergast Machine* (New York: Oxford University Press, 1968). Quotations are from pp. 14, 26, 59, 60.

The Origins of Machine Politics

The rise of the urban party machines was made possible by two factors: The emergence of a mass electorate and industrialization.[5] When the Constitution was ratified in 1789, only about 5 percent of adult white males were eligible to vote, and it took well over a century for the political systems of American cities to begin to resemble a fully democratic system, although many Americans, and especially people of color remain disenfranchised by means of overtly restrictive voting laws, ID requirements, too few (understaffed) polling sites, etc. Property qualifications for voting began to be eased after 1776, and by 1850 virtually all free white males were eligible to vote in city elections.[6] Until the 1820s, most mayors were appointed by governors or city councils. Beginning with Boston and St. Louis in 1822, charter revisions gradually transformed the office into a popularly elected post, and by 1840 this practice had become almost universal.[7] In the presidential election of 1840, 80 percent of adult white males went to the polls, the highest rate in any major democracy.[8] The spread of universal (white) male suffrage coincided with the explosive growth of cities. From the 1830s to the 1920s, more than 30 million immigrants came to the United States, most of them pouring into the cities. As soon as they were citizens, if they were male, they could vote. A new breed of enterprising politician learned to profit from this circumstance.

In most of the industrial cities, a "friends and neighbors" or "local follow-ings" style of politics evolved that fit perfectly with the decentralized nature of local governmental structures. Aldermen were elected from wards, and because these electoral units tended to be small, politicians were able to enter politics as a natural consequence of their personal connections. No one benefited from this arrangement more than pub owners. Saloons were central to the day-to-day life of working-class neighborhoods. Pub owners were considered reliable sources of information and advice. The density of pubs in immigrant neighborhoods was astonishing. In 1915, for example, there was a saloon for every 515 residents in New York, but the ratio was even greater in Chicago, which had a saloon for every 335 of its inhabitants.[9] In most cities there was at least one pub for every 50 males.[10] In late-nineteenth-century Chicago, half the city's total population entered a saloon every day.[11] Many machine politi-cians got their start as pub owners. Of New York City's 24 aldermen in 1890, 11 were pub owners. Pub owners made up a third of Milwaukee's city council members in 1902 and a third of Detroit's aldermen at the turn of the century.[12]

Party machines managed to combine two seemingly incompatible qualities: The absence of formal rules and a disciplined organization. Machine politicians were not "hired" into party organizations, and they did not have a formal job description. Their ability to deliver votes and their skill at forging alliances with other politicians determined their standing within the organization. Normally, a machine politician started at the bottom and worked his way up. Precinct captains, who were responsible for getting out the vote in the smallest and most basic political unit of the city, knew each voter personally, often as a friend and neighbor. To secure a following at this level, a politician had to be known not only as a person involved in politics but as someone who participated in local community life. Politicians climbed the political ladder only if they demonstrated they could reliably deliver the vote. If they did, the next rung they reached for was an alderman.

Most machine politicians came from backgrounds that offended silk-stocking elements. Schooled in rough-and-tumble political competition, they generally were men of incredible energy, quick temper, and rough manners. At the least, they loved what they were doing; they felt no alienation from their job. Politics was everything the machine politicians knew and did—it was their social life, their profession, their first love. They pursued political power, not high social standing.[13] George Washington Plunkitt, a member of the Tammany Hall organization in New York, advised against what he called the "dangers of the dress suit in politics." "Live like your neighbors," Plunkitt admonished aspiring politicians, "even if you have the means to live better. Make the poorest man in your district feel that he is your equal, or even a bit superior to you."[14]

Disciplined political organizations emerged when skillful leaders succeeded in persuading enough of their fellow politicians that everyone would benefit if they cooperated. When enough of them came together, a military-style hierarchy emerged, with those lower in the organization waiting for their chance to move up. This structure was once described by Frank Hague, the Jersey City boss, to columnist Joseph Alsop, who wrote, "He [Hague] was talking in the dining room of one of the local hotels. He took the squares on the tablecloth to illustrate precincts and wards, tracing them out with his finger, and he explained the feudal system of American politics, whereby the precinct captain is governed by a ward lieutenant, the lieutenant by a ward leader, and each ward leader by the boss."[15]

As shown in Figure 3.1, precincts and precinct captains constituted the foundation of the typical machine organization. The average precinct had 400–600 voters, and precinct captains were expected to know them by name. Around 30–40 precincts were generally included within a ward. The captains of the precincts were chosen by and worked for the ward's alderman. The alderman served as the chair of the ward's party committee, unless he selected a committeeman to supervise the precinct captains on his behalf. Finally, the aldermen reported to the machine boss, who was usually but not always the mayor.

The organization of local political machines, or parties, parallels the formal structures of government but is also separate from them. Like the mayor, the party leader or boss controls the entire city, or perhaps the county. The alderman represents a ward in the city council or on the board of aldermen. The alderman may or may not serve as ward leader of the party. Each ward consists of many precincts or election districts. Precinct captains are responsible for delivering the vote in their precinct.

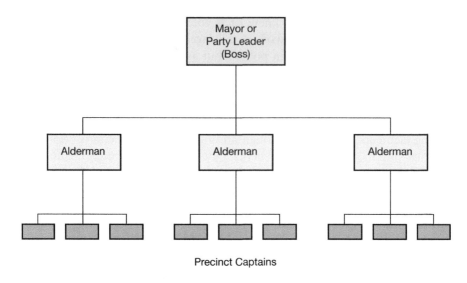

FIGURE 3.1 The Organization of Machine Politics

   In principle, power flows from the bottom up: Precinct captains elect the ward leaders, and the ward leaders elect the party boss. But in fact, power flows from the top.

   The hierarchical structure of the machine held together because everyone gained by cooperating in what was, in essence, a "system of organized bribery."[16] Bosses and individual aldermen had at their disposal patronage jobs in police, fire, sanitation, and streets departments—and occasionally even in private industry. Construction projects, such as levee construction or road building, could give a boss control over hundreds of permanent and temporary jobs. Precinct captains usually held low-level jobs arranged through the machine, perhaps serving as supervisors on street crews. Ward committeemen were rewarded with higher-paying administrative posts in the city government. Aldermen and other elected officials often owned lucrative insurance companies, ran their own construction firms, or owned saloons. The most menial jobs were passed along to some of the loyal voters who turned out faithfully on election day.

   An understanding of the patronage ladder can be gained by examining one of the last machines to exist in any American city, the one run by Richard J. Daley, mayor of Chicago, from 1953 until his death in 1976. In the early 1970s, the Cook County Central Committee (which contains Chicago) had about 30,000 positions available for distribution. Most of these jobs were unskilled; 8,000 were available through Chicago's departments and commissions, including street cleaners, park supervisors, and the like.[17] The jobs ranged from $3,600-a-year elevator operators and $6,000-a-year stenographers to $25,000-a-year department directors (in the early 1970s, a skilled factory worker in a union plant made approximately $9,000 per year). Individual ward committeemen controlled as many as 2,000 jobs. (Richard J. Daley had begun his career as committeeman of his ward.) There were (and still are) 50 wards in the city of Chicago, with an average of 500–600 patronage jobs available in each of them in the 1970s.[18]

The election-day result determined the number of jobs available for distribution by individual precinct captains and ward committeemen. A precinct captain in Chicago was expected to know all the voters in the precinct and to be known by them. "When a man is given a precinct, it is his to cover, and it is up to him to produce for the party. If he cannot produce for the party, he cannot expect to be rewarded by the party. 'Let's put it this way,' [one alderman said] 'if your boss has a salesman who can't deliver, who can't sell his product, wouldn't he put in someone else who can?'"[19]

Alderman Vito Marzullo was a member of the Chicago organization. Every week he scheduled a formal audience with his constituents. Flanked on each side by a precinct captain, he heard their complaints:

> A precinct captain ushered in a black husband and wife. "We got a letter here from the city," the man said. "They want to charge us twenty dollars for rodent control in our building." "Give me the letter, I'll look into it," Marzullo replied. The captain spoke up. "Your daughter didn't vote on November fifth. Look into it. The alderman is running again in February. Any help we can get, we can use."[20]

In the course of hearing his constituents, Marzullo exclaimed, "Some of those liberal independents in the city council, they can't get a dog out of a dog pound with a ten-dollar bill. Who's next?" Marzullo then arranged to have a traffic ticket fixed, agreed to recommend someone for a job at an electric company, refused to donate money to the Illinois Right to Life Committee ("Nothing doing …. I don't want to get into any of those controversies. People for it and people against it."), agreed to try to find a job for an unemployed truck driver and gave $50 to a mother receiving public assistance. Responding to several more requests, he offered to "see what I can do."[21]

During the Richard J. Daley years, the Chicago machine was structured like a political pyramid. Committeemen and the aldermen directed the captains of the precincts within their wards; they, in turn, reported to the Cook County Central Committee. Although most of the city machines that operated a half-century before were similarly organized, some were directed from the top with an iron hand, as in Daley's Chicago; others were little more than loose confederations of politicians jealous of their own turf. However tightly run the individual machines were, they all revealed the same qualities: They were rooted in neighborhoods, personal interaction, and a combination of material incentives and ethnic and community attachments held them together.

Being close to constituents did not necessarily mean the machines can be regarded as a model of democracy at work. Although all machines provided something to their supporters, most of them also engaged in election fraud. Because so many opportunities were available, few machine politicians could resist the temptations offered by bribes and backroom deals. But as an answer to the impression that machines were nothing but cesspools of corruption, some historians and social scientists called attention to some of their positive achievements. They have offered three main arguments in defense of the machines: That they (1) centralized power and "got the job done," (2) served as vehicles of upward mobility for immigrants, and (3) helped assimilate the immigrants into American life. In the next three sections, we examine these claims.

Did Machines "Get the Job Done"?

It has generally been assumed that political machines evolved in the late nineteenth century to fill a vacuum left by the absence of effective local governments. City governments were often inept and inefficient because they relied on a chaotic division of responsibilities among a multitude of separate officials, boards, and departments. The mayor generally wielded little authority. The city council or board of aldermen typically controlled the budget and made most of the important decisions. Day-to-day administrative responsibilities were generally assumed by committees whose members were appointed by the city council, or sometimes by some combination of the mayor, state legislature, governor, or other state or local official. At election time, a long list of names on the ballot made it impossible for voters to know anything about the candidates. Edward Sait wrote in 1933 that "when the people or particular groups among them demanded positive action, no one had adequate authority to act. The machine provided an antidote."[22] In other words, he was saying that machines were necessary if anything was to get done.

If it is true that machines arose mainly to fill a void left by disorganized and inefficient government, then we would expect to find that machines prospered best in cities where governments were the most politically and administratively fragmented. The problem with this idea is that by the time most machines came into being, reformers devoted to the cause of streamlining municipal governance had already achieved their goal of concentrating more power in the hands of mayors and a cadre of full-time civil service administrators.[23] The municipal reformers had imagined that these changes would make officeholders more accountable to the electorate and that informed voters would elect a "better class" of refined and educated leaders to office. They were sorely disappointed with the results. As it turned out, it was easier to build disciplined machine organizations where local government had been streamlined and centralized than where it remained fragmented and chaotic. Jersey City, New Jersey, supplies an instructive example. In 1913, reformers there persuaded the voters to fuse legislative and executive functions into one five-member commission. When the machine mayor, Frank Hague, gained control of the city commission, he was able to accomplish something he had tried many times before: Consolidate his power over a faction-ridden Democratic Party and become the uncontested boss of Jersey City.[24]

Control of municipal government was a prize worth pursuing. Between 1870 and 1900, municipal workforces grew even faster than urban populations,[25] and local governments spent more money than either the federal government or the state governments.[26] Cities ran up debts at a feverish pace to finance water systems, lay sewers lines, pave streets, build parks and public buildings, deepen harbors, and improve public health.[27] Even cities with fractious and divided politics, such as Los Angeles, made huge investments in infrastructure.[28] The political support for urban infrastructure and services was sufficiently strong that city budgets and workforces were bound to expand, regardless of how a city was run.[29] A study of cities from 1890 to 1940 found no difference between machine and nonmachine cities in the overall level of public expenditures.[30]

Corruption could make the price of "getting the job done" astonishingly high. Probably the most notoriously corrupt machine in American history was led by William Marcy "Boss" Tweed, who ran the infamous Tweed Ring in New York City from 1868 to 1871. In three years, Tweed took $30 million to $100 million of public funds for himself and his cronies. Under his regime, the machine's traditional take of 10 percent on construction contracts ratcheted upward. A courthouse project originally estimated to cost $250,000 ended up costing taxpayers $14 million. At least 90 percent of this cost overrun went to pay payoffs, bribes, and fake contracts.[31] Tweed's rule has been called the politics of "rapacious individualism" because everyone in the machine seemed to be after personal wealth. Ultimately, the availability of so many spoils undermined the discipline of his organization. Because Tweed was not able to count on the loyalty of his fellow politicians, he was forced to buy it directly, and therefore his authority was fragile and short-lived.[32] In 1869 and 1870, the city's debt increased from $36 million to $97 million. By 1871, when Tweed was arrested, the city was bankrupt.

Machine bosses realized that the artful distribution of spoils was the key to holding their organizations together. The rapid growth of city services guaranteed there would be plenty of largesse to spread around. Mayors and city councils negotiated lucrative multiyear contracts for streetcar operations and utility services (such as electricity, gas, and telephone). Cities issued tavern and liquor licenses and regulated gambling and prostitution (or had the option of looking the other way when they were illegal). They engaged in a continuous stream of public works projects, including the building of roads, bridges, public buildings, sewer and water systems, streetlights, and parks. There was money to be made on both ends of these transactions.

The operations of Abraham Reuf's regime, which ruled San Francisco just after the turn of the century, provide some insight into the wealth of opportunities available to people who entered politics.[33] Reuf was an attorney who never held public office, but his law practice gave him access to those who did. In October 1901 his handpicked candidate took over the mayor's office, and within days Reuf spread the word that the city's laws against prostitution would be strictly enforced. He advised the brothel owners that it would be wise to have an attorney—specifically himself—who could effectively represent their interests. The owners quickly got the point and agreed to pay him a fourth of their business profits, half of which Reuf split with the mayor. This arrangement allowed the brothels to continue operating without fear of prosecution. Reuf also provided his professional "advice" to saloon owners that it would be wise to pay premium prices for a low-quality whiskey supplied by one of Reuf's legal clients. In return, the saloon owners were protected from police raids.

San Francisco invested huge resources in municipal services, and businesses competed for the contracts. A lot of money was at stake. The mayor, the city council, or a utilities commission could, in a single stroke of a pen, enrich a business owner by awarding a contract to build trolley lines, install streetlights, supply gas, or install telephones. The temptation to make decisions secretly in smoke-filled rooms was overwhelming. The chair of the public utilities committee of the San Francisco Board of Supervisors reminded a group of business leaders in January 1906:

> It must be borne in mind that without the city fathers there can be no public service corporations. The street cars cannot run, lights cannot be furnished, telephones cannot exist. And all the public service corporations want to understand that we, the city fathers, enjoy the best of health and that we are not in business for our health. The question at this banquet board is: "How much money is in it for us?"[34]

There seemed to be plenty of money for everyone. When two telephone companies submitted competing bids to supply service to the citizens of San Francisco, Reuf collected a $1,200 monthly "attorney's fee" from one company while secretly accepting a $125,000 bribe from the other. Reuf persuaded the board of supervisors to award the contract to the company that paid the biggest bribe. Keeping $63,000 for himself, he used a loyalty test to distribute the remainder of the $125,000 to the individual supervisors: $6,000 each to those who had taken no independent bribes (showing they were not trying to compete with Reuf), $3,500 to those voting correctly despite bribes to do the opposite, and nothing at all to those who did not cooperate.

Reuf's tenure as the power behind the mayor's throne ended when he was indicted and tried for corruption. Ironically, his downfall was precipitated by too much success. After seeing how lucrative local politics could be, more and more of the politicians around him struck out on their own in search of profit and opportunity, and before long the feeding frenzy attracted attention and the jackals began to turn on one another.

Reuf's behavior was more reckless than usual, but in almost all cities, machine leaders forged alliances with illicit business owners. The relationship benefited both sides in the partnership: The businesses were free to operate without having to worry about the law, and the politicians could count on a steady flow of favors and bribes. One of the reasons that machines flourished so much in the 1920s is that the national prohibition of liquor sales opened unprecedented opportunities for selling police protection to speakeasies and bootleggers. Prohibition facilitated a cooperative arrangement between machines and organized crime not only in Chicago, where the collusion was especially notorious, but all over the country, in big cities and small. In many cases, the level of flagrant corruption and rising levels of violence brought a reaction that brought the machines down for good.

Machines took bribes from legitimate enterprises, too. The machines governed the cities during a period of explosive growth in population, services, and construction. Even if local politicians tried to be honest, business tycoons eager to expand their empires were eager to spread their money around to get what they wanted. They found it convenient to work with politicians who could make decisions expeditiously behind the scenes. Big businesses paid bigger bribes than anyone else, and this put them in a position to negotiate monopoly contracts on favorable terms. The franchises typically were granted for periods of 50–100 years, and some specified no terminal dates at all.[35] In the 1880s and 1890s, national financial syndicates made millions of dollars by gaining control of street railway franchises. In 1890, there were 39 street railway companies in Philadelphia, 19 in New York City, 24 in Pittsburgh, 19 in St. Louis, and 16 in San Francisco.[36] There was simply not enough business for all of them, and by the turn of the century only one or two major street railway companies operated in most cities.

In light of the numerous opportunities for personal enrichment, it may seem surprising that a number of machine leaders refused to cash in to enrich themselves. The extent and style of corruption varied considerably from one city to the next. In the 1930s, Boss George Cox was credited with bringing "positive and moderate reform government to Cincinnati."[37] In the years when Richard J. Daley was boss (1955–1976), Chicago was known as "the city that works" because the mayor saw to it that services were delivered effectively. Daley was popular with voters both because they felt he was responsible for getting things done and because there was never any evidence that he took money for himself.[38] For all of his life he and his family lived in a modest bungalow in an old Irish neighborhood close to the stockyards.

Were Machines Vehicles of Upward Mobility?

A leading sociologist once proposed that the machines succeeded partly because they provided "alternative channels of social mobility for those otherwise excluded from the more conventional avenues of 'advancement.'"[39] In the nineteenth century, many employers refused to hire the Irish; "Irish need not apply" was printed on many an employment notice. For the ethnics who found public employment, local politics was "like a rope dangling down the formidable slope of the socioeconomic system" that poor immigrants could grab to pull themselves up.[40]

Ample evidence supports the thesis that the urban machines aided the upward mobility of their immigrant supporters. Although it is not exactly a typical story, politics was a key element in the rise of the Kennedy clan from poverty to wealth and national power. President John F. Kennedy's grandfather on his mother's side, John "Honey Fitz" Fitzgerald, rose from a ward heeler running errands for an alderman to the office of mayor of Boston. Kennedy's grandfather on his father's side was a respected ward politician and saloon-keeper whose contacts helped the early career of the president's millionaire father, Joseph P. Kennedy, who made a fortune in bootleg liquor.[41]

Despite the many stories describing how boys from poor immigrant families rose through the ranks of local machines, the evidence supporting the idea that the machines enhanced the upward mobility of immigrants is mixed. Mostly, political machines provided only petty favors for their working-class constituents, and their pyramid-shaped hierarchy did not allow for an upward trajectory for the majority of immigrants. It is important to realize that these tales are colorful partly because they are exceptional, and in any case they apply to the Irish more than to any other immigrant group. In most cities Irish politicians mastered the art of machine politics before anyone else, and they incorporated other ethnic groups into their coalitions only if it was absolutely necessary for winning elections. Later-arriving immigrants generally found it hard to get a toehold into the political system. In New York City, for example, the machine organization called *Tammany Hall* was run by and for the Irish. Although Jews and Italians represented 43 percent of New York's population by 1920, in the same year only 15 percent of the city's aldermen and assemblymen were Jewish and only 3 percent were Italian.[42]

Most of the big-city machines were dominated by Irish politicians from the beginning, and they stayed that way.[43] Between 1900 and 1930, the machines in New York City, Jersey City, and Albany, New York, added nearly 100,000 municipal jobs. Close to two-thirds of these jobs went to Irish constituents, even though the Irish accounted for only about one-third of the population in these cities. The Irish were especially vigilant about maintaining iron-fisted control over police forces. As late as 1970, for instance, 65 percent of police officers in Albany were still of Irish descent, even though no more than 25 percent of the city's population could trace their ancestry to Ireland.[44]

Eventually, some skilled politicians managed to challenge the control wielded by Irish machine bosses by appealing to the groups that had been left out. Fiorello LaGuardia, elected mayor of New York City in 1933, smashed the Tammany organization, which had dominated the city's politics for almost a century. LaGuardia was a master at ethnic politics, perhaps because "half Jewish and half Italian, married first to a Catholic and then to a Lutheran of German descent, himself a Mason and an Episcopalian, he was practically a balanced ticket all by himself."[45] This rich ethnic heritage helped him to assemble an electoral coalition composed of disgruntled Jews, Italians, and other excluded groups. Likewise, in the 1920s Anton Cermak became mayor of Chicago by building "a house of all peoples."[46] By reaching out to Italians, Jews, Czechs, and Poles, Cermak won the 1931 mayoral election with 65 percent of the vote, and once in office he solidified his authority by adeptly distributing patronage, recruiting candidates for machine positions, and fighting against Prohibition, which almost all ethnics opposed. La Guardia and Cermak's success revealed that any political organization built on an overly narrow base was vulnerable to challenge.

The common wisdom among urban scholars has been that Black Americans remained excluded from most of the urban machines. However, this is not universally true. Chicago became one notable exception because in the 1920s the city's machine leaders recognized that they could reliably secure the vote in the segregated South Side wards simply by creating "sub-machines" run by Black politicians.[47] William Dawson, a member of Congress from 1942 until his death in 1970, ran a submachine in Chicago's South Side ghetto, but white politicians kept him carefully in check. Dawson reliably delivered huge pluralities for machine candidates from the Black wards, but Black voters received relatively little in return.[48] Throughout Chicago's history, often inexperienced Black politicians who accepted a devil's bargain were recruited into the machine: In exchange for a measure of freedom to pursue their own ambitions, they delivered the vote and kept a Black leadership focused on equal rights and more self-determination from emerging.[49] The legacy of such practices was still apparent in the Richard J. Daley years. Although Black Americans made up 40 percent of Chicago's population in 1970, they held only 20 percent of the government jobs in the city, and most of those jobs were the least desirable.[50] A study of a typical ward in Chicago found that the machine consistently over-rewarded middle-class voters at the expense of loyal working-class voters, severely disadvantaging African American voters.[51]

Disaffected Black voters did finally successfully challenge the Chicago machine organization in the 1980s. In 1983 a charismatic Black politician, Harold Washington, assembled a now famous "rainbow coalition" of poor people, Blacks, Hispanics, and white liberals to defeat the machine's mayoral candidate.[52] His victory set off a prolonged racial tug-of-war in the city council between Washington's supporters and the Old-Guard members of the machine, but when Washington died in his office of a heart attack on November 15, 1987, the new groups he had brought into politics continued to exert a voice. In 1989, Richard M. Daley, the son of Richard J., won the mayor's race by successfully reassembling the remnants of his father's organization while implementing the lessons from Washington's brilliant coalition-building tactics: He forged alliances with African American and Latino politicians and established a close relationship with the downtown business establishment. He was elected to office five times because he learned from the Washington coalition the principle that to govern effectively, he needed to build a broad base of support.

Ray Jones in New York City similarly understood the need for broad-based coalitions among Democratic politicians if they wanted to cement lasting influence. A former red cap and businessman, Jones started building "New Democrat" political coalitions among African Americans and West Indian constituencies in Harlem, resulting in the successful election of two Black municipal judges.[53] Although they had different approaches to political coalition building and were not always of the same mind, Jones and Adam Clayton Powell started working together in political organizing and coalition-building in Harlem and beyond, resulting in Powell's election as Harlem's first Black city council member, and New York's first Black member of Congress.[54] After World War II, following a fallout with Powell, Jones became a close ally of New York City mayor Robert Wagner, building key Democratic coalitions between African American, Puerto Rican, and working-class voters. Through his important alliance with Wagner, by 1964, Jones moved on to become New York County leader and the first Black politician to be "Tammany Chief."[55] As Vaz writes aptly:

> While Jones was not free to dispense jobs and contracts and contracts en masse, [as did the Tammany chiefs of old] and while he did not sit atop a tightly controlled political organization, his most significant accomplishments came in cultivating and elevating a generation of Black political leadership. Most notably, he was crucial to the rise of Constance Baker Motley, the first Black woman appointed as a federal judge, and Charles Rangel, who unseated Adam Clayton Powell and went on to serve for more than four decades in Congress. When Jones finally retired for good in 1969, his handpicked successor to lead his Harlem political club was David Dinkins, who was later elected as New York's first African American mayor.[56]

Traditional machine leaders had believed it made perfect sense to keep their coalitions only as big as necessary.[57] The more groups making up the alliance, the greater the interethnic squabbles over the distribution of patronage and the thinner the distribution of rewards. As a consequence, "once minimal winning coalitions had been constructed, the machines had little incentive to naturalize, register, and mobilize the votes of later ethnic arrivals."[58] For entrenched machines, expanding the electoral base past the minimum number of voters needed for winning elections just complicated things. The art was to strike a balance to ensure a coalition that was just large enough, and sometimes they miscalculated. The contributions of Black political leaders to the machine system have been largely overlooked, perhaps because they do not fit neatly into the traditional, Irish machine concept. Yet, their strategic and innovative efforts in coalition-building laid the basis for broader Democratic leadership coalitions to emerge in many cities across the country, and the consolidation of the Great Migration into a solid, Northern Black urban vote, which became increasingly impactful in Democratic electoral politics later in the twentieth and early in the twenty-first centuries.

The machines distributed benefits that were of great value to their supporters. According to Jessica Trounstine, in the early years of the twentieth century, "public jobs frequently paid better wages than private employment," and access to public jobs allowed the Irish and sometimes other groups to escape the discrimination they faced in the private marketplace.[59] The problem was that the number of public jobs was pitifully small compared to the jobs available in the private economy. In 1900, Tammany's vaunted patronage army made up 5 percent of New York City's workforce. It is true that from 1900 to 1920 local governments grew so fast that public employment accounted for 20 percent of all urban job growth,[60] but for most people, including the immigrants, private industry rather than patronage provided the best opportunities for upward mobility.

Although for decades the Irish laid claim to a disproportionate share of the jobs provided by the municipal government, it took a long time for them to catch up to the gains made by some other ethnic groups. Scandinavians, Germans, and Jews, for example, participated relatively little in machine politics, and yet they joined the American middle class faster than the Irish did. The Irish did not achieve economic parity with these groups until the 1960s and 1970s. This disparity is mainly due to the circumstances of immigration, as well as immigrants' socio-economic situation in their countries of origin. For instance, Germans and Jews did not come to the United States primarily for socio-economic reasons. They were often middle-class immigrants who fled discrimination in their home countries in Europe (Jews) and religious and political unrest (Germans). Despite this mixed record, however, the benefits supplied by the machines to their loyal supporters were better than nothing, and for the individuals who received them they were precious indeed. On the whole, immigrant voters got back about as much as they could have expected for what they could give in return.

Did the Machines Help Immigrants Assimilate?

Without doubt, the urban party machines helped to assimilate millions of impoverished immigrants into a culture that was fearful of and hostile to almost every newly arriving ethnic group. Machine politicians nurtured a sense of community and belonging in the immigrant wards. They sponsored picnics, patriotic gatherings (such as Fourth of July celebrations), baseball teams, choirs, and youth clubs. The local party organization was an important community institution and one of the main alternatives to the pubs: The Democratic Club was a place where men played cards and checkers or just talked.[61]

With the material resources at their disposal already devoted to their core constituency, machine politicians learned to satisfy immigrants who arrived later with largely symbolic benefits. In New York City, Tammany leader "Big Tim" Sullivan, an Irishman, ruled the Lower East Side even though as early as 1910 it was 85 percent Jewish and Italian. He retained the loyalty of his constituents through a mixture of favors and artful gestures:

> He and his Irish lieutenants distributed coal, food, and rent money to needy Jews and Italians on the Lower East Side. Tammany's police department opened up station houses as temporary shelters for the homeless. Sullivan expedited business licenses for ethnic shopkeepers and pushcart peddlers. He shamelessly "recognized" the new immigrants with symbolic gestures and donned a yarmulke to solicit Jewish votes. Sullivan solicited Italian votes by sponsoring legislation to make Columbus Day a holiday.[62]

Many immigrants felt like outsiders in the dominant Protestant and middle-class culture of the United States. One of the secrets of the machines' appeal was that they tolerated the immigrants' "strange" practices and defended them from the dominant culture.[63] This was an important benefit that machine politicians could deliver at little cost. Although working-class communities in American cities were not economically independent, they were, to a remarkable degree, socially independent. Immigrants built their own churches, mutual aid societies, and clubs for drinking and gambling. Machine politicians supported such activities because they were handy venues for campaigning and political organizing.[64]

Machine politicians appealed to and were supported by immigrant voters, in part, because they represented the possibility of success in this strange new country. Almost all machine politicians came from lower-class immigrant origins. One study of 20 bosses found that 15 were first- or second-generation immigrants; 13 had never finished grammar school; and most had gone into politics at a young age, serving as messengers or detail boys at rallies and meetings.[65] Machine leaders, therefore, became symbols of success. Immigrants may not have read the Horatio Alger stories, but in machine bosses they could see men who had risen out of poverty. Aspiring politicians often accepted this interpretation of themselves, too; they viewed themselves as examples of what could be done with hard work and a little luck along the way. These real-world examples of upward mobility were sources of pride and hope for the masses of immigrants who lived and worked under incredibly difficult conditions. However, symbol exceeded substance, especially for later-arriving southern and eastern European immigrants. Irish politicians would shrewdly pick a handful of men from other immigrant groups and place them in lesser positions on the ballot to demonstrate their generosity. Meanwhile, the bread-and-butter patronage stayed home.

The immigrants paid a high price for assimilation on these terms. Machines rarely attempted to address the collective needs of their constituents. They were not interested in implementing lasting social reforms, because machines benefitted, to a certain extent, from social inequality. Immigrant voters were encouraged to "cast their ballots on the basis of ethnicity rather than policy considerations."[66] The immigrants gave their support not as an act of consciousness about group goals but because it was easy to do and plausible alternatives were few. The vote was a minimal commitment for the immigrant but a sufficient one for the machine. Constituents could hardly expect miracles in return.

The operating principles and structures of the urban machines encouraged the politicians who ran them to steer clear of ideological battles. To deal with their constituents' requests effectively, machine politicians had to learn the art of manipulating power within the framework of a political and economic order that they did not control. A premium was placed on simple pragmatism, the ability to pull strings to get things done. Idealism was scorned. If a constituent came to complain about a building inspector, the politician's job was to make things nice with the inspector. Changing the building code was irrelevant and even counterproductive because it might reduce the need for the politician's services and would offend local property owners as well.

Machines were hostile to political movements that tried to reform the system because such movements threatened their control of the immigrant vote. Until the 1930s, most machines vigorously opposed labor unions. In the first years of the twentieth century, Irish machine politicians ordered the police to attack labor organizers in Lawrence, Massachusetts, and in New York City.[67] In Pittsburgh's 1919 steel strike, the machine likewise ordered police to harass strikers.[68] After Franklin D. Roosevelt's landslide victory in the presidential election of 1932, some of the big-city machines forged alliances with the moderate trade unions, but the relationship was never easy to maintain. The machines expected the unions to respect their turf by keeping out of local politics and focusing mainly on state and national politics and on labor–business relations.

On balance, it may be argued that the machines stunted the immigrants' potential as a political force. Working-class immigrants desperately needed reforms such as widows' pensions, better working conditions, laws regulating hours and wages (especially for women and children), and workers' compensation. On occasion, machine politicians supported these reforms as well as the regulation of utilities, the legal recognition of labor unions, and the regulation of insurance companies.[69] But the selective and often halfhearted support for a few reform measures did not exactly transform machine politicians into crusading reformers. Machine politicians were willing to declare their support for reform legislation at the state level if it made them look good, but they never became active advocates for progressive causes. Machine politicians could be quite capricious, for immediate political circumstances always took precedence over principle.

Machine politicians rarely considered how things could be changed. They often referred to reformers as "goody-goodies" or "goo-goos" who, they thought, were in politics for a few thrills. ("Goo-goo" was derived from "good government," often the reformers' rallying cry.) Much of their disdain was rooted in the social differences between themselves and middle- and upper-class reformers. As a result, they had an excessive respect for the pragmatic fix.

The Social Reform Alternative

Defenders of the machines have argued that there were few alternatives to their pragmatic style of politics, that in the face of the vast economic and political resources held by corporations and wealthy elites, machine politicians milked the system on behalf of their constituents as effectively as they could. From this way of thinking, criticizing machine politicians for what they failed to do is an exercise in wishful thinking about what might have been.

The view that the machines accomplished as much as they could for their constituents fails to take into account the full range of opportunities available to them. The Progressive Era got its name because a generation of reformers were intent on improving the quality of life for immigrants and workers. They campaigned for support from both working-class immigrants and middle-class voters, but at every turn they encountered resistance both from machine politicians and members of the business community.[70] The examples of mayors who went in a different direction show, however, that it was possible to overcome such opposition. Mayors Tom L. Johnson of Cleveland, Ohio (1901–1909), Samuel "Golden Rule" Jones of Toledo, Ohio (1897–1903), and Brand Whitlock of Toledo (1906–1913) all won election by fighting against high streetcar and utility rates and for fair taxation and better social services. Their campaigns became models for like-minded reformers across the country. Reform-oriented mayors in Jersey City, Philadelphia, and Cincinnati attempted to increase municipal revenue by raising taxes on businesses and wealthy property owners and by renegotiating streetcar and utility franchises. But machine bosses bitterly fought reform in these cities, just as they had a few years earlier when similar efforts were mounted in Cleveland and Toledo.[71]

The career of Hazen S. Pingree, who served as Detroit's mayor from 1890 to 1898, shows there were enormous possibilities for accomplishing reforms that would benefit ordinary people. Born in Maine to a poor farmer and itinerant cobbler, Pingree's background did not suggest he would one day become a political reformer. After fighting in the Civil War, Pingree moved to Detroit, where he worked as a leather cutter in a shoe factory. After a few years, he and a partner pooled their savings to purchase the outdated factory. By modernizing the machinery and producing a new line of shoes that fit current fashions, Pingree managed to become independently wealthy. He was picked as the Republican candidate for mayor in 1889, mostly because he was the only member of the exclusive Michigan Club who could be persuaded by its members to run. The business leaders who controlled Republican politics trusted him, as a member of the club, to advocate the usual program of low taxes and a minimal array of municipal services. In any case, few of them imagined he would win, and they had grown accustomed to working with the reliably cooperative Irish-dominated Democratic machine.

To their deep disappointment, Pingree was not a typical business candidate. He campaigned in the ethnic wards and even kicked off his campaign by drinking whiskey in an Irish saloon. Pingree was a big hit with German and Polish voters, who had long been ignored by the Irish politicians. He called attention to the endemic corruption of the machine and advocated an eight-hour workday for city employees. His willingness to seek the ethnic vote was the foundation on which he built his subsequent political success.

Pingree's programs, and the strategies he used to implement them, reveal how much might have been accomplished in other American cities. When Pingree took over city hall, Detroit had one of the worst street systems in the nation. Many of the streets were made of wooden blocks, which caught fire in the summer and sank into the mire in the winter. The few paved streets were pocked with ruts and potholes. Pingree quickly realized that collusion between paving contractors and machine politicians was at the heart of the street problem. He launched an aggressive campaign against this arrangement, appealing to his business supporters by pointing out that the prosperity of the city depended on good streets. His insistent efforts led the city council to adopt strict paving specifications; as a result, by 1895 Detroit had one of the best street systems in the United States.

It was not long before Pingree understood that the local business establishment was responsible for many of Detroit's problems. He challenged the high fare charged for a ferry ride across the Detroit River to Belle Isle Park. The company dropped its rate from 10 cents to 5 cents after the mayor threatened to revoke its franchise or put into operation a municipal ferry service. Pingree also found that private companies had located along the Detroit River waterfront, often on municipal property, which choked off public access to water and recreation. He took action to open up waterfront areas for public use.

Pingree's fight with the Detroit City Railway Company turned him into a true social reformer willing to use public authority to curb private power to benefit the city's residents. At a time when streetcar companies in other cities were converting from horses to electric power, Detroit's company refused to make the change. In April 1891 the company's employees went on strike, presenting a perfect opportunity for Pingree to begin a battle for modernization and lower fares. The three-day strike culminated in a riot in which workers and citizens tore up the tracks, stoned the streetcars, and drove off the horses. Pingree ignored the company's request to call in the state militia and instead took the position that privately owned public services were "the chief source of corruption in city governments."[72] Pingree's stance precipitated a protracted, bitter fight to regulate the streetcars. This conflict vaulted him to national prominence.

Many business leaders had supported the strike, believing the street railway was so badly run that it was hurting local business. The business community was mainly interested in more reliable service, but Pingree went further and pressed for lower fares and municipal ownership. Such a position ran afoul of business leaders when the company passed into the hands of an eastern business mogul. The new owner's first action was to pack the company's board of directors with prominent businessmen from Detroit. The company then demanded that the city negotiate a more favorable franchise. Pingree countered with a lawsuit meant to terminate the existing company in favor of municipal ownership. At that point, the company bought Pingree's own attorney away from him and proceeded to offer bribes to city council members, including a $75,000 bribe to Pingree himself. The Preston National Bank dropped Pingree from its board of directors; he lost his family pew in the Baptist church; and he and his friends were shunned in public. The lesson Pingree learned from all this was that business supported reform only on its own terms. And he also began to form his own analysis about what was wrong with America's cities.

In 1891, Pingree began attacking the tax privileges of the city's corporations. The railroad, he observed, owned more than one-fifth of the property value in the city but paid no taxes at all because of the tax-free status granted to it by the state legislature. Shipping companies, docks, and warehouses, and other businesses escaped local taxation by claiming that their principal places of business existed outside the city. The city's biggest employer, the Michigan-Peninsula Car Company, paid only nominal taxes. Although he was not successful in equalizing the tax burden, Pingree was able to modify some of its worst features, especially the practice of assessing, for tax purposes, real estate owned by wealthy people at rates far below its value. Pingree earned the special enmity of the city's elite by successfully campaigning for a personal property tax on home furnishings, art objects, and other luxury items.

On April 1, 1895, Detroit began operating a municipal electric plant to supply power for its streetlights. This ended a five-year running battle between Pingree and the private lighting company. Pingree's main argument against the private control of electricity was that it cost too much. Pingree gathered voluminous information to show that Detroit's service was more expensive and less reliable than service in other cities. Despite the merits of his case he would have lost, but a scandal tipped the scales in his favor. In April 1892, Pingree walked into a city council meeting waving a roll of bills and dramatically accused the Detroit Electric Light and Power Company of bribing council members. The mayor had been sure to pack the room with his working-class supporters. With Pingree's followers whipped into a dangerous mood, the council members hastily capitulated.

Pingree used similar tactics in his fights with the gas and telephone interests. To force the Detroit Gas Company to lower its natural gas rates, he initiated a campaign to inform the public about the high price of Detroit's gas. When his attempt to force lower prices stalled in the courts, he persuaded the public works board to deny permits to excavate streets for the purpose of laying gas lines. When the gas company attempted to dig anyway, Pingree saw to it that the owners were arrested. "Possession is a great point," argued Pingree. "Let them get their gas systems connected and then they could float their $8,000,000 of stock in New York City and become too powerful for the city to control.

Detroit would be helpless in the hands of corporations as never before in her history."[73]

The battle raged on, with Pingree next encouraging users not to pay their gas bills. As public resistance against the Detroit Gas Company mounted, investors' confidence in the company plummeted, precipitating a plunge in the company's stock values. Even after Southern Pacific Railroad magnate Samuel Huntington became the company's principal investor, stock prices continued to fall, and Huntington negotiated an agreement to lower the price of gas from $1.50 per cubic foot to $0.80.

In his fourth term, Pingree took on the Bell Telephone Company. Again, the issue was high prices and inadequate service. This time he helped organize a competing phone company that charged less than half of Bell's rate, and in only a few months the newly formed Detroit Telephone Company was serving twice as many customers as Bell. In response, Bell Telephone initiated a rate war and began to improve its equipment and service. By 1900, when Michigan Bell bought out Detroit Telephone, Detroit had the lowest telephone rates and the most extensive residential use among large American cities.

No other mayor in America accomplished such a broad program of social reform. In his last two terms, Pingree traveled around the country making speeches and gathering ideas about what to do next. He wrote prolifically. He inspired reformers all over the country, and his national prominence helped him bring more reform to his own city. After winning four terms as the mayor of Detroit, Pingree went on to serve two terms as the governor of Michigan, where he continued to fight for reform.

Hazen Pingree recognized the necessity of building a broad-based coalition of support. He so assiduously courted ethnic voters that by his fourth term he had even won the dependable Irish away from the Democratic machine. In effect, he pieced together his own machine, filling patronage jobs with his own supporters and firing his opponents. However, "he absolutely refused to tolerate dishonesty or theft."[74] Unlike Detroit's machine politicians, who regularly exploited ethnic hostilities to win votes in their wards, Pingree tried to unify working-class Poles, Germans, Irish, and the middle class. In short, he was aware that to accomplish reform it was necessary to "recruit a coalition of power sufficient for his purpose."[75] A great many political machines had likewise constructed powerful electoral coalitions, but the politicians who built them were more interested in furthering their own careers than in making the economic and political system more just.

Ethnic Politics in Today's Cities

Cities are once again magnets for millions of immigrants, and as a consequence, struggles over racial and ethnic political participation have become highly charged. Despite their shortcomings, the machines showed respect for the newcomers and distributed highly valued resources. Considered in this light, an intriguing question arises: What strategies can the more recent immigrant groups employ to gain a voice in local political systems? Would recent immigrants and ethnic and racial minorities benefit if they were able to build political machines much like those that existed a century ago? The historical record indicates that the answer is "not much." And in any case, the rules of the game that regulate political processes have changed so much that such a strategy would be impractical.

The early urban machines brokered a deal with both poor immigrants and economic elites, and each of these groups gave up something and got something in return. Business elites ceded control over local governments to working-class ethnic politicians who controlled armies of patronage workers, supported in part by income from bribes paid by businesses and corporations. In return, machine politicians essentially promised to leave business alone. In effect, the two sides struck a bargain by recognizing a sharp separation between the market and the public sphere. This compromise was important in managing the tension between capitalism, with its attendant inequalities, and popular democracy.[76]

On the whole this turned out to be a bad bargain for the machines' ethnic supporters. Rather than passing out favors and low-paying jobs, machine politicians could have emulated Hazen Pingree by attacking the practices that inflated the cost of urban services and infrastructure. They could have gone farther, too, and forged alliances with labor unions to pursue programs designed to modify dangerous working conditions, long hours, child labor, and low pay. Instead, they discouraged immigrants from organizing around their common interests.

There is reason to believe that today's urban residents could expect even less even if well-oiled machine organizations came into power. The machines prospered in rapidly growing industrial cities that required massive expenditures on roads, bridges, sewers, streetcar systems, schools, and parks.[77] The resulting government jobs, contracts, and franchises were traded for the political support necessary to sustain the party organizations. By contrast, in today's cities it would be extremely difficult to assemble the patronage and other material rewards necessary to build and maintain disciplined organizations. City services are now administered through civil service bureaucracies, and merit employment systems have been put in place so patronage can no longer be regularly delivered on the basis of personal or political relationships. Federal prosecutors would quickly sniff out patronage and vote-buying arrangements, which were outlawed long ago.

The last of the old-style machines, presided over by Chicago's Mayor Richard J. Daley, died along with him in 1976. From April 1989 to April 2011 his son, Richard M. Daley, assembled a disciplined political organization, and in a few respects it resembled his father's. The "rubber stamp" city council almost always endorsed his proposals; even on controversial issues, few aldermen dared to vote no.[78] Even so, the political style and policy priorities of the younger Daley were utterly different from his father's. The elder Daley ran campaigns primarily through aldermen and precinct captains; for his son, the most effective techniques involved direct mail and television ads crafted by the best political consultants that money could buy. To pay for media campaigns, new sources of money were tapped. In his father's day, machine workers provided critical financial support for the machine. By contrast, the contributions for Richard M.'s campaigns came primarily from the sectors making up the new global economy—lawyers, bankers, insurance agencies, and the conventions, tourism, and entertainment industry. For the 1999 mayoral campaign, the financial services industry contributed roughly 10 percent of the cost of the campaign and the legal community produced 5.5 percent. The tourism, entertainment, and hospitality industry, which had given very few dollars to previous mayors, emerged as a significant supporter for Daley, accounting for 4 percent of his campaign contributions in 1999. The owner of the Chicago Blackhawks hockey team threw in $10,000, and another $10,000 came from a livery firm from Frankfort, Illinois (which sponsors carriage rides in tourist areas of the city). The union representing hotel employees gave Daley's campaign $30,000. By contrast, government officials produced less than 2 percent of Daley's financial support.[79]

The second Daley maintained his authority by distributing a new kind of white-collar "pinstripe" patronage to lawyers, brokers, financial consultants, advertising and public relations firms, and lobbyists. The big volumes of money required for mayor's campaigns went more to media advertising than to grassroots campaigning. Media-centered campaigns have replaced door-to-door and face-to-face campaigns at all levels of the American political system. The election of media mogul Michael Bloomberg as mayor of New York City in 2002 suggested that media-based politics has increasingly become common in the larger cities of the United States. National issues such as abortion rights, gay rights, and social welfare spending have also become important in local politics almost everywhere.[80] Because voters care about many national issues, it is difficult to imagine how an old-style party machine oriented to ethnic voters or to a politics of immediate material rewards would again emerge in any city.

Richard M. Daley ran a tight-knit political organization in the five terms he served as mayor, but whether it should be called a "new machine" or not is subject to debate.[81] Even though it clearly had some of the elements of the classic machines, it operated in a very different fashion. As a way of securing support among a new generation of ethnic voters, City Hall distributed as many jobs as possible to pro-Daley groups, but changing circumstances made the job difficult and even hazardous. The problem with the long-standing practice of fixing job applications for favored applicants was revealed late in 2005, when federal prosecutors began looking into the city's hiring practices. On July 6, 2006, the former director of the mayor's Office of Intergovernmental Affairs and three other former employees of the mayor's office were convicted in federal court of doctoring job applications, which violated a 1969 court decree forbidding the city from making patronage appointments. (The so-called Shakman decree carried the name of Michael Shakman, a Chicago lawyer who had filed suit against the city to stop patronage hiring.) Although Mayor Daley denied any knowledge of the practices, the corruption investigation threatened to spread out of control when the convicted employees and others fearing they might be prosecuted began talking to investigators. Federal prosecutors and the FBI promised that more was to come. Some people thought at the time it might even bring the mayor down.[82] By the end of 2007, two of the mayor's aides were serving terms in federal prison, and the investigation was still going on in 2010. The string of highly publicized cases kept Chicago's special style of politics in the news, and the presidential campaign of 2008 brought it to a national audience. But the truth is that the long era of the classic party machine ended when the father, Richard J. Daley, died of a heart attack in his office in 1976. With his death, the last remnants of a colorful era slipped into the past.

Endnotes

1 Jessica Trounstine, "Challenging the Machine-Reform Dichotomy," in *The City in American Political Development*, ed. Richardson Dilworth (New York: Routledge, 2009), pp. 77–97.

2 Raymond Wolfinger, "Why Political Machines Have Not Withered Away and Other Revisionist Thoughts," in *Readings in Urban Politics: Past, Present, and Future*, ed. Harlan Hahn and Charles H. Levine (New York: Longman, 1984), p. 79. Wolfinger makes the distinction that we draw here between machine politics and a centralized machine. See also Roger W. Lotchin, "Power and Policy: American City Politics between the Two World Wars," in *Ethnics, Machines, and the American Urban Future*, ed. Scott Greer (Cambridge, MA: Schenkman, 1981), p. 9.

3 M. Craig Brown and Charles N. Halaby, "Machine Politics in America, 1870–1945," *Journal of Interdisciplinary History* 17, no. 3 (Winter 1987): 598. To qualify as a dominant political machine, a machine-style party had to control both the executive and the legislative branches of the city for an uninterrupted series of three elections.

4 One of the last classic machines, the O'Connell machine in Albany, New York, lost its grip in the 1980s. See Swanstrom and Ward, "Albany's O'Connell Organization: The Survival of an Entrenched Machine," paper delivered at the American Political Science Association Convention (Chicago, September 1987). In Chicago, Richard M. Daley, the son of Richard J., still presides over a disciplined machine, but it relies on well-funded media campaigns and a high level of amenities and services, rather than on patronage and spoils, for its support. For a comprehensive history of machine politics in Chicago, see Dick Simpson, *Rogues, Rebels, and Rubber Stamps: The Politics of the Chicago City Council, 1863 to the Present* (Boulder, CO: Westview Press, 2001).

5 Amy Bridges, *A City in the Republic* (Cambridge, UK: Cambridge University Press, 1984), p. 8.

6 Donald S. Lutz, *Popular Consent and Popular Control: Whig Political Theory in the Early State Constitutions* (Baton Rouge, LA: Louisiana State University Press, 1980), p. 105; Advisory Commission on Intergovernmental Relations, *Citizen Participation in the American Federal System* (Washington, DC: U.S. Government Printing Office, 1979), p. 41.

7   William Bennett Munro, *Municipal Government and Administration* (New York: Macmillan, 1923), p. 94.

8   William N. Chambers, "Party Development and the American Mainstream," in *The American Party System: Stages of Political Development*, 2nd ed., ed. William Nisbet Chambers and Walter Dean Burnham (New York: Oxford University Press, 1975), p. 12.

9   Jon M. Kingsdale, "The 'Poor Man's Club': Social Functions of the Urban Working-Class Saloon," in *The Making of Urban America*, ed. Raymond A. Mohl (Wilmington, DE: Scholarly Resources, 1988), p. 123.

10 Ibid.

11 Ibid.

12 Ibid., p. 130.

13 "He [the boss] does not seek social honor; the 'professional' is despised in 'respectable society.' He seeks power alone, power as a source of money, but also power for power's sake." Max Weber, "Politics as a Vocation," in *From Max Weber: Essays in Sociology*, ed. H. H. Gerth and C. Wright Mills (New York: Oxford University Press, 1946), p. 109.

14 William L. Riordan, *Plunkitt of Tammany Hall* (New York: Dutton, 1963), p. 50.

15 Quoted in Dayton McKean, *The Boss* (Boston, MA: Houghton Mifflin, 1940), p. 132.

16 Edward C. Banfield and James Q. Wilson, *City Politics* (New York: Vintage Books, 1963), p. 125.

17 Milton Rakove, *Don't Make No Waves ... Don't Back No Losers: An Insider's Analysis of the Daley Machine* (Bloomington, IN: Indiana University Press, 1975). The following material on Daley's machine is drawn from Rakove.

18 Ibid., pp. 114–115.

19 Ibid., p. 115.

20 Ibid., p. 120.

21 Ibid., p. 122.

22 Edward McChesney Sait, "Political Machines," in *Encyclopedia of the Social Sciences*, ed. Edwin R. A. Seligman (New York: Macmillan, 1933), p. 658. See also Robert M. Merton, *Social Theory and Social Structure* (New York: Free Press, 1949), pp. 126–127. For decades, Merton's functional analysis of political machines was widely accepted, but it has been seriously challenged in recent years. See Steven P. Erie, *Rainbow's End: Irish-Americans and the Dilemmas of Urban Machine Politics, 1840–1985* (Berkeley: University of California Press, 1988); Alan DiGaetano, "The Rise and Development of Urban Political Machines," *Urban Affairs Quarterly* 24, no. 2 (December 1988): 247, Table 3; M. Craig Brown and Charles N. Halaby, "Functional Sociology, Urban History, and the Urban Political Machine: The Outlines and Foundations of Machine Politics, 1870–1945," Unpublished conference paper (Albany: Department of Sociology, State University of New York at Albany, n.d.).

23 A. DiGaetano, "The Rise and Development of Urban Political Machines," pp. 257–262. See also M. Craig Brown and Charles N. Halaby, "Bosses, Reform, and the Socioeconomic Bases of Urban Expenditure, 1890–1940," in *The Politics of Urban Fiscal Policy*, ed. Terrence S. McDonald and Sally K. Ward (Beverly Hills, CA: Sage), p. 90.

24 DiGaetano, "The Rise and Development of Urban Political Machines," p. 261. Urban politics is often portrayed as a morality play in which reformers are pitted against

machine politicians. In fact, machines often used reforms to consolidate their power and put reformers on the ballot in order to legitimate their rule. On the other side, reformers often created their own type of political machines. For a critique of the dichotomy between bosses and reformers, see David P. Thelen, "Urban Politics: Beyond Bosses and Reformers," *Reviews in American History* 7 (September 1979): 406–412. For an example of a reformer who created a new type of political machine, see Robert Caro's masterful biography of Robert Moses, *The Power Broker: Robert Moses and the Fall of New York* (New York: Vintage Books, 1974).

25   DiGaetano, "The Rise and Development of Urban Political Machines," p. 247, Table 3. For more information on the expansion of city governments in the late nineteenth century, see Jon C. Teaford, *The Unheralded Triumph: City Government in America, 1870–1900* (Baltimore: Johns Hopkins University Press, 1984); Eric H. Monkkonen, *America Becomes Urban: The Development of U.S. Cities and Towns, 1780–1980* (Berkeley: University of California Press, 1988).

26   Terrence J. McDonald and Sally K. Ward, eds., *The Politics of Urban Fiscal Policy* (Beverly Hills, CA: Sage, 1984), Introduction, p. 14.

27   Ibid.

28   Lotchin, "Power and Policy," p. 11.

29   Stanley K. Schultz, *Constructing Urban Culture: American Cities and City Planning, 1800–1920* (Philadelphia, PA: Temple University Press, 1989).

30   Brown and Halaby, "Bosses, Reform, and the Socioeconomic Bases of Urban Expenditure, 1890–1940," p. 87. Interestingly, the authors found that machine cities, after reform—such as the establishment of a city manager form of government—spent more than other cities (p. 89).

31   Many sources of information are available on the Tweed Ring. The two books used here are Alexander Callow Jr., *The Tweed Ring* (New York: Oxford University Press, 1966), and Seymour J. Mandelbaum, *Boss Tweed's New York* (New York: Wiley, 1965). For a provocative yet ultimately unpersuasive defense of Tweed, see Leo Hershkowitz, *Tweed's New York: Another Look* (Garden City, NY: Anchor Books, 1977).

32   Martin Shefter, "The Emergence of the Political Machine: An Alternative View," in *Theoretical Perspectives on Urban Politics,* ed. Willis D. Hawley et al. (Upper Saddle River, NJ: Prentice Hall, 1976), p. 21.

33   The information presented here on Abraham Reuf's machine is taken from Walter Bean, *Boss Reuf's San Francisco* (Berkeley: University of California Press, 1952; reprinted 1972). Only direct quotations from Bean are cited by page in subsequent notes.

34   Ibid., pp. 93–94.

35   Paul Kantor, with Stephen David, *The Dependent City: The Changing Political Economy of Urban America* (Glenview, IL: Scott Foresman, 1988), p. 104.

36   Ernest S. Griffith, *A History of American City Government: The Conspicuous Failure, 1870–1900* (New York: Praeger, 1974), p. 183.

37   Zane Miller, *The Urbanization of Modern America: A Brief History* (New York: Harcourt Brace Jovanovich, 1973), p. 121.

38   Ester R. Fuchs and Robert Y. Shapiro, "Government Performance as a Basis for Machine Support," *Urban Affairs Quarterly* 18, no. 4 (June 1983): 537–550.

39   Merton, *Social Theory and Social Structure,* p. 130.

40   Robert A. Dahl, *Who Governs? Democracy and Power in an American City* (New Haven, CT: Yale University Press, 1961), p. 34.

41   See Doris Kearns Goodwin, *The Fitzgeralds and the Kennedys: An American Saga* (New York: Simon & Schuster, 1987).

42   Martin Shefter, "Political Incorporation and the Extrusion of the Left: Party Politics and Social Forces in New York City," in *Studies in American Political Development*, vol. 1, ed. Karen Orren and Stephen Skowronek (New Haven, CT: Yale University Press, 1986), p. 55.

43   Erie, *Rainbow's End*, p. 69.

44   Terry Nichols Clark, "The Irish Ethic and the Spirit of Patronage," *Ethnicity* 2 (1975): 341–342.

45   Caro, *The Power Broker*, p. 354.

46   John Allswang, *A House for All Peoples* (Lexington, KY: University Press of Kentucky, 1971).

47   For a useful review of the relationships between African Americans and political machines, see Hanes Walton Jr., *Black Politics: A Theoretical and Structural Analysis* (Philadelphia, PA: Lippincott, 1972), Chapter 4.

48   William J. Grimshaw, *Bitter Fruit: Black Politics and the Chicago Machine, 1931–1991* (Chicago, IL: University of Chicago Press, 1992).

49   Ibid.

50   Erie, *Rainbow's End*, p. 165.

51   Thomas M. Guterbock, *Machine Politics in Transition: Party and Community in Chicago* (Chicago, IL: University of Chicago Press, 1980).

52   See Paul Kleppner, *Chicago Divided: The Making of a Black Mayor* (DeKalb: Northern Illinois University Press, 1985).

53   Matthew Vaz, "Tammany Hall and the Machine Style in Black Politics," *Modern American History* 4, no. 1 (2021): 103–107.

54   Ibid., p. 105.

55   Ibid., p. 106.

56   Ibid.

57   Michael Johnston, "Patrons and Clients, Jobs and Machines: A Case Study of the Uses of Patronage," *American Political Science Review* 73, no. 2 (June 1979): 385–398.

58   Erie, *Rainbow's End*, p. 218.

59   Jessica Trounstine, *Political Monopolies in American Cities: The Rise and Fall of Bosses and Reformers* (Chicago, IL: University of Chicago Press, 2008), p. 11.

60   Ibid., pp. 48, 242.

61   For a discussion of the role of political clubs in the evolution of Tammany Hall, see Shefter, "The Emergence of the Political Machine," p. 35.

62   Erie, *Rainbow's End*, pp. 102–103.

63   Kenneth D. Wald argues that ethnics supported machines not so much in response to socioeconomic disadvantage but out of an awareness of their social marginality and in the belief that machines would defend them from external pressures; see his "The Electoral Base of Political Machines: A Deviant Case Analysis," *Urban Affairs Quarterly* 16, no. 1 (September 1980): 3–29.

64   It would be misleading to say that such practices simply reflected the desires of poor immigrants. Irish family life was disrupted by the easy availability of illicit entertainment. Catholic priests and a significant proportion of the immigrant population opposed vice activities.

65   Harold Zink, *City Bosses in the United States* (Durham, NC: Duke University Press, 1930).

66 Wolfinger, "Why Political Machines Have Not Withered Away," p. 70.

67 Allan Rosenbaum, "Machine Politics: Class Interest and the Urban Poor," paper delivered at the annual meeting of the American Political Science Association (September 4–8, 1973), pp. 25–26.

68 Ibid., p. 26.

69 John D. Buenker, *Urban Liberalism and Progressive Reform* (New York: Scribner, 1973). Joseph J. Huthmacher also provides evidence of machine legislators' support for reform; see his "Urban Liberalism and the Age of Reform," *Mississippi Valley Historical Review* 44 (September 1962): 231–241.

70 For the distinction between social and structural reformers, see Melvin G. Holli, *Reform in Detroit: Hazen S. Pingree and Urban Politics* (New York: Oxford University Press, 1969), Chapter 8. We discuss the social reformers in this chapter; in Chapter 4, we discuss the structural reformers.

71 Martin J. Schiesl, *The Politics of Efficiency: Municipal Administration and Reform in America, 1880–1920* (Berkeley: University of California Press, 1977), pp. 80ff.

72 Quoted in Holli, *Reform in Detroit*, p. 42.

73 Ibid., p. 92.

74 Ibid., p. 195.

75 Peter Marris and Martin Rein, *Dilemmas of Social Reform* (New York: Atherton Press, 1967), p. 7.

76 Kantor, *The Dependent City*, pp. 117–118. Machine politicians appealed to voters on the basis of where they lived (their ethnic identification), not on the basis of where they worked (their class identification). Thus machine politics reflected the "city trenches" that have divided the American political landscape into community politics and workplace politics and blunted political action by the working class. See Ira Katznelson, *City Trenches: Urban Politics and the Patterning of Class in the United States* (New York: Pantheon, 1981).

77 See James C. Scott, "Corruption, Machine Politics, and Political Change," *American Political Science Review* 63 (December 1969): 1142–1158; Clarence N. Stone, Robert K. Whelan, and William J. Murin, *Urban Policy and Politics in a Bureaucratic Age*, 2nd ed. (Upper Saddle River, NJ: Prentice Hall, 1986), Chapter 7.

78 Simpson, *Rogues, Rebels, and Rubber Stamps*, p. 280.

79 Ibid., pp. 280–290.

80 Elaine Sharp, ed., *Culture Wars and Urban Politics* (Lawrence: University Press of Kansas, 1999).

81 Larry Bennett, "The Mayor among His Peers: Interpreting Richard M. Daley," unpublished paper (June 2008).

82 Rudolph Bush and Dan Mihalopoulos, "Daley Jobs Chief Guilty"; Dan Mihalopoulos and Charles Sheehan, "Jurors Kept Focus on Case"; Gary Washburn, "Daley's Plans for Re-election Turn Murky"; and John Chase, "Things Are Not Over, FBI Boss Here Says," *Chicago Tribune* (July 7, 2006), pp. 1, 6.

CHAPTER 4

The Reform Crusades

The Reformers' Aims

In 1902, George Washington Plunkitt, a veteran of New York's legendary Tammany Hall machine organization, pontificated that reformers "were mornin' glories—looked lovely in the mornin' and withered up in a short time, while the regular machines went on flourishin' forever, like fine old oaks."[1] At the time Plunkitt delivered that pearl of homegrown wisdom, he had a valid point, but just barely. Even as he spoke, reform movements were springing up in cities all across the country. The reformers aimed to dismantle the party organizations that thrived on immigrant votes, but these movements tended to be short-lived, exactly as Plunkitt observed. Reformers were often successful in persuading state legislatures to enact some reforms intended to undermine the machines; for example, some states took the administration of services out of the hands of boards of aldermen and city councils and put them under the control of professional administrators. But despite such measures, they found it hard to destroy the basic foundation of machine politics. This was not easy to do because machine politicians had a close and often personal relationship with their constituents. Their firm grip on the reins of municipal government gave them the power to decide such matters as hiring for public jobs, streetcar and utility franchises, construction contracts, and the provision of city services. Plenty of patronage and money, the lifeblood of machine politics, were bound up in these decisions.

In the estimation of the reformers, the cities were at the mercy of criminals who plundered the public purse for personal gain, but their efforts to change this state of affairs were often frustrated. Although reformers in Cleveland, New York, Chicago, and other cities sometimes succeeded at throwing machine politicians out of office and getting some of them prosecuted in the courts for corruption, the offending politicians were easily replaced by men cut from the same cloth. Commenting on this fact of life, Englishman James Bryce expressed the view that "the government of cities is the one conspicuous failure of the United States."[2] Reformers shared his

opinion. Writing in 1909, the author of a textbook on municipal government made this assessment:

> The privilege seeker has pervaded our political life. For his own profit he has
> willfully befouled the sources of political power. Politics, which should offer
> a career inspiring to the noblest thoughts and calling for the most patriotic
> efforts of which man is capable, he has ... transformed into a series of
> sordid transactions between those who buy and those who sell governmental
> action.[3]

Concerns about political corruption were closely connected to a rising fear of
immigrants. The reaction against the "Great Unwashed" had been building for
a long time. As early as 1851, an article in the *Massachusetts Teacher* asked,

> The constantly increasing influx of foreigners ... continues to be a cause of
> serious alarm to the most intelligent of our people. What will be the ultimate
> effect of this vast and unexampled immigration ...? Will it, like the muddy
> Missouri, as it pours its waters into the clear Mississippi and contaminates
> the whole united mass, spread ignorance and vice, crime and disease, through
> our native population?[4]

The earlier generations of immigrants were scandalized by lurid newspaper
accounts of prostitution, gambling, and public drunkenness in the immigrant
wards. Religious moralists secured state and local laws abolishing prostitution,
gambling, and Sunday liquor sales. To teach immigrant children middle-class
versions of dress, speech, manners, and discipline, reformers passed laws requiring school attendance and raised the upper age limit for mandatory schooling.
Truant officers were hired to search for wayward youth.

The vicious reaction against immigrants aggravated the racial, class, and
religious tensions that had divided America for almost a century. Immigrants
were compared to the Goths and Vandals who invaded the Roman Empire in
the second century A.D. In his book *Our Country*, the Reverend Josiah Strong
accused them of defiling the Sabbath, spreading illiteracy and crime, and corrupting American culture and morals. Gathered into the cities, he said, immigrants provided "a very paradise for demagogues" who ruled by manipulating
the "appetites and prejudices" of the rabble.[5]

The spatial segregation that separated neighborhoods provided fuel for the
fears and prejudices of the more privileged members of society. By the turn
of the century, all large cities contained sprawling, overcrowded immigrant
neighborhoods near the waterfronts and factories, with middle- and upper-
class neighborhoods located farther from the urban center. Jobs, though, were
concentrated in downtown districts, and affluent city residents could hardly
escape seeing, on their way to work and to shop, the rundown tenements, dirty
streets, and littered alleys where the immigrants lived.

The fight to reform the urban political system was mounted by an alliance that brought together wealthy industrialists and other members of the upper class, well-educated members of the middle class, and middle-class voters. Andrew Carnegie and John D. Rockefeller initially financed the New York City Bureau of Municipal Research, founded in 1906. The U.S. Chamber of Commerce provided office space and paid the executive secretary of the City Managers Association for several years. Civic clubs and voters' leagues generally contained names from elite social directories, and the professionals involved in reform tended to be the most prestigious members of their professions. They succeeded in selling their message to growing numbers of middle-class voters. Between 1870 and 1910, the number of clerical workers, salespersons, government employees, technicians, and salaried professionals multiplied 7.5 times, from 756,000 to 5,609,000.[6] The growing middle class constituted a formidable political force, and with their support, the reformers accomplished most of their major aims within a couple of decades. The way Americans elect their leaders, hire public employees, and administer public services still reflects the politics of the reform era.

OUTTAKE

Municipal Reform Was Aimed at the Immigrants

The municipal reforms of the early nineteenth century were designed to undercut the electoral influence of working-class and immigrant voters. Virtually all machine politicians came from working-class, immigrant origins. Most machine bosses, like their followers, had little formal education; typically, they had started out in politics by carrying messages and working on Election Day. Reformers were at the other end of the social spectrum. Most of the prominent reformers of the Progressive Era were upper-class people, and many, in fact, were wealthy industrialists, with names like McCormick, du Pont, Pinchot, Morgenthau, and Dodge. Most of them had a college education in a day when this fact marked a very select social stratum.

Machine politicians, ethnic voters, and working-class groups usually opposed reform because they correctly perceived that these were designed to make it more difficult for working-class candidates to win public office. In the big cities where they exerted a commanding electoral presence, immigrant voters were generally successful in opposing key features of the reform agenda, but elsewhere the reformers managed to reduce the political influence of those they called the Great Unwashed. The reformers' aims were laid bare in the 1938 municipal elections in Jackson, Michigan. The local chamber of commerce persuaded voters to approve a charter that replaced wards with an at-large election system. Working-class and immigrant candidates now had to compete for votes outside their own neighborhoods; no longer could they win a council seat simply by winning enough votes in their own wards. The slate of candidates sponsored by the chamber of commerce swept into office. The new mayor and the council members celebrated with a reception in the Masonic hall, which excluded Catholics from membership, and once in power, they dismissed most of the city's Roman Catholic employees.

Sources: George Mowry, *The Era of Theodore Roosevelt, 1900–1912* (New York: Harper & Row, 1958); James Weinstein, *The Corporate Ideal in the Liberal State, 1900–1918* (Boston, MA: Beacon Press, 1968).

The Fertile Environment for Reform

In the first decades of the twentieth century, a reform impulse swept the nation, energized in equal measure by concerns about corruption at all levels of government and the enormous power wielded by corporate moguls. Several developments ushered in the period known as the Progressive Era. Ostentatious displays of wealth contrasted starkly with grinding poverty in the city and countryside. Newspapers, magazines, and books created a keen awareness about these conditions among upper-class and educated middle-class readers. By the turn of the century, falling paper prices and technical advances in rapid printing made it possible to produce high-quality mass-circulation newspapers and magazines. During the 1890s, newspaper circulation doubled and then tripled. A multitude of new periodicals appeared. All that was required to develop a mass audience was a way to popularize the press. Muckraking was such a technique. Crusading journalists investigated and reported "inside stories" exposing organized vice and the corruption of the urban machines. They also wrote sensational accounts about pervasive corruption in the national government, big business, the stock market, and the drug and meatpacking industries.

Beginning with its September 1902 issue, *McClure's* magazine printed a series of seven articles by Lincoln Steffens that told lurid stories of municipal corruption in the nation's big cities. In October, *McClure's* carried an article by Ida Tarbell exposing corporate corruption and profiteering by John D. Rockefeller's Standard Oil Company. Colorful stories of this kind attracted a large readership because they fed an insatiable appetite for shocking accounts of wrongdoing in business and government. Over the next few years, *Munsey's, Everybody's, Success, Collier's, Saturday Evening Post, Ladies' Home Journal, Hampton's, Pearson's, Cosmopolitan,* and dozens of daily newspapers published stories that contributed to a popular feeling that America's political, economic, and social institutions had become corrupt. Big business was accused of producing unsafe and shoddy goods, fixing prices, and crushing the competition. There were exposés of fraudulent practices in banking; heartrending accounts of women and children working at long, tedious, and dangerous jobs in factories and sweatshops; and stories about urban poverty, prostitution, white slavery, and business–government collusion to protect vice.

An outpouring of books played on the same themes. In 1904, Steffens gathered his *McClure's* articles together into a best-selling volume, *The Shame of the Cities*. Other popular titles included *The Greatest Trust in the World*, an exposé of price-fixing and collusion in the steel industry; *The Story of Life Insurance*; and *The Treason of the Senate*, which detailed systematic bribery of U.S. senators. Several novelists entered the field. In his novel *An American Tragedy*, Theodore Dreiser described the corrupting influence of greed on a self-made small-town boy. Dreiser's *Sister Carrie* and David Graham Phillip's *Susan Lenox* vividly portrayed how the impersonal forces of urban life victimized young women. In *The Financier*, Dreiser's story revolved around the ruthless drive for power and wealth, using the Chicago streetcar magnate Charles Yerkes as his model.

The literature produced by the muckrakers—an epithet applied to them in 1906 by President Theodore Roosevelt, referring to a character in John Bunyan's 1645 book *Pilgrim's Progress* who was too busy raking muck to look up and see the stars—was influential in building popular interest in reform. Although the details of reform were often dull and unexciting to the average citizen, the muckrakers' stories gave a feeling of drama and urgency to the cause of reform. No work was more influential than Upton Sinclair's *The Jungle*, a classic work still assigned in college courses. Sinclair tells a riveting story of a Lithuanian immigrant's fight to survive in a corrupt and chaotic Chicago. Beaten down by destitution and poverty, eventually, his wife becomes a prostitute, his children die, and he becomes a socialist revolutionary. Sinclair's nauseating accounts of the conditions in Chicago's meatpacking industry (the rats, feces, chopped fingers, and spoiled meat swept into sausage vats) catalyzed a national crusade that prompted Congress to establish the U.S. Food and Drug Administration in 1905.

The political backlash created by the muckrakers catalyzed the formation of organizations dedicated to the goals of regulating business practices, improving working conditions, imposing standards on the professions, and reforming government. Business leaders organized the National Civic Federation in 1900. By advocating workers' compensation and other modest social insurance schemes, the founders of the federation hoped to undermine more militant demands proposed by union organizers.[7] The National Child Labor Committee was organized in 1904 to fight for child labor legislation. In 1910, the National Housing Association brought together housing reform groups from many cities to campaign for building codes. Numerous public officials' associations and municipal research bureaus came into existence specifically to promote municipal reform: The National Association of Port Authorities, the Municipal Finance Officers Association, the American Association of Park Superintendents, the Conference of City Managers, and the National Short Ballot Association.

Although flagrant corruption energized campaigns to "throw the rascals out" in a few cities in the 1870s and 1880s, the issues tended to be local and the remedies specific to an immediate circumstance. But in the 1890s, the reform cause was transformed into a national crusade. Citizens' groups sprang up all across the country to lobby for improved public services and honesty in government. The problems faced by the reformers varied little from one city to the next. Like-minded reformers from different cities soon began to exchange advice and information about their efforts. It did not take long before these informal networks became transformed into national organizations.

In 1894, delegates to the First Annual Conference for Good City Government met in Philadelphia to establish the first national municipal reform organization, the National Municipal League. The delegates to the conference were united in the belief that machine politicians and their immigrant constituents had corrupted democratic institutions in the cities. But they disagreed about the measures that should be taken to change this situation. "We are not unlike patients assembled in a hospital," one of the participants put it, "examining together and describing to each other our sore places."[8] After the formation of the National Municipal League, the nationalization of reform proceeded quickly. Within two years, 180 local chapters were affiliated with the league, and, by the turn of the century member organizations had sprung up all across the country. In their annual meetings, reformers got a chance to compare notes, and by the time they met in November 1899, the members of the National Municipal League were able to reach agreement on a model municipal charter they could use as a blueprint for "good government."

As a strategy for undermining the close relationship between politicians and their immigrant constituents, the Municipal League's model charter recommended that electoral wards be abolished; instead, each city council member would be elected "at-large," that is, by all the voters of the city. It recommended the abolition of the party label on election ballots, on the premise that uneducated voters cast their ballots for a symbol, but not a name. The charter urged reformers to fight for civil service appointment procedures so that party officials would not be able to use public jobs for patronage. The league also said that local elections should be held in different years than national and state elections, so that the national political parties would find it more difficult to influence local affairs.[9]

The reformers wanted to kick the rascals out, but they also wanted to make local government more efficient and accountable to the tastes and preferences of middle-class voters. The model charter drawn up by the league urged reformers to give the mayor the power to appoint top administrators and to veto legislation. The assumption behind this reform—called "strong mayor government"—was that with authority centralized in the hands of the mayor, voters would be able to hold the mayor accountable for the city's overall governance, and the spoils system presided over by city councils would be disrupted. As they saw it, the main problem was the style of politics in which city council members or aldermen cut deals behind the scenes. Finally, the league urged city reformers to seek home rule, which would give cities, and their voters, broad powers to control their own affairs without meddling from state legislatures.

Through all these reforms, the municipal reformers intended to place the affairs of the city into the hands of educated upper- and middle-class voters and, increasingly, in a cadre of professionally trained and credentialed administrators. Within a few decades, the municipal reform movement managed to build a bureaucratic mode of governance that generations of Americans have often complained about, but which has expanded the public sector, and moved important services out of the realm of politics and into the hands of professionals.

The Campaigns against Machine Rule

The intense enmity shared by the reformers toward the urban machines and their immigrant constituents motivated them to cast about a variety of remedies for the ills they observed. Some reformers went so far as to question the wisdom of universal suffrage, claiming the immigrants were too ignorant and illiterate to vote intelligently. The Tilden Commission, appointed by the New York legislature to investigate the Tweed Ring scandals in New York City, recommended in 1878 that suffrage be restricted to those who owned property.[10] The commission's report was reprinted in an 1899 issue of *Municipal Affairs*, the National Municipal League's magazine, and many reformers read it approvingly. Andrew D. White, the first president of Cornell University, summed up the case for disenfranchising the immigrants in an 1890 issue of *Forum:*

> A city is a corporation; ... as a city it has nothing whatever to do with general political interests .... The questions in a city are not political questions .... The work of a city being the creation and control of the city property, it should logically be managed as a piece of property by those who have created it, who have a title to it, or a real substantial part in it, ... [and not by] a crowd of illiterate peasants, freshly raked in from the Irish bogs, or Bohemian mines, or Italian robber nests.[11]

However attractive the idea of attaching property qualifications to the vote might have been, such a drastic remedy was simply impractical. To wage a campaign on this issue would certainly have provoked a negative reaction, even from some of the groups that supported reform. From the constitutional period until the Jacksonian reforms of the 1820s and 1830s, most states had restricted the vote to owners of property. The abolition of these restrictions had been celebrated as a triumph for popular democracy. Virtually everyone understood that the time had passed when the ownership of property could be required as a condition for voting, but a few reformers tried to do it anyway. The 1912 charter of Phoenix, in the new state of Arizona, restricted voting in municipal elections to taxpayers, but the state courts invalidated the restriction as unconstitutional.[12] Even before Phoenix's attempt to restrict the vote, it was clear that the reformers would have to find less direct and more crea-tive methods to reduce the influence of the immigrants and the working class.

Few reformers seriously questioned the idea that immigrants should par-ticipate in the democratic system. They were convinced the real problem with elections was that they were run by machine politicians who took advantage of their immigrant constituents, and they were not entirely wrong. Municipal elections were notoriously chaotic and corrupt, conducted, as they were, in the absence of well-established rules and regulations. Because the political parties were considered private organizations, their nominating procedures were not regulated at all. To select candidates for public office, political parties held nominating conventions and ward caucuses according to their own change-able and unwritten rules, often on short notice and at locations known only to insiders. It was not unusual for caucuses to be held in the back rooms of saloons owned by ward bosses. According to one scholar,

> This was the period of massive voting frauds. In the elections of 1868 and 1872, 8 percent more people voted in New York state than were registered. In 1910, when the New York City vote was challenged and recounted, half of the votes were found to be fraudulent. In New Jersey, the stuffing of ballot boxes was so common that the state legislature replaced the wooden boxes with glass ballot jars. In Pennsylvania and Michigan, gangs of thugs moved from polling place to polling place beating up the opposition and voting at will. Fictitious and repeat voters, false counting, and stuffed ballot boxes were such regular features of city elections that voting statistics from this period are suspect.[13]

A Philadelphia politician once boasted that the signers of the Declaration of Independence were machine loyalists: "'These men,' he said, 'the fathers of American liberty, voted down here once. And,' he added with a sly grin, 'they vote here yet.'"[14]

Machine workers sometimes completed the ballot for voters or accompa-nied them into the voting booth. "Farmer Jones," a member of the Chicago machine in the 1890s, revealed to an inquiring reformer how he guaranteed voter loyalty:

> [The reformer asked,] "When you got the polling stations in your hands, what did you do?"
>
> "Voted our men, of course."
>
> "And the negroes, how did they vote?"
>
> "They voted as they ought to have voted. They had to."
>
> "… how could you compel those people to vote against their will?"
>
> "They understood, and besides," said he, "there was not a man voted in that booth that I did not know how he voted before he put the paper in the judges' hands."[15]

On the chance that other methods were not sufficiently reliable, some machines directly paid for the vote. The 1896 election in the First Ward of Chicago provides a good example:

> The bars were open all night and the brothels were jammed. By ten o'clock the next morning, though, the saloons were shut down, not in concession to the reformers, but because many of the bartenders and owners were needed to staff the First Ward field organization. The Bath, Hinky Dink and their aides ran busily from polling place to polling place, silver bulging in their pockets into which they dug frequently and deeply. The effort was not in vain, and the outcome was gratifying.[16]

Not trusting in fraud alone, machine politicians sometimes resorted to intimidation and violence. In his 1898 campaign for alderman, the Chicago ward boss John Powers threatened voters and told business owners they would lose their business licenses unless they supported him.[17] "Hinky Dink" Kenna and "Bathhouse John" Coughlin of Chicago's First Ward defended their loyal constituents but routinely harassed opponents. In the bootleg era of the 1920s, organized crime and machine politics became closely coupled in Chicago. Gangland hits were visited on meddling politicians who stood outside the inner circle of men controlling and protecting illegal liquor, speakeasies, prostitution, and gambling.

Flagrant election-day corruption energized those who opposed such abuses. Ed Crump, the boss of Memphis, Tennessee, won his first mayoral election in 1909 by watching the polls himself. He personally stopped the use of marked ballots by a machine organization he was opposing, in one case by hitting a voter in the face.[18] In Pittsburgh's state and city elections of 1933, the Democrats and Republicans—both rightly fearing fraud by the other party—mobilized opposing armies of poll watchers. The state police were called in to keep the peace, and lawyers and judges stood by to provide quick court action.[19]

In the late 1890s, reformers introduced several measures intended to reduce election fraud. The key reforms included:

- *Voter registration and literacy requirements*. These requirements reduced repeat voting and stopped the practice of importing voters for an election. By 1920, almost all states had imposed registration laws.
- *Australian ballot*. This was a ballot that could be marked only by the voter, and it was cast in secret. Before the Australian ballot was introduced in the 1880s, the parties printed the ballots and often marked and placed them in a ballot box in front of observers. The ballots were even handed to voters already marked. The use of the Australian ballot became universal after the turn of the century.
- *Nonpartisan elections*. Reformers fought hard to remove party labels of any kind from municipal, election ballots. Where they succeeded, voters

had only one clue as to how they should vote: The printed name of the individual candidate.

Although these reforms brought a measure of order and honesty to urban elections, they also had the effect of reducing voting participation by immigrants who did not speak English, and less educated voters, who could not read. Where there were no precinct captains and party workers to help voters register or look over a sample ballot, even those, who were allowed to vote in theory (white males who were U.S. citizens) were effectively disenfranchised. Twenty-five percent of the white males of voting age in the United States in 1900 were first-generation immigrants, and two-thirds of them had come from non-English-speaking countries. In the industrial cities, typically, more than two-thirds of the voters were foreign-born immigrants. Illiterate voters often asked for help in reading and filling out the ballot, or requested one that was already completed. When they showed up at the polling place, no one questioned their right to cast a vote. After reforms were adopted, they were required to register in writing, often months before an election. And when they went to the polling station, they now faced an election judge, a voting booth, and a printed ballot they could not read. Machine politicians were often able to get around the problems of the secret ballot by controlling the polling places, but these actions exposed them to the possibility of criminal prosecution.

African Americans became enfranchised for good—with some caveats and many setbacks—after the passage of the 15th Amendment in 1870, and they played a vital role in local politics in many Northern cities. Their many important contributions remain remarkably understudied, especially during the time period between the passage of the 15th Amendment and the Great Migration. Despite the fact that Black males gained the right to vote in 1870, there were continuous efforts to suppress the Black vote in many cities. In response, federal troops watched over the polls in 1870 in the nation's bigger cities, in order to prevent any such efforts. However, over the course of the following years, federal oversight waned, which left many Black voters vulnerable to suppression, continuing disenfranchisement, and even violence.

Unlike the immigrant voters, who were more easily won over by machine politicians, the Black vote was divided and fluid in many cities. In Philadelphia, for instance, an established class of educated, Black Philadelphian activists, among them Octavius Catto, Fanny Jackson Coppin, Charlotte Vadine Forten, Lucrecia Mott, and Jacob White, Jr., had traditionally supported Republican candidates and generated a Black vote significant enough to push local Republican politicians toward key issues, such as, for instance, protections from harassment by the city's Irish Democratic machine.[20] Post-reconstruction, however, Northern Blacks were more concerned with getting politicians elected, who would prioritize racial equality over mainstream Republican issues that were not directly important to them—such as government corruption. Continued focus on reform on the side of the Republicans upset Northern Black voters, who, to that point, had felt a strong loyalty to the Party of Lincoln. Calls for the foundation of a Black Independence Party became more commonplace.[21] In the long run, the strife of African Americans for equal rights and more recognition on a local level led many political activists to part ways or at least loosen their allegiance with the Republican Party. In Philadelphia, Democratic mayoral candidate Samuel G. King successfully ran on a platform of racial equality against Republican three-term incumbent, William S. Stokley. The Black activist vote helped defeat Stokley, and his defeat became symbolic as a turning point for Northern Blacks: At the local level, Democratic candidates were no longer off-limits for African American voters. Yet, at the same time, this turn in electoral allegiance led to a significant decline in motivation among Republican candidates in Philadelphia to address issues of racial equality.[22] On the other hand, as the size of the Black voting bloc grew due to the increasing influx of newcomers from the South during the Great Migration, local Democratic Party organizations and machine politicians in many cities started to see civil rights issues as a mobilization tool for the Black vote.[23]

In New York City, the Tammany Machine recognized by the late 1800s that the Black vote was a bloc they had to recon with. In response, they created segregated political clubs, among them the United Colored Democracy (UCD), established in 1898, in order to capture the Black vote.[24] Initially, the Tammany organization worked hard to dilute the impact of these Black political clubs by forcing them to consult machine leadership in neighborhood-based decision-making processes.[25] Still, over time, Black New Yorkers slowly shifted their allegiance from the Republican to the Democratic Party. This process was not without its drawbacks and frustrations for Black political activists, Black politicians, and Black voters alike, but it eventually led to a consolidation of the Black vote with the Democratic Party at the local level in the Northern cities, long before the Great Party Realignment shifted the demographic balance of the Black vote at the national level. As one observer wrote:

> Whenever Democrats were out of power or faced a threat from reform factions, they turned to Black New Yorkers [...]. [...] The transition into the Democratic Party was rocky because many Black people believed that it was foolish to align with the Democrats. Further, Tammany was viewed as unhelpful to Black causes because its members participated in and/or remained silent about issues of police brutality in the city (Lewinson, 1974: 45). Nonetheless, by the 1940s, most Black people and Black political clubs and consolidated into the mainstream, Democratic Party.[26]

The growing appeal of the machines to the Black vote became an additional point of contention for the reformers.

By 1905, voter registration laws had been placed on the books in most of the states.[27] In the next few years, states and localities set up election boards, made it illegal to vote more than once, and tried to define the legitimate uses of campaign funds. Although enforcement was uneven, especially in the cities—the machines continued to control prosecutors and the courts in many places—the existence of new laws provided the basis for investigations and prosecutions when the middle- and upper-class public became disturbed about corruption.

Once electoral reforms were put in place, municipal reformers focused their attention on the machine organizations. It was obvious that machine politicians derived their strength from ethnic neighborhoods and that the machines relied upon the ability of uneducated voters to easily identify a party label printed on the ballot. By voting a straight party ticket, the voter did not have to read the candidates' names. To make it harder for the voters to support machine candidates in this way, the reformers fought hard for two reforms—nonpartisan ballots and at-large elections.

Reformers argued that party labels encouraged blind loyalty to a political organization. They wanted a more "rational" informed voter who possessed the ability to "accumulate and carry in his head the brief list of personal preferences and do without the guidance of party names and symbols on the ballot."[28] The reformers asserted it was the responsibility of citizens to educate themselves and to vote for the best candidates strictly on their merits, not on the basis of party loyalty or ethnic solidarity. Brand Whitlock, the famous reform mayor of Toledo, Ohio, observed,

> It seems almost incredible now that men's minds were ever so clouded,
> strange that they did not earlier discover how absurd was a system which,
> in order to enable them the more readily to subjugate themselves, actually
> printed little woodcuts of birds—roosters and eagles—at the heads of the
> tickets, so that they might be more easily and readily recognize their masters
> and deliver their suffrages over to them.[29]

Just as the reformers intended, the nonpartisan ballot made it harder for immigrants to vote as a bloc. Reading their alderman's printed name could be hard for illiterate voters. Recognizing the party symbol on the ballot was infinitely easier than reading the names of candidates.

The reformers also believed that nonpartisan elections would change the types of candidates seeking public office. The party organization supplied campaign money and workers and freed working-class candidates from the necessity of holding a normal job, which would have denied them time to participate in politics. Few politicians in the cities could have started or stayed in politics without the resources supplied by a party organization. Local parties pooled resources and built cooperative relationships among politicians; without them, people of wealth and social standing tended to hold an overwhelming advantage. This result was, in fact, the objective of the nonpartisanship crusade—to make politics once again a calling appropriate to the educated and cultured classes.[30]

The proposal to replace wards with at-large elections was designed to break the link between neighborhoods and machine politicians. Andrew White complained that "wards largely controlled by thieves and robbers can send thieves and robbers" into public office, and "the vote of a single tenement house, managed by a professional politician, will neutralize the vote of an entire street of well-to-do citizens."[31] The remedy was to require every candidate for the city council to campaign for support from voters wherever they lived in the city; rarely, in such a system, could one neighborhood or ethnic group produce enough votes to carry an election. Gone would be the politics of trade-offs, logrolling, and compromise among legislators representing their own wards:

> For decades the election of councils by wards had superimposed a network of search for parochial favors, of units devoted to partisan spoils, and of catering to ethnic groups that time and again had either defeated comprehensive city programs or loaded them with irrelevant spoils and ill-conceived ward projects. The ward and precinct were the heart of machine control, and the councils so elected were usually also infested with corruption, however acceptable the councilors may have been to the voters of their wards.[32]

Wards potentially gave even relatively small ethnic and racial groups some leverage. Lithuanian voters, for example, might be able to send a Lithuanian alderman to the city council, even if they constituted a tiny proportion of a city's total population. Wards multiplied the points of access through which groups and individuals could influence public officials. At-large elections had an opposite effect. If the city is one big electoral district, candidates representing ethnic and racial groups clustered in specific neighborhoods are handicapped; in order to be elected, they are forced to broaden their appeal to groups distributed over many neighborhoods. Because campaigns covering a city are costly and time consuming, wealthier candidates have a built-in advantage. In such a system, personal wealth and social status become the ingredients of political success.

Civil service hiring systems constituted the last big plank in the reform platform. Civil service rules were crucial because they stopped the machines from rewarding loyal supporters with patronage jobs; instead, written and oral civil service examinations would become the sole basis for hiring municipal employees, and a system of tenure and seniority would make employees safe from political firings. Reformers thought of civil service as the silver bullet because without patronage, they expected the machines to quickly wither away.

The package of reform proposals generally was rejected in the industrial cities where ethnics made up a large proportion of the electorate. In smaller places, even when the machine threat did not seem plausible, reformers were often successful in making the sale. A melodramatic rhetoric of corruption and venality turned the machines into a scary bogeyman hiding just around the corner, ready to pounce at the first opportunity.[33] Such stories could just as well be, and often were, imported from cities hundreds of miles away. The reformers' job was made all the more easier because the residents of small urban places tended to share their view that local government should do little else but provide essential public services such as water, sewage disposal, streets, and perhaps libraries.

The electoral rules installed in the era of reform are much in evidence in contemporary cities. Before 1910, nonpartisan elections were almost unknown, but by 1929, they were utilized in 57 percent of the cities with populations of more than 30,000.[34] By the 1960s, a large number of states required their cities to use nonpartisan elections; these included Minnesota, California, Alaska, and most of the western states. In 10 more states, nonpartisan ballots were used in 90 percent or more of the cities (the exceptions usually being cities above a specified size). In the West, 94 percent of cities used nonpartisan elections. The eastern seaboard is the only region of the country where more cities use partisan than nonpartisan elections. The big cities managed to buck the trend: Among those with more than 500,000 people, 85 percent still print party labels on the ballot.

Reformed electoral systems were designed to reduce the influence of working-class ethnic voters, and plenty of evidence indicates that they accomplished their intended purpose. In the first years of the twentieth century, working-class candidates, some of them socialists, were elected to city offices in dozens of cities.[35] The spread of at-large elections made it much harder for candidates of this stripe to win. In Dayton, Ohio, socialists elected two aldermen and three assessors from working-class wards in the 1909 elections. This shocking outcome motivated local elites to mount a furious campaign to install an at-large system. By the 1913 election, it was in place. In that year's election, the socialists received 35 percent of the popular vote and, in 1917, 44 percent, but because all candidates were elected at-large, in neither year were the socialists able to elect a single candidate. Similarly, in 1911 Pittsburgh adopted at-large elections, with the result that upper-class business leaders and professionals pushed lower- and middle-class groups out of their places on the city council and the school board.[36]

St. Louis provides a graphic example of these two electoral systems at work. The members of the city's board of aldermen compete for office through partisan elections in each of the city's 28 wards (see Figure 4.1). In a city that was 41 percent African American in 1970, race had become a hotly contested terrain. Because of St. Louis's ward system, 10 Blacks won seats on the city's board of aldermen in the 1977 municipal elections (and 11 by 2000). All of them represented predominantly African American wards located in the northern half of the city. By contrast, all of the 18 wards with a majority of white voters elected white aldermen. (As in many cities, *alderman* is an official term in the St. Louis city charter and does not refer exclusively to males.)

These results differed sharply from the outcome of the St. Louis school board elections because all the candidates were required to compete in at-large

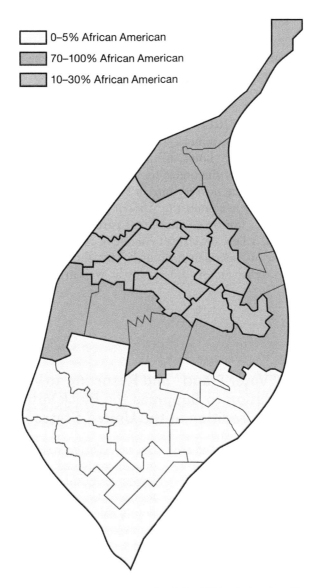

0–5% African American

70–100% African American

10–30% African American

FIGURE 4.1 Racial Composition of Municipal Wards in the City of St. Louis, 1977

Source: Racial composition of each ward estimated on the basis of the 1970 census data.

contests. In 1977, at a time when 70 percent of the public school enrollment was African American, not a single Black candidate made it onto the school board. All five of the seats on the ballot went to white middle-class candidates because few white voters would support an African American candidate. The ward system ensured that African Americans would be represented in the city's legislative body, but the rules governing school board elections produced a different outcome.

However, the structure of the electoral system is only one factor that can help determine minority representation. The fact remains that, in comparison to white turnout, minority turnout is often low, with the major exception of the 2008 and 2012 presidential elections, where African American turnout equaled (2008) or even surpassed (2012) white turnout.[37] Socio-economic status is a strong determining factor in minority turnout, especially in local elections.[38] In Ferguson, just outside St. Louis, 67 percent of the population is African American, but 94 percent of the police force is white, as are five out of its six city council members.[39] The poverty rate in Ferguson, however, is 22 percent, and it is particularly high among the African American population.[40] Low socio-economic status is known to curb voter participation, especially in local elections. In addition, a lack of African American candidates is an additional factor to lower African American turnout.[41] This shows that, in addition to the electoral system, other factors are at play as well in determining minority representation.

OUTTAKE

Claiming "Voter Fraud" and Resorting to Violence and Intimidation to Suppress the Black Vote Has a Long Tradition in the United States

In the aftermath of the 2020 election and former President Trump's false claims of voter fraud, Republicans engaged in efforts to discredit or disregard the lawfully cast votes of millions of voters—the vast majority of them African Americans in the nation's major cities: On Tuesday, November 17, two weeks after the 2020 presidential elections, the two Republican members of the bi-partisan board of canvassers (consisting of two Democrats and two Republicans) in Wayne County, MI (the country in which Detroit is located), voted not to certify the election results of the City of Detroit and its metro area. One of the Republican board members claimed to not have "complete and accurate information" in order to verify which ballots originated in which precincts.[42] In truth, the issues described by the Republican board member, Monica Palmer, only concerned 387 ballots, or 0.15 percent, out of Detroit's more than 250,000 ballots cast in the 2020 presidential election. Tellingly, Palmer then moved to certify the election results in Wayne Country's majority-white suburbs as well as the county's "communities other than the city of Detroit."[43] The city of Detroit's population in 2020 was over 78 percent Black. In a Zoom meeting that night, intended to allow citizens to comment on the board's vote, the Rev. Wendell Anthony, head of the Detroit branch of the NAACP, famously called the board's two Republican members' refusal to certify the election results a "disgrace." He noted: "You have extracted a Black city out of a county and said the only ones that are at fault is the City of Detroit where 80% of the people who reside here are African Americans. Shame on you!"[44]

In Wisconsin, another "swing state" in 2020, where the Trump campaign had hoped to win and, after losing the state to Biden, had claimed "election fraud," Republicans filed a petition to recount *only* ballots cast in Milwaukee and Dane counties, where the cities of Milwaukee and Madison are located, and where the state's largest concentration of African Americans live.[45] In Milwaukee County, Biden had won over Trump by 53 points, in Dane County by 40 points.[46] Republicans had no interest to recount the results in the rest of the state of Wisconsin, which is majority white and whose rural and suburban areas had voted for Trump. The Trump team also claimed voter fraud and targeted election results in Philadelphia and Atlanta, two other cities with a plurality or majority of Black voters, located in states that Republicans had hoped to win but narrowly lost in 2020. Kristen Clarke, president and executive director of the Lawyers' Committee for Civil Rights Under Law said of the Trump campaign's focus on discrediting election results in majority Black cities, such as Detroit, Philadelphia, and Atlanta: "It is difficult for me to think of another president in modern time who has literally driven a national scheme to disenfranchise Black voters and other voters of color en masse, in the way that we see with these post-election lawsuits."[47] While Clarke is not wrong, efforts to throw out, discredit, or suppress the Black vote in the United States date as far back as the 15th Amendment.

In Wilmington, NC, on November 10, 1898, a democratically elected government was overthrown and replaced with white supremacists, culminating in one of the country's many race massacres that are rarely spoken about in history classes. One observer simply called it a violent coup d'etat.[48] Originally referred to as the "Wilmington Race Riot," the event was framed as a violent uprising by Wilmington's Black population, which was then successfully "subdued" by the white supremacist instigators.

One of the first cities in the nation to elect African Americans to local office, Wilmington's bi-racial Republican party had managed to elect three Black aldermen. In addition, African Americans held important positions in the city's bureaucracy, and the Black community had significant economic influence over the city's private sector. By the end of the century, the North Carolina Fusion Party, an interracial coalition of mostly Black Republicans and white Populists had managed to establish significant political strength in the state and started to dismantle the segregationist, Democratic position, by chipping away at their institutionalized position of power, much to the disdain of the state's white supremacists. In 1898, the newly elected Democratic State Party Chairman, Furnifold Simmons, summed up the Democrat's party platform thus: "North Carolina is a white man's state, and white men will rule it, and they will crush the party of negro domination beneath a majority so overwhelming that no other party will ever dare to attempt to establish negro rule here."[49] Leading up to election day, there had already been ample intimidation of Blacks and Republicans by Democrat white supremacists. This escalated on the day of the election itself, when Democrats attempted to drive Blacks from the polls with gunfire and violence. The Democrats "won" the statewide election, most likely by simply letting many Republican and Fusionist ballots disappear, but since Wilmington's local government had not been up for election, it remained in power. On the morning of November 9, 1898, North Carolina's white supremacist leadership issued an obnoxious "White Declaration of Independence" in which they "asserted the supremacy of white men" and called for an end to Black voting rights and political participation, giving Wilmington's African American citizenry 12 hours for compliance. When they received no response by 7:30 am the next morning, a mob of hundreds of white businessmen marched to the building that housed *The Daily* Record, the city's Black newspaper, vandalized it, and set it on fire. Following this act of violence, thousands of white "vigilantes" swarmed the streets of the city rioting, shooting, and eventually forcing Wilmington's political leadership to resign. After installing a white supremacist government in Wilmington, the perpetrators marched the city's Black leadership to the train station and expelled them to the North. As the Rev. Allen J. Kirk, a contemporary observer, recounted: "The streets were dotted with their [African Americans'] dead bodies. A white gentleman said that he saw ten bodies lying in the undertaker's office at one time. Some of their bodies were left lying in the streets until up in the next day following the riot. Some were found by the stench and miasma that came forth from their decaying

bodies under their houses. Every colored man who passed through the streets had either to be guarded by one of the crowd or have a paper (pass) giving him the right to pass. All colored men at the cotton press and oil mills were ordered not to leave their labor but stop there, while their wives and children were shrieking and crying in the midst of the flying balls and in sight of the cannons and Gatling gun. All the white people had gone out of that part of the City, this army of men marched through the streets, sword buckled to their sides, giving the command to fire. Men stood at their labor wringing their hands and weeping, but they dare not move to the protection of their homes."[50]

It is estimated that 60–300 people died that day in Wilmington. After the coup, North Carolina effectively came under one-party (Democratic) rule. The events of that day reflect the continuing assault on racial equality and Black voting rights post-Reconstruction. In combination with the aftermath of the 2020 election, they should also serve as an eerie warning sign for what is still possible in the twenty-first Century.

Sources: Matt Stieb, "Republicans Keep Trying to Throw Out Black Votes After the Election," *New York Magazine* (November 18, 2020); "Trump Push to Invalidate Votes in Heavily Black Cities Alarms Civil Rights Groups," *All Things Considered, NPR* (November 24, 2020); Adrienne LaFrance and Vann R. Newkirk II, "The Lost History of an American Coup D'Etat," *The Atlantic* (August 12, 2017); Richard Wormser, *The Rise and Fall of Jim Crow* (New York: Macmillan, 2004), pp. 85–86; Rev. Allen J. Kirk, "A Statement of Facts Concerning the Bloody Riot in Wilmington, N.C. Of Interest to the United States." Electronic Edition. Wilmington, NC (1898). North Carolina Collection, The University of North Carolina at Chapel Hill.

Over time, virtually all cities in the southwestern United States adopted some combination of nonpartisan and at-large elections. Partly as a result, a style of politics evolved in that region that was tilted heavily in favor of business elites. "Frugality, efficiency, and professionalism in public administration" have always been the themes guiding the governance of southwestern cities, but a multitude of governmental units have been willing to take on a great many responsibilities to promote local development.[51] For decades, legions of bureaucrats and professionals have found employment in special districts and authorities devoted to developing land, providing water, dredging harbors, supplying electricity, and lobbying the federal government so that business could grow.[52] Until the 1960s, candidates for public office tended to be selected by business associations. As a result, the cities of the Southwest produced a distinctive type of machine politics, though of course its participants did not give it that label. Voters tended to turn out for elections at a much lower rate than in the industrial cities of the North.[53] This state of affairs began to change in the 1960s only when civil rights and neighborhood groups mobilized in several Sunbelt cities to challenge the tightly knit regimes that had long been dominated by white business interests.

"Efficiency and Economy" in Municipal Affairs

In the earliest years of the movement for municipal reform, "efficiency and economy" became code words for good government. When Theodore Roosevelt addressed the delegates to the First Annual Conference for Good City Government in 1894, he urged them to go beyond their moral outrage at the way things were being run to find ways of streamlining and improving government: "There are two gospels I always want to preach to reformers .... The first is the gospel of morality; the next is the gospel of efficiency .... I don't think I have to tell you to be upright, but I do think I have to tell you to be practical and efficient."[54] In truth, it is doubtful the reformers needed such advice. Municipal reformers were hard at work searching for guideposts marking the way to good governance. If they succeeded at kicking the rascals out, they needed to know what to do with their inheritance.

The extreme disorganization of city governments gave the reformers a big target to aim at. All through the nineteenth century, cities had tended to add new responsibilities and services piecemeal, one small step at a time. By the late century, every city was governed by a multitude of independent boards and commissions administering municipal services. Organization charts had never been drawn up, making it impossible to make sense of how any individual city was run. This state of affairs seemed like a perfect recipe for chaos and corruption. Typically, a city was governed by a city council, with each of the aldermen representing a ward. Reformers claimed that this system produced a political culture of logrolling and vote-trading. Aldermen also got in the habit of filling the multitude of committees, boards, and commissions with their political cronies, who also took bribes when the opportunity arose. What was to be done? The reformers agreed that the best solution was to replace ward-based with at-large elections. The idea was that individuals with the personal resources to run citywide campaigns would tend to win, and that therefore a better class of person would end up occupying the mayor's office. This assumption was often, but not always, borne out. Campaigns covering an entire city were expensive, and in the late nineteenth century, candidates for mayor paid most of their own campaign costs.[55] As a result, mayors generally came from prominent, even upper-class, backgrounds. Working-class ethnic candidates came to the office mainly in cities with a disciplined party organization with a broad and diverse base.

To enhance the authority of mayors and administrators, state legislatures regularly intervened to take budgetary and supervisory authority from elected councils and to give these powers to mayors or to full-time boards and commissions whose members were appointed by the mayor. In 1891, the Indiana legislature gave the Indianapolis comptroller the authority to draft the budget; the council retained the authority to lower, but could not increase, appropriations. New charters granted the mayors of Cleveland and Indianapolis the right to remove executive officials, a feature that was also adopted in charters approved in other states: New Orleans in 1896 and Baltimore in 1898.[56] In 1892, New York's legislature mandated a Board of Estimate and Apportionment, modeled on New York City's, for all cities over 50,000 in population. In the 1870s and 1880s, state legislative committees assumed financial or administrative control of the police departments of Detroit, Baltimore, Boston, St. Louis, Kansas City, and New York.

Reformers became accustomed to lobbying legislatures to enact legislation that would favor the reform cause. When they intervened in this way, legislatures became, in effect, referees among the contending interests that were trying to control local politics. Even if they had wanted to, state legislatures could not have been completely insulated from the political battles occurring in the cities. Local governments provided key public services, and representatives to state legislatures answered to local constituents; as a consequence, local and state affairs were closely entwined: "The ordinary work of state politics was local affairs, and an ordinary branch of local government was the state legislature."[57] Most legislators were not inclined to interfere actively in issues arising from local governments outside their legislative districts, and rules governing the apportionment of legislative districts limited the number of legislators coming from big cities. Research has shown that "virtually all bills affecting big cities were introduced by representatives from those cities."[58] Nonlocal representatives "routinely deferred to local governments."[59] Therefore, the important question became: Who, if anyone, spoke for local governments?

Ordinarily, the legislators who represented the biggest cities came from the more privileged sectors of society, and this occurred even where machines governed.[60] They were business leaders, bankers, lawyers, and other men of professional and social standing. The men of wealth and social prestige refused to run in the ethnic wards against immigrant saloonkeepers and party loyalists, but they possessed the personal resources to compete and win in state legislative districts. In addition, members of many of the boards and commissions of city government were appointed by governors, legislative committees, and mayors, and thus they were "protected from popular control, insulated from the undue influence of the city's aldermen, and dominated by those perched proudly on the top rung of the urban social ladder."[61]

By these means, reformers achieved some check on the ward-based city councils, but they were looking for a more comprehensive approach that might transform the governance of the city from top to bottom. To accomplish this, they thought, they needed to agree on a coherent theory of governance to guide their efforts. By the late 1890s, such a theory began to take shape, built around the premise that a singular "public interest" could be defined that benefited all citizens equally and objectively. The reformers rallied around four sacred principles of reform: (1) *low taxes*: There must be strict budgetary controls to ensure taxes would be kept as low as possible and public services delivered at the lowest possible cost; (2) *no politics*: The day-to-day administration of city government should be strictly separated from "politics"; (3) *administrative expertise*: Experts with training, experience, and ability should run city services; and (4) *efficiency*: Government should be run like a business, with cost efficiency being the ultimate touchstone for good government. This last plank in the "good government" platform was derived from the principles guiding the scientific management movement that swept the country during the Progressive Era. As businesses became ever larger, accountants, engineers, and corporate managers were busily inventing the structure of the modern corporation. What emerged was a quasi-military model of hierarchical administrative control.

In 1911, Frederick Winslow Taylor became a household name with the publication of his book *The Principles of Scientific Management*.[62] Taylor's life work was devoted to the application of military discipline and hierarchy to the workplace, factory, and even daily life. He urged employers to study the movements of individual workers to discover how work tasks could be organized to achieve maximum output with a minimum expenditure of each worker's time and energy. Taylor promised that the application of his efficiency principles would bring progress, prosperity, and happiness to society and material wealth to all. By making management into a science, Taylor said, it would be possible to achieve harmony and cooperation between owners and workers because both had the same interest in maximizing output. There was even a spiritual side; principles of efficiency would allow each worker to develop "his greatest efficiency and prosperity."[63] The essence of the Taylor catechism was that "In the past, the man has been first; in the future the system must be first."[64] Taylor and his disciples spread an urgent message: "Soldiering" (slow work) and inefficiency should be stamped out at home as well as at work. Popular magazines featured articles on efficient housework—describing, for instance, how a homemaker could sequence her daily chores and arrange appliances and furniture to minimize wasted movement while doing household work. By playing upon a universal desire for prosperity and social harmony, the efficiency movement quickly achieved the status of a secular religion; the scientific management movement swept across the country.

To its disciples, scientific management seemed to promise a bloodless revolution, a solution to hostile employer–worker relations, disastrous economic panics, and poverty and want. Efficiency societies sprang up in cities all over the country, and efficiency experts were in great demand as speakers.[65] Taylor's followers invaded the factories to spread the gospel of efficiency. Efficiency and scientific management—"business methods"—also became the model for municipal reform. The advantages of applying efficiency principles to the workings of government seemed obvious: "The rising prestige of technicians in industry and the increasing demand for new public works and municipal services strengthened the desire for more technical efficiency in local government."[66]

In 1912, Henry Brueré, the first director of the privately funded New York Bureau of Municipal Research, published a book applying efficiency principles to municipal management.[67] Brueré argued that much of the mismanagement in New York City "formerly attributed to official corruption and to popular indifference was really due to official and popular ignorance of ... orderly and scientific procedures."[68] What these procedures amounted to were elaborate accounting and reporting devices designed to codify the responsibilities of city officials, the actions taken by them to carry out their duties, the costs of equipment and personnel, and other details. Brueré invented a scoring system whereby the efficiency of cities could be rated and compared, and with the performance of a city reduced to a number. Cities were to be rated on the basis of such items as: "Is a record kept of all city property?" "How often are the treasurer's books audited?" "Twenty questions on the protection of milk supply." "Is the location of houses of prostitution known and recorded?"[69] In all, Brueré and his aides used a list of 1,300 standardized questions to rate cities from the "worst governed" to the "best."

In 1913, Brueré was given the opportunity to make New York City efficient. In November of that year, one of Brueré's closest confidants, John Purroy Mitchell, was elected New York's mayor. Mitchell appointed Brueré to the office of city chamberlain (the mayor's policy adviser). Brueré immediately launched an attack on Tammany Hall's patronage system and managed to push through the first fully fledged civil service system in the nation. Brueré assigned the task of designing the details of the civil service system to Robert Moses, a young staff member at the New York Bureau of Municipal Research. Moses carried out his assignment with the enthusiasm of a Taylorite fanatic. He proposed a system in which every municipal employee would be closely and constantly monitored at work by efficiency experts trained to rate each worker's efficiency by applying an elaborate mathematical formula. The responsibilities of employees were codified and "given a precise mathematical grade. These grades would ... be used as a basis for salary increase and promotion."[70] To implement his system, Moses instructed his assistants to draw up rating forms, which he then distributed to supervisors. The idea was that each day, the supervisors would hand a scorecard containing a mathematical score to every employee. City workers would be paid, promoted, or fired on the basis of their performance.

Such a system, if implemented fully, would have fallen of its own weight. There was no way to ensure objective ratings. The amount of time required to rate employees would have resulted in a truly enormous civil service administrative staff. Instead of spending the prodigious amounts of money required to hire hundreds of specially trained supervisors, Moses tried to rely on existing city employees. The 50,000 city employees steadfastly refused to use the reporting forms, objecting that the system was hopelessly time consuming and unwieldy, and arbitrary and capricious to boot.

The elaborate system established during Mitchell's mayoral tenure illuminates the values, assumptions, and foibles of the reformers. As Taylor had put it, "The natural laziness in men is serious, but by far the greatest evil from which both workmen and employers are suffering is the systematic soldiering which is almost universal."[71] Reformers were taking on the formidable task of remaking human beings. Such an ambition could only be based on a fundamental distrust of people as they were. An essential human element was lacking. Mayor Mitchell, while trying to reorganize city departments and implement civil service procedures, tried to reduce all "unnecessary" programs and expenditures. He instituted cutbacks in school expenditures, asked teachers to work without salaries in the summers, tried to close down special schools for persons with mental disabilities, and reduced park and recreational expenditures.[72]

New York's civil service proposals were too draconian even for most reformers, but some of the abstract principles made sense. Streamlined administration and better-trained city workers clearly could save money and improve services. Cities across the country adopted civil service systems but omitted New York City's impossibly complicated reporting system. In addition to the cities, the federal government and the states soon entered the field. President William Howard Taft appointed a Commission on Economy and Efficiency, and President Woodrow Wilson later created the Bureau of Efficiency. Between 1911 and 1917, 16 states established efficiency commissions. These commissions generally recommended streamlining budgeting procedures, centralizing more power in the governor's office, consolidating state agencies, and establishing civil service systems.[73]

The Business Model

The principles of scientific management suggested that municipal government should be modeled as closely as possible on the business corporation. Reformers pointed out that the municipal governments inherited from the past were terribly cumbersome and dysfunctional. A history of reform written by scholars

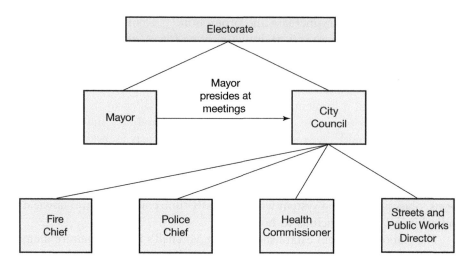

FIGURE 4.2 Weak Mayor Government

sympathetic with this view described the problem in these terms: "The reformers, who tried to get good men into office, found ... that, even if they elected a mayor or council, they were intolerably handicapped by the existing systems of municipal government. [Due to] the principles of separation of powers and of checks and balances ... there was no single elective official or governing body that could be held responsible for effecting reform."[74] Reformers claimed that the "weak mayor" form of government that existed in most cities dispersed authority among too many politicians—elected aldermen plus the legions of appointed members of boards and commissions. Trying to make sense of it all, they employed organizational charts like the one shown in Figure 4.2. In this "weak mayor" organizational chart, the mayor presides over meetings of the city council, but the council presides over the departments that provide city services. The question being asked was simple: who could the voters blame if they were dissatisfied with the way the city was being run?

It was supposed that businesses operated efficiently because there was a clear separation between policymaking, which was located in a board of directors, and the tasks of day-to-day administration, which was left in the hands of professional executive officers and their employees. Applied to cities, this model would leave policymaking to elected officials, who represented their constituents, just as a board of directors in a business answered to stockholders. The policies they enacted, however, were to be implemented by professional administrators schooled in the principles of cost accounting and personnel management.

The business model required an executive with sufficient authority to run the company. Applying this insight to city government, advocates of reform lobbied for city charters that would reduce the number of elected officials and

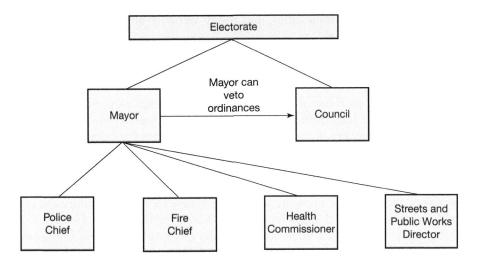

FIGURE 4.3 **Strong Mayor Government**

create a "strong mayor" with authority to appoint most city officials and veto legislation. In 1899, the National Municipal League published a model city charter that contained charts much like the one displayed in Figure 4.3. In this scheme, the mayor presides at the top of a hierarchical chain of command with clear lines of authority and accountability. A city council of five to nine members, each elected at-large, replaces the boards of aldermen that were typical of the time. Reformers thought that with this arrangement in place, voters would be able to clearly understand who was in charge of the affairs of the city, and thus hold them accountable for how well they did their jobs.

Now that the reformers felt confident they knew what to do if they won control of the cities, they launched a crusade for "home rule." They asked state legislatures to grant the cities the authority to set their own tax rates, regulate their internal affairs, and decide how and where to provide services. In this way, the cities would be free to realize the full potential offered by their new and efficient governmental structures. At its state constitutional convention in 1875, Missouri became the first state to write a general home rule charter for its cities, although the legislature retained control of St. Louis's police budget. The state still retained ultimate legal power, but Missouri's cities would not have to seek approval for their every action, as long as they stayed within their broad charter authority. Cities were now permitted to hire new sanitation workers and firefighters, for example, or build a new street without consulting with members of the legislature. The general charter spelled out the range of services to be provided, but not such details as salary levels, the location of firehouses and streets, and the number of city employees. The home rule movement, pushed hard by the National Municipal League and other organizations, quickly spread across the country. By 1925, 14 states had granted home rule to their cities, and today virtually all cities are governed by "home rule" charters.

Commission and Manager Government

Galveston, Texas, established the first municipal government derived explicitly from the model of the business corporation. In 1894, Galveston's business and professional leaders organized a campaign to elect business leaders to the most significant positions in the city government. The following year, a coalition of city council members and business leaders secured a charter amendment from the Texas legislature that abolished wards and created at-large elections. To the reformers' great disappointment, however, this new election procedure did not result in the sweeping changes its sponsors had hoped for. Over the next few years, a few businessmen were elected to the city council, but on important matters, they were regularly outvoted.[75]

A natural disaster provided the pretext for business and corporate leaders to assert themselves decisively. On September 8, 1900, hurricane-driven waves breached the seawall protecting Galveston, and the inrushing sea washed over the town, killing 6,000 of the town's 37,000 residents. Half of the property in the city was destroyed. In an effort to rebuild the city, business leaders organized the Deepwater Committee and set out to gain control of the local government. The members of the committee argued that if "a municipality is largely a business corporation,"[76] then it follows that it should be run like one, with the voters acting in the role of stockholders and a board of directors—an elected commission—responsible to them. Guided by this principle, the Deepwater Committee drafted an outline of a commission form of government and asked the state legislature to approve it. Their proposal was promptly enacted.

The Galveston Plan created a five-member commission that exercised the legislative powers previously assigned to the city council, as well as the administrative authority to oversee the city's services. Each of the commissioners assumed responsibility for a department of government. Such a concentration of authority seemed entirely appropriate, and even necessary, in the context of the emergency that followed the hurricane. Initially, the commission was even granted jurisdiction over criminal and civil law enforcement in the city, although a state court subsequently struck down this authority. Even so, the commission exercised sweeping powers. Headed by five leading members of the business community, Galveston initiated a vigorous rebuilding program, and, in the process, the city reduced its debts and restored and improved public services.

The notable success of Galveston's experiment in commission government gained national attention. The new idea spread like wildfire. Its appeal was obvious: It seemed to streamline government, make public service attractive to upper- and middle-class people, and offer a straightforward plan around which reformers could rally in challenging the machines and party bosses.

Galveston's performance so impressed business leaders in other Texas cities that they pressed the Texas legislature to allow them to follow Galveston's example and install a commission government. By 1907, seven major cities in the state had imitated Galveston's charter, including Houston, Dallas, and Fort Worth.

In 1908, voters in Des Moines, Iowa, gave the commission concept a shot in the arm by placing it within an entire package of reform. In addition to a five-member commission, Des Moines adopted the initiative, referendum, and recall; nonpartisan and at-large elections; and a civil service system. This package, which reformers labeled the Des Moines Plan, caught on rapidly. The Plan was adopted by 23 cities in different parts of the nation in 1909 and by 66 cities in 1910.[77] By September 1915, at least 465 cities were governed by a commission, and by 1920, about 20 percent of all cities with populations of more than 5,000 had adopted the model.[78] During these years, a few states made commission government compulsory for their cities, and in most states, it became an option for cities that wanted to adopt it.

Reformers promoted the Des Moines Plan as a cure for every ill, sure to bring less taxation, more efficient public services, and a "better class of men" to the government. In city after city, it was promoted as a means of making government more businesslike. Accordingly, chambers of commerce and other organized business groups became the strongest backers. The Commercial Club succeeded in pushing through Des Moines's new charter in 1907, although, interestingly, the first commissioners voted into office represented a working-class slate—much to the dismay of the charter's sponsors.[79] In Pennsylvania, the Pittsburgh Chamber of Commerce organized a statewide convention of business organizations to persuade the state legislature to require cities above a minimum size to adopt commission government. The coalition of bankers, merchants, and manufacturers secured the legislation in 1913.[80]

Despite its appeal, the commission government had some problems. To its critics, its worst feature was that it did not fit the business model faithfully enough. A commission was not truly like a board of directors because commissioners engaged in both policymaking and administration. Because each of the commissioners headed a separate administrative department, they often refused to cooperate. Sometimes they built personal empires by handing out jobs and contracts, thereby acting a lot like the machine politicians they had replaced. It was hard for the mayor to prevent such practices because each of the commissioners was a "first among equals." This defect was the chief complaint of the secretary of the National Short Ballot Association, Richard S. Childs. Noting that commission government was "an accident, not a plan" (referring to the Galveston emergency that brought it into being), he addressed the problem of having five coequal executives: "The theory that the commission as a whole controlled its members in their departmental activities became neglected—the commission could not discipline a recalcitrant member."[81] Childs noted that commissioners typically ignored one another ("You attend to your department and quit criticizing mine") or exchanged favors and support ("I'll vote for your appropriation if you'll vote for mine").[82] This was not the model of efficiency that reformers like Childs had in mind.

The crusaders for reform responded to these criticisms by putting forward a new idea: Place administrative authority into the hands of a professional manager specifically trained for the job. As elected officials, the mayor and the council would continue to make policy decisions, but the city manager would be responsible for the day-to-day operations of the government. "The reform leaders realized that technical ability could not be expected of elected officials, and they hoped that a strong mayor could appoint trained technicians and administrators as department heads."[83] In this way, the reformers hoped, the city manager would bring to local government administrative expertise and accountability.[84]

This time, the reformers intended to get the business model right. In 1913, the National Municipal League issued a report (written by Childs) recommending that the commission government be abandoned in favor of the city manager plan. Only six years later, in 1919, the league amended its model charter to recommend that cities adopt the city manager form of government. In only a few years, the city manager plan replaced the commission model, and by the 1920s, the commission form was regarded as a failed experiment.

Between 1908 and 1912, several Midwestern cities hired city managers. The idea caught on in earnest when Dayton, Ohio, changed its city charter. As in Galveston, a natural disaster served as the catalyst. In 1913, John H. Patterson, president of the National Cash Register Company, persuaded the Dayton Chamber of Commerce to draft a new city charter. The chamber established the Bureau of Municipal Research to promote the idea, and the Committee of One Hundred, a group funded by the business community, sponsored a slate of candidates. By organizing a campaign ward by ward, the business slate put several Republican candidates on the city council, but they were still outnumbered by politicians representing the local Democratic machine. It appeared that charter reform had failed to accomplish its purpose. Two months later, however, the Miami River flooded the town, and the municipal government was slow to organize emergency services. Patterson turned his factory into a shelter for flood victims, and virtually overnight, he became the town's leading citizen. Business leaders pressed the state governor to put Patterson in charge of an effort to draw up a new city charter. A few months later, the committee headed by Patterson recommended the city manager model, and the voters soon registered their approval.[85]

The results were spectacular. The new government improved public services, retired most of the city debt, instituted new budget-making procedures, enforced a uniform eight-hour day for city employees, and established civil service. Because of its widely advertised success, the Dayton Plan, with its city manager system, quickly became the nation's most popular "good reform" reform model. Although rarely instituted in the big industrial cities, it became the most common form of government in smaller cities around the country.

In the five years before 1918, some 87 cities adopted manager charters, and 153 did so between 1918 and 1923. During the next five years, 84 more cities were added to the list.[86]

The city manager plan became popular because it appeared to be the best expression of the reformers' desire to find an objective, nonpolitical, efficient way to run local government. Almost all arguments for reform were founded upon analogies to business organizations. The *Dallas News* promoted the manager plan in 1930 by asking, "Why not run Dallas itself on a business schedule by business methods under businessmen? ... The city manager plan is after all only a business management plan. The city manager is the executive of a corporation under a board of directors. Dallas is the corporation. It is as simple as that. Vote for it."[87]

Despite the references to the business model, it was hard to hide the fact that the city manager plan was designed not only to bring efficient government but also to ensure the election of a different class of people who would insulate government from the influence of the Great Unwashed. A few participants in the reform crusades recognized the issue this raised about democratic processes. A delegate to the 1913 meeting of the League of Kansas Municipalities, after listening to his colleagues orate about the necessity of treating the city as a business, protested that "a city is more than a business corporation" and "good health is more important than a low tax rate."[88] However, the vast social chasm dividing municipal reformers from the rest of the urban populace made such sentiments anathema to most reformers.

Reformers made ambitious claims about the benefits to be realized by adopting businesslike models of government. Without doubt, some of their promises were overblown. Studies have shown that the adoption of city manager government had little, if any, effect on the level of city expenditures.[89] Machine and reform cities taxed at about the same rate and spent similar amounts on key public services. The major difference between them was that they distributed services and other valuable governmental benefits to different constituencies. Reform governments tended to neglect lower-income neighborhoods so that they could reward their supporters in more affluent parts of the city. They built libraries, increased services to homeowners (such as free refuse collection), and zoned land to maximize new housing developments. Above all, they promoted policies that benefited downtown businesses and corporations. Bureaucratic rules made it easy to control the distribution of rewards, as well. In the 1980s, for instance, citizens in the city of New Haven found that, "acquiring delivery of some services like tree pruning or waste disposal required attaining a series of permits from offices open at irregular, infrequent times."[90]

Bureaucratic systems often make things difficult for workers who do not have flexible hours and for people not skilled at filling in forms and following formal rules. Wouldn't it be a lot easier if a person could just tell their local alderman what they need? As convenient as that might seem, there are disadvantages for that system, too. Political appointees tend to be less professional,

insiders get better treatment than anyone else, and some level of petty corruption is more or less inevitable. Whatever its frustrations, government by
bureaucracy is generally less biased than any system based on political favors.[91]

Did Reform Kill the Machines?

Admirers of the reform crusades always assumed the party machines died out
because the reformers succeeded in cleaning up local politics. A large number
of machines had short lives of only a decade or so before they went into
slow decline or the politicians that ran them suddenly lost their grip. Between
1909 and 1918, machines fell apart in Dayton, Ohio; Detroit and Grand
Rapids, Michigan; Los Angeles; Portland, Oregon; Milwaukee; Minneapolis;
San Francisco; and Seattle. In each case, some variety of reform was adopted
and civil service systems changed hiring rules.[92] Most of the machines that
survived this era died by the mid-1950s, if not before, including New York's
Tammany Hall. By World War II, it would have been impossible to find a city
left completely untouched by reform. Voter registration was universal and
civil service hiring was nearly so; at-large, nonpartisan elections were used
in most cities. Even in the big industrial cities where reform was generally
less successful, election rules underwent some degree of change. Boston, New
Orleans, and Pittsburgh had switched to at-large elections; Memphis and
Detroit had adopted both at-large and nonpartisan elections. Denver, New
Orleans, Philadelphia, Cleveland, and Pittsburgh also became nonpartisan
before World War II.[93]

There can be little doubt that these reforms made a difference, but it is also
clear that they did not "cause" the big-city machines to collapse. The scholarly
evidence confirms the observation that "The adoption of structural reform was
not sufficient to eliminate or preclude the appearance of machine politics."[94]
Machines were often adept at adjusting to the new rules of the game. In 15 cities,
machines actually benefitted from strong mayor and city manager systems.[95] The
reformers accomplished their goal of making someone accountable to voters,
but the voters did not always respond as the reformers hoped. After Cleveland
adopted the city manager plan in the 1920s, the machine put a party hack into
the post.[96] Richard J. Daley built his powerful machine in Chicago, beginning
with his election in 1955, despite the fact that the city's elections were nonpartisan and the vast majority of its employees were civil servants.

In most cases, the machines died because they were unable to adapt to the
population and economic transformations that were changing the cities. Over
time, the immigrant base began to shrink. Irish immigration dropped sharply
after the turn of the century; the bulk of new immigrants came from Italy and
Eastern Europe. The Irish had been the mainstay groups for most machines,
and, as their numbers declined, machines found their support gradually erod-
ing. If they were to continue to exist at all, machines would have to adapt to
the times. In New York City, Fiorello LaGuardia put together a coalition of

Italian and Jewish voters to defeat Tammany Hall's candidate in 1933, and in the process, he built his own, more inclusive version of machine politics. In Chicago, Anton Cermak transformed the machine by bringing Italians, Jews, Czechs, and Poles into its orbit. James Michael Curley, Boston's longtime boss, lasted longer than most other bosses, probably because the Irish were such a dominant force in the city, but he was finally defeated for reelection in 1949.[97] When he was elected mayor in 1955, Richard J. Daley was able to keep the Chicago machine from fracturing by adding middle-class white voters and the downtown business elite to its traditional base in the ethnic neighborhoods, and by rebuilding ties to African American politicians who could deliver the vote in the sprawling black-belt neighborhoods of south and west Chicago.

The second decisive blow to the machines occurred when their immigrant supporters began moving up the economic ladder. As immigrants joined the ranks of the middle class, the petty favors and patronage offered by the machines carried less weight, both in material and symbolic terms, than they had in an earlier era. After World War II, immigrants and the children of immigrants joined the mass movement to the suburbs. Precinct captains saw their neighbors moving out of the city, and sometimes they moved, too. Machines were not generally successful in reaching out to the new generation of immigrants, poor whites, and Blacks who streamed into the cities during and after World War II.[98]

The Reform Legacy

Although the municipal reform movement has long since passed, the reforms adopted in that era still reverberate throughout the American political system. Rules governing elections and representation continue to be battlegrounds because they involve disputes over the role of government in determining who will reap the benefits of public policy.[99] Conflicts over the "rules of the game" were rekindled in the 1960s and in the decades to follow because of clear evidence that racial and ethnic minorities were consistently underrepresented at all levels of the American political system. The Voting Rights Act of 1965 was enacted as a way of incorporating Blacks into the national political system. Federal registrars were sent into jurisdictions to register Blacks, and in some cases, Hispanics and Native Americans. At the local level, lawsuits were filed in the federal courts challenging the electoral rules inherited from the Progressive Era. Groups such as the National Association for the Advancement of Colored People (NAACP) and the United Latin American Citizens, who had, in many cases begun to chip away at racist and xenophobic voting regulations at the local level for decades, now sought to invalidate at-large electoral systems on a national scale, arguing that they violated the Fourteenth Amendment guarantee of equal protection of the laws. They also asked the courts to review the boundaries of state legislative and congressional districts because, they claimed, many of them had been expressly drawn to place hurdles in the way of minority participation. The courts sometimes upheld challenges to at-large elections but issued inconsistent rulings on the constitutionality of legislative boundaries drawn to dilute minority representation (a practice known as racial gerrymandering).[100] The intensity of the battles fought in and out of the courts serves as a reminder that the rules of governing participation in the political system are as crucial today as they were during the reform crusades 100 years ago.

Research has consistently shown that at-large elections reduce the influence of racial and ethnic minorities.[101] In response to the accumulating evidence and over the strenuous objections of the Reagan administration, in 1982, Congress amended the 1965 Voting Rights Act to make it easier for minorities to challenge local election practices. Congress passed the amendments, contained in Section 2 of the new act, in reaction to a 1980 U.S. Supreme Court decision that had required litigants to demonstrate an *intent* to discriminate before an election rule could be declared invalid.[102] In Section 2, Congress specified that challenges to local election rules could meet a much easier standard than before: They would be considered illegal if they merely had the *effect* of under-representing minorities in elected positions.

On June 30, 1986, the Supreme Court handed down a landmark decision, *Thornburg v. Gingles*, interpreting the 1982 amendments.[103] This case came to the Court after the U.S. Justice Department brought suit against the state of North Carolina, arguing that several multimember state legislative districts in North Carolina violated the voting rights of Blacks because in those districts white candidates invariably won all seats.[104] The Court ordered North Carolina to create single-member districts and laid down standards for deciding when at-large and multimember district systems would be considered suspect: (1) When litigants could show it would be possible to create at least one single-member electoral district that would give a minority group an electoral majority; (2) when it could also be demonstrated that the minority group seeking more representation was politically cohesive; and (3) when it could be shown that whites had previously voted as a bloc to prevent minority candidates from being elected.[105]

At-large district systems have since been successfully challenged throughout the United States. In 1986, after finding that at-large elections made it impossible for African American candidates to win, a federal court ordered several Alabama counties to institute single-member districts for electing county commissioners.[106] In a 1987 lawsuit filed against the city of Springfield, Illinois, a federal judge ordered the city to expand the number of its electoral districts from five to ten. Because only 10.8 percent of the city's population was African American, the expansion to ten districts was necessary if any one of them was to contain a majority of Black voters.[107] (Interestingly, a different federal judge did not require this solution in a similar suit filed against the Springfield Park District.[108]) In the same year, the city of Danville, Illinois, expanded its city council to 14 members elected from seven wards after a federal judge threw out its previous system in which a three-member commission and a mayor were all elected at-large.[109]

The numerous court decisions arising from the 1982 amendments to the Voting Rights Act produced an extraordinary amount of confusion about local election rules. All through the 1980s and into the 1990s, court decisions called into question the electoral systems of hundreds of cities, counties, townships, and special districts. To preempt court action, some local governments voluntarily redrew district and ward boundaries to facilitate minority representation. Frequently, this required devising districts with tortuously meandering boundaries.[110] The attempt to redraw boundaries, however, is not a solution available to every city. It may, in fact, be available only to those whose minority populations live in highly segregated circumstances rather than in several distinct but unconnected neighborhoods, because in segregated cities, it is easier to draw boundaries that seem coherent. In a series of decisions beginning in 1993, the U.S. Supreme Court invalidated congressional district boundaries that did not meet standards of "compactness, contiguity, and respect for political subdivisions."[111]

Although the courts seemed to be enforcing the compactness standard for a time, it did not necessarily signal an end to all redistricting meant to achieve representation for particular racial or ethnic groups.[112] The Court's standard could be met simply by increasing the number of legislative districts; smaller districts to ensure that even small minority neighborhoods could exercise influence in some of them. For several years, it was unclear whether there was some upper limit to the number of districts a local government might have to draw to achieve the equitable representation of minorities. By 1987, however, it seemed likely (despite the city of Springfield case) that, under normal circumstances, the number of districts already existing would be left alone.[113]

The courts took up more technical considerations as well. For example, in drawing legislative boundaries was it sufficient to count the entire minority population, or only the voting-age minority population? Most courts decided that a majority voting-age population was required.[114] Could two or more minority groups be combined so that the two together constituted the majority of voters in a district? Only, the courts said, if it could be shown that the groups were politically cohesive—and research makes it clear, for example, that Blacks and Latinos do not generally vote similarly.[115]

In 1991, the issue of minority representation was placed at the forefront of the political infighting over congressional reapportionment required as a result of the decennial census of 1990. Because state legislatures approve the boundaries for congressional districts, party control at the state level was crucial. In 1990, there were 37 Blacks and Latinos in Congress. In 1992, as a result of redistricting, 19 additional Blacks and Latinos were elected to Congress. In many states, it was Republicans, working with the Congressional Black Caucus, who promoted the formation of districts safe for minority candidates. This move not only increased the number of minority representatives in Congress but also the number of districts where a Republican candidate was competitive.[116] Complicated gamesmanship of this sort became a standard feature of legislative apportioning.

In June 1991, the Supreme Court ruled that judicial elections in Louisiana and Texas violated the 1982 Voting Rights Act because at-large election districts diluted the electoral strength of minorities. A flurry of lawsuits followed that challenged election procedures for state and local judges. Traditionally, nearly all state and local judges have been elected at-large—that is, multiple positions are filled in each electoral district. This perhaps explains why, as of 1985, only 3.8 percent of judges in state courts were African American and only 1.2 percent were Latino.[117]

The court decisions brought a revolution in local electoral practices. In 1981, 66.5 percent of cities used at-large electoral systems. By 1986, in a space of only five years, the proportion had fallen to 60.4 percent.[118] This very significant change can be traced to research demonstrating that changing from at-large to district elections did, as anticipated, improve the representation of Blacks and Latinos.[119] Cities almost everywhere came under pressure to institute a ward system or to redraw existing ward and district boundaries. In 1991, for example, African American leaders in St. Louis threatened to go to court to force a redrawing of the boundaries of the city's 28 wards. At the time, 11 of the 28 aldermen were African American, but a new ward map would have made it mathematically possible to give half of the wards a majority of African American voters.[120]

Court cases in the 1990s seemed to signal that except in extreme circumstances, the courts wanted to get out of the business of telling state and local governments how to draw their electoral districts. In an interesting twist, the courts also indicated that electoral districts that were gerrymandered to excessively increase or decrease minority representation now would be treated as suspect. In *Shaw v. Reno* (1993), the U.S. Supreme Court ruled that a very oddly shaped district in North Carolina made up almost entirely of Blacks was illegally gerrymandered, calling such districts "political apartheid." Speaking for the majority, Sandra Day O'Connor wrote, "When a district obviously is created solely to effectuate the perceived common interests of one racial group, elected officials are more likely to believe that their primary obligation is to represent only the members of that group, rather than the constituency as a whole."[121] The Court left the door open for modest attempts to take race into account in redistricting by declaring that race could not be the "predominant factor" in drawing district boundaries, and in 1996, it declared that each case would be decided on its own merits and that minority districting might be permissible if the boundaries were sufficiently compact and coherent.[122] These rulings had the effect of discouraging the drawing of tortuous boundaries but otherwise did not change the status quo significantly. Over the subsequent years, courts have been very reluctant to take on such issues.

In 2013, things changed significantly, and for the worse. The Supreme Court, in a 5:4 decision, struck down the preclearance requirement of the 1965 Voting Rights Act, dealing a fatal blow to efforts to make access to the ballot box more equitable for minorities. The preclearance requirement had applied to nine Southern states—Alabama, Alaska, Arizona, Georgia, Louisiana, Mississippi, South Carolina, Texas, and Virginia—and required clearance with the United States Attorney General, as well as a panel at the United States District Court for the District of Columbia, for any changes in the voting laws. The district attorney and the district court were then to determine whether any proposed changes in the voting laws would impede with the right to vote of any minority group. In 2011, Shelby County, Alabama sued the United States Attorney General, Eric Holder, in the District Court for Washington, D.C., claiming that the preclearance requirement was unconstitutional. In 2013, the Supreme Court decided to hear the case, and subsequently struck down Section 4(b) of the Voting Rights Act in *Shelby v. Holder.* In its majority opinion, the Supreme Court saw the coverage formula inherent in Section 4(b), which mandated the federal review of changes in voting laws for the nine states, where less than 50 percent of the population of voting age was registered to vote on November 1, 1964,[123] in conflict with the federalism principle, and states' rights to sovereignty.[124] Chief Justice John G. Roberts noted that the provision in Section 4(b) was "based on 40-year-old facts having no logical relationship to the present day."[125] Roberts further noted that the country had fundamentally changed. In reference to the two hotspots of the Civil Rights Movement—Philadelphia, Mississippi, where several civil rights activists were murdered during the summer of 1964, while seeking to help register African Americans to vote, and Selma, Alabama, where civil rights protesters were severely beaten by police during a demonstration in 1965, Justice Roberts noted: "Today, both of those towns are governed by African-American mayors. Problems remain in these states and others, but there is no denying that, due to the Voting Rights Act, our nation has made great strides." In her dissenting opinion, Justice Ruth Bader-Ginsberg mourned the end of an era:

> For a half century, a concerted effort has been made to end racial discrimination in voting. Thanks to the Voting Rights Act, progress once the subject of a dream has been achieved and continues to be made. […] The court errs egregiously by overriding Congress's decision.[126]

In 2020, the Supreme Court solidified its conservative majority after the death of Justice Ruth Bader Ginsberg in September, and the subsequent appointment of Amy Coney Barrett, a conservative Catholic judge, as her replacement by the outgoing President Trump only seven days before the 2020 presidential election. Just before the end of the Supreme Court's summer recess the following year, in July 2021, this new conservative majority dealt another fatal blow to the Voting Rights Act in *Brnovich v. Democratic National Committee*: Along with other conservative state legislatures, the State of Arizona had passed two restrictive voting laws earlier in the year claiming that they would help prevent voter fraud—both of them were struck down by a federal appeals court based on the reasoning that they were having a disparate impact on minority voters, and that the provisions were not based on any instances of voter fraud. The first of these laws made it illegal for anyone but a relative of a caregiver to collect absentee ballots. The second provision made any ballots cast in the wrong precinct inadmissible. The Supreme Court, however, ruled in a 6:3 decision to reinstate both provisions, arguing that their impact on minority groups was small enough to be acceptable and that, since other states had similar voting laws, the State of Arizona did not need to prove that the provisions had been enacted in response to actual election fraud. Justice Alito, writing for the majority argued: "the mere fact that there is some disparity in impact [on minority groups] does not necessarily mean that the system is not equally open or that it does not give everyone an equal opportunity to vote."[127]

After the 2013 Shelby County decision, which had gutted the 1965 Voting Rights Act by striking down the preclearance requirement set in Section 4(b), the heart of the law, this decision meant an even deeper cut into the few protections that were left for minorities. Section 2 of the Voting Rights Act was intended to (a) protect the minority vote from dilution by redistricting and to (b) prevent the implementation of any voting laws that "result in a denial or abridgement of the right of any citizen of the United States to vote on account of race or color." Clearly, the new Arizona voting laws describe circumstances in which the state would engage in denial of voting or vote counting. Therefore, the 2021 decision represented an important indicator of how broadly the Court would interpret Section 2. In the dissenting opinion, Justice Elena Kagan sharply condemned the Court's decision, accusing the majority of remaking Section 2 against its original intent:

> The Court always says that it must interpret a statute according to its text—that it has no warrant to override congressional choices. But the majority today flouts those choices with abandon. The language of Section 2 is as broad as broad can be. It applies to any policy that "results in disparate voting opportunities for minority citizens. It prohibits, without any need to show bad motive, even facially neutral laws that make voting harder for members of one race than of another, given their differing life circumstances. [...] But the majority today lessens the law—cuts Section 2 down to its own preferred size. [...] This Court has no right to remake Section 2. Maybe some think that vote suppression is a relic of history – and so the need for a potent Section 2 has come and gone. [...] But Congress gets to make that call. Because it has not done so, this Court's duty is to apply the law as written.[128]

The Supreme Court's two subsequent decisions in *Shelby v. Holder* (2013) and *Brnovitch v. Democratic National Committee* (2021) under a solid conservative majority have led to a significant weakening of the Voting Rights Act and will bear some very serious consequences for voting rights in the future, especially as political polarization grows, and voting rights for minorities are, once again, under siege in the United States.

The Battles Continue

As bitter conflicts over the rules of the game continue, the main battleground has shifted from electoral districts to voter registration rules and restrictive provisions supposedly preventing voter fraud. These recent claims of voter fraud, especially by Republicans after the 2016 and 2020 presidential elections, are particularly vindictive, given the fact that scholars place the instances of voter fraud between 0.0003 and 0.00025 percent.[129]

Especially since the razor-thin and controversial presidential election decision in 2000, Republicans and Democrats have become locked in a protracted struggle over voter registration requirements. Both parties have a lot at stake. As in the Progressive Era, strict voter registration rules tend to reduce participation for minorities, the poor, and others who find it more difficult to negotiate the bureaucratic labyrinth. The outcome of the presidential election of 2000 was decided before Election Day in the state of Florida, when the Republican secretary of state invalidated the registration of more than 70,000 Black voters because of technical problems with their applications, such as a misspelled name or failure to change their address. Several hundred were invalidated mistakenly because their names matched those on a list of convicted felons. These actions proved to be decisive; ultimately, the election was determined by a little more than 500 voters.

Both parties took the lesson to heart. Democrats redoubled efforts to make it easier to register and to mobilize voter registration drives. The Republican Party fought such reforms in a state-by-state skirmish. When immigration became a contentious national issue, their attempts to impose stricter rules of registration began to bear fruit. In 2008, a major battle erupted over whether states should impose proof of citizenship as a condition of registration and a photo ID as a condition to vote. Previously, in most of the 25 states that required a form of identification at the polls, identification could come in several forms, including utility bills, paychecks, driver's licenses, or student or military IDs. A wave of new laws were proposed that would require passports, birth certificates, or naturalization papers as a condition of voting. Democrats charged that these proposals were thinly veiled attempts to discourage low-income and minority voters from coming to the polls; Republicans countered by asserting they were merely measures to reduce voting fraud.[130] The aftermath of the 2020 presidential election, which, in spite of myriad recounts yielding the same results, former President Trump refused to concede to his successor, Joseph Biden, inciting anger and even violence, cumulating in the Capitol Riots of January 6, 2021, has only increased contention between partisans.

It is hazardous to take any of these claims at face value. It is clear that conflicts over voter participation reflect the political interests of the antagonists, a point driven home by controversies over the registration of college students in the period leading up to the 2008 presidential election. In September 2008, a local elections registrar in Virginia (a Republican) announced that Virginia

Tech students who registered to vote in Blacksburg might lose scholarships or become subject to Virginia state taxes if they listed their campus as their voting address. His announcement clearly contradicted a U.S. Supreme Court decision granting students the right to vote where they go to school, but it nevertheless provoked confusion on the Virginia Tech campus. As it turns out, the Virginia case was not an exception. Eleven states discourage student voting by refusing to treat P.O. boxes and dormitories as legitimate mailing addresses for determining a permanent residency. Others have specified that out-of-state driver's licenses cannot be used to vote. All of these cases virtually invite election officials to throw out votes in close elections, as occurred in Florida in 2000.[131]

In the two years following the 2010 elections, 180 new voting restrictions were introduced in 41 states, and Republican state legislators have continued to support new voting restrictions. In January 2013, the Virginia Senate passed a redistricting map designed to reduce Democratic representation by at least eight seats. The map was defeated in the House but set a tone on voting rights for the legislative session.[132] The first three months of 2013 saw 55 new voting restrictions proposed in 30 states. At the end of March 2013, Republican lawmakers unveiled a new idea to cut the early-voting window in half, thereby eliminating same-day voter registration and Sunday voting. Critics argue that Republican policymakers are determined to place obstacles between voters and the ballot box as a way of reducing voting participation by minorities.[133]

Republicans in North Carolina were particularly active in proposing voter restrictions in 2013. Senate Bill 721 proposed reducing early voting to six days, eliminating same-day voter registration, and imposing a five-year delay on the eligibility of persons with a past felony conviction to vote and new voter ID restrictions.[134] Florida had already taken the lead in denying ex-felons voting rights; after taking office in 2011, Governor Rick Scott eliminated the automatic restoration of voting rights for nonviolent ex-offenders. The African American population in Florida stood at 16.5 percent in 2010, but Black inmates made up 31.5 percent of the state prison population. Citing such statistics, activists asserted that Florida's rules had the effect (and probably the intent) of suppressing the minority vote. Howard Simon, the executive director of ACLU Florida stated, "this is one of the few government programs that has worked precisely as it was designed, namely to try to suppress the vote of as many African Americans as possible. It was designed that way in 1868, and it continues to have that effect in 2013."[135]

In 2013, the Commonwealth Institute estimated that 869,000 registered voters in Virginia would lack the new forms of identification required by new voter ID bills. Whereas in the 2012 election, voters in Virginia were able to vote by showing a form of ID from a variety of sources such as a utility bill or a concealed handgun permit, the new law restricted acceptable ID to a driver's license, passport, state-issued ID card, a student photo ID or an employee photo ID.[136] Studies have shown that restrictions like these reduce voting turnout for young people and minority voters.[137] A report by political scientists at the University of Chicago and Washington University found that "17.3 percent of black youth and 8.1 percent of Latino youth said their lack of adequate ID kept them from voting, compared with just 4.7 percent of white youth."[138] Even in states with no voter ID laws, 65.5 percent of Black youth were asked to show ID at the polls, compared to 42.8 percent of white youth.[139]

In 2012, Viviette Applewhite, a white 93-year-old female and former hotel housekeeper in Philadelphia, had her pocketbook stolen in a supermarket, thereby losing her only form of identification, her Social Security card. When she was not allowed to vote in the presidential election, she initiated a lawsuit against the state of Pennsylvania. In her view, "They're trying to stop black people from voting so Obama will not get re-elected."[140]

Students have also been affected by the proposed restrictions. In North Carolina, Senate Bill 666, which was introduced in 2013, proposed a tax penalty for parents whose children registered to vote at a college address by stipulating that they would not be able to claim that child as a dependent for state income tax purposes. Bill 667 proposed that student voters who changed their voting registration would be required to register their new address within 60 days and pay local property taxes.

While advocates of restrictions like these asserted that the laws are designed to ensure the integrity of elections by preventing voter fraud, opponents point to the fact that nearly every state legislature that had passed voter ID laws was Republican-run and that the constituencies which were most affected are new requirements tended to vote Democratic.[141] Whatever side one takes in such controversies, it is clear that voting rules are not (and cannot be) neutral and that they can determine the outcome of elections.

For the 2016 presidential elections, around 40 observers were sent to the United States by the Organization of American States (OAS) to monitor the polls, and the Organization for Cooperation and Security in Europe (OSCE) increased its amount of observers that year, sending several hundred monitors to the United States.[142] Usually, the United States is one of the sending countries for such election monitors, who get dispatched to countries with instable political systems and a shaky democratic track record. This illustrates the current level of political polarization, but also the high level of the salience of U.S. elections to the rest of the world.

The aftermath of the 2020 presidential elections, in which Republicans openly tried to overturn a democratic election, which was among the most secure in American history, as confirmed by key members of the Trump cabinet, and conservative judges, among them the FBI, the Department of Homeland Security's Cybersecurity and Infrastructure Security Agency (CISA), the Department of Justice under Attorney General William Barr, a devoted Trump follower, the U.S. Election Assistance Commission, and the Courts, such as the United States District Court for the Middle District of Pennsylvania, the Third Judicial Circuit Court of Michigan, the United States Court of Appeals for the Third Circuit, the Wisconsin Supreme Court, and a flurry of election experts and officials, many of them Republicans.[143]

How can it be, more than a century after voter registration and polling rules were first enacted, that issues of political participation continue to be so divisive? Indeed, the debate surrounding voter registration rings particularly odd to citizens and residents of other established democracies, where voting is simply a right that comes with citizenship and does not require the extra step of registration. Citizens simply go to the polls and cast their votes without having to register to do so. So, what brings about the intense level of contestation around this issue in the United States? The era of municipal reform suggests the answer. Reform, even in established democracies, is always motivated by political goals and purposes, however noble the stated principles may seem. In politics, the rules governing participation matter more than almost anything else because they determine who will govern and therefore who will benefit. Accordingly, they will always be the object of conflict and contention. After all, political power is the most sought-after commodity, even in established democracies.

Endnotes

1   William L. Riordon, *Plunkitt of Tammany Hall* (New York: Dutton, 1963), p. 17.

2   James Bryce, *The American Commonwealth*, 3rd ed., vol. 1 (New York: Macmillan, 1924), p. 642.

3   H. E. Deming, *The Government of American Cities: A Program of Democracy* (London and New York: Putnam, 1909), p. 194.

4   Quoted in Michael B. Katz, *School Reform: Past and Present* (Boston, MA: Little, Brown, 1971).

5   Josiah Strong, in *Our Country*, ed. Jurgen Herbst (Cambridge, MA: Belknap Press, Harvard University Press, 1963; first published in 1886), p. 55.

6   Samuel P. Hays, *The Response to Industrialism, 1885–1914* (Chicago, IL: University of Chicago Press, 1957), p. 73.

7   James Weinstein, *The Corporate Ideal in the Liberal State, 1900–1918* (Boston, MA: Beacon Press, 1968).

8   Melvin G. Holli, "Urban Reform in the Progressive Era," in *The Progressive Era*, ed. Louis L. Gould (Syracuse, NY: Syracuse University Press, 1974), p. 137.

9   Frank Mann Stewart, *A Half Century of Municipal Reform: The History of the National Municipal League* (Berkeley: University of California Press, 1950), Chapter 1.

10 Samuel Haber, *Efficiency and Uplift: Scientific Management in the Progressive Era, 1890–1920* (Chicago, IL: University of Chicago Press, 1964), p. 99.

11 Andrew D. White, "City Affairs Are Not Political," originally titled "The Government of American Cities," *Forum* (December 1890), pp. 213–216; reprinted in Dennis Judd and Paul Kantor, eds., *The Politics of Urban America*, 2nd ed. (New York: Addison Wesley Longman, 2002).

12 Amy Bridges, "Winning the West to Municipal Reform," *Urban Affairs Quarterly* 27, no. 4 (June 1992): 511.

13 Arthur T. Hadley, *The Empty Polling Booth* (Upper Saddle River, NJ: Prentice Hall, 1978), p. 61.

14 Alexander B. Callow Jr., ed., *The City Boss in America* (New York: Oxford University Press, 1976), p. 158.

15 William T. Stead, *If Christ Came to Chicago* (Chicago, IL: Laird and Lee, 1894), pp. 56–57.

16 Lloyd Wendt and Herman Kogan, *Bosses in Lusty Chicago* (Bloomington: Indiana University Press, 1967), p. 169.

17 Allan F. Davis, *Spearheads for Reform* (New York: Oxford University Press, 1967), pp. 156–162.

18 William D. Miller, *Mr. Crump of Memphis* (Baton Rouge: Louisiana State University Press, 1964), p. 74.

19 Bruce M. Stave, *The New Deal and the Last Hurrah: Pittsburgh Machine Politics* (Pittsburgh, PA: University of Pittsburgh Press, 1970), p. 77.

20 Julie Davidow, *"Citizens in the Making": Black Philadelphians, The Republican Party and Urban Reform, 1885–1913.* Doctoral Dissertation, Department of History, The University of Pennsylvania (2017). p. 25.

21 August Meier, "The Nego and the Democratic Party, 1975–1915," *Phylon (1940–1956)*, 2nd Qtr. 1956, pp. 173–191.

22 Julie Davidow, *"Citizens in the Making": Black Philadelphians, The Republican Party and Urban Reform, 1885–1913.* Doctoral Dissertation, Department of History, The University of Pennsylvania (2017).

23 Keneshia N. Grant, *Relocation & Realignment: How the Great Migration Changed the Face of the Democratic Party.* Doctoral Dissertation, Department of Political Science, Syracuse University (2014). p. 51.

24 Keneshia N. Grant, *The Great Migration and the Democratic Party. Black Voters and the Realignment of American Politics in the 20th Century* (Philadelphia, PA: Temple University Press, 2020). p. 97.

25 Ibid.

26 Ibid., p. 98.

27 Ernest S. Griffith, *A History of American City Government: The Conspicuous Failure, 1870–1900* (New York: Praeger, 1974), p. 71.

28 Richard S. Childs, *Civic Victories: The Story of an Unfinished Revolution* (New York: Harper and Brothers, 1952), p. 299. In this passage, Childs was referring to the short ballot reform in conjunction with nonpartisanship. The short ballot reformers advocated fewer elected officials so voters would not be confused and elected officials would be held accountable to voters.

29 Edward C. Banfield, ed., *Urban Government: A Reader in Administration and Politics* (New York: Free Press, 1969), p. 275. Selection from Brand Whitlock, *Forty Years of It*, preface by Allen White (New York and London: Appleton, 1925; first published in 1914).

30 Haber, *Efficiency and Uplift*, pp. 99–101.

31 White, "City Affairs Are Not Political," pp. 213–216.

32 Griffith, *A History of American City Government*, p. 130.

33 Amy Bridges, *Morning Glories: Municipal Reform in the Southwest* (Princeton, NJ: Princeton University Press, 1997), Chapter 8.

34 Willis D. Hawley, *Nonpartisan Elections and the Case for Party Politics* (New York: Wiley, 1973), p. 14. Subsequent information on the use of nonpartisan elections is from Hawley, pp. 15–18.

35 Weinstein, *The Corporate Ideal*, p. 109. Subsequent information on the Dayton election is from Weinstein.

36 Samuel P. Hays, "The Politics of Reform in Municipal Government in the Progressive Era," in *Social Change and Urban Politics: Readings*, ed. Daniel N. Gordon (Englewood Cliffs, NJ: Prentice Hall, 1973), pp. 107–127.

37 Jens Manuel Krogstad and Mark Hugo Lopez, "Black voter turnout fell in 2016, even as record number of Americans cast ballots," *FactTank—News in Numbers*, The Pew Research Center, May 12, 2017. Accessed online: http://www.pewresearch. org/fact-tank/2017/05/12/black-voter-turnout-fell-in-2016-even-as-a-record-number-of-americans-cast-ballots/.

38 Jordan Weissmann, "Ferguson Is Mostly Black. Why Is Its Government So White?" *Slate*, August 14, 2014. Accessed online: http://www.slate.com/blogs/moneybox/ 2014/08/14/ferguson_missouri_government_why_is_it_so_white.html.

39 Ibid.

40 Ibid.

41 Ibid.

42 Matt Stieb, "Republicans Keep Trying to Throw Out Black Votes After the Election," *New York Magazine* (November 18, 2020). Accessed online: https://nymag.com/ intelligencer/2020/11/gop-keeps-trying-to-throw-out-black-votes-after-the-election. html.

43 Ibid.

44 Colin Dwyer, "Michigan's Wayne County Certifies Election Results after Brief GOP Refusal," *NPR* (November 18, 2020). Accessed online: https://www.kcrw.com/news/ shows/npr/npr-story/936120411.

45 Matt Stieb, "Republicans Keep Trying to Throw Out Black Votes After the Election," *New York Magazine* (November 18, 2020). Accessed online: https://nymag.com/ intelligencer/2020/11/gop-keeps-trying-to-throw-out-black-votes-after-the-election. html.

46 Ibid.

47 "Trump Push to Invalidate Votes in Heavily Black Cities Alarms Civil Rights Groups," *All Things Considered, NPR* (November 24, 2020). Accessed online: https://www.npr.org/2020/11/24/938187233/trump-push-to-invalidate-votes-in-heavily-black-cities-alarms-civil-rights-group.

48 Adrienne LaFrance and Vann R. Newkirk II, "The Lost History of an American Coup D'Etat," *The Atlantic* (August 12, 2017). Accessed online: https://www.theatlantic. com/politics/archive/2017/08/wilmington-massacre/536457/.

49 Richard Wormser, *The Rise and Fall of Jim Crow* (New York: Macmillan, 2004), pp. 85–86.

50 Rev. Allen J. Kirk, "A Statement of Facts Concerning the Bloody Riot in Wilmington, N.C. Of Interest to the United States." Electronic Edition. Wilmington, NC (1898). North Carolina Collection, The University of North Carolina at Chapel Hill. Accessed online: https://docsouth.unc.edu/nc/kirk/kirk.html.

51 Bridges, *Morning Glories*, p. 146.

52 Ibid., Chapter 7.

53 Ibid., pp. 144–145.

54 Quoted in Holli, "Urban Reform in the Progressive Era," p. 144.

55 Ibid., p. 47.

56 Ibid., p. 45.

57 Nancy Burns and Gerald Gamm, "Creatures of the State: State Politics and Local Government 1871–1921," *Urban Affairs Review* 33, no. 1 (September 1997): 90.

58 Ibid., p. 86.

59 Scott Allard, Nancy Burns, and Gerald Gamm, "Representing Urban Interests: The Local Politics of State Legislatures," *Studies in American Political Development* 12 (Fall 1998): 294; see also Nancy Burns, Laura Evans, Gerald Gamm, and Corrine McGonnaughy, "The Local Politics of State Legislatures," paper delivered at the annual meeting of the Midwest Political Science Association (April 25, 2002).

60 Allard, Burns, and Gamm, "Representing Urban Interests," p. 68.

61 Ibid., p. 76.

62 Frederick Winslow Taylor, *The Principles of Scientific Management* (New York: Harper and Brothers, 1919; first published in 1911).

63 Ibid., p. 140.

64 Ibid., p. 7.

65 Haber, *Efficiency and Uplift*, p. 56.

66 Harold A. Stone, Don K. Price, Kathryn H. Stone, *City Manager Government in the United States: A Review After Twenty-Five Years* (Chicago, IL: Public Administration Service, 1940), p. 5.

67 Henry Brueré, *The New City Government: A Discussion of Municipal Administration Based on a Survey of Ten Commission-Governed Cities* (Upper Saddle River, NJ: Prentice Hall, 1912).

68 Ibid., p. v.

69 Ibid., pp. 27–29.

70 Robert A. Caro, *The Power Broker: Robert Moses and the Fall of New York* (New York: Oxford University Press, 1969), p. 75.

71 Taylor, *The Principles of Scientific Management*, p. 20.

72 Melvin B. Holli, *Reform in Detroit: Hazen S. Pingree and Urban Politics* (New York: Oxford University Press, 1969), p. 167.

73 Haber, *Efficiency and Uplift*, p. 115.

74 Stone, Price, and Stone, *City Manager Government*, p. 4.

75 Martin J. Schiesl, *The Politics of Municipal Reform: Municipal Administration and Reform in America, 1880–1920* (Berkeley: University of California Press, 1977), pp. 134–135.

76 Quoted in Weinstein, *The Corporate Ideal*, p. 96.

77 Clinton R. Woodruff, ed., *City Government by Commission* (Upper Saddle River, NJ: Prentice Hall, 1911), pp. 293–294.

78 Childs, *Civic Victories*, p. 138.

79 Hays, "The Politics of Reform," p. 116.

80 Weinstein, *The Corporate Ideal*, p. 99.

81 Childs, *Civic Victories*, p. 137.

82 Ibid.

83 Stone, Price, and Stone, *City Manager Government*, p. 5.

84 Griffith, *A History of American City Government*, p. 167.

85 Ibid., p. 166; Schiesl, *The Politics of Municipal Reform*, pp. 175–176.

86 Weinstein, *The Corporate Ideal*, pp. 115–116.

87 Quoted in Stone, Price, and Stone, *City Manager Government*, p. 27.

88 Quoted in Weinstein, *The Corporate Ideal*, pp. 106, 107.

89 Anirudh V. S. Ruhil, "Structural Change and Fiscal Flows: A Framework for Analyzing the Effects of Urban Events," *Urban Affairs Review* 38, no. 3 (January 2003): 396–416.

90 Jessica Trounstine, *Political Monopolies in American Cities: The Rise and Fall of Bosses and Reformers* (Chicago, IL: University of Chicago Press, 2008), pp. 162–163.

91 Ibid., p. 163.

92 Alan DiGaetano, "Urban Political Reform: Did It Kill the Machine?" *Journal of Urban History* 18, no. 1 (November 1991): 37–67.

93 Ibid.

94 Ibid.

95 Ibid.

96 Ibid., p. 67.

97 Ibid.

98 Steven P. Erie, *Rainbow's End: Irish-Americans and the Dilemmas of Urban Machine Politics, 1840–1985* (Berkeley: University of California Press, 1988).

99 Karen M. Kaufmann, *The Urban Voter: Group Conflict and Mayoral Voting Behavior in American Cities* (Ann Arbor: University of Michigan Press), p. 19.

100 Jay M. Shafritz, *The Dorsey Dictionary of American Government and Politics* (Homewood, IL: Dorsey Press, 1988), pp. 244–246. A legislative district is considered gerrymandered when it is drawn with tortuously meandering boundaries as a means of advancing the interests of a party or group. The term comes from a district drawn in Massachusetts in 1811 and signed into law by Governor Elbridge Gerry.

101 Robert L. Lineberry and Edmond P. Fowler, "Reformism and Public Policies in American Cities," *American Political Science Review* 61 (September 1967): 701–716; Chandler Davidson and George Korbel, "At-Large Elections and Minority Group Representation: A Re-Examination of Historical and Contemporary Evidence," *Journal of Politics* 43 (November 1981): 982–1005; Jerry L. Polinard, Robert D. Wrinkle, and Thomàs Longoria Jr., "The Impact of District Elections on the Mexican American Community: The Electoral Perspective," *Social Science Quarterly* 71, no. 3 (September 1991): 608–614; Richard L. Engstrom and Michael D. McDonald, "The Effect of At-Large versus District Elections on Racial Representation in U.S. Municipalities," in *Electoral Laws and Their Political Consequences*, ed. Bernard Grofman and Arend Liphart (New York: Agathon, 1986), pp. 203–225; W. E. Lyons and Malcolm E. Jewell, "Minority Representation and the Drawing of City Council Districts," *Urban Affairs Quarterly* 23 (1988): 432–447; Delbert Taebel, "Minority Representation on City Councils: The Impact of Structure on Blacks and Hispanics," *Social Science Quarterly* 59 (1982): 729–736; Jeffrey S. Zax, "Election Methods, Black and Hispanic City Council Membership," *Social Science Quarterly* 71 (1990): 339–355.

102 *City of Mobile v. Bolden*, 446 U.S. 55 (1980).

103 *Thornburg v. Gingles*, 106 S. Ct. 2752 (1986).

104 A multimember legislative district is just like an at-large system that covers an entire city. All candidates for city council seats must run in the same district; by contrast, in a ward system, a single alderman or council member represents each ward.

105 C. Robert Heath, "*Thornburg v. Gingles*: The Unresolved Issues," *National Civic Review* 79, no. 1 (January–February 1990): 50–71.

106 *Dillard v. Crenshaw County*, 649 F.Supp. at 289 (C.O. Ala. 1986).

107 *McNeal v. Springfield*, 658 F.Supp. at 1015, 1022 (C.D. Ill. 1987).

108 *McNeal v. Springfield Park District*, 851 F.2d at 937 (7th Cir. 1988).

109 *Derrickson v. City of Danville*, 87–2007 (C.D. Ill. 1987).

110 Joseph F. Zimmerman, "Alternative Local Electoral Systems," *National Civic Review* 79, no. 1 (January–February 1990): 23–36.

111 The quotation is from *Shaw v. Reno* 509 U.S. 630 (1993), commonly known as Shaw I. Other cases are *Miller v. Johnson*, 63 U.S.L.W. 4726 (1995); *Shaw v. Hunt*, 64 U.S.L.W. 4437 (known as Shaw II); *King v. Illinois Board of Elections*, 65 U.S.L.W. 3353 (1996); and *Abrams v. Johnson*, 65 U.S.L.W. 4478.

112 Carmen Cirincione, Thomas Darling, and Timothy O'Rourke, "Does the Supreme Court Have It Right?" paper delivered at the 1997 annual meeting of the American Political Science Association, Washington, D.C. (August 28–31, 1997).

113 Heath, "*Thornburg v. Gingles*," pp. 51–53.

114 Ibid., pp. 54–55.

115 Ibid., pp. 55–59; Charles S. Bullock III, "Symbolics or Substance: A Critique of the At-Large Election Controversy," *State and Local Government Review* 21, no. 3 (Fall 1989): 91–99.

116 Edward Blum and Roger Clegg, "The GOP's 2002 Racial Redistricting Dilemma," *Weekly Standard* (October 17, 1992).

117 Scott Armstrong, "Minorities Seek More Clout on the Bench," *Christian Science Monitor* (October 1, 1991), pp. 1–2.

118 International City Management Association, "Municipal Election Processes: The Impact on Minority Representation," *Baseline Data Report* 19, no. 6 (November–December 1987): 3–4.

119 Ibid., pp. 6–9; Polinard, Wrinkle, and Longoria, "The Impact of District Elections," pp. 608–614.

120 Tim O'Neil, "Blacks Want Half of City's Wards in Redistricting," *St. Louis Post-Dispatch* (June 8, 1991), p. 3A.

121 *Shaw v. Reno*, 92 357 (1993). In 1996, the Court rejected a somewhat redrawn 12th congressional district in North Carolina yet again.

122 *Miller v. Johnson*, 515 U.S. 900 (94 631), 1995; *Bush v. Vera*, 571 U.S. 900 (94 805), 1996.

123 *The United States Department of Justice*, "Section 4 of the Voting Rights Act." Accessed online: https://www.justice.gov/crt/section-4-voting-rights-act.

124 Adam Liptak, "Supreme Court Invalidates Key Part of the Voting Rights Act," *The New York Times* (June 25, 2013). Accessed online: http://www.nytimes.com/2013/06/26/us/supreme-court-ruling.html.

125 Quoted in Ibid.

126 Quoted in Ibid.

127 Quoted in Nina Totenberg, "The Supreme Court Deals A New Blow To Voting Rights, Upholding Arizona Restrictions," *NPR, Morning Edition* (July 1, 2021), https://www.npr.org/2021/07/01/998758022/the-supreme-court-upheld-upholds-arizona-measures-that-restrict-voting.

128 Kagan, J., Dissenting, *Brnovitch v. Democratic National Committee; Arizona Republican Party v. Democratic National Committee*, July 1, 2021.

129 Justin Levitt, "The Truth About Voter Fraud," *The Brennan Center for Justice* (November 9, 2007), https://www.brennancenter.org/our-work/research-reports/truth-about-voter-fraud.

130 Ian Urbina, "Voter ID Battle Shifts to Proof of Citizenship," *The New York Times* (May 12, 2008), www.nytimes.com/2008/05/12/us/politics/12vote.html.

131 Nikki Schwab, "Confusing Voter Registration Laws Could Affect Presidential Election," *U.S. News and World Report* (September 24, 2008), www.usnews.com/articles/campaign-2008/09/2008/09/24.

132 Ari Berman, "New Voter Suppression Efforts Prove the Voting Rights Act is Still Needed," *The Nation* (March 28, 2013), http://www.thenation.com/blog/173562/new-voter-suppression-efforts-prove-voting-rights-act-still-needed#.

133 Steve Benen, "Three Months, 30 States, 55 New Voting Restrictions," *MSNBC: The Maddow Blog* (March 29, 2013), http://www.projectvote.org/news/three-months-30-states-55-new-voting-restrictions/.

134 Chris Kromm, "Art Pope-Backed Lawmaker Leads Push for New Voting Restrictions In NC," *The Institute for Southern Studies: Facing South* (April 3, 2013) http://www.southernstudies.org/2013/04/art-pope-backed-lawmaker-leads-pushfor-new-voting-restrictions-in-nc.html.

135 Bill Kaczor, "Florida Leads in Denying Ex-Felons Voting Rights," *The Associated Press* (April 14, 2013), http://www.tallahassee.com/viewart/20130414/POLITICSPOLICY/304140029/Florida-leads-in-denying-ex-felons-voting-rights.

136 Berman, "New Voter Suppression Efforts Prove the Voting Rights Act Is Still Needed."

137 Benen, "Three Months, 30 States, 55 New Voting Restrictions."

138 Berman, "New Voter Suppression Efforts Prove the Voting Rights Act Is Still Needed."

139 Emily Schultheis, "Study Finds Voter ID Laws Hurt Young Minorities," *POLITICO* (March 12, 2013), http://www.politico.com/story/2013/03/study-finds-voter-idlaws-hurt-young-minorities-88773.html.

140 Ethan Bronner, "Legal Battles Erupt Over Tough Voter ID Laws," *The New York Times* (July 19, 2012).

141 Ibid.

142 Carol Morello, "Foreign Election Observers to Cast Their Eyes on U.S. Presidential Vote," *The Washington Post* (October 5, 2016). Accessed online: https://www.washingtonpost.com/world/national-security/foreign-election-observers-to-cast-their-eyes-on-the-us-presidential-vote/2016/10/05/2fb0646e-8666-11e6-ac72-a29979381495_story.html?utm_term=.e45f78dd8edb.

143 The Brennan Center for Justice, "It's Official: The Election Was Secure." (December 11, 2020), https://www.brennancenter.org/our-work/research-reports/its-official-election-was-secure.

CHAPTER 5

Urban Voters and the Rise of a National Democratic Majority

City and Nation in the Twentieth Century

From today's perspective, it may be hard to imagine a time when there was political support for programs to help the cities. In the 1980s, at the tail-end of the suburbanization movement, representatives from both major parties started losing interest in making explicitly urban policies—based on the assumption that cities were permanently in decline and, eventually, would simply wither away. This, as we know now, has clearly not happened. Quite to the contrary: Many—though not all—cities have since resurged in economic and population growth. They feature bastions of tremendous wealth—while pockets of poverty have deepened at the same time. But in spite of their resurgent population growth, cities, according a team of researchers at Portland State University, have some of the lowest turnout rates in the country. In the country's three largest cities, New York City, Los Angeles, and Chicago, turnout was significantly below 50 percent: Chicago led the way with 32.68 percent turnout, followed by L.A. at 18.6 percent, and New York City at 13.79 percent.[1] Three growing Sunbelt metropoles had turnout rates below 10 percent: Las Vegas (9.4 percent), Fort Worth (6.48 percent), and Dallas (6.14 percent).[2] Only one major U.S. city had turnout rates above 50 percent: Portland (59.43 percent), followed by Louisville (45.43 percent), and Seattle (44.49 percent).[3] And in spite of the fact that Black voters in the country's major metropoles today are the Democrat's most solid and reliable voting bloc, cities and their key issues, since the 1980s, remain largely ignored, even by the Democrats.

Attention to the problems of the cities emerged at a time when the calculation was different. Voters living the industrial belt stretching from New England and through the Midwest and in some cities beyond were important to Democratic candidate Franklin D. Roosevelt's landslide victory in the presidential election of 1932, and for decades after, they continued to play a decisive role in determining the national balance of power between the two parties. The nation's 11 largest cities accounted for 27 percent of the popular vote in 1932 and a commanding majority in several of the industrial states with the largest numbers of electoral college votes.[4] For the first time in the nation's history, in the 1930s the politicians representing urban voters began to wield influence in national politics. Their loyalty to the Democratic Party fundamentally shaped American politics until the election of Republican Ronald Reagan in 1980.

Modern American liberalism, as expressed in the New Deal programs of the 1930s and the Great Society programs of the 1960s (these terms were borrowed from the campaign slogans of Presidents Roosevelt and Lyndon Baines Johnson), can be traced to the mobilization of the urban electorate during the years of the Great Depression. The alliance that became the foundation for the Democratic Party's ascendancy was made up of two wings, the urban North and the "solid South." Urban voters in northern cities voted Democratic because they benefited from the outpouring of programs enacted during the New Deal years. Legislation proposed by Roosevelt and supported by the big Democratic majorities in Congress granted powers to regulate the economy and to assist citizens in times of need. Urban working-class people were helped by labor legislation such as Section 7a of the National Industrial Recovery Act and the Wagner Labor Act, which established workers' compensation for death or injury, safety and workplace regulations, and the right of workers to organize unions. As a result, union members became reliable Democratic voters. The African American electorate also became important to the northern wing of the party. Even in the 1930s, decades before civil rights legislation became politically viable, the Roosevelt administration took steps to ensure that Black citizens received some appointments to federal posts and a share of the benefits from job and relief programs. In addition, Black intellectuals and Black political activists had made significant inroads into northern urban machines on their own, as explained in Chapter 4. Although southern voters would eventually become estranged from the party, until the civil rights legislation of the 1960s they stayed in the fold because a lot of the New Deal legislation benefited them too, and the bitterness of the Civil War and reconstruction years had not yet faded enough to allow them to make the leap to the Republican Party. The odd coalition between urban voters in the North and the one-party Democratic South was forged as an alliance of convenience that began to break apart in the 1960s, when racial tensions around the push for civil rights eventually forced Democrats to take a stand on the national level and thus started to politically amplify the wedge of racism that existed between inner-city Black communities, white working class and suburban voters, and southern conservatives. When the New Deal coalition dissolved for good in the 1980s, the cities' influence in national politics almost vanished.

OUTTAKE

Urban Ethnics Became a Mainstay of the Democratic Party

It is often supposed, mistakenly, that voters in the central cities have always voted Democratic. But until the New Deal years, about half of the party machines that ruled the cities were Republican. The Democratic machines did little to deliver votes to the national ticket, because their leaders had little connection either to the national or even to the state party organizations. At the state level, party organizations were dominated by rural, not city, politicians. Machine politicians had gotten into politics through their precincts and wards, and they specialized in a politics of ethnicity and trade-offs, not abstract principles. The machines were strictly local organizations, a product of the segregation of ethnic voters from the rest of American society.

When ethnic politicians from the cities ended up in the state legislature, they found that they received little pay and even less respect. It was often a kiss of political death to be sent away to small upstate or downstate towns like Albany, New York, or Springfield, Illinois, away from friends, family, community, and constituents. When New York City's machine organization, Tammany Hall, sent Al Smith to the state legislature at the age of 30, he had scarcely been outside lower Manhattan. He felt as if he were exiled, sent away to a foreign country:

> Al Smith went to Albany unprepared to be legislator—or even to sleep away from home .... [O]vercome by the intricacies of the legislative process, he sat day after day in the high-ceilinged chamber in silence.

As he sat there staring down at the desk, a page boy would deposit another pile of bills on it. The wording was difficult enough for the expert. It might have been designed to mock a man whose schooling had ended in the eighth grade, who had never liked to read even the simple books of childhood, who, he had once said, had in his entire life read only one book cover to cover: *The Life of John L. Sullivan.**

Before Al Smith, who was later elected governor of New York and nominated as the Democratic presidential candidate in 1928, Tammany politicians had never prospered in Albany.

Personal loyalties and their pocket books motivated urban ethnic voters. When precinct captains took them to the polls, they voted for the local party organization, not for a cause. What in their background would excite them about complicated national issues such as tariff policy or child labor legislation? The upshot was that even when a powerful machine dominated a city, the party bosses and their loyal constituents mostly ignored gubernatorial and presidential elections.

All this changed quickly in the 1930s, when urban ethnic and labor union workers became important to the New Deal coalition.

Source: Robert A. Caro, *The Power Broker: Robert Moses and the Fall of New York* (New York: Knopf, 1974), pp. 118–119.

*John L. Sullivan was a famous boxing champion.

A New Political Consciousness

In 1912 a Harvard political scientist wrote, "before many years have passed, the urban population of the United States will have gained numerical mastery."[5] He based this prediction on a simple calculation of demographic trends.[6] In the 30 years from 1890 to 1920, more than 18 million immigrants poured into America's cities. These immigrants came mainly from Italy, Poland, Russia, Greece, and Eastern Europe. They were overwhelmingly Roman Catholic and Jewish. They made up the preponderance of the workforces in the iron and steel, meatpacking, mining, and textile industries. Few spoke English when they arrived, and many were illiterate even in their native languages.

The ever-present nineteenth-century nervousness about the "strangers in the land" escalated into a national phobia in the next century. The viciousness of the campaigns launched against immigrants gradually made them aware that they had a stake in national, and not only local, politics. Immigrant voters had been brought into politics by the urban party machines, but these were strictly local organizations that stayed away from big political issues. But they could scarcely remain neutral when the cultural values and customs they and their constituents held dear came under attack.

The campaigns for prohibition were aimed squarely at immigrants and their cultural values. Proposed to the states by Congress in 1917 and ratified in 1919, the Eighteenth Amendment prohibited the sale and distribution of alcoholic beverages. Small-town Methodists and Baptists—joined in their crusade by upper- and middle-class Protestants in the cities and in the privileged suburbs—claimed that if the immigrants were forced to abstain from alcohol it would reduce poverty, improve workers' efficiency and family life, and end immorality and crime. Prohibition became the most compelling political issue of the first two decades of the century because it gave middle-class Protestants and rural voters a practical way to express their hostility toward the foreign immigrants crowded into the industrial cities:

> [Drinking] was associated with the saloonkeepers who ran the city machines and who used the votes of the whiskey-loving immigrant … with the German brewers and their "disloyal" compatriots who drank beer and ale …. The cities, which resisted the idea that "thou shalt not" was the fundamental precept of living, were always hostile to prohibition. The prohibitionists, in turn, regarded the city as their chief enemy, and prohibitionism and a pervasive antiurbanism went hand-in-hand.[7]

To the members of the Protestant middle class, the sins of liquor were indistinguishable from what they saw as the depraved cultural customs of Catholic immigrants. Southern and western newspapers reflexively connected crime, national origin, and liquor. When it was not legitimate to attack foreigners directly, it was easy to attack them indirectly through the surrogate liquor issue, allowing "prohibition partisans to talk about morality when in reality they were worried about cultural dominance and political supremacy."[8]

Prohibition and religion were intimately connected. To most Protestant Americans, the Roman Catholic Church represented evil incarnate. It signified ostentatious authority—the robes, the ceremony, and the architecture of Catholic churches seemed like an affront to the simplicity and informality of small-town life. Like the right-wing groups of the 1950s obsessed by the idea that an international communist conspiracy was poised to subvert the American political system, religious fundamentalists of the early twentieth century were convinced that the Roman Catholic Church was dedicated to the goal of worldwide domination.

By exploiting such fears, the Ku Klux Klan attracted millions of followers. Revived in Atlanta in 1915, for a few years the Klan enjoyed spectacular growth in both the North and the South. Klan membership skyrocketed in California, Oregon, Indiana, Illinois, Ohio, Oklahoma, Texas, Arkansas, and throughout the South. In 1924, at its peak, 40 percent of the Klan's membership resided in Ohio, Indiana, and Illinois. Half of its membership was located in cities of more than 50,000, with chapters of hundreds of members in such cities as Chicago, Detroit, Indianapolis, Pittsburgh, Baltimore, and Buffalo.[9] The Klan remained a powerful political force until at least the mid-1920s. It helped elect a member of the Senate; governors in Georgia, Alabama, Oregon, and California; and 75 members of the House of Representatives.

Although the Klan found its most enthusiastic support among less-educated fundamentalist Christians, its message also reached a broader audience. In 1916, Madison Grant, curator of New York City's Museum of National History, published *The Passing of the Great Race*, in which he worried that Aryans might someday be overwhelmed by dark-skinned races. His book was elevated to the status of a scientific work, along with Lothrop Stoddard's *The Rising Tide of Color against the White World-Supremacy* (1921).

Congress responded to the rising xenophobia with the Emergency Quota Act of 1921 and the National Origins Act of 1924. Both laws drew support from intellectuals, labor leaders, rural people from all sections of the country, and anxious middle-class voters. The Emergency Quota Act reaffirmed the total exclusion of Chinese, which had been legislated by Congress in 1882, and established a national origins quota of 3 percent of the population of other nationality groups as recorded in the 1910 census. The law succeeded in cutting immigration from 805,228 in 1920 to 309,556 in 1921–1922.[10] Three years later, the National Origins Act reduced the origins quota to 2 percent and established the 1890 census as the new baseline. The effect of the legislation was to drastically reduce immigration by ethnic groups that had come to the United States primarily since 1890. Italian immigration was reduced by 90 percent; British and Irish immigration, by contrast, declined by just 19 percent.[11] The overall immigrant flow fell sharply, from 357,803 in 1923–1924 to 164,667 in 1924–1925.

In floor debates on the two immigration bills, members of Congress reviled the foreign-born of the cities in language that could have been lifted from Ku Klux Klan pamphlets. This furious assault taught immigrant voters that national politics affected them, and in the 1920s they began to express their new understanding. Before long, it became apparent they "were not going to support candidates who wanted them to stop drinking, Protestantize their schools, or tell them as often as possible that they were inferior."[12] Opposition to prohibition was the one political issue that unified Catholic immigrants, regardless of national origin.

Earlier, when the State of Illinois began enforcing restrictive drinking laws in 1906, immigrants had launched protests and launched efforts "to endorse political candidates and lobby city and state governments to protect the free sale and consumption of liquor."[13] Over the next three decades, the number of naturalized immigrants registered to vote rose sharply, and they turned out at very high rates for local elections.[14] They were clearly becoming a political force to be reckoned with, and one of the causes that could motivate them was Prohibition. Anton Cermak, the future mayor of Chicago, began his political career in the 1920s by becoming one of the leaders of the campaign for repeal.[15] Al Smith, the Democrats' nominee for president in 1928, gained support among immigrant voters because he opposed Prohibition and he was, as an Irish Catholic, one of them. In effect, Prohibition taught immigrants that politics was not only local but also national.

The Changing Political Balance

Before the 1930s, neither the Republicans nor the Democrats paid much attention to the cities. The Republicans, the triumphant party of Abraham Lincoln, emerged from the Civil War as the dominant party controlling Congress and the presidency. Between 1860 and 1928, the Republicans won 14 of 18 presidential contests and controlled both houses of Congress more than half of the time. Because the party's main base of support was made up of financial, industrial, and commercial interests, it opposed taxes on business, enacted high tariffs on foreign imports, encouraged private exploitation (mineral, grazing, homesteading) of federal lands in the West, and used federal troops to quell strikes. At the same time, the Republicans gained support from middle- and working-class voters in the North because the party presided during a long-term economic expansion tied closely to frontier development and industrial production.

For several decades after the Civil War, the Democratic Party tried to hold together an uneasy alliance made up of Southerners and an assortment of groups opposed to economic domination by east-coast "big money." The party's presidential candidates appealed for support from urban workers, but a lot of other interests jostled for attention too. The chronic problem for the Democrats' coalition was its fragility. The issues that held it together arose from the abiding enmity of Southerners to the party of Lincoln, the insecurities of small farmers about credit and prices, and the tensions between business and industrial workers, but aside from their resentments, these groups had little if anything in common. The party did better during the periodic downturns but lost ground when the economy improved.

The fragile nature of this alliance was revealed at the 1924 Democratic Convention, held in Madison Square Garden in New York City. The Democrats treated the first radio audience of a national convention to a futile 16-day, 103-ballot marathon that listed 19 candidates on the first ballot and 17 on the 100th. The galleries booed the speeches of Southerners and Westerners, especially when William Jennings Bryan, a three-time failed candidate for president, asked the convention to reject a proposed resolution condemning the Ku Klux Klan by name. The motion to condemn the Klan brought forth such heated oratory that police were brought onto the convention floor in case a riot broke out. Delegates shouted at and cursed one another. When the final vote on the resolution was taken, it lost by one vote, 542 3⁄20 to 541 3⁄20. Demands for a recount were drowned out when the band struck up "Marching through Georgia," which incited the southern delegates to paroxysms of rage. After 16 days, the convention finally nominated a presidential candidate, John W. Davis, who almost nobody wanted and few of the delegates even knew.[16]

The crowds and the din of New York City confused and frightened the delegates from the towns and farms of the South and West. They found New Yorkers unfriendly and rude, and the city seemed all too easy to get lost in. Delegates who "wandered downtown to Fourteenth Street to gawk at Tammany Hall with its ancient Indian above the door reacted as if they expected to see an ogre come popping out. Almost all delegates were dismayed by the New York traffic, the noise and hustle."[17] Their antagonism toward the city was reaffirmed every day the convention dragged on through the stifling July heat. Small-town reporters filled their hometown newspapers with vivid accounts of the horrors of the city.[18]

Only four years later the Democrats named Al Smith, the four-term governor of New York, their presidential candidate. The convention was held in Houston, Texas, the first time either of the parties had met in the South since the Civil War. The nomination laid bare bitter divisions. Smith represented everything that was anathema to the city haters. He was the first Roman Catholic nominated for the presidency and an ardent opponent of Prohibition and the Ku Klux Klan. He was a self-made member of the nation's most notorious machine, Tammany Hall. He said "foist" instead of "first" and wore a brown derby, which only accentuated his bulbous nose and ruddy complexion. Smith proudly reminisced about his past: Swimming in the East River and working at the Fulton Fish Market as an errand boy. Considering these fractious conflicts, how could he have been nominated? Once he was nominated, why did the party not simply break apart?

Southern and aggrieved farmers had little choice but to stay within the fold because they had come to share, however crudely, a class interest. The party had become—mostly by default because the Republicans took an uncompromising probusiness stand—the "little man's" party. Those who opposed Republican policies could never hope to have a voice in national politics unless they cooperated with one another. Despite their differences, most of the delegates to the 1928 convention wanted to avoid a repeat of the Madison Square Garden debacle. Few delegates thought Smith could win, but no other candidate was available who was capable of bridging the divisions in the fractious party. As the four-term governor of New York, he had gained national prominence as a progressive leader who had created state parks and beaches, sponsored workers' safety legislation, and financed public improvements throughout the state. He had reorganized state government, making New York the model for progressives who believed in efficiency principles. Admired by progressives for his record as governor and supported by Democratic organizations and their ethnic supporters, his nomination could be denied by rural delegates, but only at the cost of another fiasco like 1924—multiple ballots and a guaranteed loss for the presidential nominee. There was even reason to believe Smith might have a chance. In his victorious gubernatorial run in 1924, he had received 100,000 more votes than the losing Democratic presidential ticket in New York.

In 1928, the Democrats gave the nomination to Al Smith. He lost several southern and border states and won only 41 percent of the national vote, but his candidacy marked the beginning of the party's increasing reliance on the urban electorate. Both in 1920 and 1924, the 12 largest cities in the United States had, taken together, given a decisive majority to the Republicans. Now the tables were turned, and the Democrats gained ground. As later elections were to prove, this marked the beginning of a long-term trend in which voters in the cities cast most of their ballots for Democrats.[19]

For the Roman Catholic ethnics in the cities, Smith's campaign educated them about the national issues of Prohibition, ethnicity, and religion. Smith campaigned with his brown derby and his theme song, "The Sidewalks of New York." Protestants shuddered at the idea of a Catholic in the White House. His stand on Prohibition made drinking the leading issue of the campaign. Blue-blood upper-class Protestants found him beneath them. The campaign highlighted the issues of race, religion, culture, and social class so clearly that never again would the urban ethnics be unmindful of their stake in the national political system.

The election of 1928 brought a Democratic electoral plurality to the industrial cities where immigrant voters lived. In 1920, the Republican presidential ticket carried the 12 largest cities by more than 1.5 million votes, and in 1924 the ticket did almost as well. But in 1928, with Al Smith as the Democratic candidate, the Republican margin in the cities shrank to a narrow 210,000 votes. In the 1932 election, the Democrats beat the Republicans in the big cities for the first time, and decisively, by almost 1.8 million votes.[20] Franklin Delano Roosevelt's landslide demonstrated that the Democrats now had a firm lock on the urban electorate. Since then, the old industrial cities have normally voted heavily Democratic, and this fact proved to be especially decisive in the outcomes of two presidential elections. In 1948 Harry S. Truman barely won the national popular vote, but he carried the cities by nearly 1.5 million votes. Urban voters again provided the crucial difference in the 1960 election, when they put John F. Kennedy over the top.

The Depression and the Cities

The Great Depression came as a shock to Americans and to their public leaders. Especially for the rapidly growing middle class, the 1920s had been a decade of prosperity and optimism. Business leaders and politicians promoted the idea that sustained economic growth was virtually limitless. A strong undertow of poverty ran below the surface in the immigrant slums and on farms alike, but for the growing middle class an air of prosperity prevailed. It was an age that extolled mass consumption and complacency. For a time, the discontents of the industrial age seemed long past.

October 24, 1929, is the symbolic beginning of the Great Depression. On that day—Black Thursday—disorder, panic, and confusion reigned on the New York Stock Exchange. Stock prices virtually collapsed. For several months prices had sagged, then rallied, then sagged again, with each trough lower than the previous one and each peak less convincing. When the bottom fell out, "the Market ... degenerated into a wild, mad scramble to sell, ... the Market ... surrendered to blind, relentless fear."[21] In one morning, 11 well-known speculators committed suicide. From Wall Street the economic catastrophe rippled outward, with global and domestic consequences that fundamentally reshaped American politics.

Over the next three years, the nation sank ever deeper into economic stagnation. In the spring of 1929, the unemployment rate stood at 3.2 percent. Within a few months, the number of unemployed exceeded 4 million, representing 8.7 percent of the labor force.[22] By 1932, 24 percent of all workers—more than 12 million in all—could not find jobs. In the depths of the Depression, during the spring of 1933, the number of unemployed reached 13 million workers, fully one-fourth of the labor force.[23]

The Depression dragged on for a decade. Unemployment levels remained above 20 percent in both 1934 and 1935 and dropped below 15 percent only in 1937. Most of those who managed to find work made less than before. From 1929 to 1933, the average income of workers fell by 42.5 percent.[24] Weekly wages dropped from an average of $28 in 1929 to $17 by 1934, and workers faced the constant threat of layoffs. Many jobs were reduced from full-time to part-time status, and employers cut wages and hours to meet payrolls. For example, the payroll of the nation's largest steel company, U.S. Steel, was cut in half from 1929 to 1933, and in 1933 the company had no full-time workers at all.[25] Steel mills operated at only 12 percent of capacity by 1932.[26]

The basic structure of the capitalist system seemed irreparably damaged. In the three years following the stock market collapse, national income fell by 44.5 percent. By the summer of 1932, stocks had fallen 83 percent below their value in September 1929.[27] By the end of 1932, 5,096 commercial banks had failed. Farm income declined from $7 billion in 1929 to $2.5 billion in 1932.[28] For many farmers whose incomes had been sharply dropping throughout the 1920s, the Depression came as a final blow.

The statistics of disaster painted a portrait of human suffering. Between 1 million and 2 million men rode the rails and gathered in hobo jungles or camped in thickets and railroad cars. Others lived in "Hoovervilles," clusters of cardboard, scrap wood, and scrap metal shacks in empty lots and city parks. Hoovervilles varied greatly in terms of size and governance. Seattle had as many as eight Hoovervilles—New York City had two, one in Central Park and one in Riverside Part on the west side of the island of Manhattan. St. Louis, which was especially hard hit by the Great Depression and far surpassed the national unemployment rate, had the biggest Hooverville in the nation. It even had a church and a mayor. However, this did not mean that its residents were better off. As Hooverville residents in other cities, they barely got by. Those who had been chronically poor in the 1920s were now hungry and destitute. They stood in bread lines, ate from garbage cans, or went begging from door to door. One-quarter of all homeowners lost their homes in 1932, and more than 1,000 mortgages a day were foreclosed in the first half of 1933.[29] By March 1933, when Franklin D. Roosevelt was inaugurated as president, 9 million savings accounts had been lost.[30]

Never before had the nation faced an economic catastrophe of this magnitude, nor was there a tradition of federal government assistance for the unemployed and destitute.[31] However, unemployment and poverty were certainly not new. In the period from 1897 to 1926, unemployment levels in four major industries fluctuated around the 10 percent level,[32] and poverty was a chronic condition of industrialization and immigration. What made the Great Depression unique were its depth, persistence, and broad reach. In earlier depressions, including the panics of the 1870s and 1890s, production and employment declined much less severely, and recovery began within a year or two.[33] The Great Depression of the 1930s lasted for over a decade, it touched all classes, and people at all income levels felt its effects. The measure of the crisis of the 1930s was not just unemployment and poverty but also the breakdown of economic institutions.

No one knew how to respond. President Herbert Hoover firmly resisted intervention by the federal government and instead launched two national drives to encourage private relief. Late in 1930 he appointed the President's Emergency Committee for Employment. Its main charge was to encourage state and local committees to expedite public construction and coordinate public and private funding for relief efforts. In August 1931 he formed the President's

Organization on Unemployment Relief, whose job was to help organize private unemployment committees in states and communities.

Despite Hoover's stubborn opposition to federal assistance, two programs were funded during his administration. First, the Federal Home Loan Bank Act supplied capital advances to a small number of mortgage institutions so they could forbear rather than foreclose on mortgages in default. This program saved a few banks. Second, the Emergency Relief and Construction Act extended $300 million in loans to state and local governments so they could continue to provide relief to indigent people.

Hoover was hardly alone in opposing aggressive federal action. Until 1932 most governors took a "we'll do it ourselves" attitude toward solving unemployment and its associated problems.[34] Two governors refused to work with the President's Organization on Unemployment Relief, even though federal funds were not involved.[35] The officials of financially strapped local governments were also skeptical of federal aid. In July 1931 the socialist mayor of Milwaukee wrote to the mayors of the largest 100 cities, asking them to come to a conference to discuss a joint request for a national relief program. He got no response at all from many of the major cities, and several mayors criticized the idea, arguing that federal aid would constitute "an invasion of community rights."[36]

In the 1932 campaign, the Democrats accused Hoover of doing too much rather than too little. Their nominee, Roosevelt, promised to balance the budget while accusing Hoover of having presided over "the greatest spending administration in peace times in all our history."[37] It was apparent that the weight of the past lay heavily on both political parties. Against a cultural tradition that extolled individualism and free enterprise, there was great reluctance to expand the powers of government—especially the federal government—to meet the crisis. Nevertheless, when Roosevelt was inaugurated on March 4, 1933, he set in motion a concentrated period of reform that vastly increased the powers of the federal government in areas of business regulation, farm policy, and social insurance. Why did Roosevelt break so thoroughly from the American tradition of limited national government?

The new president's change of heart was motivated by the overwhelming sense of crisis that ushered him into the White House. Between his election in November and his inauguration in March, the nation passed through the worst months of the depression.[38] The economy teetered on the brink of utter collapse. In February 1933, some of the nation's biggest banks failed. "People stood in long queues with satchels and paper bags to take gold and currency away from the banks to store in mattresses and old shoe boxes. It seemed safer to put one's life's savings in the attic than to trust the financial institutions in the country."[39] Roosevelt wondered if anything would be left to salvage by the time he assumed office. By Inauguration Day, 38 states had closed their banks, and on that day the governors of New York and Illinois closed the nation's biggest banks.[40] The New York Stock Exchange stopped trading. The Kansas City and Chicago Boards of Trade closed their doors. "In the once-busy grain pits of Chicago, in the canyons of Wall Street, all was silent."[41]

It was also one of the harshest winters on record. In desperation, people overran relief offices and rioted at bank closings. Relief marchers invaded state legislative chambers. Farmers tried to stop foreclosure proceedings and blockaded roads. Amid marches, riots, arrests, and jailings, many people feared there might be a revolution against the capitalist system. The demands for some kind of response became almost impossible to resist.

In its first 100 days, Roosevelt's administration presented Congress with a flood of legislative proposals.[42] On March 9, Roosevelt signed the Emergency Banking Act. The act extended financial assistance to bankers so they could reopen their doors and gave the government authority to reorganize banks and control bank credit policies. It received a unanimous vote from a panicked Congress, sight unseen. A flurry of legislation followed: The Civilian Conservation Corps (CCC) (March 31), the Agricultural Adjustment Act and the Federal Emergency Relief Act (FERA) (May 12), the Tennessee Valley Authority (May 18), the Federal "Truth in Securities" Act (May 27), the Home Owners' Loan Act (June 13), the National Industrial Recovery Act (June 16), and more than a score of other bills.

Most of the legislative onslaught was designed to stimulate, regulate, and stabilize the most important economic institutions of the economy. But the benefits filtered down. After the Emergency Banking Act was passed, depositors gained enough confidence to put their money back into the banks. After passage of the National Housing Act (signed into law in 1934), homebuyers were able to secure long-term mortgages from banks, whose loans were guaranteed by the federal government. Foreclosures on farms and homes fell sharply when the government, through the Farm Credit Administration and Home Owners' Loan Corporation, agreed to buy up defaulted mortgages. New Deal programs affected millions of lives by salvaging savings, houses, and farms. Nevertheless, the New Deal's attempts to reform the economy were designed more to bring stability to financial institutions than to fight poverty and destitution in a more fundamental way. Home lending and farm credit programs primarily helped the nation's important economic institutions and secondarily aided the heavily mortgaged middle class.

The other side of the New Deal included its public works and relief programs. Between 1933 and 1937, the federal government administered public works programs for several million people and supplied direct relief to millions more. The earliest of the public works programs was the CCC. Overall, the CCC employed more than 2.5 million boys and young men. In 1935 alone, 500,000 men were living in CCC camps. They planted trees, built dams, fought fires, stocked fish, built lookout towers, dug ditches and canals, strung telephone lines, and built and improved bridges, roads, and trails. Their contribution to conservation was enormous; the CCC was responsible for more than half of all the forest planted in the United States up to the 1960s.[43]

The Civil Works Administration (CWA) was much larger and broader in scope. Established in November 1933, it employed 4.1 million by the third week of January 1934, and within a few months it employed almost a third of the unemployed labor force.[44] Although the CWA lasted for less than a year—Roosevelt ended it in the spring of 1934 because he thought it was too costly—it enabled many families to survive the bitter winter of 1934. The CWA was "immensely popular—with merchants, with local officials, and with workers," and its demise was resisted in Congress.[45] The Public Works Administration (PWA) enjoyed a longer run, and its impact was more lasting. In six years, from 1933 to 1939, the PWA built 70 percent of the new school buildings in the nation and 35 percent of the hospitals and public health facilities.[46]

The FERA, which Roosevelt signed into law on May 12, 1933, was never as popular as public works legislation because it undercut the cherished principles of work and independence by making relief money directly available to the destitute. Roosevelt himself viewed the Federal Emergency Relief Administration with distaste, thinking it would sap the moral strength of the poor. Roosevelt constantly sought ways to cut its budget, but the destitution and the civil disorder that prevailed in Roosevelt's first term made the program necessary. In the winter of 1934, 20 million people received FERA funds.[47]

The FERA was treated as an embarrassing necessity. The government's response was understood to be an emergency measure, comparable to helping victims of catastrophes such as floods, earthquakes, and tornadoes. Congressional debate on the FERA received little coverage by the media. When the act was passed on May 9, 1933, the *New York Times* only mentioned it on page 3 in a column listing legislation passed by Congress. The day after President Roosevelt put his signature to it, it made page 21 of the *Times* but only in reference to the appointment of the administrator. In a culture that extolled individualism, competition, and hard work, people were uncomfortable with the idea of relief.

Roosevelt frequently expressed doubts about relief and public works programs. He preferred economic recovery to government spending, but his response to the economic emergency vastly broadened the electoral base of the Democratic Party. Public works and relief created a loyal following among middle- and working-class people who benefited. By the 1936 election, and for decades thereafter, voting in small towns split between the Republicans on the wealthier side of the tracks and the working class and poor on the other. The most reliable new Democratic following, however, could be found in the cities. Urban ethnics, especially if they were union members, learned to vote Democratic. The New Deal programs also broke African American voters away from the Republican Party. Before the 1936 election, a prominent Black publisher counseled, "My friends, go turn Lincoln's picture to the wall. That debt has been paid in full."[48] In that election, Black Americans gave Roosevelt

75 percent of their votes, indicating the early stages of a change in voting behavior at the national level, which would become amplified with the Democrats' (reluctant) support of the Civil Rights Movement and the subsequent party realignment of the 1960s.

The Great Depression fundamentally altered the group composition of the party system in the United States. In addition to its traditional base in the South, the Democratic Party now claimed solid support among workers, African Americans, and the poor in the northern cities, where large numbers of the working class and the poor were concentrated. The party's electoral coalition broadened sufficiently to ensure that Democratic candidates would be competitive in presidential contests and that Democrats would hold majorities in Congress in most years. In 1936, the Gallup poll found that 59 percent of farmers favored Roosevelt (Agricultural Adjustment Act, Farm Credit Administration, Farm Mortgage Corporation, abolition of the gold standard); 61 percent of white-collar workers (bank regulation, Federal Housing Administration, savings deposit insurance); 80 percent of organized labor (government recognition of collective bargaining, unemployment insurance, work relief); and 68 percent of people under age 25 (CCC, National Youth Administration). Among lower-income groups, 76 percent favored Roosevelt, compared with 60 percent of the middle class.[49] By contrast, upper-income groups identified overwhelmingly with the Republican Party, and they did so for the remainder of the century. Only in the second decade of the twenty-first century did this begin to change.

Cities Gain a Voice

The Great Depression marked a turning point in American politics. To secure the votes of urban ethnics, Democratic candidates reliably supported the New Deal's initiatives. The voice of the cities in national politics was also amplified in these years by another development: The forging of a direct relationship between the federal government and the cities. Three elements stand out as key factors in this development: (1) A fiscal and social crisis in the cities, (2) indifference by the states, and (3) the forging of an alliance among city officials for the purpose of securing a federal response to their problems.

Even before Roosevelt took office, the cities had exhausted their resources. In the 1920s they had borrowed heavily to finance public improvements and capital construction. They were already deep in debt when the onset of the depression confronted them with rising unemployment and poverty. Local officials could not avoid seeing the misery and want on their streets. Faced with a manifest emergency, they provided relief funds as rapidly as they could, but it was not enough. Municipal governments simply lacked the financial resources to cope with the emergency.

Cities entered the depression after they had already financed a multitude of new public improvement programs. In the 1920s cities had built roads to accommodate the millions of automobiles flooding onto the streets. The auto imposed heavy new costs on local governments. Cities invested in traffic signals, police cars, garbage trucks, school buses, snowplows, roads, and bus and airline terminals. In response to demands from the rapidly expanding middle class, cities increased spending for education, built new school buildings and public libraries, and invested heavily in improving parks and recreational facilities.

Local governments made heavier investments in these areas than either the state or the federal governments. During the 1920s counties and municipalities spent 55–60 percent of all public funds in the nation, and their total debts mounted to $9 billion.[50] From 1923 to 1927, while the states increased expenditures by 43 percent, spending by the largest 145 cities rose by 79 percent, and cities of 100,000 or more increased their budgets by 82 percent.[51] In the latter cities expenditures for work relief and welfare shot up by 391 percent from 1923 to 1932; during the same period, states increased their relief and welfare budgets by only 63 percent. In the last year of the Hoover administration, the 13 cities with populations above 100,000 spent $53 million more than all the states combined for public welfare. Over the decade of the 1920s federal grants actually declined from 2 to 1.3 percent of all public expenditures.[52] The 13 biggest cities incurred 50 percent more debt in the 1920s, and many of them were hard pressed, even early in the Depression, to pay for government services and public improvements.[53]

The Great Depression placed unprecedented responsibilities on city officials at the very time that fiscal resources were drying up. Cities were unable to generate enough tax revenues to keep pace with their additional responsibilities. Two-thirds of the revenue for city budgets came from property taxes. Falling property values brought a 20 percent decline in property tax revenues from 1929 to 1933.[54] At the same time, the rate of tax delinquency increased from 10 to 26 percent in cities of over 50,000 in population.[55] Between 1931 and 1933, tax losses resulted in a reduction in the budgets of the largest 13 cities from $1.8 to $1.6 billion.[56] State-imposed debt limitations did not allow cities to borrow for day-to-day services. In principle, cities were allowed to borrow for capital improvements, but this option soon evaporated as well. By 1932, because of their high debt loads, cities found it impossible to sell long-term bond issues to investors. In 1932 and 1933, many states and municipalities, including Mississippi, Montana, Buffalo, Philadelphia, Cleveland, and Toledo, were unable to market any bond issues at all.[57] Temporary loans with high interest rates replaced long-term notes.

When the cities financed public works programs to help the unemployed, their budgets quickly ran dry. Municipal governments lacked sufficient resources to treat the depression's symptoms, yet many mayors saw this as their principal mission. Detroit's experience revealed the impossibility of the task. In the fall of 1930, Frank Murphy won a surprise victory in a special mayoral election on a campaign promising unemployment relief.[58] His efforts to provide relief by expanding public jobs and welfare in Detroit attracted national attention.

He appointed an unemployment committee, operated an employment bureau, sponsored public works projects, raised private donations for poor relief, and consulted with private firms about rehiring workers. Detroit did more than any other city for its unemployed, but its compassion was costly. With over 40,000 families receiving relief and one-third of the workforce out of work, it was spending $2 million a month for relief in 1931, far more than second-place Boston.[59]

The burden soon brought financial ruin to the city, and by the spring of 1931, Detroit faced municipal bankruptcy. To avoid default on its debts and payroll, Murphy curtailed the city's health and recreational services and slashed the fire and police department budgets. Only an emergency bank loan allowed Murphy to meet the June 1931 payroll, but even this measure was not enough. Under pressure from the New York banks that held most of Detroit's bonds, Murphy was forced to cut relief expenditures in half during 1932. Thousands of families were dropped from the relief rolls as it became painfully obvious that Detroit could not single-handedly solve the local problems caused by a national economic calamity.

The mayors of other cities were learning the same lesson. Finally, their sense of desperation galvanized them to take action. In the spring of 1932, Murphy issued invitations to the mayors of the major cities to attend a conference. In June, representatives from 29 cities met in Detroit with a single purpose in mind. Murphy stated the cities' case succinctly: "We have done everything humanly possible to do, and it has not been enough. The hour is at hand for the federal government to cooperate."[60] New York City's mayor likewise pleaded for assistance:

> The municipal government is the maternal, the intimate side of government; the side with heart. The Federal Government doesn't have to wander through darkened hallways of our hospitals, to witness the pain and suffering there. It doesn't have to stand in the bread lines, but the time has come when it must face the facts and its responsibility.

We of the cities have diagnosed and thus far met the problem, but we have come to the end of our resources. It is now up to the Federal Government to assume its share. We can't cure conditions by ourselves.[61]

The mayors' demands for federal assistance represented a turning point in federal–local relations. Historically, there had been no direct relationship between cities and the federal government. Many local officials felt it was illegitimate to ask the federal government for help, and others feared any aid, thinking it might cause their cities to lose their independence. Only a few months before, most of the mayors had declined to attend a similar mayors' conference suggested by the mayor of Milwaukee.[62] Desperation finally made them reconsider.

The situation was made worse by the fact that state governments refused to respond to the cities' plight. While municipal governments' expenditures on jobs and relief skyrocketed, the states sharply cut back; "As tax revenues dwindled and unemployment increased, economy in government became a magic word."[63] Beginning in 1932, several states slashed their budgets: Arizona by 35 percent; Texas, Illinois, Vermont by 25 percent; South Carolina by 33 percent. As state tax revenues declined, public works and construction programs were curtailed. In 1928 the states had spent $1.35 billion for public works projects, mainly in the form of road building, but this amount was reduced to $630 million by 1932 and to $290 million for the first eight months of 1933.[64] On average, per capita spending for highways and education fell only slightly from 1927 to 1932,[65] but some states made drastic cuts. Tennessee, for example, failed to provide funds for its rural schools for much of 1931.[66] State educational institutions, especially universities, were hard hit. During 1933, education budgets had dropped by 40 percent in Maryland, 53 percent in Wyoming, and more than 30 percent in several other states.[67] All of these cutbacks reduced public payroll and thus aggravated the unemployment crisis.

Relief spending by the states went up in the early years of the depression, from $1.00 per capita in 1927 to $3.50 four years later.[68] But the amount of welfare provided by the states was small and failed to come close to what was needed even in those few states willing to increase their effort. From mid-1931 to the end of 1932, welfare spending by the states increased from $500,000 to $100 million, but almost all of the money was provided by a few states, principally New York, New Jersey, and Pennsylvania. When the New Deal began, only eight states provided any money at all for relief.[69]

Local officials petitioned the states for help, as the depression wore on their pleas sounded increasingly desperate.[70] Except for the very few states that provided relief payments to the unemployed, no response was forthcoming. State governments were slow to respond to the needs of their cities because rural representatives controlled their legislatures. In state after state, legislative districts were drawn up to ensure that rural counties would outvote cities in the state legislative chambers. In Georgia, each county was represented equally in the legislature, regardless of its population.[71] Likewise, Louisiana granted each parish at least one representative in the state senate and house. Rhode Island applied this standard to every town.[72] Without exception, all the states made sure that representatives from rural areas would continue to hold legislative majorities, no matter how much a state's population might become concentrated in the cities.

There were important political stakes in this pattern of underrepresentation. If cities were allowed to gain majorities in legislatures simply because of their growing populations, political alignments and party structures would fundamentally change. Incumbent rural legislators would be unseated, and it is likely that a shift in legislative power would have favored more generous policies for the cities. The persistent underrepresentation of urban areas resulted in indifference to urban problems. Traffic congestion, slums, inadequate park space, and smoke pollution did not interest rural and small-town legislators. Governors, too, tended to be insensitive to urban issues; indeed, they were remarkably indifferent to the social calamity unfolding all around them. Governors' and legislators' national conferences ignored the depression. At the 1930 governors' conference in Salt Lake City, for example, the major topics of discussion included such topics as the essentials of a model state constitution, the need for constitutional revisions, constitutional versus legislative home rule for cities, and the extent of legislative control of city governments.[73] Likewise, the 1931 conference studiously avoided any mention of the economic crisis. In the face of such indifference, the cities had nowhere to go but to the federal government.

There was a danger that the special plight of the cities would disappear from view because the gathering disaster of the Great Depression affected the entire nation. Conditions in many rural areas were even worse than in the cities. Grinding poverty was pervasive in the Appalachian region and throughout the South; families lived in one-room hovels, children walked around with bellies distended by malnutrition, and some parents could not afford to clothe their children to send them to school. A drought from the Midwest to the Rockies turned much of the Plains into a vast dust bowl; in the winter of 1934, New England's snow turned red from the huge billowing clouds of dust blowing from Texas, Kansas, and Oklahoma. Families left the ravaged land by the thousands. The experiences of those heading for California provided the grist for John Steinbeck's moving novel *The Grapes of Wrath*.

Roosevelt and his advisers instinctively distrusted city politics and urban culture. Roosevelt's first public works program, the CCC, was inspired by his feeling that the moral character of unemployed youth in the cities would be improved by living in the country.[74] Roosevelt felt "small love for the city."[75] One of the president's closest advisers confessed that "since my graduate school days, I have always been able to excite myself more about the wrongs of farmers than those of urban workers."[76] In its first two years, the New Deal accomplished a comprehensive farm policy of guaranteed price supports, crop allotments to reduce supplies and increase prices, and federally guaranteed mortgages. By contrast, it was not until 1937 that it produced its first specifically urban program. The Public Housing Act (also called the Wagner-Steagall Public Housing Act after the names of its legislative sponsors) provided slum clearance and public housing on a very limited scale.

Despite the indifference they initially encountered, city officials managed to forge close relationships with politicians and administrators in Washington, D.C. The New Deal's first relief and recovery programs were administered through the states, but federal programs were later enacted that put local officials in charge. Federal officials administered the three largest public works programs—the PWA, CWA, and the Works Progress Administration—in cooperation with both state and local officials. The Federal Emergency Relief funds were channeled through the states, but local relief agencies actually administered the funds. In several cities, such as New York, Pittsburgh, and Kansas

City, local Democratic machines found that the new federal resources allowed them to rebuild their strength.[77] Local officials found themselves testifying to congressional committees about programs that affected the cities. By 1934 a southern mayor observed, "Mayors are a familiar sight in Washington these days. Whether we like it or not, the destinies of our cities are clearly tied in with national politics."[78]

The Urban Programs of the New Deal

The first hint of any national concern about the problems of urban America came in 1892 when Congress appropriated $20,000 to investigate slum conditions in cities with more than 200,000 people.[79] In the report that followed, the commissioner of labor informed Congress that all of the nation's big cities contained block after block of rundown tenement districts that packed immigrants together into often unsafe and unsanitary conditions. The commissioner made much of the fact that these areas had a higher incidence of arrests and saloons than anywhere else in the country. In effect, the report amounted to a moral condemnation of city life.

Federal assistance for the construction of urban housing can be traced to the entry of the United States into World War I. In 1918, Congress authorized direct federal loans to local realty companies.[80] At the cost of $69.3 million, 8 hotels, 19 dormitories, 1,100 apartment units, and approximately 9,000 houses were constructed to house wartime shipyard workers in 27 cities and towns.[81] Later the same year, Congress approved the nation's first public housing program, designed to accommodate defense plant workers who needed housing near wartime factories. The U.S. Housing Corporation was created to manage the program. In the brief three months of the program's existence, the Housing Corporation built 6,000 single-family dwellings, plus accommodations for 7,200 single men, on 140 project sites scattered around the country.[82] As soon as the war was over, all of these federally owned housing units were sold to private owners, and in this way, the government removed itself from the housing business.

The first significant federal intervention into housing came during the Great Depression. Even during the prosperous 1920s, the nation's cities contained rundown business districts and residential slums. As the depression wore on, the situation deteriorated; landlords and owners invested little or no money in repairs and renovation, and the construction of new housing slowed to a crawl. The solutions to the problems of housing and slums lay beyond the financial capacity of local governments. The slums that had long plagued the nation's cities slowly became defined as a national and not only local problem, and urban officials and business elites who were concerned about the condition of their business and residential districts looked to the national government for help.

In 1932, the last year of Herbert Hoover's presidency, Congress created the Reconstruction Finance Corporation (RFC) and authorized it to extend loans to private developers for the construction of low-income housing in slum areas.[83] Only two projects were actually ever undertaken, with over 98 percent of the money spent in three slum blocks of Manhattan to construct Knickerbocker Village, with its 1,573 apartments.[84] This program had two purposes. On the one hand, it was supposed to help revive the construction industry; on the other hand, it was supposed to increase the supply of low-income housing in New York. In the case of Knickerbocker Village, the first goal won out. Eighty-two percent of the slum families who initially moved into the apartments were soon forced to move back to the slums they had left because of the escalating rents charged by the owners.[85]

Franklin D. Roosevelt implemented a long list of national programs designed to stimulate the economy and bring the depression to an end. One of the first of these, the National Industrial Recovery Act of 1933, included a minor provision authorizing "construction, reconstruction, alteration, or repair, under public regulation or control, of low-rent housing and slum clearance projects."[86] The Housing Division of the PWA was charged with administering this provision. At first, the PWA tried to entice private developers into constructing low-income housing by offering them low-interest federal loans. This strategy reflected one of the major purposes of the program, which was "to deal with the unemployment situation by giving employment to workers ... [and] to demonstrate to private builders the practicability of large-scale community planning."[87] But contractors and home builders did not find low-interest loans sufficiently attractive, and only seven projects ever met specifications and were approved. As a result, the PWA decided to bypass the housing industry altogether and finance and construct its own federally owned housing. The U.S. Emergency Housing Corporation was established for this purpose in 1933, and it asserted the right to use eminent domain to force the owners of slum property to sell so that the land could be prepared for construction.

Federal administrators ran into a problem when court decisions in Kentucky and Michigan declared that the federal government could not use eminent domain if it usurped the authority of state and local governments.[88] In response, they tried another tack. The Emergency Housing Corporation decided to make low-income housing grants to local public housing authorities. States could legally charter local authorities, and previous court cases made it clear that the states could use eminent domain to accomplish a variety of public purposes. With the offer of federal money dangled before them, city officials lobbied their state legislatures to allow them to create local housing authorities to receive the funds. By the end of the PWA public housing program in 1937, 29 states had passed enabling legislation allowing local governments to operate local public housing authorities, and 46 local housing agencies had already come into existence.[89] These authorities built almost 22,000 public low-income housing units in 37 cities.[90]

For all the effort to get the PWA program off the ground, the eventual results were mixed, at best. More low-income units were torn down through slum clearance than were ever built. Local public housing authorities were closely tied to the housing industry in their communities, and as a result, a substantial proportion of PWA funds was used not to build housing but to help politically connected owners sell their properties at inflated prices.[91] These properties were then slated for clearance, even though there were no plans to replace the housing units that were to be razed. In all these respects, the PWA experience provided a warning for the future: Program goals were easily subverted if local communities were allowed to make all of the important decisions.

The PWA experience became the administrative model for future housing programs. It was accepted that if federal grants were made available for public housing in the future, local public housing agencies would become the recipients of the funds and federal agencies would not try to build public housing units themselves. When the Public Housing Act of 1937 replaced the PWA program, it was based on the principle that housing programs would be implemented through federal grants-in-aid to local housing authorities. Under the legislation, public housing would be built and administered by local agencies, not by the federal government, and real estate agents and contractors would handle land sales and construction. Its stated purposes were:

> To provide financial assistance to the states and political subdivisions thereof for the elimination of unsafe and unsanitary housing conditions, for the eradication of slums, for the provision of decent, safe, and sanitary dwellings for families of low-income and for the reduction of unemployment and the stimulation of business activity, to create a United States Housing Authority, and for other purposes.[92]

The Public Housing Act of 1937 was "designed to serve the needs of low-income families who otherwise would be unable to afford decent, safe, and sanitary dwellings."[93] Because real estate agents, builders, and banks could not make much profit by constructing public housing projects, they steadfastly opposed the program. As far as they were concerned, government-owned housing competed with the private real estate market, and its only redeeming virtue was that public housing provided jobs in the construction industry. But this benefit failed to outweigh the unpopularity of providing housing subsidies to the bottom third of the population. As explained by the president of the National Association of Real Estate Boards, the housing industry's philosophy was that low-income housing should become available through a filter-down process:

> Housing should remain a matter of private enterprise and private ownership. It is contrary to the genius of the American people and the ideals they have established that government become landlord to its citizens. There is a sound logic in the continuance of the practice under which those who have the initiative and the will to save acquire better living facilities and yield their former quarters at modest rents to the group below.[94]

To make sure middle-class families could not opt out of the private housing market by moving into public housing, the legislation contained specific limitations on the costs and quality of rental units and a restriction that occupancy be strictly limited to low-income families. A requirement was also added that the number of new housing units constructed could not exceed the number of slum dwellings torn down.[95]

The 1937 act authorized the U.S. Housing Administration (USHA) to extend low-interest loans to local public housing agencies. The loans could cover up to 100 percent of the cost of financing slum clearance and building low-income housing units. The USHA was also authorized to make grants and annual subsidies to local housing agencies for the operation and maintenance of housing units after they were built. The USHA and its successor agencies, the Federal Public Housing Authority (1942–1946) and the Public Housing Administration (1946–the present), completed a total of 169,451 low-income public housing units under the authority of the 1937 housing act.[96]

World War II was the third national emergency (the others were World War I and the Great Depression) recognized by Congress as requiring the production of publicly built and financed housing. In addition to 50,000 housing units built during the war through the 1937 housing act authorizations, 2 million more units were provided through temporary and emergency programs to house workers who streamed into cities to take jobs in defense industry plants. Around a million of these were privately built with federal financial assistance, and another million were completed under programs that left ownership in the hands of the federal government.[97] As soon as the war ended, these government-owned units were sold on the private market.

The New Deal Legacy

The New Deal transformed American politics. The Great Depression persuaded local officials that it was legitimate to seek federal assistance. To help them do so, they formed an enduring urban lobby organized specifically to represent cities in the federal system. Through the United States Conference of Mayors (USCM), formed in 1932, mayors met annually to discuss their mutual problems. The USCM financed a permanent office in Washington to lobby for urban programs. Together with the International City Management Association (now the International City and County Management Association), the National Municipal League, the American Municipal League, and other organizations representing local public officials, cities developed the capacity to lobby federal administrators, Congress, and the White House.

The nation's first urban programs reflected the political pressures that local officials were able to bring to bear on Washington. Through the 1937 Housing Act, the federal government undertook slum clearance and built public housing. In the late 1930s, federal policymakers expressed a concern about urban problems. In 1937 the National Resources Committee, composed of federal administrators and experts appointed by the president, published a pamphlet titled *Our Cities: Their Role in the National Economy*.[98] The report asserted that slums and urban blight threatened a hoped-for economic recovery and recommended federal action to improve the economic performance of cities. Four years later, the National Resources Planning Board issued a report, *Action for Cities: A Guide for Community Planning*, which recommended that cities devise local plans to combat blight and the federal government provides assistance for this purpose.[99] In 1944, a federally assisted highways bill was enacted; unlike highway legislation passed in the 1930s, this time, the cities got their fair share of construction money. Five years later, in 1949, Congress passed a massive program to build public housing and clear slums in the inner cities.

Between 1953 and 1961, when a Republican president, Dwight Eisenhower, occupied the White House, urban interests were able to push through only one significant new program, the Interstate Highway Act of 1956, an accomplishment made possible because Republicans wanted it too. From 1959 to 1961, President Eisenhower even eliminated public housing requests from the federal budget. But in the wake of the election of John F. Kennedy in 1960, the urban lobby again found a receptive environment, and it did not take long for it to seize the moment. The New Deal experience had convinced city officials they had a right to argue for their interests in Washington, and they were already organized for the task. For years to come, Democrats in the White House and Congress would ignore the concerns of groups representing the cities and the urban voters they spoke for at their peril.

Endnotes

1   "Who Votes For Mayor?" *Portland State University*, 2016, http://whovotesformayor. org/.
2   Ibid.
3   Ibid.
4   Samuel J. Eldersveld, "The Influence of Metropolitan Party Pluralities in Presidential Elections since 1920: A Study of Twelve Key Cities," *American Political Science Review* 43, no. 6 (December 1949): 1200.
5   W. B. Munro, *The Government of American Cities* (New York: Macmillan, 1913), p. 27.
6   In the first significant suburban movement of the twentieth century, which lasted from the late 1890s to about 1914 (the outbreak of World War I), the rate of growth in the suburbs exceeded the rate of growth in many central cities, but the total population gains in those cities were much larger than the population gains in the suburbs. Growth rates can be deceptive when expressed as percentage increases on a small original population base.
7   William E. Leuchtenburg, *The Perils of Prosperity, 1914–1932* (Chicago, IL: University of Chicago Press, 1958), pp. 213–214.
8   Robert K. Murray, *The 103rd Ballot: Democrats and the Disaster in Madison Square Garden* (New York: Harper & Row, 1976), p. 9.

9 Kenneth T. Jackson, *The Ku Klux Klan in the City, 1915–1930* (New York: Oxford University Press, 1967).

10 Murray, *The 103rd Ballot*, p. 7.

11 Ibid.

12 Kenneth Finegold, *Experts and Politicians: Reform Challenges to Machine Politics in New York, Cleveland, and Chicago* (Princeton, NJ: Princeton University Press, 1995), p. 174.

13 Jessica Trounstine, *Political Monopolies in American Cities: The Rise and Fall of Bosses and Reformers* (Chicago, IL: University of Chicago Press, 2008), p. 87.

14 Ibid., p. 98.

15 Ibid, p. 87.

16 Murray, *The 103rd Ballot*.

17 Murray, *The 103rd Ballot*, p. 103.

18 For good accounts of the 1924 convention, see Murray, *The 103rd Ballot*; Edmund A. Moore, *A Catholic Runs for President: The Campaign of 1928* (New York: Ronald Press, 1956); and Arthur M. Schlesinger Jr., *The Crisis of the Old Order, 1919–1933* (Boston, MA: Houghton Mifflin, 1956).

19 John D. Hicks, *Republican Ascendancy, 1921–1933* (New York: Harper, 1960), p. 212.

20 Samuel Lubell, *The Future of American Politics*, 3rd revised ed. (New York: Harper & Row, 1965).

21 John Kenneth Galbraith, *The Great Crash, 1929*, revised ed. (Boston, MA: Houghton Mifflin, 1979; first published in 1961), p. 99.

22 Lester V. Chandler, *America's Greatest Depression, 1929–1941* (New York: Harper-Collins, 1970), p. 5.

23 Ibid.

24 Ibid., p. 35.

25 William E. Leuchtenburg, *Franklin D. Roosevelt and the New Deal, 1932–1940* (New York: Harper & Row, 1963), p. 19.

26 Ibid., p. 1.

27 Chandler, *America's Greatest Depression*, p. 19.

28 Ibid., p. 57.

29 Arthur M. Schlesinger Jr., *The Coming of the New Deal* (Boston, MA: Houghton Mifflin, 1957), p. 3.

30 Leuchtenburg, *Franklin D. Roosevelt*, p. 18.

31 Most relief was given by local public and private agencies. Although many states had programs for relief to designated categories of people—dependent children, people who are blind or disabled—few of these were actually funded.

32 Arthur E. Burns and Edward A. Williams, *Federal Work, Security, and Relief Programs* (New York: Da Capo Press, 1971), pp. 1–2; first published as *Research Monograph 24* (Washington, D.C.: Works Progress Administration, Division of Social Research, 1941).

33 James T. Patterson, *The New Deal and the States: Federalism in Transition* (Princeton, NJ: Princeton University Press, 1969), p. 30.

34 Ibid., p. 15.

35 Ibid.

36 Mark I. Gelfand, *A Nation of Cities: The Federal Government and Urban America, 1933–1965*, Urban Life in America Series (New York: Oxford University Press, 1975), p. 35.

37 Leuchtenburg, *Franklin D. Roosevelt*, p. 11.

38 Inauguration Day was changed to January by the Twentieth Amendment to the Constitution, ratified in 1933.

39 Leuchtenburg, *Franklin D. Roosevelt*, p. 39.

40 Ibid.

41 Ibid., p. 40.

42 For a thorough account of New Deal programs, see Burns and Williams, *Federal Work*.

43 Leuchtenburg, *Franklin D. Roosevelt*, p. 174.

44 Burns and Williams, *Federal Work*, pp. 29–36.

45 Leuchtenburg, *Franklin D. Roosevelt*, pp. 122–123.

46 Ibid., p. 133.

47 Josephine Chapin Brown, *Public Relief, 1929–1939* (New York: Holt, Rinehart & Winston, 1940), p. 249.

48 Quoted in William E. Binkley, *American Political Parties: Their Natural History* (New York: Knopf, 1943), p. 284.

49 Ibid., pp. 380–381.

50 Patterson, *The New Deal and the States*, p. 26.

51 Calculated from James A. Maxwell, *Federal Grants and the Business Cycle* (New York: National Bureau of Economic Research, 1952), p. 23, Table 7.

52 Ibid.

53 Gelfand, *A Nation of Cities*, p. 49.

54 U.S. Department of Commerce, Bureau of the Census, *Historical Statistics on State and Local Government Revenues, 1902–1953* (Washington, D.C.: U.S. Government Printing Office, 1955), p. 12.

55 Maxwell, *Federal Grants and the Business Cycle*, p. 27, Table 11.

56 Ibid., p. 24, Table 8.

57 Ibid., p. 29.

58 Gelfand, *A Nation of Cities*, p. 31.

59 Ibid., p. 32.

60 Ibid., p. 36.

61 Ibid.

62 Ibid., p. 34.

63 Patterson, *The New Deal and the States*, p. 39.

64 Ibid., p. 40.

65 Ibid.

66 Ibid., p. 44.

67 Ibid., p. 47.

68 Ibid., p. 40.

69 Brown, *Public Relief*, pp. 72–96.

70 George C. S. Benson, *The New Centralization: A Study in Intergovernmental Relationships in the United States* (New York: Holt, Rinehart & Winston, 1941), pp. 104–105.

71 Robert G. Dixon Jr., *Democratic Representation: Reapportionment in Law and Politics* (New York: Oxford University Press, 1968), p. 174.

72 Ibid., pp. 71–75, 80, 86–87.

73 Patterson, *The New Deal and the States*, p. 45.

74 Leuchtenburg, *Franklin D. Roosevelt*, p. 52.

75 Ibid., p. 136.

76 Guy Rexford Tugwell, quoted in ibid., p. 35.

77 Finegold, *Experts and Politicians*, p. 12; Bruce M. Stave, *The New Deal and the Last Hurrah: Pittsburgh Machine Politics* (Pittsburgh, PA: University of Pittsburgh Press, 1970); Lyle W. Dorsett, *Franklin D. Roosevelt and the City Bosses* (Port Washington, NY: Kennikat, 1977); Dorsett, *The Pendergast Machine* (New York: Oxford University Press, 1968).

78 Quoted in Gelfand, *A Nation of Cities*, p. 66.

79 Public Law 65–102, 65th Cong. (1918); refer to Congressional Quarterly Service, *Housing a Nation* (Washington, D.C.: author), p. 166; Edith Elmer Wood, *Recent Trends in American Housing* (New York: Macmillan, 1931), p. 79.

80 Congressional Quarterly Service, *Housing a Nation*, p. xiii.

81 Joint Resolution 52–22, 52d Cong. (1892); refer also to U.S. Congress, House, *Your Congress and American Housing—The Actions of Congress on Housing*, 82d Cong., 2d sess., 1952, H. Doc. 82–532, p. 1.

82 Public Laws 65–149 and 65–164, 65th Cong. (1918); refer also to Twentieth Century Fund, *Housing for Defense* (New York: Twentieth Century Fund, 1940), pp. 156–157; Congressional Quarterly Service, *Housing a Nation*, p. 18.

83 Refer to the Emergency Relief and Reconstruction Act, Public Law 72–302, 72d Cong. (1932).

84 The only other loan made under this authorization was $155,000 for rural housing in Ford County, Kansas.

85 Edwin L. Scanton, "Public Housing Trends in New York City" (Ph.D. dissertation, Graduate School of Banking, Rutgers University, 1952), p. 5.

86 Public Law 73–67, 72d Cong. (1933).

87 From a statement by Harold L. Ickes, Secretary of Interior and Public Works Administrator, quoted in Bert Swanson, "The Public Policy of Urban Renewal: Its Goals, Trends, and Conditions in New York City," paper delivered at the American Political Science Association Meeting (New York, September 1963), p. 10.

88 *U.S. v. Certain Lands in City of Louisville, Jefferson County, Ky., et al.*, 78 F.2d 64 (1935); *U.S. v. Certain Lands in City of Detroit et al.*, 12 F. Supp. 345 (1935).

89 Refer to Glen H. Boyer, *Housing: A Factual Analysis* (New York: Macmillan, 1958), p. 247.

90 Richard D. Bingham, *Public Housing and Urban Renewal: An Analysis of Federal-Local Relations*, Praeger Special Studies in U.S. Economics, Social, and Political Issues (New York: Praeger, 1975), p. 30.

91 Nathaniel S. Keith, *Politics and the Housing Crisis since 1930* (New York: Universe Books, 1973), p. 29.

92 Public Law 75–412, 75th Cong. (1937). Also found in U.S. Congress, House Committee on Banking and Currency, *Basic Laws and Authorizations on Urban Housing*, 91st Cong., 1st sess., 1969, p. 225.

93 Roscoe Martin, "The Expended Partnership," in *The New Urban Politics: Cities and the Federal Government*, ed. Douglas Fox (Pacific Palisades, CA: Goodyear, 1972), p. 51.

94 Keith, *Politics and the Housing Crisis*, p. 33.

95 The restriction limiting participation to low-income families, seen from a comparative perspective, is a root cause of the failure of public housing in America. See Arnold J. Heidenheimer, Hugh Heclo, and Carolyn Teich Adams, *Comparative Public*

Policy: The Politics of Social Choice in Europe and America (New York: St. Martin's Press, 1975), pp. 69–96.

96   Public Law 76–671, 76th Cong. (1940), relating to defense housing needs; Public Law 80–301, 80th Cong. (1946), suspended cost limitations for some low-income housing projects.

97   U.S. Housing and Home Finance Agency, *Fourteenth Annual Report* (Washington, D.C.: U.S. Government Printing Office, 1961), p. 380.

98   U.S. Department of the Interior, National Resources Committee, Urbanism Committee, *Our Cities: Their Role in the National Economy* (Washington, D.C.: U.S. Government Printing Office, 1937).

99   Philip J. Funigiello, "City Planning in World War II: The Experience of the National Resources Planning Board," *Social Science Quarterly* 53, no. 1 (June 1972): 91–104.

PART II

The Urban Crisis of the Twentieth Century

CHAPTER 6

Federal Policy, Race, and the Emerging Urban/Suburban Divide

A Century of Demographic Change

In order to understand American urban politics in the twentieth century, it is vital to understand the suburban movement and the manifestation of suburbia as a somewhat quintessential American phenomenon, inextricably connected to developments within American culture and society. The twentieth-century movement of millions of people from the central cities to the suburbs constitutes one of the "great population migrations in American history."[1] The suburbs had begun drawing affluent families from the densely packed neighborhoods of the industrial cities as early as the turn of the century, and in the prosperous 1920s, the suburbs began growing in earnest.[2] The suburban movement paused for a time in the years of the Great Depression and World War II but turned into a gathering stampede as soon as postwar prosperity made it possible. The 1970 census revealed that, for the first time, more Americans lived in the suburbs than in either rural areas or the central cities. And the suburbs just kept on growing. All through the 1980s and 1990s, suburban communities continued to sprawl in ever-widening arcs around the historic urban centers.

A second great story of the twentieth century involved the several successive waves of migration in the opposite direction, into the cities. From the turn of the century to the 1930s, African Americans left the South and poured into the industrial cities of the North, Mexican immigrants made their way to cities of the Southwest, and the great rural-to-urban migration that had begun in the nineteenth century continued to unfold. After World War II, these restless waves of movement reached flood tide. White families living in desperate poverty fled the Appalachian coal fields and depressed areas scattered across rural areas of the country. They were joined by millions of African Americans who pulled up roots and struck out for the cities of the North. Mexicans continued to filter

DOI: 10.4324/9781003175315-8

161

across the border but in larger numbers than before, and by the late century, their presence had ignited an anti-immigrant backlash.

Measured in social and political turmoil, the postwar migration of 5 million African Americans out of the South was clearly the most significant of all these population movements.[3] In the mid-1960s, a new phrase, "the urban crisis," was coined as a way of referring to the rapidly emerging geography of extreme segregation that separated whites, who now lived primarily in the suburbs, from Black Americans, who were concentrated in the central cities. In the popular imagination, the phrase came to signify the collision of two powerful cultural stereotypes: "The Black ghetto," on the one hand, and, on the other, the American dream of homeownership and upward mobility. These contrasting images called attention to a fundamental fact of American life: In a single generation, racial segregation had become the transcendent and visceral issue in national politics and culture, in the North as well as in the South. Americans became accustomed to thinking in these stereotypical dichotomies—city/suburban, Black/white, poor/affluent—and these stereotypes consistently cast cities in a dismal light.[4] The suburbs became identified, in the popular imagination, with tranquil subdivisions with cul-de-sacs and green expanses of lawn; at the same time, images of poverty and crime symbolized the inner cities. By the 1970s, stories of murder, mayhem, and drugs in urban neighborhoods became a means by which local news stations could shore up their ratings. For white Americans, crime and violence became racialized stereotypes for the inner city and the people who lived there.[5]

Since the mid-1980s, the United States has been undergoing still another demographic transformation. Millions of immigrants have been making their way to the United States from countries all over the world, but for the first time in the nation's history, most of them are bypassing the cities entirely and moving directly into the suburbs or beyond. This movement has been transforming both the geography and the politics of urban areas in unexpected ways. The tensions of urban society are no longer rooted mainly in differences between city and suburb. Today, the racial and ethnic groups that make up urban society are spread throughout metropolitan regions. As of 2006, the Hispanic population in the United States exceeded the African American population,[6] and by mid-century, Latinx Americans are expected to outnumber Black Americans by more than two to one.[7] Already, these trends are bringing about profound social and political changes to the nation and to its urban areas.

OUTTAKE

Anti-Immigrant Passions Have Reached a Fever Pitch

Unlike any period in the past, immigrants are now moving nearly everywhere in the United States. It was once assumed, correctly, that immigrants tended to concentrate into a few gateway cities and from there, spread out to older inner-city neighborhoods. In recent years, however, this pattern has changed so much that many suburbs have become as ethnically diverse as the historic cities at the metropolitan core. In the 1990s, for example, immigrants from an impressive number of countries moved to the suburbs of Long Island: Japanese, Koreans, Vietnamese, Indians, Pakistanis, and Iranians from Asia, and Guatemalans, Cubans, Haitians, and Salvadorans from the Caribbean and Latin America. Immigrants are also moving to cities of all sizes and small towns and rural areas in almost every region of the country. Some rural areas have been changed almost overnight as immigrant workers moved to be near meat packing plants, poultry operations, and agribusinesses devoted to raising livestock or processing agricultural products.

Such massive changes have spawned fear and resentment, and it is clear that the most inflamed passions have been aimed at undocumented immigrants from Mexico. Hundreds of measures have been introduced into state legislatures to curb and regulate immigration. In 2007, state legislatures considered 1,562 immigration-related measures and enacted 240 of them, a threefold increase over 2006. Among other things, these laws made it a felony for an employer to hire an undocumented immigrant, even unknowingly, or for an undocumented immigrant to hold a job; made it harder for undocumented immigrants to get state ID papers or driver's licenses; and barred undocumented immigrants from receiving unemployment insurance or other public services. Over the next two years, local governments adopted literally thousands of anti-immigrant ordinances, many of them of doubtful legality, and police departments took measures to

rid their communities of undocumented immigrants—and, critics charged, of all Hispanics. As a pretext for deportation, local police departments targeted Hispanic people they thought might be immigrants by arresting them for minor crimes or detained Hispanics merely on the suspicion that they might be in the country without papers—a clear case of racial profiling and a potential violation of the protection against "unreasonable search and seizure" under the Fourth Amendment, and the equal protection clause of the Fourteenth.

The hostility toward immigrants was inflamed by the economic crisis that began to unfold in 2008. By 2010, it had reached a fevered pitch not seen since the anti-immigrant hysteria that swept the country almost 100 years before. When Arizona's governor signed into law the nation's strictest anti-immigration law on April 23, 2010, it unleashed a firestorm of protest. The legislation made it a crime to fail to carry identification proving citizenship and empowered police to arrest anyone if they had a "reasonable cause" to suspect a person was in the country without documents. While conservatives in the Republican Party praised the law, critics called for boycotts on Arizona travel, hurried to prepare legal challenges, and sponsored street protests and rallies. Opponents charged that the law would encourage racial profiling and harassment. President Obama also criticized it, saying that the legislation "threatened to undermine basic notions of fairness that we cherish as Americans ...." Meanwhile, a series of unintended consequences from the law's passage began to unfold. Hundreds of thousands of undocumented immigrants and Hispanic citizens began an exodus that had already been taking place since 2008. The number of foreclosures and vacant homes skyrocketed. It was estimated that the impact on the housing market alone could run into hundreds of millions of dollars and that the state's economy would lose more than $26 billion if all undocumented immigrants were to leave. Nevertheless, it was unclear if economic realities could much influence the course of a controversy stirred up by such emotions.

Immigration has remained among the most prominent issues on the federal agenda, and it was a key presidential campaign issue for the Trump campaign in 2016. Among the presidents in American history most vigorously opposed to immigration, while in office, President Trump made anti-immigration legislation one of his top priorities, issuing two executive orders and one presidential proclamation, which restrict the entry to the United States for the citizens of certain countries, many of the majority Muslim. These "Muslim Bans" spurred a legal battle that continued all the way up to the United States Supreme Court. In *Trump v. Hawaii,* the Supreme Court let stand the final iteration of the former president's Muslim ban, arguing that it did not, as originally charged, exceeded his authority under the Immigration and Nationality Act (INA), nor did it violate the Establishment Clause of the U.S. Constitution, which renders unconstitutional any government attempts to make laws "respecting an establishment of religion." President Trump, during his time in office, also attempted to overturn President Obama's

2012 Deferred Action for Childhood Arrivals (DACA) program, which was also implemented by executive order and provided undocumented immigrants who arrived in the United States as minors with a 2-year, renewable visa. The program was due to expire in March 2018 unless Congress implemented a more permanent policy. Without the protection of DACA around 800,000 educated youth, who are currently working and paying taxes, would have fallen back into undocumented status. However, the United States Supreme Court dealt a blow to the Trump administration in 2020. In a 5:4 decision in *Department of Homeland Security v. Regents of the University of California,* the Court argued that the administration had violated procedure in attempting to end DACA by failing to provide "a reasoned explanation for its action." The battle around immigration rages on, as borders were shut in March 2020 in the wake of the COVID-19 pandemic, and the incoming Biden administration, which had promised big changes on immigration and more open borders, initially let many travel bans stand.

Sources: Dan Anderson, "Times Topics: Immigration and Refuges," *The New York Times* (June 9, 2008), 20; Randal C. Archibald, "Arizona Enacts Stringent Law on Immigration," *The New York Times* (April 23, 2010); Seth Hoy, "Another Unintended Consequence of AZ Immigration Law: More Foreclosures and Vacant Homes," *AlterNet,* www.alternet.org/rights/147211; Nina Totenberg, "Supreme Court Rules for DREAMers, against Trump," *NPR* (June 18, 2020), https://www.npr.org/2020/06/18/829858289/supreme-court-upholds-daca-in-blow-to-trump-administration.

Streams of Migration

Three periods of migration and foreign immigration and the subsequent racist reactions of certain white ethnics led to several crises of segregation, race, and poverty that beset America's cities by the second half of the twentieth

TABLE 6.1 Rural-to-Urban Migrant Streams in Twentieth-Century America

Migrant Group	Principal Migration Period	Approximate Number of Migrants[a]	Origin	Destination
Appalachian whites	1940–1970	1,600,000	Southern Appalachian Mountains (Kentucky and West Virginia)	North-central states
Mexicans	1910–1930	700,000	Mesa Central primarily, also Mesa del Norte	Texas and southwestern states
	1940–1970	700,000	Mesa Central primarily, also Mesa del Norte	Texas and California
African Americans	1910–1930	1,250,000[b]	Mississippi Delta, Atlantic Black belt, coastal plain	Illinois, Ohio, Michigan, New York, and Pennsylvania
	1940–1970	5,000,000[b]	Mississippi Delta, Atlantic Black belt, coastal plain	Cities everywhere

Note: [a] These figures are approximate. The data for the Mexican migration, for example, are obscured by contract labor, two-way migration, and illegal entrants. [b] U.S. Bureau of the Census, *Historical Statistics of the United States: Colonial Times to 1970* (Washington, D.C.: U.S. Government Printing Office, 2002). Greenberg's original table lists 1 million Blacks, 1910–1930, and 3.5 million Blacks, 1940–1965.

Source: Adapted from Stanley B. Greenberg, *Politics and Poverty: Modernization and Response in Five Poor Neighborhoods* (New York: Wiley, 1974), p. 19.

century.[8] The data in Table 6.1 reveal that the first wave began in the early twentieth century and crested just before the Great Depression. Between 1910 and 1930, some 700,000 Mexicans moved into Texas, New Mexico, Arizona, and California, and more than a million African Americans left the southern states for Chicago, Detroit, Cleveland, New York City, Pittsburgh, Philadelphia, and other cities of the industrial Midwest and Northeast. The second, much bigger wave washed over the cities during World War II and did not ebb until the late 1960s. From 1940 to 1970, up to 5 million African Americans and 700,000 Mexicans uprooted themselves in search for better lives and poured into the industrial cities in the north. During this same period, more than a million and a half impoverished whites also left rural and small-town life, although their migration received little attention as it, unsurprisingly, did not lead to the same racist reactions by urban whites.

Between 1910 and 1926, the bloody and protracted violence of the Mexican Revolution drove Mexicans into the southwestern states. Although the revolution released millions of peasants from their feudal relationship with landholders, it left many of them without a way to make a living. Bloody confrontations between a Mexican government dedicated to land reform and landowners who resisted change drove the newly liberated peasants into Texas, Arizona, and California. During World War II and its aftermath, employment opportunities in the southwestern states induced still more Mexicans to cross the border. In 1970, 5.5 million Mexican Americans were living in the American Southwest, accounting for more than 90 percent of all the people of Mexican descent in the United States.[9] By 2000, 17.9 million Mexican Americans were spread out in the South and throughout the western states, about 87 percent of the nation's total.[10] Hispanic immigrants from several other Latin American countries streamed into the states of the Southwest in even larger numbers in the 1980s and 1990s, pushed by political repression and poverty and pulled by the availability of jobs. By 2019, the Hispanic population in the United States had continued to grow but also further dispersed and diversified. Immigrants from Central and South America are now a major group among Hispanic immigrants: Venezuelans, Guatemalans, and Dominicans were the fastest-growing Hispanic immigrant groups between 2010 and 2019.[11] In addition, while the largest proportion of Hispanics, about 50 percent of the nation's total, is concentrated in the four border states, California, Texas, New Mexico, and Arizona (California and Texas alone account for 45 percent of the United States' Hispanic population), there is also explosive population growth is elsewhere[12]: Florida is the state with the third-largest concentration of Hispanics in the country. Between 2010 and 2019, Latinx populations in Georgia, North Carolina, and Pennsylvania passed the one million mark.[13] Southern states as a group saw by far the biggest increase in their Hispanic population—26 percent between 2010 and 2019, accounting for almost 48 percent of the total growth among Latinx people in the United States in the past decade.[14]

The inexorable decline of the coal industry from the 1930s to the 1960s in the southern Appalachian Mountains and the Cumberland Plateau of Virginia, West Virginia, and Kentucky forced the desperately poor families in mining communities to flee year by year by the thousands. The exodus reached such proportions after World War II that some counties in Appalachia were almost depopulated. In his moving book *Night Comes to the Cumberlands*, Harry Caudill describes the abject poverty that forced families and entire communities to pick up and leave their marginal farm plots and shabby towns. Families could trace their roots in Appalachia several generations back. Homesickness for the hills and hollows left behind became a lament often expressed in folk and bluegrass music. In the 1950s alone, a quarter of the population deserted the Cumberland Plateau, settling in cities and towns of Kentucky, Tennessee, Maryland, Virginia, and the industrial belt of the upper Midwest.[15] A steady stream of impoverished white families living in the smaller coal fields of southern Illinois, Kentucky, and Arkansas joined them. The new migrants, who were scarcely more welcome than Blacks and Hispanics, were derisively called Hoosiers, Okies, and Arkies. Like the flood of African Americans and the lesser stream of Hispanics, they crowded into rundown urban neighborhoods, although unlike these groups, they had the option of moving into small towns or trailer parks located at some remove from the inner city. More than class origins or poverty, race was the great dividing line of American urban life.

The two great waves of African American migration, one before the Depression and the other in the years after World War II, were by far the largest regional population movements of the twentieth century, and they had the most enduring effects. Historians have referred to the exodus of Blacks from the South between 1910 and 1930 as "the Great Migration" because it was "one of the largest and most rapid mass internal movements of people in history—perhaps the greatest not caused by the immediate threat of execution or starvation."[16] In the decade from 1910 to 1920, 450,000 Blacks moved out of the South, followed by another 750,000 in the 1920s.[17] In the 20 years between 1910 and 1930, about a million African Americans—one-tenth of all Black Americans living in the South—moved to cities in the Northeast and Midwest. In just 20 years, the Black population living outside the South shot up by 134 percent, and the proportion of the nation's Black population residing in the South dropped from 89 to 79 percent.[18]

Like the generations of European immigrants who preceded them, African Americans were pushed by crisis and pulled by opportunity. Poverty and unemployment in the South provided the push, jobs in the North the pull. Beginning in southern Texas in the late 1890s and sweeping eastward through Georgia by 1921, boll weevil infestations wiped out cotton crops, forcing Black sharecroppers off the land. In the same period, an abrupt decline in European immigration occasioned by World War I, combined with the sudden rise of armaments industries, produced labor shortages in the industrial cities of the North.

Almost all the African Americans leaving the South settled into densely packed neighborhoods in northern cities. Only 10 percent of the nation's African Americans lived in cities of 100,000 or more in 1910; this percentage increased to 16 percent in 1920 and to 24 percent by 1930.[19] The biggest cities lured most of the migrants. The proportion of Blacks living in cities smaller than 100,000 declined from 1910 to 1930, but the proportion increased substantially in cities of over 100,000.[20] Thus, the Great Migration was made up of two principal components: Blacks were becoming northern, and they were becoming urban.

African Americans made up more than 2 percent of the population in only a handful of northern cities in 1910. By 1930, however, they accounted for 18 percent of the population of Gary, Indiana, and 16 percent in East St. Louis, Illinois, with its stockyards, rail yards, and heavy industry. As shown in Table 6.2, in the same two decades, Black populations had grown two to three times as large in the big cities. By 1930, percentages ranged from almost 5 percent in New York City to 7 percent in Chicago and 8 percent in Cleveland,

TABLE 6.2 **Growth of Black Population in Several Cities, 1910–1930**						
			Total Population		Percentage Increase	
City	1910	1920	1930	1910–1930	1910	1930
New York	91,709	152,467	327,706	257.3	2	5
Chicago	44,103	109,458	233,903	429.3	2	7
Philadelphia	84,459	134,229	219,599	160.0	5.5	11
St. Louis	43,960	69,854	93,580	112.9	6	11
Cleveland	8,448	34,451	71,889	751.0	1.5	8

Source: U.S. Bureau of the Census, Negroes in the United States, 1920–1932 (Washington, D.C.: U.S. Government Printing Office, 1935), p. 55.

to just over 11 percent in St. Louis and Philadelphia. African Americans became concentrated in well-defined and increasingly segregated neighborhoods due to the growing efforts of white urban populations to isolate Black migrants. In north Harlem in New York City, about one-third (36 percent) of the population was African American in 1920, but this proportion increased to 81 percent by the 1930 census.[21]

The North was not the "promised land" that it is often made out to be by [white] narratives of American racism, offering an escape from the violent racism of the South and the opportunity for economic advancement. While it may be true that some Black migrants from the south began their trek to northern cities and states as a means of escaping the shackles of the southern caste system, the treatment that awaited them in the northern gateway cities was often no better than what they had experienced in the south. It was merely different.

The migration northward had already commenced when, in May 1917, the publisher of the *Chicago Defender* launched "The Great Northern Drive" to persuade African Americans to move. Founded in 1905, by World War I, the *Defender* already had reached a circulation of 100,000, and African Americans read it avidly throughout the South. The *Defender*'s editorials exhorted Black southerners to come north to the land of opportunity, where they could find employment and, if not equality, at least an escape from harassment and violence. Its columns of job advertisements added substance to the vision of the "promised land." At the same time, the *Defender* exposed the terrible conditions experienced by Black southerners. Lynchings and other forms of intimidation were regularly highlighted in lurid detail. Moving out of the South was portrayed as a way to advance the cause of racial equality for all Black southerners.[22]

The *Defender* was only one of many voices encouraging African Americans to abandon the South. Those who had already moved wrote letters to relatives and friends describing their new life in glowing terms. Throughout the South, African Americans had lived under a reign of terror. From 1882 to 1930, there were 1,663 lynchings in the five states of the Cotton Belt alone—Alabama, Georgia, Louisiana, Mississippi, and South Carolina—and 1,299 Blacks were executed by the legal system.[23] In the 10 southern states, more than 2,500 Blacks—an average of about one person per week—were lynched between 1880 and 1930.[24] The legal systems of the southern states were so completely rigged that the difference between lynching and legalized murder by police and the courts was not much more than a technicality. Blacks who failed to obey the racial caste system, even inadvertently, could expect immediate retribution in the form of beatings or worse. Failing to step off the sidewalk, forgetting to say "sir" or "ma'am," or looking a white person in the eye could bring a sudden and violent reaction. As a way of enforcing strict obedience, lynchings had long been a way of life throughout the southern states. Frequently these descended into orgies of depravity, the victims slowly tortured to death with blowtorches or other devices, and the mobs carrying off clothing and body parts as souvenirs.[25] Truly integrated towns, such as Wilmington, North Carolina, did exist. So did Black elites in places like the Greenwood District of Tulsa, Oklahoma. If they did exist, they were perceived as a threat by whites and sooner or later, on the pretext of election fraud when no election was actually taking place, like in Wilmington, or that of alleged inappropriate behavior of a single individual, destroyed.

The opportunities for leaving such conditions improved in proportion to labor shortages in northern factories. After war broke out in Europe in 1914, factory owners found themselves with lucrative armaments contracts but too few workers. They sent labor agents into the South with free train tickets in hand, which could be exchanged for a labor agreement. Southern white employers and planters took steps to prevent the exodus of their cheap labor. Magazines, newspapers, and business organizations decried the movement, as in this October 5, 1916, editorial in the Memphis *Commercial Appeal*:

> The enormous demand for labor and the changing conditions brought about by the boll weevil in certain parts of the South have caused an exodus of negroes which may be serious. Great colonies of negroes have gone north to work in factories, in packing houses and on the railroads ....

> The South needs every able-bodied negro that is now south of the line, and every negro who remains south of the line will in the end do better than he will do in the North ....

> The negroes who are in the South should be encouraged to remain there, and those white people who are in the boll weevil territory should make every sacrifice to keep their negro labor until there can be adjustments to the new and quickly prosperous conditions that will later exist.[26]

States and communities went to great lengths to discourage migration. Jacksonville, Florida, passed an ordinance in 1916 levying heavy fines on unlicensed labor agents from the North. Macon, Georgia, made it impossible for labor agents to get licenses and then outlawed unlicensed agents. The mayor of Atlanta talked to Blacks about the "dreadfully cold" northern winters.[27] In some communities, police were sent to railroad stations to harass Blacks near the stations, keep them from boarding trains, or even drive them off the trains.

But despite all obstacles, the exodus continued. What the new arrivals found was an opportunity—but not equal opportunity—and persistent and often violent discrimination. Whenever African Americans attempted to move into white neighborhoods, they were harassed or violently assaulted. In the workplace, they were the last hired and the first fired. They were kept in the most menial occupations. Job opportunities were limited not only by employers but even more so by labor unions, which generally prohibited Blacks from membership. Because the North was more heavily unionized than the South, there were actually fewer opportunities in some occupations, especially for skilled laborers.[28] In both union and nonunion shops, white workers often refused to work alongside Blacks. To avoid trouble, employers assigned Blacks to the least desirable jobs.

The urbanization of Black Americans was not unique to the North, however. The proportion of African Americans living in urban areas grew steadily in the South as well: In 1900, 17 percent of African Americans in the South lived in urban areas, whereas by 1970, that number had swelled to 67 percent.[29] Metropolitan areas in both the North and the South experienced steadily rising rates of residential segregation during the time of the Great Migration, but overall, residential segregation was even higher in Northern cities than in the South.[30]

African Americans found it hard to adjust to urban life. Hardly any of them had previously lived in a city. Many had never even participated directly in the cash economy. Sharecroppers had often worked under contracts with provisions that they buy only from the planters' stores and then with scrip and credit rather than cash. Some of them had never even seen U.S. currency, and they were often cheated and overcharged. On the whole, however, recent research shows that Black southern migrants to the North did comparatively better socio-economically than their northern counterparts:[31] Once settled in northern cities, Black southerners were more likely to be employed and in full-time jobs,[32,33,34] were stronger earners than Black northerners,[35,36,37,38] and were less likely than Black northerners to experience divorce.[39,40,41,42] By the second generation, these differences between Black northerners and Black southerners in northern cities had dissipated,[43] but it is evident from their initial socio-economic differences that the hypersegregation experienced by African Americans in northern industrial cities tore at the very social fabric of their communities, and turn the "promised land" into a nightmare for many.

The intense, federally organized segregation of African Americans into dilapidated, overcrowded housing in increasingly hypersegregated neighborhoods led to astonishing levels of social disparity. The arrest rate for African Americans in Detroit in 1926 was four times that for whites. Blacks constituted 31 percent of the nation's prison population in 1923, although they made up only 9 percent of the total population. The death rate in Harlem between 1923 and 1927 was 42 percent higher than in New York City as a whole, even though Harlem's population was much younger than the overall city population. Harlem's infant mortality rate was 111 per 1,000 births, compared with the city's rate of 64 per 1,000. Tuberculosis, heart disease, and other illnesses also far exceeded the rates for the city's general population.[44]

Blacks moving into northern cities were often surprised when they encountered a level of hostility, racism, and discrimination that was as bad as in the South. Restaurants and stores refused to serve them; banks typically refused to give them loans. Cemeteries, parks, bathing beaches, and other facilities were put off limits or divided into "white" and "colored" sections. Many dentists, doctors, and hospitals refused to treat Blacks. Worse, the violence that had plagued them in the South followed them everywhere they went. On July 2, 1917, 39 Blacks and 5 whites died in a race riot in East St. Louis, Illinois.[45] In the infamous "Red Summer" of 1919, race riots broke out in more than 20 cities, all of them involving attacks by white mobs on African Americans. Chicago's riot of that summer started when a Black teenager inadvertently swam across a strip of water separating the beach designated "For Coloreds Only" from the one reserved for whites. A crowd stoned the boy to death and then terrorized Blacks throughout the city for days. From July 1, 1917, to March 1, 1921, Chicago experienced 58 racial bombings.[46] Unemployed Blacks were forced out of Buffalo by city police in 1920. That same year, in perhaps the worst mass murder of Blacks in U.S. history, more than 300 Blacks were killed by white mobs in Tulsa, Oklahoma—an incident covered up for almost 80 years before it was brought to light.[47] Almost everywhere, Blacks who attempted to move into white neighborhoods were terrorized by cross burnings, vandalism, and mob violence.

In all cities, restrictive covenants were attached to property deeds to keep African Americans from buying into white neighborhoods. Deeds with racial restrictions were filed in the office of the county clerk or the register of deeds and enforced by the courts. Chicago, with more than 11 square miles covered by restricted deeds in 1944, was typical of northern cities.[48] Neighborhood improvement associations sprung up in new subdivisions and, by legal prosecution and social persuasion, they forced homeowners to accept and abide by restrictive covenants. The result was that racial segregation in northern cities had become firmly fixed even before the second great wave of Black migration, which was many times larger than the first.

Exclusive Residential Access to Recreational Facilities in Many Suburbs Continues to Reinforce Segregation

Residential segregation is only the most common phenomenon in a wide array of segregational tactics. Another common but less covered one is access to public facilities. In the year 2021, access to suburban beaches and swimming pools in New York City's affluent suburbs remains as exclusive as in the 1970s. "Parks and recreational facilities under county jurisdiction should be used solely by county residents who are taxed for them. To open them up to everyone would mean that they would serve no one, because we are now barely able to take care of our own population." This statement was made in 1974 by Ralph Caso, a Nassau County Executive, who became known for the "Caso Doctrine," which explicitly aimed to restrict access to recreational facilities to county residents. This has led to huge discrepancies in access facilities based on race, ethnicity, and class: Westchester county is 73.2 percent white, Nassau county 73.4 percent. Manhattan, on the other hand, as the "whitest" borough was 64.4 percent white, while other NYC counties were 44.7 percent (Bronx) and 49.8 percent (Kings) white. The median household income in the three New York City counties (New York, Bronx, Kings, and Richmond counties) was $86,553, $40,088, $60,231, and $82,783, respectively, whereas Westchester and Nassau counties had a median household income of $96,610, and $116,100, respectively.

The doctrine and the argument, which date back almost 50 years have aged well: Similar policies remain in place in New York City's affluent suburbs, and arguments similar to Caso's remain the key justification. Residents of counties such as Nassau and Westchester that still maintain exclusive access to their recreational facilities for county residents only, on the other hand, enjoy free access to all recreational facilities in the Five Boroughs—among them the City's great public library and parks systems. In neighboring New Jersey, in 1972, two residents of Neptune City had filed a lawsuit against the city of Avon-by-the-Sea, demanding equal access to the town's exclusive beaches. The state's highest court had sided with the plaintiffs and ordered Avon-by-the-Sea's beaches opened "on equal terms." The dire predictions of unusable, overcrowded beaches that followed proved completely unwarranted. Instead, the decision caused other towns across New Jersey with equally exclusive beach access to open up their beaches to the general public. At the same time, as reported by *The New York Times*, counties, towns, and municipalities across neighboring New York and Connecticut went the opposite way and further restricted access to beaches and other recreational facilities. In New York, such exclusive residency requirements to access, for instance, public pools and beaches remain in place 50 years on.

The COVID-19 pandemic exacerbated the very visceral disadvantages that emerge from such segregation tactics: In the wake of the pandemic, the Mayor of the City of Chicago, Lori Lightfoot, closed down the city's public beaches in an effort to prevent the spread of the virus among beachgoers that tightly pack city beaches during the summer months. Suburban beaches, on the other hand, remained open. The already existing fees, which are imposed on Chicago residents at suburban beaches, were suddenly combined with new, pandemic-related restrictions and virtually shut off all beach access to Chicagoans. As the Chicago Council on Global Affairs noted poignantly, "[t]he result is a regional geography of racial and class inequality manifested in—and amplified by—access to the shoreline."

Sources: John Darnton, "Suburbia's Exclusive Beaches," *The New York Times* (June 2, 1974), https://www.nytimes.com/1974/06/02/archives/suburbias-exclusive-beaches-the-keepout-syndrome-is-under-legal.html; Samuel King and Lucas Stephens, "The Right to the Shoreline: Race, Exclusion, and Public Beaches in Metropolitan Chicago," *The Chicago Council on Global Affairs,* Working Paper (September 22, 2020), https://www.thechicagocouncil.org/research/working-paper/right-shoreline-race-exclusion-and-public-beaches-metropolitan-chicago; *United States Census Bureau* Quick Facts: Bronx County; Kings County; Nassau County; New York County; Richmond County; Westchester County (2019), https://www.census.gov/quickfacts/fact/table/US/PST045219.

Racial Conflict in the Postwar Era

Although the movement to the North slowed to a crawl in the years of the Great Depression, during World War II, it picked up momentum and soon reached levels far exceeding anything that came before. As in the years of the Great Migration, factory jobs pulled Blacks into northern cities, and conditions in the South provided a push. The mechanization of southern agriculture, in particular the widespread adoption of the mechanized cotton picker, threw hundreds of thousands of sharecroppers and farm laborers out of work. From Texas, Louisiana, and Arkansas, African Americans streamed into cities of the West, especially in California; from the middle South, they moved to St. Louis, Chicago, Detroit, Cleveland, and other cities of the Midwest; and from Mississippi and eastward in the Deep South, they moved to Washington, D.C., New York, Boston, and other cities in the East. In 1940, 77 percent of the nation's Black population still lived in the southern states, but by 1950, only 60 percent lived in the South. Over the next two decades, the South's share declined to 56 percent (in 1960) and to 53 percent (in 1970).[49] Almost all the northward-bound migrants ended up in cities.

Recent research has added important nuances for understanding the motivations, as well as the demographics of African Americans leaving the South for the Northern cities. Several researchers have started to question the dominant narrative that most African American migrants to the North were rural sharecroppers, displaced by the mechanization of agricultural labor.[50] In fact, research findings seem to indicate that a significant proportion of Black migrants from the South was urban and had received professional training beyond agricultural labor.[51,52] Therefore, it is important not to describe and perceive Black migrants of the Great Migration as one homogeneous group with similar motivations and outcomes.

As Black migrants continued their trek out of the South, the pressure on the urban housing stock intensified. The African American families crowded into segregated areas expressed resentment about the discriminatory tactics that kept them out of the more desirable areas inhabited by whites.[53] At the other end of the scale, virtually all whites wanted to keep their neighborhoods segregated.[54] Realtors were complicit in this ploy by refusing to show homes in white neighborhoods to African Americans or by rejecting their business altogether. Oftentimes, however, realtors made money by doing exactly the opposite. To induce white homeowners to sell their homes at bargain prices, some realtors distributed handbills or went door-to-door announcing that Black neighbors were moving onto the block. Panicked homeowners were eager to sell out cheap, and at the other end of the process, the realtor was able to charge a premium for Black newcomers who wanted to buy homes in the "busted" neighborhood.[55]

The tactics employed by homeowners to resist the movement of Black residents into their neighborhoods assumed some of the aspects of war. In the 1950s, a homeowners' movement swept through the neighborhoods of Detroit. Neighborhood associations organized meetings to urge their neighbors not to sell to Blacks and to discuss strategies of resistance. At night, when they could most effectively terrorize their victims, crowds gathered in front of houses newly purchased by Black families, shouting racial epithets and insults; strewing garbage on the lawn; breaking windows with stones, bricks, and bottles; tearing down fences; breaking car windshields; and, if all else failed, setting fire to the house.[56] Racial change occurred in block-by-block skirmishes, with whites making a slow retreat until panic precipitated a sudden exodus. By the mid-1960s, resistance had given way to "white flight," and white families were "fleeing" from the neighborhoods of central cities.

These racial wars shattered lives and left an enduring legacy of bitterness. Whites who fled in self-induced panic sold their homes at bargain-basement prices. Blacks who had to abandon their houses in the face of intimidation often lost their investments and any hope of moving to a neighborhood they liked. Many neighborhoods never recovered from the turmoil; for others, it would take decades, if it happened at all. In 2005, Detroit was a city in which 11 percent of the population was white, and 82 percent was African American. The contrast to its suburbs was stark: There, African Americans comprised less than 10 percent of the population.[57]

As a result of the two streams flowing in opposite directions—African Americans moving into the cities, whites fleeing to the suburbs—the demographic composition of the central cities changed almost overnight. By the mid-1960s, a yawning racial chasm separated the central cities from the suburbs. In the wake of urban riots in 1965 and 1966, a series of presidential commissions gave expression to the rising concern that the extreme segregation of urban areas had developed into a national crisis. The National Commission on Civil Disorders of 1967 (called the Kerner Commission after its chair, Illinois governor Otto B. Kerner) warned of "two nations, one Black, one white—separate and unequal."[58] With this phrase, the commission was merely acknowledging a reality that anyone could easily observe. Table 6.3 shows that in 1940, Black

TABLE 6.3 Percentage of Black Americans in Central Cities and Suburban Rings in 12 Selected Standard Metropolitan Statistical Areas (SMSAs), 1940, 1970, 2000[a], and 2019[c]

	Central City				Suburban Ring			
	1940	1970	2000	2019	1940	1970	2000	2019
New York[b]	6	23	29.5	24.3	5	6	10	12.4
Los Angeles–Long Beach	6	21	12	9.3	2	7	6	5.7
Chicago	8	34	37	29.6	2	4	11	11
Philadelphia	13	34	45	42.1	7	7	12	13.6
Detroit	9	44	83	78.3	3	4	9	12
San Francisco–Oakland	5	33	12	11.3	4	9	6	2.2
Boston	3	18	28	25.2	1	2	3.5	5.5
Pittsburgh	9	27	28	23	4	4	5	5.7
St. Louis	13	41	52	46.4	7	8	13	14.2
Washington, D.C.	28.5	72	61	46	14	9	23	23.8
Cleveland	10	39	52	48.8	1	1	11	11
Baltimore	19	47	65	62.4	12	6	14.5	25
All 12 SMSAs	10.7	36.1	42	37.2	4	6	10	11.8

Note: [a] Except for St. Louis, Baltimore, and Washington, D.C., figures refer to the consolidated metropolitan statistical areas (CMSAs), which are not strictly comparable to the standard metropolitan statistical areas (SMSAs) used in earlier years. For 2000, additional central cities are included for some urban areas: Oakland for San Francisco–Oakland; Bridgeport (Connecticut), Newark, Jersey City, and New Haven for New York. As of 2000, Washington, D.C. and Baltimore were considered central cities of a single metropolitan area, but they are kept separate to facilitate accurate comparisons with earlier censuses. Camden has also been deleted as a separate central city for the Philadelphia region. Calculated from U.S. Bureau of the Census, *Census of 2000*, www.census.gov. [b] Includes data from the Nassau–Suffolk SMSA, which was deleted from the New York City SMSA in 1971. They are included to maintain comparability across time periods. [c] The data for 2019 was calculated from census data and data for CMSAs from the American Community Survey. The same adjustments that were made for 2010 were not made for 2019, as suburban metro areas, in general, have been getting more diverse, and this data allows for the most authentic reflection of this development.

Source: Data for 1940 and 1970 adapted from Leo F. Schnore, Carolyn D. André, and Harry Sharp, "Black Suburbanization, 1930–1970," in *The Changing Face of the Suburbs*, ed. Barry Schwartz (Chicago: University of Chicago Press, 1976), p. 80. Reprinted by permission. The figures here were transposed to yield data on Black percentages.

Americans accounted for more than 10 percent of the population in just 4 of 12 big cities; on average, the proportion was 9 percent. Only 30 years later, African Americans made up 72 percent of the population in Washington, D.C., 47 percent in Baltimore, 44 percent in Detroit, 39 percent in Cleveland, and 41 percent in St. Louis.

Although the opposing streams of movement began to slow in the 1970s, the racial gap continued to grow more extreme right up to the end of the century. By the 2000 census, African Americans accounted for large majorities in several cities even while the suburbs contained relatively fewer African Americans. The data displayed in Table 6.3 reveal that even as late as the census of 2000, African Americans accounted for barely more than 10 percent of the suburban population (and sometimes less) in most of the leading metropolitan areas: 11 percent in Chicago's suburbs, 9 percent in Detroit's, and 5 percent in Pittsburgh's; 3.5 percent in Boston's, and 11 percent in Cleveland's. By 2019, there is a small but noticeable upward trend among most suburban metros displayed in Table 6.3. However, despite a growing number of people of color entering the suburbs, high levels of residential segregation among suburban jurisdictions indicate that the racial disparities inherited from the era of the urban crisis continue to persist.

The Emergence of a New Kind of Poverty

Inevitably, the mass migration of Black Americans from the South to the inner cities and their concentration into densely packed urban neighborhoods yielded intractable social problems. African Americans were not only forced to crowd into segregated neighborhoods, but their unequal access to employment caused high poverty rates. A large proportion of Black migrants from the South found themselves in areas in which almost everyone was poor. Ironically, the problem of concentrated poverty worsened at the same time that housing opportunities for middle-class African Americans improved. As the African American middle class started to move out of segregated urban neighborhoods, they left behind the families that lacked the resources to make the same move. As a result, poverty became more concentrated, even than before, and it was concentrated in the nation's industrial cities. In 1970, the Census Bureau classified more than one-fourth (27 percent) of the census tracts located in the 100 largest cities as officially designated "poverty" tracts where at least 20 percent of the residents lived in households with incomes that fell below the federal government's poverty line. Two decades later, the percentage of poverty tracts had reached 39 percent.[59] In 2005, the poverty rate in large cities (18.8 percent) was twice as high as in the suburbs (9.4 percent), and this ratio had not changed for decades.[60] By the first decade of the twenty-first century, however, the concentration of poverty had started to change: Between 2000 and 2018, poverty rates grew the sharpest in the suburbs[61]; while urban poverty rates grew by no insignificant amount (31 percent), suburban poverty rates grew by 51 percent, rendering overall poverty rates in cities (18 percent) and suburbs (17 percent) virtually the same.[62] Among other factors, this is one significant indicator that implies growing similarities between cities and suburbs.

African Americans, Hispanics, and American Indians are far more likely to live in high-poverty neighborhoods than whites.[63] A 2011 survey study found that overall, African American and Hispanic households live in neighborhoods with more than one and a half times the national poverty rate. The differences, though, may be even more extreme than that statistic seems to suggest—for example, in 2010, African American and Hispanic households earning more than $75,000 lived in less affluent and resource-rich neighborhoods than white households earning less than $40,000.[64] However, by 2019, poverty rates for Black and Hispanic families had declined significantly compared to a decade earlier, falling from the mid-twenties for both groups to 18.8 percent for African Americans and 15.7 percent for Hispanics. Poverty rates for Asian Americans fell as well—from the mid-teens to 7.3 percent, the same rate as for white Americans.[65] In spite of the significant gains made by Black and Hispanic Americans, substantial gaps in poverty rates remain in comparison to white Americans. In 2019, the number of Black Americans living in poverty was 1.8 times higher than those for the general population.[66] African Americans only make up 13.2 percent of the total U.S. population, but they represented 23.8 percent of the U.S. population living in poverty.[67] Similarly, Hispanics represent 18.7 percent of the population of the United States but 28.1 percent of its poverty population.[68] Meanwhile, white, non-Hispanic Americans comprised 59.9 percent of the total U.S. population, but only 41.6 percent of its poverty population.[69] The slow transition out of poverty for many African Americans in the United States carries two significant implications: (1) The nation's general economic success has been paid for by the continuous exploitation and disadvantaging of minority groups, and specifically of African Americans, and (2), as indicated by the overall decline in poverty rate, Black Americans have showed tremendous resilience in the face of continuous socio-economic disadvantage, often not only tolerated but instigated at the highest levels of government.

In the 1980s, the sociologist William Julius Wilson used the term *underclass* to refer to people who were concentrated in low-income areas and who were chronically out of work and out of the social mainstream.[70] The media, politicians, and social scientists quickly appropriated the term, using it to refer loosely to "a constellation of behaviors or conditions, including being poor and living in the inner city, being chronically unemployed, on welfare, homeless, residing in a single-parent family, having a criminal record, or using drugs (especially crack cocaine)."[71] Although this list clearly included behaviors that might be exhibited throughout society or by poor people regardless of where they lived, the term was normally used to refer to African Americans exclusively. Frequently, "underclass" was defined so broadly that it included Blacks not living in poverty areas at all, but who allegedly exhibited a single characteristic (such as unemployment or single parenthood) that was thought of as "underclass." In short, the underclass concept became a way of speaking about race without actually admitting that race was the topic of conversation.[72]

Because the underclass concept was widely exploited for ideological purposes and as a media stereotype, most scholars abandoned it. Wilson stopped using the term and began instead to refer to the harmful effects that result from segregating the poor together as "concentration effects."[73] Later, he used the term *the new urban poverty*, and his main focus turned to the high proportion of unemployed males in areas with high poverty rates. Wilson linked the persistent joblessness among African Americans to the steep decline of manufacturing jobs in the 1970s and 1980s. In the past, African Americans held a disproportionate share of blue-collar jobs, and even though their employment in the service sector rose sharply in the period of deindustrialization, full-employment wages declined by 25–30 percent by the mid-1990s.[74] Wilson's research was alarming because it appeared that the conditions of life in the inner-city ghettos were getting worse, with no end in sight. It was a dismal conclusion to reach fully a quarter century after the civil rights legislation and the programs of the Great Society.

OUTTAKE

Racism is an Insufficient Term to Describe an American History Based in Enslavement, Systemic Exploitation, and Violence against Minorities

By the second decade of the twenty-first century, the conversation around race and racism in the United States has once again evolved among researchers and activists. The two terms of Barack Obama's presidency seemed to insinuate to many Americans that racism was a thing of the past and they now lived in a "post-racial society." This, of course, was a fallacy. As several researchers demonstrated in studies conducted during Obama's first term, while people of different racial and ethnic backgrounds came together to support the nation's first Black president, "his 'Blackness' is sanctioned by established White power structures [...] Obama, like most mainstream post-racial leaders, has been 'racially vetted' and is welcomed by all political parties because he does not seek to confront White supremacy."

The Trump presidency, which followed Obama's two terms, cured anyone of any hopes of living a post-racial society. "Racism has been a festering wound on America since emancipation. Patchwork policies have haphazardly bandaged that wound – but now, in 2020, the bandage has been ripped off, and the infection is exposed," Otis Taylor, Jr. noted in the San Francisco Chronicle: "There's no denying anymore that racism is alive and well in America. We have President Trump to thank for that. [...] In Black communities, the conversation about racial atonement has been ongoing for generations, but now the conversation has expanded to other communities."

The four tumultuous years of the Trump presidency culminated in a global pandemic, which disproportionately affected communities of color, and a country-wide resurgence of the Black Lives Matter movement in the aftermath of several racist incidents, most prominently, the murder of George Floyd in Minneapolis by police officer Derek Chauvin. Chauvin had knelt on Floyd's neck for almost nine minutes, supposedly to subdue him and subsequently killing him. Chauvin was later tried, found guilty of second-degree unintentional murder, third-degree murder, and second-degree manslaughter. He was sentenced to 22.5 years in prison in 2021.

The COVID-19 pandemic laid bare persisting racial and ethnic disadvantages, as communities of color were especially hard hit. Zip code-based data compiled by the City of New York and the New York Times revealed that "[B]lack and Latino New Yorkers were dying at twice the rate of white residents when the data is adjusted for age." Housing that allows for the possibility of social distancing or isolation in case of an infection, access to healthcare, and the ability to work remotely were all significant factors in whether and how severely people would get infected with the Coronavirus.

In combination, the Trump presidency's blatant endorsement of racism, the COVID-19 pandemic's disproportionate toll on communities of color, and the resurgence of the Black Lives Matter movement in the face of the persistence of institutionalized police violence against people of color sparked one of the most explicit conversations on race and racism in the country's history that even went beyond communities of color alone.

Isabel Wilkerson published her book *Caste* in September 2020, in which she described the racial history of the United States as akin to a caste system, arguing that race, on its own, is not sufficient to describe the deep embeddedness of race-based violence throughout American history and the institutions of American democracy: "Caste and race are neither synonymous nor mutually exclusive. They can and do coexist in the same culture and serve to reinforce each other. Race, in the United States, is the visible agent of what we can see, the physical traits that have been given arbitrary meaning and become shorthand for who a person is. Caste is the powerful infrastructure that holds each group in place. [...] We cannot fully understand the current upheavals or most any turning point in American history, without accounting for the human pyramid encrypted into us all. The caste system, and the attempts to defend, uphold, or abolish the hierarchy, underlay the American Civil War and the civil rights movement a century later and pervade the politics of twenty-first-century America. Just as DNA is the code of instructions for cell development, caste is the operating system for economic, political, and social interaction in the United States from the time of its gestation."

Any conversation about race and racism at any given moment in time of the history of the United States must take into consideration what came before and the way that the system of caste has institutionalized racial hierarchies. Concentrated Black poverty in America's industrial cities did not happen in a vacuum, nor was racism and race-based violence and conflict specific to the mid-twentieth century. Instead, it was a small part of a larger pattern of systematic and institutionalized racial violence that has been part of the country since its inception. In fact, as Wilkerson noted in an interview, the term "Black" does not predate the transatlantic slave trade: "It is only when they enter into a multilayered caste structure ... a hierarchy such as this, do they then have to think of themselves as Black. But back where they are from, they do not have to think of themselves as Black, because Black is not the primary metric of determining one's identity." Similarly, Wilkerson notes that "whiteness" is an American invention. National identity and language were the primary identifiers to European immigrants to the New World. Yet, upon their arrival, the unifying "American" element became their skin color. The racial identifier, as Wilkerson illustrates, is so powerful that it is absorbed, along with the hierarchical caste system it lives in, even by young children. "Colorblindness," therefore, is a privilege intrinsic to white Americans, as only those who remain unoppressed by the caste system itself can claim not to see it.

Many attempts of conceptualizing the root of segregation and concentrated poverty in mid-century American cities, therefore, fall short of pointing to the more fundamental and pervasive racial hierarchy that spans throughout the history of the United States.

Sources: Bettina L. Love and Brandelyn Tosolt, "Reality or Rhetoric? Barack Omaba and Post-Racial America," *Race, Gender & Class* 17, no. 3–4 (2010): 19–37; Michael Schwirtz and Lindsey Rogers Cook, "These NYC Neighborhoods Have the Highest Rates of Virus Deaths," *The New York Times* (May 18, 2020), https://www.nytimes.com/2020/05/18/nyregion/coronavirus-deaths-nyc.html; Otis Taylor, Jr., "Thanks to Trump, U.S. No Longer in Denial of Racism," *The San Francisco Chronicle* (November 1, 2020), https://www.sfchronicle.com/bayarea/otisrtaylorjr/article/Thanks-to-Trump-U-S-no-longer-in-denial-of-15692294.php; Isabel Wilkerson, *Caste. The Origins of Our Discontents* (New York, NY: Random House, 2020); Terry Gross, "It's More Than Racism: Isabel Wilkerson Explains America's 'Caste' System," *Fresh Air, NPR* (August 4, 2020), https://www.npr.org/2020/08/04/898574852/its-more-than-racism-isabel-wilkerson-explains-america-s-caste-system.

Health and health care in inner-city poverty areas continued to deteriorate after the 1970s. Families in poverty generally lacked health insurance and so were forced into overcrowded health clinics and emergency rooms. For these reasons, in 1990, the United States had among the highest infant mortality rates in the industrialized world.[75] The overall national rate was about 10 deaths for every 1,000 live births in the late 1980s, but the rate for inner-city poverty neighborhoods approached that of developing countries. In 1988–1989, for example, the infant mortality rate in central Harlem was 23 per 1,000 births, about the same as in Malaysia.[76] In the 1980s, the drug epidemic began to devastate inner-city minority neighborhoods. The murder rate among young Black males tripled between 1984 and 1991, in part because of crack cocaine and heroin use.[77]

Fueled by turf wars between gangs engaged in the drug trade, violent crime soared in American cities in the late 1980s and early 1990s.[78] In 1990, New York City set a record with 2,262 murders, yet its per capita homicide rate ranked it only slightly above average for the country's 25 largest cities.[79] Violent death reached pandemic proportions among young Black and Latino males in inner-city areas. Citing the fact that homicide was the leading cause of death for Black males aged 15–24 in 1990, the federal Centers for Disease Control and Prevention (CDC) stated the casualty rate was approaching that of war. According to a study in the *New England Journal of Medicine*, young men in Harlem, primarily because of high homicide rates, were less likely to survive to the age of 40 than their counterparts in Bangladesh.[80] A late-1980s survey of schoolchildren in Chicago found that an astonishing 24 percent of them had personally witnessed a murder.[81]

Despite the fact that overall crime rates fell after 1990, there continued to be a high level of random violent crime in low-income minority areas. Gang warfare had become a fact of life in low-income communities, and innocent bystanders frequently got caught up in street-level violence. This trend has continued in recent years. For instance, although 2009 was the safest year in New York in more than four decades, in the first 11 weeks of 2010, the city-wide murder rate increased 22.8 percent over the same period as in 2009, and most of this occurred in a few high-poverty areas.

Stereotypes about "inner city neighborhoods" in the late twentieth century bred a national obsession with crime and violence. In 1990, approximately 20 percent of front-page news stories and local news broadcasts focused on violent crime.[82] A 10:00 p.m. newscast typically contained live footage of a reporter standing at a crime scene in front of a minicam, the talking head soon giving way to a video collage of a bloodstained street or sidewalk, shocked spectators, and perhaps grief-stricken friends and relatives. The discourse about the inner cities became "our … national morality play," a performance made up of sensationalized and exaggerated narratives of good and evil, the "good" in the suburbs, and the "evil" in the cities.[83]

In the 1990s, the stark divide between cities and suburbs began to melt away, and thus the main defining characteristic of the postwar urban crisis began to disappear. At the national level, other issues—terrorism, economic crisis, immigration, and the environment—have largely displaced concern about the cities and their problems. As suburbs have become more diverse, they have also become more "urban," and the revitalization of the central cities has restored a sense that they are vital and interesting places. These momentous developments tend to obscure the fact that many of the social problems associated with the urban crisis are long predate it and persist to the current day. Violence and discrimination against Black Americans have been part and parcel of American society since its inception. Today, African Americans still remain more highly segregated than any other racial or ethnic group in American society, though segregation is no longer limited to the cities and now also exists throughout suburban America. The discourse on how to address and remedy our nation's racial history continues.

The Suburban Exodus

In order to understand the social dynamics of the twentieth-century city, it is important to understand the social dynamics of the twentieth-century suburbs, as both are inextricably connected. It is also insufficient to focus solely on the segregation of African Americans into inner-city neighborhoods. The mass exodus of the white population from the city is the other side of the coin. Wealthy people began leaving the cities in the nineteenth century, but only in small numbers. Hardly anyone noticed because the industrial cities appeared prosperous and crowded. In the twentieth century, urban America underwent a historic sea change when the movement to suburbs accelerated at the same time that the industrial cities began to lose their economic vitality. The denouement to this process came in the years after World War II when white families of all social classes began to desert the cities en masse.

The movement to the suburbs came in four great bursts, each fueled by some combination of middle-class prosperity, transportation innovations, a desire for a larger house and a higher standard of living—and a growing rejection of the city. Although a few suburbs began to form as early as the mid-nineteenth century, when railroads made it possible for a few affluent urban dwellers to escape the teeming masses in the densely packed cities, the first burst of suburban development began later in the century, with the building of a streetcar network. A second surge, which came in the 1920s, was energized by middle-class prosperity, the adoption of the automobile, and the building of paved roads. But the two suburban movements that truly altered the geography of urban America and redefined its national politics have come over the past half-century or so: first, in the 1950s and 1960s, with the flight of middle- and working-class white families from the city, and second, the movement of minorities and immigrants not only to the cities but throughout metropolitan areas. As we shall see, these successive periods of suburban growth changed the contours of American urban politics in their own distinctive ways.

The Romantic Suburban Ideal: 1815–1918

The first faint hint of a city/suburban split became evident quite early in the nation's history. The desire to escape from the maddening crowd can be traced not only to the conditions in the industrial cities but also to a deeply ingrained hostility to urban life that dates to the nation's founding. Historians have often noted Thomas Jefferson's suspicion that cities undermined the democratic impulse. According to Jefferson, "The mobs of great cities add just so much to the support of pure government, as sores do to the strength of the human body."[84] In the 1830s and 1840s, the disdain for urban life was reinforced by the literature of the Romantic Movement, whose writers admired nature and abhorred cities, technology, and modernism.

A series of nineteenth-century transportation innovations allowed an increasing number of city dwellers to leave the crowded streets of the historic city center. In 1814, Robert Fulton began operating a steam ferry service between Manhattan and Brooklyn, thus making Brooklyn the nation's first commuter suburb.[85] A few years later, a select class of wealthy people rode in luxury cars pulled by steam locomotives to mansioned districts a few miles from the built-up city, but for most of them, these residences served as weekend and country homes. In the years after the Civil War, rail improved connections enabled wealthy families to live in pristine isolation from the problems of industrial society. Some railroads lost money on day-to-day operations, but that did not prevent railroad entrepreneurs from amassing fabulous fortunes through suburban land speculation.[86] Llewellyn Park, located 13 miles outside the boundary of New York City, was founded in 1853 by a wealthy entrepreneur who thought that placing people in a natural setting would revive religious and moral values. Lake Forest, founded in 1857 as a railroad suburb a few miles north of Chicago, was designed around a picturesque village square surrounded by tree-shaded lanes winding among the hills and bluffs along Lake Michigan. After the Civil War, more suburbs modeled on the picturesque landscaping ideal of the Romantic Movement made their appearance: "gracefully-curved lines, generous spaces, and the absence of sharp corners, the idea being to suggest and imply leisure, contemplativeness and happy tranquility."[87] Even today, most of the suburbs built on this model retain their exclusive character: In contrast to the grid-patterned streets of cities, these suburbs look like "scattered buildings in a park," the homes integrated with nature, with no hint of the grimy factories on which this suburban wealth was based.[88]

The image of the suburb as a romantic idyll reflected a growing disenchantment with urban life. At the turn of the century, a back-to-nature movement, built on a romanticized version of nature and rural environments, swept the country. Boy Scouts, Campfire Girls, Woodcraft Indians, and several other organizations sought to expose children to the healthy influence of nature study. Children's literature was filled with stories of adventure in "natural" settings. Adults, too, were thought to be purified and rejuvenated by visits to the countryside. Bird-watching and nature photography became major pastimes. Tourism to national parks boomed, especially after the turn of the century, when automobiles became available to the middle classes.

Although the suburban ideal was intimately linked with a yearning for an idealized version of nature, suburban residents had no intention of giving up the amenities and advantages of the cities they had left behind. Instead, they attempted a fusion of both worlds—the urban and the rural—in the suburbs. Magazines and newspapers of the day were filled with articles on the advantages of suburban life as an amalgam of city conveniences and rural charm. In 1902, one magazine writer claimed that suburban living could "offer the best of chances for individualism and social cooperation."[89] The next year, *Cosmopolitan* carried an article hailing the "new era" of suburban living:

> The woeful inadequacy of facilities of communication and transportation which formerly rendered every suburbanite a martyr to his faith have, in great measure, been remedied; and moreover, residents in the environs have now reached the happy point where they consider as necessities the innumerable modern conveniences of the city house which were little short of luxuries in the suburban residence of yesterday.[90]

The turn of the century brought a flood of advertisements describing suburban living as a dreamland landscape of springs, orchards, and forests, where the inhabitants enjoyed bathing, fishing, and shooting, all while living in houses with the modern conveniences of hot water, gas lighting, and telephones.[91] One ad promised "A Country Home with All City Comforts," while another talked of crops of oats and hay, orchards, trees and shrubbery, fruit trees, and other accompaniments of the rural environment.[92] The lush ads featured drawings and photographs of wide expanses of lawn, trees, and meticulously tended gardens.

When horse-drawn streetcars began to run on city streets in the 1850s, the opportunity to escape the noise and anarchy of the industrial city filtered down the social ladder; now, professionals and small businessmen were able to commute up to 3 miles from the downtown precincts. Cities still remained quite compact, but all that changed with the coming of the electric trolley in the 1890s. By tripling the distance of a practical commute, the trolley increased the amount of land available for residential use by an incredible 900 percent. American's urban areas began to spread inexorably outward.

By the 1890s, the electric streetcar had quickened the pace of suburban development, and it did not take long for a more affordable version of the suburban dream to emerge. A new generation of suburbs sprang up along the boundaries of the older cities, such places as University City, Missouri, just outside St. Louis, and Oak Park, 8 miles west of Chicago. These suburbs preserved the basic idea of the romantic ideal even while incorporating physical elements of the city, with grid street patterns, houses planted in rows along a sidewalk, and yards in the back. The quickened pace of suburban development was tied to an intellectual and sentimental reaction against the city. Academic writers promoted the idea that "our great cities, as those who have studied them have learned, are full of junk, much of it human."[93] A Boston University professor called city life "a self-chosen enslavement" and indicated that "the psychological causes of urban drift are socially most sinister."[94] Already, it was possible to discern a presentiment of the attitudes that would later be directed at African Americans in the post–World War II era. Cities were thought to nurture every conceivable sort of evil, as evidenced by such titles of sociological research as *The Social Evil in Chicago*; *Five Hundred Criminal Careers*; *The City Where*

Crime Is Play; *Family Disorganization*; *Sex, Freedom and Social Control*; and *The Ghetto*.[95] Cities had few defenders and a host of critics.

The Automobile Suburbs: 1918–1945

For a while, it seemed that suburban development posed no threat to the vitality of the industrial city. In hindsight, though, it is clear that this state of affairs could not last. The data in Table 6.4 can be read as a narrative revealing that even before the automobile became popular, the suburbs around several big cities were growing fast enough to suggest that suburban growth might eventually pose a problem. Between 1900 and 1910, New York City's population increased by 39 percent, but in the same decade, its suburbs grew even faster, by 61 percent. Meanwhile, the number of people living in Chicago's suburbs skyrocketed, growing by 88 percent in the first decade of the century. Meanwhile, St. Louis's suburbs grew at an even faster pace of 91 percent. As more and more people took to the streetcars and the early automobile, the trend accelerated. A new kind of urban form began to emerge, too. Los Angeles, which began to grow in the era of the automobile, began to spread out even before the city was fully formed.

Still, the day when suburban growth might be regarded as a problem was some way off. The cities were madhouses of activity, and on their borders, a few people lived their quieter lives. Between 1900 and 1920, for instance, New York City grew by 2.2 million people; over the same period, the suburbs beyond the city limits increased by 190,000. This meant that the suburbs had more than doubled in 20 years, but this hardly mattered when considered in the larger context: in 1920, New York City's population was 5.6 million people, making the suburban population of 379,000 seem awfully small.

The same could be said for all of the big cities. Almost everything was concentrated close to downtown. Industrial and manufacturing facilities remained near the water and rail transportation facilities located at or near the historic center. Between 1904 and 1914, St. Louis lost some industry to its suburbs (its share of industrial employment fell from 95 to 90 percent of the area's manufacturing establishments), as did Baltimore (96 to 93 percent) and Philadelphia (91 to 87 percent), but these cities were the exception rather than the rule.[96] The industrial cities overwhelmingly dominated the economies of their urban regions. Men left the suburbs in the morning to commute to their jobs downtown, and at night they returned home. Suburban residents went downtown to shop for cars, appliances, and practically everything else. Railroad and streetcar suburbs prospered, but the people who lived in them were still dependent on downtown jobs and downtown businesses. Downtown streets were constantly jammed with traffic.

Though it took a few decades for the process to unfold, ultimately, the automobile utterly transformed the urban landscape. When it first made its appearance, the car was mainly an expensive toy for the rich. Henry Ford

TABLE 6.4 Metropolitan Area Population, 1900–1940 (Increases in Population Expressed as Percentage Growth and Number of People Added)

Districts	1900–1910		1910–1920		1920–1930		1930–1940	
	Central City	Outside Central City	Central City	Outside Central City	Central City	Outside Central City	Central City	Outside Central City
Boston	20	23	9	21	4	21	−1	3
Chicago	29	88	23	79	25	74	0.6	10
Cleveland	46	46.5	40	140	12	126	−1	13
Los Angeles	206	553	81	108	115	158	−3	30
New York City[a]	39	61	18	35	23	67	8	18
St. Louis	19	91	12.5	26	7	71	−1	16
Mean for all metro districts (nation)	34	38	25	32	21	47	4	14

Note: [a] Includes growth of population in New York City proper and in satellite areas of New York State. New Jersey population is excluded.

Source: U.S. Bureau of the Census, *The Growth of Metropolitan Districts in the United States, 1900–1940*, by Warren S. Thompson (Washington, D.C.: U.S. Government Printing Office, 1947), especially Table 6.2.

changed that equation: He made it affordable in 1908 when he introduced the Model T, a car for the masses that was reliable and easy to operate. After he introduced the moving assembly line in 1913, Ford managed to reduce the cost of a Model T each year, from $950 in 1910 to $290 by 1924. Car ownership skyrocketed. American car production increased from 63,000 automobiles in 1908 to 550,000 by 1914. After World War I, car production reached new highs, rising from 2.27 million automobiles in 1922 to 4.45 million in 1929.[97] The construction of adequate roads lagged seriously behind car ownership, but this problem was eventually solved when the driving public successfully pressed for more state and federal funding.

The automobile allowed an increasing number of middle-class Americans to make a move to the suburbs. The streetcar suburbs had sprung up along the rail tracks, leaving big patches of undeveloped land in between. The car made it possible to fill in the gaps. Vast new tracts of land were opened to land speculation and suburban development, and the upper-middle-class invested much of its newfound money in suburban real estate. Total national wealth doubled in the ten years from 1912 to 1922, and from 1915 to 1925 average hourly wages climbed from 32 to 70 cents.[98] Residential land followed suit by doubling in value during the 1920s.[99]

These circumstances conspired to push suburban development to unprecedented levels. In the 1920s, the cities of Boston, St. Louis, and Cleveland grew more slowly than ever in their history, but their suburbs boomed, both in total population and rates of growth. The truck and the automobile began to change well-established economic patterns as well. The proportion of factory employment in the cities of more than 100,000 residents declined between 1920 and 1930. This trend continued steadily because the new assembly line production techniques required a lot of land rather than vertical buildings, and this land was most easily found in the suburbs. Still, it would take decades for the process of decentralization to fully work itself out. The volume of downtown office space tripled in the 1920s, and employment continued to soar in most central cities.[100] For the old industrial cities, the day of reckoning was still a ways off.

The Great Depression of the 1930s signaled the twilight of the city-building era. As the data in Table 6.4 reveal, Boston, Los Angeles, St. Louis, and Cleveland all lost population in the 1930s; so did Philadelphia, Kansas City, and the New Jersey cities—Elizabeth, Paterson, Jersey City, and Newark (the latter cities are not shown in the table). San Francisco, which had added 27 percent to its population in the 1920s, suddenly stopped growing. Small manufacturing cities of New England and the Midwest slid into decline—Akron and Youngstown, Ohio; Albany, Schenectady, and Troy, New York; Joplin, Missouri; and New Bedford, Massachusetts.

The Great Depression hit the suburbs hard, too, because now most upper-middle- and middle-class people lacked the means to buy a new home. Some suburban development still occurred, but it was slow and uncertain. The rate of growth in New York's suburbs fell from 67 percent in the 1920s to only

18 percent in the 1930s. In the same decade, Chicago's suburban expansion slowed from 74 percent in the 1920s to 10 percent in the 1930s; Cleveland's dropped from 74 to 13 percent and Los Angeles's from 158 to 30 percent. All through the 1930s, the effects of the Great Depression stubbornly lingered. With the coming of World War II, materials needed for housing construction were commandeered for the war effort. Suburban growth came to a standstill.

The Bedroom Suburbs: 1946–1970

The slowdown in housing construction during depression and war would have caused a serious housing shortage all by itself, but the postwar baby boom made the situation worse. After falling to a low point in the years of the Great Depression, the birth rate began to rise in 1943 and climbed rapidly in the post-war years, when 16 million GIs returned to civilian life.[101] By 1947, 6 million families were doubling up with relatives or friends because they could not find a home of their own.[102] The housing industry geared up to meet the demand, pushing single-family housing starts from only 114,000 in 1944 to 1,692,000 by 1950.[103] Virtually all of this new construction occurred in the suburbs.

Utilizing mass-production methods and sophisticated marketing techniques, big construction companies began to dominate the industry. Big firms accounted for only 5 percent of all houses built in 1938 but increased their share of the market to 24 percent by 1949, and a decade later, they produced 64 percent of all new homes.[104] The preferred method was to buy tracts of land on the out-skirts of cities and to create entire new subdivisions by bulldozing everything to an even surface and constructing houses quickly using standardized production techniques. The emergence of cookie-cutter residential developments stimulated a boom in suburban construction. In the ten years between 1940 and 1950, the suburbs experienced a 36 percent gain; in the same decade, the core cities they surrounded grew by only 14 percent. In fact, however, postwar suburban growth had occurred much faster than these statistics suggest because no sub-divisions at all were built until 1946 when wartime restrictions on building materials finally ended. After the war, the pent-up demand for housing ignited a virtual gold rush to new suburban subdivisions. In earlier decades, suburban development had been mainly an upper- and middle-class phenomenon, but now it filtered down to embrace working-class families, too. Federally insured home loans, cheap energy, and new, efficient building technologies made it less expensive to build a new house in the suburbs than to rehabilitate a home or rent an apartment in the city. The nation's homeownership rate increased from 44 percent in 1940 to 63 percent by 1970.[105]

The suburban boom accelerated during the prosperous years of the 1950s. Virtually all the cities that had prospered in the industrial era were losing popu-lation, some at a dramatic pace. Cities all through the industrial belt stretching from New England through the Great Lake states were hemorrhaging popu-lation. Between 1950 and 1960, Boston's population shrunk by 13 percent;

by comparison, the population losses in that decade were 12.5 percent in St. Louis and 4 percent in Cleveland. From there, things got quickly worse. In the 1960s, St. Louis lost 17 percent of its population, 17 percent in the 1970s, and an extraordinary 27 percent in the following decade. In 1950, before it started its long slide, 857,000 people resided within the city, but by the century's end, only 335,000 people were left.[106]

In the 40 years from 1950 to 1990, virtually all of the old industrial cities hemorrhaged population. Even after the 1970s, when the first hints that things might turn around began to appear in some places, some cities continued their long slide. The downtowns and neighborhoods of most of the industrial cities were clearly on the rebound by the end of the century, but even so many of them continued to lose population, though at a slower rate than before. Between the 2000 census and 2003, Cleveland, Baltimore, Flint (Michigan), Detroit, and Cincinnati all shrank by 3.5 percent or more, an experience shared by 30 other older cities.

Table 6.5 shows that as the central cities continued to shrink, their share of the metropolitan population rapidly declined. Already by 1940, only 29 percent of the people in metropolitan Boston resided in the city, a reflection of the fact that suburbanization there had begun earlier than in most places. Before the war, Chicago still had 70 percent of its region's population, compared to

TABLE 6.5 Share of Metropolitan Population Living in Selected Central Cities, 1940–2000[a]

	Percentage Living in Central City			
	1940	**1960**	**1980**	**2000**
Boston	29.0	21.8	11.0	10.1
Chicago	70.4	51.5	37.0	31.6
Cleveland	64.1	32.1	19.5	16.2
Los Angeles	51.6	32.0	25.8	22.6
New York	64.3	50.5	37.8	37.8
St. Louis	57.0	35.0	18.8	13.4

Note: [a] It is difficult to calculate precise figures over time of city/suburban ratio because the Census Bureau's definition of metropolitan areas has changed from time to time. Corrections have been made to minimize this problem. Although Lorain–Elyria counties were not included in the 1940 Cleveland metropolitan area, they have been added because these counties were included from 1960 and thereafter. For Boston, the four major counties are included for 1940 and 1960, which is comparable to the regional definition from 1970 to 2000.

Sources: U.S. Bureau of the Census, *Statistical Abstract of the United States* (Washington, D.C.: U.S. Government Printing Office, various years): 1987, pp. 29–31, Table 34; 1993, pp. 37–39, Table 42; 2003, p. 32, Table 27.

64 percent for Cleveland and New York and 57 percent for St. Louis. Even in metropolitan Los Angeles, which had begun sprawling in the early years of the century, more than half of the population still lived within the city limits. But the postwar suburban exodus changed regional geographies very quickly. When the 2000 census was conducted, just 10 percent of the population of metropolitan Boston lived within the city in the St. Louis region, only 13 percent still claimed the city as their home, and in the Cleveland metropolitan area, only 16 percent did so. Among older industrial cities, New York and Chicago stood out as exceptions because they still captured as high as one-third of their region's population in 2000.

The suburbs of the 1950s and 1960s were by no means all cut from the same cloth. The legacy of the past was plain to see, with middle-class housing tracts, a sprinkling of working-class blue-collar subdivisions, a few isolated areas populated by Blacks, and, of course, the enclaves inhabited by the wealthy. But most of the housing tracts built in the postwar years were marketed to white middle-class families. Some suburbs were remarkably uniform, with row after endless row of houses looking as if they had been produced on the same assembly line, an impression that turned out to be close to the truth. Suburbia came to be portrayed in the popular media as a place of look-alike streets and regimented people, where bored couples with small children spent their free time watching television and picking crabgrass out of their lawns, and where the men commuted to office jobs, leaving behind lonely housewives to care for the children in culturally sterile environments. This image of suburbia was captured in three best-selling novels published during the period: *The Man in the Gray Flannel Suit* (1955), *The Crack in the Picture Window* (1956), and *The Split Level Trap* (1960). Although the cultural images of suburbia undoubtedly traded on stereotypes, they were close enough to the truth to strike a responsive chord.[107]

By the mid-twentieth century, civic elites in the central cities were thoroughly alarmed that the suburbs threatened the vitality and even viability of the urban core. It was not only that the suburbs were growing so fast. As affluent and middle-class white families deserted, they were leaving behind African Americans and poor people who remained trapped in the cities. Increasingly, suburbanization was understood in racial terms; the phrase "white flight" started to be heard, implying that suburban development was motivated to a large part by racism, a suggestion for which there is abundant evidence.[108]

The riots of the mid-1960s called attention to the fact that racial segregation on this scale might legitimately be regarded as a national problem. After all, it was not only the individual motivations by white Americans to live in racial segregated communities that led to white flight. Individual racism was backed by federal policies, which were specifically aimed at racial segregation. In fact, the Federal Housing Administration (FHA) specifically endorsed the emergence of segregated suburbs: The history of American homeownership was, from the beginning, riddled with racialized motivations, and this only became amplified in the early post-war years when rates of homeownership soared, especially in the booming suburbs. The Veteran's Home Loan Program, especially Title III of Servicemen's Readjustment Act of 1944 and the Housing Act of 1934, by the FHA, laid the foundation for this. As government agencies, they served as powerful backers of mortgages, which significantly reduced the risk for lending institutions in providing home loans to middle-class Americans and opening the door to suburban homeownership. Key scholars have found that these government agencies strongly prioritized white homeownership while implementing discriminatory criteria that severely limited homeownership opportunities for African Americans.[109],[110] In addition, Census data document the persisting racial gap in homeownership, which was exacerbated by federal policies in the post-war era, but predated the mid-twentieth century suburban movement: In fact, "double-digit disparities in ownership had been documented by each census, beginning in 1900 when racial ownership rates began to be reported."[111] Recent scholarship, based on Census data, documents that homeownership rates for whites and African Americans would grow and decline simultaneously while maintaining a significant gap even throughout the decades before World War II, but that the racial gap started to significantly widen during the post-war period.[112] This was the consequence of targeted federal programs that were intended to discriminate by race.

Redlining, or the refusal of loan insurance in majority Black neighborhoods by federal agencies, such as the VA or the FHA, who had started to insure the majority of home loans in the post-war boom era, caused property values in those areas to decline. In the meantime, property values in suburban [white] neighborhoods were booming. This had serious consequences for the racial wealth gap, and the racialized effects of these policies can still be felt today. In addition, the central role of the FHA and the VA as the insurers of home loans for the general public made them powerful arbiters of homeownership. The VA, for instance, did not itself administer home loans but only co-sign any loan advanced by a financial institution. Financial institutions, on the other hand, would openly discriminate against Black veterans looking to secure a home loan by simply refusing them.[113] "These impediments [to securing home loans] were not confined to the South. In New York and the northern New Jersey suburbs, fewer than 100 of the 67,000 mortgages insured by the GI bill supported home purchases by non-whites."[114] In addition, the U.S. military still implemented recruiting quotas for African Americans,[115] limiting the Black population eligible for VA loan assistance. The FHA tied its argument for racial discrimination in insuring home loans to real estate values. It argued that if Black Americans were to purchase homes in white suburbs or their vicinity, this would negatively impact real estate values and the home values of those homes already insured by the FHA, putting all FHA-insured loans at risk.[116] In an interview, scholar Richard Rothstein strongly rebukes this FHA claim: "There was no basis for this claim on the part of the Federal Housing Administration. In fact, when African-Americans tried to buy homes in all-white neighborhoods or in mostly white neighborhoods, property values rose because African-Americans were more willing to pay more for properties than whites were, simply because their housing supply was so restricted and they had so many fewer choices."[117]

In short, the predatory practices of federal government agencies against Black Americans played one of the most significant roles in the systematic racial segregation of cities and suburbs in the post-World War II era. In 1967, when the National Commission on Civil Disorders called attention to the stark dichotomy between the cities and suburbs, the suburbs had already become far removed from the conditions that attracted the commission's concern. All of the ingredients that defined the twentieth-century urban crisis had come together into an explosive mixture.

The Rise of the Multiethnic Metropolis

By the end of the 1960s, the momentous movements that had brought millions of African Americans to northern cities had pretty much ran their course; indeed, in the decade of the 1990s, 579,000 Blacks returned to the South.[118] The biggest demographic change, however, involved the movement of large numbers of African Americans to the suburbs, and this occurred at exactly the same time that white flight had begun to ebb. A surge of foreign immigration added another ingredient to the mix. After the 1960s, the pace of immigration steadily gained momentum, and by the last decade of the century, it had reached a level not experienced for 100 years. By the new millennium, the systematic, state-sponsored segregation of Black and white Americans was being supplanted by a new reality: The politics of urban America was becoming multiracial and multiethnic. Unlike any previous period of immigration, more immigrant groups were settling in the suburbs than in the central cities. Ethnic enclaves began springing up in a lot of unlikely places.

The number of immigrants entering the country from abroad in the 1990s exceeded every other decade of the twentieth century except 1910–1920, and the movement continued until recently when the number of persons obtaining legal permanent residence status began a steady decline. From 2000 to 2005, the immigrant flow increased 16 percent, and the newcomers were showing up in all regions of the country. In the same five-year period, Indiana experienced a 34 percent rise, and several other states also far exceeded the national rate: South Dakota, with a 44 percent increase, compared to 32 percent in Delaware, 31 percent in Missouri, and 26 percent in New Hampshire.[119] According to census estimates, in September 2004, there were 11.6 million legal permanent residents in the United States, with 8 million of them eligible to be naturalized; in addition, more than 5 million undocumented immigrants were thought to reside within the nation's borders.[120] In 2019, the last year before the COVID-19 pandemic brought much of immigration to a virtual standstill with shuttered borders and travel bans, 1,031,765

TABLE 6.6 Immigrants by Place of Origin, 1951–2019

	Percentage of Total Immigration					
Year	Europe	Asia[a]	Canada[a]	Other Western Hemisphere[b]	All Other[c]	Total Number (Thousands)
1951–1960	57	6	11	22.5	3	2,515.5
1961–1970	37	13	9	39	2	3,321.7
1971–1980	18	36	3	40	3	4,493.3
1981–1990	10	38	2	47	3	7,338.1
1991–2000	14	32	1.5	48	5	9,092.9
2011	7.9	42.5	1.2	38	9	1,062.04
2019	8.4	35.4	1.1	42.9	11.9	1,031.77

Note: [a] Cambodia, China, Taiwan, Hong Kong, India, Iran, Israel, Japan, Korea, Philippines, Thailand, Vietnam, and "other Asia." [b] Mexico, Caribbean, Central America, South America. [c] Africa, Australia, New Zealand.

Sources: U.S. Department of Justice, Immigration and Naturalization Service, *Statistical Yearbook of the Immigration and Naturalization Service, 1989* (Washington, D.C.: Government Printing Office, 1990), pp. 2–5; U.S. Bureau of the Census, *The Official Statistics, Statistical Abstract of the United States, 2003* (Washington, D.C.: U.S. Government Printing Office, 2004); "2011 Yearbook of Immigration Statistics: Table 1," *U.S. Office of Immigration Statistics*; "2019 Yearbook of Immigration Statistics: Table 3. Persons Obtaining Lawful Permanent Resident Status by Region and Country of Birth: Fiscal Years 2017–2019," *Department of Homeland Security*, https://www.dhs.gov/immigration-statistics/yearbook/2019/table3#.

immigrants obtained legal permanent status, which was quite consistent with the previous decade.[121]

The rate of immigration increased decade by decade after 1950. Table 6.6 reveals that during the 1950s, 57 percent of the foreign immigrants came from Europe, 22.5 percent from the Western Hemisphere south of the United States, and 6 percent from Asia. But the composition of the immigrant stream changed dramatically over time. Immigrants from European countries fell sharply to less than 10 percent of the total number of arrivals in the 1980s before rebounding briefly to about 14 percent because of a surge from Russia and the formerly communist countries of Eastern Europe. By 2009, the number of European immigrants fell back to slightly less than 10 percent of the total immigrant flow and has risen only slightly in the years since.[122] In the decade of the 1980s, Asian immigrants shot up from 6 percent to more than 38 percent of the total immigrant flow before settling back to 30 percent or so. The biggest surge came from the Western Hemisphere south of the United States, mostly from Mexico and Latin America. Since the turn of the century, immigrants from that region have constituted about half of all arrivals to the United States. In 2011, the leading countries of birth of new legal permanent residents were Mexico (14 percent), China (8.2 percent), and India (6.5 percent).

The laws governing immigration from the 1920s to the mid-1960s were adopted in a climate of xenophobic fear and resentment. The National Origins Immigration Act of 1924 established an annual quota that could not exceed 2 percent of the base population of foreign-born nationality groups already in the country as of 1890. This restriction accomplished its intended goal of drastically reducing immigration by all nationality groups except those from northern Europe. In debating the legislation, members of Congress made it clear that they considered Slavs, Jews, Italians, Greeks, and other people of the countries of Eastern Europe to be inferior. The new law slashed annual immigration by these nationality groups by more than 90 percent. During the Holocaust years, when European Jews, as well as political dissidents, members of the LGBTQ+ community, and many others considered "inferior" were fleeing Nazi persecution and genocide, a refugee category did not even exist in the immigration discourse—it was not until the 1951 Refugee Convention that the term was established, complete with the rights of refugees, as well as the obligations of nation-states in protecting them. During the 1930s and 1940s, the United States government alone turned back thousands of refugees fleeing the Holocaust, sending many of them to a certain death. Jewish community organizations, which were also instrumental in passing the Displaced Persons Act of 1948, worked diligently to raise money and help Jewish refugees from Europe with the complicated and expensive process of securing a visa.[123] They could, however, only save a fraction.

By the 1960s, the changing political climate made overtly racist formulas for immigration unacceptable. In the Hart-Cellar Act of 1965, Congress essentially put immigrants from all countries on an equal footing and granted a high priority to family reunification. Special provisions for political refugees from countries affiliated with the Soviet Bloc increased the rate of immigration even more, and the ethnic composition of the immigrant flow changed radically. After the 1960s, between 80 and 85 percent of the immigrants entering the United States were of Hispanic or Asian origin. (As of the 2000 census, the U.S. Census Bureau used the terms *Latinx*[124] and *Hispanic* interchangeably; we follow that practice here. In order to reflect the broader movement toward gender- and LGBT+ inclusivity, we also use the more inclusive term Latinx instead of the original Spanish gendered form.) People of both ethnic categories came from many nations—Hispanics from a vast area from the Caribbean to the tip of South America, Asians from the arc of countries from Japan to India.

In 1990, Congress again reformed the immigration laws, and as a result of the legislation, the number of documented immigrants allowed into the country increased by 40 percent. The law more than doubled the number of visas granted to foreigners with job skills needed in the United States, and it allowed the highest percentage of European-origin groups into the country since Hart-Cellar.[125] Immigration from Eastern Europe, Russia, and the nations that had been a part of the former Soviet Union increased sharply. By the mid-1990s, the United States was admitting more documented immigrants in total numbers than all the rest of the nations of the world combined.[126]

Asians were the fastest-growing ethnic group in the 1980s, with the metropolitan areas of Los Angeles, San Francisco, and New York having the largest Asian communities. The number of people coming from Asia in the 1980s almost equaled the number from all countries of the Western Hemisphere south of the U.S. border. But in the last decade of the century, Asian immigration slowed while Hispanic immigration increased.[127] In 2019, the number of persons obtaining legal permanent residence status, whose region of last residence was Asia, was 364,761 of the 1,031,765 total legal permanent residents.[128] During the same period, the number from Mexico, the Caribbean, Central, and South America rose to 450,057.[129] As a result of the rising volume of the immigrant flow and the relatively large size of Hispanic families, in 2005, Hispanics outnumbered Blacks for the first time in the nation's history, a trend which has held—in 2019, Blacks made up 13.4 percent of the total U.S. population, while persons of Hispanic or Latinx origin constituted 18.5 percent.[130]

Hispanics arriving from the Caribbean, Latin America, Central America, and South America were made up of a complex mixture of languages, cultures, and nationalities. Significant numbers from the Caribbean were Black, which thoroughly confused census categories (nearly all other Hispanics filling out the census forms fit the "white" racial category). In 2000, nearly 8 percent of Black people in the United States were foreign-born, with the figure over 200 percent in New York, Florida, and New Jersey.[131] The Census Bureau found it difficult to identify ethnic categories accurately in New Mexico (where 42 percent of the population is officially classified as Hispanic) because many families are descended from residents who lived in the region generations before most American settlers arrived; as a consequence, even if they were once citizens of Mexico (before New Mexico was ceded to the United States in 1846), they cannot accurately be classified as coming from there.

Figure 6.1 reveals that the racial and ethnic composition of the immigration stream differs remarkably among the seven metropolitan areas receiving the largest numbers of immigrants in 2004. In the Los Angeles—Long Beach—Anaheim metro area, which is composed of numerous interlocking cities, Mexicans and Filipinos are the largest immigrant groups, followed by Salvadorans, Vietnamese, and Koreans. By contrast, Cubans were the most numerous group to arrive in Miami in the same year, and nearly all the rest were from the other Caribbean and Latin American countries. While Mexicans easily led the list in Los Angeles and Houston, a significant number also came from Asia and elsewhere in Latin America. The immigrant flow to the New York region was so diverse that only Dominicans accounted for more than 15 percent of the total; the other leading groups were Chinese, Mexicans, Indians, and Jamaicans. Washington, D.C., attracted a diverse mixture of Asian and Hispanic immigrants, with a significant number of Ethiopians added to the

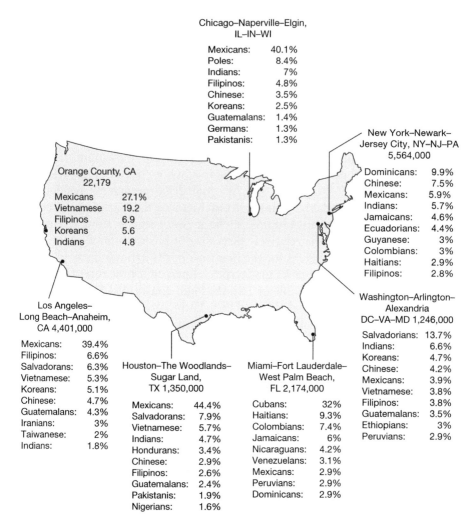

Chicago–Naperville–Elgin, IL–IN–WI

Mexicans:	40.1%
Poles:	8.4%
Indians:	7%
Filipinos:	4.8%
Chinese:	3.5%
Koreans:	2.5%
Guatemalans:	1.4%
Germans:	1.3%
Pakistanis:	1.3%

Orange County, CA 22,179

Mexicans	27.1%
Vietnamese	19.2
Filipinos	6.9
Koreans	5.6
Indians	4.8

New York–Newark–Jersey City, NY–NJ–PA 5,564,000

Dominicans:	9.9%
Chinese:	7.5%
Mexicans:	5.9%
Indians:	5.7%
Jamaicans:	4.6%
Ecuadorians:	4.4%
Guyanese:	3%
Colombians:	3%
Haitians:	2.9%
Filipinos:	2.8%

Los Angeles–Long Beach–Anaheim, CA 4,401,000

Mexicans:	39.4%
Filipinos:	6.6%
Salvadorans:	6.3%
Vietnamese:	5.3%
Koreans:	5.1%
Chinese:	4.7%
Guatemalans:	4.3%
Iranians:	3%
Taiwanese:	2%
Indians:	1.8%

Houston–The Woodlands–Sugar Land, TX 1,350,000

Mexicans:	44.4%
Salvadorans:	7.9%
Vietnamese:	5.7%
Indians:	4.7%
Hondurans:	3.4%
Chinese:	2.9%
Filipinos:	2.6%
Guatemalans:	2.4%
Pakistanis:	1.9%
Nigerians:	1.6%

Miami–Fort Lauderdale–West Palm Beach, FL 2,174,000

Cubans:	32%
Haitians:	9.3%
Colombians:	7.4%
Jamaicans:	6%
Nicaraguans:	4.2%
Venezuelans:	3.1%
Mexicans:	2.9%
Peruvians:	2.9%
Dominicans:	2.9%

Washington–Arlington–Alexandria DC–VA–MD 1,246,000

Salvadorans:	13.7%
Indians:	6.6%
Koreans:	4.7%
Chinese:	4.2%
Mexicans:	3.9%
Vietnamese:	3.8%
Filipinos:	3.8%
Guatemalans:	3.5%
Ethiopians:	3%
Peruvians:	2.9%

FIGURE 6.1 Seven U.S. Metropolitan Areas with Largest Immigrant Flows, Pooled Data from 2009–2013

Source: Compiled and calculated with data from the *Migration Policy Institute* (MPI), Data Hub: "Top Immigrant Origins by Metropolitan Statistical Area (MSA), 2009–2013," https://www.migrationpolicy.org/programs/data-hub/charts/top-immigrant-origins-metropolitan-statistical-area.

mix. In the Chicago region, Mexicans overwhelmingly dominated all nationality groups, with Poles and Indians next.

In 1987, more than 93 percent of legal immigrants coming to the United States settled in urban areas, and more than half of them moved into just seven metropolitan areas. Notably, many of these immigrants bypassed the central cities and moved directly to the suburbs. The statistics displayed in Table 6.7 show recent trends for the nation's 14 most diverse metropolitan areas (for

TABLE 6.7 **City and Suburban Minority Shares, Year 2000 Metropolitan Areas with Populations Over 500,000 (in Percentage)**

		Share of Suburban Population			
Metro Area	City	Suburban	Latino	Black	Asian
Los Angeles	69	69	45	8	14
New York	65	32	13	12	4
Chicago	65	26	11	8.5	5
Washington, D.C.	61	40.5	8.5	22	7
Houston	68	40	23	10	5
Dallas	62	31	15	9	4
Riverside	51	53	38	7	4
Phoenix	37	30	21	3	2
Orange County	70	40	22	1	14
San Diego	50	40	27	4	6
Oakland	67	48	19	8	17
Miami	82	78.5	56	19.5	1.5
Newark	86	34	11	17	4.5
San Francisco	56	43	19	3	17

Source: Adapted from William H. Frey, *Melting Pot Suburbs: A Census 2000 Study of Suburban Diversity* (Washington, D.C.: Center on Urban and Metropolitan Policy, Brookings Institution Press, June 2001), p. 14.

areas of more than 500,000). In all of the 14 central cities listed there, minorities comprised half or more of the population when the census of 2000 was taken.

In all but four of these same urban regions, more than 40 percent resided in the suburbs. In the Washington, D.C., and Newark areas, Blacks still outnumbered Hispanics, but the differences were much smaller in the New York and Chicago metropolitan regions. In the other Sunbelt urban regions shown in Table 6.7, Hispanics constituted the largest racial or ethnic group by far. Asians constituted less than 10 percent in all metro areas of the Sunbelt except for those clustered around Los Angeles, Orange County, Oakland, and San Francisco.

Increasingly, we also see that immigrant destinations are changing. While throughout the twentieth century, the vast majority of immigrants was settling in the nation's largest cities, recent census data shows that immigrant destinations have moved beyond just the largest metros, and settlement patterns have become more complicated. A larger percentage of immigrants now reside in the suburbs than in cities, and a growing percentage is settling in small metros and rural areas.

The census of 2011 showed that two-thirds of all Hispanics in the United States reside in only five states. Almost half (47%) of all Hispanics lived in only two states, California and Texas,[132] despite the fact that all but two of the cities with the largest Hispanic populations, Chicago and New York, are located in other states (the other three leading cities are Los Angeles, Houston, and San Antonio).[133] Approximately 80 percent of the Hispanics in the southwestern states came originally from Mexico, compared to 60 percent for the United States as a whole. But in the 1990s, Mexican-origin immigrants began to spread across the nation, with the largest percentage occurring in North Carolina (479 percent increase), Arkansas (388 percent), Georgia (374 percent), Tennessee (327 percent), and Nevada (271 percent).[134] By 2011, new trends of Hispanic immigrant settlement were apparent: Based on 2011 census data, five non-traditional immigrant states have experienced the fastest growth of their Hispanic population: Alabama (158 percent South Carolina (154 percent), Tennessee (154 percent), Kentucky (132 percent), and South Dakota (129 percent).[135] What was once mainly a regional phenomenon has become a truly national trend. By 2019, persons of Hispanic or Latino origin composed 18.5 percent of the total U.S. population, making people of Hispanic origin the nation's largest ethnic or race minority.[136] Regional variations are substantial. In New Mexico, 49.3 percent of the state's population was Hispanic in 2019, the highest of any state, and Hispanics constituted over one-third of the population in California and Texas.[137]

Adverse economic conditions in Mexico and poverty and political repression in other countries pushed most of the Hispanic immigrants northward. Economic opportunity in the United States exerted the necessary pull. The minimum wage in the United States was approximately six times the prevailing wage in Mexico in 1990, which was higher than in most other Latin American countries.[138] Undocumented immigration helps account for persistently low wages and low levels of education among Latinos. Undocumented immigrants are willing to take (or are coerced into taking) jobs paying less than the minimum wage, and they often end up in sweatshops, meat-processing plants, or agricultural jobs working under abysmal conditions. Beginning with the Clinton administration, there have been frequent and serious efforts to further fortify the border, especially along urban areas, where most of the crossings were occurring. This kind of fortification has pushed undocumented immigrants into more hostile but less fortified border territory, such as the Arizona desert, leading to a drastic increase in immigrant deaths. According to the United Nations' migration agency's report, there were 232 deaths along the U.S.-Mexico border during the first seven months of 2017 alone, marking a 17 percent increase compared to the first seven months of the previous year.[139] Most border crossers die from exposure to the elements, given the extreme conditions in the desert and dehydration, but some also drown in the Rio Grande. Frequently

led across the border by professional smugglers, called *coyotes* for their predatory habits, undocumented immigrants live at the margins of American society.
Because they live in constant fear of detection by the United States Citizenship
and Immigration Services (USCIS), a bureau of the Department of Homeland
Security, they are in no position to bargain with employers.

To address the issue of undocumented immigration, Congress enacted
the Immigration Reform and Control Act (IRCA) in 1986, which established
stiff penalties for employers who knowingly hired undocumented workers. At
the same time, the law made it possible for undocumented immigrants who
had already entered the country to achieve citizenship by registering with the
Immigration and Naturalization Service (INS). Within four years of the passage of the IRCA, more than 2 million undocumented immigrants attained
legal status, and the INS stepped up efforts to find employers who violated the
law. One of the unintended effects of the 1986 reform is that many employers
began to discriminate against anyone who looked or sounded like they came
from anywhere south of the U.S. border.[140] Reflecting a growing national
anxiety about undocumented immigration, the successor agency to the INS,
the USCIS, began to round up undocumented immigrants in spectacular,
well-publicized raids. After the U.S. Senate failed to pass an immigration bill
in 2006, several states adopted legislation requiring employers to check the
backgrounds of employees; in addition, by 2008, 15 states had passed laws
that established criminal penalties for smugglers who bring immigrants into
the country.[141]

The reactions against immigrants prompted towns and cities across the
nation to adopt an extraordinary variety of laws that required, for example,
business owners to check the identity of potential employees, property owners
to check the backgrounds of renters, public buildings to post "English only"
signs, and other measures. Local police departments rounded up anyone looking like immigrants for minor violations, such as, in Georgia, fishing without a
license.[142] These actions, many of doubtful legality, gave police the pretext for
beginning deportation orders. Arizona took this strategy a step further when
the state senate passed legislation in April 2010 that empowered the police,
when interacting with people on a routine basis, to question anyone suspected
of being in the country without papers.[143]

California, on the other hand, went a different route. In September 2017,
the California legislature passed the California Values Act, which prohibits
police departments state-wide from arresting immigrants for their lack of status
in the United States and precludes any undocumented immigrants from being
handed over to federal authorities at Immigration and Customs Enforcement
(ICE) unless they have been convicted of a specific list of felonies or misdemea-
nors.[144] In addition, the act puts a limit on the amount of personal information
on undocumented immigrants, which can be shared with federal immigration
authorities. The bill, which was signed by California Governor Jerry Brown
in early October 2017, went into effect on January 1, 2018, and was widely

interpreted to be a direct reaction to the Trump administration's efforts to crack down on undocumented immigrants.

Has the Urban Crisis Disappeared?

The twentieth-century urban crisis of city versus suburb is coming to an end. In the past, most immigrants settled in central cities, often moving into neighborhoods already occupied by the same ethnic group, but the recent pattern of settlement has become more complex and less predictable. In a break from historic patterns of settlement, many of the immigrants are bypassing the central cities entirely and moving directly into suburbs. By 2000, 55 percent of Asians, 50 percent of Latinos, and 39 percent of Blacks lived in the suburbs, and the proportions were much higher in many Sunbelt metropolitan urban regions.[145] Several of the communities that minorities moved into are now ethnically diverse, which reduces the extreme polarization between central city and suburb that characterized urban areas only a few years ago.

The movement to the suburbs has had the effect of moderating the extremely rigid pattern of racial and ethnic segregation that was the defining feature of the twentieth-century urban crisis. Research shows that in the 1990s, the level of segregation declined in 272 metropolitan statistical areas (MSAs) and increased in only 19 MSAs.[146] Most of the metropolitan areas where segregation increased were located in second-tier older industrial cities in the Northeast and Midwest, which tend to be less diverse than the faster-growing metropolitan areas elsewhere. In one study, the authors found that between 1970 and 2000, all ethnic groups had become more spatially assimilated, although Black Americans remained more segregated than Asians or Latinos.[147] The dismal findings from earlier studies of residential segregation were distilled into a book titled *American Apartheid*,[148] but census data from the late 1990s and early 2000s seemed to suggest that change may be afoot.

In the 1990s, the number of people living in neighborhoods of concentrated poverty—which researchers define as areas where 40 percent or more of the residents are under the poverty line—fell dramatically in the 1990s, by 24 percent, or 2.4 million people.[149] The proportion of people living in high-poverty neighborhoods fell among all racial and ethnic groups, and the sharpest declines were in cities in the Midwest and South, such as Detroit, Chicago, St. Louis, Milwaukee, Memphis, New Orleans, Houston, San Antonio, and Dallas. Researchers referred to the decline in concentrated poverty as "stunning progress."[150] It should be noted that these figures changed little when the effects of the Great Recession were reported in the 2010 census.

By the late 1990s, there was also evidence to suggest that poverty had become less concentrated than before. The clustering of poverty in a few areas fell so dramatically in the 1990s that the scholars conducting the research called the trend "nothing short of profound." The researchers drew the conclusion that "many fewer neighborhoods now resemble the depressing descriptions of the inner city that were commonplace in journalistic and scholarly accounts of previous years."[151]

These patterns, however, reversed once again in the 2010s. Several social scientists concluded that during the past decade, concentrated poverty has returned to its peak levels from the 1990s or even surpassed those levels. However, poverty patterns seem to have changed. For instance, high-poverty tracts seem to be more racially and ethnically diverse, smaller cities and metros appear to have the most explosive growth of such high-poverty areas, and within bigger cities and metros (which typically had the largest ratio of high-poverty census tracts in the past), high-poverty neighborhoods tend to be increasingly remote and disconnected.[152] In other words, poverty is returning with a vengeance, but in different geographic patterns than previously known.

Even though in the 2010s, high-poverty neighborhoods tended to be more racially and ethnically diverse than during the twentieth century, the residents of high-poverty neighborhoods are still disproportionately members of ethnic and racial minority groups.[153] Racial and ethnic segregation still prevail as well. However, the demographic patterns of poverty are growing increasingly complex: One recent study found that the proportion of non-Hispanic white people living in high poverty neighborhoods almost doubled between 2000 and 2007–2011, from 1.4 million to 2.9 million.[154] On the other hand, the proportion of Black and Hispanic residents in high-poverty neighborhoods grew from 39 percent to 51 percent during that time.[155] Within that high-poverty population, the Hispanic proportion has grown, in comparison Black high-poverty residents.[156] In total, the proportion of Black residents of high poverty neighborhoods declined since the 1990s, from 40 percent to 37 percent, still making up a plurality of high-poverty residents, while the proportion of white high-poverty residents has grown from 20 percent to 26 percent, and the proportion of Hispanics in such neighborhoods has remained about the same, at 30 percent.[157]

Crime rates in urban areas went into a steep decline. For the nation as a whole, violent crime per 100,000 persons decreased by 29 percent from 1990 to 2000 (after an increase of 20 percent from 1987 to 1990), and the murder rate fell by 41 percent (after a 13 percent increase).[158] The drop in crime was even more dramatic in big cities than elsewhere; homicide rates, for example, fell by 75 percent in New York City from 1990 to 2003 (from more than 2,200 in 1990 to 597 in 2003).[159] Although the rate of violent crime has increased in some cities since then, overall crime rates have continued to drop, often to levels not seen in decades. In 2009, there were 1,318,398 violent crimes, a decrease of 5.3 percent from 2008, 5.2 percent from 2005, and 7.5 percent from the 2000 level.[160] The trend continued into the next decade—in 2011, an estimated 1,203,564 violent crimes occurred nationwide, a decrease of 3.8 percent from 2010.[161] By 2014, the national homicide rate, as well as violent crime rates overall had reached a historic low, reaching 4.4 per 100,000: New York City's murder rate had fallen 90 percent from its all-time high, and researchers, baffled, referred to the phenomenon "the great crime decline."[162] By the next year, those trends seemed to be reversing slightly, with a spike in homicides in many major American cities throughout the years 2015 and 2016. This sudden increase, however, seemed to be temporary and had largely dissipated in 2018 and 2019. The COVID-19 pandemic seems to have changed the equation on violent crime in cities once again—though researchers are still not quite certain as to why and whether the trend will last. The overall homicide rate across the country increased by an astonishing 25 percent during the pandemic, as the *Washington Post* reported in July of 2021, to 6.2 homicides per 100,000.[163] The reasons for this increase seem difficult to pin down exactly. The trend appears to be unique to the United States, even though the entire world has been affected by the pandemic. The most likely reason for the unique situation of the United States seems to be the availability of guns in the United States and the fact that an unprecedented amount of people across the country obtained firearms during the pandemic. As commentators from the *Washington Post* hypothesized, "Beneath it all, the ready availability of guns looms. Put simply, social disruptions and de-policing probably have higher stakes in American cities – where a small but persistent number of criminal offenders carry guns – than they do in countries where firearms are not as easy to get."[164]

Despite the accumulating evidence that some things have changed in urban regions, it would be premature to conclude that the urban problems of the twentieth century—high levels of segregation, inequality and poverty, and racial and ethnic tensions—are disappearing. The urban crisis was defined by reference to the great city/suburban divide. This geographic pattern is slowly changing, and in that important sense, the old urban crisis is mostly a thing of the past. But some of the problems previously associated with broad swatches of urban neighborhoods are now cropping up all over the place.

The prospects for the central cities have improved, but the benefits from this turnaround have been selective. By many measures, downtowns and residential areas in the central cities have been on the rebound since sometime in the 1990s. Fifteen large older industrial cities—including, for example, St. Louis, Gary, Baltimore, Buffalo, Pittsburgh, Cincinnati, and Detroit—continued to lose population in the 1990s, but the rate of loss slowed. A declining population could no longer be interpreted as a reliable measure of decline. Many cities were becoming less densely populated, and single and childless households were replacing larger families. In effect, the cities were exporting social problems to the suburbs by replacing poorer families with more affluent single professionals who have led the gentrification of old neighborhoods.[165]

The inequalities between the downtown professional class and the residents of minority neighborhoods have become transparently obvious in cities tied closely to the global economy. Global cities have attracted a more diverse profile of immigrants than any other cities.[166] Jobs are the lure. The concentration of multinational businesses, financial services corporations, and the businesses connected to them draws highly educated workers from all over the globe.

But the greatest demand for jobs (at least expressed in numbers) is found at the other end of the job market. Lower-status service workers are indispensable to the working of a global city—clerical workers, janitors and cashiers, nannies, cooks and busboys, maintenance and security workers, hotel maids, and a multitude of personal-service specialists from masseuses and personal shoppers to dog walkers: These kinds of jobs are taken disproportionately by immigrants and minorities. The jobs generally pay little, with the result that inequality escalates upward. New York's experience is revealing. In the late 1980s, the poorest 20 percent of the population in the New York metropolitan region accounted for 5 percent of incomes, but the top 20 percent of wage earners had a 45 percent share. By 1997, the percentage of earnings claimed by the poorest quintile had fallen to just above 2 percent, whereas the richest quintile received 56 percent of all earnings. While New York was becoming more affluent, it was also becoming poorer; between 1990 and 2000, the poverty rate rose from 29 to 32 percent of households.[167]

Rising inequality is occurring not only in global cities but throughout American society. In 1980, the bottom one-fifth of the population earned 4.3 percent of all earned income, but only a few years later, in 1998, the poorest fifth of wage earners accounted for just 3.6 percent. Meanwhile, from 1980 to 1998, the richest fifth increased its share from 44 to 49 percent. Perhaps even more telling, the top 5 percent of wage earners had increased its share of earnings in the same period from 16 to 21.4 percent.[168] As of 2020, the United States has the highest level of income inequality among all G-7 nations, ranking first, with a Gini coefficient above 0.4, followed by the U.K. (0.392), Italy (0.373), Japan (0.363), Canada (0.352), Germany (0.351), and France (0.326).[169] Gini coefficients, which denote gross income inequalities, rank around 0.25 among some European countries and can reach 0.5 or 0.6 in some countries in the south of the African continent.[170]

In 2011, the richest 1 percent of Americans took home almost 24 percent of the total national income, an increase of almost 9 percent from 1976. As a reporter for *The New York Times* wrote, "… you no longer need to travel to distant and dangerous countries to observe such rapacious inequality. We now have it right here a home …"[171] From 1980 to 2005, the richest 1 percent took away more than four-fifths of the total increase in the national income. Such a concentration of income at the top tier of earners has only occurred three times in the twentieth century: in 1915 and 1916, at the end of the Gilded Age, and again in the late 1920s prior to the stock market crash.[172]

Minorities continue to significantly lag behind in income and wealth. Indicators of economic well-being show that Hispanics, as a group, have a long way to go to catch up with the general U.S. population. The real median household income for Hispanic families in 2019 was 73.7 percent of the average earnings for non-Hispanic white families (down from 75 percent in 2001 but up from 72 percent in 2006). It remained above the average earnings of Black families, which was 61 percent of white family income.[173] While the

2020 census showed that nearly 23.4 percent of Americans 25 and older had bachelor's degrees, it also showed the great racial disparity in education. The rate for Black Americas was 18 percent, and only 14 percent for Hispanic Americans. The lag in educational qualifications, plus a measure of discrimination, has meant that Hispanics have occupied lower rungs on the job ladder. Even though they held 12 percent of all jobs in 2000, only 6 percent of Hispanics worked in managerial or professional positions.[174] The economic crisis that began in 2008 affected Hispanics and Blacks disproportionately. By March 2009, the unemployment rate for whites reached 7.3 percent, but for Hispanics, it had climbed to 12.9 percent and 13.8 for Blacks.[175] During the recovery, unemployment rates for whites have fallen far faster than for any either of these groups.

It is unrealistic to expect that inequality on this scale can occur without an increase in social problems. Within urban areas, extreme inequality has always been expressed in two ways: social disorder (in the form of crime, violent protest, and family disorganization, for instance) and residential patterns of segregation. No one knows whether the crime rates or the incidence of concentrated poverty will continue to fall. Especially in the aftermath of a global pandemic, which has disproportionately affected Black and Hispanic Americans, the jury is still out on the long-term consequences this will have for the socio-economic future of communities of color. In 2020, the United States once again started a national conversation about the historical injustices experienced by people of color throughout American history. It also, perhaps for the first time in its history, started a conversation about the fact that the success at the roots of the American economy is inextricably tied to the institution of slavery—something that the country as a whole will need to continue to reckon with much more substantively in the future. Whether it is reparations or a different kind of substantive action to acknowledge not only the deep, historical injustices committed by this country against minority groups but also their fundamental contributions to the success of the American economy—the conversation must continue, hopefully resulting in some definitive action.

Endnotes

1 Barry Checkoway, "Large Builders, Federal Housing Programs, and Postwar Suburbanization," in *Marxism and the Metropolis: New Perspectives in Political Economy*, ed. William K. Tabb and Larry Sawers (New York: Oxford University Press), p. 156.

2 Population growth on the outskirts probably exceeded population growth in the center before the 1920s. However, before 1920, the annexation of suburban land by central cities obscured the statistical trend. See John D. Kasarda and George V. Redfearn, "Differential Patterns of City and Suburban Growth in the United States," *Journal of Urban History* 2, no. 1 (November 1975): 53.

3 Nicolas Lemann, *The Promised Land: The Great Migration and How It Changed America* (New York: Vintage Books, 1991), p. 6.

4 Robert A. Beauregard, *Voices of Decline: The Postwar Fate of U.S. Cities* (Cambridge, MA: Blackwell, 1993).

5 Dennis Judd, "Urban Violence and Enclave Politics: Crime as Text, Race as Subtext," in *Managing Divided Cities*, ed. Seamus Dunn (Keele, Staffordshire, UK: Ryburn Publishing, Keele University Press, 1994), pp. 160–175.

6 U.S. Bureau of the Census, *Statistical Abstract of the United States* (2005), www.census.gov/prod/2005pubs/06statab/pop.pdf.

7 Pew Research Center, *Social and Demographic Trends* (Washington, D.C.: Pew Charitable Trusts, 2008).

8 A brief but excellent account of these movements may be found in Stanley B. Greenberg, *Politics and Poverty: Modernization and Response in Five Poor Neighborhoods* (New York: Wiley, 1974), pp. 15–27.

9 See ibid., pp. 15–27; and Leo Grebler, Joan W. Moore, and Ralph C. Guzman, *The Mexican-American People* (New York: Free Press, 1970), p. 113.

10 U.S. Bureau of the Census, *Statistical Abstract of the United States*.

11 Luis Noe-Bustamente, "Facts about U.S. Latinos and Their Diverse Origins," *PEW Research Center* (September 16, 2019), https://www.pewresearch.org/fact-tank/2019/09/16/key-facts-about-u-s-hispanics/.

12 Jens Manuel Krogstad, "Hispanics Have Accounted for More Than Half of Total U.S. Population Growth since 2010," *Pew Research Center* (July 10, 2020), https://www.pewresearch.org/fact-tank/2020/07/10/hispanics-have-accounted-for-more-than-half-of-total-u-s-population-growth-since-2010/.

13 Ibid.

14 Ibid.

15 Harry M. Caudill, *Night Comes to the Cumberlands* (Boston, MA: Little, Brown, 1962).

16 Lemann, *The Promised Land*, p. 6.

17 Stewart E. Tolnay and E. M. Beck, "Rethinking the Role of Racial Violence in the Great Migration," in *Black Exodus: The Great Migration from the American South*, ed. Afrerdteen Harrison (Jackson: University Press of Mississippi, 1991), p. 20.

18 Robert B. Grant, ed., *The Black Man Comes to the City: A Documentary Account from the Great Migration to the Great Depression, 1915–1930* (Chicago, IL: Nelson-Hall, 1972), p. 27; see pp. 16–30 for a complete set of statistics on black migration from 1890 to 1930. These data are used throughout this section.

19 Ibid., p. 22.

20 Ibid., p. 23.

21 Winfred P. Nathan, *Health Conditions in North Harlem, 1923–1927*, Social Research Series No. 2 (New York: National Tuberculosis Association, 1932), pp. 44–45, excerpted in Grant, *The Black Man Comes to the City*, pp. 59–61.

22 *Chicago Defender*, reprinted in Grant, *The Black Man Comes to the City*, pp. 31–40.

23 Tolnay and Beck, "Rethinking the Role of Racial Violence," p. 27.

24 Philip Dray, *At the Hands of Persons Unknown: The Lynching of Black America* (New York: Random House, 2002).

25 A collective amnesia has erased much of this past from America's consciousness. A recent book of photographs from the period is shocking but an effective antidote to cultural denial. See James Allen, *Without Sanctuary: Lynching Photography in America* (Sante Fe, NM: Twin Palms Publishers, 2000).

26 Memphis *Commercial Appeal* (October 5, 1916), reprinted in Grant, *The Black Man Comes to the City*, pp. 43–44.

27 *Chicago Defender* (August 12, 1916), reprinted in Grant, *The Black Man Comes to the City*, p. 45.

28 Herbert Northrup, *Organized Labor and the Negro* (New York: Kraus Reprint, 1971).

29 Christine Leibbrand, Catherine Massey, J. Trent Alexander, Katie R. Genadek, and Stewart Tolnay, "The Great Migration and Residential Segregation in American Cities during the Twentieth Century," *Social Science History* 44, no. 1 (Spring 2020), https://www.ncbi.nlm.nih.gov/pmc/articles/PMC7297198/.

30 Ibid.

31 Ibid.

32 Ibid.

33 Stewart Tolnay, "The Great Migration Gets Underway: A Comparison of Black Southern Migrants and Nonmigrants in the North, 1920," *Social Science Quarterly* 82, no. 2 (2001): 235–252.

34 S. Lieberson and CA Wilkinson, "A comparison between Northern and Southern Blacks Residing in the North," *Demography* 13, no. 2 (May 1976): 199–224.

35 Christine Leibbrand, Catherine Massey, J. Trent Alexander, Katie R. Genadek, and Stewart Tolnay, "The Great Migration and Residential Segregation in American Cities during the Twentieth Century," *Social Science History* 44, no. 1(Spring 2020), https://www.ncbi.nlm.nih.gov/pmc/articles/PMC7297198/.

36 Stanley Lieberson, "A Reconsideration of the Income Differences Found between Migrants and Northern-Born Blacks," *American Journal of Sociology* 83, no. 4 (1978): 940–966.

37 Larry Long and Lynne Heltman, "Migration and Income Differences between Black and White Men in the North," *American Journal of Sociology* 80, no. 6 (1975): 1391–1409.

38 Stanley Masters, "Are Black Migrants from the South to the Northern Cities Worse Off Than Blacks Already There?" *The Journal of Human Resources* 7, no. 4 (1972): 411–423.

39 Christine Leibbrand, Catherine Massey, J. Trent Alexander, Katie R. Genadek, and Stewart Tolnay, "The Great Migration and Residential Segregation in American Cities during the Twentieth Century," *Social Science History* 44, no. 1 (Spring 2020), https://www.ncbi.nlm.nih.gov/pmc/articles/PMC7297198/.

40 Stewart Tolnay, "The Great Migration and Changes in the Northern Black Family, 1940–1990," *Social Forces* 75, no. 4 (1997): 1213–1238.

41 Stewart Tolnay, "Migration Experience and Family Patterns in the 'Promised Land'," *Journal of Family History* 23, no. 1 (1998): 68–89.

42 Stewart Tolnay and Kyle Crowder, "Regional Origin and Family Structure in Northern Cities: The Role of Context," *American Sociological Review* 64, no. 1 (1999): 97–112.

43 Christine Leibbrand, Catherine Massey, J. Trent Alexander, Katie R. Genadek, and Stewart Tolnay, "The Great Migration and Residential Segregation in American Cities during the Twentieth Century," *Social Science History* 44, no. 1(Spring 2020), https://www.ncbi.nlm.nih.gov/pmc/articles/PMC7297198/.

44 These statistics are from several sources excerpted in Grant, *The Black Man Comes to the City*, pp. 58–61.

45 See Elliott M. Rudwick, *Race Riot at East St. Louis, July 2, 1917* (Carbondale: Southern Illinois Press, 1964), for a discussion of this event.

46 Chicago Commission on Race Relations, *The Negro in Chicago: A Study of Race Relations and a Race Riot* (Chicago, IL: University of Chicago Press, 1922), p. 122.

47 Tom Kenworthy, "Okla. Starts to Face up to, '21 Massacre," *USA Today* (February 18, 2000), p. 4A.

48 Grant, *The Black Man Comes to the City*, p. 71.

49 U.S. Department of Commerce, Bureau of the Census, *Census of Population 1970: General Social and Economic Characteristics* (Washington, D.C.: U.S. Government Printing Office, 1972), pp. 448–449, Table 3.

50 Stewart Tolnay, "The African American 'Great Migration' and Beyond," *Annual Review of Sociology* no. 29 (2003): 209–232.

51 J.T. Alexander, "The Great Migration in Comparative Perspective," *Social Science History* 22 (1998): 349–376.

52 C. Marks, *Farewell—We're Good and Gone: The Great Black Migration* (Bloomington: Indiana University Press, 1989).

53 Douglas Massey and Nancy Denton, *American Apartheid: Segregation and the Making of the Underclass* (Cambridge, MA: Harvard University Press, 1993), pp. 89, 91.

54 Ibid., p. 91.

55 Rosalyn Baxandall and Elizabeth Ewen, *Picture Windows: How the Suburbs Happened* (New York: Basic Books, 2000), p. 202; Ray Suarez, *The Old Neighborhood: How We Lost in the Great Suburban Migration, 1966–1999* (New York: Free Press, 1999), pp. 40–41.

56 Quoted in ibid., pp. 252–253.

57 U.S. Bureau of the Census, *American FactFinder* (2005), http://factfinder.census.gov/home/saff/main.html?_lang=en.

58 National Advisory Commission on Civil Disorders, *Report of the National Advisory Commission on Civil Disorders* (New York: Bantam Books, 1968), p. 1.

59 John Kasarda, "Inner-City Concentrated Poverty and Neighborhood Distress: 1970 to 1990," *Housing Policy Debate* 4, no. 3 (1993): 253–302.

60 Alan Berube and Elizabeth Kneebone, *Two Steps Back. City and Suburban Poverty Trends 1999–2005* (Washington, D.C.: Brookings Institute, 2006).

61 Kim Parker, Juliana Menasce Horowitz, Anna Brown, Richard Fry, D'Vera Cohn, and Ruth Igielnik, "What Unites and Divides Urban, Suburban, and Rural Communities," *Pew Research Center* Report (May 22, 2018), https://www.pewresearch.org/social-trends/2018/05/22/what-unites-and-divides-urban-suburban-and-rural-communities/.

62 Ibid.

63 Rolf Pendall, Elizabeth Davies, Lesley Freiman, and Rob Pitingolo, *A Lost Decade: Neighborhood Poverty and the Urban Crisis of the 2000s* (Washington D.C.: The Urban Institute, for the Joint Center on Political and Economic Studies, September 2011).

64 John R. Logan, *Separate and Unequal: The Neighborhood Gap for Blacks, Hispanics and Asians in Metropolitan America* (Providence, RI: Brown University, July 2011).

65 John Creamer, "Inequalities Persist Despite Decline in Poverty For All Major Race and Hispanic Origin Groups," *United States Census Bureau*, Income and Poverty (September 15, 2020), https://www.census.gov/library/stories/2020/09/poverty-rates-for-blacks-and-hispanics-reached-historic-lows-in-2019.html.

66 Ibid.

67 Ibid.

68 Ibid.

69 Ibid.

70 William Julius Wilson, *The Truly Disadvantaged. The Inner City, the Underclass, and Public Policy* (Chicago, IL: The University of Chicago Press, 1987).

71 Michaela di Leonardo, "White Lies/Black Myths: Rape, Race, and the Black Underclass," *The Village Voice* (September 22, 1992), p. 31.

72 Norman Fainstein, "Race, Class, and Segregation: Discourses about African-Americans," *International Journal of Urban and Regional Research* 17, no. 3 (1993): 384–403.

73 Wilson, *The Truly Disadvantaged.*

74 Ibid., p. 31.

75 Lisa W. Foderaro, "In Harlem, Children Reflect the Ravages U.N. Seeks to Relieve," *The New York Times* (September 30, 1990), p. 1.

76 Walter J. Jones and James E. Johnson, "AIDS: The Urban Policymaking Challenge," *Journal of Urban Affairs* 11, no. 1 (1989): 85.

77 Joel A. Devine and James D. Wright, *The Greatest of Evils: Urban Poverty and the American Underclass* (New York: De Gruyter, 1993), p. 167.

78 Robert D. McFadden, "New York Leads Cities in Robbery Rate, But Drops in Murders," *The New York Times* (August 11, 1991), p. 1.

79 See James Diego Vigil, *Barrio Gangs: Street Life and Identity in Southern California* (Austin, TX: University of Texas Press, 1988).

80 Ronald Kotulak, "Study Finds Inner-City Kids Live with Violence," *Chicago Tribune* (September 28, 1990), p. 1.

81 Jonathan Kozol, *Rachel and Her Children: Homeless Families in America* (New York: Crown, 1988), p. 9.

82 Margaret T. Gordon and Claudette Guzan Artwick, "Urban Images in the Mass Media" (research proposal, Urban University Research Consortium, June 17, 1991), p. 2.

83 di Leonardo, "White Lies/Black Myths," p. 31.

84 Quoted in James A. Clapp, ed., *The City: A Dictionary of Quotable Thoughts on Cities and Urban Life* (New Brunswick, NJ: Center for Urban Policy Research, Rutgers University, 1984), p. 129.

85 Ibid., pp. 25–30. Robert Fishman dates the first true suburb somewhat earlier, in the 1790s in Clapham and other villages outside London; see Robert Fishman, *Bourgeois Utopias: The Rise and Fall of Suburbia* (New York: Basic Books, 1987), p. 53.

86 For accounts of railroad suburbs and land speculation, see Kenneth T. Jackson, *Crabgrass Frontier: The Suburbanization of the United States* (New York: Oxford University Press, 1985), Chapter 5; Fishman, *Bourgeois Utopias*, Chapter 5; and Harry C. Binford, *The First Suburbs: Residential Communities on the Boston Periphery, 1815–1860* (Chicago, IL: University of Chicago Press, 1985).

87 John W. Reps, *The Making of Urban America: A History of City Planning in the United States* (Princeton, NJ: Princeton University Press, 1965), p. 344.

88 The phrase "scattered buildings in a park" is Lewis Mumford's; see his *The City in History: Its Origins, Its Transformations, and Its Prospects* (New York: Harcourt, Brace and World, 1961), p. 489.

89 Editorial, (New York) *Independent* (February 27, 1902), p. 52.

90 Weldon Fawcett, "Suburban Life in America," *Cosmopolitan* (July 1903), p. 309.

91 Advertisement in *Country Life in America* (November 1906), p. 3.

92 Advertisement in *Country Life in America* (March 1908), p. 474.

93 Robert Park, Ernest W. Burgess, and Roderick D. McKenzie, *The City* (Chicago, IL: University of Chicago Press, 1925), p. 109.

94 Quoted in Peter J. Schmitt, *Back to Nature: The Arcadian Myth in Urban America* (New York: Oxford University Press, 1969), p. 180; original quotation found in Ernest Groves, "The Urban Complex," *Sociological Review* 12 (Fall 1920): 74, 76.

95 A more complete list of titles can be found in Schmitt, *Back to Nature*, pp. 180–182.

96 Gary A. Tobin, "Suburbanization and the Development of Motor Transportation: Transportation Technology and the Suburbanization Process," in *The Changing Face of the Suburbs*, ed. Barry Schwartz (Chicago, IL: University of Chicago Press, 1976), p. 100. See also U.S. Bureau of the Census, *Industrial Districts: 1905, Manufactures and Population*, Bulletin 101 (Washington, D.C.: U.S. Government Printing Office, 1909), pp. 9–80; and U.S. Bureau of the Census, *Census of Manufactures: 1914*, vol. 1, *Reports by States with Statistics for Principal Cities and Metropolitan Districts* (Washington, D.C.: U.S. Government Printing Office, 1918), pp. 564, 787, 1292.

97 These data are cited in Tobin, "Suburbanization and the Development of Motor Transportation," pp. 102, 103, and are also available in National Industrial Conference Board (NICB), *The Economic Almanac 1956: A Handbook of Useful Facts about Business, Labor and Government in the United States and Other Areas* (New York: Crowell for the Conference Board, 1956).

98 Tobin, "Suburbanization and the Development of Motor Transportation," pp. 102, 103.

99 Ibid.

100 Jackson, *Crabgrass Frontier*, pp. 174, 184.

101 The birth rate (the number of live births per 1,000 population) increased from 18.4 in 1936 to 26.6 in 1947. U.S. Bureau of the Census, *Historical Statistics of the United States, Colonial Times to 1970*, Bicentennial ed., pt. 2 (Washington, D.C.: U.S. Government Printing Office, 1975), p. 49.

102 Jackson, *Crabgrass Frontier*, p. 232.

103 Ibid., p. 233.

104 Checkoway, "Large Builders, Federal Housing Programs, and Postwar Suburbanization," pp. 155–156.

105 U.S. Bureau of the Census, *Historical Statistics of the United States, Colonial Times to 1970*, p. 646.

106 U.S. Department of Commerce, *Bureau of the Census, Census of Population, 1950*, vol. 1 (Washington, D.C.: U.S. Government Printing Office, 1952), p. 69, Table 17; *Census of Population, 1970*, vol. 1, *Characteristics of the Population*, pt. A, p. 180, Table 34; *Census of Population, 1980*, suppl. reports, *Standard Metropolitan Statistical Areas and Standard Consolidated Statistical Areas*, p. 2, Table B, p. 6, Table 1, and p. 49, Table 1; *State and Metropolitan Areas Data Book*, 1991, Table D; Bruce Katz and Robert Lang, ed., *Redefining Urban and Suburban America: Evidence from Census 2000* (Washington, D.C.: Brookings Institution Press, 2003), pp. 47–50.

107 For criticisms of the 1950s stereotype of suburbia, see Bennett M. Berger, *Working-Class Suburb: A Study of Auto Workers in Suburbia* (Berkeley: University of California Press, 1968); and Herbert J. Gans, *The Levittowners: Ways of Life and Politics in a New Suburban Community* (New York: Pantheon Books, 1967).

108 Thomas M. Guterbock, "The Push Hypothesis: Minority Presence, Crime, and Urban Deconcentration," in *The Changing Face of the Suburbs*, ed. Barry Schwartz (Chicago, IL: University of Chicago Press, 1976), p. 26.

109 Ira Katznelson, *When Affirmative Action Was White: An Untold History of Racial Inequality in Twentieth-Century America* (New York: W. W. Norton & Company, 2006), p. 113.

110 Douglas S. Massey and Nancy A. Denton, *American Apartheid: Segregation and the Making of the Underclass* (Cambridge, MA: Harvard University Press, 1998).

111 Amanda Tillotson, "Race, Risk, and Real Estate: the Federal Housing Administration and Black Homeownership in the Post World War II Home Ownership State," *DePaul Journal for Social Justice* 8, no. 1 (2014): 28.

112 Ibid.

113 Erin Blakemore, "How the GI Bill's Promise Was Denied to a Million Black WWII Veterans," *The History Channel Stories* (June 21, 2019), https://www.history.com/news/gi-bill-black-wwii-veterans-benefits.

114 Katznelson, *When Affirmative Action Was White: An Untold History of Racial Inequality in Twentieth-Century America*, p. 140.

115 Tillotson, "Race, Risk, and Real Estate: the Federal Housing Administration and Black Homeownership in the Post World War II Home Ownership State," 29.

116 Terry Gross, "A 'Forgotten History' of How the U.S. Government Segregated America," *Fresh Air on NPR* (May 3, 2017), https://www.npr.org/2017/05/03/526655831/a-forgotten-history-of-how-the-u-s-government-segregated-america.

117 Ibid.

118 William H. Frey, "Census 2000 Shows Large Black Return to the South, Reinforcing the Region's 'White-Black' Demographic Profile," U.S. Bureau of the Census, PSC Research Report No. 02-473 (May 2001).

119 Rick Lyman, "Census Shows Growth of Immigrants," *The New York Times* (August 15, 2006), www.nytimes.com.

120 Department of Homeland Security, Office of Immigration Statistics, www.uscis.gov/graphics/shared/statistics/publications/LPRest2004.pdf.

121 "2019 Yearbook of Immigration Statistics: Table 3. Persons Obtaining Lawful Permanent Resident Status by Region and Country of Birth: Fiscal Years 2017–2019," *Department of Homeland Security*. https://www.dhs.gov/immigration-statistics/yearbook/2019/table3#.

122 "2009 Yearbook of Immigration Statistics: Table 1," *U.S. Office of Immigration Statistics*; "2011 Yearbook of Immigration Statistics: Table 1," *U.S. Office of Immigration Statistics*.

123 Libby Garland, *After They Closed the Gates: Jewish Illegal Immigration to the United States, 1921–1965* (Chicago, IL: The University of Chicago Press, 2014).

124 According to a recent Pew survey, the vast majority of Latinx adults in the United States does not know of or use the term Latinx: Of a total of 23 percent of the Hispanic population in the United States who know about the term, only 3 percent use it, while 20 percent do not. The remaining 77 percent of the U.S. Hispanic population said to not have heard about the term. According to the Pew study, many Hispanics reject the term based on the fact that as an "American invention" it rejects the traditional gendered form of the Spanish language. Proponents, on the other hand, note that LatinX is a specifically gender- and LGBTQ+-inclusive term, which is part and parcel of a general effort in the United States toward inclusivity. See: Luis

Noe-Bustamante, Lauren Mora, and Mark Hugo Lopez, "About One-in-Four U.S. Hispanics Have Heard of Latinx, but Just 3% Use It," *Pew Research Center Report* (August 11, 2020), https://www.pewresearch.org/hispanic/2020/08/11/about-one-in-four-u-s-hispanics-have-heard-of-latinx-but-just-3-use it/. We use the term in this book for that reason.

125 Robert Pear, "Major Immigration Bill Is Sent to Bush," *The New York Times* (October 29, 1990), p. A1; see also Stephen Castles and Mark J. Miller, *The Age of Migration: International Population Movements in the Modern World* (New York: Guilford Press, 1993), p. 249.

126 Rodman D. Griffin, "Illegal Immigration," *CQ Researcher* 2, no. 16 (1992): 364.

127 U.S. Bureau of the Census, *1990 to 1998 Annual Time Series of Population Estimates by Age, Race, Sex, and Hispanic Origin* (January 2000), http://www.census.gov/population/estimates/county/casrh_doc.txt.

128 Ryan Baugh, "Table 3. New Lawful Permanent Residents by Region and Country of Birth: Fiscal Years 2017 to 2019," *Department of Homeland Security Immigration Statistics Annual Flow Report* (September 2020), p. 6, https://www.dhs.gov/sites/default/files/publications/immigration-statistics/yearbook/2019/lawful_permanent_residents_2019.pdf.

129 Ibid, p. 6.

130 "Quick Facts: USA, 2019" *U.S. Bureau of the Census.* Accessed online: https://www.census.gov/quickfacts/fact/table/US/PST045221.

131 Frey, "Census 2000 Shows Large Black Return to the South, Reinforcing the Region's 'White-Black' Demographic Profile."

132 Pew Hispanic: "A Statistical Portrait of U.S. Hispanics," *Pew Research Center* (February 2013). Accessed online: http://www.pewhispanic.org/2013/02/15/hispanic-population-trends/ph_13-01-23_ss_hispanics1/.

133 U.S. Census Bureau News, "Census 2000 Paints Statistical Portrait of the Nation's Hispanic Population," www.census.gov/press-release/www/releases/archives/population/00434/html.

134 Ibid.

135 Pew Hispanic: "A Statistical Portrait of U.S. Hispanics," *Pew Research Center* (February 2013). Accessed online: http://www.pewhispanic.org/2013/02/15/hispanic-population-trends/ph_13-01-23_ss_hispanics1/.

136 "Percentage of Hispanic Population in the United States in 2019, by State," *Statista*, https://www.statista.com/statistics/259865/percentage-of-hispanic-population-in-the-us-by-state/.

137 Ibid.

138 Alejandro Portes and Ruben Rumbaut, *Immigrant America: A Portrait* (Berkeley: University of California Press, 1990), p. 10.

139 Amanda Holpuch, "Migrant Deaths at US-Mexico Border Increase 17% This Year, UN Figures Show," *The Guardian* (August 5, 2017). Accessed online: https://www.theguardian.com/us-news/2017/aug/05/migrants-us-mexico-border-deaths-figures.

140 As reported in Charles Kamasaki and Paul Yzaguirre, "Black-Hispanic Tensions: One Perspective," paper delivered at the annual meeting of the American Political Science Association (Washington, D.C., August 29–September 1, 1991), p. 5. See also Castles and Miller, *The Age of Migration.*

141 Julia Preston, "Surge in Immigration Laws around the U.S.," *The New York Times* (June 23, 2008), www.nytimes.com/2007/08/06/washington/06immig.html.

142 Dan Anderson, "Times Topics: Immigration and Refugees," *The New York Times* (June 9, 2008), www.nytimes.com.

143 Randal C. Archibald, "Arizona Enacts Stringent Law on Immigration," *The New York Times* (April 24, 2010), p. 1.

144 Harriet Sinclair, "More Than 2 million Undocumented Immigrants Will Now Be Protected under California's Sanctuary Law," *Newsweek* (October 5, 2017). Accessed online: http://www.newsweek.com/more-2-million-undocumented-immigrants-will-now-be-protected-californias-679150.

145 Logan, "The New Ethnic Enclaves in America's Suburbs," a report by the Lewis Mumford Center for Comparative Urban and Regional Research (Albany, NY, 2002), p. 2; William H. Frey, *Melting Pot Suburbs: A Census 2000 Study of Suburban Diversity* (Washington, D.C.: Center for Urban and Metropolitan Policy, Brookings Institution Press, June 2001).

146 Edward L. Glaeser and Jacob L Vigdor, "Racial Segregation: Promising News," in *Redefining Urban & Suburban America: Evidence from Census 2000.*, ed. Bruce Katz and Robert E. Lang (Washington, D.C.: Brookings, January 31, 2003), pp. 211–234.

147 Jeffrey M. Timberlake and John Iceland, "Change in Racial and Ethnic Residential Inequality in American Cities, 1970–2000," *City & Community* 6, no. 4 (December 2007): 335–365.

148 Massey and Denton, *American Apartheid.*

149 Paul Jargowsky, *Stunning Progress, Hidden Problems: The Dramatic Decline of Concentrated Poverty in the 1990s* (Washington, D.C.: Brookings Institution Press, 2004), pp. 1–2.

150 Ibid., p. 1.

151 Paul A. Jargowsky and Rebecca Yang, "The 'Underclass' Revisited: A Social Problem in Decline," *Journal of Urban Affairs* 28, no. 1 (2006): 76.

152 Paul A. Jargowsky, "Concentration of Poverty in the New Millennium: Changes in Prevalence, Composition, and Location of High-Poverty Neighborhoods" (New York, NY: The Century Foundation & Camden, NJ: Rutgers Center for Urban Research and Education, 2015), p. 1.

153 Ibid., p. 4.

154 Ibid.

155 Ibid.

156 Ibid.

157 Ibid.

158 U.S. Bureau of the Census, *Statistical Abstract of the United States 2003*, Table 305, Crimes and Crime Rates, by Type of Offense: 1980 to 2001, p. 199.

159 Federal Bureau of Investigation, *Uniform Crime Reports, 1990–2003*. Accessed online: https://www.fbi.gov/services/cjis/ucr/publications.

160 "Violent Crime in the United States, 2009," *U.S. Department of Justice.*

161 "Crime in the United States: 2011," FBI Uniform Crime Reports (2011), http://www.fbi.gov/about-us/cjis/ucr/crime-in-the-u.s/2011/crime-in-the-u.s.-2011/violent-crime/violent-crime.

162 Ames Grawert, Cameron Kimble, "Takeaways from 2019 Crime Data in Major American Cities," *Brennan Center for Justice* (December 18, 2019), https://www.brennancenter.org/our-work/analysis-opinion/takeaways-2019-crime-data-major-american-cities.

163 Aaron Chalfin and John MacDonald, "We Don't Know Why Violent Crime Is Up. But We Know There's More Than One Cause," *The Washington Post* (July 9, 2021),

https://www.washingtonpost.com/outlook/we-dont-know-why-violent-crime-is-up-but-we-know-theres-more-than-one-cause/2021/07/09/467dd25c-df9a-11eb-ae31-6b7c5c34f0d6_story.html.

164 Ibid.

165 William H. Frey and Alan Berubé, "City Families and Suburban Singles: An Emerging Household Story," in *Redefining Urban & Suburban America: Evidence from Census 2000.*, ed. Bruce Katz and Robert E. Lang (Washington, D.C.: Brookings, January 31, 2003), p. 265.

166 Mark Abrahamson, *Global Cities* (New York: Oxford University Press, 2004), pp. 99–100.

167 Ibid., p. 101.

168 U.S. Bureau of the Census, *The Changing Shape of the Nation's Income Distribution, 1947–1998*, p. 3, Table 1 (published June 2000), http://www2.census.gov/prod2/popscan/p60-204.pdf.

169 Katherine Schaeffer, "6 Facts about Economic Inequality in the U.S.," *Pew Research Center* (February 7, 2020), https://www.pewresearch.org/fact-tank/2020/02/07/6-facts-about-economic-inequality-in-the-u-s/.

170 Ibid.

171 Nicholas Kristof, "Our Banana Republic," *The New York Times* (November 6, 2010).

172 Louis Uchitelle, "The Richest of the Rich, Proud of a New Gilded Age," *The New York Times* (July 15, 2007).

173 Calculated from "Figure A: Real Median Household Income by Race And Ethnicity," EPI Analysis of Current Population Survey Annual Social and Economic Supplement Historical Poverty Tables, cited by Valerie Wilson, "Racial Disparities in Income and Poverty Remain Largely Unchanged Amid Strong Income Growth in 2019," *Economic Policy Institute Working Economics Blog* (September 16, 2020), https://www.epi.org/blog/racial-disparities-in-income-and-poverty-remain-largely-unchanged-amid-strong-income-growth-in-2019/.

174 U.S. Bureau of the Census, *Table 11, Employment Status of Civilian Population, Sex, Race, and Hispanic Origin* (2005), www.bls.gov/html.

175 Ibid., Table A-2.

CHAPTER 7

Federal Programs, the Democrats, and the Politics of Racism

The Consequences of National Policies

By the end of World War II, there was a growing national concern about the condition of the nation's cities. The neglect of basic infrastructure brought about by the Great Depression and the war could be observed in the decay of business districts, the dilapidation of older housing stock, and the tattered state of roads, bridges, parks, and urban amenities. These problems seemed all the more urgent because of overcrowding. The wartime boom had brought a crush of new residents to cities, but housing was hard to find. At first, the suburban subdivisions seemed like a welcome safety valve, but while they grew, the cities slid ever deeper into decline. This was alarming because the industrial cities had always been the engines of the American economy, and thus their fate seemed inextricably tied to the nation's well-being.

Even before the war was over, congressional leaders from both political parties began to consider ways to address the sorry state of the cities. After several years of haggling over details, in 1949, Congress approved ambitious urban renewal and public housing programs, and over the next few years, these programs leveraged an astonishing amount of private investment—$35.8 billion by 1968.[1] Despite the best of intentions, however, the federal effort to help the cities failed in considerable measure because other federal policies were, at the same time, igniting a suburban housing boom and actively encouraging racial segregation. These deep contradictions virtually guaranteed policy failure because the left hand was trying to revive the cities while the right hand was undermining that effort.

Even the federal programs designed to help the cities often had exactly the opposite effect. The massive slum clearance projects financed by the urban renewal program razed low-income housing units faster than public housing

214

DOI: 10.4324/9781003175315-9

could be produced. The effect was to sharply reduce the supply of housing available to African American homebuyers and renters. All through the 1950s and 1960s, hundreds of thousands of low-income Black Americans were displaced, and they were forced either to play a game of musical slums or move into high-rise public housing projects that ultimately turned into architectural eyesores and deeply segregated neighborhoods. Because they were denied access to the suburbs by discriminatory policies implemented by the real estate industry and federal administrators, middle-class African Americans were forced into an intense competition for housing in neighborhoods already occupied by white homeowners. Meanwhile, federally insured loans made it possible for millions of white middle-class families to find new housing in the suburbs. Still, another federal program financed a national system of freeways that made it easy for suburbanites to commute long distances. When considered in their entirely, the mix of federal policies that affected metropolitan development intensified racial segregation in the cities and simultaneously subsidized white flight to the suburbs.

Although the federal government shifted course in the 1960s, the changes came too little and too late. Racial discrimination in the buying and selling of real estate was outlawed by the 1968 Civil Rights Act, and federal programs were enacted to make funds available to minority homeowners. But the pattern of extreme racial segregation between city and suburb was, by then, too firmly established to be easily reversed. A metropolitan pattern of rigid racial segregation was fixed in place, and the national government had helped to create it.

OUTTAKE

Highway Programs Contributed to the Decline of the Cities

It is inaccurate to use the phrase "national urban policy" when referring to the policies that have influenced urban development in the United States. There has never been a national policy for the cities. Instead, a mixed bag of uncoordinated programs has been adopted at different times and for different purposes. Although some of these programs profoundly impacted cities and urban regions, their urban effects were rarely given serious consideration, and even if they had, the political forces at work and the complexity of the governmental system in the United States would have made it virtually impossible to achieve a comprehensive and well-coordinated strategy of urban development.

Highway programs serve as an enlightening example. For decades, the federal government devoted massive resources to build a national highway system, but the powerful effects of that program on cities and urban areas were mostly ignored. Early in the twentieth century, the federal government began providing aid for state-constructed roadways as a way of connecting farmers to the national economic system and opening up rural areas for settlement. By the 1930s, federal aid had become focused on a more abstract objective of promoting the use of the automobile. The political muscle of the automobile industry expanded in step with its economic importance. The states established trust funds that relied primarily upon gasoline taxes, and federal legislation in 1934 established penalties for any state that used any auto taxes for other purposes than building and maintaining highways.

The federal role expanded enormously in 1956 when Congress declared the intention to create a 42,000-mile national system of interstate highways. As in previous years, the taxes used to finance the system were "disproportionately collected in cities and disproportionately spent outside of cities," which reflected the power of rural interests in state legislatures and the aims of the highway engineers. It also accorded with the thinking of President Eisenhower, who thought that an integrated system

of highways was important to the national defense because, in times of war, it would be easier to move troops and equipment. There was another consideration as well. It was widely thought that the concentration of populations and economic activity in cities made the United States vulnerable if nuclear warfare broke out. An influential city planner warned that urban areas had to decentralize or face disaster, saying that "If we delay too long, we may wake up some morning and find that we haven't any country, that is, if we wake up at all that morning." The lesson to be drawn is that even when the policymakers took some notice of the urban impacts of their policies, they considered these to be secondary if they mattered at all.

Sources: Quotations are from Owen D. Gutfreund, *20th Century Sprawl: Highways and the Reshaping of the American Landscape* (New York: Oxford University Press, 2004), p. 56; Robert M. Fogelson, *Downtown: Its Rise and Fall, 1880–1950* (New Haven, CT: Yale University Press, 2001), p. 392.

The Politics of Slum Clearance

Following World War II, a powerful and diverse coalition lobbied Congress to enact a federally funded slum clearance program. Local public officials and business leaders were alarmed by the condition of downtown business districts and nearby residential areas. Public housing administrators, labor unions, social workers, and liberal Democrats were concerned about the plight of the poor and argued that the residents of dilapidated neighborhoods had a moral right to adequate housing. Realtors, developers, financial institutions, and local business elites had entirely different reasons for favoring slum clearance. They were concerned not so much about the conditions of life in the slums as for the security of their own investments in inner-city property. Clearly, the widespread deterioration of commercial and residential areas threatened the economic vitality of the central cities. For this reason, the National Association of Real Estate Boards (NAREB) favored a federally funded program of urban renewal even though it maintained a venomous opposition to public housing programs, in large part because of the real estate industry's interest in preventing government competition with private developers and landlords.[2]

A coalition of groups important to the Democratic Party fought for the principle that public housing must be included in any urban renewal program funded by the federal government. Organized labor led the way in criticizing the real estate industry's fixation on its own bottom line. Local government officials represented by the U.S. Conference of Mayors, the National League of Cities, and the American Municipal Association lined up behind a program of urban renewal that included public housing. These groups formed an alliance powerful enough to prevent the legislation before Congress from being sabotaged by bickering over details. In the spring of 1949, Congress approved the Housing Act. Despite intense lobbying by real estate agents and their allies to throw out the public housing provision, it was kept in the final bill, but only by a razor-thin five-vote margin. The final version of the legislation was then passed by a bipartisan majority of northern Democrats, urban Republicans, and a few southern Democrats.[3]

In the 1949 Housing Act, Congress declared a national commitment to rebuild the cities, eliminate slums and blight, and provide decent housing for the nation's citizens. The preamble to the act, titled "Declaration of National Housing Policy," offered a sweeping statement about the need for a housing program:

> The general welfare and security of the Nation and the health and living standards of its people require housing production and relating community development sufficient to remedy the serious housing shortage, eliminate substandard and other inadequate housing through the clearance of slums and blighted areas, and the realization as soon as feasible of the goal of a decent home and suitable living environment for every American family.[4]

Business interests and the housing industry got what they wanted in the bill but were forced to accept public housing in the bargain. In the end, the housing bill received the endorsement of key business, real estate, and housing interests because the legislation gave control over the urban renewal and public housing programs to local public authorities. The result was a piece of legislation full of internal contradictions, with dire consequences.

Title I of the act empowered the Housing and Home Finance Agency (HHFA) to distribute grants-in-aid to help local urban renewal agencies absorb the cost of buying and clearing renewal sites. After this process was complete, urban renewal agencies were allowed to "write-down" the cost of the properties so they could be sold to developers at bargain prices. Because part of the "write-down" was covered by federal grants, it amounted to a direct subsidy to well-connected developers.

Tenants and slum dwellers displaced by renewal programs were supposed to be supplied with "decent, safe and sanitary dwellings." Title III of the bill, which funded low-rent public housing, authorized (but did not appropriate money for) the production of 810,000 government-subsidized housing units over a six-year period. This amounted to 10 percent of the estimated national need for new low-cost dwellings. Occupancy preferences were given for veterans and families displaced by Title I (clearance) activities. Federal administrators imposed per-room and per-unit cost limitations to prevent "extravagance and unnecessary" amenities and imposed tenant eligibility requirements to minimize competition with the private housing market and to ensure that public housing benefited only the neediest families. This provision was intended to keep the real estate industry content and in support of the Housing Act, as many private landlords were critical of federal funding for housing and the concept of public housing as such. Title III also did not appropriate any federal money for the maintenance of the units that were to be produced. Instead, it intended to finance maintenance through rental incomes. This proved to make sense while the cities were full and the demand for public housing was high. However, Title II of the Housing Act encouraged white families to leave the cities en masse.

In 1937, the Home Owners' Loan Corporation (HOLC) had created a rating system for neighborhoods throughout the United States, based on which the federal government would assess its "risk" for guaranteeing loans for new homeowners. The maps, which resulted from HOLC's risk assessment system, were not only used by the federal government itself but by the entire real estate industry, which included appraisers, loan officers, and real estate agents. They also coined the term "redlining," as HOLC would color-code neighborhoods on its maps based on its assessment of investment- and credit-risk: Green stood for "best," blue for "still desirable," yellow for "definitely declining," and red for "hazardous."[5] Potential home buyers interested in homes in these "hazardous" or redlined neighborhoods would be denied loans, and general structural investment projects would not be financed. Neighborhoods were persistently redlined based on the amount of minority residents.[6] HOLC's 1937 underwriting manual was more or less adopted in full by the FHA for determining the risk in mortgage insurance under Title II of the 1949 Housing Act. In it, the federal government clearly and openly discriminated against neighborhoods located in urban settings, as well as against communities of color. In terms of risk assessment, the underwriting manual stated:

"In general, factors which are vital in mortgage risk measurement in larger communities are sometimes of less significance in smaller communities. [...] Identical conditions, acceptable in smaller towns, are frequently unacceptable in larger communities."[7]

The manual did not go into specifics as to why exactly community size mattered for risk measurement, but it clearly implies an early preference for investment in small, suburban communities.

Even more disturbing, however, are the manual's criteria for its "rating of location," or, more specifically, its rating of "quality of neighborhood development":

> Areas surrounding a location are investigated to determine *whether incompatible racial and social groups are present, for the purpose of making a prediction regarding the probability of the location being invaded by such groups.* If a neighborhood is to retain stability, it is necessary that properties shall continue to be occupied by the same social and racial classes. A change in social or racial occupancy generally contributes to instability and a decline in values.[8]

Here, in essence, the FHA spelled out, verbatim, HOLC's redlining policy and adopted it as a key determination for who exactly would have access to the American Dream of homeownership and where these homes should be located. It thereby served a central function in laying the foundation for not just racial segregation but for the kind of hypersegregation which followed and which afflicted American cities and their residents for decades to come. In other words, the federal government was deeply complicit in race-based residential segregation across the country.

A 2018 study traced the persistent consequences of redlining over the past 80 years into the present day. The researchers found that redlining maps serve as direct predictors for a concentration of poverty in those same neighborhoods today. "Homeownership is the number-one method of accumulating wealth, but the effect of these policies that create more hurdles for the poor is a permanent underclass that's predominantly minority," John Taylor, president of the National Community Reinvestment Coalition, which conducted the 2018 study, told the *Washington Post*.[9] He added, "I think most people believe the problem is not with the rules but with the people. Most middle-class whites in America don't have empirical observations of what happens in underserved neighborhoods or understand the historical treatment of poor and minority communities."[10]

The trajectory of federal government policies had powerful consequences for communities of color across the United States that still reverberate today. For centuries, it prevented Black Americans from owning property at all, regarding their own bodies as property instead. In the twentieth century, when African Americans were finally entitled, on paper at least, to the same rights and liberties as white Americans, it still found ways to deny them access, among many other things, to one of the key factors for socioeconomic upward mobility: homeownership. With long-lasting effects: The wealth gap, even today, between Black and white families is significant: The net worth of white families was nearly ten times that of Black families in 2016.[11]

To add insult to injury, in 2018, the U.S. Congress passed a bill rolling back a portion of the 2008 Dodd-Frank Act, which had required credit unions and banks to disclose more specific data about their lending practices in order to root out any discrimination that might occur.[12] The surprising conviction, within the legislative and judicial branches of the United States government, that race-based discrimination is a thing of the past does not bode well for the future.

How Local Politics Shaped Urban Renewal

Local political and economic elites were far more concerned about the economic decline of central business districts (CBDs) than they were about slum residents. Business leaders and politicians were convinced that encroaching slums were responsible for the steady decline in property values and retail activity in the downtown areas. Despite the fact that the legislation seemed to favor residential development, right from the beginning, local renewal agencies placed a much higher priority on commercial development than low-income housing, a practice made possible by the flexible way federal administrators interpreted the provisions of the housing act. Guidelines issued by the HHFA defined any renewal project that allocated 51 percent or more of its funds to housing as a "100 percent housing" project. In its effect and intent, this standard gave local authorities permission to emphasize commercial development over other uses despite the "predominantly residential" language contained in the original legislation.

Public housing immediately ran into trouble. In the abstract, housing for low-income people might seem worthwhile, but at the local level, it ran into determined opposition. Experiences with housing legislation passed in the 1930s had already showed that it was likely there would be problems. In December 1946, when the Chicago Housing Authority (CHA) tried to move a few families of African American veterans into a public housing project built with funds from the housing act of 1937, white mobs jeered and threw stones. In August 1947, menacing mobs gathered to keep Blacks from moving into a project on the city's southwest side. A contingent of police was assigned to protect the Black families, and they stayed six months.[13] The CHA learned its lesson well and backed off any further attempts to integrate housing projects.

After the passage of the 1949 housing act, the Chicago experience was repeated in cities across the country. In city after city, local chapters of the NAREB organized opposition to public housing projects. In vitriolic campaigns, the opponents of subsidized housing played on fears that public housing might be used to promote racial integration. Between 1949 and the end of 1952, public housing programs were rejected by referenda in Akron, Houston, Los Angeles, and almost 40 other cities. Social and political realities at the local level made public housing a volatile issue. Local officials were acutely aware "there could hardly be many votes to be gained in championing the cause—and perhaps a great many lost."[14]

By contrast, slum clearance and economic redevelopment were programs that local political interests were happy to embrace. Seizing on redevelopment as a way to secure federal funds, in city after city, enterprising mayors managed to assemble powerful alliances to support the cause of redevelopment. Corporate executives were the most important members of the coalition, but other crucial participants were involved as well. Real estate and small business owners, metropolitan newspapers, and the construction trades unions lent their support. A prominent urban scholar, Robert Salisbury, observed that this "new convergence of power" that brought public power and private resources together turned urban renewal into an almost irresistible force capable of overwhelming all opposition.[15]

The programs financed by the Housing Act were perfect vehicles for mayors who wished to secure their personal political futures. After he was elected mayor of Chicago in 1955, Richard J. Daley forged a powerful civic coalition to launch an ambitious program to revitalize Chicago's downtown Loop and lakefront. In Boston, the candidate selected by the business-sponsored New Boston Committee defeated longtime machine boss James Michael Curley in the 1951 mayoral race, then backed the massive clearance of Boston's Italian West End and the construction of a government center. Ultimately, Boston's renewal program took 10 percent of the city's land area.[16] In 1950, St. Louis's mayor, Joseph Darst, received national publicity when his city became the nation's first to secure federal funding for urban renewal. Raymond Tucker, who replaced him in 1953, was even more aggressive in pushing clearance projects. He assembled a broad coalition that included all of the major corporations in the city—69 businesses in all—and managed to persuade them to raise $2,000,000 in private capital to help fund the local urban renewal agency. An almost identical alliance came together in New Haven, Connecticut, where the young Democrat Richard Lee won several terms by leading an ambitious renewal effort. Lee's political capital derived from his ability to marry the public resources made available through the program with the political and financial support of business leaders. Mayor Lee referred to this coalition as

> the biggest set of muscles in New Haven .... They're muscular because they control wealth, they're muscular because they control industries, represent banks. They're muscular because they head up labor. They're muscular because they represent the intellectual portions of the community. They're muscular because they're articulate, because they're respectable, because of their financial power, and because of the accumulation of prestige they have built up over the years as individuals in all kinds of causes.[17]

Mayors and business leaders tended to share the view that the economic fortunes of their cities depended on the health of the downtown. In the 1950s, the flight of the middle class to the suburbs was seriously undermining the economic viability of the inner cities. Because the CBD was the center of activity where the local business establishment held heavy real estate and business investments, it was only logical that businesses would try to protect their investments. The need for political visibility and campaign contributions from wealthy donors ensured that elected officials would favor downtown sites. Those areas were generally the oldest in the cities and therefore easily designated as officially "blighted" by the local urban renewal authority, the first step in a process that led to condemning and clearing property.

The members of the urban renewal coalition needed one another. Local officials coveted the investment capital and the public prestige the business community possessed. In turn, leaders in the business community realized that governmental authority was a necessary ingredient for a successful redevelopment effort. Public authority was, in the first instance, called on to apply for federal funds through an officially constituted urban renewal agency. The government's power of an eminent domain, which allowed it to condemn "blighted" property for a "higher" public use, was crucial for land assembly because individual property owners could not otherwise be compelled to sell. Finally, the unique ability of local renewal agencies to secure the necessary write-down subsidies and loans from the federal government made local officials and agencies indispensable to business leaders who wanted urban redevelopment. In this way, "this strange coalition"[18] became a singularly dominant force in local politics.

Over the years, the urban renewal program "engineered a massive allocation of private and social resources" in cities all over the United States.[19] Public funds were used to make downtown areas more desirable to investors. By 1968, private institutions had committed $35.8 billion in 524 renewal projects across the nation.[20] From 1953 to 1986, when the last money left in the pipeline was finally exhausted, over $13 billion in direct federal spending had been committed to urban renewal.[21] At the same time, the huge federal expenditures authorized by the National Defense Highway Act of 1956 provided hundreds of thousands of jobs and considerable profits to construction firms building limited-access highways through urban neighborhoods.

The clearance of neighborhoods associated with urban renewal and highway building soon ignited resistance and controversy. Although business leaders talked glibly about benefiting all the residents of the city through the provision of jobs and increases in business investment, it became painfully apparent that viable and even thriving neighborhoods were often destroyed in the process. In Boston, block after block of well-kept bungalows and row houses, grocery stores, barber shops, bakeries, and taverns—all the elements making up historic, safe, thriving Italian neighborhoods in Boston's West End—were leveled. *Blight* was such an ambiguous term that it could be and often was, applied even to healthy neighborhoods.[22]

All across the country, community protests called attention to the destruction caused by urban renewal and highway construction projects. According to one scholar, "development issues ... dominated the neighborhoods" in the 1950s and 1960s in the four cities he studied.[23] Despite the intensity and frequency of protests, however, in the end, neighborhoods won few victories. This poor record of success reflected the fact that the groups opposing renewal were small and often easily divided. The residents of neighborhoods put a priority on protecting their own turf but rarely saw any reason to expend scarce resources to help someone else. By astutely selecting renewal and redevelopment sites, urban renewal administrators found it easy to pursue a strategy of divide and conquer.

Atlanta provides an excellent example of how this kind of politics worked. Beginning in 1952, Atlanta's Metropolitan Planning Commission became concerned about the movement of African Americans into neighborhoods close to the CBD. In its report of that year, *Up Ahead*, the commission maintained that "from the viewpoint of planning the wise thing is to find outlying areas to be developed for new colored housing." The commission recommended, "public policies to reduce existing densities, wipe out blighted areas, improve the racial pattern of population distribution, and make the best possible use of central planned areas."[24] The actual goal, which was only thinly disguised by this rhetoric, was to move Blacks into areas farther from the downtown area and to secure land near the CBD for redevelopment.

The Central Atlanta Improvement Association, an organization that represented corporate interests, energetically promoted clearance. Corporate leaders took special care to obtain the support of the Chamber of Commerce, which represented smaller businesses. The Atlanta Real Estate Board was brought on board with reassurances that renewal would help maintain segregated housing patterns and that no public housing would be built on properties cleared by urban renewal. At the same time, the corporate and public leadership gained support from leaders of the Black community by promising that land would be made available for the construction of single-family, owner-occupied housing for Blacks well away from the downtown. Years later, downtown Atlanta was still undergoing massive clearance and reconstruction, and a huge enclosed mall called the Peachtree Center was slowly replacing the historic downtown.

The local renewal coalitions born in the 1950s used their political muscle to crush opponents. Although almost any city could be selected as a suitable example, San Francisco's single-minded pursuit of downtown renewal is especially revealing.[25] In 1953, the San Francisco Board of Supervisors approved a plan to clear several blocks adjacent to the financial district and south of Market Street. This area, with its market stalls, narrow passageways, and constant bustling activity, stood in the way of plans to remake the downtown into a collection of corporate, cultural, and tourist facilities. By the late 1950s, civic leaders had settled on a plan to clear the area for a sports arena and convention center that would be named the Yerba Buena Center. Planners envisioned that Yerba Buena would help support the city's financial district and become a magnet for further development.

This vision appealed to the scores of corporate giants located in the heart of the city, including Standard Oil of California, Southern Pacific, Transamerica

Corporation, Levi Strauss, Crown Zellerbach, Del Monte, Pacific Telephone and Telegraph, Bethlehem Steel, and Pacific Gas and Electric. Among the many financial institutions located in downtown San Francisco were Bank of America, Wells Fargo, Crocker National Bank, Bank of California, Aetna Life, John Hancock, and Hartford Insurance. During the 1960s, the buildings that housed these institutions utterly changed San Francisco's skyline. Twenty-three high-rises were constructed in downtown San Francisco between 1960 and 1972.[26]

The director of the San Francisco Redevelopment Agency, M. Justin Herman, became the "chief architect, major spokesman, and operations commander" for the massive renewal project. Under his leadership, the redevelopment agency hired several hundred professionals and dozens of consultants and applied for millions of dollars in federal urban renewal subsidies. Herman regarded even the mildest criticism of his project as an attempt by parochial interests to stand in the way of progress. In 1970, he was quoted as saying, "This land is too valuable to permit poor people to park on it."[27] He was cited in a major publication in 1970 as "one of the men responsible for getting urban renewal" renamed "the federal bulldozer" and "Negro removal":

> He was absolutely confident that he was doing what the power structure wanted insofar as the poor and the minorities were concerned. That's why San Francisco has mostly luxury housing and business district projects— that's what white, middle-class planners and businessmen envision as ideal urban renewal.[28]

Federal administrators turned a blind eye to the fact that the Yerba Buena Center project was being planned with no thought of building replacement housing for the people who lived in the area. During the summer of 1969, local residents challenged the project in federal court, arguing that the 1949 Housing Act required the renewal agency to find safe and suitable housing for people displaced by clearance. The judge who heard the case concluded that the secretary of the Department of Housing and Urban Development (HUD) "had not been provided with any creditable evidence at all" in regard to the redevelopment agency's plan to relocate residents.[29] Temporarily stopped in its tracks, the agency eventually agreed to increase the hotel tax in San Francisco in order to finance the construction of some low-income housing to absorb the area residents displaced by the Yerba Buena Center. Eventually, a series of court battles, plus the escalating costs of building the center doomed the project, and it was never built. It was a rare and widely celebrated victory for the opponents of urban renewal.

Organized opposition at the national level emerged in the early 1960s. Liberal critics viewed urban renewal as a "federally financed gimmick to provide relatively cheap land for a miscellany of profitable, prestigious [private] enterprises."[30] Conservatives were equally appalled by the results of the program. At its inception and through its early years, business leaders and politicians expected a miraculous reversal of central-city decline. The optimism soon turned into frustration. By the late 1960s, it took an estimated four years to plan a typical clearance project and an additional six years to clear the site. Frequently, by the time it was ready for redevelopment, the original plans had long been abandoned.[31] Even generous write-downs to lower the cost of acquisition often failed to entice developers. Meanwhile, blighted and slums continued to spread; indeed, it appeared that the displacement of residents only accelerated the deterioration of nearby neighborhoods.

Racial Segregation and "The Projects"

The public housing program turned out to be a cruel hoax because it promised to improve the lives of slum dwellers but instead made things worse. African Americans who moved to the cities in the great migrations of the twentieth century were often forced to crowd into rundown neighborhoods clustered near the urban core. Because much of the oldest and most dilapidated housing was located near CBDs, clearance projects displaced Black Americans more than anyone else. Critics coined the phrases "Black removal" and "Negro clearance" as a way of referring to the fact that two-thirds of the people displaced in the first eight years of the program were Black.[32] Economic and racial barriers left them no choice other than to move to another area much like the slum they had left behind: "Given the realities of the low-income housing market … it is likely that, for many families, relocation [meant] no more than keeping one step ahead of the bulldozer."[33] Thus a new game was added to the harsh realities of urban life—"musical slums."

Black families displaced by urban renewal clearance found their options to be few. They had the choice of either moving into public housing projects or to other slum areas, where they paid higher rents because the overall supply of low-rent housing units was rapidly dwindling. By the end of 1961, clearance projects had eliminated 126,000 housing units. The 28,000 new units that replaced them could house less than one-fifth of the 113,000 families and 36,000 individuals displaced by clearance.[34] There was a 90 percent decline in the supply of low-income housing within redevelopment areas during the first ten years of the program's operation.[35] Only $34.8 million of the urban renewal funds—less than 1 percent—was used for relocation assistance, placing a disproportionate share of the cost of the program on the slum residents who were forced to move.[36]

Their status as displaced slum residents conferred on Blacks "the dubious privilege of eligibility for public housing."[37] For potential renters, the problem was that public housing was basically designed to fail. The first and perhaps most important impediment was that eligibility was restricted to those who could not afford to rent on the private housing market. The real estate lobby would have tolerated no other policy. The insidious result was to concentrate those poor families together who had to fulfill eligibility conditions for public housing that made it almost impossible for them to improve their circumstances. Tenants who got jobs and increased their incomes were evicted. Already, in the 1950s, the concentration of families in poverty and the often punitive nature in which they were treated by the local housing authorities caused some residents of public housing projects to be prone to high levels of violence and juvenile crime. Over the years, public housing tenants were increasingly made up of "broken families, dependent families, and welfare families."[38] This was because the housing authorities were under pressure from the private housing market to prohibit better-off tenants from living in public housing. Until the Supreme Court struck down the requirement in 1968, some local housing authorities would also deem married couples of two-parent families ineligible for public housing.[39] The consequences of this were manifold: If the families whose incomes went up had been able to stay in their apartments by paying higher rents, the rise in social pathologies might have been moderated,[40] and the rental income they paid would have helped make public housing more economically viable. In retrospect, the clustering of poor families in public housing and the resulting concentration of poverty has been the root of criticism of public housing by many free-market proponents, who saw such housing as a "communist" ideation of sorts, and it gave conservatives in the 1980s ammunition to push harder against federally funded welfare programs, which, they argued, led to broken families and an inherent reliance on public assistance. In the end, however, it was the private market that restricted public housing so severely that it was never in a position to fulfill its social promises to its residents.

The second flaw was related to the fact that public housing projects almost always were built on sites carefully separated from more desirable parts of the city. This meant that "the projects" were often built in majority-Black neighborhoods. From the beginning, most public housing projects were segregated by the explicit policy in all but a few northern states. It is true that, nationwide, nonwhites accounted for only 38 percent of all public housing tenants in 1952 and 46 percent by 1961. Significant portions of the buildings were occupied by whites and were, for a time, considered desirable by young families headed by veterans, who received first priority.[41] However, strict racial segregation between projects was the universal norm. But by the time President John F. Kennedy signed an executive order forbidding the racial segregation of public housing projects in 1962, it could have little practical effect because by then the overwhelming majority of tenants in large cities were African American anyway; white families found it easy to find other housing, especially after the suburban boom ended the national housing shortage, but Black families did not. Thus, the public housing program had the perverse effect of reinforcing and intensifying the racial segregation that prevailed before it was adopted.

The third fatal flaw of the public housing program was that the units themselves were cheap and shoddily built. Everything about public housing served as a constant reminder to its tenants and to everyone else that this was a grudging welfare program. To save money on site preparation and construction costs, cities built clusters of high-density high-rise buildings. The African American writer James Baldwin might have been describing almost any of these projects when he referred to those in Harlem as "colorless, bleak, high and revolting."[42] Of course, big American and European cities are full of high-rises that command steep rents from affluent clientele, but such structures, especially when built cheaply, "were not suitable for poor people with big families."[43] It was difficult for parents to supervise children even when play facilities were available. Elevators were often broken and stuck, laundry rooms were many floors removed from tenants' apartments, and dark hallways and stairwells were poorly lighted even when bulbs were available. In addition, the housing authorities were expected to cover all operating costs through rental incomes from the tenants. Federal loans were only to cover the construction period and were unavailable thereafter. It was not until 1970, as many public housing authorities began to fail, and shortly before the famous Pruitt-Igoe public housing complex in St. Louis was demolished on national television, that the federal government agreed to contribute to operating costs of public housing.

The Cabrini-Green projects north of Chicago's Loop began as two-story brick row houses built to house war workers in World War II. All of the occupants were white. In 1958, these houses were replaced by 15 high-rise buildings, and another 8 were constructed in 1962. These 19-story rectangular monstrosities loomed over the surrounding neighborhoods. The same situation existed in New York City, where public housing typically rose to more than 20 stories. The Pruitt-Igoe project in St. Louis, built between 1954 and 1959, was composed of 2,762 apartments in 33, 11-story buildings on a 57-acre site. By the time the last building was completed, the project was already a community scandal.[44] By 1973, it had become an international symbol for the failure of American public housing. In that year, photographs that made *Life* magazine's "The Year in Review" showed the shocking spectacle of one of the buildings imploding from hundreds of charges of carefully placed dynamite. As a monument to a policy failure, the episode could hardly have been more dramatic and fitting: Explosives experts got the opportunity to hone their demolition skills on buildings that had been completed, with awards to the architectural firm, just 15 years before.

In 1965, Congress approved rent supplement programs as an alternative to public housing construction. The idea was that if the government paid part of the rent, low-income families would be able to choose their own housing on the private market. The Housing and Urban Development Act of 1968 required that a majority of privately constructed housing units built on redevelopment sites be reserved for low- and moderate-income families.[45] These steps began a long-term trend away from governmentally constructed public housing. Public housing and urban renewal met their effective demise in the 1970s. In 1974, urban renewal was merged into the Community Development Block Grant program. During the Nixon administration, public housing was allowed to wither away; dropping from 104,000 starts in 1970 to only 19,000 by 1974.[46]

A few years later, public housing was essentially abandoned when the Reagan administration eliminated low-income housing built by the government in favor of programs that subsidized landlords by giving housing vouchers to prospective tenants.

By the early 1970s, finally, some legal resistance to many housing authorities' blatant segregation tactics materialized. During the 1960s, civil rights activists in Chicago started to document patterns of segregation in the site selection for public housing construction by the CHA. In 1966, the Illinois chapter of the American Civil Liberties Union (ACLU) filed a class-action lawsuit against the CHA's site selection methods in federal district court. It argued that the vast majority of public housing sites selected by the CHA since at least 1950 had been in majority-Black neighborhoods, charging that the CHA had "deliberately chosen sites for such projects which would avoid the placement of Negro families in white neighborhoods."[47] This policy, the ACLU lawyers argued, violated the policy of the Department of HUD, as well as the 1964 Civil Rights Act. Dorothy Gautreaux, after whom the suit was named, was one of the four Black CHA tenants on whose behalf, along with two Black CHA housing applicants, the ACLU had filed the suit. Gautreaux was a civil rights activist herself. She had applied for CHA housing in 1953, and she argued that tenants were well aware of the CHA's policy of preventing Black tenants from moving into public housing in white neighborhoods, keeping a strict cap on the number of Black tenants allowed to move into the few "integrated" housing projects in the city. After the federal court found in Gautreaux's favor in 1969 and ordered the CHA to build "scattered site" housing throughout the city, in majority-white neighborhoods, HUD entered the lawsuit as a defendant, and it was litigated all the way up to the Supreme Court, as *Hills v. Gautreaux*. In 1976, the Supreme Court issued a consent decree, in which both parties came to an understanding without any admission of guilt on either side and ordered the CHA to move tenants from segregated housing projects with a high concentration to scattered sites throughout the city and the suburbs.

From this court-ordered desegregation of several Chicago public housing projects emerged the "Gautreaux Project." Since not all public housing families chose to move out of racially segregated projects in Chicago, researchers at Northwestern University started to compare the two groups—those who left the segregated projects on Section 8 vouchers and those who remained. While initial Gautreaux findings seemed to indicate that especially single mothers who left segregated CHA housing projects experienced significant social upward mobility, a follow-up study was more nuanced in its conclusions:

> Merely changing neighborhoods, even changing to much better
> neighborhoods, does not produce the kind of achievement-oriented successes
> in either generation that many had hoped for, although Gautreaux One
> children were able to sustain the residential successes of their mothers.
> Perhaps mobility programs need to go beyond merely placing families in

better neighborhoods and provide them with needed family and personal services and supports. But here it makes sense to think more broadly, since low-income families involved in mobility programs are not the only ones in need of these kinds of family-based supports.[48]

While, in general terms, the psychological factors that impact the well-being of Black Americans remain utterly under-researched, some scholars have found that African Americans residing in the south report higher levels of happiness well-being than their non-southern, urban counterparts.[49] This may seem surprising given the persistence of Jim Crow laws in the American South, and the general hostility to racial equality. At the same time, however, as discussed in earlier chapters, Black Americans experienced, and continue to experience, high levels of hostility by whites in the northern states as well. Instead of any big differences in behavior by the white population, for Black Americans, the proximity of close family and friends, which was by far the strongest predictor of personal happiness and satisfaction for Black Americans in a recent study, seems to be the key factor to determine comfort.[50] The Great Migration caused many Black families to leave tight-knit communities in the south and migrate to cities where they became more socially isolated. It therefore makes sense that we cannot only look at neighborhood quality as a predictor for social upward mobility for Black Americans. Instead, we also need to take into consideration the existence (or absence) of intimate social networks when determining well-being and social upward mobility.

National Policy and Suburban Development

In the decades after World War II, millions of white families moved from the cities to the suburbs. Suburban growth would have occurred with or without government policies that hurried it along. Operating on its own, the private real estate market would have supported, as it did in the past, a movement to the urban periphery. But by accelerating the pace of suburban development, the federal government guaranteed that central cities would quickly empty even while the suburbs prospered. The National Housing Act of 1934 and the Serviceman's Readjustment Act of 1944 made it possible for millions of American families to purchase their first suburban home. These programs were an unalloyed blessing for the white families who poured into the suburbs, but they also had other important consequences.

Until the Great Depression of the 1930s, the government played little direct role in housing provision. The notable exception was that the federal and state courts enforced restrictive covenants attached to property deeds; usually, such attachments restricted the sale of homes in urban neighborhoods to whites only. Restrictive covenants exerted a huge impact on the housing market, but the role of the courts was not considered to be a matter of government policy; rather, enforcement of the covenants was considered a private contractual matter between buyer and seller that the courts were occasionally called upon to mediate.

During the Great Depression, the federal government was prompted to intervene in the nation's housing market because it constituted a significant sector of the national economy. Second only to agriculture as an employer, during the depression, the housing industry experienced a sudden, devastating contraction. Before the stock market crash of October 1929, 900,000 new housing units came on the market each year, but in 1934 this number had fallen to one-tenth as many. Throughout the 1930s, housing starts lagged far behind the demand for new housing.[51] In Chicago, only 131 new housing units were constructed in all of 1933, compared with 18,837 in 1929 and 41,416 in 1926.[52] Across the nation, 63 percent of the workers in the housing industry were unemployed in 1933. Foreclosures on millions of mortgages brought hardship to homeowners and drove thousands of banks out of business. Something had to be done to keep millions of people from becoming homeless and to save the banking system.

The National Housing Act of 1934 created both the Federal Housing Administration (FHA) and the Federal Savings and Loan Insurance Corporation (FSLIC). The FHA assumed much of the risk in the housing market by insuring most of the value of home loans made by banks. The FSLIC insured individual savings accounts up to $5,000 (this level has since risen in a series of steps to more than $250,000). It was hoped that such insurance would inspire confidence by potential savers and investors, so people would be encouraged to put their savings into banks instead of in shoeboxes and under their mattresses. These savings accounts, in turn, would enable savings and loan institutions to invest more capital in the floundering housing market.

The most important provision of the housing act is Section 203, the basic home mortgage insurance program under which the bulk of FHA insurance has been written up to the present day. Fully 79 percent of all FHA-insured units from 1934 to 1975—about 9.5 million units representing a face value of more than $109 billion—came under the provisions of Section 203.[53] The act specified that 80 percent of the value of the property financed by banks would be insured through the FHA. (Later, through the Housing and Urban Development Act of 1974, this share was increased to 97 percent of the first $25,000 and 80 percent of the remaining value. Since then, the formula has been changed from time to time.) Under FHA guidelines, the low risk assumed by the lending institution permits the borrower to pay a low down payment, with the remaining principal and interest spread over a period of up to 30 years.

There were many different interpretations about the main purpose of the 1934 National Housing Act. Title I of the act provided FHA insurance for loans used for "permanent repairs that add to the basic livability and usefulness of the property."[54] Social welfare liberals saw Title I as a means of eliminating substandard living conditions in the central cities by providing low-interest, low-risk loans. City officials hoped Title I would entice affluent people to stay within the city limits and remodel their homes rather than move to new homes in the suburbs. Downtown business interests had a different goal in mind: They favored it because they thought it could shore up downtown property values. Most banks, savings and loan institutions, real estate agents, and contractors had another thing in mind entirely. They regarded Section 203 as a way to finance new construction in the suburbs. In lobbying for the housing act, they had agreed to Title I only as a compromise to facilitate quick congressional action.

Despite the impression one might get from reading the 1934 legislation, over the years, almost all the government's resources were devoted to promoting suburban housing development. Congress never appropriated much money to finance Title I repairs for existing property, but it provided generous support for the home insurance provisions of Section 203. Freed of most of the risk entailed in making a loan, banks were quick to liberalize loan terms. Table 7.1 shows how much more difficult it was to buy a home before the passage of the FHA program. In the 1920s, banks ordinarily required down payments of 30–50 percent and amortized the loan over a maximum of five years, often with a balloon payment (the remainder of the loan) due at the end. Savings and loan institutions, which amortized loans for up to 11 years, were slightly more generous. The FHA program changed all that, and in 1944, when Congress approved legislation making veterans eligible for special loan terms, loan terms for new housing became even more liberal. Under the FHA, a home buyer could get a 30-year mortgage with only 5 percent down. The VA allowed banks to finance a mortgage with no down payment at all. The FHA and VA

TABLE 7.1 Relative Burden of Loan Terms, 1920s and 1960s[a]

Decade and Lender	Terms
1920s	
Savings and loan association	60 percent of house value loaned for 11 years fully amortized
Bank or insurance company	50 percent of house value loaned for 5 years unamortized (balance due at end)
1960s	
Conventional lender	75 percent of house value loaned for 20 years fully amortized
FHA	95 percent of house value loaned for 30 years fully amortized

Note: [a] For a house equal to approximately 2.5 times the purchaser's annual salary.

Source: From *Shelter and Subsidies: Who Benefits from Federal Housing Policies,* Table *Studies in Social Economics* by Henry J. Aaron (Washington, D.C.: Brookings Institution Press, 1972), p. 77. Copyright © 1972. Reprinted with permission.

programs helped increase the federally insured share of the mortgage market from 15 percent in 1945 to 41 percent by 1954, and these programs provided an incentive for the banks to ease loan terms on conventional loans as well.[55] By the 1960s, the typical home loan could be obtained with a 25 percent down payment and was amortized over 30 years.

The FHA loan guarantee program fundamentally changed the home credit market. Between 1935 and 1974, more than three-fourths of the FHA-insured home mortgages financed new (as opposed to existing) housing.[56] The proportion of all homes that were owner occupied rather than rented increased from 44 percent in 1940 to 63 percent in 1970 and to 68 percent in 2002.[57] As shown in Table 7.2, more than one-third of all homes purchased in 1950 and

TABLE 7.2 Use of FHA- and VA-Insured Loans in the United States, 1950–2002

Year	Percentage of Private Housing Financed through the FHA or VA[a]
1950	35
1955	41
1960	26
1965	30
1970	50
1980	36
1990	26
1995	19
2002	14
2016	22.8

Note: [a] Data from 1950, 1955, and 1960 for all private-sector housing. Data from 1965 to 2002 for newly built, private-sector, single-family homes actually built and sold within the reporting year. These new methods are not strictly comparable; the percentages for all private-sector housing will tend to be somewhat smaller than for private-sector, single-family housing built and sold within the reporting year. This bias will tend to understate FHA/VHA financing for 1950, 1955, and 1960.

Sources: U.S. Bureau of the Census, Historical Statistics of the United States to 1970, Colonial Times to 1970, pt. 2 (Washington, D.C.: U.S. Government Printing Office, 1975), pp. 369, 641 (for 1950, 1955, 1960); Historical Statistics of the United States (Washington, D.C.: U.S. Government Printing Office, various years) 2003: pp. 611–612, Tables 943–945; 2002: pp. 591–592, Tables 921–923; 1999: pp. 724–725, Tables 1201–1202; 1998: pp. 718–719, Tables 1199–1201; 1993: pp. 718–719, Tables 1221, 1224; 1989: p. 715, Tables 1262–1263; 1987: p. 706, Tables 1273–1274; 1982–1983: p. 748, Tables 1341–1342; 1973: pp. 684–685, Tables 1156–1158; 1969: pp. 697, 698, Tables 1071, 1075; 2016: The Urban Institute, Housing Finance Policy Center, "Housing Finance at a Glance: A Monthly Chartbook" (Washington, D.C., February 2017), p. 8.

1955 were financed through the FHA or VA programs, and the proportion of new single-family home sales financed under these programs varied from a low of 26 percent (in 1960 and 1990) to a high of 50 percent (in 1970). In 1995, FHA/VA financed 19 percent of mortgages, and the proportion fell to 14 percent in 2002.[58] The declining reliance on FHA and VA loans in the 1990s occurred mainly because lending institutions began offering variable-rate and other creative forms of mortgage financing that made buying a home easier for almost everyone.

Virtually all of the new homes bought with FHA/VA loans were built in the suburbs. Throughout the 1940s and 1950s, the FHA displayed an overwhelming bias in favor of the suburbs; for instance, in its first 12 years, it did not insure a single dwelling in Manhattan. In part, this bias reflected a widespread cultural preference for less dense, single-family neighborhoods, which were normally found in the suburbs, over the denser, multiunit neighborhoods in the cities. But the roots of the FHA policy went beyond a simple matter of architectural form or geography. The real agenda was racial. FHA administrators were convinced that neighborhoods should be racially and ethnically segregated.

FHA mortgage insurance programs relied upon the private-sector lending institutions that processed the actual loans. From the beginning, the FHA absorbed the values, policies, and goals of the real estate and banking industries.[59] The staff of the FHA was drawn from the ranks of those industries, and it was only logical that the FHA's philosophy would parallel theirs. On the surface, it might seem that the "FHA's interests went no farther than the safety of the mortgage it secured."[60] This is a bit misleading because in the minds of FHA administrators, the soundness of a neighborhood and its racial makeup could not be separated. The FHA administrators took some pains to make sure that banks understood the connection. When it issued its underwriting manual to banks in 1938, one of the guidelines instructed loan officers to steer clear of changing or racially mixed areas.

Even the language itself was despicable, apart from the content it described. The underwriting manual tied property values and neighborhood stability to whether or not "incompatible racial and social groups" were present in any one neighborhood or whether there was any likelihood of them "invading" it. Neighborhood stability, according to the government's manual, was intimately dependent upon its ethnic [read white] homogeneity. It further suggested that the influx of people of color into any neighborhood would lead to "instability and a decline in values."[61] Once again, the federal government was not only tolerating but, in fact, mandating race- and ethnicity-based segregation and discrimination when it came to access to property and property ownership.

A revealing glimpse into how nuanced FHA administrators were in their race- and ethnicity-based discrimination can be gained by reading the language of a 1933 report submitted to the agency by one of its consultants, Homer Hoyt, a well-known sociologist and demographer at the time. He offered his view that land values and the racial composition of a neighborhood were closely linked and that it was possible to determine the desirability/undesirability of racial and ethnic groups with some precision. His list was, he said, an accurate representation of each group's "beneficial effect upon land values":

> If the entrance of a colored family into a white neighborhood causes a general exodus of the white people it is reflected in property values. Except in the case of Negroes and Mexicans, however, these racial and national barriers disappear when the individuals of the foreign nationality groups rise in the economic scale or conform to the American standards of living .... While the ranking may be scientifically wrong from the standpoint of inherent racial characteristics, it registers an opinion or prejudice that is reflected in land values; it is the ranking of races and nationalities with respect to their beneficial effect upon land values. Those having the most favorable effect come first in the list and those exerting the most detrimental effect appear last:
>
>   1. English, Germans, Scotch, Irish, Scandinavians
>   2. North Italians
>   3. Bohemians or Czechoslovakians
>   4. Poles
>   5. Lithuanians
>   6. Greeks
>   7. Russian Jews of lower class
>   8. South Italians
>   9. Negroes
>   10. Mexicans[62]

FHA administrators advised the developers of residential projects to draw up restrictive covenants barring sales to nonwhites before they applied for FHA-insured financing.[63] Banks were made to understand that even "a single house occupied by a black family in an urban neighborhood, even one tucked away on an inconspicuous side street, was enough for the FHA to label a predominantly white neighborhood as unfit for mortgage insurance."[64] Through such policies, the federal government required the banks to ensure that new subdivisions were strictly segregated. Thus, federal policy acted as a powerful instrument to establish the social and racial patterns that emerged in urban America in the postwar years.[65] Between 1946 and 1959, Blacks purchased less than 2 percent of all of the housing financed with the assistance of federal mortgage insurance.[66] In the Miami area, only one Black family received FHA backing for a home loan between 1934 and 1949, and there is "evidence that he [the man who secured the loan] was not recognized as a black" at the time the transaction took place.[67]

When the U.S. Supreme Court ruled in 1948 that racial covenants attached to property deeds could not be constitutionally enforced in courts of law, the

FHA was forced to amend its official policies. In 1950, the FHA revised its underwriting manual so it no longer openly recommended racial segregation or restrictive covenants. However, it did nothing to reverse the effects of its previous policies and took no actions to discourage real estate agents, developers, or lending institutions from discriminating against Blacks. Until the passage of the Housing Act of 1968, it was still legal and customary for real estate agents and mortgage institutions to discriminate on the basis of race. Indeed, any real estate agent who broke the industry's unwritten code on this issue was liable to be barred from membership in the local real estate association and from its listings services.

Under Title VIII of the Civil Rights Act of 1968,[68] Congress outlawed racial discrimination in housing. Its provisions were sweeping, barring discrimination in rentals and sales and in the provision of information about cost and availability, advertising, purchasing, construction and repair, and real estate services and practices. The statute mandated that each of the federal regulatory agencies involved with the real estate industry take affirmative steps to enforce both the spirit and the letter of the law.[69]

The 1968 legislation opened the suburban housing market to African Americans. Between 1970 and 1980, the number of Black Americans who lived in the suburbs grew by almost 50 percent, an increase of 1.8 million persons.[70] One in ten Black Americans living in the central cities in 1970 moved to the suburbs during this period, and the percentage of Black urban residents living in the suburbs increased from 16 to 21 percent.[71] In the 1980s, the trend continued. By the 1990 census, about 25 percent of urban Black families lived in the suburbs; about 85 percent of white families did so.

Black Americans who moved to the suburbs tended to have higher incomes than those who stayed behind.[72] Suburbanization undoubtedly expanded housing choices for Blacks, but those who moved to the suburbs in the 1970s and 1980s remained about as segregated from whites as they were before.[73] Black families moved mostly into older inner-ring suburbs, where they displaced white residents, much as they had previously in central cities.[74] These older suburbs tended to have many of the same problems as central-city neighborhoods. In general, the suburbs to which Black Americans moved had lower tax bases, higher debts, poorer municipal services, lower socioeconomic status, and higher population densities than did suburbs that were mostly white.[75]

Most suburban whites had little contact with suburban Blacks. In the mid-1980s, 86 percent of the white residents of suburbs lived in jurisdictions with a Black population of less than 1 percent.[76] Even those suburbs that were statistically mixed tended to be segregated internally, and there is evidence that segregation intensified in the 1980s.[77] Why was the racial segregation characteristic of the cities being replicated in the suburbs? Research indicated that discrimination, not social class or income, tended to determine residential location.[78] Socioeconomic differences between Blacks and whites accounted for less than 15 percent of the segregation among suburbs in 1980.[79] Research conducted in the St. Louis area indicated that in the 1980s, nonracial factors such as housing cost and economic factors seemed to be less important in explaining patterns of residential segregation than in any previous decade,[80] and this pattern persisted into the 1990s.[81]

Racial discrimination in housing continued even though the legislation had outlawed it, in part because the enforcement provisions of the 1968 legislation were weak. Rather than being granted positive responsibilities for identifying discrimination, the Department of HUD was permitted only to receive complaints initiated by individual citizens. By thus assuming a passive rather than an active enforcement role, it was easy for HUD to avoid controversy by treating each case as an isolated occurrence rather than as part of a general pattern. For citizens, the time and red tape involved in initiating a complaint were daunting, and thus all through the 1970s, the volume of HUD-processed complaints remained low. Interestingly, enforcement improved somewhat under a Republican president, Ronald Reagan, when HUD took steps to publicize the remedies available under the 1968 civil rights legislation. Partially, as a result, the number of complaints that HUD received rose sharply in the 1980s. Still, most citizens bypassed HUD and state and local civil rights agencies and went directly to the courts.[82] By focusing on individual remedies rather than on positive efforts to enforce compliance, the governmental role in fair housing enforcement remained small and inconsequential.

Some of the policies initiated by the federal government to eliminate housing discrimination benefited Blacks but in very limited ways. The Equal Credit Opportunity Act of 1974, the Mortgage Disclosure Act of 1975, and the Community Reinvestment Act of 1977 (CRA)[83] were intended to ensure that Black Americans receive equal consideration for home loans and that banks stop redlining areas where Black Americans lived. Following enactment of the 1974, 1976, and 1977 legislation, banks became the targets of protests and litigation of community groups challenging redlining practices. Rather than contest a blizzard of litigation and to avoid problems with federal regulators, many banks entered into negotiations with community groups. According to one estimate, by 1991, approximately $18 billion in urban reinvestment commitments had been negotiated in more than 70 cities across the country.[84] However, just as it would be premature to conclude that all redlining stopped, it would be inaccurate to assume all individual loan applications were judged strictly on their merits. Social change rarely comes that easily or rapidly. A 1992 study by the Federal Reserve Bank of Boston found that minorities were roughly 60 percent more likely to be turned down for a mortgage, even after controlling for 38 factors affecting creditworthiness, such as credit history and total debt.[85]

The spatial configuration of today's metropolitan areas still reflects a generation of policies that encouraged suburbanization and fostered racial segregation and discrimination. These policies had tremendous and long-lasting effects because they altered the dynamics of housing markets decisively in favor of suburban development and racial segregation. This did not only have immediate effects on the housing market itself but it also had many other far-reaching consequences for communities of color in terms of school districts, job opportunities, and general social upward mobility. There have been no sweeping attempts by the federal government to rectify this. The series of legislative remedies enacted in the 1960s and 1970s brought about a change in long-established practices, but these remedies could not be expected to work miracles. Social customs, racial attitudes, and socioeconomic path dependency still influence how social, racial, and ethnic groups become sorted out on the urban landscape and how many odds are stacked against them when it comes to accumulating wealth.

Suburbs, Highways, and the Automobile

As we have seen, for several decades, federal housing and urban renewal policies facilitated the racial and socioeconomic segregation of America's urban areas. The National Defense Highway Act of 1956 amplified the effects of these policies. The highway act financed the construction of a massive system of limited-access freeways that ensured the triumph of the automobile over urban mass transit. "Automobility" enabled Americans to implement a version of Henry Ford's solution to urban problems: "We shall solve the problems of the city by leaving the city."[86] Metropolitan highway systems made Ford's abandonment strategy practical, but mainly for affluent white families able to make the suburban move.

As its title implies, the 1956 National Defense Highway Act was justified partly on military grounds—two of its stated purposes were to aid the movement of troops and supplies and to help evacuate American cities in case of a nuclear attack. The main rationale, however, was that freeways would stimulate the economy by creating a national system of superhighways linking all of the major metropolitan areas in the nation. Within urban areas, the new expressways were expected to solve the growing problem of traffic congestion. A committee appointed by President Eisenhower asserted that suburbs were superior to cities and recommended that the new freeway system be used to decentralize American urban areas.[87] That is exactly what the new freeways did.

The 1956 legislation placed federal gasoline taxes and new excise taxes on tires and heavy vehicles into a Federal Highway Trust Fund. Congress established a grant-in-aid formula of a 90 percent federal and a 10 percent state share for construction. The federal government agreed to distribute the funds for the 42,500-mile system on the basis of need. Because costs in built-up urban areas were greater, urban areas got the lion's share of the funds.

In the years leading up to the legislation, urban planners debated with highway engineers about how a national highway system should be built. Urban planners wanted to design highway systems that would shape regional development and revitalize declining central cities. By contrast, highway engineers believed the new interstate system should be designed with one goal in mind: To move people and goods in the most efficient manner from point A to point B. This meant, in effect, that freeways would be routed directly from the suburbs to the central cities, and whatever got in the way would have to go. The engineers got their way. The 1956 act was written so that the funds allocated by the federal government would be administered by state highway departments with no input from urban planners. As one historian put it, "Since federal and state road engineers controlled the program, they had few incentives to include urban renewal, social regeneration, and broader transportation objectives in the programming."[88] When highways were built through urban areas, state highway planners chose routes without reference to their effects on existing neighborhoods.

Laying wide ribbons of concrete had different effects in crowded cities than in the open countryside. As the highway builder Robert Moses said in a speech before the National Highway Users Conference in 1964, "You can draw any kind of picture you like on a clean slate ... but when you operate in an overbuilt metropolis, you have to hack your way with a meat axe."[89] The meat axe approach turned out to be the main method Moses used to build his highways, displacing 250,000 people in the New York City area alone.[90] Because the highway engineers wanted to cause the least disruption to private commercial land values, highways were routed through residential areas, especially those with the cheapest housing occupied by poor people and minorities.[91] The program was justified not only as highway building but also as slum clearance. According to one estimate, the uncompensated loss to city residents who were displaced averaged 20–30 percent of one year's income.[92]

The methods used to ram freeways through urban areas left a damaging imprint that lingers to the present day. The highways took land off the tax rolls, destroyed intact neighborhoods, and separated downtown areas off from their waterfronts. In St. Louis, Interstate 70 erected a barrier between the Mississippi River waterfront from its downtown that made downtown revitalization difficult. By dividing the South Bronx from the rest of the city, the Cross-Bronx Expressway in New York helped turn the South Bronx into one of the most disadvantaged neighborhoods in the country. Scholars estimate that the unsightliness of the Fitzgerald Expressway in Boston reduced surrounding property values by about $300 million.[93] In 2004, after more than 15 years of work and more than $15 billion in funding, Boston completed a massive project to tear down the expressway and replace it with an underground tunnel. The land once occupied by the freeway was turned into a park.

The meat axe approach favored by the engineers provoked "freeway revolts" all across the nation.[94] One of the first victories for opponents came in 1959 when San Franciscans successfully prevented the completion of the Embarcadero Freeway. If the protests had failed, a freeway would today run along the shores of the San Francisco Bay, making the later development of such tourist attractions as Ghirardelli Square and the Wharf almost impossible.

Protests forced highway planners to become more sensitive to aesthetic and social considerations, but not before irreversible harm had been done to hundreds of urban neighborhoods and waterfronts.

By the 1980s, the price tag for building the interstate system exceeded $100 billion. While highway building received huge subsidies year in and year out, urban mass transit was starved. Unlike Europe, where gasoline taxes had always been used to help support mass transit, federal gas taxes in the United States could not be allocated for that purpose until 1975. Funding for urban mass transit gradually increased after the mid-1970s but remained small. Senator Gaylord Nelson of Wisconsin estimated that up to the 1980s, 75 percent of government expenditures for transportation in the United States in the postwar period had been spent on highways and roads, but only 1 percent was allocated to urban mass transit (most of the rest was spent for railroads and shipping).[95]

The result of these policies is that Americans depend on the automobile for urban travel more than people in any other nation. Although other advanced industrial nations such as Germany, Britain, and Japan embraced the automobile, they also maintained modern systems of mass transit as workable alternatives, despite the fact that automobile use has increased sharply in those countries. In the United States, by contrast, between 1950 and 1977, as the volume of automobile traffic on urban roads more than tripled, urban mass transit ridership declined by over half, and it has not rebounded since. For the United States as a whole, only 4 percent of workers used public transit to commute to work in 2000—a decline from a peak of 5.4 percent in 1983.[96] In all but a handful of cities in the Northeast, notably New York City, which has higher public transit ridership rates but is grappling with a 100-year old subway system in dire need of updating, less than 5 percent of workers use mass transit.

In the 1990s, concerns about urban air pollution and long commuting patterns emerged on the national policy agenda, in considerable part because Democrats enjoyed majorities in Congress. In 1992, Congress passed the Intermodal Surface Transportation Efficiency Act (ISTEA, commonly referred to as "ice tea").[97] The significance of ISTEA is that it took substantial authority over interstate highway funds from politically insulated state transportation departments, which had always been dominated by highway engineers, and put decisions about urban transportation systems into the hands of metropolitan planning organizations (MPOs). Governed by delegates representing municipal governments within urban regions, MPOs assumed authority over funding categories designed to reduce auto congestion and improve air quality.

The ISTEA legislation encouraged regional transportation planning by "flexing" federal highway funds, a process that allowed a portion of motor vehicle taxes to be spent on mass transit and even bicycle and pedestrian uses if local transportation planners chose to. Between the fiscal year 1992 and fiscal year 1999, $33.8 billion was available for transfer from transportation programs to transit projects, but local planners decided to transfer only 12.5 percent, or

TABLE 7.3 Commuting Patterns 1990–2006, Selected Metropolitan Areas		
	Percentage Public Transit 1990	**Percentage Public Transit 2006**
Boston	10.6	8.9
Chicago	13.7	10.8
Dallas	2.4	1.6
Denver	4.2	4.2
Los Angeles	4.6	4.9
New York	26.6	26.2
St. Louis	3.0	2.4
San Francisco	9.3	9.2

Note: Urban area definitions in 2006 are slightly larger than those previously used, and therefore include more low-transit ex-urban areas than before. However, this method does not change ridership statistics significantly.

Source: 1990 data, U.S. Bureau of the Census, Summary File 3, Transit Ridership Share 1990 (July 2004), www.census.gov.

$4.2 billion, of this amount. Some states, such as New York, Massachusetts, California, and Oregon, transferred more than one-third of highway funds available to them to transit use; others transferred little or none.[98]

The precedent set for local flexibility was carried over in the 1998 Transportation Equity Act for the Twenty-first Century (TEA-21), which replaced ISTEA. Under this legislation, highway builders were required to submit studies of the air quality effects for major new federally funded projects. But despite the new efforts to encourage the funding of public transportation, as shown in Table 7.3, the proportion of commuters using automobiles rose only slightly from 1990 to 2006, and for most metropolitan areas, less than 4 percent of commuters used mass transit. Improvements in mass transit systems might improve these numbers, but even after the 1998 legislation, adequate funding for that purpose was not made available to most transit authorities. On average, state and local governments still provided 90 percent of the funds for mass transit systems.

In 2008, sharply rising gasoline prices provided incentives for people to reduce the use of their cars. As gas prices climbed to a national average of more than $4 for regular gasoline during that summer, buses, interurban trains, and light-rail systems became packed with riders. Cities such as New York and Boston, with their well-developed transit systems, showed an increase of 5 percent or more, but by far the largest increases in ridership, in the 10–15 percent range, occurred in urban areas that have been the most dependent on the automobile. However, in most metropolitan areas, it will be difficult to significantly change transit patterns. Mass transit systems are not developed well enough to conceivably absorb more than a very small fraction of commuters, even if they run full all the time. In places like Denver, St. Louis, and any number of other cities, light-rail systems are important for transporting visitors to and from airports and for bringing fans to downtown ball games and other events, but they do not and cannot carry a large proportion of daily commuters. As a result of decades of investment in highway systems, urban transportation systems are well established, and commuting habits are basically fixed. Any significant changes will require very costly infrastructure investments that will take years to complete.

Mass transit systems tend to be chronically underfunded. During the financial crisis of 2008–2009, several metropolitan areas reduced service on their transit systems. The irony is that fiscal problems were occurring at the same time that ridership had increased. This was because only about one-fifth of the revenues from mass transit systems come from fares; the remaining portion is raised through state and local taxes, and these were sharply declining. In early 2009, the Metropolitan Transit Authority of New York City was trying to close a $1.2 billion budget gap. In the St. Louis area, officials were temporarily closing 2,300 bus stops, a move that threatened to raise unemployment levels by stranding workers who relied on the system. Likewise, transit authorities, almost everywhere, were considering fare increases and service cuts.[99]

The summer of 2017 in New York City was dubbed the "MTA's Summer of Hell," after a mass amount of derailings and massive delays throughout the summer months, especially for commuters from the outer boroughs, and New York Governor Cuomo's declaration of a state of emergency at the state of the MTA's subway system. Cuomo pledged one million dollars in subway repair funds for the MTA,[100] which will hardly be enough to foot the bill for the necessary improvements.

Local officials looked to the federal government with high expectations that help was on the way. The American Recovery and Reinvestment Act of 2009, signed into law by President Obama on February 17, 2009, made $27.5 billion available for surface transportation, highways, roads, and bridges. As part of the administration's "green" initiative, about $12 billion was reserved for mass transit. Because the program was regarded mainly as a jobs initiative, federal administrators indicated that the funds had to be spent only on infrastructure projects such as new train cars, track repair, and station renovations.[101] These measures were likely to improve the quality of service, but they would do nothing for the most basic long-term problem for mass transit in the United States: A funding system that worked against investments in systems that might appreciably alter transit patterns in metropolitan areas.

President Biden's 2021 massive infrastructure bill is expected to allocate $39 billion to public transit networks across the country, many of which are in dire need of updating. According to a report by the Associated Press, the Department of Transportation currently estimates a massive repair backlog within public transit systems across the country, which includes "more than 24,000 buses, 5,000 rail cars, 200 stations, and thousands of miles of track and power systems."[102] In addition, it would allocate an additional $66 billion to address Amtrak's maintenance backlog, with a special focus on Amtrak's most active section of rail—the Northeast Corridor. Taken together, the $39 billion for public transit systems and the $66 billion to be allocated to Amtrak cannot rival the whopping $110 billion earmarked in the bill for the repair of roads and bridges.[103] The Biden administration stated in August 2021 that the $40 billion out of that $110 billion reserved for bridge repair represents the largest financial investment by the federal government toward bridges since the 1956 Interstate Highway Act. As of August 2021, the bill has passed the Senate with a bipartisan majority but still faces some challenges in the House. If passed, it would mean a huge relief, especially to the budgets of public transit systems across the country, which have been financially strained even more than before by the COVID-19 pandemic, which cost them additional ridership. Whether the bill would be enough to help combat the ever more serious consequences of climate change is another question.

The Damaging Effects of National Policies

It is a tragic irony that the urban programs initiated after World War II contributed to racial segregation and discrimination. While urban renewal clearance programs bulldozed slum housing, public housing projects segregated Black Americans more than ever. Meanwhile, white middle-class Americans were paid, in essence, to move to the suburbs, and expensive new freeway systems eased their commute to their jobs in the center city. For decades, millions of white middle-class families were able to secure loans guaranteed by the federal government. It allowed them to move into new suburban developments, where housing values appreciated. For white middle-class America in the postwar period, the home became the principal source of family worth and savings, money that could be invested in a child's education, in a bigger or newer house, or saved for retirement. Until the late 1940s, the federal policy excluded African Americans from federal home loan programs, and it took until the late 1960s, when open-housing legislation was passed, for African American families to be able to enter the real estate market in any meaningful sense.

With or without federal programs, a high degree of residential segregation would have evolved in metropolitan areas, as there had never been any meaningful effort, locally or federally, to address systemic racism, let alone begin to combat it. But if federal housing programs had not actively discouraged banks from lending to African Americans, middle-class African American homeowners would have been able to find affordable and desirable housing by buying new homes. With this dynamic in operation, the presence of African Americans in a neighborhood would not have become so automatically equated, as signaled by the federal government, with neighborhood changes and declining property values. Equally important, if African Americans had been able to buy homes wherever they chose much sooner, they also would have been able to invest in the future. For decades, most African Americans were denied this crucial means of life savings and upward mobility.

Endnotes

1 John H. Mollenkopf, "The Post-War Politics of Urban Development," in *Marxism and the Metropolis: New Perspectives on Urban Political Economy*, ed. William K. Tabb and Larry Sawers (New York: Oxford University Press, 1978), p. 140.

2 Mark Gelfand, *A Nation of Cities: The Federal Government and Urban America, 1933– 1965*, Urban Life in America Series (New York: Oxford University Press, 1975), p. 14.

3 See Nathaniel S. Keith, *Politics and the Housing Crisis since 1930* (New York: Universe Books, 1973), pp. 41–100.

4 Housing Act of 1949, Public Law 81–171, Preamble, sec. 2, 81st Cong. (1949).

5 Bruce Mitchell and Juan Franco, "HOLC Redlining Maps: The Persistent Structure of Segregation and Economic Inequality," *NCRC Research* (March 20, 2018), p. 5, https://ncrc.org/wp-content/uploads/dlm_uploads/2018/02/NCRC-Research-HOLC-10.pdf.

6 Ibid.

7 *Underwriting Manual: Underwriting and Valuation Procedure Under Title II of the National Housing Act*, Federal Housing Administration (Washington, D.C.: Revised 1938), 604.

8 Ibid, 937, emphasis added.

9 Tracy Jan, "Redlining Was Banned 50 Years Ago. It's Still Hurting Minorities Today," *The Washington Post* (March 28, 2018), https://www.washingtonpost.com/news/wonk/wp/2018/03/28/redlining-was-banned-50-years-ago-its-still-hurting-minorities-today/.

10 Ibid.

11 Tracy Jan, "White Families Have Nearly 10 Times the Net Worth of Black Families. And the Gap Is Growing," *The Washington Post* (September 28, 2017), https://www.washingtonpost.com/news/wonk/wp/2017/09/28/black-and-hispanic-families-are-making-more-money-but-they-still-lag-far-behind-whites/.

12 Tracy Jan, "The Senate Rolls Back Rules Meant to Root Out Discrimination by Mortgage Lenders," *The Washington Post* (March 14, 2018), https://www.washingtonpost.com/news/wonk/wp/2018/03/14/the-senate-rolls-back-rules-meant-to-root-out-discrimination-by-mortgage-lenders/.

13 Martin Meyerson and Edward C. Banfield, *Politics, Planning, and the Public Interest* (New York: Free Press, 1955).

14 Leonard Freedman, *Public Housing: The Politics of Poverty* (New York: Holt, Rinehart and Winston, 1969), p. 55.

15 Robert H. Salisbury, "The New Convergence of Power in Urban Politics," *Journal of Politics* 26, no. 4 (November 1964): 775–797.

16 Mollenkopf, "The Post-War Politics of Urban Development," p. 138.

17 Quoted in Robert A. Dahl, *Who Governs: Democracy and Power in an American City* (New Haven, CT: Yale University Press, 1961), p. 136. For another insightful example of the use of urban renewal by political entrepreneurs, see Jewel Bellush and Murray Hausknecht, "Urban Renewal and the Reformer," in *Urban Renewal: People, Politics and Planning,* ed. Jewel Bellush and Murray Hausknecht (Garden City, NY: Doubleday, Anchor Books, 1967), pp. 189–197.

18 Gelfand, *A Nation of Cities,* p. 161.

19 Mollenkopf, "The Post-War Politics of Urban Development," p. 140.

20 Ibid., p. 138.

21 Williamson, Imbroscio, and Alperovitz, *Making a Place for Community,* p. 76.

22 Herbert J. Gans, *The Urban Villagers: Group and Class in the Life of Italian-Americans* (New York: Free Press, 1962), Chapter 13.

23 John H. Mollenkopf, "On the Causes and Consequences of Neighborhood Political Mobilization," paper delivered at the Annual Meeting of the American Political Science Association (New Orleans, September 4–8, 1973).

24 Quoted in Clarence N. Stone, *Economic Growth and Neighborhood Discontent: System Bias in the Urban Renewal Program of Atlanta* (Chapel Hill: University of North Carolina Press, 1976), pp. 48–49.

25 See Chester Hartman et al., *Yerba Buena: Land Grab and Community Resistance in San Francisco* (San Francisco: Glide, 1974). The following material on the Yerba Buena controversy draws on this excellent book. In most cases, citations are limited to quotations or specific data.

26 Ibid., p. 31.

27 Ibid., p. 19.

28 Ibid., p. 190.

29 Ibid., p. 128.

30 National Commission on Urban Problems, *Building the American City* (New York: Praeger, 1969), p. 153. This commission, appointed by the president, was established in January 1967 and headed by former Illinois senator and longtime urban policy advocate Paul H. Douglas.

31 Ibid., pp. 164–165.

32 See Martin Anderson, *The Federal Bulldozer: A Critical Analysis of Urban Renewal, 1949–1962* (Cambridge, MA: MIT Press, 1964), p. 65; compare Rossi and Dentler, *The Politics of Urban Renewal,* p. 224.

33 Chester Hartman, "The Housing of Relocated Families," in *Urban Renewal: The Record and the Controversy,* ed. James Q. Wilson (Cambridge, MA: MIT Press, 1966), p. 322, as reprinted from *Journal of the American Institute of Planners* 30, no. 4 (November 1964): 266–286.

34 Anderson, *The Federal Bulldozer,* pp. 65–66; see also Bellush and Hausknecht, "Urban Renewal and the Reformer," p. 13.

35 Anderson, *The Federal Bulldozer,* p. 65.

36 Mollenkopf, "The Post-War Politics of Urban Development," p. 140.

37 Freedman, *Public Housing,* p. 140.

38 Lawrence M. Friedman, *Government and Slum Housing: A Century of Frustration* (Chicago, IL: Rand McNally, 1968), p. 121.

39 Cynthia Gordy, "Welfare, Fathers and Those Persistent Myths," *The Root* (June 17, 2011), https://www.theroot.com/welfare-fathers-and-those-persistent-myths-1790864434.

40 Freedman, *Public Housing,* p. 111.

41 Friedman, *Government and Slum Housing,* p. 123.

42 James Baldwin, *Nobody Knows My Name* (New York: Dial Press, 1961), p. 63, quoted in Freedman, *Public Housing,* p. 117.

43 Friedman, *Government and Slum Housing,* p. 121.

44 Lee Rainwater, *Behind Ghetto Walls: Black Families in a Federal Slum* (Chicago, IL: Aldine, 1970).

45 Housing and Urban Development Act of 1968, Public Law 90–448, 90th Cong. (1968).

46 U.S. Department of Housing and Urban Development, *1974 Statistical Yearbook of the U.S. Department of Housing and Urban Development* (Washington, D.C.: U.S. Government Printing Office, 1976), p. 104.

47 Quoted in: Debra Shore, "The Houses That Gautreaux Built," *The University of Chicago Magazine* 87, no. 3 (February 1995), https://magazine.uchicago.edu/9502/ Feb95Gautreaux.html.

48 Anita Zuberi and Greg J. Duncan, "Mobility Lessons from Gautreaux and Moving to Opportunity," *Northwestern Journal of Law & Social Policy* 1, no. 1 (Summer 2006): p. 119.

49 Robert Joseph Taylor, Linda M. Chatters, Cheryl Burns Hardison, and Anna Riley, "Informal Social Networks and Subjective Well-Being among African Americans," *Journal of Black Psychology* 27, no. 4 (November 2001): 452.

50 Ibid., p. 453.

51 Stephen David and Paul Peterson, eds., *Urban Politics and Public Policy: The City in Crisis* (New York: Praeger, 1973), p. 94.

52 Charles Abrams, *The Future of Housing* (New York: HarperCollins, 1946), p. 213.

53 Bureau of National Affairs, *The Housing and Development Reporter* (Washington, D.C.: Bureau of National Affairs, 1976).

54 Ibid.

55 Calculated from data in Congressional Quarterly Service, *Housing a Nation,* p. 6.

56 U.S. Department of Housing and Urban Development, *1974 Statistical Yearbook of the Department of Housing and Urban Development,* pp. 116–117.

57 U.S. Bureau of the Census, *Historical Statistics of the United States, Colonial Times to 1970,* pt. 1, Bicentennial ed. (Washington, D.C.: U.S. Government Printing Office, 1975), p. 646; for 2002 data, Danter Company, www.danter.com/statistics/homeown. htm.

58 Compiling reliable statistics on FHA/VA loans is difficult because of inconsistent data over time. The most accessible source is the *Statistical Abstract of the United States* (Washington, D.C.: U.S. Government Printing Office) for various years.

59 For a discussion of this phenomenon, see Murray Edelman, *The Symbolic Uses of Politics,* 7th ed. (Champaign: University of Illinois Press, 1976), pp. 44–76. We are indebted to Jeffrey Gilbert for several of the ideas contained in this section.

60 Michael Stone, "Reconstructing American Housing" (unpublished manuscript), quoted in Chester W. Hartman, *Housing and Social Policy,* Prentice Hall Series in Social Policy (Upper Saddle River, NJ: Prentice Hall, 1975), p. 30.

61 Quoted in Brian J. L. Berry, *The Open Housing Question: Race and Housing in Chicago, 1966–1976* (Cambridge, MA: Ballinger, 1979), p. 9.

62 Quoted in ibid., pp. 9, 11.

63 Luigi M. Laurenti, "Theories of Race and Property Value," in *Urban Analysis: Readings in Housing and Urban Development*, ed. Alfred N. Page and Warren R. Seyfried (Glenview, IL: Scott Foresman, 1970), p. 274.

64 Richard Moe and Carter Wilkie, *Changing Places* (New York: Henry Holt, 1997), p. 48.

65 Charles Abrams, quoted in Norman N. Bradburn, Seymour Sudman, and Galen L. Gockel, *Side by Side: Integrated Neighborhoods in America* (Chicago, IL: Quadrangle Books, 1971), p. 104.

66 Gelfand, *A Nation of Cities*, p. 221.

67 Nathan Glazer and David McEntire, eds., *Housing and Minority Groups* (Berkeley: University of California Press, 1960), p. 140.

68 Public Law 90–284, 90th Cong. (1968), Title VIII ("Fair Housing"), sec. 805.

69 D.C. Public Interest Research Group (DCPIRG), Institute for Self-Reliance, and Institute for Policy Studies, *Redlining: Mortgage Disinvestment in the District of Columbia* (Washington, D.C.: Authors, 1975), p. 3.

70 U.S. Department of Housing and Urban Development, *1974 Statistical Yearbook of the Department of Housing and Urban Development*, pp. 116–117.

71 Thomas A. Clark, "The Suburbanization Process and Residential Segregation," in *Divided Neighborhoods: Changing Patterns of Racial Segregation*, ed. Gary A. Tobin (Newbury Park, CA: Sage, 1987), p. 115; Larry Long and Diane Deare, "The Suburbanization of Blacks," *American Demographics* 3 (1981), cited in Douglas S. Massey and Nancy A. Denton, "Suburbanization and Segregation in U.S. Metropolitan Areas," *American Journal of Sociology* 94, no. 3 (November 1988): 592–626.

72 Kenneth T. Jackson, *Crabgrass Frontier: The Suburbanization of the United States* (New York: Oxford University Press, 1985), p. 205.

73 John R. Logan and Harvey L. Molotch, *Urban Fortunes: The Political Economy of Place* (Berkeley: University of California Press, 1987), p. 195.

74 Clark, "The Suburbanization Process and Residential Segregation," pp. 115–137.

75 Massey and Denton, "Suburbanization and Segregation in U.S. Metropolitan Areas," pp. 592–626.

76 Logan and Molotch, *Urban Fortunes*, p. 194.

77 Douglas S. Massey and Mitchell L. Eggers, "The Spatial Concentration of Affluence and Poverty during the 1970s," *Urban Affairs Quarterly* 29, no. 2 (December 1990): 299–315. See also S. Roberts, "Shifts in 80's Failed to Ease Segregation," *The New York Times* (July 15, 1992), pp. B1–B3.

78 John F. Kain, "Housing Market Discrimination and Black Suburbanization in the 1980's," in *Divided Neighborhoods: Changing Patterns of Racial Segregation*, ed. Gary A. Tobin (Newbury Park, CA: Sage, 1987), p. 68.

79 John Farley, *Segregated City, Segregated Suburbs: Are They Products of Black-White Socioeconomic Differentials?* (Edwardsville: Southern Illinois University, 1983), cited in Joe T. Darden, "Choosing Neighbors and Neighborhoods: The Role of Race in Housing Preference," in *Divided Neighborhoods: Changing Patterns of Racial Segregation*, ed. Gary A. Tobin (Newbury Park, CA: Sage, 1987), p. 16.

80 John F. Farley, "Race Still Matters: The Minimal Role of Income and Housing Cost as Causes of Housing Segregation in St. Louis, 1990," *Urban Affairs Review* 31, no. 2 (November 1995): 244–254.

81 Public Policy Research Centers, University of Missouri-St. Louis, *Analysis of Impediments to Fair Housing: St. Louis County* (St. Louis: Author, 1995).

82 William E. Nelson and Michael S. Bailey, "The Weakening of State Participation in Civil Rights Enforcement," in *Public Policy across States and Communities*, ed. Dennis R. Judd (Greenwich, CT: JAI Press, 1985), p. 160.

83 Public Law 94–200, 94th Cong. (1975), Title III, and Public Law 95–128, 95th Cong. (1977), Title VIII.

84 Calvin Bradford, *Community Reinvestment Agreement Library* (Des Plaines, IL: Community Reinvestment Associates, 1992), as cited in Gregory D. Squires, "Chapter 1: Community Reinvestment: An Emerging Movement," in *From Redlining to Reinvestment: Community Responses to Urban Disinvestment*, ed. Gregory D. Squires (Philadelphia, PA: Temple University Press, 1992), p. 2.

85 Mitchell Zuckoff, "Study Shows Racial Bias in Lending," *Boston Globe* (October 9, 1992), p. B1.

86 Henry Ford, quoted in J. Allen Whitt and Glenn Yago, "Corporate Strategies and the Decline of Transit in U.S. Cities," *Urban Affairs Quarterly* 21, no. 1 (September 1985): 61.

87 Alan Lupo, Frank Colcord, and Edmund P. Fowler, *Rites of Way: The Politics of Transportation in Boston and the U.S. City* (Boston, MA: Little, Brown, 1971), p. 184.

88 Mark Rose, *Interstate Express Highway Politics, 1941–1956* (Lawrence: Regents Press of Kansas, 1979), p. 97.

89 Quoted in Helen Leavitt, *Superhighway—Superhoax* (Garden City, NY: Doubleday, 1970), p. 53.

90 Robert A. Caro, *The Power Broker: Robert Moses and the Fall of New York* (New York: Random House, 1974), p. 19.

91 Between 1951 and 1974, for example, 89 percent of the 10,000 households displaced by public projects in Baltimore were Black. See Anthony Downs, *Urban Problems and Prospects* (Chicago, IL: Marsham, 1970), pp. 204–205.

92 Ibid., p. 223.

93 John R. Meyer and Jose A. Gomez-Ibanez, *Auto Transit and Cities* (Cambridge, MA: Harvard University Press, 1981), p. 177.

94 By 1970 there were 400 struggles under way by community groups to oppose highway construction. Harry C. Boyte, *The Backyard Revolution: Understanding the New Citizen Movement* (Philadelphia, PA: Temple University Press, 1980), p. 11.

95 Jackson, *Crabgrass Frontier*, p. 250.

96 U.S. Federal Transportation Administration (USFTA), *Summary of Travel Trends, 1995 National Personal Transportation Survey*, December 1999; USFTA and U.S. Bureau of Transportation Statistics, *National Household Travel Survey*, 2001.

97 This account of ISTEA relies on Paul G. Lewis, "The Politics of Structure in Transportation Policy: Resuscitating Metropolitan Planning Organizations Under ISTEA," paper delivered at the Annual Meeting of the Urban Affairs Association (Toronto, Canada, April 17, 1997).

98 Pietro S. Nivola, *Laws of the Landscape: How Policies Shape Cities in Europe and America* (Washington, D.C.: Brookings Institution Press, 1999), p. 15.

99 Michael Cooper, "Rider Paradox: Surge in Mass, Drop in Transit," *The New York Times* (February 3, 2009), www.nytimes.com/2009/02/04/us/04trans.html.

100 Nick Baumgarten, "Public Transit's Summer of Hell," *The New Yorker* (July 24, 2017). Accessed online: https://www.newyorker.com/magazine/2017/07/24/public-transits-summer-of-hell.
101 Michael Cooper, "Rider Paradox: Surge in Mass, Drop in Transit," *The New York Times* (February 3, 2009), www.nytimes.com/2009/02/04/us/04trans.html.
102 Mary Clare Jalonick, "What's Inside the Senate's Bipartisan Infrastructure Bill," *The Associated Press* (August 11, 2021), https://apnews.com/article/joe-biden-business-bills-38b84f0e9fcc8e68646eedf6608c4c70.
103 Ibid.

CHAPTER 8

Federal Programs and the Divisive Politics of Race

The Brief Life of Inner-City Programs

The problems of racial segregation and discrimination, poverty, and inner-city decline burst onto the nation's political agenda in the 1960s. For a brief time, urban problems became the main focus of national policy. The National Commission on Urban Problems (1958), the National Commission on Civil Disorders (1967), the President's Task Force on Suburban Problems (1967), President Nixon's Commission on Population Growth and the American Future (1972), and a host of state and city task forces decried the segregation of Black Americans in neighborhoods of the central cities. A great deal of hope was invested in the social and urban policies of the 1960s, but many of these programs became embroiled in political controversy and proved to be short-lived.

In the 1964 presidential race, the Democratic candidate, Lyndon Johnson, promised to build a Great Society by launching an aggressive effort to solve the pressing social problems of the time. The Democratic landslide that year gave him the legislative majority needed to implement literally hundreds of programs in only the two-year period from 1965 to 1967. By the 1968 election, spending for the Vietnam War had already begun to undermine support for the Democratic agenda, but racial divisions proved to be even more decisive. The landslide win by the Democrats in 1964 masked a development that would soon compromise the party's ability to win presidential elections. The issue of race was tearing apart the coalition the Democrats had fashioned in the 1930s. Although President Johnson won by historic margins elsewhere, he lost in the one part of the country where Democrats had never been challenged, the Deep South. The Republican standard-bearer, Barry Goldwater, received 87 percent of the popular vote in Mississippi, close to 70 percent in Alabama, and substantially more than 50 percent in Louisiana, Georgia, and South Carolina.

DOI: 10.4324/9781003175315-10

After 1964, Republican candidates regularly carried the South for the first time since the carpetbagger governments imposed on southern states in the years after the Civil War.

Richard Nixon's victory in the 1968 election made it clear that it was impossible to separate the issue of race from the political fate of social welfare and urban programs. This had become obvious as early as the 1930s when southern Democrats in Congress often expressed their concern that New Deal programs might be used to upset "traditional racial relationships," by which they meant Jim Crow style segregation and discrimination that pervaded in the southern states. In the postwar years, they successfully fought to ensure that public housing would not be used to promote racial integration. As long as the programs advanced by Democratic liberals did not challenge race relations in the South, southern Democrats were willing to go along. But this tacit bargain ended with the civil rights legislation and the social programs of the 1960s.

OUTTAKE

Racism Eventually Doomed Urban Programs

The federal urban programs of the 1960s were adopted in response to civil disorders in the cities and the serious social problems highlighted by racial turmoil. The federal response fractured the Democratic Party, which relied upon urban voters from the North and reliable support in the southern and border states. The urban vote had been essential to the Democrats for decades. Time after time, overwhelming Democratic majorities in the big cities balanced out Republican pluralities in the suburbs and small towns, providing the margin of victory in key states holding large blocs of electoral votes. The Democrats would have lost the presidency in 1940, 1944, and 1948 without the big turnout in 12 big cities in the nation. The urban electorate was essential to John F. Kennedy's victory in the close election of 1960. Kennedy beat Nixon by a razor-thin 112,000 votes, a margin of less than one-tenth of 1 percent, but he carried 27 out of the 39 largest cities. In 1964, Lyndon Johnson won by an unprecedented landslide, with the cities delivering lopsided results that exceeded the national average by 10 percent or more.

The attempt to address the longstanding grievances of African Americans alienated white Southerners and white working-class voters almost everywhere. In 1968, the Republicans capitalized on resentment provoked by the successes of the civil rights movement. The Democratic presidential candidate, Hubert Humphrey, carried only one southern state, Texas. Across the South, he won just 31 percent of the vote, running behind both Republican Richard Nixon (34.5 percent) and Alabama governor and third-party (Dixiecrat) candidate George Wallace (34.6 percent), who ran as an avowed segregationist. In 1968, the Nixon campaign adopted law and order as its main theme. This had also been the campaign slogan of the Republican nominee in 1964, Barry Goldwater, but he had handled it crudely and ineptly. Goldwater's television ads tried to convey an impression that America's cities were in ruins by showing scenes of Black Americans rioting. In the scenes meant to portray Goldwater's vision of the American past he would like to restore, African Americans were shown picking cotton. The ads that Nixon aired four years later were less blatant, although they were not subtle either. One of his television spots showed scenes of urban riots, with a Nixon voice-over calling for "some honest talk about the problem of order."

Richard Nixon won 32 percent of the African American vote in 1960 when he lost to Kennedy, but even though his share fell to 12 percent in the 1968 election, he still beat Hubert Humphrey. One of the president's closest advisers, John Ehrlichman, told civil rights administrators that "blacks are not where the votes are, so why antagonize the people who can be helpful to us politically?" After the 1960s, the Republican Party mostly wrote off the African American vote. The Republican base became increasingly conservative, embracing working-class whites, a (now) solid Republican South under the guise of "states' rights" (a way of implying that southern states would be left alone by Republicans if they chose to hold on to Jim Crow practices), suburban and Sunbelt Republican voters, and the religious right. The results of the 2000 presidential election, which George W. Bush lost by 500,000 popular votes, suggested that the Republican coalition was losing some of its energy. Bush entered the White House only because the Electoral College favors small and less populated states. Nevertheless, it is clear that cities did not figure much in the overall tally. Democrats have drawn the logical conclusion that programs meant for the cities cannot get them much political mileage.

The 2020 presidential election demonstrated that it is time to rethink this contention. In 2020, the Democrats successfully "flipped" the state of Georgia for the first time since 1992. Since 1972, the Democrats had only been able to win Georgia's electoral votes three times: Georgian Jimmy Carter had managed to turn Georgia blue in 1976 and 1980, and Bill Clinton with his Arkansan drawl and his fiscally conservative political agenda had managed to do it one more time in 1992. In 2020, Georgia's electoral votes went to the Democrats thanks in large part to an active Black electorate in Atlanta and an extremely dedicated and successful grassroots campaign by state assemblywoman Stacey Abrams, who had run for governor of Georgia in 2018 and lost to then-secretary of state Brian Kemp. Kemp, in his former position, was in charge of voter registration and elections and refused to resign from his position until two days after the election. Before and during the campaign for governor, Kemp engaged in some dubious voter suppression practices, purging from voter rolls more than 50,000 Georgians, about 80 percent of them Black. This not only prompted a lawsuit against Kemp, which is still being litigated but also compelled Abrams to engage in a massive grassroots voter registration campaign. The campaign paid off, as, in 2020, Atlanta's urban districts successfully provided the votes the Democrats needed to win the state's electoral votes and, ultimately, the presidency. According to *The New York Times*, the Biden campaign made the biggest gains in "well-educated, wealthy and increasingly diverse precincts around Atlanta, while making relatively few gains elsewhere in the state." Similarly,

Wisconsin, which had gone to the Trump column in 2016, went for Biden in 2020 only because of very strong turnout in cities like Milwaukee, Green Bay, Madison, and Kenosha. In Pennsylvania, Biden's home state, and another swing state, which the Republicans had taken in 2016, Biden won Philadelphia, as well as its four collar counties, and Allegheny County, where Pittsburgh is located, along with its wealthy suburbs. The 2020 presidential election, if anything, should give Democrats strong cause to speak specifically to urban electorates once more.

Sources: Statistics and quotations from Theodore H. White, *The Making of the President, 1960* (New York: Atheneum, 1961), p. 1201; John Mollenkopf, *The Contested City* (Princeton, NJ: Princeton University Press, 1983), p. 83; Kathleen Hall Jamieson, *Packaging the Presidency: A History and Criticism of Presidential Campaign Advertising* (New York: Oxford University Press, 1984), pp. 202–203; Joseph McGinnis, *Selling the President, 1968* (New York: Trident Press, 1969); Numan V. Barley and Hugh D. Graham, *Southern Politics and the Second Reconstruction* (Baltimore, MD: Johns Hopkins University Press, 1975), pp. 126–127; Everett Carl Ladd Jr., "The Shifting Party Coalitions, 1932–1976," in *Emerging Coalitions in American Politics,* ed. Seymour Martin Lipset (San Francisco: Institute for Contemporary Studies, 1978), p. 98; A. James Reichley, *Conservatives in an Age of Change: The Nixon and Ford Administrations* (Washington, D.C.: Brookings Institution Press, 1981), pp. 145, 186; Myrydd Wells, "Georgie Goes Blue for the First Time since 1992," *Atlanta Magazine* (November 13, 2020); Meagan Flynn, "Georgia's GOP Gubernatorial Candidate Brian Kemp Is Sued over Claims of Suppressing Thousands of Minority Voters," *The Washington Post* (October 12, 2018); Nate Cohn, Matthew Conlen and Charlie Smart, "Detailed Turnout Data Shows How Georgia Turned Blue," *The New York Times* (November 17, 2020); *Wisconsin Public Radio,* "Joe Biden Wins Wisconsin, Thanks to Late-Breaking Lead from Milwaukee, Green Bay, Kenosha" (November 4, 2020); Jonathan Tamari and Julia Terruso, "How Joe Biden Won Pennsylvania," *The Philadelphia Inquirer* (November 9, 2020).

In the public's imagination, the Great Society became identified as a constellation of programs that primarily benefited inner-city Black Americans. The truth is that no significant programs were aimed so narrowly. Funds for Head Start and the War on Poverty, for example, were spread broadly across the country to urban and rural areas alike, and social programs such as Medicare and Medicaid benefited people regardless of where they lived. But impressions mattered. From 1969 to 1976, when Republican presidents Richard Nixon and Gerald Ford occupied the White House, many of the Democratic-sponsored programs came under attack, and Ronald Reagan's victory in the 1980 presidential election quickly brought an end to most urban programs. Most of the Great Society programs lasted for 20 years or less, and they never received enough resources to plausibly remedy the problems they were meant to address.

The Democrats and the Cities

When President Kennedy took office on January 20, 1961, his administration was already committed to helping the cities. Even before his campaign, Kennedy had concluded that the problem of the cities was "the great unspoken issue in the 1960 election."[1] During the campaign, the Democrats discussed doing something about the urban crisis, whereas the Republicans tried to avoid such issues. "If you ever let them campaign only on domestic issues," confided presidential nominee Richard M. Nixon to his aides, "they'll beat us."[2] President Kennedy "emerged as an eloquent spokesman for a new generation. In presidential message after message Kennedy spelled out in more detail than the Congress or the country could easily digest the most complete programs of domestic reforms in a quarter century."[3]

The Kennedy administration mapped out an ambitious agenda. Poverty, racial segregation, juvenile delinquency and crime, bad schools, and a host of other social problems were discovered in the 1960s only in the sense that they were no longer "out of sight, out of mind." They had existed for a long time and were no worse and little different by the beginning of the Kennedy administration than they had been under Presidents Roosevelt, Truman, and Eisenhower. What made them seem worse was their greater visibility. Martin Luther King Jr. understood the task of creating visibility during the civil rights demonstrations in 1963. "I saw no way," he later commented, "of dealing with things without bringing the indignation to the attention of the nation."[4]

King turned the civil rights issue into a national crisis in Birmingham, Alabama, in the summer of 1963. What started in Birmingham spread across the South and even filtered into northern cities. During the summer, there were 13,786 arrests of demonstrators in 75 cities of the 11 southern states.[5] In the ten weeks that followed nationally publicized police attacks on demonstrators in Birmingham, the Justice Department counted 758 demonstrations across the nation. It quickly became clear that the administration could no longer avoid dealing with civil rights. The brutal treatment of civil rights demonstrators throughout the South was being televised in the living rooms of millions of American homes. By mid-June, 127 civil rights bills had been introduced in the House of Representatives. The Kennedy administration, like it or not, was being drawn into the nation's most significant and divisive internal conflict since the Civil War.

The political pressures applied by the civil rights movement were reinforced by the influence of the Black electorate. As John C. Donovan observed in his book *The Politics of Poverty*, "The greatest strength of the Negro communities lies in its voting power, in its numbers, and in their strategic location."[6] In the South, the Black population was geographically diffused and systematically denied the right to the vote. When they moved to northern cities, Black Americans gained the franchise. Their votes were concentrated in the cities of the states holding a majority of the electoral college votes—Illinois, California, Massachusetts, Ohio, Michigan, New Jersey, New York, Texas, and Pennsylvania. Kennedy targeted his campaign on these key states, and the 68 percent plurality that Black voters gave him was crucial to his razor-thin victories in Illinois, Missouri, and other states. In 1956, Adlai Stevenson, the liberal Democratic candidate from Illinois, had received 61 percent of the Black vote.[7] If Kennedy had not done better, he would have lost the election: "It is difficult to see how Illinois, New Jersey, Michigan, South Carolina, or Delaware (with 74 electoral votes) could have been won had the Republican Democratic split of the Negro wards and precincts remained as it was, unchanged from the Eisenhower charm of 1956."[8]

On June 11, 1963, President Kennedy overruled his advisers and announced he would propose a civil rights bill. When Kennedy was assassinated on November 22, the bill had just reached the House Rules Committee. The assassination created an emotionally charged atmosphere that the new president, Lyndon Baines Johnson, adroitly exploited. Opinion polls indicated overwhelming public support for civil rights legislation. Seizing the moment, Johnson added new provisions to the legislation and harried Congress into acting quickly. When Republicans joined with northern Democrats to move the bill out of the House Rules Committee, the bill was sent to the floor, where it passed by a vote of 290 to 130. On June 6, 1964, the Senate mustered the necessary two-thirds vote to overcome a filibuster mounted by Southerners, and the legislation passed.

The Civil Rights Act of 1964 outlawed discrimination in public accommodations, thus effectively striking down the South's Jim Crow laws that had denied Black Americans equal access to bus stations, restaurants, lunch counters, theaters, sports arenas, gasoline stations, motels, hotels, and lodging houses. It outlawed racial discrimination in the hiring, firing, training, and promoting of workers. It barred discrimination in the administration of federal grants. A year later, Congress passed the Voting Rights Act, which not only outlawed literacy tests and other discriminatory voting restrictions but also provided that federal registrars could replace local registrars in counties where there had been a history of discrimination against Black voters.

Taking advantage of the post-assassination atmosphere, President Johnson also pressed for a program to redress economic inequalities.[9] Kennedy's advisers had persuaded him that the time had come for his administration to devise a program to attack poverty and unemployment. In June 1963, Kennedy had told Walter Heller, the chair of his Council of Economic Advisors, to appoint a task force of officials who would be responsible for proposing a program to attack poverty. Although Kennedy's commitment to a program was almost certain by the time of his assassination, it was not clear how hard he would have fought for it.

President Johnson was told about the proposed antipoverty program only two days after assuming office, but he quickly responded, "That's my kind of program. It will help people. I want you to move full speed ahead."[10] The idea of an ambitious, highly visible program appealed to Johnson's desire to be perceived as a second Roosevelt, as a president who would go down in history as the one who completed the social agenda left unfinished in the 1930s. In his first State of the Union address, on January 10, 1964, President Johnson announced he would seek a "total effort" to end poverty in the United States. Using a grandiose military analogy, he said, "This Administration here and now declares unconditional war on poverty in America, and I urge this Congress and all Americans to join me in that effort."[11] When Johnson signed the Economic Opportunity Act on August 8, he had two big legislative victories, the civil rights act and his "war on poverty," to carry into the presidential campaign.

The 1964 campaign provided the setting for a contentious national debate over the federal government's role and responsibilities. The Republican nominee, Barry Goldwater, was one of the few non-Southerners to vote against the civil rights act in the Senate. He attacked the welfare programs funded through the Social Security Act of 1935 and even questioned the immensely popular old-age insurance program established through that legislation. The Republican Party's platform warned that "individual freedom retreats under the mounting assault of expanding centralized power."[12] Lyndon Johnson, by contrast, called for a Great Society that would eliminate poverty and treat other social ills through federal action on civil rights, the cities, health care, welfare, education, and employment.

Johnson won the election by a historic landslide, receiving 61 percent of the popular vote and picking up 486 electoral college votes to Goldwater's 53. The dimensions of the landslide allowed the Democrats to ignore the fact that Goldwater had swept several southern states that Democrats had always carried. The president's coattails were long; Democrats commanded a 289-to-146 majority in the House to go along with a 67-to-33 majority in the Senate.

The Democrats' overwhelming victory set the stage for a period of legislative activism not seen since Roosevelt's fabled First Hundred Days of 1933. Between 1964 and 1966, Congress authorized 219 new programs, which included some of the most important and enduring social initiatives of the 1960s. In 1965, Congress approved Medicare for the elderly and Medicaid for welfare recipients. The Elementary and Secondary Education Act provided federal grants to schools. Food stamps, an experimental program tried during the Kennedy years, became permanent in 1966. New and expanded educational and job-training assistance was made available for individuals with mental and physical disabilities. The public housing and urban renewal programs were expanded, and a new "Model Cities" program to treat the problems of cities was initiated. In 1966, Congress also created a new cabinet-level department, the Department of Housing and Urban Development (HUD), to administer urban programs.

Figure 8.1 shows that spending on federal grants for regional and community development hit a high point in the 1960s, and, after another high point in the 1970s, it started a continuous decline into the present day. The same figure also shows, however, that the composition of federal grants for local communities has changed dramatically over the years, with spending in areas such as community and regional development, education, transportation, and income security continuously declining since the 1980s, but health-related grants seeing a continuous increase over the decades, with its most dramatic increase due to the Obama administration's implementation of the Affordable Care Act in 2010. In 1962, the federal government spent $3.8 billion on these

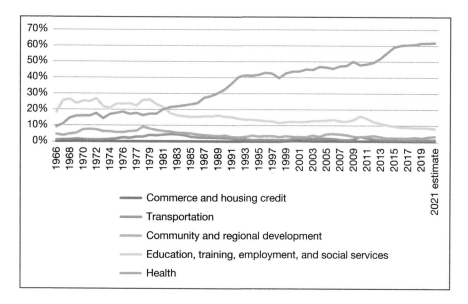

FIGURE 8.1 Federal Grants to State and Local Governments, 1966–2019

Source: Office of Management and Budget/Government Publishing Office, Budget FY 2021, Historical Tables, Budget of the United States Government, Fiscal Year 2021, Table 12.2—Total Outlays for Grants to State and Local Governments by Function and Fund Group, 1940–2025. https://www.govinfo.gov/app/details/BUDGET-2021-TAB/BUDGET-2021-TAB-13-2.

programs (in constant 2008 dollars; the actual figure that year was $445 million), and $24.2 billion by 1980 (2008 dollars; $9.2 billion in actual dollars). Local governments became increasingly dependent on intergovernmental transfers from federal and state governments. In 1950, grants from states and from the federal government accounted for only 10 percent of the revenues making up local budgets, but this proportion rose to over 26 percent of municipal revenues by 1978. But then the bottom fell out, and by the end of the 1990s, only 7 percent of city budgets came from intergovernmental revenues. This proportion rose slightly to 10 percent in 2008. During the fiscal year of 2017, that figure had risen 36 percent.[13]

The explosion in federal spending was energized by the conviction that the national government should take the nation in a new direction. Not since the closing of the frontier in the 1870s had the federal government attempted so forcefully to chart a course for the nation. The Louisiana Purchase of 1803, a succession of township and homestead acts, generous land grants to railroad companies, and an aggressive military policy toward the Indians supported the federal government's intention to open up the West in the nineteenth century.[14] In the 1960s, the president and Congress pursued a national agenda of comparable ambition. This time, the national government set out to eliminate poverty, erase racial discrimination, provide equal opportunity in education and jobs, and revitalize cities and communities.

A stronger focus on equality and social justice within the national discourse was reflected in clear terms in the case of the Civil Rights Act of 1964 when the federal government served notice that its new civil rights statutes would override state and local racial practices. The preambles to the grant programs of Kennedy's New Frontier and Johnson's Great Society articulated a variety of national goals. Consider this example from the Manpower Development and Training Act of 1962:

> It is in the national interest that current and prospective manpower shortages be identified and that persons who can be qualified for these positions through education and training be sought out and trained, *in order that the nation may meet the staffing requirements of the struggle for freedom.*[15]

Or the Economic Opportunity Act of 1964:

> The United States can achieve its full economic and social potential as a nation only if every individual has the opportunity to contribute the full extent of his capabilities and to participate in the workings of our society. *It is, therefore, the policy of the United States* to eliminate the paradox of poverty in the midst of plenty in this nation.[16]

And the Demonstration Cities and Metropolitan Development Act of 1966 (the so-called Model Cities legislation):

> The Congress hereby finds and declares that *improving the quality of urban life is the most critical domestic problem facing the United States.*[17]

Imagine such statements of intention introducing hundreds of pieces of legislation, ranging from rent supplements to federal school aid to crime control, and the complexity of the new system of grants becomes readily apparent. Hardly an economic or a social problem escaped attention, and each program specified its own complicated methods of implementation. Recipient institutions were subjected to complex rules and close scrutiny. After all, it makes no sense to fund a national priority unless the money is going to be used carefully, according to prescribed guidelines and standards.[18]

The War on Poverty and Model Cities programs attracted attention because they were sold with grandiose promises about what they would accomplish. In 1964, when Lyndon Johnson proposed the War on Poverty, he announced his objective was "total victory."[19] Such a promise could not possibly be fulfilled no matter how well the program might be implemented. As it turned out, the War on Poverty became a lightning rod for controversy, as did the Model Cities program, which was funded through the Demonstration Cities and Metropolitan Development Act of 1966. Under the terms of the War on Poverty, community action agencies were instructed to operate with the "maximum feasible participation" of the poor. Likewise, Model Cities agencies were supposed to galvanize participation by local residents by giving them a role in planning. City halls and other agencies of local government were cut out of the loop. The idea was to create new institutions in the cities capable of mobilizing the energies of people outside the established power structure. An early program guide distributed by the Office of Economic Opportunity said that to qualify for funding, local antipoverty programs should involve the poor from the very first "in planning, policy-making, and operation."[20]

These programs were, in effect, a means of fomenting a revolution in local politics. According to two scholars, Frances Fox Piven and Richard A. Cloward, many of the Great Society programs were formulated to preserve and strengthen the Democratic Party's advantage in the industrialized states holding the largest blocs of Electoral College votes.[21] Frustrated that local politicians had repeatedly shown an unwillingness to mobilize the votes of Black Americans living in the nation's cities, federal administrators tried to work directly with organizations and leaders in Black communities. The expectation was that Blacks would vote Democratic in return.

A multitude of new agencies was established to receive and distribute federal dollars. Of all the community action funds the Office of Economic Opportunity spent by 1968, only 25 percent was given to public agencies. The remainder went to organizations such as universities, churches, civil rights groups, settlement houses, family services agencies, United Way programs, and newly established nonprofit groups.[22] Likewise, only 10 percent of the funds distributed through programs administered by the Department of Health, Education, and Welfare was passed through to state and local governments.[23]

The War on Poverty and the Model Cities programs continued to receive congressional support mainly because the funds were distributed in a large number of states and congressional districts. Politicians of both parties were able to take credit for delivering federal dollars to local constituencies. To broaden the base of support in Congress, the Johnson administration abandoned its original intention to restrict the antipoverty and Model Cities programs to a few "demonstration" projects. Instead, the federal funds were spread as thinly as thought necessary to secure annual program budgets. The deleterious effect of this strategy was that it virtually guaranteed that no program in any city could deliver on its promises.

Within the context of what had come before them, the Great Society Programs were a huge improvement to the status quo in many ways: The Johnson administration outlawed the literacy tests that many Southern states were still requiring as a prerequisite for voting. Partially as a result of that (and other Civil Rights legislation), Black voter registration in the southern states increased by 67 percent between 1964 and 1968.[24] Civil Rights legislation also made illegal any discrimination based on race, color, national origin, religion, or sex. The federal government created the Equal Employment Opportunity Commission and instructed the attorney general to engage in lawsuits those institutions (such as schools) employing discriminatory practices.[25] For a government that had not only condoned but mandated race-based segregation, discrimination, and even violence for centuries, this was almost a revolutionary step. For many communities of color, on the other hand, it was only a first step on a long road to equal treatment that is still littered with massive setbacks, such as the Supreme Court's 2013 and 2021 rollbacks of major aspects of the Voting Rights Act, and subsequent moves, in many southern states, to implement unreasonable and dangerous voting restrictions that will have strong impacts on the voting rights of communities of color.

The Republicans and the New Federalism

When Richard Nixon assumed the presidency in January 1969, it seemed likely that the Great Society programs would be dismantled. Somewhat surprisingly, however, from 1969 through 1976, when Republicans held the presidency, aid to state and local governments actually climbed, from $20 to $59 billion, staying well ahead of inflation.[26] Funding continued to rise because the Democrats controlled Congress and a powerful constellation of interest groups influential with both parties rallied to the cause. Even some Republican congressional representatives, governors, and local officials wanted the flow to continue. After a failed attempt to kill the War on Poverty in 1969, President Nixon bowed to political realities and set a middle course by trying to reform rather than eliminate urban programs.

Nixon signaled his desire to fundamentally change how federal programs were administered. He spoke of the grant programs as producing a "gathering of the reins of power in Washington," which he saw as "a radical departure from the vision of federal-state relations the nation's founders had in mind." He proposed a New Federalism, meant to restore "a rightful balance between the state capital and the national capital."[27] To reduce federal authority, Nixon wanted to take the decisions about how to spend money out of the hands of federal bureaucrats and give the authority to local governments. A revenue-sharing program was the first major initiative of the New Federalism. Revenue sharing gave local officials extraordinary latitude in deciding how to spend federal money. Because of the lack of detailed federal oversight, revenue-sharing dollars were intermingled with other monies that flowed into the treasuries of the more than 39,000 state, county, township, and municipal governments across the nation. As a consequence, they could not be traced beyond the reports filed with the Treasury Department by local officials.

Revenue-sharing monies constituted a small supplement to the tax revenues of state and local governments. In 1974, the $4.5 billion apportioned among 35,077 local governments accounted for an average of 3.1 percent of their revenues for that year.[28] Financially strapped big cities were under pressure to use revenue-sharing funds just to keep things going; as a consequence, they spent nearly all of their revenue-sharing dollars on day-to-day operations and maintenance.[29] Congressional Democrats complained that the programs ignored the needs of historically disadvantaged populations, but for Republicans, that was the whole point. The program continued at a low level until 1986 when President Reagan killed it.

The Community Development Block Grant (CDBG) program, enacted by Congress in 1974 and signed into law by President Gerald Ford in January 1975, remains today as the only significant survivor of the major urban policies enacted in the pre-Reagan era. It has survived so long because it has been useful to so many people. For local officials, it is a source of much-needed funding. It has enjoyed broad bipartisan support because CDBG funds go to thousands of communities. Unlike for general revenue sharing, cities were required to submit an annual application for CDBG funds even though they were automatically eligible. But the process was quite painless. By the end of the program's first year, HUD Secretary Carla Hills reported that her department had reduced the average review period from two years for the programs that the Community Development Act replaced to 49 days and that applications averaged 50 pages, compared with an average of 1,400 pages for the old urban renewal applications alone.[30]

In the first few years, a recurring issue was that communities were spending their CDBG money in violation of program guidelines. The original legislation included a requirement that cities give "maximum feasible priority" to low- and moderate-income areas.[31] Communities were often accused of ignoring this requirement, a fact documented by the Department of Housing and Urban Development.[32] That community development funds would be spent in affluent areas was hardly a surprising turn of events because local political elites exerted a controlling voice in the allocation process. In most local communities, poorer residents had little influence. As a result of this circumstance, Little Rock, Arkansas, for example, spent $150,000 of the city's block grant funds to construct a tennis court in an affluent section of town. When questioned about this use of funds, the director of the local Department of Human Resources unpersuasively claimed that "ninety-nine percent of this money is going to low- and moderate-income areas." But he revealingly continued, "You cannot divorce politics from that much money. We remember the needs of the people who vote because they hold us accountable. Poor people don't vote."[33]

President Carter and the Democrats' Last Hurrah

In the four years that he was in office, Democratic President Jimmy Carter attempted to give urban programs some of the attention they had received in the past, but his difficulties showed just how much the contours of national politics had changed since the 1960s. There was good reason for Carter to respond favorably to the older industrial cities. Inner-city voters had remained faithful to the Democrats for decades, and they gave Carter his margin of victory in several states in the 1976 presidential election. Accordingly, the administration tried to develop policies that would shore up support among urban voters. The president persuaded Congress to pass an amendment to the revenue-sharing program that added an "excess unemployment" factor to the distribution formula.[34] Cities with high unemployment levels received all the money. He successfully sought increases in CDBG funding and significantly amended the program in 1978 to help the big cities. Large increases were legislated for Comprehensive Employment and Training Act (CETA) programs, which gave money to local training centers and to local governments to put people to work repairing parks and public facilities. Despite these accomplishments, however, by the time Carter left office, he seemed to be abandoning urban policy altogether, a process that would reach its logical conclusion under his Republican successor, Ronald Reagan.

Soon after Carter assumed office in January 1977, his administration began efforts to reward key members of his electoral base. An effort was launched to amend the Community Development Act so that more aid would flow to the older industrial cities. As it happened, the original distribution formula adopted in 1974 discriminated against the worst-off cities of the Northeast and Midwest. The older industrial cities were destined to receive a declining share of CDBG funds over time, whereas fast-growing Sunbelt cities were going to receive more.[35] This was mainly because the formula for distributing the money was partially tied to each city's total population. The older cities would lose funds over time simply because they were rapidly shrinking; by contrast, Sunbelt cities were growing.

The administration initiated efforts to persuade Congress to revise the formula to take into account population *loss* in a city.[36] As soon as the legislation was introduced, a bitter feud broke out between representatives from the Northeast and Midwest and the congressional delegations from southern and western states. Ultimately, the new formula won in a vote that divided along regional, not party, lines: Representatives from the East and Midwest voted overwhelmingly in favor, while almost all of those from the South and West voted against. Although the legislation passed the house in May 1977, the battle within Congress showed that in the future, regional divisions were likely to become fundamentally important factors in national politics.

The fight over the block grant program marked a watershed. In the Great Society years, urban programs had emphasized social purposes. By contrast, during the Carter administration, urban programs began to stress a different goal: Leveraging private investments in troubled cities and neighborhoods. Because it relied upon the dynamics of the private market, it attracted support from local officials in both the North and South, regardless of their partisan affiliation. The first test of this bipartisan strategy came in 1978 when Congress approved the Urban Development Action Grants (UDAG) program. Over the years, UDAG were used to build festival malls such as Union Station in St. Louis and Harborplace in Baltimore; to expand convention centers; to repair historic buildings; to support neighborhood improvements; and to build public infrastructure (such as improved streets, new lighting, landscaping, and fountains) that might leverage private investment.

As time went on, it became apparent that the administration was retreating from any emphasis at all on social, as opposed to economic, development goals. On March 28, 1978, President Carter announced, with great fanfare, a comprehensive new urban policy that emphasized private investment. Asserting "the deterioration of urban life in the United States is one of the most complex and deeply rooted problems of our age," The president stated that "the federal government has the clear duty to lead the effort to reverse that deterioration."[37] The centerpiece of President Carter's proposal was a national development bank, which would be authorized to guarantee loans to businesses in depressed urban and rural areas; in addition, the administration wanted to offer tax credits for businesses hiring youths from high-poverty neighborhoods, a labor-intensive public works program, and more money for housing rehabilitation. The amount of additional money requested was relatively modest (about $4.4 billion), but this did not deter Carter from promising a "new Partnership involving all levels of government, the private sector and neighborhood and voluntary organizations."[38]

President Carter's ringing call for a comprehensive urban policy raised hopes in city halls, but it quickly turned into an abject political failure. The only major legislative proposal enacted into law was the Targeted Employment Tax Credit. The timing was bad for any new legislative initiative.[39] In 1978, California voters passed Proposition 13, which sharply reduced local property taxes. The gathering strength of a tax revolt across the nation helped shape a mood of fiscal conservatism in Congress and a go-slow approach in the White House.[40] Sensing a change in the political climate, Carter did an about-face in the last two years of his term, turning his attention away from urban policy toward the problems of the national economy and the cost and availability of energy. A sharp decline in manufacturing jobs and the flight of manufacturing outside the country became the leading domestic issues of the 1980 presidential campaign.

After Carter's election in 1976, Mayor Kenneth A. Gibson of Newark had spoken for many Democratic mayors when he remarked, "we have every reason to believe that this is the beginning of a new relationship between the White House and the nation's mayors."[41] The new relationship, however, proved to be short-lived. Even if Carter had won the 1980 presidential race, it is doubtful any significant urban programs would have emerged in a second term.

Republicans and the End of Federal Assistance

In the campaigns of 1980 and 1984, the Republicans virtually wrote off the African American vote. Richard Wirthlin, Ronald Reagan's campaign strategist, advised before the 1980 election that the "Reagan for President 1980 campaign must convert into Reagan votes the disappointment felt by Southern white and rural voters."[42] Reagan won only 10 percent of the Black vote in 1980 and slightly less in 1984. In 1984, however, three out of four southern whites supported him. The Reagan White House actively worked to undo civil rights guarantees, slashing the budgets of civil rights enforcement units and slowing or stopping enforcement.[43] The Reagan administration also set out to dismantle federal programs designed to help the cities, and over the course of eight years, it largely succeeded.

President Reagan's agenda mapped out a radical new departure in federal policy. Philosophically, Reagan believed that the federal government should stop helping the cities altogether. Instead, he thought, they, and the people who lived within them, should help themselves. In a press conference held in October 1981, President Reagan suggested the residents of cities where unemployment was high should "vote with their feet" and move to more prosperous areas of the country.[44] His remark ignited an instant political controversy, but, in fact, it was consistent with the recommendations of a presidential commission appointed by his predecessor, Jimmy Carter. In a report issued only a few weeks after Reagan took office, the Presidential Commission on the National Agenda for the Eighties urged that the national government stop helping cities. The commission emphasized that federal policies should be used to promote national economic growth, but these policies should be neutral about where that growth occurred:

> It may be in the best interest of the nation to commit itself to the promotion of locationally neutral economic and social policies rather than spatially sensitive urban policies that either explicitly or inadvertently seek to preserve cities in their historical roles.[45]

Recommending that the federal government let the process of decay in some areas and growth in others take its natural course, the commission noted that cities adapt and change in response to economic and social forces. This process of adaptation, said the commission, should be facilitated, rather than altered, by governmental policy:

> Ultimately, the federal government's concern for national economic vitality should take precedence over the competition for advantage among communities and regions.[46] To attempt to restrict or reverse the processes of change—for whatever noble intentions—is to deny the benefits that the future may hold for us as a nation.[47]

The policies subsequently pursued by the Reagan administration signaled a historic turn. For the first time since the urban policy was first enacted in the 1930s, policymakers operated on the assumption that cities were valuable only if they contributed in a positive way to the national economy. Three researchers at the University of Delaware called the new policy direction "a form of Social Darwinism applied to cities."[48] Cities would survive if they could manage to regenerate their local economies. Otherwise, they would be allowed to wither away.

The Reagan administration began to slash federal urban aid, proclaiming "the private market is more efficient than federal program administrators in allocating dollars."[49] Cities were instructed to improve their ability to compete in a struggle for survival in which "state and local governments will find it is in their interests to concentrate on increasing their attractiveness to potential investors, residents, and visitors."[50] The assumption was that free enterprise would provide a bounty of jobs, incomes, and neighborhood renewal, and such local prosperity would make federal programs unnecessary. The CDBG and UDAG programs were spared deep cuts in the 1983 budget, as was revenue sharing. The administration had wanted to reduce these programs too, but the White House heard the pleas of governors and mayors, quite a few of them Republican. Local government representatives came away relieved that the budget cuts were less drastic than they had feared. Only two years later, however, the administration realized its goal of eliminating most urban programs.

Urban programs gave way to a new priority: cutting taxes. On February 18, 1981, President Reagan proposed a massive tax cut to stimulate the economy. The legislation quickly sailed through Congress, and when Reagan signed the Economic Recovery Tax Act on August 13, 1981, he proclaimed "a turnaround of almost a half a century of ... excessive growth in government bureaucracy, government spending, government taxing."[51] In its final version, the act reduced individual tax rates by 25 percent over three years and also substantially reduced business tax liability. The revenue losses were huge. In just the first two years, $128 billion was lost to the federal treasury, and by 1987 this figure rose to more than $1 trillion.[52] In combination with massive increases in military spending, the 1981 tax cuts created huge budget deficits.

The Tax Reform Act of 1986 reduced federal revenues even further. Tax rates fell only modestly or not at all for most taxpayers, but they were cut drastically for the rich. In subsequent years, a perception that tax burdens fell unfairly on the middle class helped fuel a tax revolt. George H. W. Bush won the presidency in 1988 partly with the promise, "Read my lips: no new taxes." Within a few months, the administration slashed spending for programs for education, housing, health, and welfare. (It should be pointed out, however, that later in his term, President Bush went along with a bill raising some taxes in order to reduce the accumulating federal deficit. By some accounts, this cost him his bid for a second term.)

President Reagan initiated the first reductions of consequence in grants-in-aid expenditures since the 1940s. Broad entitlement programs with middle-class recipients, such as the old-age and survivors' benefits funded through the Social Security Act of 1935, veterans' benefits, and Medicare, were affected only marginally. By contrast, deep cuts and new eligibility restrictions were imposed on public assistance programs for the poor. Medicaid, which was available through the states to welfare recipients, was subjected to tighter eligibility requirements, but Medicaid outlays soared anyway because of rising medical costs. Enrollment in Aid to Families with Dependent Children (AFDC) fell by half a million. A million people lost food stamps. It became harder to get unemployment benefits; whereas 75 percent of the unemployed received benefits during the recession of 1975, only 45 percent were able to qualify during the 1982–1983 recession.[53]

Several urban programs were also killed off by the end of Reagan's first term, including revenue sharing and federally assisted local public works. The UDAG grants were eliminated in 1986, although a trickle of money continued to flow in the administrative pipeline for several years (the total spending fell from an annual level of between $400 and $500 million for the first ten years of the program [fiscal years 1978–1987] to $200 million in fiscal 1988 and dried up to a nominal $3 million by fiscal 1994).[54] Other budget cuts also affected the cities. Most subsidies for the construction of public housing were eliminated. Only 10,000 new units a year were authorized after 1983, compared with the 111,600 new or rehabilitated units authorized for 1981.[55]

Despite his opposition to urban programs of almost any kind, President Reagan moved to put his stamp on a "Republican" approach to the cities by proposing legislation meant to stimulate private investment in troubled inner-city neighborhoods. On March 7, 1983, Reagan sent his draft of the Urban Enterprise Zone Act to Congress and asserted that the legislation represented a sharp departure from the past policy:

> Enterprise zones are a fresh approach for promoting economic growth in
> the inner cities. The old approach relied on heavy government subsidies
> and central planning. A prime example was the model cities program in the
> 1960s, which concentrated government programs, subsidies and regulations
> in distressed urban areas. The enterprise zone approach is to remove
> government barriers, bring individuals to create, produce and earn their own
> wages and profits.[56]

Although the president claimed that the enterprise zone legislation was a "fresh approach," it was actually built on concepts pioneered by the Carter Administration. Since at least 1974, the federal policy had stressed the role of the government in subsidizing private investment. In the Reagan years, the enterprise zones idea surfaced from time to time, but it was far down on the president's policy agenda. After George H. W. Bush's election to the presidency in 1988, the idea continued to receive an occasional nudge from the White House, but urban policy of any kind did not surface as a meaningful item on the president's legislative agenda until very late in his term.

The administration of George H. W. Bush was not motivated by its electoral base or its ideology to propose any kind of urban legislation. In the 1988 presidential election, Bush used racial issues to mobilize his base. Republicans ran an attack ad that featured a police photograph of Willie Horton, who had raped a woman in Maryland and stabbed her fiancé while on a weekend pass from a Massachusetts prison. The Democratic candidate, Michael Dukakis, had been the governor of Massachusetts at the time. According to Bush's campaign director, Lee Atwater, the fact that Willie Horton was Black was the key element explaining the ad's emotional impact.

In the 1992 election, the Bush campaign refined its racial appeals by resorting to a code language that used attacks on cities as a signifier of race and welfare-state liberalism. In one of the opening salvos of the campaign, Vice President Dan Quayle attacked New York City by saying, "The liberal vision of a happy, productive and content welfare state hasn't even worked on 22 square miles of the most valuable real estate in the world."[57] A later Quayle attack prompted a *New York Times* headline: "Everyone to City: Drop Dead!"[58]— akin to the famous 1972 *Daily News* headline "Ford to City: Drop Dead!" in response to then-President Ford's unwillingness to bail out New York City. An editorial in *The New York Times* called Quayle's attacks an attempt to make New York City "The Willie Horton of 1992."[59]

Despite the administration's rhetoric, late in his term, President Bush made some faint gestures in the direction of urban policy. The pressure to do so came on April 29–May 3, 1992, when serious street protests broke out in Los Angeles over the acquittal of four police officers, three of them white, after brutally beating a Black man, Rodney King. The scene was incidentally caught on camera by a passerby, and people across the country and around the world were able to see the incident in all its brutality. This made the acquittal even more unbelievable to many onlookers. As a criminal justice and law professor at the University of Southern California told NPR 25 years after the verdict: "My jaw dropped. There was ocular proof of what happened. It seemed compelling. And yet, we saw a verdict that told us we couldn't trust our lying eyes. That what we thought was open and shut was really 'a reasonable expression of police control' toward a Black motorist."[60] King had been on parole for robbery and had been engaged in a police chase around the city. Once the police managed to stop him, they made him exit his car and proceeded to kick and beat him with their batons for a full 15 minutes while other officers stood by looking on. They only later charged King with driving under the influence. From the incident, King suffered a fractured skull and permanent brain injury, as well as other bone fractures and broken teeth.

In response to the not-guilty verdict issued in favor of the four police officers who had beaten King, a year later, on April 29, 1992, by a majority-white, suburban jury from Ventura County, almost 80 miles away, Los Angeles exploded with anger. Measured by the number of deaths (53), injuries (2,383), property damage (over $700 million), and the response required to reestablish order, to some, the Los Angeles riot was the country's worst episode of civil disorder in the twentieth century.[61] To others, it was yet another one in a long line of reactions against the disproportionate use of force by police, especially against people of color. In spite of big protests in the decades to come and the more organized attempts of the Black Lives Matter movement to call attention to the issue of police violence, the problem remains unresolved in the twenty-first century.

Many people thought the riot could be used as an opportunity to call attention to the problems of urban America. Two weeks after the riots, 150,000 people descended on Washington for a Save Our Cities/Save Our Children rally. As the atmosphere of crisis faded, however, urban issues got lost in election-year politics. Democratic candidate Bill Clinton initially blamed the riots on "twelve years of denial and neglect" by Presidents Bush and Reagan, but fearing he might be accused of advocating new spending programs, Clinton soon muted his criticisms.[62] On Monday, May 5, 1992, Bush's press secretary, Marlin Fitzwater, said the Great Society's programs of the 1960s were to blame for the rioting. Nevertheless, in an attempt to look like he was responding positively, President Bush proposed an emergency aid package. In June, Congress passed $1.3 billion in emergency aid that allocated $500 million for summer jobs, $382 million for loans to businesses damaged or destroyed in the riot areas, and some flood relief for the city of Chicago.

Through the summer and early fall of 1992, Congress worked on a larger and more permanent urban aid bill. A version was finally approved by the House on October 6 and the Senate on October 8. The legislation would have created 25 urban and 25 rural enterprise zones and financed so-called weed and seed programs that combined enhanced law enforcement with job training and education programs. The bulk of the legislation, however, was made up of an array of items that had nothing to do with cities, including liberalized (tax-free) retirement accounts for upper-income people and a provision for the repeal of luxury taxes on yachts, furs, jewels, and planes (Democrats backed this amendment as enthusiastically as Republicans). It was estimated that of the $30 billion the bill would cost over five years, about $6 billion would be used to help depressed areas in cities.[63] By the time the legislation was passed and sent to the White House for President Bush's signature, the election was over. Bush vetoed it, using the excuse that it was contaminated by pork-barrel amendments.

The CDBG program was the only major urban program to survive the Reagan/Bush years. CDBG spending fell from $4 billion in the 1981 fiscal year to $2.8 billion in fiscal 1990 before rebounding slightly in fiscal 1992, the year the Democrats reclaimed the White House. Under President Clinton, CDBG spending rose modestly to $4.6 billion by the 1996 fiscal year[64] and to $5.1 billion by Clinton's last budget, the 2001 fiscal year (when adjusted for inflation, however, funding for the program actually stayed even). Under President George W. Bush, the level of funding fell, but the program was not eliminated entirely.[65]

Political Reality and Urban Policy

As a self-styled "new Democrat" who wanted to project an image as a friend of the "forgotten middle class," Bill Clinton could not be expected to place aid to cities or to the poor on the front burner. In the 1992 presidential election, the Clinton campaign decided to concentrate on appealing to the white suburban middle class and to assume that inner-city voters would support him anyway because they had no place else to go. Clinton's electoral strategy succeeded in making him the first Democrat to be elected to two full terms since Franklin D. Roosevelt. Clinton succeeded by winning back many of the white suburban voters who had deserted the party in 1980. Even so, he still lost the overall white vote by a 39–41 percent margin. He carried huge pluralities in the cities, coming out of New York City, for example, with almost a million-vote lead. His ability to capture 82 percent of the African American vote was crucial to his victory.

A compelling logic informed Clinton's suburban strategy. By the 1990 census, 48 percent of the nation's population lived in the suburbs. Because they tended to turn out for elections at a relatively high rate, it seemed certain they would cast a majority of the national vote in the 1992 election.[66] In addition, large proportions of suburban voters were so-called Reagan Democrats, blue-collar and middle-class voters who had abandoned the party to vote Republican in the three previous presidential elections. They were heavily concentrated in the older suburbs in key states such as New Jersey, Michigan, and California, which could deliver the big blocs of electoral college votes coveted by every presidential candidate. To bring them back to the fold, Clinton wanted to avoid identifying himself with policies that were targeted to cities, and especially to benefit African Americans.

In developing his strategy, Clinton followed the advice of a well-known African American sociologist, William Julius Wilson, whose 1987 book, *The Truly Disadvantaged*, warned against race-specific policies. Wilson, who was a friend and adviser of the president, recommended a "hidden agenda" in which inner-city minorities might be helped "by emphasizing programs to which the more advantaged groups of all races and classes can positively relate."[67] In an interview before the election, Wilson praised Clinton's programs for targeting "all low- to moderate-income groups, not just minorities."[68]

Clinton ended up devising what two scholars called a "stealth urban policy" composed of programs that were not specifically targeted to cities but would be beneficial to them.[69] In their campaign book, *Putting People First*, Bill Clinton and Al Gore advocated policies designed to help the middle class and the disadvantaged equally. Clinton's highly successful campaign bus tours avoided the inner cities and gave the media ample opportunities to photograph the candidate against small town and rural backdrops. After winning the nomination, Clinton did attend a meeting of the United States Conference of Mayors (USCM) and lent his support to a public works initiative. Clinton stressed, however, that the principal goal was to stimulate the economy and that aiding cities would be a secondary effect.

Clinton began his presidency with the intention of rewarding the cities that had voted lopsidedly for him. To accomplish this, he put together a $19.5 billion economic stimulus bill that included $4.4 billion for public works (mostly in cities), $2.5 billion for community development grants, and $735 million for inner-city schools and jobs. Led by minority leader Bob Dole (R.-Kansas), Senate Republicans filibustered the bill, refusing to let it come up for a vote. Lacking the 60 votes necessary to end the filibuster, the Democrats were forced to back down. Eventually, all that was passed was a very modest bill not targeted at the cities at all, a $4 billion extension of unemployment benefits for the chronically unemployed.[70]

The only significant new urban initiative that the Clinton administration could claim was the Empowerment Zones/Enterprise Communities (EZ/EC) program, which was included as Title XIII of the Omnibus Budget Reconciliation Act of 1993. Republicans and even many conservatives had supported the enterprise zones idea in the Reagan and Bush years because it was based on a strategy of cutting taxes and regulations in inner cities, with the intention of stimulating investment in depressed neighborhoods. Conservatives liked it because it mirrored the Republicans' national-level policies. The Clinton administration adopted this same free-market approach. To promote investment in EZ/EC zones, tax credits were provided for employers who hired workers who lived in the zone, and businesses located within the zones became eligible for accelerated depreciation on business property and tax-exempt bond financing for new construction. Grant money was also made available to assist zone residents in obtaining education, job training, and child care so that they could work. Ultimately, 31 Empowerment Zones were created across the country, and 74 additional distressed areas (33 in rural areas) also won grants, but these were small in comparison to the full-fledged Empowerment Zones.

Empowerment Zones proved to be the only politically viable urban program left. The midterm 1994 elections dealt a near deathblow to urban policies. Led by House Speaker Newt Gingrich and his Contract with America (labeled Contract on America by detractors), the Republicans won control of both houses of Congress for the first time in 40 years. The Republicans were hostile to the little that remained of federal urban programs. Speaker Gingrich called for the elimination of the Department of Housing and Urban Development, asserting, "You could abolish HUD tomorrow morning and improve life in most of America." He was blunt about why HUD was being singled out for especially harsh treatment: Its "weak constituency," he said, "makes it a prime candidate for cuts."[71]

In a desperate attempt to stave off disaster, HUD secretary Henry Cisneros proposed to "reinvent" his department in ways pleasing to conservatives. Announced a month and a half after the 1994 election, HUD issued a *Reinvention Blueprint* calling for a consolidation of the department's programs into three flexible block grants that would be administered by cities and states. The plan also proposed converting all public housing aid to vouchers, which would allow recipients to find housing wherever private landlords would take them. Reinventing HUD became the centerpiece of Clinton's National Urban Policy Report, issued in July 1995.[72]

The decline in public housing and urban programs began well before Clinton came into office, but the fact that a Democrat was now in the White House, in large part thanks to the Black urban vote, did not change things very much. In the Reagan and Bush years, HUD experienced the largest cuts of any cabinet-level department in the federal government. HUD budget authority (what Congress authorizes it to spend) fell from 7.5 percent of the total federal budget in 1978 to 1.3 percent by 1990. During the Clinton administration, annual HUD spending recovered slightly, but this only enabled HUD to meet past commitments for housing subsidies. Four programs of special interest to city governments, General Revenue Sharing, Urban Development Action Grants, Local Public Works, and Antirecession Fiscal Assistance, were zeroed out—were eliminated entirely.

The welfare reform bill Clinton signed in August 1996 also hurt the cities. The Personal Responsibility Act of 1996 converted Aid to Families with Dependent Children into a block grant run by the states. In addition to a 64 percent decline in welfare spending from 1990 to 1998, food stamps and community services programs were sharply reduced. Three programs—child nutrition, supplemental (infant) feeding, and housing assistance—increased somewhat only because they were linked to welfare reform efforts. Medicaid costs climbed substantially (by 146 percent), but the big winner was justice assistance, which skyrocketed 1,250 percent in less than a decade. Although some of this money went to cities, the states used most of it to build prisons. Obviously, crime control trumped any other social purpose.

The Cities' Fall from Grace

Until the election of Barack Obama to the presidency in November 2008, both political parties had largely abandoned the cities. It was a matter of making a political calculus. In the case of the Republicans, party leaders had long sought to capitalize on white suburbanites' disaffection from the Democratic-sponsored civil rights and antipoverty policies of the 1960s. What is more interesting is the way the past friend of the cities, the Democratic Party, has shied away from urban issues. In 1968 the Democrats used the word *city* 23 times in the party platform adopted at their presidential nominating convention. It did not appear even once in the 1988 platform. The substitute term, *hometown America*, signaled a recognition that the suburban vote had grown in importance. In 1992 and 1996, Clinton avoided policies targeted to cities and concentrated his appeals on the suburban middle class. Notably, in the 2000 campaign, Democratic candidate Al Gore mentioned urban sprawl as a significant national issue. By the new century, urban policy no longer referred to central cities but to urban regions.

The near-invisibility of cities in national politics can be explained by a simple fact: Today, central-city voters are a very small fraction of the national electorate. The central cities of the 32 largest metropolitan areas reached a high-water mark of 27 percent of the electorate in 1944, but by 1992 they accounted for just 14 percent of the national vote[73] and 12 percent by the 2000 election. As shown in Figure 8.2, the share of their states' votes cast by their largest cities has fallen steadily for half a century in New York, Illinois, Pennsylvania, Michigan, and Massachusetts.[74] In 1952, New York City voters represented 48 percent of the statewide electorate, but by the 2000 presidential election, their proportion of the statewide vote had fallen to 32 percent. Chicago claimed 41 percent of the Illinois presidential vote in 1952 but only 20 percent by 2000. Between 2000 and 2020, those numbers have remained remarkably stable.

Cities also lost representation in the U.S. House of Representatives. Between 1963 and 1994, the number of congressional districts with a majority of the

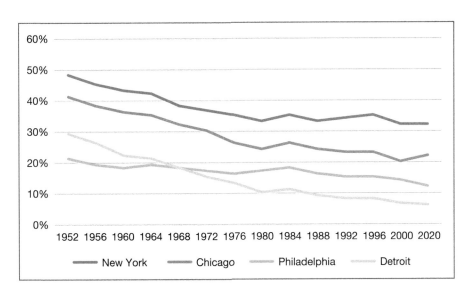

FIGURE 8.2 Cities as Percentage of Statewide Total Vote, 1952–2020

Sources: Richard Scammon, *America Votes* (various issues); U.S. Bureau of the Census, *Census of Population and Housing,* various years; and reports of actual city votes from county boards of elections (and newspapers for 1996 election). Data compiled by Richard Sauerzopf. Data from 2000 from Peter Dreier, John Mollenkopf, and Todd Swanstrom, *Place Matters,* 2nd ed. (Lawrence, KS: University Press of Kansas, 2004), p. 282; figures for 2020 compiled from 2020 Census data, data from *The New York City Campaign Finance Board* 2020–21 Voter Analysis Report, https://www.nyccfb. info/media/reports/voter-analysis-report-2020-2021/ and "Estimates of the Voting Age Population for 2020," *Federal Register: The Daily Journal of the United States Government* (published May 6, 2021), *United States Department of Commerce,* Office of the Secretary, https://www.federalregister.gov/ documents/2021/05/06/2021-09422/estimates-of-the-voting-age-population-for-2020.

population coming from central cities fell from 94 to 84, and over the same period, the number of districts with a majority of suburban voters increased from 94 to 214. In 1994, after the Republicans took control of the House, the proportion of leadership positions held by representatives from districts with a sizable proportion of central-city voters fell precipitously, from 30 to 10 percent.[75] Similar trends reduced the influence of the big cities in state governments as well.[76] The number of states with suburban electoral majorities climbed from 3 in 1980 to 14 in 1990 and increased again when seats were reapportioned as a result of the 2000 census.

It is generally assumed the suburbs now hold the key to winning national elections. Suburban votes were critical to the presidential victories of Presidents Ronald Reagan and George H. W. Bush; Reagan won huge landslides in 1980 and 1984 even though he only carried about a third of the central-city vote. In the 1988 election, suburban voters gave Bush such a comfortable cushion that he could have carried almost all of the northern industrial states without a single vote from the big cities in those states. By contrast, the central-city electorate was an important part of Bill Clinton's winning coalition in 1992 and 1996. In 1992 New York City provided Clinton with 92 percent of his nearly 1-million statewide vote margin, and Clinton lost to Bush in suburban Long Island (Nassau and Suffolk counties). In 1996, Clinton did even better in the cities, winning 67 percent of the vote in Milwaukee, 74 percent in Boston, 76 percent in St. Louis and New York, and 80 percent in Chicago.[77] In the 2000 presidential election, Al Gore won similar pluralities in the cities, but it was not enough to overcome George W. Bush's near-sweep of southern and less urban, less populated states of the Plains and the West. Gore won the national popular vote by more than 500,000 votes, but Bush was able to win the election by commanding a bare majority of votes in the Electoral College.

Even though President Clinton owed a debt to big-city voters for his two election victories, he did not make urban issues a priority. During his presidency, federal spending for the cities continued to fall. Clearly, Clinton felt he could take his urban base for granted, and he was right. This strategy did impose a potential cost on the Democrats, however, because as the federal government turned away from the cities, voter turnout in them went into a steep slide. Indeed, in the past half-century, 40 percent of the loss in the proportion of votes cast in the 32 largest cities can be traced to falling turnout and not to a shrinking population.[78]

The End of Urban Policy

At first blush, it would appear that Barack Obama's election put the voters of central cities and their constituency groups into a more favorable position than they had enjoyed for decades. For the first time since the Carter administration, the president signaled that he might pay attention to urban problems. Only a few weeks after taking office, the Obama administration announced the appointment of Adolfo Carrion, the president of Borough of the Bronx, as its "urban czar," with the charge to coordinate the urban-related programs then on the books. That goal was not realized. It would be a daunting job merely to identify the programs that influence cities and urban regions. An even harder task would follow. These programs are located in dozens of agencies operating under almost all of the cabinet-level departments. Even with a lot of attention and political muscle from the White House, it is not clear what "coordination" would amount to. Probably for this reason, as time passed, little was heard from the urban czar, and there was no prospect that urban issues would be able to compete in a crowded political agenda any time soon.

Still, it should be noted that more than at any time in decades, programs initiated by the Obama administration significantly influenced metropolitan development and improved the fiscal condition of states and cities. The American Recovery and Reinvestment Act, which authorized the expenditure of $787 billion over a 10-year period, was critically important to states and localities. The act allocated $79 billion to provide fiscal assistance to states, an important initiative because the states were imposing deep budget cuts that threatened to make the post-2007 recession worse. In addition, the legislation authorized $144 billion for infrastructure projects, which included $32 billion for transportation projects, $10 billion for rail and mass transit, and $2 billion for airports.[79] School districts were slated to receive $41 billion in grants for construction projects and other activities. The legislation set aside money for a wide array of activities to promote clean energy and conservation. Among other initiatives, the administration also announced a $1 billion program to put 5,500 more police officers on the streets.[80]

Organizations representing urban interests, broadly defined, were invigorated by these programs. On March 14–18, 2009, the National League of Cities convened its Annual Congressional City Conference, a gathering of local officials from across the country. By contrast to previous years, the conference revolved around a wide-ranging agenda featuring discussions of new federal initiatives in many areas, including infrastructure investment, jobs programs, green energy, and transportation. Local officials needed to share information because they found themselves involved in administering a broader variety of new federal programs than they have since the 1960s.

However, all of these programs taken together do not add up to an urban policy or even a collection of policies with similar aims. Even in the heyday of urban and social welfare programs, when federal administrators of the Great Society showered the cities with money, a coherent urban policy never existed. Programs were created for different reasons and for different purposes and to satisfy a variety of political needs and influential constituencies. There are still a large number of programs that influence cities, suburbs, and the people that live within them, but hardly any of these actually have "urban" aims. The stimulus package illustrates this fact perfectly: Although local governments were deeply affected, the main policy objective was to stimulate the national economy. For a long time, "urban" has not been a category that the federal government cares very much about, and that is unlikely to change.

"American Carnage": Trump's War on Cities

If cities did not see the much hoped-for improvements under the Obama administration, the Trump administration, after taking office in early 2017, all but declared war on cities. Cities morphed into the enemy trope for the urbanite Donald Trump, who is from Queens and has always identified as a New Yorker. But New York City neither gave its native son any electoral support in the November 2016 presidential elections, nor did it remain silent amid his offensive style and anti-urban, anti-immigrant, and anti-minority policies: Protests erupted in New York City upon his first visits as the country's new president. In September 2019, Trump decided to turn his back on New York City once and for all: He filed a "declaration of domicile," making his Palm Beach property his permanent residence, as did his wife, Melania Trump. It was generally assumed that the primary reason for this move was Florida's lower tax rate (unlike New York, the state does not have a state income tax or an inheritance tax), but in typical Trump fashion, the former president blamed public officials in New York for his departure, claiming, "I have been treated very badly by the political leaders of both the city and the state. Few have been treated worse."[81]

Already during his campaign, Trump had talked about "inner cities" in a fashion that more resembled the urban crisis of 1970s and 1980s than cities of the twenty-first century. In his description, "inner cities" were dark dystopian places of crime and prostitution rather than the complex, gentrifying giants of innovation and inequality that they are today. In his inaugural address, in which Trump vowed to put an end to what he referred to as "American Carnage," the former president painted a bleak picture of the state of the nation:

> Mothers and children trapped in poverty in our inner cities, rusted out factories scattered like tombstones across the landscape of our nation, an education system flush with cash but which leaves our young and beautiful students deprived of all knowledge. And the crime, and the gangs, and the drugs that have stolen too many lives and robbed our country of so much unrealized potential. This American carnage stops rights here and stops right now.[82]

Trump had already threatened repeatedly during the first six months of 2017 to drastically reduce or cut entirely funding for services for the homeless, housing, as well as critical social safety net programs in his 2018 budget proposals.[83] This threat was realized, along with threats of more and deeper funding cuts to cities, after the administration's clash with urban leaders around the country over undocumented immigrants and the sanctuary city movement.

In 2017, the Trump White House issued an executive order in which he directed government agencies to withhold millions in federal funding from urban jurisdictions who refused to cooperate with federal immigration authorities. While state and local jurisdictions wield no independent authority to issue immigration mandates or to amend or alter federal law, they have some limited rights to refuse cooperation with federal immigration enforcement, especially when it comes to so-called detainer requests issued by Immigration and Customs Enforcement (ICE). Detainer requests notify local agencies that ICE has a separate interest in individuals currently held in custody by local law enforcement. In them, ICE usually requests that they be notified 48 hours in advance before a person of interest is being released from local custody. Local jurisdictions have no set obligation under the law to honor these detainer requests. Detainer requests are interpreted merely as an "ask," not an order, for cooperation. The federal government awards grants, mostly in law enforcement, to local jurisdictions on a regular basis. In 2017, Trump attempted to punish so-called Sanctuary Cities for their lack of cooperation with ICE on detainer requests by withholding such funds from them. A federal district court in San Francisco issued a temporary injunction against the Trump administration's withholding of such funds to sanctuary jurisdictions that same year. In 2020, the Trump White House also announced that it would withhold COVID-19 related federal aid from Sanctuary Cities. That same spring, a federal appeals court in Chicago upheld several lower court decisions that had blocked the Trump administration from withholding COVID relief funds from sanctuary jurisdictions, noting that its ruling would apply nation-wide, and not just in the specific case it was deciding, which had been brought by the City of Chicago.[84] In a separate decision regarding federal grants for local law enforcement, however, the U.S. Appeals Court for the Second Circuit had decided to side with the Trump administration in February of 2020, allowing it to withhold millions in funding. The plaintiffs in that case, which included New York State, New York City, and six other states, appealed to the Supreme Court in 2020, but the case was withdrawn after Joseph R. Biden won the 2020 presidential election, and his justice department, under the new attorney general, Merrick Garland, reversed the Trump administration's punitive policies vis-à-vis Sanctuary Cities.[85]

Trump's tax bill, which was signed into law in December 2017 and went into effect during the 2018 fiscal year, was another explicit affront toward high-cost urban areas, along the nation's coasts—the economic engine of the country, and the places where Trump saw the greatest electoral defeats in 2016.[86] This tax bill further increased taxes in high-cost areas in the country, as it does not allow for deductions of city- and state income taxes and is likely to depress housing prices in those places, as the cost of living will increase.[87] The bill was interpreted by many urban leaders and dwellers alike as another punishment for their political opposition to the president.

By the end of its term, the Trump administration, along with many social safety regulations, also rolled back several key provisions implemented by the

Obama White House, which had been intended to fight pervasive segregationist housing policies in the suburbs. In several tweets, Trump noted that rolling back these policies would allow "people living their Suburban Lifestyle Dream" to "no longer be bothered or financially hurt by having low income housing built in your neighborhood."[88]

Besides the aggressive and racist political rhetoric by the former president, the Trump family has a personal history in housing discrimination: In the 1970s, the Justice Department brought a case against Donald Trump and his father, Fred Trump, who had considerable real estate holdings across New York City, alleging that they were engaging in discriminatory practices against Black tenants. The Trumps won the lawsuit, but in a 2016 in-depth investigation into old Justice Department records and court documents, as well filings from the New York City Commission on Human Rights, and interviews with tenants, civil rights activists, and prosecutors, *The New York Times* revealed what it called "a long history of racial bias at his [Trump's] family's properties, in New York and beyond."[89]

In 2020, the then-president issued a "warning" to "the Suburban Housewives of America," a term that seemed more appropriate in the 1950s than in the 2020s, claiming that, if elected, "Biden will destroy your neighborhood and your American Dream."[90] In reaction to Trump's recurring fear-mongering and racist rhetoric, a Democratic pollster, Jef Pollock noted, "Trump is playing old New York politics from the 1990s. The reality is that more and more suburban voters have embraced diversity as a positive thing for their community."[91] Even though Pollock's statement sounds somewhat naively optimistic in twenty-first-century America, the suburbs are changing, and in 2020, they largely provided Trump's Democratic challenger, Joseph R. Biden, with the necessary votes for the presidency—a significant shift from 2016.

Better Days Ahead? The Biden Administration's "Non-Urban" Urban Policy

The Biden campaign's 2020 election victory marked yet another shift in voting patterns across the nation. This time, a significant shift among suburban voters was the most impactful. In the 2020 election, especially those suburban counties located in larger metro areas contributed most notably to Biden's victory. This was particularly evident in the swing states in the North and Midwest, such as Wisconsin, Michigan, and Pennsylvania, but also in some Sunbelt states, most notably Georgia, North Carolina, Arizona, and even Texas.[92] Though the Trump campaign still won Texas and North Carolina, their margins in suburban counties shrunk quite significantly, especially in the suburbs of large metros, such as Dallas, Houston, San Antonio, and Austin.[93] Trump's solid victories in rural areas are testament to the growing rural-urban divide, where cities (and increasingly suburbs) appear to be swinging toward the Democrats, with rural areas remaining staunchly Republican, earning Trump a 34 percent margin in 2020.[94] While large cities continued to remain powerful Democratic strongholds in 2020, suburban areas within large metros saw a swing toward the Democrats as well in 2020 for the first time since 2008.[95] Either the Democrats were actually able to flip those suburbs to a majority blue vote, or they were able to significantly shrink Republican margins there. The Obama campaign had started to make those areas competitive for the Democrats in 2008, but that shift had seemed short-lived after Trump was able to gain back some of the Obama-era advantages, especially in the suburbs. On the other hand, the Biden campaign's gains in the suburbs and smaller cities across the country, but especially in key states (even in the South), seem to indicate a larger shift, which is in line with the demographic changes that have been occurring in the suburbs for some time now: The suburbs, especially those that are part of larger metro areas, seem to be increasingly approximating cities in terms of their demographic makeup: They are becoming more diverse, but also more unequal—with areas of strong wealth and deeper and more segregated pockets of poverty.

After a scathing election season and a grueling pandemic year during which the nation lost more than half a million (and counting) of its citizens to COVID-19, the new Biden administration took office in January 2021. The inauguration took place only two weeks after the outgoing president, on January 6, had instigated his followers to break into the United States Capitol and, using violent force, overturn the results of the 2020 presidential election. Congress, under the leadership of Vice President Mike Pence, was supposed to certify the results of the presidential election that day. The country, still ravaged by the COVID-19 pandemic, looked on in shock as Capitol Police appeared helpless and outnumbered amid the violent mob, which made its way into the sacred heart of American democracy—seemingly without resistance, and temporarily laid siege to the Capitol building. Lawmakers had to interrupt their session to be evacuated through the underground tunnels of the building. This was by no means an overreaction: "You could have literally had open air executions in Washington on January 6," the executive director for the Institute for Research and Education on Human Rights told the media: "It's clear from the rhetoric they were using inside the halls, their intentions, given things like noose hanging out in front or the fact that they brought zip ties and weapons into the halls, it could have been disastrous."[96] Despite the fact that the attempted coup d'etat failed in the end, it left five dead in the immediate aftermath of the riots, including one officer of the Capitol Police.

The new president's inauguration took place under the strictest security protocols, making it the most secured inauguration since the Lincoln inaugurations, which occurred before and after the Civil War, including barbed wire fences and thousands of National Guard troops, heavily armed.[97] In spite of the somewhat muted beginnings, the Biden administration has a political agenda promising for cities—even if it is not an urban agenda per se. However, after four years of aggressively anti-urban policies from the Trump administration, one should also keep in mind that any policy agenda is prone to look more promising for cities than what they had to contend with during Trump's term.

The administration's infrastructure bills, which, as of August 2021, made it through the Senate but are likely to face more challenges in the House, can be expected to have a beneficial impact on cities. Even before the pandemic, many of the nation's urban transit systems were severely underfunded and in dire need of updating. The first bill to pass the Senate (which remains up for debate in the House) earmarked $39 billion for public transportation systems. More specifically, transit systems are supposed to be expanded, their accessibility for people with disabilities is intended to be improved, and transit at the state and local levels is targeted to be converted to low- and zero-emission buses.[98] The funding represents a big boost for many cities, whose transit systems, already underfunded, struggled even harder during the pandemic year, and who were facing the most dire consequences, such as having to reduce service and increasing fares.

In terms of housing, the administration has, via executive order, extended Congress' pandemic eviction moratoria (which expired on July 30, 2021) for homeowners whose properties were financed or insured by the U.S. Department of Agriculture (USDA) (until September 30, 2021), as well as for renters (until October 3, 2021), and it is expected to help cover about 90 percent of the nation's renters.[99]

Beyond what it has implemented in its first 200 days in office, the new Biden administration has made a lot of campaign promises that could, in the long and short run, benefit cities. Among those promises are opening up the Section 8 housing voucher program to anyone who needs it, beyond the strict qualification criteria; a $100 billion Affordable Housing Fund to support public housing authorities to rebuild and modernize their partially dilapidated housing stock, as well as $10 billion increase to both, the Low Income Housing Tax Credit program, which helps incentivize and fund more low-income housing, and the Community Development Block Grants, which have been on the decline for decades.[100] As part of the administration's infrastructure bill, it is also pushing for widely available internet access, though this is something that primarily small towns and rural areas, which are currently lacking such infrastructure, will benefit from. In addition, the administration wants to set aside $65 billion in infrastructure funds aside to help modernize the electric grid to prevent frequent power outages, $25 billion to help improve airport infrastructures, such as runways, terminals, and air traffic control towers, and $55 billion to improve water and wastewater infrastructure.[101]

None of the Biden administration's proposed improvements are specifically aimed at cities, nor are they promoted to be. Urban dwellers and governments alike can expect to benefit, in one way or another, from many of the Biden administration's plans and proposals, but they all fall short of addressing cities and their unique challenges in particular. What is certain is that we live in a time of change—demographically, electorally, and in terms of party politics. Things are changing once again throughout the country. It remains to be seen how these developments will impact the United States' urban future in the long run.

Endnotes

1 As reported in *The New York Times* (December 1, 1959), p. 27, quoted in Mark I. Gelfand, *A Nation of Cities: The Federal Government and Urban America*, Urban Life in America Series (New York: Oxford University Press, 1975), p. 295. See also John F. Kennedy, "The Great Unspoken Issue," in *Proceedings, American Municipal Congress 1959* (Washington, D.C.: American Municipal League, n.d.), pp. 23–28; and John F. Kennedy, "The Shame of the States," *The New York Times Magazine* (May 18, 1958).

2 Quoted in Theodore H. White, *The Making of the President, 1960* (New York: Atheneum, 1961), p. 206. Nixon's strategy, which White contends was no strategy at all, was a "national" one, in which he committed himself to visit all 50 states; Kennedy, in contrast, used an urban strategy centered on the industrial states with large blocs of electoral votes (see pp. 267–352).

3 John C. Donovan, *The Politics of Poverty*, 2nd ed. (New York: Bobbs-Merrill, Pegasus, 1973), p. 19.

4 Quoted in White, *The Making of the President*, p. 165.

5 Donovan, *The Politics of Poverty*, p. 225.

6 Ibid., p. 104.

7 Nelson W. Polsby and Aaron Wildavsky, *Presidential Elections: Contemporary Strategies of American Electoral Politics*, 7th ed. (New York: Free Press, 1988). The statistics given are for "nonwhite" voters.

8 White, *The Making of the President*, p. 354.

9 For good recent summary accounts, see ibid.; also James A. Morone, *The Democratic Wish: Popular Participation and the Limits of American Government* (New York: Basic Books, 1990), Chapter 6.

10 Quoted in Richard Blumenthal, "The Bureaucracy: Antipoverty and the Community Action Programs," in *American Political Institutions and Public Policy*, ed. Allan P. Sindler (Boston, MA: Little, Brown, 1969), p. 149.

11 *Message of the President to Congress*, reprinted in *Congressional Quarterly Weekly Report* 32, no. 2 (January 11, 1964).

12 *Congress and the Nation, 1945–1964* (Washington, D.C.: Congressional Quarterly Service, 1965), p. 1379.

13 *Tax Policy Center Briefing Book*, "The State of State (and Local) Tax Policy: What Are the Sources of Revenue for Local Governments?" https://www.taxpolicycenter.org/briefing-book/what-are-sources-revenue-local-governments.

14 Refer to Daniel J. Elazar, *The American Partnership: Intergovernmental Cooperation in the Nineteenth Century United States* (Chicago, IL: University of Chicago Press, 1962).

15 Manpower Development and Training Act of 1962, Public Law 87–415, 87th Cong. (1962); emphasis added.

16 Economic Opportunity Act of 1964, Public Law 88–452, 88th Cong. (1964); emphasis added.

17 Demonstration Cities and Metropolitan Development Act of 1966, Public Law 89–754, 89th Cong. (1966); emphasis added.

18 See James L. Sundquist and David W. Davis, *Making Federalism Work: A Study of Program Coordination at the Community Level* (Washington, D.C.: Brookings Institution Press, 1969), pp. 3–5.

19 Lyndon B. Johnson, "Total Victory over Poverty," Message to Congress, March 15, 1964, reprinted in *The Failure of American Liberalism: After the Great Society,* ed. Marvin E. Gettleman and David Mermelstein (New York: Vintage Books, 1970), p. 181.

20 U.S. Office of Economic Opportunity, *Community Action Program Guide* (Washington, D.C.: U.S. Government Printing Office, 1965).

21 Frances Fox Piven and Richard A. Cloward, *Regulating the Poor: The Functions of Public Welfare* (New York: Pantheon, 1971).

22 Ibid., p. 295.

23 U.S. Advisory Commission on Intergovernmental Relations, *Fiscal Balance in the American Federal System,* vol. 1 (Washington, D.C.: U.S. Government Printing Office, 1967), p. 169.

24 Karen Tumulty and Kennedy Elliott, "Evaluating the Success of the Great Society: Lyndon B. Johnson's Visionary Set of Legislation Turns 50," *The Washington Post,* May 17, 2014, https://www.washingtonpost.com/sf/national/2014/05/17/the-great-society-at-50/.

25 Ibid.

26 U.S. Office of Management and Budget, *Special Analyses: Budget of the United States Government: Fiscal Year 1981* (Washington, D.C.: U.S. Government Printing Office, 1982), p. 254.

27 Michael D. Reagan, *The New Federalism* (New York: Oxford University Press, 1972), p. 97.

28 U.S. Department of the Treasury, Office of Revenue Sharing, *Reported Uses of General Revenue Sharing Funds, 1974–1975: A Tabulation and Analysis of Data from Actual Use,* Report 5 (Washington, D.C.: U.S. Government Printing Office, 1966), p. 5.

29 Ibid., p. 25.

30 "New Directions Cited in First Annual Block Grant Reports," *Housing and Development Reporter* (January 12, 1976), p. 761.

31 Housing and Community Development Act of 1974, sec. 104(a).

32 Reported in *Housing and Development Reporter* (January 10, 1977), p. 684.

33 Interview by Sharon Cribbs (investigator for the Southern Governmental Monitoring Project) with Nathaniel Hill, Director, Department of Human Resources, Little Rock, Arkansas (Summer 1975), quoted in Southern Governmental Monitoring Project, *A Time for Accounting: The Housing and Community Development Act in the South: A Monitoring Report,* ed. Raymond Brown with Ann Coil and Carol Rose (Atlanta, GA: Southern Regional Council, 1976), p. 53.

34 Ann R. Markusen and David Wilmoth, "The Political Economy of National Urban Policy in the U.S.A.: 1976–81," *Canadian Journal of Regional Science* 5, no. 1 (Summer 1982): 145–163.

35 Rochelle L. Stansfield, "Federalism Report: Government Seeks the Right Formula for Community Development Funds," *National Journal* (February 12, 1977): 242.

36 Ann R. Markusen, "The Urban Impact Analysis: A Critical Forecast," in *The Urban Impact of Federal Policies,* ed. Norman Glickman (Baltimore, MD: Johns Hopkins

University Press, 1979); see also discussion by Ann R. Markusen, Annalee Saxenian, and Marc A. Weiss, "Who Benefits from Intergovernmental Transfers?" in *Cities Under Stress: The Fiscal Crises of Urban America,* ed. Robert W. Burchell and David Listokin (New Brunswick, NJ: Center for Urban Research, 1981), p. 656; and Stansfield, "Federalism Report."

37　Quoted in Robert Reinhold, "President Proposes a Broad New Policy for Urban Recovery," *The New York Times* (March 28, 1978).

38　"Excerpts from the President's Message to Congress Outlining His Urban Policy," *The New York Times* (March 28, 1978).

39　F. J. James, "President Carter's Comprehensive National Urban Policy: Achievements and Lessons Learned," *Environment and Planning C: Government and Policy* 8 (1990): 34.

40　Markusen and Wilmoth, "The Political Economy of National Urban Policy," p. 15.

41　"Washington Update: Administration Officials, Mayors Have Love Fest," *National Journal* (January 29, 1977): 189.

42　Quoted in Theodore H. White, *America in Search of Itself: The Making of the President, 1956–1980* (New York: Harper & Row, 1982), p. 381.

43　D. Lee Bawden and John L. Palmer, "Social Policy: Challenging the Welfare State," in *The Reagan Record,* ed. John L. Palmer and Isabel V. Sawhill (Cambridge, MA: Ballinger, 1992), p. 200.

44　Ronald Reagan, "Interview with Reporters on Federalism," *Ronald Reagan Presidential Library & Museum* (November 19, 1981). https://www.reaganlibrary.gov/archives/speech/interview-reporters-federalism.

45　President's Commission for a National Agenda for the Eighties, *A National Agenda for the Eighties* (Washington, D.C.: U.S. Government Printing Office, 1980), p. 66.

46　Ibid., p. 4.

47　Ibid., p. 66.

48　Timothy K. Barnekov, Daniel Rich, and Robert Warren, "The New Privatism, Federalism, and the Future of Urban Governance: National Urban Policy in the 1980s," *Journal of Urban Affairs* 3, no. 4 (Fall 1981): 3.

49　U.S. Department of Housing and Urban Development, *The President's National Urban Policy Report* (Washington, D.C.: U.S. Government Printing Office, 1982), pp. 2, 23.

50　Ibid., p. 14.

51　Ibid., p. 135.

52　Ibid., p. 138.

53　Robertson and Judd, *The Development of American Public Policy,* p. 233.

54　U.S. Office of Management and Budget, *Budget of the United States Government, Fiscal Year 1996, Historical Tables* (Washington, D.C.: U.S. Government Printing Office, 1996), Table 12.3.

55　Henry J. Aaron and Associates, "Nondefense Programs," in *Setting National Priorities: The 1983 Budget,* ed. Joseph A. Pechman (Washington, D.C.: Brookings Institution Press, 1982), p. 119.

56　White House press release, March 7, 1983.

57　Quoted in Robert Pear, "Quayle Criticizes New York as Proof of Welfare's Ills," *The New York Times* (February 28, 1992), p. 1.

58　Bruce Weber, "Everyone to City: Drop Dead," *The New York Times* (June 21, 1992), p. 27.

59 "The Willie Horton of 1992," *The New York Times* (March 3, 1992), p. 3.

60 Anjuli Sastry and Karen Grigsby Bates, "When LA Erupted in Anger: A Look Back at the Rodney King Riots." *NPR Special Series: The Los Angeles Riots, 25 Years On* (April 26, 2017), https://www.npr.org/2017/04/26/524744989/when-la-erupted-in-anger-a-look-back-at-the-rodney-king-riots.

61 James H. Johnson Jr., Cloyzelle K. Jones, Walter C. Farrell Jr., and Melvin L. Oliver, "The Los Angeles Rebellion: A Retrospective View," *Economic Development Quarterly* 6, no. 4 (November 1992): 356–372.

62 Robert Pear, "Clinton, in Attack on President, Ties Riots to 'Neglect,'" *The New York Times* (May 6, 1992), p. 1.

63 Clifford Krauss, "Congress Passes Aid to Cities," *The New York Times* (June 9, 1992), p. A20.

64 U.S. Office of Management and Budget, *Budget of the United States Government, Fiscal Year 1996, Historical Tables*, Table 12.3.

65 U.S. Office of Management and Budget, *Budget of the United States Government, Fiscal Year 2003* (Washington, D.C.: U.S. Government Printing Office, 2003), Appendix, p. 485.

66 William Schneider, "The Suburban Century Begins," *Atlantic Monthly* (July 1992), pp. 33–44.

67 William Julius Wilson, *The Truly Disadvantaged: The Inner City, the Underclass, and Public Policy* (Chicago, IL: University of Chicago Press, 1987), p. 155.

68 "A Visit with Bill Clinton," *Atlantic Monthly* (October 1992); and William Julius Wilson, "The Right Message," *The New York Times* (March 17, 1992).

69 Bernard H. Ross and Myron A. Levine, *Urban Politics: Power in Metropolitan America*, 5th ed. (Itasca, IL: F. E. Peacock, 1996), p. 434.

70 Adam Clymer, "G.O.P. Senators Prevail, Sinking Clinton's Economic Stimulus Bill," *The New York Times* (April 22, 1993), p. 1.

71 Quoted in Kenneth J. Cooper, "Gingrich Pledges a Major Package of Spending Cuts Early Next Year," *Washington Post* (December 13, 1994), p. 1.

72 U.S. Department of Housing and Urban Development, *Empowerment: A New Covenant with America's Communities* (Rockville, MD: HUD USER, July 1995).

73 Peter F. Nardulli, Jon K. Dalager, and Donald E. Greco, "Voter Turnout in U.S. Presidential Elections: An Historical View and Some Speculation," *PS: Political Science and Politics* 23, no. 9, (September 1996): 484.

74 Calculations are from Richard Sauerzopf and Todd Swanstrom, "The Urban Electorate in Presidential Elections, 1920–1992: Challenging the Conventional Wisdom," paper delivered at the annual meeting of the Urban Affairs Association (Indianapolis, April 22–25, 1993). Updated by authors.

75 Hal Wolman and Lisa Marckini, "Changes in Central City Representation and Influence in Congress," paper prepared for delivery at the annual meeting of the Urban Affairs Association (Toronto, Canada, April 17, 1997). See also Demetrios Caraley, "Washington Abandons the Cities," *Political Science Quarterly* 107, no. 1 (1992): 20.

76 Margaret Weir, "Central Cities' Loss of Power in State Politics," *Cityscape: A Journal of Policy Development and Research* 2, no. 2 (May 1996): 23–40.

77 From CNN.com, http://www.cnn.com/ALLPOLITICS/1996/.

78 Nardulli, Dalager, and Greco, "Voter Turnout in U.S. Presidential Elections," p. 484.

79 "Stimulus Package Unveiled," *Wall Street Journal*, http://online.wsj.com/article/SB123202946622485595.html.

80 National League of Cities, "NLC Applauds Announcement of COPS Hiring Recovery Program," http://www.nlc.org/documents/Utility%20Navigation/News%20Center/NCW/2009/NCW032309.pdf.

81 Maggie Haberman, "Trump, Lifelong New Yorker, Declares Himself a Resident of Florida," *The New York Times,* (October 31, 2019), https://www.nytimes.com/2019/10/31/us/politics/trump-new-york-florida-primary-residence.html.

82 "President Trump's Inaugural Address, Annotated," *NPR Special Series Fact Check* (January 20, 2017), https://www.npr.org/2017/01/20/510629447/watch-live-president-trumps-inauguration-ceremony.

83 Mary K. Cunningham, "The Cost of Homelessness Will Spike If Congress Adopts Trump's 2018 Budget Proposal," *The Urban Wire: The Urban Institute* (June 6, 2017). Accessed online: https://www.urban.org/urban-wire/cost-homelessness-will-spike-if-congress-adopts-trumps-2018-budget-proposal.

84 Ted Hesson, "U.S. Appeals Court Rules against Trump Attempt to Withhold Funds from 'Sanctuary' Cities," *Reuters* (April 30, 2020), https://www.reuters.com/article/us-usa-immigration-court/u-s-appeals-court-rules-against-trump-attempt-to-withhold-funds-from-sanctuary-cities-idUSKBN22C408.

85 Sarah N. Lynch, "EXCLUSIVE U.S. Justice Department Ends Trump-Era Limits on Grants to 'Sanctuary Cities,'" *Reuters* (April 28, 2021), https://www.reuters.com/world/us/exclusive-us-justice-department-ends-trump-era-limits-grants-sanctuary-cities-2021-04-28/.

86 Shane Goldmacher, Maggie Haberman, and Kate Kelly, "On Tax Bill, It's Trump vs. His Hometown," *The New York Times* (December 7, 2017). Accessed online: https://www.nytimes.com/2017/12/07/nyregion/tax-bill-republican-trump-new-york.html.

87 Ibid.

88 Quoted in Annie Karni, Maggie Haberman, and Sydney Ember, "Trump Plays on Racist Fears of Terrorized Suburbs to Court White Voters," *The New York Times* (July 29, 2020), https://www.nytimes.com/2020/07/29/us/politics/trump-suburbs-housing-white-voters.html.

89 Jonathan Mahler and Steve Eder, "'No Vacancies' for Blacks: How Donald Trump Got His Start, and Was First Accused of Bias," *The New York Times* (August 27, 2016), https://www.nytimes.com/2016/08/28/us/politics/donald-trump-housing-race.html.

90 Quoted in Annie Karni, Maggie Haberman and Sydney Ember, "Trump Plays on Racist Fears of Terrorized Suburbs to Court White Voters," *The New York Times* (July 29, 2020), https://www.nytimes.com/2020/07/29/us/politics/trump-suburbs-housing-white-voters.html.

91 Quoted in Ibid.

92 William Frey, "Biden's Victory Came from the Suburbs," *Brookings Report* (November 13, 2020), https://www.brookings.edu/research/bidens-victory-came-from-the-suburbs/.

93 Ibid.

94 Ibid.

95 Ibid.

96 Quoted in: Kelly McLaughlin, "5 People Died in the Capitol Insurrection. Experts Say It Could Have Been So Much Worse." *Business Insider* (January 23, 2021), https://www.businessinsider.com/capitol-insurrection-could-have-been-deadlier-experts-say-2021-1.

97 Daniel Newhauser, "US Tightens Security before Joe Biden's Inauguration," *Al Jazeera* (January 16, 2021), https://www.aljazeera.com/news/2021/1/16/a-sad-day-for-america-inauguration-will-be-militarised.

98 Mary Clare Jalonick, "What's Inside the Senate's Bipartisan Infrastructure Bill?" *The Associated Press* (August 11, 2021), https://apnews.com/article/joe-biden-business-bills-38b84f0e9fcc8e68646eedf6608c4c70.

99 Alicia Adamczyk, "The CDC Extending the Federal Eviction Moratorium Is Expected to Cover about 90% of Renters," *CNBC* (August 4, 2021), https://www.cnbc.com/2021/08/03/cdc-will-extend-the-federal-eviction-moratorium-through-oct-3.html.

100 Jack Blumgart, "A City Leaders' Guide to Joe Biden's Policy Agenda," *City Monitor* (January 20, 2021), https://citymonitor.ai/government/budgets/a-city-leaders-guide-to-joe-bidens-policy-agenda.

101 Ibid.

CHAPTER 9

Changing Demographics: The Rise of the Sunbelt, the Changing Suburbs, and the Emerging "Rural-Urban Divide"

A Historic Shift

Over the past half-century, regional population shifts have brought radical changes to the nation's politics, economics, and culture. Historically, the center of gravity for the nation's politics had been located in the big industrial states and cities of the Northeast and the heartland. Because of its continued reliance on an agricultural economy, the South remained marginalized. Democratic politicians from the southern states could influence national politics only by voting as a bloc in the House and Senate and by maintaining a tenuous alliance with Northern Democrats. Most Northerners regarded southern culture as a curious relic of a faded past. But at least its participation in the national party system allowed the South to maintain a presence in national politics. By contrast, until mid-century, the Southwest was almost invisible. Its population, small and dispersed, was still defined largely by its frontier legacy. Except for Los Angeles, as late as the middle of the twentieth century, there were no other cities of significant size in the vast region stretching from New Mexico to the southern California coast. Over 1.5 million people lived in Los Angeles in 1940, compared to San Diego, with its population of 203,000, Phoenix, at 65,000, and tiny Las Vegas, with just 8,500 residents. But over the next few decades, population growth would be so rapid in cities of the South and the Southwest that these two regions would become fused into a vast region that became known as the Sunbelt.

DOI: 10.4324/9781003175315-11

This historic redistribution of the national population irreversibly changed the contours of national politics. The rise of the Sunbelt brought about a conservative shift in American politics. Beginning in the 1950s, business corporations began to move to southern and western states to escape higher labor costs in the industrial North and to take advantage of a vast pool of low-wage, non-unionized labor. Twelve of 15 Sunbelt states have right-to-work laws that allow employers to hire workers in a plant even if they refuse to join the plant's union. By contrast, two of the 14 states in the old industrial belt stretching from the Midwest and up through New England have a right-to-work law. These laws have discouraged unionization and kept wages lower than in states where unions are stronger.[1] In the Sunbelt, these policies have reflected a political culture that is highly individualistic and generally hostile to governmental action, unless that action is geared toward helping business, supporting military bases, or financing water and other federal projects that promote economic development. Due in part to the rising influence of Sunbelt politicians in both parties who represented such values, the nation's political culture began to move rightward in the second half of the twentieth century, and in many respects, the Sunbelt became the driving force in the nation's politics.

OUTTAKE

The Electoral College Favors the Sunbelt

The term *Sunbelt* was popularized in the mid-1970s, and it quickly became almost indispensable in everyday discourse about national development and politics. Even though the geographic boundaries of the Sunbelt were rather vague in most people's minds, the term generally conveyed a positive image of a region of the country that was prosperous and growing: "When a person hears the term on radio or on television, or reads it in a magazine or book, or sees it in the telephone book or on a firm's letterhead, it is likely to conjure up an image of growing cities and booming economies in Southern or Southwestern cities with pleasant climates." It would be possible to regard the term as merely a "rhetorical ruse," as one scholar commented, or a "public relations coup," as the president of a corporation helping other companies move to the Sunbelt claimed, were it not for the fact that the long-term population growth in the region has resulted in a fundamental realignment of political power in the nation. Until Barack Obama, all the winning presidents since John F. Kennedy came from the Sunbelt. Over the past half-century, the reapportionment that follows each decennial census has shifted the balance of power in Congress toward the congressional delegations that represent southern and western states. Without doubt, this realignment of power explains the shift toward conservative social policies in recent decades.

Over time, the Sunbelt was able to flex its muscles in Washington because population equals votes. Politicians could scarcely ignore this reality. The

Republicans were strongest in the suburbs of urban regions in the West and, after 1964, the South, all of which were booming. Each decennial census was followed by a reapportionment of seats in the House of Representatives, which, together with the two senators from each state, determines the number of Electoral College votes each state casts in a presidential election. The Sunbelt states increased the number of their votes in the Electoral College every time the country was reapportioned after 1928; over the same period, states in the Midwest and Northeast steadily lost Electoral College votes. In 1928, the 15 Sunbelt states were able to cast 146 votes in the Electoral College, compared to the 237 cast by electors representing 14 Midwestern and northeastern states. By the 2000 presidential election, the situation was reversed: The Sunbelt states held 222 votes, but by then, the 14 northern states could cast only 180 votes in the Electoral College balloting. If Al Gore had won the same states but run for the presidency in 1960 instead of 2000, he would have carried the election by 275 to 262 Electoral College votes; likewise, John Kerry would have won the presidency in 2004. Barack Obama's victory in 2008 was achieved mainly because he added some border and western states, plus Florida, to the Democratic tally. By 2024, the Sunbelt states will have an estimated eight more electoral votes, making it all the more important to Democratic candidates that their party continues to make inroads there.

Sources: Bradley R. Rice, "Searching for the Sunbelt," in *Searching for the Sunbelt: Historical Perspectives on a Region*, ed. Raymond A. Mohl (Knoxville, TN: University of Tennessee Press, 1990), p. 217: David R. Goldfield, *Cotton Fields and Skyscrapers: Southern City and Region, 1706–1980* (Baton Rouge, LA: Louisiana State University Press, 1982), p. 192, cited in Rice, "Searching for the Sunbelt," p. 218; Edward M. Burmila, "The Electoral College after Census 2010 and 2020: The Political Impact of Population Growth and Redistribution," *Perspectives on Politics* 7, no. 4 (December 2009): 839.

In the last couple of decades, however, the politics of the Sunbelt has been changing, so much so that the term is beginning to lose much of its meaning. African Americans have been moving back into the South from northern states, and millions of immigrants have been moving into southern and southwestern metropolitan regions and into smaller towns. The new demographic realities have created a shifting and unpredictable political landscape. Since the 1990s, Hispanics have accounted for almost 40 percent of the population growth in the United States, and Sunbelt cities and suburbs have attracted the largest numbers. In the first decade of this century, the Hispanic population accounted for more than half of the nation's growth. The 2010 census indicated that the U.S. Hispanic population grew 43 percent, from 35.5 million in 2000 to 50.5 million by 2010. By the 2020 census, it had grown to 62.1 million, a 23 percent increase over the past decade. This trend is expected to continue. The Census Bureau predicts that the non-Hispanic white population will drop to 50.8 percent of the total population by 2040 and even lower, to 46.3 percent, by 2050.[2]

Twelve of the 18 U.S. cities whose populations changed from a majority of non-Hispanic whites to a majority of minority residents during the 1990s were located in the South and Southwest.[3] In addition, the fast-growing suburbs of Sunbelt cities have attracted large numbers of highly educated professionals, and this group is not as reliably conservative as Sunbelt voters have been in the past.[4] The 2000, 2004, 2008, 2012, and 2020 presidential elections revealed that Democratic and independent-leaning voters had turned Arizona (and, by 2020, Georgia and Texas) from solidly Republican into potential swing states, and Virginia and California from Republican to solidly Democratic states. By 2020, it became apparent that parts of the South may have tipped into the Democratic-leaning column. The Sunbelt appears to be is breaking apart as a regional political force. Despite the fact that the 2016 elections turned the South almost solidly red again and marked the breakdown of the "blue wall" of the Midwestern states, Michigan, Wisconsin, and Iowa, which had traditionally gone for the Democrats, by 2020, Virginia had turned solidly Democrat, and Georgia had become a blue state for the first time since 1992, continuing the 2008 trend and indicating that change is on the way in the Sunbelt in the future.

If the ongoing sea change in national electoral alignments ultimately favors the Democratic Party, there is likely to be increasing support for an active national presence in health care, urban transportation and infrastructure, and other initiatives that people think of as "liberal." As in the past, changes in the regional balance of power will be of great consequence.

The Concept of the Sunbelt

Kevin Phillips, the chief political analyst for the 1968 Republican presidential campaign, is generally credited for coining the term *Sunbelt*. In his book *The Emerging Republican Majority*, published in 1969, Phillips asserted that the United States was going through a historic electoral realignment that was transforming the Republican Party into the nation's majority party. The basis of this national political realignment, he said, was the movement of millions of Americans out of the old industrial cities of the North to the suburbs and to the South and West. Phillips sometimes lumped the South and the West into an area he called the Sunbelt, although he never actually defined its boundaries; indeed, of the 47 maps in his book, none portrays such a region.[5]

Phillips's prediction that regionalism would increasingly influence the direction of national politics turned out to be correct. In 1973, an embargo on the sale of oil imposed by the Arab oil-producing nations drove the world price of oil sharply upward. The economies of oil-producing states such as Texas, Louisiana, Oklahoma, and Colorado boomed, and new jobs were created throughout the southern and western states. At the same time, energy-dependent industries and consumers in the northern states were hit hard. In 1974 and 1975, northern states went through an economic depression that saw hundreds of thousands of layoffs in industrial jobs. By the spring of 1975, New York City was facing bankruptcy and had to ask the federal government for loan guarantees. President Gerald Ford initially refused to help.[6] Congressional legislative battles began to divide along regional lines, pitting a prosperous South and West against an economically troubled North.

In this atmosphere, Kirkpatrick Sale's book *Power Shift*, published in 1975, quickly became a national bestseller.[7] Sale wrote that the states of the South and West—a region he called the Southern Rim—were gaining national political power at the expense of the older industrial states. Trying to find a way to report on the political issues raised by the new regional antagonisms, the media revived Phillips's notion of the Sunbelt, and the term soon came into common use. In February 1976, *The New York Times* published a five-part series documenting the demographic and political trends favoring the Sunbelt. In May, *BusinessWeek* devoted its feature article to "The Second War between the States."[8] The regional war became one of the hot topics helping sell newspapers and magazines in 1976 and 1977.

Although the concept of the Sunbelt quickly became part of the everyday language of Americans (the term has been included in dictionaries since the late 1970s), the precise boundaries of the region were hard to pin down. In a letter to a scholar researching the politics of the Sunbelt, Kevin Phillips defined it as the "territory stretching from the eastern Carolina lowlands down around (and excluding) Appalachia, picking up only the Greater Memphis area of Tennessee, omitting the Ozarks and moving west to Oklahoma, thence virtually due west," possibly also including Colorado.[9] It is understandable that Phillips would want to draw his boundaries to exclude pockets of poverty in the Border States, but his description was extremely imprecise. Sale's definition, displayed in Figure 9.1, encompassed the entire portion of the United States below the

FIGURE 9.1 The American Sunbelt and Frostbelt

Source: Adapted from Richard M. Bernard and Bradley R. Rice, eds., *Sunbelt Cities: Politics and Growth Since World War II* (Austin, TX: University of Texas Press, 1985), p. 7.

37th parallel, extending across the country from North Carolina to the West Coast, including southern California and part of southern Nevada.[10] (For statistical purposes, we include all of California and Nevada in our discussion.) Thus, Sale's map put 15 states in the Sunbelt. The 14 states of the Northeast and the upper Midwest were lumped together into a region that for a time was called the *Frostbelt*, a term that has since pretty much disappeared from the national political discourse.

Right from the beginning, a significant number of scholars considered the concept of the Sunbelt to be suspect. For one thing, the vast region encompassed by Sale's definition was far from uniformly prosperous. The most rapid economic and population growth was occurring in Florida, parts of Texas, Arizona, Southern Nevada, and Southern California. Rural areas all across the Sunbelt and many urban areas of the South remained untouched by the prosperity that was proclaimed as the Sunbelt's principal defining feature, a fact that led two scholars to note that the Sunbelt had "collapsed into only a few 'sunspots.'"[11]

A second problem with the Sunbelt concept was that it assumed the South and the Southwest were similar enough to be lumped together under a single label. Until its image was burnished by its rhetorical association with the prosperous Sunbelt, the South was often thought of as a backward, poverty-ridden, violent region with a peculiar caste system. Most political studies of the South focused on issues of race, the enduring effects of the Civil War and Reconstruction, and the dominance of a single, authoritarian party (until the 1960s, the Republican Party rarely ran candidates in most southern states)—the elements making up a conservative political culture that had changed little since the Civil War. The main industries that had located in the South were those associated with low-wage labor. In the 1930s, Franklin Roosevelt and the New Deal administrators looked at federal programs as a way to bring economic development to this backward region.[12]

The image of the West, by contrast, tended to be "urban, opulent, energetic, mobile, and individualistic, a region of economic growth and openness to continual change which matched America's self-image."[13] If the image of perpetual sunshine gave the Sunbelt its name, then certainly this image fit the West better than the South. Because Los Angeles was the home of the movie and television industries, America's popular culture became increasingly identified with western images. Los Angeles served as a vision of America's future, with its sprawling suburbs, freeways, shopping centers, and even its smog.

Some observers argued thought that the idea of the Sunbelt was overplayed. Nicholas Lemann, who edited the *Texas Monthly* in the 1980s, observed that "millions of people were living in the Sunbelt without one of them realizing it. They thought of themselves as Southerners or Texans, or Los Angelenos."[14] The concept of the Sunbelt was regarded with suspicion not only because there were so many differences within it but also because all regions of the United States seemed to be becoming more alike. The industrial belt was becoming less industrial, urban populations were spreading out into suburbs in all parts of the country, and a media-based national culture was replacing regional cultural differences. "Just try to find a town anywhere in the United States without a McDonald's or a television happy-news format featuring an anchorperson with an unidentifiable accent."[15]

Despite the shortcomings of the Sunbelt/Frostbelt dichotomy, it remains useful as a starting point for understanding the regional demographic movements of the past half-century, and how these population shifts have contributed to the conservative turn in American national politics. The move away from urban and social welfare policies has occurred both because people moved out of the central cities and because large numbers of people left the old industrial heartland. For a variety of reasons, both the South and the Southwest have produced a political culture that is suspicious of government. For a brief time, it seemed that the 2008 presidential election may have signaled a decisive change in direction, but the Republican gains in the congressional elections of 2010 made that very doubtful, though it still appears that population shifts have moved the region into a political uproar. After significant Democratic gains in states like Georgia and Texas in the 2020 presidential election, the jury on political shifts in the sunbelt is still out.

Regional Shifts

For the past half-century, population and economic activities in the United States have been moving away from older urban areas. This population movement contrasts sharply with a long-standing pattern of national growth. Since the early years of the nineteenth century, the industrial cities had acted as magnets, drawing millions of immigrants from abroad and luring a steady stream of people from the countryside. The industrial cities were the engines of the nation's economy, and population movements reflected this fact. In 1950, 65 percent of the nation's metropolitan population lived in or near the industrial belt that reached from Boston and New York in the Northeast across to the Great Lakes and down to St. Louis.[16] More than two-thirds of the manufacturing jobs and 10 of the nation's 14 urban areas of more than a million people were stretched across this industrial zone. Over the next half-century, however, a decisive shift in the regional distribution of population occurred.

In the five decades between 1940 and 1990, the population of the 15 Sunbelt states increased by 163 percent (to 103,868,000), compared to a population gain in the 14 Frostbelt states of 48 percent (to 92,818,000).[17] Over this half-century, the fastest-growing states were Nevada (+50 percent), Arizona (+35 percent), Florida (+33 percent), and California (+26 percent). The only Frostbelt state to show a significant gain was New Hampshire (+20.5 percent), which grew because it was attracting commuters from elsewhere in the Northeast urban corridor.[18] As shown in Figure 9.2, these trends continued

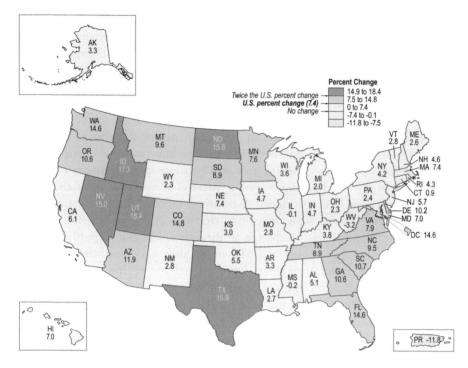

FIGURE 9.2 Population Growth in States, 2010–2020

Source: United States Census Bureau: "2020 Census: Percent Change in Resident Population for the 50 States, the District of Columbia, and Puerto Rico: 2010–2020" (April 27, 2020), https://www.census.gov/library/visualizations/2021/dec/2020-percent-change-map.html.

into the twenty-first century. Every state with a growth rate faster than 7.4 percent for the decade (the national average) was located in the West or in the Sunbelt, with the exception of Virginia, Delaware, Minnesota, and the District of Columbia. Five states that gained more than 15 percent in population—Utah, Idaho, Nevada, North Dakota, and Texas—were either located in the West or were part of the Western Sunbelt.

Most metropolitan areas of the Sunbelt expanded so quickly after World War II that it was difficult to build infrastructure fast enough. Table 9.1 compares the growth rates for seven Sunbelt metropolitan areas with population change in six Frostbelt urban regions from 1950 to 2000. All seven of the Sunbelt metropolitan areas boomed in the half-century from 1950 to 2000, in many cases growing by more than 40 percent per decade. Phoenix had a population of 107,000 in 1950 but morphed into a metropolitan region of more than 3 million people in half a century. Las Vegas was transformed from a dusty, seedy gambling town of 24,000 in 1950 to a major metropolis (and entertainment city) of 1.4 million by 2000. Several smaller metropolitan areas in the Sunbelt grew even faster than the larger urban areas. For example, Fort

TABLE 9.1 Population Growth of Selected Metropolitan Areas, 1950–2020

Metropolitan Area (Ranked by % Growth in 1970s)	Percentage Increase in Population							
	1950–1960	1960–1970	1970–1980	1980–1990	1990–2000	2000–2008	2010–2020	
Sunbelt and West								
Denver–Boulder	52	32	31	44	32	15	20[a]	
Houston	52	40	45	21	25	21.5	9.8	
Las Vegas	123	115	69	61	85.5	35.6	16.1[b]	
Los Angeles–Long Beach	45.5	16	6	18.5	10	4.1	2.8[c]	
Phoenix	100	46	55	40	45	31.7	11.2	
San Diego	85.5	32	37	34	12.6	6.7	6.1	
Frostbelt								
Boston	7.5	6	–5	6.5	6	3	9.4	
Chicago	20	12	2	0.2	11	5.2	1.9	
Detroit	28	12	–2	–2	5	–0.6	–10.5	
New York City	12	8	–4.5	3	9	3.7	7.7	
Pittsburgh	9	20	–5	–7	–1.5	–3.3	–0.89	
St. Louis	20	12	–2	3	4.6	4.4	–5.9	

Notes: Due to the 2020 Census results not being completely available by August 2021, the data presented here have the following limitations: [a] The currently available 2020 census data is for Denver alone, not Denver–Boulder. [b] The Las Vegas data from 2020 is for the Las Vegas–Henderson–Paradise metro area. [c] The currently available data is for Los Angeles City alone, not Los Angeles–Long Beach.

Sources: U.S. Bureau of the Census, 1970 Census of Population, vol. 1, Characteristics of the Population, pt. A (Washington, D.C.: U.S. Government Printing Office, 1973), p. 171, Table 32; U.S. Bureau of the Census, 1980 Census of Population, Supplementary Reports, Standard Metropolitan Statistical Areas and Standard Consolidated Statistical Areas (Washington, D.C.: U.S. Government Printing Office, 1981), p. 3, Table 1; U.S. Bureau of the Census, State and Metropolitan Area Data Book: 1991 (Washington, D.C.: U.S. Government Printing Office, 1991), Table A; U.S. Bureau of the Census, Standard Metropolitan Area Data Book: 1997–1998 (Washington, D.C.: U.S. Government Printing Office, 1999), pp. 60–65, Table B-1; U.S. Bureau of the Census, *Statistical Abstract of the United States: 2010* (129th Edition) (Washington, D.C.: U.S. Government Printing Office), Table 21: 50 Largest Metropolitan Statistical Areas in 2008—Components of Population Change: 2000 to 2008.

Myers, Cape Coral, Ocala, Sarasota, and Naples (all in Florida) attracted large numbers of retirees. Other smaller cities in the Sunbelt and the West, such as Austin, Texas; San Diego and San Jose, California; Boise, Idaho; and Provo, Utah, thrived because of an influx of high-tech industries.

Meanwhile, the six Frostbelt metropolitan areas listed in Table 9.1 went in exactly the opposite direction. Until the late 1960s, the Chicago, Detroit, and St. Louis regions continued to prosper as industrial centers even though their central cities were losing populations. But the bottom fell out during the deindustrialization of the 1970s and 1980s. Modest gains in the 1950s and 1960s were followed by stagnation or population loss; indeed, five of the six Frostbelt metropolitan areas shown in Table 9.1 lost population in the 1970s. Manufacturing firms picked up and moved abroad or to cheaper sites in the South or Southwest, where labor unions were weak. Older metropolitan areas were able to reverse this trend in the late century only by attracting the same kinds of service or high-tech firms that had already brought growth to the Sunbelt.

The old manufacturing cities fared much worse than their regions. In the 1970s, as deindustrialization reached its zenith, St. Louis lost 27 percent of its population, but the St. Louis region shrunk just 2 percent because the suburbs were growing significantly, by more than 6 percent. All of the cities in the industrial belt were going through a similar process; for example, in the 1970s, Chicago's population fell by 11 percent, Detroit's by 20.5 percent, and Cleveland's by 24 percent, but the suburbs in each of these urban regions continued to grow (although slowly). Most of these cities hemorrhaged population in the 1980s, but in most cases, the rate of loss slowed in the last decade of the century. In fact, during the 1990s, New York, Chicago, and a few other older industrial cities held their own or even added population for the first time in 20 or 30 years.

By contrast, in the Sunbelt, most central cities grew in step with their metropolitan regions. One reason Sunbelt cities did well was that many of them were newer and less built-up than the cities in the North. Another is that they were not usually encircled by suburbs. David Rusk has categorized cities according to their degree of "elasticity"—their ability to add population either by filling in undeveloped land or by annexing new territory. Of the 52 metropolitan areas of more than 200,000 populations that Rusk rated as having "high" or "hyper" elasticity in 1990, 49 were located in the Sunbelt. No Frostbelt city made the list.[19]

By 2020, the population shifts in urban and metro areas have changed their dynamics once again, indicating the fluidity and flexibility of the process as such. Contrary to previous trends, in the decade between 2010 and 2020, some old industrial cities along the east coast, mostly those that are centers for tech and knowledge industries, like Boston and New York City, grew at rates approximating and even surpassing some sunbelt cities. Still, according to the 2020 Census, the strongest population growth among metro areas was in the South and West, with The Villages, FL exhibiting the fastest population growth since 2010, marking a 38.9 percent population increase over the past decade. Other places among the top ten fastest-growing metros were exclusively in the sunbelt, featuring Austin, TX (33 percent), St. George, UT (30.5 percent), Greeley, CO (30.1 percent), and Myrtle Beach-Conway-North Myrtle Beach, NC/SC (29.5 percent) among the top five.

Why the Sunbelt Prospered

The movement of people to the Sunbelt has been matched by a redistribution of the nation's economic resources. In recent decades, job growth has heavily favored the South and West. Table 9.2 shows that in 1960, 58 percent of the nation's workforce was located in the Northeast and Midwest. The West still lagged behind, with only 15 percent of U.S. employment. By the 1980s, the share of jobs located in the Northeast and Midwest had slipped to 49 percent and to 46 percent by 2000. Meanwhile, big gains were registered in the South and West, which together accounted for 56 percent of U.S. employment by 2000 (21 percent in the West).

The reasons for the Sunbelt's economic success are many and complex. Economic and technological factors played a major role.[20] The urban infrastructure of the older Frostbelt cities was geared to the high-density patterns of production of the industrial period. Sunbelt cities had an advantage because they could start afresh to build infrastructure suited to the postindustrial economy. The building of the interstate highways network provided the foundation for

TABLE 9.2 Comparison of Regional[a] Shares of U.S. Employment and Shares of U.S. Job Growth 1960–2000 (in Percentages)

	Share of U.S. Employment			Share of Job Growth	
	1960	**1980**	**2000**	**1960–1980**	**1980–2000**
Northeast	29	23	21	13.5	12
Midwest	29	26	25	21.5	20
South	27	32	34	39.5	42
West	15	19	20	25.5	26

Note: [a] Regions defined according to Bureau of the Census definition; North Central changed to Midwest in 1989.

Sources: Adapted from U.S. Bureau of the Census, *Statistical Abstract of the United States, 1973* (Washington, D.C.: U.S. Government Printing Office, 1973), using 1960 and 1970 census data, p. 227; U.S. Bureau of the Census, *U.S. Statistical Abstract of the United States, 2001* (Washington, D.C.: U.S. Government Printing Office, 2001), using 1990 and 2000 census data; U.S. Bureau of the Census, *Statistical Abstract of the United States, 1996* (Washington, D.C.: U.S. Government Printing Office, 1996), using 1980 census data.

a national economy that favored the decentralization of economic activities. The adoption of air conditioning made the Sunbelt more attractive both for living and for white-collar work.[21] The materials used in manufacturing shifted from heavy metals such as iron and steel to lighter materials such as aluminum and plastic, and the newer manufacturing plants could be located on relatively cheap, easily available land in Sunbelt metropolitan areas. Most important, the source of energy for industry and for homes shifted from Frostbelt coal to Sunbelt oil. Oil jumped from meeting less than half of the nation's energy needs in 1940 to almost 78 percent by 1975. By the mid-1970s, coal supplied no more than 17 percent of the nation's energy.[22]

Changing demographics and lifestyles favored the Sunbelt as well. More leisure time and a greater emphasis on recreation lured people to warmer climates. After World War II, tourism accounted for a larger share of the national economy. Major recreational and tourist facilities developed in Florida and California (homes of Disney theme parks) and in New Orleans and Las Vegas. Entire communities, such as Lake Havasu, Arizona, arose to serve the needs of an expanding class of retired people who preferred Sunbelt lifestyles and the lower cost of living found there.

However, demographic and economic trends do not explain why the Sunbelt prospered as much as it did. Federal spending exerted a powerful impact in stimulating local economies. In particular, the Pentagon budget induced military-dependent sectors to migrate to the Sunbelt. No other major industrialized nation used military spending so forcefully to relocate economic activity from one region to another.[23] The Great Depression ended in the United States when government spending for military procurement climbed steeply in 1940 in response to the stunning success of the Nazi blitzkrieg in Europe. As military contracting soared, the War Production Board made a policy decision to spread out defense installations and productive capacity to make bombing and a potential invasion more difficult. The South and West possessed the advantage of favorable weather for aircraft training facilities. Overall, an estimated 60 percent of the $74 billion wartime expenditures went into the 15 states of the Sunbelt at a time when those states contained less than 40 percent of the national population.[24]

The metropolitan areas of the South experienced the most rapid growth of any region. World War II jumpstarted the urbanization of the South and West by pulling thousands of workers into the cities in search of relatively well-paid industrial employment. In the three years between 1940 and 1943, the population of the metropolitan counties of the South grew by 4 percent and those of the West by 3 percent; by contrast, the metropolitan counties in the upper Midwest increased by only 2 percent and the northeastern metropolitan areas contracted by 0.6 percent.[25] Some cities, most of them located in the South and West, became overnight boomtowns. Between April 1940 and October 1941, 150,000 people poured into Los Angeles, which increased the city's population by a third. During the war years, San Diego's population shot up by 27 percent and Wichita, Kansas, by 20 percent.[26] The wartime boom taxed the housing stock, infrastructure, and public services in these cities to the breaking point.

Near the end of World War II, war production began to shift from heavy industry (tanks and guns) to high-tech weaponry such as missiles, jet airplanes, and sophisticated communications systems. All through the Cold War, the nation's military spending remained high, and most of it went to the Sunbelt. One study showed a "definite regional shift" from the Northeast to the Sunbelt between 1950 and 1976 in the awarding of defense contracts.[27] During that period, the total number of defense employees in the nation increased by more than 35 percent; even so, their numbers fell by 3 percent in the 16 northeastern and upper Midwestern states.[28] By 1975, the defense budget contributed only 4 percent to personal incomes in the Northeast, compared to 9 percent in the states comprising the Sunbelt.[29]

Defense spending shifted to the Sunbelt not just because the region was an efficient location for some kinds of military production. For a long time, Democratic senators and representatives from the South had a lock on their seats because of uncontested one-party elections. Their long service in Congress gave them control of powerful committees because assignments were made on the basis of seniority. Congressional representatives from the South used their positions as committee chairs to steer defense spending and major infrastructure investments, such as dams and water projects, to their states and districts. Perhaps the best example is Mendell Rivers, who represented Charleston, South Carolina, for 40 years, from 1930 to 1970. As chair of the House Armed Services Committee, Rivers succeeded in getting the federal government to build in his hometown "an Army depot, a Marine Corps air base, a Marine boot camp, two Navy hospitals, a Navy shipyard, a Navy base, a Navy supply center, a Navy weapons center, a Navy submarine base, a Polaris missile base, two Air Force bases, and a federal housing development."[30] Because senators and representatives from more pluralistic and diverse Frostbelt districts usually served fewer terms in Congress before being defeated for reelection, they were not able to accumulate comparable seniority and congressional clout.[31]

Other federal spending programs also benefited the Sunbelt. Federal subsidies for highway building favored the Sunbelt because the long distances between cities and the larger size of metropolitan areas increased federal expenditures. Federal grants for the construction of sewer and water systems and for dams and water projects were also critically important to Sunbelt development. Some federal spending programs such as public employment programs and social welfare spending were biased toward the older industrial cities, but these did not tend to stimulate sustained economic development. By contrast, federal spending in the Sunbelt created permanent federal payrolls and infrastructure to support whole new industries, such as microelectronics. One of the most important ingredients of economic growth is a skilled labor force. The military actively recruited highly trained white-collar workers, engineers, and scientists to areas near Sunbelt military installations. Writing in the late

1980s, one scholar noted that "Every year the Department of Defense pays a number of companies a large sum of money to move college-educated (often at the public expense) engineers and scientists from the Midwest and other regions to the Southwest."[32]

In addition to direct spending, provisions in the federal tax code also favored the Sunbelt. In 1954, accelerated depreciation allowances deducted from corporate income taxes provided tax breaks for constructing new commercial and industrial structures but not for rehabilitating old buildings. Accelerated depreciation thus speeded up the flow of capital out of older industrial cities to suburban and Sunbelt locations.[33] Between 1954 and 1980, this subsidy was worth $30 billion in reduced taxes to corporations. The investment tax credit, which President Kennedy introduced in 1962, granted a dollar-for-dollar reduction in corporate taxes for investments in new plants and equipment. In this way, the federal tax code encouraged companies to abandon older plants in the Frostbelt and build new plants in the Sunbelt. Between 1962 and 1981, this subsidy was worth $90 billion,[34] and in 1982 alone, it was worth $20 billion.[35] A study conducted in the early 1980s of nine tax subsidies that promoted the mobility of investment (such as accelerated depreciation allowances on old plant and equipment and allowances for new equipment) found they were worth more than twice the total budget of the U.S. Department of Housing and Urban Development.[36]

Regional inequities in federal policy attracted the attention of public officials in the Midwest and Northeast. In June 1976, a group of governors formed the Coalition of Northeast Governors, and in September 1976, congressional representatives from 16 states formed the Northeast-Midwest Economic Advancement Coalition (today called the Northeast-Midwest Institute). To counter the influence of the Frostbelt politicians, the Southern Growth Policy Board, which had been formed in 1971, stepped up its lobbying efforts.[37] Regional disparities in federal spending narrowed somewhat between 1975 and 1979,[38] but Ronald Reagan's election in 1980 decisively shifted the momentum the other way.[39] Once in office, Reagan sharply cut programs targeted to older central cities.[40] Between 1980 and 1987, grant programs of special importance to cities, such as mass transit, public housing, social welfare, and job training, were cut by 47 percent.[41] At the same time, his administration increased defense and highway programs that disproportionately benefited the Sunbelt.

The federal budget became a way to redistribute national resources from other regions of the country, in the process rewarding the constituencies that favored Republicans the most. Between 1983 and 1998, the citizens of just two states, New York and New Jersey, paid $500 billion more into the federal treasury than they received back in benefits.[42] In 1997, the citizens of nine southern and Border States paid $45 billion less in federal taxes than they paid into the federal treasury; in the same year, eight northern states paid an $82 billion surplus. Put simply, northern taxpayers subsidized much of the economic prosperity of the Sunbelt.

The Changing Politics of Sunbelt Cities

Since the 1980s, the culture and the politics of Sunbelt cities have been undergoing a sea change. Only half a century ago, the South was an economically backward, generally poor region mired in a racist political tradition. The Southwest was an area of the country heavily dependent on military installations and agriculture, with a politics mainly devoted to securing more federal dollars for water projects and military bases. Today, from Florida to southern California, cities that have been growing rapidly since the 1950s are still on an upward trajectory. The population increases have been driven by the growth of services and high-tech industries, and the workers drawn to them; retirees; and a huge influx of immigrants, mainly from the Western Hemisphere. The politics of the Sunbelt have changed in step with these historic processes.

Before World War II, most Sunbelt cities were governed by caretaker governments presided over by politicians from long established, sometimes prominent, families. The leadership structures looked a lot like party machines led by bosses or cliques that had been around for a long while, but in other respects, they bore little resemblance to the turn-of-the-century machines of the northern cities. Working-class voters of the South were manipulated by scare-mongering about race and the alleged influence of outsiders. The political leadership of these cities wanted, above all, to protect local culture against change. Such organizations governed Tampa, Florida; San Antonio, Texas; and many other cities until well after World War II. New Orleans was run by a longtime machine, the Regular Democratic Organization until de Lesseps S. Morrison was elected mayor in 1946.[43]

These tight-knit political machines were ill prepared for the changes set in motion by the defense buildup during World War II. After the war, a new generation of political activists came onto the scene. In city after city, "G.I. revolts" sprang up in which "bright young candidates marched against corrupt or inept city hall cliques under the banner of progress."[44] They appealed to middle-class voters who had few ties to the existing political establishment. Coalitions of white-collar professionals, business leaders, and growth-oriented city managers and bureaucrats came together to form business-dominated reform governments committed to modernization, new infrastructure, and growth.

This wave of reform transformed the political landscape throughout the Sunbelt, especially in cities of the Southwest. Between 1945 and 1955, San Antonio, Houston, Dallas, Oklahoma City, Albuquerque, Phoenix, and San Jose all adopted significant reforms, usually installing non-partisan city-manager systems with at-large electoral arrangements.[45] These movements, instigated by such organizations as the Phoenix Charter Government Committee, the Albuquerque Citizens Committee, and San Antonio's Good Government League, were led by middle- and upper-class Anglo professionals and business leaders.

These postwar business-dominated coalitions campaigned for support from white middle-class voters, and minorities were as strictly excluded as they had been in the past. Over the years, whites had used various methods, both legal and extralegal, to discourage African Americans and Latinos from voting. The white primary, which kept Black Americans from casting ballots in Democratic primary elections, worked as an effective means of keeping Black citizens completely out of politics. In the southern states, the white primary was tantamount to disenfranchisement because where Democratic candidates always ran unopposed in general elections. In 1944, the U.S. Supreme Court struck down the white primary as a violation of the Fifteenth Amendment of the Constitution.[46]

Other methods continued to be used to dilute the electoral influence of Black and Latinx Americans. Many cities used at-large election districts to ensure that minority neighborhoods would be outvoted in the citywide totals. The 1965 Voting Rights Act, however, gave federal judges the power to strike down voting systems that systematically reduced minority representation. In 1975, the act was extended to Latinx people. Both Houston and Dallas were forced to modify their at-large systems by adopting ward boundaries that would maximize representation for Black and Latinx Americans. Likewise, Los Angeles was forced to redraw its ward boundaries. Minority voters helped pass new city charters that provided for ward-based representation in San Antonio, Fort Worth, Albuquerque, San Francisco, Atlanta, Richmond, and several other cities.[47]

These measures began opening up political systems all across the Sunbelt, but even without reform, the growing populations of African Americans and Hispanics would have made political change impossible to resist. By 1990 Black and Latinx Americans made up a majority of the population in many cities in Florida and in a belt stretching from Texas to California, with Hispanics outnumbering African Americans about two to one. In Miami, more than 90 percent of the population was minority, compared to 60 percent in Los Angeles, Houston, and San Antonio. Minorities constituted more than 50 percent in most Sunbelt cities with populations of more than 500,000.

Minority populations in the suburbs of Sunbelt metropolitan areas shot upward in the 1990s—by more than 18 percent in the Fort Lauderdale area and by more than 11 percent in the Oakland, Las Vegas, Atlanta, San Jose, Houston, Orange County (California), Miami, and Dallas areas, among others.[48] Within Sunbelt areas, the biggest increases were in the suburbs. As a result of three decades of immigration, by the census of 2000, minorities made up at least 40 percent of the population of the suburbs in 20 metropolitan areas in the Sunbelt. Tables 9.3 and 9.4 show that the urban areas with the largest numeric gains in minority population in the suburbs are located in the Sunbelt. The largest percentage increases in minority population in the suburbs, on the other hand, were in metro areas in the old industrial north. Hispanic populations, in particular, have grown explosively in some of the metro suburbs throughout the Old South. Since 2010, the South (not including the Southwest) has seen larger increases in its Latinx population than any other region in the United States,

TABLE 9.3 Largest Black Population Increases, Metropolitan Suburbs, 2000–2010

	Highest Numeric Gains (Suburbs of Metro Area)		Highest Growth Rates (Percent) (Suburbs of Metro Area)	
Rank	Metro Area	Numeric Gain	Metro Area	Percentage
1	Atlanta–Sandy Springs–Marietta, GA	503,239	Indianapolis–Carmel, IN	150
2	Houston–Sugar Land–Baytown, TX	216,823	Des Moines–West Des Moines, IA	146
3	Washington–Arlington–Alexandria, DC–VA–MD–WV	193,524	Phoenix–Mesa–Scottsdale, AZ	137
4	Dallas–Fort Worth–Arlington, TX	192,576	Syracuse, NY Minneapolis–St. Paul–Bloomington, MN–WI	129
5	Miami–Fort Lauderdale–Pompano Beach, FL	183,381	Allentown–Bethlehem–Easton, PA–NJ	104
6	Detroit–Warren–Livonia, MI	133,488	Milwaukee–Waukesha–West Allis, WI	90
7	Chicago–Naperville–Joliet, IL–IN–WI	116,622	Scranton–Wilkes-Barre, PA	87
8	Baltimore–Towson, MD	98,195	Austin–Round Rock, TX	84

Source: Adapted from William Frey, "Melting Pot Cities and Suburbs: Racial and Ethnic Change in Metro America in the 2000s," *State of Metropolitan American, Metropolitan Policy Program at Brookings* (May 2011), p. 11, Table 4, https://www.brookings.edu/wp-content/uploads/2016/06/0504_census_ethnicity_frey.pdf.

with a percentage increase of 26 percent (as compared to the Northeast and the Midwest with 18 percent, respectively, and the West with 14 percent).[49] The counties with the highest number of Hispanics in the country are still almost exclusively located in the South and Southwest—with one exception: Cook County, the county in which Chicago is located, ranked fifth among the metro counties with the highest amount of Hispanic residents in the country, with a total population of 1,320,000, or 26 percent of its population identifying as Latinx.[50] Los Angeles County still topped the list with 4,880,000 Hispanic residents—49 percent of the county's total population.[51]

One demographic scholar predicted in 2014 that there will be a profound suburban population shift over the next two decades, leaving whites

TABLE 9.4 Largest Hispanic Population Increases, Metropolitan Suburbs, 2000–2010

Rank	Highest Numeric Gains (Suburbs of Metro Area)		Highest Growth Rates (Percent) (Suburbs of Metro Area)	
	Metro Area	Numeric Gain	Metro Area	Percentage
1	Riverside–San Bernadino–Ontario, CA	659,355	Scranton–Wilkes Barre, PA	416
2	New York–Northern New Jersey–Long Island, NY–NJ–PA	572,337	Knoxville, TN	214
3	Houston–Sugarland–Baytown, TX	557,132	Nashville-Davidson–Murfreesboro–Franklin, TN	192
4	Miami–Fort Lauderdale–Pompano Beach, FL	549,675	Indianapolis–Carmel, IN	183
5	Los Angeles–Long Beach–Santa Ana, CA	443,170	Columbia, SC	177
6	Dallas–Fort Worth–Arlington, TX	417,175	Charleston–North Charleston–Summerville, SC	177
7	Chicago–Naperville-Joliet, IL–IN–WI	412,255	Birmingham–Hoover, AL	176
8	Washington–Arlington–Alexandria, DC–VA–MD–WV	331,555	Charlotte–Gastonia–Concord, NC–SC	171

Source: Adapted from William Frey, "Melting Pot Cities and Suburbs: Racial and Ethnic Change in Metro America in the 2000s," *State of Metropolitan American, Metropolitan Policy Program at Brookings* (May 2011), p. 11, Table 4, https://www.brookings.edu/wp-content/uploads/2016/06/0504_census_ethnicity_frey.pdf.

in the minority in the suburbs across the country, even in the Northeast and Midwest.[52]

This marks a new trend for the Frostbelt: In the past, fewer minorities lived in the suburbs of the Frostbelt regions. In fact, in the middle-sized urban areas in the industrial belt—anchored by such areas as Scranton, Allentown, and Harrisburg, Pennsylvania; Youngstown, Akron, Toledo, and Columbus, Ohio; and Buffalo, Albany, and Rochester, New York—minority suburban populations used to be in the single digits. By 2030, the Urban Institute predicts significant population losses among whites in all regions across the country, making the Sunbelt a trendsetter for the nation as a whole.[53]

The number of Black and Latinx Americans winning public office has kept pace with population change. Nationwide, the number of Black elected officials increased from 1,469 in February 1970 to 9,040 in January 2000,[54] and to then 10,500 in 2011.[55] African Americans were elected mayors in some of the largest Sunbelt cities, including Los Angeles, New Orleans, Atlanta, and Birmingham, as well as in suburban and non-metropolitan cities and counties. With about 20,000 Latino immigrants gaining citizenship and the right to vote each year, Hispanic gains have been especially dramatic, with the number of Hispanic public officials increasing from 3,147 in September 1985 to 5,205 in September 2000[56]; by 2008, the number was 5,240.[57] In the 1990s, Hispanics were elected mayor in Miami, Denver, San Antonio, and many smaller cities.

The incorporation of minorities into the political systems of Sunbelt cities has brought significant policy change. Atlanta is a good example. African American mayors have governed Atlanta since 1973. The majority of the city council and of the school board is Black, and Blacks hold a majority of the key appointed and civil service positions in the city government. Under the city's first African American mayor, Maynard Jackson, the African American proportion of the police department rose from 19 to 35 percent in only four years, and complaints about police brutality fell.[58] The city established 24 neighborhood councils, each with professional staff so that neighborhoods could influence city planning and development decisions. A preferential program begun under Jackson's first term raised the percentage of minority firms holding city contracts from one-tenth of 1 percent to 35 percent by 1988.[59]

Similar gains have been achieved in Birmingham, Alabama, and New Orleans, which have had African American mayors since 1979 and 1977, respectively. In both cities, political participation by people of color has increased significantly, and community organizations have become active in local politics. As a consequence, in both cities, police brutality has become less important as a policy issue.[60]

Hispanics have become incorporated into local political structures as well. In Miami, Hispanics have become the most important electoral constituency in the city because they are the largest population group and have become successful economically. In the 1990s, Hispanics succeeded in overturning at-large election systems that had disadvantaged them in Miami and surrounding counties. As a result, they have been able to win public offices at all levels, and Hispanics and African Americans have been well represented on boards and commissions and in public employment.[61] Similarly, African Americans and Hispanics have become powerful forces in the political system of Denver (a city with many Sunbelt characteristics). In 1983, with the election of Frederico Peña, Denver became the first American city without a Hispanic majority to elect a Hispanic mayor (at the time, 18 percent of Denver's population was Latino). After Peña's two terms, Wellington Webb was elected as the city's first Black mayor at a time when Blacks made up 11 percent of the city's population. Hispanics and African Americans have become well represented on the city council and on city boards and commissions, in public employment, and on the civilian police board.[62]

Lessons from the 2020 Presidential Election: Diversifying Suburbs and the Hispanic Vote

The 2020 presidential election has been touted as a landmark election decided, among others, by the suburbs, which shifted away from their 2016 support for Republican Donald J. Trump and turned increasingly blue. In doing so, the suburbs helped to flip back states that had turned "red" in 2016, such as Wisconsin, Michigan, and Pennsylvania, and make competitive former Republican bastions, such as Georgia, North Carolina, Texas, and Arizona. The growing diversity of the suburbs is certainly one explanatory factor for this phenomenon. It does, however, not tell the whole story. Some scholars have suggested that educational attainment among white people, who, as a group, vote majority Republican, may play an important role as well: Many suburban communities also exhibit rising levels of educational attainment among whites, which can serve as an indicator for their openness to racial diversity, as well as their inclination to vote Democratic.[63] The fact that in spite of an increased diversification of the suburbs, not all diversifying suburbs swung Democratic seems to underpin this theory. As a team of researchers from *FiveThirtyEight* noted,

> some suburbs that grew more racially diverse over the past decade saw a smaller swing toward Biden than others – or even moved slightly into Trump's column. And other suburbs that didn't diversify much at all still became much bluer in 2020. Rather, it was education—and particularly how much more educated a place has gotten over the past 10 years—that was more closely related to increased support for Biden (especially once accounting for how educated a county was in 2010).

The researchers found that diversity still matters for voting behavior, it just cannot be used as the sole indicator. In combination, education level and diversity seemed to be the greatest predictor for whether suburban counties lent their support to Trump or whether they swung Democratic.

In part, this uncertainty about diversity and voting behavior may be related to the fact that researchers have used the term "diversity" much too generally, without breaking down different groups of people of color and looking into their voting behavior and social values more specifically. Hispanic or Latinx voters, in particular, are a highly diverse group, with vastly different voting behaviors, depending on their countries of origin, their race, and ethnicity, as well as their social background(s).

In 2020, much was made of former president Trump's gains among the Hispanic vote in the Miami-Dade area—an urban county, which Democrats had traditionally carried with comfortable margins. Biden still carried Miami-Dade County for the Democrats in 2020, but by only 7 points, compared to Hillary Clinton's 30 points in 2016.[64] However, Cuban Americans dominate Miami's Hispanic community and the city's overall political climate: In 2017, Cuban Americans constituted 25.7 percent of the county's total residents and 48.5 percent of its foreign-born population, making Miami's Hispanic community somewhat unique among the United States' Hispanic immigrant communities.[65]

In electoral terms, Cuban Americans constitute a very particular subset of Hispanic voters, whom the Trump campaign may have singled out as a potential constituency that could be drawn toward the Republican Party. The Trump campaign's outreach to Cuban voters in South Florida was more or less constant during the former president's four years in office. Their main campaign item with Cubans was their (false) claim that a Biden administration would enter office pushing a socialist agenda, which resonated particularly well with established Cuban Americans, who fled Cuba in the wake of a communist government takeover. Other Hispanic groups in Florida, such as Puerto Ricans, did not seem as drawn to that message. In the end, and despite his gains with Miami's Hispanic population, Trump still lost Dade County, in which Miami is located, which is a testament to the fact that Republicans overall had a tougher time making inroads with urban populations.

The Trump campaign in 2020 also made gains among Hispanic voters as a whole, not just Cuban Americans, but when considering these gains, scale is key: Relatively speaking, Trump made some gains among Hispanic voters in 2020, but that was also due to the fact that he did extremely poorly among Hispanics, more so than other Republican candidates, winning a mere 18 percent of the Latinx vote.[66] In 2020, he won 27 percent of the Hispanic vote, which was a closer approximation to other Republicans running for the presidency in recent decades, but still a loss vis-à-vis the Democrats.[67]

In its 2020 election eve poll, *Latino Decisions* presented a detailed analysis of the Hispanic vote by national origin. Overall, the poll showed Democrats with a significant edge over Republicans among all groups of Hispanic voters. Cuban Americans were the only significant outlier, as can be seen in Figure 9.3, whereas Puerto Rican Americans represent the national Latinx average, giving Democrats a comfortable 44-point lead, with 73 percent of Puerto Ricans supporting the Democrats and 27 percent of Puerto Ricans supporting the Republicans.

Broken down by demographic subgroup, the differences among Hispanics in terms of voting behavior are even less stark than they appear to be between Cuban Americans and other Latinx national groups, with rural Hispanics (67 percent), Hispanic men (67 percent), and those in the 30–39 age group (64 percent) showing the lowest rates of support for the Democrats. On the other hand, as shown in Figure 9.4, Cuban Americans were the only demographic group among Hispanic voters that Trump ended up (narrowly) winning.

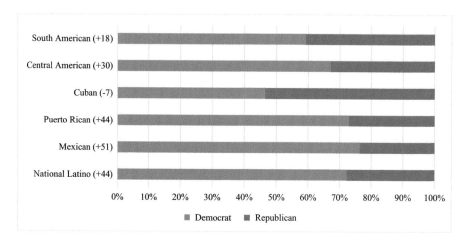

FIGURE 9.3 Latinx Vote in the 2020 Presidential Election for by National Origin

Source: Adapted from "Latino Voters in the 2020 Election National Survey Results," *The American Election Eve Poll, Latino Decisions*, 8, Presidential Latino Vote By National Origin (November 2020), https://latinodecisions.com/wp-content/uploads/2020/11/Latino-EE2020-Deck.pdf.

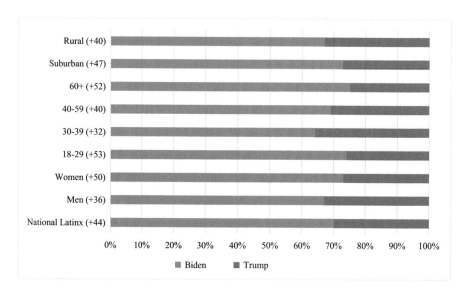

FIGURE 9.4 Latinx Support for Biden/Trump in the 2020 Presidential Election, by Demographic Subgroup

Source: Adapted from "Latino Voters in the 2020 Election National Survey Results," *The American Election Eve Poll, Latino Decisions*, 7, Presidential Latino Vote By Subgroup (November 2020), https://latinodecisions.com/wp-content/uploads/2020/11/Latino-EE2020-Deck.pdf.

The polling results on voting behavior among different Hispanic groups in the 2020 presidential election demonstrate some variation among the different groups—most significantly between Cubans and other Hispanics, though the Democrats, and then-candidate Joe Biden in particular, seemed to still receive solid support from Hispanics overall during the 2020 election cycle. The results also show a rural-suburban difference in voting behavior. This is significant because it indicates that location is increasingly having an impact on voting behavior, regardless of race and ethnicity. The growing rural-urban divide across the nation is something policy makers and urban leaders appealing to the federal government for funding and support will increasingly have to reckon with.

The Growing Rural-Urban Divide

In his now-famous 2004 Democratic National Convention speech, with catapulted him overnight to the national stage of politics, Barack Obama, then Illinois State Senator, said the following about the country's national political divisions:

> The pundits like to slice and dice our country into red states and blue states: red states for Republicans, blue states for Democrats. But I've got news for them, too. We worship an awesome God in the blue states, and we don't like federal agents poking around our libraries in the red states. We coach little league in the blue states and, yes, we've got some gay friends in the red states. There are patriots who opposed the war in Iraq, and there are patriots who supported the war in Iraq. We are one people, all of us pledging allegiance to the stars and stripes, all of us defending the United States of America. In the end that's what this election is about. Do we participate in a politics of cynicism, or do we participate in a politics of hope?[68]

By the third decade of the twenty-first century, Obama's rhetoric seems almost naïve. A decade and a half later, at the end of Trump's term, the country seems more ideologically divided than ever. Today, many scholars and pundits have come to think of the country's divisions less in terms of states and more in terms of location and lifestyle: Enter to rural-urban divide.

Over the past few election cycles, a trend seems to have manifested according to which higher population density coincides with the higher turnout for Democrats and lower density with the higher turnout for Republicans. Similar to the red-state-blue-state narrative, the rural-urban divide presupposes a binary that separates the country into two distinct versions of itself. In reality, things are much more complicated.

During the 2016 and 2020 presidential elections, for instance, rural counties in the Sunbelt tended to behave quite differently from rural counties in the North. A *FiveThirtyEight* analysis found, for example, that while exurban counties in the Sunbelt have been trending toward the Democrats since the 2012 presidential election, former President Trump's breaking of the "blue wall" in the Midwest seemed to be a sudden anomaly of 2016. That anomaly partially reversed itself again in 2020, but it remains to be seen which way exurban areas in the industrial North will swing in the long run. In addition to that, rural communities, too, are becoming more diverse. Researchers from the Brookings Institution wrote in late 2020, after the presidential election, that the narrative about the rural-urban divide of ethnically and racially diverse and economically successful suburbs and cities and poor, "left behind," white rural towns, was not only shamefully inaccurate but also harmful. They noted that this narrative erases the existence of any kind of poverty beyond white, rural poverty. It also ignores the fact that many rural areas are no longer majority-white:

> Prioritizing calls to 'heal' the rural-urban divide conceals the real divide of American racism, acts as if there are no working-class Black and brown people living in small towns, and furthers 'the unstated assumption that the country can't heal if white Americans aren't accommodated first.' [...] conflating 'rural' with 'white' propagates an incomplete story of rural America that centers white political anxieties. This incomplete story furthers myths about race and poverty in America that cater to white supremacy, and the longer it remains dominant, the more severe consequences it engenders for people across America.[69]

The researchers argued that the simplified narrative of the rural-urban divide also invites oversimplified policy measures aimed at alleviating poverty.[70] In rural areas across the country, about 20 percent of residents are now people of color.[71] It may certainly be the case that for some communities of color residing in rural communities, their voting patterns may be more conservative in comparison to urban or suburban residents of their same race or ethnicity. However, communities of color still vote overwhelmingly Democratic, while the majority of whites vote Republican. Thus, the rural-urban divide is the most pronounced among white Americans, as is the education gap: Overall, Trump won almost all demographic groups among white people, but he lost most demographic groups among Black and Hispanic Americans. While Trump lost all demographics with education levels past college, the "college plus" group was the *only* white demographic he lost (he had a 12-point edge among white voters overall in 2020—17 points among men and 7 points among women)![72] The key reason for why Trump lost his decisive edge in suburban counties in 2020 seems to be a general increase in education level among all voters there, but white voters were the only demographic group where education level was a significant factor in whether they would support Trump or not.

In terms of residence, the American Communities Project[73] provides some insight into the specific voting behaviors and demographic compositions of specific segments along the lines of the urban-rural divide. Based on their classifications, Trump only had a decisive edge within those rural and exurban communities, which were almost exclusively white: He carried "Aging Farmlands" (94 percent white), "Evangelical Hubs" (82 percent white), "Working Class Country" (95 percent white), and "Rural Middle America" (91 percent white) with the highest margins in the country.[74] All four community types were not only rural—they were mostly characterized by their whiteness and their low education levels. In three out of four of these community types, Trump had an advantage of around 50 points or more over Biden, except for "Rural Middle American," where Trump led Biden with 28 points.[75] Comparatively poor, rural and exurban communities that were not overwhelmingly white only provided Republicans with a small advantage over Democrats in 2016, and, in many cases, no advantage at all in 2020: Researchers of the American Communities project found that rural and exurban communities, which they characterized as the "African American South," where the median Black population accounted for 37 percent of the community, Democrats had the edge over Republicans in 2008 and 2012, and Trump won them, if at all, by a mere percentage point in 2016.[76] Geography, therefore, is not destiny in terms of voting behavior for all rural communities.

In other words, the "rural-urban divide" seems to be a result of a growing gap within the white voter demographic: More highly educated voters, who cluster in more diverse communities in the cities and urban suburbs, tend to vote more Democratic, but that educational and geographic gap is only highly pronounced among white voters, who skew Republican, while people of color tend to vote overwhelmingly Democratic, regardless of their geographic location and education level.

Regional Convergence and National Politics

For a long time, scholars have predicted that the different regions of the nation would become increasingly similar.[77] At least to some degree, their predictions have turned out to be accurate. Economic forces have diversified the economies as well as changed the demographic profiles of cities all over the nation. In the Frostbelt, corporate white-collar employment, services, and tourism have become critically important to urban regions and to downtown economies. Frost-belt metropolitan regions are less heavily blue collar and union than in the past, and central cities in the North have been attracting a significant proportion of affluent households. At the same time, many of the characteristics traditionally associated with older industrial cities—rapid immigration, concentrated poverty, and racial and ethnic conflict—have come to the cities of the Sunbelt. Cities all over the country are now multiracial and multiethnic.

Reflecting this convergence in demographics and politics, over time, the public policies of cities have become more alike. Older industrial cities of all sizes have moved aggressively to become more "entrepreneurial" in their pursuit of business investment.[78] Accordingly, many of them have shifted resources away from social services and toward developmental programs that subsidize investment.[79] Large volumes of public money have been devoted to building facilities such as sports stadiums, convention centers, and redevelopment districts.[80] By investing in high-tech and corporate services and developing an infrastructure to support tourism and recreation, Frostbelt cities have become more like the cities of the Sunbelt.

Likewise, regional differences in voting behavior and party identification have become less extreme. In the past, the Sunbelt favored the Republican Party and pulled the country in a conservative direction. Recent research, however, shows that Democrats are gaining in metropolitan areas in both the North and the South and in suburbs as well as central cities.[81] This trend is supported, in part, by immigration flows; African Americans, Latinos, and Asians, when combined, are about 75 percent Democratic. White-collar professionals, heavily concentrated in the suburbs and in central cities with high-tech sectors, made up 21 percent of the electorate in 2000. They tend to be moderate on social issues and to support environmental protection, civil rights, and women's rights, and their numbers are rapidly growing throughout the Sunbelt.

Their predictions seemed to come to fruition in the 2008 presidential election. A tier of southern states still went heavily Republican, but the electoral map showed big gains for the Democratic Party almost everywhere else. Four southern, four Midwestern, and three western states supported John McCain by more than 55 percent margins, while California, Nevada, Colorado, New Mexico, and Florida voted as blue states. Republicans made a big comeback in the congressional elections of 1910, but this happened in all regions of the country. Whatever utility the Sunbelt concept had in the past, in 2008 and 2010, it did not seem to explain the election result. Even in the 2016 presidential election, which saw massive gains for the Republicans in many states across the nation (especially in the Midwest) which were thought to be securely in Democratic hands, showed that certain changes in Sunbelt voting behavior are solidifying: New Mexico and Nevada seem to be relatively reliable blue states, and much of that is due to immigration. By 2020, Georgia, North Carolina, Texas, and Arizona showed significant losses for the Republicans, mostly thanks to a growing number of people of color in those states.

It would be tempting to interpret the Arizona anti-immigration law signed by Governor Jan Brewer on April 32, 2010, as a step backward to an earlier time in Sunbelt politics. Doubtlessly the law, which requires people to carry immigration papers and empowers police officers to determine immigration status, was motivated by deep resentments against not only illegal immigrants but against all Hispanics in the state. Indeed, a June 2012 Huffington Post article asked: "Is Arizona the worst place in the country to be a Latina?"[82] Texas followed suit in June 2011, when the state Senate passed a bill giving police officers broad powers to ask those detained regarding their citizenship status. In fact, 2011 was a record year for anti-immigration legislation. Alabama, Georgia, Indiana, South Carolina, and Utah all passed anti-immigration bills modeled after Arizona's 2010 law. Sunbelt states were no exception; from 2010 to 2011, all Sunbelt states passed at least one anti-immigration law, with the average number ranging between three and six laws.[83]

In other places, there was a strong reaction to these kinds of measures. On May 13, 2010, the Los Angeles city council passed a resolution banning the expenditure of any city funds for travel to Arizona. The debate over the resolution was highly emotional, with speakers mentioning the Holocaust and the World War II internment of Japanese Americans. From Miami to Los Angeles, cities with large Hispanic populations are sprinkled throughout the Sunbelt. Clearly, the Sunbelt—if there is any longer such a thing—does not speak with one voice but with many.

In October 2017, in reaction to the Trump administration's crackdown on undocumented immigration, California governor Jerry Brown signed a statewide "sanctuary bill," California Senate Bill 54, into law. The bill takes effect in January 2018 and limits the cooperation of any state authority with federal immigration authorities. This means that individuals' immigration statuses will not be investigated by California state authorities or reported to federal immigration authorities, except if they have committed serious crimes.[84,85]

The economic meltdown that began in the fall of 2008 put into question the vaunted economic advantages of the Sunbelt. More than anywhere else, much of the wealth of Sunbelt cities depends upon real estate and construction. These sectors were hit the hardest in the economic downturn, and as a result, the nation's highest home foreclosure rates and declines in housing values occurred in metropolitan areas of the South and Southwest: In the year from October 2007 to October 2008, housing values in Phoenix and Las Vegas fell by a third, compared to a decline in the New York region of 7.5 percent.[86] People in the Sunbelt must have been startled to see that after years of feeling sorry for those left behind in the frozen North, the shoe was on the other foot, at least for a time.

Endnotes

1   Robert Goodman, *The Last Entrepreneurs: America's Regional Wars for Jobs and Dollars* (New York: Simon & Schuster, 1979), p. 42.
2   Sudeep Reddy, "Latinos Fuel Growth in Decade," *The Wall Street Journal* (March 25, 2011), http://online.wsj.com/article/SB10001424052748704604704576220603247344790.html.
3   Alan Berube, "Racial and Ethnic Change in the Nation's Largest Cities," in *Redefining Urban & Suburban America: Evidence from Census 2000*, ed. Bruce Katz and Robert E. Lang (Washington, D.C.: Brookings Institution Press, 2003), p. 142.

4   John B. Judis and Ruy Teixeira, *The Emerging Democratic Majority* (New York: Scribner/A Lisa Drew Book, 2002).

5   Kevin P. Phillips, *The Emerging Republican Majority* (New Rochelle, NY: Arlington House, 1969).

6   Prompting the famous headline, "Ford to City: Drop Dead!" *New York Daily News* (October 29, 1975), p. 1.

7   Kirkpatrick Sale, *Power Shift: The Rise of the Southern Rim and Its Challenge to the Eastern Establishment* (New York: Random House, 1975).

8   "The Second War between the States," *Business Week* (May 17, 1976).

9   Quoted in Carl Abbott, *The New Urban America: Growth and Politics in Sunbelt Cities* (Chapel Hill, NC: University of North Carolina Press, 1987), p. 6.

10   Sale, *Power Shift*, p. 11.

11   Bernard Weinstein and Harold Gross, interview quoted in Abbott, *The New Urban America*, p. 4.

12   Bruce J. Schulman, *From Cotton Belt to Sunbelt: Federal Policy, Economic Development, and the Transformation of the South, 1938–1980* (New York: Oxford University Press, 1991), Chapter 2.

13   Abbott, *The New Urban America*, p. 22.

14   Quoted in David R. Goldfield and Howard N. Rabinowitz, "The Vanishing Sunbelt," in *Searching for the Sunbelt: Historical Perspectives on a Region*, ed. Raymond A. Mohl (Knoxville: University of Tennessee Press, 1990), p. 224.

15   Ibid., p. 231.

16   William H. Frey, "Metropolitan America: Beyond the Transition," *Population Bulletin* 45, no. 2 (July 1990): 14.

17   U.S. Bureau of the Census, *Statistical Abstract of the United States, 1980*, 101st ed. (Washington, D.C.: U.S. Government Printing Office, 1981), p. 10; U.S. Bureau of the Census, *Statistical Abstract of the United States, 1992*, 112th ed. (Washington, D.C.: U.S. Government Printing Office, 1992), p. 22.

18   U.S. Bureau of the Census, *Statistical Abstract of the United States, 1992*, p. 22.

19   David Rusk, *Cities without Suburbs* (Washington, D.C.: Woodrow Wilson Center Press, 1993).

20   For a thorough analysis of the growth of the Sunbelt that emphasizes economic and technological factors, see John D. Kasarda, "The Implications of Contemporary Redistribution Trends for National Urban Policy," *Social Science Quarterly* 61, no. 3 (December 1980): 373–400.

21   Raymond Arsenault, "The End of the Long Hot Summer: The Air Conditioner and Southern Culture," in *Searching for the Sunbelt*, ed. Mohl, pp. 176–211.

22   Kirkpatrick Sale, "Six Pillars of the Southern Rim," in *The Fiscal Crisis of American Cities*, ed. Roger E. Alcaly and David Mermelstein (New York: Random House, Vintage Books, 1977), p. 174.

23   Ann R. Markusen, *Regions: The Economics and Politics of Territory* (Totowa, NJ: Rowman and Littlefield, 1987), p. 113.

24   Sale, "Six Pillars of the Southern Rim," p. 170.

25   Phillip J. Funigiello, *The Challenge to Urban Liberalism, Federal-City Relations during World War II* (Knoxville, TN: University of Tennessee Press, 1978), pp. 12–13.

26   Abbott, *The New Urban America*, p. 103.

27   Maureen McBreen, "Regional Trends in Federal Defense Expenditures: 1950–76," in *Selected Essays on Patterns of Regional Change: The Changes, the Federal Role, and*

the Federal Response, submitted by Senator Henry Bellmon to the Senate Committee on Appropriations (Washington, D.C.: U.S. Government Printing Office, 1977), p. 527.

28 A report issued by the Northeast-Midwest Economic Advancement Coalition, cited in Edward C. Burks, "16 Northeast and Midwest States Find Inequities in Defense Outlays," *The New York Times* (September 22, 1977).

29 Richard S. Morris, *Bum Rap on America's Cities: The Real Causes of Urban Decline* (Upper Saddle River, NJ: Prentice Hall, 1978), pp. 148–149.

30 Sale, *Power Shift*, p. 149.

31 Since the early 1970s, both parties have permitted exceptions to the seniority rule, and the power of committee chairs has been reduced.

32 Ann R. Markusen, "Regional Planning and Policy: An Essay on the American Exception," Working Paper No. 9 (Brunswick, NJ: Center for Urban Policy Research, Rutgers University, July 1989).

33 See George Peterson, "Federal Tax Policy and Urban Development," in *Central City Economic Development*, ed. Benjamin Chinitz (Cambridge, MA: Abt Books, 1979), pp. 67–78.

34 Michael I. Luger, "Federal Tax Incentives as Industrial and Urban Policy," in *Sunbelt/Snowbelt: Urban Development and Regional Restructuring*, ed. Larry Sawers and William K. Tabb (New York: Oxford University Press, 1984), pp. 204–205.

35 John F. Witte, "The Growth and Distribution of Tax Expenditures," in *The Distributional Impacts of Public Policies*, ed. Sheldon H. Danziger and Kent E. Portney (New York: St. Martin's Press, 1988), p. 179.

36 Peter Marcuse, "The Targeted Crisis: On the Ideology of the Urban Fiscal Crisis and Its Causes," *International Journal of Urban and Regional Research* 5, no. 3 (1981): 339.

37 See Markusen, *Regions*, Chapter 8. The Southern Growth Policy Board relinquished its federal monitoring activities to the Congressional Sunbelt Council in January 1981.

38 "Neutral Federal Policies Are Reducing Frostbelt-Sunbelt Spending Imbalances," *National Journal* (February 7, 1981): 233–236.

39 For evidence on the Sunbelt bias in direct federal military expenditures during the Reagan administration, see the data compiled in *The New York Times* (December 20, 1983), cited in Michael Peter Smith, *City, State, and Market: The Political Economy of Urban Society* (New York: Blackwell, 1988), p. 57.

40 Harold Wolman, "The Reagan Urban Policy and Its Impacts," *Urban Affairs Quarterly* 21, no. 3 (March 1986): 311–336.

41 Peggy L. Cuciti, "A Nonurban Policy: Recent Public Policy Shifts Affecting Cities," in *The Future of National Urban Policy*, ed. Marshall Kaplan and Franklin James (Durham, NC: Duke University Press, 1990), p. 243.

42 Thad Williamson, David Imroscio, and Gar Alperovitz, *Making a Place for Community: Local Democracy in a Global Era* (New York: Routledge, 2002), p. 56.

43 See Gary Mormino, "Tampa: From Hell Hole to the Good Life," in *Sunbelt Cities: Politics and Growth Since World War II*, ed. Richard M. Bernard and Bradley R. Rice (Austin: University of Texas Press, 1983), pp. 138–161; and Abbott, *The New Urban America*.

44 Abbott, *The New Urban America*, p. 247.

45 Amy Bridges, "Politics and Growth in Sunbelt Cities," in *Searching for the Sunbelt*, Historical Perspectives on a region. ed. Raymond A. Mohl, Knoxville, TN: University of Tennessee Press, 1990, p. 2.

46 *Smith v. Allwright*, 321 U.S. 649 (1944). See the discussion in V. O. Key, *Politics, Parties, and Pressure Groups*, 5th ed. (New York: Crowell, 1964), p. 607.

47 Abbott, *The New Urban America*, p. 217.

48 William Frey, *Melting Pot Suburbs: A Census 2000 Study of Suburban Diversity* (Washington, D.C.: Center for Urban and Metropolitan Policy, Brookings Institution Press, June 2001), p. 8.

49 Luis Noe-Bustamente, Mark Hugo Lopez, and Jens Manuel Krogstad, "U.S. Hispanic Population Surpassed 60 million in 2019, but Growth Has Slowed," *Pew Research Center* (July 7, 2020), https://www.pewresearch.org/fact-tank/2020/07/07/u-s-hispanic-population-surpassed-60-million-in-2019-but-growth-has-slowed/.

50 Ibid.

51 Ibid.

52 Kriston Capps, "White People Aren't Driving Growth in the Suburbs," *CityLab* (July 29, 2015). Accessed online: https://www.citylab.com/equity/2015/07/white-people-arent-driving-growth-in-the-suburbs/399659/.

53 Ibid.

54 Joint Center for Political and Economic Studies, *Black Elected Officials: A Statistical Summary, 2001* (April 2001), p. 250, www.jointcenter.org/databank/graphs/99beo.pdf.

55 *Roster of Latino Elected Officials* (Washington, D.C.: National Association of Hispanic Elected and Appointed Officials, annual).

56 Ibid., citing original source as *National Roster of Latino Elected Officials* (Washington, D.C.: National Association of Hispanic Elected and Appointed Officials, annual).

57 U.S. Bureau of the Census. *Hispanic Public Elected Officials by Office, 1985 to 2008, and State, 2008*. Table 421.

58 Michael Leo Owens and Michael J. Rich, "Is Strong Incorporation Enough? Black Empowerment and the Fate of Atlanta's Low-Income Blacks," in *Racial Politics in American Cities*, 3rd ed., ed. Rufus P. Browning, Dale Rogers Marshall, and David H. Tabb (New York: Longman, 2003), pp. 209–210.

59 Timothy Bates and Darrell Williams, "Preferential Procurement Programs and Minority-Owned Business," *Journal of Urban Affairs* 17, no. 1 (1995): 1.

60 Huey L. Perry, "The Evolution and Impact of Biracial Coalition and Black Mayors in Birmingham and New Orleans," in *Racial Politics*, 3rd ed., ed. Browning, Marshall, and Tabb (London, New York & New Jersey: Pearson, 2003), pp. 228–254.

61 Christopher L. Warren and Dario V. Moreno, "Power without a Program: Hispanic Incorporation in Miami," in *Racial Politics*, 3rd ed., ed. Browning, Marshall, and Tabb (London, New York & New Jersey: Pearson, 2003), pp. 281–306.

62 Rodney E. Hero and Susan E. Clarke, "Latinos, Blacks, and Multiethnic Politics in Denver: Realigning Power and Influence in the Struggle for Equality," in *Racial Politics*, 3rd ed., ed. Browning, Marshall, and Tabb (London, New York & New Jersey: Pearson, 2003), pp. 309–330.

63 Geoffrey Skelley, Elena Mejia, Amelia Thomson-DeVeaux, and Laura Bronner, "Why the Suburbs Have Shifted Blue," *FiveThirtyEight* (December 16, 2020), https://fivethirtyeight.com/features/why-the-suburbs-have-shifted-blue/.

64 Beth Reinhard and Lori Rosza, "Miami-Dade Hispanics Helped Sink Biden in Florida," *The Washington Post* (November 4, 2020), https://www.washingtonpost.com/politics/biden-miami-dade-vote-drop/2020/11/04/ec06f13e-1ebd-11eb-ba21-f2f001f0554b_story.html.

65 Rob Wile, "Miami's Biggest New Wave of Immigrants Looks a Lot Like Its Previous Ones," *Miami Herald* (August 5, 2019), https://www.miamiherald.com/article232514327.html.

66 Amelia Thomson-DeVeaux, Geoffrey Skelley, and Laura Bronner, "What We Know about How White and Latino Americans Voted in 2020," *FiveThirtyEight* (November 23, 2020), https://fivethirtyeight.com/features/what-we-know-about-how-white-and-latino-americans-voted-in-2020/.

67 Ibid.

68 Quoted in Charlotte Alter, "How Obama's Final State of the Union Echoed His 2004 Convention Speech," *Time* (January 12, 2016), https://time.com/4178469/state-of-the-union-obama-convention/.

69 Hanna Love and Tracy Hadden Loh, "The 'Rural-Urban Divide' Furthers Myths about Race and Poverty—Concealing Effective Policy Solutions," *The Avenue, Brookings* (December 8, 2020), https://www.brookings.edu/blog/the-avenue/2020/12/08/the-rural-urban-divide-furthers-myths-about-race-and-poverty-concealing-effective-policy-solutions/.

70 Ibid.

71 Ibid.

72 Ruth Igielnik, Scott Keeter, and Hannah Hartig, "Behind Biden's 2020 Victory," *Pew Research Center* Report (June 30, 2021), https://www.pewresearch.org/politics/2021/06/30/behind-bidens-2020-victory/.

73 Dante Chinni, "The 2020 Results: Where Biden and Trump Gained and Lost Voters," *American Communities Project* (November 9, 2020), https://www.americancommunities.org/the-2020-results-where-biden-and-trump-gained-and-lost-voters/.

74 Ibid.

75 Ibid.

76 Ibid.

77 Theodore J. Lowi, "The State of Cities in the Second Republic," *Fiscal Retrenchment and Urban Policy*, ed. J. P. Blair and D. Nachmias (Beverly Hills, CA: Sage, 1979), pp. 43–54; John H. Mollenkopf, *The Contested City* (Princeton, NJ: Princeton University Press, 1983); Paul Kantor, *The Dependent City Revisited: The Political Economy of Urban Development and Social Policy* (Boulder, CO: Westview Press, 1995).

78 Peter K. Eisinger, *The Rise of the Entrepreneurial State: State and Local Economic Development Policy in the United States* (Madison, WI: University of Wisconsin Press, 1988).

79 For evidence of this shift, see Kenneth K. Wong, *City Choices: Education and Housing* (Albany, NY: State University of New York Press, 1990), p. 16.

80 Dennis R. Judd, ed., *The Infrastructure of Play: Building the Tourist City* (Armonk, NY: M. E. Sharpe, 2003).

81 Judis and Teixeira, *The Emerging Democratic Majority*.

82 Jessica Gonzales-Rojas, "Is Arizona the Worst Place in the Country to Be a Latina?" *Huffington Post* (June 20, 2010), http://www.huffingtonpost.com/jessica-gonzalezrojas/arizona-worst-for-latinas_b_1612776.html.

83 Ian Gordon and Tasneem Raja, "164 Anti-Immigration Laws Passed Since 2010? A MoJo Analysis," *Mother Jones* (March 1, 2010), http://m.motherjones.com/politics/2012/03/anti-immigration-law-database.

84 The California Legislature, *Senate Bill No. 54*, Chapter 495 (October 5, 2017). Accessed online: https://leginfo.legislature.ca.gov/faces/billNavClient.xhtml?bill_id=201720180SB54.

85 Jazmine Ulloa, "California Becomes 'Sanctuary State' in Rebuke of Trump Immigration Policy," *The Los Angeles Times* (October 5, 2017). Accessed online: http://www.latimes.com/politics/la-pol-ca-brown-california-sanctuary-state-bill-20171005-story.html.

86 Richard Florida, "How the Crash Will Reshape America," *The Atlantic* (March 1, 2009), p. 54.

PART III

The Fractured Metropolis

CHAPTER 10

The Changing Metropolis

Metropolitan Turf Wars

A deeply ingrained distrust of cities has long been an important feature of American culture. Only a few years after the Constitution was ratified, Thomas Jefferson wrote, "I view great cities as pestilential to the morals, the health, and the liberties of man."[1] In the 1970s, John V. Lindsay, the former mayor of New York, observed that "in the American psychology, the city has been a basically suspect institution."[2] Although the harshest judgments have slowly melted away, a distrust of urban life has persisted despite the fact that, according to the 2000 census, 80 percent of Americans live in metropolitan areas.[3] But it is unclear what it means to observe that America is an urban nation. Residents of Phoenix or Dallas may feel they have little in common with residents of New York City or Boston or even with the city just a few miles away. The feeling of separation is one of the important effects of the fragmented American metropolis.

Even before the suburban movements of the twentieth century, people living in the cities were sorting themselves out into different neighborhoods. New developments in transportation technology (from trolleys to streetcars to, eventually, the automobile) accelerated social and income segregation by making it possible for the wealthy to live further away from urban production zones and commuting to work and play. These developments culminated in the proliferation of the car as a middle-class commodity and explosive construction of the interstate highway system in the 1950s. The Suburban Movement that followed accentuated this tendency in two respects: It drastically increased the geographic distances between social and ethnic groups, and it gave the residents of the more privileged neighborhoods a set of tools for excluding racial and ethnic groups they considered undesirable. Suburban governments employed a variety of means to protect themselves from unwanted change. Early in the twentieth century, zoning laws emerged as the principle device for preserving land values and maintaining social class and racial segregation. A sharp separation among residential areas was also enforced by developers, who routinely imposed deed restrictions forbidding property owners from selling to Blacks and other groups they deemed to be a threat to property values. It took decades, but eventually, deed restrictions were overturned by the courts. Zoning laws, however, have continued largely unchanged, and suburban governments still use them as a means of determining patterns of development.

If they have the choice, suburban jurisdictions try to attract mainly affluent homeowners and the kinds of economic development that contribute positively to the local tax base. This calculus sets up an intensely competitive metropolitan game that often pits one local government against another. People living in the suburbs with high property values and/or plenty of business investment are able to pay lower taxes even while they enjoy higher levels of public services than the residents of poorer municipalities. In the past, central cities were disadvantaged in this game, and as a consequence, they became "the receptacle for all the functions the suburbs [did] not care to support."[4] Originally, the strategies used by suburbs to maintain residential segregation were aimed specifically at people of color, new immigrants, and the poor, most of whom remained clustered in decayed neighborhoods in central cities and, sometimes, in nearby older suburbs. But with the rise of multiethnic suburbs in the 1980s, the metropolitan turf wars have become more complicated. In many urban regions, higher-income residents have been moving to the historic central city even while some older suburbs have attracted poor people and waves of foreign immigrants. Some scholars have termed this phenomenon "The Great Inversion," essentially, a significant population shift of the poor, as well as ethnic and racial minorities away from the gentrifying cities, into the older suburbs, and the white upper- and upper-middle classes from the suburbs back to the cities.[5] Alan Ehrenhalt, who coined the term, argues that American metros are moving toward increasingly resembling European metros, with wealthy urban areas surrounded by poor and working-class suburban rings.[6] This description, however, oversimplifies the complicated demographic developments in American metro areas. It also masks the fact that there are significant country- and region-specific differences among European metros. What is clear, however, is that the ethnic, racial, and social composition of and distribution of people in the American metropolis has become much more complicated at the advent of the twenty-first century. For instance, Alan Berube and Elizabeth Kneebone of the Brookings Institution found that poverty in Atlanta's suburbs grew by 159 percent between 2000 and 2011.[7] Paul Jargowsky, who studies urban poverty in the American metropolis, finds a reconcentration of poverty in metro areas throughout the United States. However, he finds the redistribution of poverty changed:[8] Jargowsky reports that poverty throughout American metros has declustered: High-poverty tracts can now be found in urban, suburban, and rural communities.[9] This creates a highly complicated metropolitan mosaic of poverty and wealth.[10] These developments have had the predictable consequence of keeping the metropolitan game and the metropolitan fragmentation that it sustains very much alive.

Recently, the strategies used by municipalities to attract affluent residents and "higher" land uses have been reinforced by the privatization and walling off of residential developments. By creating privately governed common interest developments (CIDs), homeowners are able to escape many of the burdens of the public realm altogether. Gated communities have become ubiquitous in all urban areas in all regions of the country. Surrounded, as they often are, by a perimeter of walls, fences, or other barriers, they have the effect of segmenting urban populations to a finer degree than was possible through the policies imposed by suburban governments. The effect they exert on metropolitan politics and geographic patterns is still evolving, but certainly, they possess the potential to create an urban landscape that is, in key respects, even more fragmented than in the past.

OUTTAKE

There Is a Debate about Gated Communities

The proliferation of gated communities (perhaps more accurately called *common interest developments*, or *CIDs*) is fragmenting the urban landscape into a mosaic of publicly governed municipalities and privatized residential enclaves. A lively debate is being fought over the question: Is privatized government a good or a bad thing? Arguments on each side of the issue should be considered.

One of the points Evan McKenzie makes in his book, *Privatopia*, is that gated communities constitute a strategy for segregating affluent urban residents from those who rely upon public services. He maintains that CIDs facilitate a "gradual secession" of the affluent from the political and social life of cities, potentially making them "financially untenable for the many and socially unnecessary for the few." He points out that the homogeneous populations that make up most CIDs also undermine any sense of shared social responsibility. Sheryll Cashin echoes this

sentiment when she notes that residents of CIDs "tend to view themselves as taxpayers rather than citizens, and they often perceive local property taxes as a fee for services they should receive rather than their contribution to services local government must provide to the community as a whole." This change in perspective has consequences: Private security guards replace police, and walled-off recreation areas replace community centers and swimming pools.

CIDs have defenders, too. Robert H. Nelson argues that they make it possible for residents to "protect their own neighborhood environment, and also provide a wider range of choice for new residents in search of a neighborhood physical and social environment corresponding to their own individual preferences." In his view, privately governed associations respect one of the most basic rights of human liberty, the right of free association. He maintains that homogeneity within individual neighborhoods is not necessarily a bad thing, since it is based upon the freedom to associate: "the special case of race aside, the right of a neighborhood association to discriminate among potential new unit owners should be protected as a basic matter of defending the right of freedom of association under the U.S. Constitution."

Gated communities, CIDs, or whatever we wish to call them, are becoming the norm in America's metropolitan regions. They are here to stay. As a result, in the next few years, the debate is likely to shift toward a middle ground, involving questions such as whether to compel neighborhood associations to respect constitutional rights and rules of procedural democracy.

To this end, one scholar has proposed a bill of rights for the private residential government. This might be an effective remedy for the rights of people living within CIDs, but it would not reduce the spatial fragmentation of metropolitan areas.

Sources: Evan McKenzie, *Privatopia: Homeowner Associations and the Rise of Residential Private Government* (New Haven, CT: Yale University Press, 1994), p. 186; Sheryll D. Cashin, "Privatized Communities and the 'Secession of the Successful': Democracy and Fairness beyond the Gate," *Fordham Urban Law Journal* 28 (2001): 1679; Robert H. Nelson, *Private Neighborhoods and the Transformation of Local Government* (Washington, D.C.: The Urban Institute Press, 2005), pp. 260–261, 400; Susan F. French, "The Constitution of a Private Residential Government Should Include a Bill of Rights," *Wake Forest Law Review* 27 (1992): 345–352.

How the Suburbs Became Segregated

Many narrative threads make up the story of how American suburbs became fragmented into a patchwork of segregated neighborhoods, subdivisions, and independent suburban jurisdictions. There is, to begin with, a cultural explanation: Beginning in the early years of the Republic, Americans nurtured a negative attitude toward cities, and this antiurban bias was reinforced by racist reactions to the concentration of immigrants in cities during the nineteenth century and the massive demographic movements, such as the Great Migration, of the twentieth century. There is an economic interpretation, too, that stresses the material benefits that the residents of suburban jurisdictions realized by gaining control of local tax and spending policies. A third explanation, which we treat in this section, links the rise of the suburbs to the actions of developers who found residential segregation to be an effective marketing strategy for selling their products. Which came first: consumer preferences or marketing? There may be no definitive answer to this question, but it is worth pondering nevertheless.

Clearly, there has been a popular preference for suburban living for a long time. The pent-up demand for housing coincided with new government policies to promote homeownership. Never before had it been so easy for white people to secure a loan. In 1934, Congress created the Federal Housing Authority to ensure the home loans made by banks. The legislation was followed in 1944 by a law authorizing the Veterans Administration (VA) to make loans to returning veterans for no money down and for long amortization periods. These policies made it possible for millions of white middle-class families to buy homes even if they had few savings—or none at all, in the case of returning veterans. The new home-buyers eagerly seized the opportunity to move out of overcrowded urban neighborhoods.

Federal policies and the real estate industry powerfully shaped the attitudes that favored suburban life. The policies of Federal Housing Administration (FHA) and VA administrators and bank loan officers encouraged builders to promote construction almost exclusively outside the cities. In this sense, it may be said that the suburbs were created first by policy makers, developers, and the housing industry and only later by the preferences of buyers. Developers influenced the character of the suburbs by selecting the clientele that could best supply profits and by molding the tastes and preferences of potential buyers. Realtors, developers, and financial institutions aggressively marketed the suburbs because new housing construction maximized their profitability, and it was easier to do than the rehabilitation of older neighborhoods.[11] Developers were quick to realize that an enormous market had been opened up, and they seized the opportunity. Within a few years, big development firms became the frontline agents that shaped the development of the suburban subdivisions that quickly spread across the urban landscape. As one scholar observed:

> The plain fact is that … the main force in our process of urban development is the private developer. The primacy of the bulldozer in transforming rural land to urban uses, the capacity of the private company to build thousands of homes on quiet rolling hills is a predominant fact of American urban life.[12]

What the developers put in place during the suburban boom of the postwar years became the foundation for the pattern of settlement that still exists in America's urban areas.

In many ways, the United States is unique among industrialized countries in its extensive suburban developments. This is, among other things, due to the low population density of the United States as a country in general: According to the World Bank, the United States ranks among the top 60 countries with the least population density in the world, the same as other former colonies, such as Australia, and Canada.[13] This fact made suburban land extraordinarily cheap and available to developers and buyers.

To market the houses they built, developers promised not only a home but also an entire way of life. They were not merely the builders of houses; they were "community builders" interested in shaping the character of entire neighborhoods.[14] In their attempt to market the new subdivisions, developers virtually invented an iconic image of the American Dream—the suburban house. The suburbs were promoted as ways to achieve instant social status, escape the problems of the cities, and live in a closely regulated social environment. Thus, the suburbs became sharply differentiated from the cities, both in people's minds and in reality. Developers were careful to target the potential homeowners who could add to their bottom line. This strategy proved to be especially effective for the developers of exclusive subdivisions, who found that the bigger the house and the higher the income of buyers, the more money they could make.

One of the first and most influential of community builders was Jesse Clyde Nichols, who pioneered the concept of planning entire communities decades before it became common practice. Born on a farm close to Kansas City, Kansas, Nichols attended the University of Kansas and later studied economics at Harvard. In 1900, Nichols took a trip to Europe, where he admired the beauty and grandeur of European cities. He saw no reason why cities in the United States could not be even more majestic than the cities of Europe. In 1905, Nichols began buying up land southwest of downtown Kansas City, where he intended to build and sell top-market residences.

Nichols was different from the typical small-time real estate operator, or "curbstoner," who bought a few small parcels of land on the edge of the city, divided them into lots, and hoped to make a speculative profit. Nichols believed in a scientific approach to land development. In a speech before a real estate convention in 1912, Nichols attracted national attention by criticizing those small-time land developers who went for the fast sale and the quick profit. Instead, he advocated a more comprehensive approach. He shocked his contemporaries by arguing that planning was not only compatible with private profit but could actually increase profits over the long run. As he later put it in a landmark article on suburban shopping centers, "good planning is good business."[15] Over the years, Nichols became a persuasive advocate for planned suburban development. He was a leader in the National Association of Real Estate Boards (NAREB), and in 1935 he founded the Urban Land Institute (ULI), which is influential in the housing industry to this day. In his lifetime, he saw the private planning he pioneered become public policy through local subdivision regulations, zoning laws, and federal loan guarantee programs.

Nichols put his principles into practice by developing the Country Club District on the edge of Kansas City, considered by many at the time to be the most beautiful suburb in the nation. Nichols appealed to his wealthy clientele with extraordinary aesthetics—he modeled the suburb's shopping center, the first in the nation, on the architecture of Seville, Spain. Nichols also applied the latest in household technology, such as piped gas and electric service, in a period when servants were becoming less common. Nichols's suburban houses promised to provide a secure haven far from the stresses and tensions of city life. Husbands could go off to work in the city secure in the knowledge that their wives and children were safe in the idyllic environment of the Country Club District.

Nichols's projects were strictly limited to affluent homeowners. To guarantee that his development would remain an exclusive preserve long after he completed his work, Nichols devised the self-perpetuating deed restriction, which required owners to follow requirements laid down by the developer.[16] The deed restrictions specified minimum lot sizes, minimum cost for houses, setbacks from the street, and even the color and style of houses. And the deeds specified that the houses could be bought by and sold to whites only.[17] These restrictions became an important marketing tool because they promised to protect exclusivity and secure property values.

Until the years after World War II, developments like those built by Nichols were available mainly to the upper middle-class homebuyers. This began to change in the postwar years. In the late 1930s, Levitt & Sons succeeded as a medium-sized developer of plain tract housing for upper-middle-class families leaving New York City for Long Island, but the company's big break came during World War II, when it won contracts to build thousands of houses for the U.S. Navy around Norfolk, Virginia. It is here that the Levitts worked on the mass-production techniques that revolutionized home building throughout the United States. Within a few years after the war, the firm founded by William J. Levitt, his father Abraham, and his brother Alfred became the largest home builder in the United States.

Unlike Nichols, William Levitt drifted into building houses. Caring little for school, Levitt dropped out of New York University after his third year because, as he put it in a *Time* magazine cover story, "I got itchy. I wanted to make money. I wanted a big car and a lot of clothes."[18] In 1936, after he passed through several jobs, Levitt and his father decided to build a house on a Long Island lot they had been unable to sell. They made a profit. From this small beginning, Levitt launched his extraordinary career.

The Levitts quietly began buying up land from Long Island farmers and building inexpensive homes by using assembly-line methods. The basic process involved laying a concrete slab for a foundation, erecting preassembled walls, then tying the structure together with a roof trucked to the site. The Levitts broke down the complex process of building a house into 26 operations and then assigned each step to a separate contractor. Because each contractor did the same job over and over again, it was possible to achieve incredible speed.[19] Levitt avoided unions and used piecework incentives to speed the process even more.[20] At the Levitt lumberyard, one man was able to cut parts for ten houses in one day.[21] By 1950, the firm was producing one house every 16 minutes.[22] By preassembling as many components as possible, Levitt reduced the amount of skilled labor necessary on the job site, and by purchasing directly from the manufacturers, he eliminated middlemen's fees. Overall, Levitt was able to build a typical house for about $6,000, an affordable amount even for some working-class families.[23]

Between 1947 and 1951, the Levitts converted 4,000 acres of potato farms in Hempstead, Long Island, into the largest housing development in the nation's history.[24] Ultimately housing 82,000 residents, Levittown, as it came to be known, became a huge success. Because of the huge pent-up demand for inexpensive housing following World War II, in the first years, people lined up and camped out for days waiting to purchase one of the homes. The basic Cape Cod model sold for $7,990. With federal guarantees for the loan and no down payment required for veterans, an ex-GI could buy a Levitt house for only $56 a month.[25]

Like Nichols, Levitt believed that tight controls over buyers and their behavior were the best way to guarantee rising real estate values. Restrictive covenants required the grass to be cut each week (if not done, one of Levitt's men would cut it and send a bill) and disallowed fences (but allowed hedges). Laundry could not be hung out on a clothesline. In addition, the covenants barred tenants or homeowners from selling to or even allowing their property to be used by African Americans. The standard lease for the first homes in Levittown, in which the tenant had an option to buy, contained this language: "The tenant agrees not to permit the premises to be used or occupied by any person other than members of the Caucasian race. But the employment and maintenance of other than Caucasian domestic servants shall be permitted."[26] Levitt argued that economic realities required him to recognize that "most whites prefer not to live in mixed communities,"[27] but his determination to enforce his own racial prejudices went beyond mere economics; he evicted two tenants who had allowed Black children to play in their homes.[28] In 1960, not a single Black family lived in Levittown,[29] and even 30 years later, only about one-fourth of 1 percent of its residents were African American.[30]

In the mid-1950s, Levitt decided to build two more Levittowns, one in Pennsylvania and one in New Jersey. Opened in October 1958 and finished in 1965, Levittown, New Jersey, provided several new features. Fearing that an unfavorable image of sterile uniformity would damage sales, the company offered several house styles and floor plans. The idea of mixing styles was offered by William Levitt's wife and implemented by him over the objections of his executives.[31] Levitt did not offer changes from a standardized model to provide more aesthetically pleasing suburban residential areas. His motives were strictly economic; in order to sell houses, he needed to ensure that the houses would continue to appeal to the aspiring middle class.

Levitt attracted purchasers by other means as well. Long-term financing with low monthly payments was made possible through the firm. He also carefully selected the buyers by excluding applicants who did not conform to middle-class values in conduct and appearance. All homes were designed for families with young children. Advertisements stressed that it was a planned community with schools, churches, swimming pools, and parks. In all of these respects, the Levitt company constructed the kind of community that fit the developer's ideas about suburban life. If middle-class homebuyers wanted something different, they would have been hard put to find any other places to live, at least in the suburbs.

Levitt's fortunes began to change in 1968 when he sold his development company to the International Telephone and Telegraph Corporation (ITT) for $60 million in ITT stock. Soon after the sale, the stock, which he used as collateral for loans, plunged in value. Because of a clause in his sales contract, Levitt was forbidden to renew his building activities for ten years, except in cities where ITT had no interest. Levitt invested $20 million in a project in Iran, but the new government took it over after the 1979 revolution. In 1987, at the age of 80, Levitt was forced to declare bankruptcy and was evicted from his New York City offices.[32]

The careers of Nichols and Levitt demonstrate the power given to private developers by federal government agencies, who implemented housing policies and financings, such as the FHA and the VA, to shape the suburbs to fit their own tastes and attitudes. Residential segregation on the basis of incomes and lifestyles was a natural result of the logic of federal policy in combination with profitability and marketing. These observations may be applied to contemporary suburbs as well. Whether a developer builds luxury single-family homes, townhouses for young middle-class homebuyers, condominiums for singles, or a gated community, the character of the community that results will reflect the developers' business plan. Buyers choose their environment before they move, but once they have decided where they are going to live, they "are very largely prisoners of that environment with but little opportunity of changing it."[33]

The Imperative of Racial Segregation

The rise of the twentieth-century American suburb went hand in hand with a cultural imperative of racial segregation. The precedents for segregation enforced by social custom, law, the federal government, and the policies of the housing industry were established very early, and by the time these practices were abandoned in the late 1970s, a metropolitan land use landscape of racial segregation had become basically fixed.

Beginning in the early twentieth century, restrictive covenants became the main instrument used by the real estate industry to enforce racial segregation. When a buyer purchased a house, the deed often came with a printed covenant that restricted its subsequent sale. Typically, African Americans were identified as a restricted group on the back of the deed, but sometimes Jews and "consumptives" (anyone with tuberculosis) were also be named. Restrictive covenants became, in effect, governmental policy when the supreme courts of 14 states upheld their legality and ruled they could be enforced in the courts.[34] It is estimated that restrictive covenants applied to homes sold in half of the subdivisions built in the United States before 1948 when the U.S. Supreme Court ruled they could not be enforced in courts of law.[35]

Restrictive covenants dating back to the 1940s and 1950s remain on many property deeds today. One from suburban Maryland, dated May 6, 1946, states that the property "shall never be used or occupied by ... negroes or any person or persons, of negro blood or extraction, or to any person of the Semitic Race, blood or origin, or Jews, Armenians, Hebrews, Persians and Syrians, except ... partial occupancy of the premises by domestic servants."[36]

None of the provisions of the restrictive covenant are enforced today, and a biracial family owns the house, but they remain part of the deed itself. In the wake of a broader reckoning with the country's racist past in 2020, the ubiquity of such restrictive covenants on the basis of race and ethnicity, which appear notoriously difficult to eliminate, was startling to policy makers, activists, and citizens alike. In October of 2020, a new law went into effect in the state of Maryland, which allows homeowners to request that courts remove such restrictive covenants on their deeds for free. Several other states, among them California, Florida, and Virginia, followed suit in eliminating bureaucratic requirements and expenses for removing restrictive covenants. Not everyone agrees that restrictive covenants should be erased completely from property records: Some scholars argue that not all records of the country's system of racist housing and lending policies should be completely erased and that keeping the records is an important warning sign for the future.[37]

The NAREB was established in 1908 to represent the interests of builders and real estate agents. Everyone involved in the housing business accepted as a fundamental principle that the value of the property was connected to the homogeneity of neighborhoods. Based on this premise, the NAREB "racialized" land use in urban areas by promoting the idea that whites and Blacks must be strictly segregated.[38] From 1924 until 1950, Article 34 of the Realtors' national code (circulated to realtors everywhere by the NAREB) read, "A Realtor should never be instrumental in introducing into a neighborhood a character of property or occupancy, members of any race or nationality, or any individual whose presence will clearly be detrimental to property values in the neighborhood."[39]

To enforce this policy, local real estate boards issued written codes of ethics prohibiting members from introducing "detrimental" minorities into white neighborhoods. The textbooks and training materials used in real estate training courses took care to emphasize that real estate agents were ethically bound to promote homogeneous neighborhoods. The leading textbook used in such courses in the 1940s compared some ethnic groups to termites eating away at sound structures:

> The tendency of certain racial and cultural groups to stick together, making it almost impossible to assimilate them in the normal social organism, is too well known to need much comment. But in some cases the result is less detrimental than in others. The Germans, for example, are a clean and thrifty people .... Unfortunately this cannot be said of all the other nations which have sent their immigrants to our country. Some of them have brought standards and customs far below our own levels .... Like termites, they undermine the structure of any neighborhood into which they creep.[40]

Any real estate agent found breaking the code by selling to members of the wrong groups was subject to loss of license and expulsion from the local board. Even brokers who were not affiliated with the national association felt compelled to accept the Realtors' guidelines because most of their business depended upon referrals.

In 1948, in the case of *Shelly v. Kraemer*, the U.S. Supreme Court ruled that racially restrictive covenants violated the Fourteenth Amendment's guarantee of equal protection of the law and that they could not therefore be enforced in the courts.[41] Despite the ruling, covenants sometimes continued to be written, but now they were enforced not by the courts but by pressure exerted by realtors, developers, homeowner associations, and neighbors. Banks refused to make loans to Blacks trying to buy in white neighborhoods; in any case, realtors refused to show them the homes. The suburbs did not begin opening up to Black Americans until Congress passed the 1968 Housing Act, which barred racial discrimination in the sale and rental of housing.

OUTTAKE

Integrating Levittown, PA: The Trauma of Deepgreen Lane

Daisy Myers and William Myers, Jr. were the first African American family to move to Levittown, PA. Residential integration, and the trauma that came with it, especially for African Americans, is somewhat more easily addressed in general terms. The particular personal trauma of the hostilities, which many African Americans experienced when attempting to enter exclusively white suburbs, is better illustrated along the lines of personal experiences. The Myers moved to Levittown in the late summer of 1957, facing staunch resistance from local residents. This resistance was vividly captured in a 1957 documentary *Crisis in Levittown, PA,* produced by Dan W. Dodson, a professor of sociology at New York University. Born in 1907, Dodson was a Texan by birth, and as the son of a sharecropper, he was raised in acceptance of Jim Crow laws but came to embrace and promote racial equality. Dodson's film documents blatant white racism: Many of the Levittown residents interviewed for the documentary claim

to be concerned about property values, but they also openly worry about mixed marriages and racial equality. Several note that among their motivations for moving to Levittown was the promise of living in an all-white community.

Daisy Myers recalls "the rocks through the windows, the taunts and name-calling and cross-burnings and the day-and-night blaring of 'Old Black Joe' that greeted her arrival as a member of the first African American family in Levittown, PA [...]."

Daisy Myers holds two MA degrees, and her husband, William, was an engineer. They did not perceive themselves as political activists for racial integration but instead were looking for a larger home as their family was expanding. Daisy Myers was first mistaken for the maid when the mailman delivered the first mail to the house. When she cleared up the mistake, the mailman informed the rest of the community of the new arrivals, and within a few hours, loiterers gathered in front of the Myers' house, throwing rocks, screaming racial slurs, and, eventually burning crosses. The community was divided, with some residents embracing the Myers as new members of the community, bringing food, and helping out. Two competing petitions were gathering signatures, one by the "Levittown Betterment Committee," protesting the potential racial integration of Levittown, and one by the "Citizens Committee for Levittown" condemning the violence against the Myers. The story drew national and even international attention in the media. When a vacant house in the vicinity of the Myers' home was turned into a "clubhouse" for the "resistance" to Levittown's integration, flying a confederate flag, and blaring racist music at all hours of the day and night, William Myers, Jr. appealed to then-Attorney General Thomas D. McBride for help. McBride charged eight residents with

"evil conspiracy" and asked the Bucks County Court to end the harassment against the Myers. The court issued an injunction on October 23, 1957. A year later, a second African American family moved into the community. The organized opposition to racial integration of Levittown, PA, had finally broken down.

Sources: Robert Mcg. Thomas, Jr., "Dan W. Dodson, 88, Foe and Scholar of Racism." Obituary. *The New York Times* (August 19, 1995). Accessed online: http://www.nytimes.com/1995/08/19/obituaries/dan-w-dodson-88-foe-and-scholar-of-racism.html; Dan W. Dodson: *Crisis in Levittown, PA.* Documentary. Dynamic Films, Inc. 1957; Lacy McCrary, "Trauma of Levittown Integration Remembered History: In August 1957, an African-American Family Moved to Deepgreen Lane and Was Greeted by a Mob Screaming Racial Epithets and Making Threats," *The Baltimore Sun* (August 21, 1997). Accessed online: http://articles.baltimoresun.com/1997-08-21/news/1997233064_1_daisy-myers-levittown-epithets; David B. Bittan, "'A Flaming Cross': Pennsylvania, August 1957–August 1958." *Reporting Civil Rights: American Journalism 1941–1963.* The Library of America.

By the time the housing act became law, patterns of racial segregation had already been firmly established, and they would have been hard to change even if racial discrimination, by some act of magic, had disappeared overnight. The change was also made more difficult because of the rise of CIDs, which proved to be a remarkably efficient device for preserving the social-class uniformity of new housing developments. When homebuyers purchase a home in a CID, they automatically agree to abide by a list of restrictions on the use of their property. They also pay fees for their share in the cost and maintenance of services and amenities held "in common" (thus the term "common interest") with other residents. The "community" of homeowners is governed by a homeowner's association, which is responsible for enforcing the long list of covenants, contracts, and restrictions (CC&Rs). Such rules can be used to enforce the homogeneity of neighborhoods even more effectively than restrictive covenants, with one principal exception—they cannot be used explicitly to sort out buyers on the basis of race, ethnicity, or gender.

The number of CIDs, which includes cooperative apartments, condominiums, and single-family housing developments, exploded from fewer than 500 in 1964 to 10,000 by 1970 and to 150,000 by 1992, when 32 million Americans lived within them.[42] CIDs were concentrated especially in the Sunbelt, with California, Florida, and Texas leading the way. All through the Sunbelt, large numbers of retired people moved into gated communities. By 2005, 54.6 million people lived in 274,000 developments governed by homeowner associations.[43] In many metropolitan areas, they have become so common that new homebuyers who do not want to live in one will find it hard to find a house anywhere else. Since 2000, 80 percent of all homes built in the United States are governed by homeowner associations that administer privately provided amenities.[44]

CIDs became the main device used by developers to become "community builders" in the tradition of Jesse Clyde Nichols. The CC&Rs that homebuyers agreed to were drawn up by the developer before the first resident moved in. Developers could point to the CC&Rs to reassure homebuyers that the future of their investment was secured against unwanted change. The CID mechanism also solved a pressing problem that immediately threatened developers' profits. By the late 1950s, suburbia had become synonymous with low-density tract housing, an equation that reflected the developers' success in marketing the suburbs as an escape from the cities. By the 1960s, however, this version of the suburban dream began to yield lower profits because the market for single houses constructed on individual lots was diminishing. Perceptive developers realized that there were huge demographic and income groups, such as retirees and young singles and married couples without children, which remained as vast untapped markets.

The problem for developers was that by the 1960s, the constantly rising price of suburban land meant that they could build homes affordable for the middle class only if they could achieve much higher densities than before. Accordingly, the housing industry initiated a campaign to market a revised version of the suburban dream that would include row houses and apartment buildings. Almost overnight, attached housing, which developers had always associated with inner-city neighborhoods, became desirable. By the late 1960s, the American Society of Planning Officials, the ULI, developers, and the FHA became sudden critics of the "gridiron" housing tracts and large-lot, low-density development they had promoted for so long. The CID idea anchored a campaign to convince local governments and consumers that higher-density development was compatible with the maintenance of property values, exclusion, and status.[45]

In a report published in 1963, the ULI pointed out that CIDs could exclude unwanted residents better than any alternative form of development: "Existing as private or semi-private areas they may exclude undesirable elements or trouble-makers drifting in."[46] The FHA agreed to insure loans for condominiums in multiunit buildings in 1961. Two years later, the FHA released its first manual explicitly encouraging developers to build planned units that would be governed by homeowner associations. In 1964, the FHA and the ULI co-published a 400-page volume describing the history of CIDs and setting forth detailed directions on how to establish CC&Rs and the homeowner associations to enforce them.[47] Since the early 1970s, the two biggest secondary mortgage purchasers, the Federal National Mortgage Association and the Federal Home Loan Corporation have insisted on formulating and reviewing guidelines for residential associations before purchasing the loans on properties that will be governed by them. In only two decades, the institutional pressures applied by the housing industry and the federal government changed the face of the suburbs.

In popular parlance, CIDs are generally referred to as "gated communities," though this term is imprecise because many privatized developments are not actually physically gated. For developers, gates and walls are often used as a marketing tool; these features allow them to play upon themes of security, seclusion, and exclusivity.[48] Developers establish the rules and regulations and set up the homeowner association even before the first property is sold; in this way, they are able to promise to buyers that all residents who move in later will follow closely prescribed norms of behavior and decorum. The list of covenants and restrictions enforced by residents' associations is typically very long and detailed. They may dictate such things as the minimum and maximum ages of residents, hours and frequency of visitors, color of paint on a house, style and color of draperies hung in windows, size of pets and number of children (if either is allowed), parking rules, patios and landscaping, and even minute details like what vehicle a resident can park in the driveway. Many CID residents no doubt find such regulations comforting. For others, the restrictions become intolerable, as evidenced by the high number of lawsuits filed against community associations.

Gated communities are planned as remarkably homogeneous environments. Some of them are developed and marketed to appeal to people on the basis of particular shared interests or life conditions; for instance, communities have been built exclusively for retirees, golfers, singles, and even nudists. Green Valley, Nevada, a massive gated community just outside Las Vegas, is segmented not only by different architectural styles but also by the cost and size of houses.[49] Each of these "villages" (as the developer calls them) carries the accoutrements of community: A name (Silver Springs or Valle Verde, for example), a community center, a school, a recreational center, and sometimes a park.[50] The separation between this private city and the outside world is, in effect, embellished by a finer-grained separation within.

The Housing Act of 1968 made it illegal to discriminate on the basis of race in the selling or rental of housing. To some degree, however, the intensified social-class segregation facilitated by CIDs acts as a partially effective substitute for earlier means of discrimination. In 2019, the median income was 61 cents for every dollar earned by non-Hispanic white, up from 59 cents in 2018.[51] Because, after centuries of race-based oppression, exploitation, and segregation of racial minorities, racial inequality is strongly reinforced by economic inequality, any effective remedy to residential segregation would require policies that directly interfere with the basic operations of the housing market. Since these would be politically and legally unacceptable, there is no practical way to fundamentally alter the patterns of segregation inherited from the past in lieu of groundbreaking legal and political changes.

Walling Off the Suburbs: Incorporation

The many suburban jurisdictions that exist in a typical metropolitan region act as a powerful force preserving racial and socioeconomic segregation. In all older metropolitan areas, exclusive suburbs dating back to the late nineteenth century dot the landscape. When the automobile made it possible for more people to make the suburban move, a ring of middle-class suburbs grew up just beyond the city limits. The suburban boom following World War II created a true patchwork of white working-class, middle-class, and upper-class suburbs—for example, Levittown was a middle-class bastion on Long Island, but it remained worlds apart from the wealthier enclaves only a few miles away. Over time, this process fragmented urban areas into a multitude of jurisdictions, each eager to preserve its character and history.

For a variety of reasons, the number of suburbs outside the big cities remained relatively small until the 1920s. Some of the people who moved beyond the city limits in the post-Civil War era sought annexation rather than separation because public services were otherwise too expensive or hard to get. At other times, suburban residents were coerced into joining the city. From the turn of the century to the 1920s, for example, Los Angeles used its monopoly over water supply to force neighboring communities, such as Hollywood, Venice, Lordsburg, Sawtelle, Watts, Eagle Rock, Hyde Park, Tujunga, and Barnes City, to become part of the city. This coercive behavior came to a stop with the formation of the Metropolitan Water District in 1927, which ended Los Angeles's monopoly over water.[52] A subsequent agreement among local governments called the *Lakewood Plan* made it possible for suburbs to obtain municipal services by contracting with the county government.[53] Almost overnight, the number of suburbs outside Los Angeles began to multiply.

There are many reasons why suburbs proliferated so rapidly. On occasion, simple economic self-interest supplied a sufficient motive to incorporate. E.J. "Lucky" Baldwin was a notorious gambler and entrepreneur in California in the early twentieth century. He got his nickname by making a fortune gambling on mining stocks,[54] and he was the defendant in a number of seduction and paternity suits that culminated in spectacular trials. Baldwin wanted to build a racetrack, but he knew he would be opposed by southern California's foes of sin, led by the Anti-Saloon League. Accordingly, Baldwin decided to create his own suburb, called Arcadia. As the name implied, he intended the town to be his personal utopia. He imported his own employees as residents and handed out free watermelons on election day. Not surprisingly, they approved incorporation unanimously and elected a city council composed of Baldwin and his employees. Baldwin realized his dream when Santa Anita raceway opened on December 7, 1907.[55]

On other occasions, suburban governments came into being to protect businesses from taxes and regulations. Efforts to incorporate were almost always successful when they were led by powerful companies.[56] In 1907, meat-packing companies incorporated National City on the northern border of East St. Louis, Illinois, to escape being taxed by East St. Louis. A few years later, Monsanto Chemical Company created the city of Sauget on East St. Louis's border for the same purpose. In the 1950s, a group of industrialists tried to form a separate suburban jurisdiction in Los Angeles County as a means of avoiding having to pay for the services of a growing suburban population. When they found that the area did not include the 500 residents required for incorporation, they redrew the boundaries to include 169 patients of a mental sanitarium, which put them over the top. Appropriately, they named their new town "Industry."[57]

In most cases, though, the desire to incorporate was driven by more complicated motives. Put simply, the people who had left the city wanted to wash their hands of it. The only effective way to ensure they could never be annexed by the city they had fled was to draw legal boundaries around themselves. The formal incorporation of a new jurisdiction turned out to be a good strategy for gaining control over taxes and services, and in the bargain, it provided a means of keeping out city dwellers. At the turn of the century, residents of Oak Park on the border of Chicago feared that the Slavic population might spill over from neighboring Austin. Their motive for incorporating, according to one author, was that "Slavic persons with little aversion for alcohol were rapidly settling the Austin area, and the native American Protestant population of Oak Park feared the immoral influences that might accompany these foreigners."[58] Between 1899 and 1902, Austin joined the city of Chicago, but Oak Park formed a separate suburban government.

People began creating independent municipalities outside the boundaries of all the big cities. In 1890, Cook County, whose principal city is Chicago, had 55 governments; by 1920, it had 109. Similarly, the number of general-purpose governments in the New York City area grew from 127 in 1900 to 204 by 1920. There were 91 incorporated municipalities in the Pittsburgh area in 1890 but 107 in 1920.[59] During the 1920s, new suburbs were formed by the score.

Legal incorporation had not always been so easy to accomplish. Local governments are not mentioned in the U.S. Constitution; legally, they are creatures of the states. In the early part of the nineteenth century, the incorporation of a local government was viewed as a privilege bestowed by state legislatures. In their fights to persuade state legislators to allow them to form their own governments, the residents of place typically claimed that smaller governments were closer to the people and were therefore the best possible expressions of democracy.[60] Because legislators tended to view the cities with a measure of distrust anyway, their pleas got a favorable reception.

Gradually, state legislatures made it so much easier for groups of citizens to create new towns and cities that incorporation shifted from a privilege to a right.[61] Eventually, the legislatures of all of the states liberalized the rules by which citizens could come together to form a municipality. "By the early twentieth century suburbanites had begun carving up the metropolis, and the states had handed them the knife."[62] By 1930, every state legislature in the country had adopted liberalized incorporation laws that put the decision of whether suburban residents would or would not be annexed by the central city firmly into the hands of those who had already fled from it.

Suburban residents have pursued incorporation with great enthusiasm. According to the census of 2002, there were 19,431 municipalities in the United States.[63] The pace slowed somewhat late in the twentieth century, but by then, it hardly made any difference. According to the 2002 census, there were more than 35,000 municipalities in the United States. St. Louis County, Missouri, had 92; DuPage County, outside Chicago, had 38. As in the past, the proponents of incorporation are motivated by a variety of concerns, but mainly they want to ensure that their communities will continue to develop in a way that fits with their own values. In June 2005, 94 percent of the affluent residents of Sandy Springs, Florida, voted to support incorporation to achieve smaller government so that "Sandy Springs can control its own destiny," or as another put it, "My major thing, let's make the decisions here rather than downtown."[64]

Mostly, the residents of Sandy Springs were upset that some of their tax money supported services supplied to less affluent people living in their home county. A simple desire for government closer to home combines with bare-knuckled economic self-interest in most incorporation proposals. The principle most often cited in these battles is the desire to gain control over tax revenues and land use decisions. In 2005, a resident supporting the incorporation of the Village of the Falls in Dade County, Florida (outside Miami), said, "We want to be able to have a say how our tax dollars are spent," and, he added, "we want to control zoning of our neighborhood to maintain and improve our quality of life."[65]

Control over land use decisions is important because these policies are directly connected to local economic growth. In the most affluent communities, residents may wish to keep out malls, big-box stores, and all other development they deem to be undesirable. The residents of less fortunate suburbs, however, are more likely to desire exactly the opposite. All but the richest suburban governments simply cannot raise revenues sufficient for providing adequate service levels unless they attract business; if they cannot do so, homeowners end up paying high property taxes. By the mid-1950s, local governments were fighting hard for the first generation of shopping centers, which later morphed into enclosed malls. Local officials encouraged development through direct subsidies to private firms, abatement of local taxes, and the provision of infrastructure such as access roads. In the process, local officials sometimes took money on the side, thus creating a culture of corruption that has cropped up in many places.[66]

The competition for growth is especially intense in the 28 states that have authorized local sales taxes. Receipts from sales taxes can generate 40 percent or more of local revenues. Accordingly, local officials go to great lengths to land a mall, big-box store, and smaller retailers. The competition is fierce; in the words of a vice president of the Utah Taxpayers Association, "It's kind of a Cold War mentality. Basically, what you have is cities competing against each other for sales tax dollars."[67] Ventura, California, provides an apt example of what local officials are willing to do. To ensure the continued viability of the Buenaventura Mall, the city agreed to a $12.6 million subsidy package that obliged it to rebate 80 percent of the sales tax revenues that would be realized by an expansion and makeover of the mall. When a neighboring municipality, Oxnard, proposed a plan to share sales tax revenues among local governments, a Ventura city official summarily rejected the offer: "Now because their shopping center deteriorated … they want to share. I haven't seen any movement from them wanting to share Wal-Mart and all those stores along the … Freeway."[68] Battles motivated by attitudes exactly like this are constantly playing out in metropolitan areas all over the country.

Walling Off the Suburbs: Zoning

Zoning is the most powerful tool that municipalities can use to control land use. It may be used for many purposes, but without a doubt, its origins are rooted in the desire to make it difficult or impossible for less affluent people to settle nearby. The nation's first zoning law was enacted in New York City on July 25, 1916. By the end of the 1920s, 768 municipalities with 60 percent of the nation's urban population had enacted zoning ordinances.[69] Quick adoption was made possible when real estate interests discovered what a useful tool zoning could be for protecting valuable land from uses deemed less desirable. As promoters of New York's ordinance explained it to audiences around the country, "The small homeowner and the little shopkeeper were now protected against destructive uses next door. Land in the lower Fifth Avenue section, which had been a drag on the market when zoning arrived, was now undergoing so successful a residential improvement that rents were on the rise. 'Blighted districts are no longer produced in New York City.'"[70] The principle claim made for zoning was that it kept land values high by segregating "better" from "inferior" land uses. In state after state, real estate groups and politicians lobbied for state laws enabling cities to zone their property.

New York City's zoning ordinance arose from the fear that fashionable sections of Fifth Avenue might be invaded by loft buildings from the garment district on the West Side. Their concerns were well founded. From 1850 to 1900, New York's population increased from 661,000 to 3,437,000. Such growth rewarded speculators and entrepreneurs who had been discerning enough to predict the path of the city's expansion. But there was a downside for the upper-class residents who kept establishing themselves at the city's edge, only to move out again with the arrival of new waves of immigrants and businesses.

By the turn of the century, the upper class had established a mansion district and an exclusive shopping area on upper Fifth Avenue. The wealthy residents of the area felt threatened by their working-class neighbors only a few blocks away. The garment district, characterized by tall loft buildings in which thousands of poorly paid immigrant garment workers and carters worked, threatened to destroy the exclusive shopping district. A way—a legal way—had to be found to protect Fifth Avenue, which was often described (especially by the wealthy residents along the avenue) as the cultural fulcrum of New York, "a unique place" in "the traditions of this city and in the imagination of its citizens," "probably the most important thoroughfare in this city, perhaps any city in the New World," an area with a "history and associations rich in memories," "the common pride, of all citizens, rich and poor alike, their chief promenading avenue, and their principal shopping thoroughfare."[71] In 1916 the Fifth Avenue Association, which employed lawyers to invent this kind of lofty rhetoric, pleaded that Fifth Avenue was a special area that should be protected from encroachment. Fifty-four years later, the rationale behind zoning had changed little: "We moved out here ... to escape the city. I don't want the city following me here," explained a Long Island resident.[72]

The Fifth Avenue Association looked for a way to keep loft buildings out. At first, they tried to limit the building height but soon hit upon a more ambitious scheme. In 1916, the Buildings Heights Commission, which had been appointed in 1913 to investigate the problems of tall buildings in New York City, proposed carving Manhattan into areas designated to ensure a "place for everything and everything in its place."[73] According to the commission, "the purpose of zoning was to stabilize and protect lawful investment and not to injure assessed valuations or existing uses."[74]

New York's law specified five zones, each defined by the uses and values of land. In the zoning pecking order, residential uses assumed first place even though commercial and industrial land was often more valuable. Next down the ladder were commercial business districts, differentiated on the basis of building height (the taller the buildings, the lower the place in the zoning hierarchy). Warehouses and industries were allotted last place.

New York City officials fanned out to other cities to publicize their law, in part to ensure it would be widely adopted before courts could challenge its constitutionality. "By the spring of 1918 New York had become a Mecca for pilgrimages of citizens and officials" who wanted to enact a similar ordinance. Within a year after the passage of the legislation, more than 20 cities had initiated "one of the most remarkable legislative campaigns in American history."[75] Zoning was literally mass produced; most cities copied the New York ordinance and adopted it virtually verbatim. Zoning soon became the chief weapon used by urban real estate interests to protect land prices. By 1924, the federal government had given zoning its seal of approval. A committee of the Department of Commerce drafted the Standard State Zoning Enabling Act, which served as a model zoning law for all of the nation's cities.

In 1926, the U.S. Supreme Court reviewed a case from Ohio, *Village of Euclid v. Ambler Realty Co.*, and in a landmark decision, it declared that zoning was a proper use of the police power of municipal authority.[76] One interesting facet of the case revealed how zoning would be used in the future. Ambler Realty had purchased property in the village of Euclid in hopes it would become valuable as commercial property. In 1922, the village zoned Ambler's property as residential, which had the effect of instantly lowering its market value. In bringing suit against the village, Ambler argued that Euclid's zoning law had lowered its property values without due process of law. In its decision, the Court set forth a classic statement in defense of restrictive zoning, arguing that the presence of apartment, commercial, and industrial buildings undermined residential neighborhoods. The justices took care to spell out the preferred hierarchy of uses:

> With particular reference to apartment houses, it is pointed out that the development of detached house sections is greatly retarded by the coming of apartment houses ... the coming of one apartment house is followed by others, interfering by their height and bulk with the free circulation of air and monopolizing the rays of the sun which otherwise would fall upon the smaller homes, and bringing, as their necessary accompaniments, the disturbing noises incident to increased traffic and business, and the occupation, by means of moving and parked automobiles, of larger portions of the streets, thus detracting from their safety and depriving children of the quiet and open spaces and play, enjoyed by those in more favored localities—until, finally the residential character of the neighborhood and its desirability as a place of detached residences is utterly destroyed.[77]

In its decision, the Court ruled that separating residential from other land uses was a legitimate use of the city's police power to promote the order, safety, and well-being of its citizens.

Zoning became popular at the very time that well-to-do suburbs began to ring the central cities—Beverly Hills, Glendale, and a multitude of other communities outside Los Angeles; Cleveland Heights, Shaker Heights, and Garfield Heights near Cleveland's city limits; and Oak Park, Elmwood Park, and Park Ridge outside Chicago. It is not difficult to understand why communities like this championed the concept of zoning. The possibility that the poor might disperse throughout metropolitan areas threatened people living in exclusive neighborhoods, both in central cities and in the suburbs. From its inception, zoning became the legal means to ensure what informal social class barriers or the housing market might not have been able to achieve—the exclusion of the city's Great Unwashed.

To accomplish this separation, restrictive residential zoning attempted to exclude apartments, to set minimum lot sizes, or to stop new construction altogether. Apartments in the suburbs represented the possibility of class, lifestyle, or racial changes. The residential character of a tree-lined, curved-street subdivision with individual homes set well back seemed to be threatened by apartment buildings. "We don't want this kind of trash in our neighborhood" was an attitude applied even to luxury apartments. Apartments symbolized the coming to suburbia of city problems:

> The apartment in general, and the high-rise apartment in particular, are seen as harbingers of urbanization, and their visibly higher densities appear to undermine the rationale for the development of the suburbs, which includes a reaction against the city and everything for which its stands. This is particularly significant, since the association is strong in suburbia between the visual characteristics of the city and what are perceived to be its social characteristics.[78]

Any proposal to build an apartment complex invariably alarmed the residents of affluent suburban communities. An executive living in Westport, an exclusive suburb in Connecticut, exclaimed, "Thank god we still have a system that rewards accomplishment, and that we can live in places where we want to live, without having apartments and the scum of the city pushed on us."[79] Most suburbs banned the building of apartments entirely. In the 1970s, over 99 percent of undeveloped land zoned residential in the New York region excluded apartments.[80] Although this did not mean apartments could not be constructed, it did require apartment builders to secure zoning variances, a process that favored opponents.[81]

Subdivision regulations and building codes made developers go through a costly review process that artificially increased the cost of new houses and gave local residents an opportunity to oppose new developments. But the most common device for raising the minimum cost of new construction was (and is) large-lot zoning. Sometimes the regulations requiring large lots also specified minimum floor-space requirements, the use of particular building materials, and minimum street setbacks. These kinds of regulations raised the cost for the homebuyer and thus helped protect exclusive neighborhoods.

Large-lot zoning is an effective device to keep out people with lower incomes. In some upper-class communities, this means keeping out the middle class; in some middle-class communities, it means excluding the working class. A defender of 4-acre lot minimums in Greenwich, Connecticut, said that large-lot zoning is "just economics. It's like going into Tiffany and demanding a ring for $12.50. Tiffany doesn't have rings for $12.50. Well, Greenwich is like Tiffany." A New Jersey legislator defended large-lot zoning as a means of making sure "that you can't buy a Cadillac at Chevrolet prices." An official of St. Louis County, where 90,000 acres were zoned for 3-acre lots in 1965, indicated that his suburban county welcomed anyone "who had the economic capacity [to enjoy] the quality of life that we think our county represents ... be they black or white."[82] The way the U.S. tax code is written in many ways invites such exclusionary zoning. Since taxes are among the few ways for municipal governments to generate direct income, residence literally comes at a price. In many suburban communities, however, this price also guarantees exclusivity.

Exclusionary zoning often makes room for industrial and commercial investment that will provide more in taxes than it consumes in services. Of course, affluent communities want the kinds of industry that do not produce bothersome pollution and traffic or bring in the wrong kind of workers. Sy Schulman, a Westchester County (New York) planning commissioner, wryly noted that the ideal industry "is a new campus-type headquarters that smells like Chanel No. 5, sounds like a Stradivarius, has the visual attributes of Sophia Loren, employs only executives with no children and produces items that can be transported away in white station wagons once a month."[83] Because the demand for such a clean industry exceeds the supply, there is a fierce competition for it.

The Challenge to Exclusionary Zoning

As a tool for perpetuating residential exclusion, zoning went largely uncontested in the federal and state courts for more than half a century.[84] But in the 1970s, it was challenged in the federal courts as a violation of the equal protection clause of the Fourteenth Amendment to the U.S. Constitution. Lawton, Oklahoma, just southwest of Oklahoma City, had attempted to use its zoning ordinance to keep out apartments, but in 1971 the federal appellate court for its circuit ruled that municipalities could not enact zoning ordinances that had the effect of excluding minorities unless they could show a non-discriminatory intent concerning their land use objectives.[85] In April 1971, another case gave even more hope to proponents of residential integration. The U.S. Court of Appeals for the Second Circuit rejected an attempt by the city officials of Lackawanna, New York, to block the building of a Black housing subdivision in a white neighborhood.[86] Clearly, suburban municipalities were under the gun to show that their zoning ordinances were not adopted simply to keep out Blacks.

In a case from Black Jack, Missouri, the courts imposed a tougher standard yet, one that made it appear that exclusionary zoning might be in danger of collapsing altogether. In September 1974, a federal appeals court ruled that the city's new zoning ordinance forbidding the construction of multiunit housing had a discriminatory *effect* even if it did not have a discriminatory intent, and therefore it violated the U.S. Constitution. In June 1975, the U.S. Supreme Court refused to review the circuit court's decision, thereby upholding it. The Black Jack decision had an enormous potential to change suburban land practices in the United States: If the court's decision stood, local governments would lose their most effective weapon for keeping "undesirables" out.

It took only two years, however, for the Supreme Court to back away from their decision. The zoning ordinance of Arlington Heights, Illinois, barred a federally subsidized townhouse project from being built, a restriction identical to Black Jack's. After agreeing to hear a challenge to the law, the Court declared that the effect of zoning laws could not be used as the only argument against them; rather, they had to be shown to have been enacted with the intent to discriminate: "Disproportionate impact is not irrelevant, but it is not the sole touchstone of an invidious racial discrimination."[87] The Supreme Court had already made it much more difficult for litigants to challenge zoning ordinances by requiring them to show a "distinct and palpable injury."[88] By 1977, then, the courts had gotten out of the business of reviewing local zoning laws except in the rare case when it could be shown that they were adopted specifically to discriminate against minorities.

The courts have consistently held that discrimination on the basis of income or class is not prohibited by the U.S. Constitution. If suburbs can show that their zoning laws are designed to protect the tax base and the exclusive residential character of the local community, their laws will not be declared unconstitutional even if they happen to discriminate against poor people. In 1971, the Supreme Court upheld an amendment to the California constitution, passed in 1950, which required that low-rent housing could not be built without prior approval by a referendum of the voters of the city. Although clearly biased against those seeking low-income housing, the Court ruled that discrimination on the basis of income was not unconstitutional under the equal protection clause of the Fourteenth Amendment.[89] In the intervening years, that Court ruling has stood the test of time.

Since the federal courts have been unwilling to use the U.S. Constitution to break down the walls of suburban exclusion, state courts have become the main avenue of redress. But two well-publicized and highly controversial cases from Mount Laurel, New Jersey, reveal the formidable hurdles that stand in the way of meaningful change. In 1970, Mount Laurel, located not far from Camden and Philadelphia, was a mostly rural community. The area contained a small African American community that had been there since before the Civil War. Quakers had made Mount Laurel a sanctuary for runaway slaves on the Underground Railroad, and their descendants still resided in the area. Many of them lived in small shacks and converted chicken coops, and when these were condemned by the city of Mount Laurel, the residents realized they would be forced to move to the slums of Camden. They formed an action committee and applied for federal funds to build a subsidized housing project, but in 1970 the local planning and zoning board turned down the committee's proposal.

The residents then turned to the courts. They found three idealistic lawyers working for the Camden Region Legal Services who agreed to pursue a challenge to Mount Laurel's zoning laws, which allowed only single-family homes and specified big lots, large building sizes (a minimum of four bedrooms), and substantial setbacks from the street. In 1972 a trial court found that Mount

Laurel's zoning laws violated language in the New Jersey constitution that guaranteed equal protection of the law for all persons. Further, the court ruled that not only Mount Laurel but all of New Jersey's 567 municipalities had an obligation to provide land uses that would meet regional housing needs. The U.S. Supreme Court subsequently refused to hear an appeal of this decision.

A few years later, in 1982, the chief justice of the New Jersey Supreme Court heard six cases showing that the city of Mount Laurel was ignoring the original trial court's decision. He combined the cases into one proceeding, and in 1983 the court issued a pathbreaking unanimous decision, widely known as *Mount Laurel II*. The court noted that the town of Mount Laurel had made no real attempt to comply with the original judicial directive; it had simply rezoned 33 of its 14,176 acres and not one of the 515 low-income housing units required to meet the court's decision had been built.[90] To compel compliance with its original decision, *Mount Laurel II* required that New Jersey municipalities set aside land for low-income housing, if necessary, and make low-income housing attractive to developers through such devices as tax incentives and subsidies. Second, to encourage builders to pursue lawsuits against exclusionary zoning, the court established "builder's remedies," which allowed developers of low- and moderate-income housing to sue cities that tried to keep them out.

As a result of *Mount Laurel II*, New Jersey's suburban municipalities were besieged with lawsuits, and politicians were increasingly pressured to do something about the situation. Republican governor Thomas H. Kean, who won office in 1981, came out against what he called an "undesirable intrusion on the home rule principle." In a 1984 interview, Kean stated, "I don't believe that every municipality has got to be a carbon copy of another. That's a socialistic country, a Communistic country, a dictatorship."[91] Kean proposed an amendment to the New Jersey constitution that would place local zoning policy beyond review by state courts. Meanwhile, he signed legislation that moved exclusionary zoning cases out of the courts and into arbitration before a nine-member Council on Affordable Housing (COAH), to be appointed by the governor.[92] Cities and towns were given a grace period to achieve their "fair share" regional housing goals.

In actuality, most communities were let off the hook completely. Municipalities were allowed, for example, to allocate up to 25 percent of their "fair share" to elderly people, and any city was allowed to transfer up to half of its fair-share obligation to another city in the region (if the receiving city approved), along with the funds to help the receiving town pay to build the housing. Older central cities were put in the position of competing against one another for subsidies from wealthier suburbs so they could obtain funds to meet the pressing housing needs of their low-income residents. What had begun as an effort to open up the suburbs ended up doing exactly the opposite.

Despite the years of political thunder and lightning, the payoff from the long, drawn-out Mount Laurel process was meager. Most New Jersey municipalities did nothing at all. In Mount Laurel, only 12 families had moved into low-cost mobile homes by the late 1980s, 12 more had put down deposits on similar units, and 20 low-cost subsidized condominiums had been completed. This was the grand total of low-income housing after 17 years and millions of dollars of litigation and protracted political uproar.[93]

The New Jersey case illustrates the difficulty of changing local land use practices when a political consensus is lacking. Mount Laurel represents the clash between two deeply held American values: Equal protection of the law, on the one hand, and local home rule, on the other. Americans are reluctant to support policies that force local governments to give up their autonomy. In an era when the federal government has cut housing subsidies drastically, even if local zoning laws could be successfully challenged, it is doubtful much low-income housing would be built in the suburbs. If the New Jersey experience offers a lesson, it is that exclusionary zoning and the residential segregation that comes with it, is here to stay.

The New Face of Enclave Politics

Over time, the suburbs have changed. People of all racial and ethnic groups have become suburban. A lot of poor people, too, have finally made the move out of the central city. Middle- and working-class suburban homes built in the immediate postwar period tended to be small tract homes or bungalows that lacked the amenities and conveniences expected by a new generation of homeowners.[94] These older subdivisions were generally located in the suburbs with depressed housing prices and a low level of public services, and some of them became a new kind of an urban slum but much more isolated from jobs and transportation networks than slums located in the urban core. Many of them are located in inner suburbs close to the central cities, but others are sprinkled in the spaces between more affluent suburbs located somewhat further out.[95]

Poor people and recent immigrants find it easier to find housing in older suburbs because there is less demand for housing in those areas, often because the homes are small and long out of fashion. In the 1990s, for example, Levittown and other 1950s-era suburbs of Long Island began to attract recently arrived immigrants from the Middle East, Central and Latin America, and Asia.[96] They remained hidden from the larger society in part because they were walled off into municipalities that had few resources—and therefore, they were unable to make effective claims on the political system. A pair of writers asked, "Suburbs are now becoming—albeit not always willingly—multiclass, multiethnic, and multiracial .... Can older suburbs accommodate these new ethnic groups, or will outmoded, decentralized government structures and prejudice keep them hidden *baja del agua*—underwater?"[97]

When poor residents—immigrants or otherwise—are pushed into the suburbs, one key issue arises: Most suburban communities are not equipped to deal with residential poverty. They were formed as middle- and upper-class communities and lacked the social service infrastructure of a big city. This may require a fundamental restructuring of many suburban bureaucracies. A 2015 article in the *Atlantic* points out:

> The problem speaks to a different kind of erosion of the American Dream, in which families strive to get to the much-vaunted suburbs, only to find out there's nothing for them there. And as suburbs see more and more poverty, they become the same traps that impoverished, urban neighborhoods once were, where someone born there has few chances to improve his economic standing.[98]

Low-income service jobs and affordable housing are increasingly located in the older, first ring suburbs, but these communities, in turn, lack transportation infrastructure, which is detrimental to new residents who may not be able to afford a car. Many suburban communities are alien to social programs, such as food stamps, which have long been available in cities.

The tendency to push marginalized groups "underwater" is reinforced by the rise of privatized enclaves of people trying to sever all connection to central cities and even with nearby neighborhoods.[99] Some gated communities built in the 1980s and 1990s seem like fortresses. The emphasis on security in some of these developments is akin to a state of war. Leisure World, a California retirement community, is surrounded by 6-foot walls topped with barbed wire. Quayside, a planned community in Florida, blends the atmosphere of a Norman Rockwell small town of the 1920s with the latest in high-tech security; laser beams sweep the perimeter, computers check the coded entry cards of the residents, and store exits and entries from the property in a permanent data file, and television cameras continuously monitor the living and recreation areas. The many trappings of security constantly remind the inhabitants that the world beyond their walls is dangerous, so that "'being inside' becomes a powerful symbol for being protected, buttressed, coddled, while 'being outside' evokes exposure, isolation, and vulnerability."[100] In 2006, a Texas developer marketed a new subdivision as a "sex-offender free" development; prospective buyers would have to pass a criminal background check.[101]

By the 1990s, fortress enclaves had become a ubiquitous feature of suburban development all across southern California. In search of high-tech security, architects for the affluent were "borrowing design features from overseas embassies and military command posts," building hardened walls, improvising secret passages and doors, and installing a dazzling array of sophisticated electronic surveillance devices.[102] The demand for gated communities in the Los Angeles suburbs was so high that they quickly replaced all other kinds of development. This same process has occurred from coast to coast, and it has led the residents of some gated communities to try to withdraw support for services supplied by local governments, on the theory that paying for privatized as well as public services constitutes "double taxation." Political movements like this make it clear that the urban crisis of the twentieth century may have come to an end only to be replaced by a different kind of politics, one that not only pits suburb against suburb but also enclave against enclave and privatized privilege against public needs.

The Byzantine (Dis)Organization of Urban Regions

Population movement from the urban core is a feature of urban development all over the world. With transportation breakthroughs such as automated rail systems and the automobile, urban areas in the advanced Western countries have been spreading out for at least a century.[103] But what distinguishes the urban pattern in the United States most clearly from that of other Western nations is not the extent of sprawl but the fracturing of metropolitan areas into a multitude of separate governments. In many countries in Europe, as well as in most other nations, there are fewer suburbs because cities tend to encompass a large part of their metropolitan areas. In addition, national and regional governments finance and administer crucial services that are, in the United States, provided by municipalities and special districts. American suburbs are autonomous entities that make taxation, spending, and land use decisions without any oversight from higher levels of government. There are a lot of them. The 2017 federal census of governments counted 90,126 local governments in the United States.[104] Statistics like these have led to a consensus that the "degree of governmental fragmentation in the United States is unique among the urban-industrial societies."[105]

The extreme fragmentation of urban regions makes it hard to find solutions to problems that are truly regional in scope. These difficulties have been overcome, to some degree, by the construction of a staggeringly complex maze of governmental responsibilities. Typically, urban counties do such things as administer building codes, run systems of parks and libraries, operate health clinics, offer police services, build roads and bridges, manage jails and courts, and sponsor 911 emergency services. Special-purpose districts also supply a variety of services that overlap municipal boundaries, and some of these, such as sewer and water and mass transit districts, are metropolitan-wide in scope. But most of the dozens of special districts within metropolitan areas are much smaller and virtually invisible. They raise taxes for and manage everything from hospitals to fire protection to mosquito abatement, plus a great number of other very specialized services. The jerry-rigged nature of these arrangements makes a degree of regional service provision possible, but a coherent system of regional governance remains out of reach. It also makes many people wish for a system of regional governance that would be more democratic, efficient, and effective.

OUTTAKE

The Costs of Sprawl Are Hotly Debated

The urban specialist Neal Peirce has called Americans "the champion land hogs of history" because the country's urban areas are growing in land area at a rate four to eight times faster than the growth of the national population. The cost of sprawl, he said, is "frightening" because it brings "despair in the inner cities, environmental degradation, undermining of old neighborhoods and suburbs."

Peirce and other critics of urban sprawl have amassed convincing evidence to demonstrate its negative effects. They cite the many studies to show that it is more expensive to supply infrastructure—new highways, streets, and bridges; schools; sewer and water systems; street lighting; gas, electric, and telephone hookups; libraries and parks—to low-density areas than to high-density areas. They demonstrate that sprawl has contributed to the decline of the central cities and the abandonment of neighborhoods in the cities and older suburbs. And finally, they show that governmental fragmentation slows the economic growth of urban regions.

Critics of sprawl also argue that it creates serious environmental problems. Evidence to support their point of view is not difficult to find, and in the era of visible climate change, the issue is all the more pressing: Thousands of acres of farmland, wetlands, and open space disappear each year. Runoff from highways, parking lots, and lawns pollutes streams and rivers; auto and truck traffic spews ozone-depleting and greenhouse gases into the atmosphere. Excess energy consumption and air pollution are deeply implicated in global climate change, which citizens of all countries and residents of all locales are now experiencing in one way or another. Urban residents in the United States consumed about four times as much gasoline per capita as did urban residents in Europe in 1990. Urban sprawl and lack of public transit infrastructure were the basic reasons for this difference. In the late 1980s, annual consumption in sprawled-out Houston was 567 gallons per person, compared to 335 gallons in New York City, where high population density facilitated the use of mass transit. (In Manhattan, gasoline consumption was only 90 gallons per person.)

A 2014 study conducted by researchers at the University of California, Berkeley, found that the massive suburban sprawl around dense urban centers is canceling out the positive effects of high-density housing in the city cores. The researchers, who compared per household carbon emissions, found that those households with the highest carbon emissions were located about 15–45 minutes outside the city center.

Despite the accumulating weight of such facts, it should not be supposed that there is only one point of view about urban sprawl. In fact, it is a hotly contested issue. Fred Siegel, a prominent scholar and writer, has argued that sprawl is a logical outcome of prosperity and the pursuit of the American dream, "an expression of the upward mobility and growth in home-ownership generated by our past half-century of economic success." Expanding on this theme, he maintains that people on the lower end of the economic scale are able to find opportunities to escape from poor neighborhoods by moving into housing left behind by the middle class. In this way, he says, the construction of new housing at the metropolitan edge helps to expand opportunities for all residents of the metropolis. There are some good points to Siegel's logic. As their incomes go up, people usually move from high-density to low-density neighborhoods in search for more space and better amenities. Low-density neighborhoods are usually located in newer communities located at some remove from the urban core. Until the Great Recession of 2008–2010, one in seven of newly constructed homes exceeded 3,000 square feet, a size reserved only for wealthy families in the past.

On the other hand, the creation of such new living spaces in the suburbs is less and less likely to make space for poorer people in the inner cities, as downtown areas are also becoming increasingly expensive places to live. And even so, the challenges of climate change will sooner or later have a strong impact on life and welfare for all people, but especially the poor in developing countries. Therefore, it is important to start the conversation about more sustainable alternatives to urban sprawl.

The two perspectives on urban sprawl suggest that there is a contradiction between freedom to choose on the one hand, and regulation and planning, on the other. When forced to choose between these two values, urban residents often seem to be of two minds. Americans have always been keenly sensitive about anything that intrudes on their individual property rights, but suburban residents have generally been willing to make an exception when it comes to land use controls such as zoning, growth control measures that impose a limit on housing permits, green belts to preserve open space, fand ordinances restricting new infrastructure development. The problem is that local control over such policies comes at the cost of metropolitan-wide planning. The paradox is that even when people are disturbed about unplanned and runaway urban growth, their deep attachment to small-scale governance makes it hard to devise metropolitan-wide solutions to unplanned urban growth.

Climate change makes such solutions a pressing need, however. In the era of runaway, human-inflicted climate change, the resource-intensive lifestyle of suburban America has become impossible to justify. If Americans desire to pass on their version of the American dream to the next generation, they urgently need to make it more sustainable.

Sources: Neal Peirce, "The Senselessness of Urban Sprawl," *National Journal* (September 25, 1993), p. 2326; Burchell et al., *The Costs of Sprawl Revisited* (Washington, D.C.: National Academy Press, 1998); Arthur C. Nelson and Kathryn A. Foster, "Metropolitan Governance Structure and Income Growth," *Journal of Urban Affairs* 21, no. 3 (1999): 309–324; Peter G. Newman and Jeffrey R. Kenworthy, "Gasoline Consumption and Cities," *Journal of the American Planning Association* (Winter 1989): 26–27; Christopher Jones and Daniel M. Kammen, "Spatial Distribution of U.S. Household Carbon Footprints Reveals Suburbanization Undermines Greenhouse Gas Benefits of Urban Population Density." *Environmental Science and Technology* 48, no. 2 (2014): 895–902; Fred Siegel, "Is Regional Government the Answer?" *The Public Interest* (Fall 1999): 86.

At a time when conversations have started shifting from "cities" to "metro regions" and "megalopolises," we have started to overlook the governmental fragmentation of our metro regions throughout the country. In a political sense, the "bigger picture" of the metropolitan region is near meaningless because barely any administrative or bureaucratic structures exist to connect such regions internally.

Over the years, there have been many attempts to bring some order to the task of governing metropolitan regions. The remedies that have been proposed may be grouped under four labels: Metro Gov, the New Regionalism, Smart Growth, and the New Urbanism. The Metro Gov movement, which began about a century ago, has been based on the ambitious idea that urban regions should be governed, as far as possible, by a single metropolitan-wide government or by a few consolidated governmental bodies. A drive through the many towns and suburban jurisdictions that make up a typical urban area makes it obvious to even the casual observer that metro reform has failed to achieve most of its aims. The *New Regionalism*, which dates back to the late 1980s, was founded on the premise that the flight from the cities to the suburbs has produced an unacceptable degree of inequality within urban areas. Rather than trying to reduce the number of governments, the advocates for a "new regionalism" have emphasized the importance of achieving cooperation among local governments to moderate the intense interjurisdiction competition for economic growth and reduce extreme differences in tax burdens and service quality. In the late 1990s, the *Smart Growth* movement came together around a collection of proposals designed to achieve "balanced" regional development by regulating land use and promoting community and environmental planning. At about the same time, the *New Urbanism* came onto the scene. This movement was energized by the idea that better urban design and architecture are the necessary ingredients for countering sprawl and achieving healthy neighborhoods and communities. Each of these movements confronts a formidable obstacle: The incredibly complicated governmental mosaic that already exists in America's urban regions.

The New Urban Form

The sprawled metropolis has spawned a set of chronic and sometimes vexing problems. Commuting is expensive and is likely to become more so over the long run. In 2021, a gallon of gasoline cost about $3.14 in the United States,[106] which is still ridiculously cheap compared to the nearly $7 per-gallon price that people paid for gas in the United Kingdom and Eurozone countries.[107] Commuters experience traffic congestion and gridlock almost every day. The public has become concerned about such issues as air pollution, the loss of open space and farmland, and polluted water. Urban sprawl has blossomed as an important public policy issue. Growth control measures began to appear in the early 1970s, and the movement to regulate the pace and location of development continued to gain momentum over time. People want the freedom to move where they please, but they are not happy when their neighborhoods seem threatened by a steady stream of newcomers.

However serious the problems associated with sprawl may be, it is here to stay. One reason is that local governments jealously guard their powers. The other equally important reason is that the geographic structure of metropolitan areas has become basically fixed. The old urban form, which found a big city surrounded by rank on rank of spreading suburbs, has given way to a metropolis organized around many nodes of activity.[108] Once the suburbs were wholly dependent satellites of cities, where most of the jobs and businesses were located. Today, however, the center is only one of several clusters of activity. For a long time, suburban development was mainly a residential movement, but by the late 1940s, jobs began to decentralize even faster than population.[109] Retailing followed when regional shopping malls began to spring up to cater to the shopping and entertainment needs of suburban consumers.[110] Suburban residents no longer needed to go downtown, and thus a historic link between cities and suburbs was severed.

Manufacturing has been moving out of the old industrial cities for almost a century because of technical innovations that freed factories from a dependence on rail connections. Electrification made single-story plants more economical than multistory buildings that housed belt-driven machinery powered by water or steam. In the twentieth century, federal tax law allowed manufacturers to take tax deductions through "accelerated depreciation of assets" when they abandoned inner-city factories; at the same time, investment tax credits allowed manufacturing firms to write off the cost of new plant and equipment. In these ways, the federal tax code subsidized the flight of industrial jobs to the suburbs and to the Sunbelt.[111] Manufacturing firms also left northern urban areas because they viewed them as hotbeds of union organizing and unrest.[112] By 1970, a majority of the manufacturing jobs in metropolitan areas were located outside the central cities, and many were moving out of older urban areas to the Sunbelt or abroad.

The service sector was the last to leave. Historically, professional and business activities were concentrated in or near central business districts, but the building of integrated urban highway systems fundamentally changed the urban landscape. As employees left the city and commuted greater distances to work, it made less sense for firms to stay downtown. Routine service employment, the so-called back-office functions such as copying and secretarial services, left expensive downtown office space. In 1975, for the first time, the volume of office construction in the suburbs exceeded the pace of construction in central cities. Higher-level and higher-paid corporate services, however, such as legal assistance, corporate consulting, accounting services, and investment services, continued to be located in the downtowns of large cities, partly for prestige reasons. Corporations, though, have many components so that even if they kept their management and professional-service functions downtown, they generally moved everything else either to suburbs or out of the country. Suburban office parks evolved as still another option. By moving their professional staff onto self-contained campuses, companies were able to recreate many of the characteristics of central business districts in the suburbs.

Within a few years, some suburbs became basically independent of their core cities. Cross-commuting became common; by 1980, twice as many people commuted from suburb to suburb as from the central city to suburb.[113] The historic urban form, in which a city is surrounded by dependent suburbs, was replaced by the "polynucleated metropolis" made up of several nodes of concentrated activity that combined residential, retail, recreational, light industry, and service firms. This geographic pattern has sometimes been called *exurbanization* or even *counterurbanization*,[114] plus a variety of odd and often confusing labels, such as "urban villages, technohubs, suburban downtowns, suburban activity centers, major diversified centers, urban cores, galactic city, pepperoni-pizza cities, a city of realms, superburbia, disurb, service cities, perimeter cities, and even peripheral centers."[115] What these entities have in common is that they keep springing up at the outer boundary of urban regions, often near freeway interchanges and airports.

Significant numbers of the new suburbs are large—in fact, some have grown bigger than their nearby central cities. Two researchers coined the term "boomburbs," which they define as suburbs that have grown by at least double-digit rates for every decade since 1970 and finally reaching a population of at least 100,000 by the census of 2000.[116] They discovered that 54 cities across the nation met this statistical standard and that 12 of them contained more than 200,000 people. The total number of boomburbs in the nation might seem small, but they held one-quarter of all residents living in small- and medium-sized urban areas.[117] The census of 2006 showed that 17 boomburbs had practically overnight joined the ranks of the 100 largest U.S. cities.[118]

Despite their sudden appearance, boomburbs have attracted little attention, probably because they tend to lack the physical form and identity that might make them stand out. They generally do not have tall buildings and heavily favor the automobile over pedestrians, office workers tend to be clustered in office parks, and a large proportion of shopping is done in strip malls and mall clusters. Perhaps the most surprising fact about boomburbs is that they often defied the suburban stereotype. Forty-five of the 54 contained a larger percentage of Hispanic residents, and 42 had a higher proportion of Asians than did the national population.[119]

Boomburbs are, in essence, fully developed cities, with a mixture of office, retail, residential, and sometimes light industry. They differ markedly from one another, but few, if any, fit the profile of the exclusive residential suburb or of the one-dimensional bedroom community. High-rise office and condominium towers are beginning to sprout in some of them, and new housing construction often favors townhouse and condominium construction over free-standing homes. The growth of the boomburbs makes it clear that urban sprawl is tightly woven into the fabric of urban regions. The multi-nodal metropolis is here to stay.

The Concerns about Sprawl

The term *urban sprawl* generally refers to low-density residential development. Research published in 1974 defined it as the residential density of two dwellings per acre, but a late 1980s study and another conducted by the Environmental Protection Agency in the early 1990s defined it as the residential density of three dwellings per acre or less.[120] Even if we use the latter definition, sprawl is rare in Europe and Asia, where land is scarcer than in the United States, and land use controls are the norm. In such contexts, urban areas may be spreading outward, but not in such a way as to create the social and political dynamic that characterizes sprawl in the United States: Low-density development at the edge of metropolitan regions that consumes huge tracts of land and entails the abandonment of older areas at the urban core.

When people move farther out, they generally are choosing lower-density suburbs as places to live. The result is that land is gobbled up at a rate all out of proportion to the population growth of urban regions—indeed, sprawl occurs even in metropolitan areas with steady-state or declining populations. For example, although the New York region's population grew by only 5 percent between 1964 and 1989, in the same years, the amount of developed land increased by 61 percent.[121] Similarly, from 1950 to 1995, the population of the St. Louis region increased by just 35 percent, but the area of developed land exploded by more than ten times that much, by 355 percent.[122] Even in slow-growth regions, people have been drifting to the outer edges. From 1986 to 2001, 73,000 people moved from St. Louis County out to St. Charles County; in the same period, St. Charles County attracted only 5,500 people from outside the metropolitan region. St. Charles County is now filling up, and its growth is outpaced by Warren County, which lies still even farther out.[123] This restless movement to the urban edge is why almost all urban regions continued to sprawl in the 1990s, regardless of their population growth rates.[124]

Why does land disappear so fast, even in slow-growth urban regions? First, families have become smaller in recent decades because of the increasing number of single-parent families, childless and unmarried couples, and singles. The smaller size of the typical suburban family requires more dwellings for a given population size and makes many of the single-family houses built only a couple of decades ago obsolete. Second, although average family sizes have been declining, the size of homes has steadily increased in step with a desire for more luxuries and amenities (although it should be noted the Great Recession arrested this trend for a time). And third, when people move within metropolitan areas, they tend to leave higher-density neighborhoods nearer the urban core for lower-density subdivisions farther out.

More recently, this third point has come under more scrutiny. A number of scholars have started to argue that since the 2000s, certain cities have started to experience a back-to-the-city movement. This encompasses the movement of wealthier people from lower-density settings "back" to urban centers, ultimately leading to neighborhood change and the possible displacement of lower-income groups. One scholar, using the example of Washington, D.C., a city that, until the year 2000, had a solid Black majority, argued that by 2010, the city had lost over 39,000 African American residents, mostly due to the in-migration of wealthy, white residents.[125] In addition, the decade between 2000 and 2010 was the first since 1950 during which Washington's population grew instead of further declining, as it had done in the decades from 1960 to 2000.[126] It also coincided with the increased gentrification of some historical African American neighborhoods, such as Shaw/U Street.[127] Whether the back-to-the-city-movement is actually a movement is debated among scholars, and it is already clear that not all cities are experiencing this phenomenon or are experiencing it uniformly. What is clear, however, is that many bigger cities around the United States have started to experience population growth after decades of decline. Neighborhood change is often a consequence of the "urban renaissance," and displacement of lower-income residents is common. The cost of living in many thriving coastal cities like New York City and Los Angeles has become prohibitive, even for many middle-income earners. On the other hand, certain mid-range cities like Detroit continue to lose population. The back-to-the-city-movement, if we can actually call it a movement, is far from universal.

Many suburban residents, meanwhile, have discovered that there is a downside to low-density development. Commuters experience some of the negative effects of sprawl every day, firsthand and close up. By the last decades of the twentieth-century highway congestion had increased to the point that the daily commute has ceased to be merely annoying. In November 1999, *USA Today*, in a special report on national gridlock, offered up one horror story after another. The average commuter's daily experience seemed to be summed up by a Chicago driver's description of a bottleneck called "the Hillside Strangler": "It's not even a traffic jam. It's my enemy. It's my daytime bad dream."[128] In 2001, the knot of off-ramps that made up the Strangler was finally eliminated, but many other gridlocked spots remained. A study conducted in 2005 ranked Chicago second in the nation as the most congested (Los Angeles had the honor of first place). The report estimated that in 2003 Chicago-area commuters spent 58 hours in traffic jams each year, an increase of 55 hours from only three years earlier. The authors concluded that the term "rush hour" had become virtually meaningless.[129] However, by 2016, Chicago had slipped down the congestion index, ranking only 10th among the most congested cities nationwide.[130] This, according to the most recent study conducted by the navigation system maker TomTom, was based on the fact that traffic congestion is strongly correlated with economic job growth.[131] In the United States, post-economic crisis recovery has been uneven, centering around the East and West coasts.[132] Therefore the latest index features almost exclusively coastal cities, with Honolulu (ranked 6th) and Chicago (ranked 10th) being the exceptions. Furthermore, the West Coast cities seem to dominate in terms of traffic congestion, with L.A. and

San Francisco ranking 1st and 2nd, respectively. New York City (ranked 3rd), Miami (ranked 7th), and Washington, DC (ranked 8th) were the only East Coast cities that featured among the top ten.[133]

By the mid-2000s, the concerns about urban sprawl had started to decline from voters' and policymakers' minds, as scholars predicted a change in growth trends in and around cities. In 2004, two researchers from Rutgers University, a demographer and an economist, published a major study using data from 31 counties in the NYC metro region.[134] They found that, after the suburbs had grown explosively for a half-century after 1945, exclusively suburban growth had come to an end in the late 1990s.[135] Since then, according to this study, growth in the urban core had increased, largely matching the growth in the suburbs.[136] While this may not end sprawl, it at the very least indicates a densification of housing developments in the suburbs and the city. While its long-term consequences are still unknown, Hughes and Seneca identified a new and important trend in their study, which continue to take shape—with slight regional modifications—in metro regions across the country.

In any case, it has become clear over the decades that urban sprawl cannot be curbed without far-reaching changes in public policies and governance arrangements. There is an obvious tension, however, between governmental regulation and the deeply held cultural values of individualism and free enterprise that define American politics. Leaders of four movements—Metro Gov, the New Regionalism, Smart Growth, and the New Urbanism—have attempted to negotiate the treacherous terrain between personal autonomy and regional planning. Over the years, there have been numerous campaigns to reform the governance of metropolitan regions, but the successes have been relatively few. The New Regionalism has been directed mainly at more modest efforts to bring about interlocal agreements, share tax burdens, and achieve a level of cooperation in providing services as a way of reducing the extreme inequalities of local governments. The proponents of Smart Growth also shy away from large-scale solutions and believe that local governments must take the lead in reducing the environmental effects of unregulated urban growth and unplanned land use. For their part, the New Urbanists focus on land use and architectural regulations meant to facilitate development on a "human scale."

The Prospect for Reform

The alleged disease of the American suburb has long been the subject of commentary. The writer James Howard Kunstler begins his book *The Geography of Nowhere* with this vivid summary:

> Eighty percent of everything ever built in America has been built in the last fifty years, and most of it is depressing, brutal, ugly, unhealthy, and spiritually degrading—the jive-plastic commuter tract home wastelands,

the Potemkin village shopping plazas with their vast parking lagoons, the Lego-block hotel complexes, the "gourmet mansardic" junk-food joints, the Orwellian office "parks" featuring buildings sheathed in the same reflective glass as the sunglasses worn by chain-gang guards, the particle-board garden apartments rising up in every little meadow and cornfield, the freeway loops around every big and little city with their clusters of discount merchandise marts, the whole destructive, wasteful, toxic, agoraphobia-inducing spectacle that politicians call "growth."[137]

In Kunstler's narrative, suburban residents have learned to live "in places where nothing relates to anything else," a landscape in which daily activities—home, work, shopping, recreation—are pulled apart into large-scale segregated developments accessible only by automobiles: "The houses are all in their respective income pods, the shopping is miles away from the houses," and schools, malls, and office parks are also set apart, together with their seas of cars glistening on massive parking lots.[138] Kunstler's storyline describes a dystopia in which human beings are forced to sit in their cars, gridlocked, or find themselves in the embrace of a gated community, school, or shopping mall—worst of all—a nameless suburban subdivision.

Like clear-cutting a forest, a parking lot, mall, or a housing subdivision can be most efficiently built by means of industrial methods; the first step is a bulldozer that removes everything in the way. Such methods link efficiency and wastefulness in an intimate dance. Urged on by advertising, constant changes in product lines and styles, and the proliferation of disposable packaging, "most consumer goods are destined for a one-night stand."[139] Applied to land and places, such a consumer habit has far-reaching social consequences—"cycling of people through places," mobility and rootlessness that replaces community with the hope of renewal that comes from moving, "a kind of magic that keeps expectations high."[140] If the new place disappoints, the answer will be found in another move, and still another one after that.

Lifeless suburbia, the most meaningful symbol of this sort of late capitalist consumer mentality, has even been a recurring theme in popular culture throughout the 1980s and 90s, which also marked the (re-)discovery of New Urbanism as a counter-movement. The 1999 movie *Office Space*, for instance, in a humorous fashion, portrays the soul-killing office park, including its cubicles and neon-light fixtures, the uninspiring, cookie-cutter restaurants, the plain suburban subdivisions, the numbing traffic jams, which accompany the commute from A to B to C.

The band Green Day, in the song *Jesus of Suburbia*, takes a similar stance:

At the center of the earth
In the parking lot
Of the 7-11 where I was taught
The motto was just a lie.

It says home is where your heart is
But what a shame
Cause everyone's heart
Doesn't beat the same
It's beating out of time.

City of the dead
At the end of another lost highway
Signs misleading to nowhere
City of the damned.[141]

Loved but also increasingly revered, suburbia, the twentieth-century symbol of the American Dream, also became associated with deadbeat capitalism and consumer culture just before the millennium, inspiring the calls for reform.

Virtually all suburban jurisdictions follow a standard zoning or planning regime that separates residential, commercial, and industrial development in big chunks. The effect is to make neighborhoods less walkable because corner stores, strip malls, barber and beauty shops, and other things that people need are rigorously zoned out of large residential subdivisions, thereby forcing people to drive a long way for basic services. Can suburban environments be designed to discourage such practices?

Suburban residents are caught in a bind, and the way out is likely to be painful. They are fed up with gridlock and runaway development, especially when these threaten the quality of life they so highly value. In trying to solve the problems of the sprawling metropolis, there are three approaches available to them. One solution is to support reforms that will make it possible to achieve metropolitan planning and a high degree of cooperation among governments. A second solution directly contradicts the first: Use the powers of municipal government as an instrument to forestall change. A third strategy they may exercise is to retreat as far as possible behind the walls of gated communities. In fact, suburban residents have used all three, but in the last few decades, the last of these options has been enthusiastically embraced. Clearly, municipal autonomy and the proliferation of privatized gated communities make it much harder than ever to build support for metropolitan reform.

New Jersey's experience with land trusts suggests how difficult it will be to find ambitious solutions that go beyond parochial interests. In 1998, Governor Christie Todd Whitman announced that New Jersey's program—with its goal of acquiring more than a million acres of open space—could serve as a national model. But in the end, New Jersey was reluctant to place environmental concerns ahead of economic development. In 2000, when Merrill Lynch announced it would leave the state unless it was granted permission to build in a rural area, politicians quickly caved. An assistant in the governor's policy office explained, "They wanted a suburban-style campus, so it was either here or Pennsylvania."[142] Even in the unlikely event that politics elsewhere might be different, land trusts can do little more than preserve islands of open space in a moving stream of development.

As the urban historian Jon C. Teaford has observed, "change appears to be the ultimate enemy."[143] Local control of land use, economic development, and local taxes and services give people a sense that they are masters of their own destiny. Governmental fragmentation will continue to be a fixture of the American metropolis, as will sprawl and its attendant problems. This is why the art of muddling through will continue to define the regional policy agenda.

Endnotes

1   Quoted in James A. Clapp, *The City: A Dictionary of Quotable Thoughts on Cities and Urban Life* (New Brunswick, NJ: Center for Urban Policy Research, Rutgers University, 1984), pp. 128–129.

2   Quoted in ibid., p. 148.

3   U.S. Bureau of the Census, *Census 2000,* www.census.gov/cens2000.

4   Robert C. Wood, *Suburbia: Its People and Their Politics* (Boston, MA: Houghton Mifflin, 1958), p. 106.

5   Alan Ehrenhalt, *The Great Inversion and the Future of the American City* (New York, NY and Toronto, ON: Random House, 2012).

6   Ibid.

7   Elizabeth Kneebone and Alan Berube, *Confronting Suburban Poverty in America* (Washington, D.C.: The Brookings Institution, 2013).

8   Paul A. Jargowsky, *Concentration of Poverty in the New Millennium. Changes in Prevalence, Composition, and Location of High Poverty Neighborhoods* (New York and Camden, NJ: The Century Foundation and Rutgers Center for Urban Research and Education, 2013).

9   Ibid.

10   Ibid.

11   See Mark Gottdiener, *Planned Sprawl: Private and Public Interests in Suburbia* (Beverly Hills, CA: Sage, 1977).

12   Robert C. Wood, "Suburban Politics and Policies: Retrospect and Prospect," *Publius, The Journal of Federalism* 5 (Winter 1975): 51.

13   Food and Agriculture Organization and World Bank Population Estimates, "Population density (people per sq. km of land area)." *The World Bank Data,* 2016. Accessed online: https://data.worldbank.org/indicator/EN.POP.DNST.

14   The term is taken from Mark Weiss, *The Rise of the Community Builders* (New York: Columbia University Press, 1987).

15   J.C. Nichols, "The Planning and Control of Outlying Shopping Centers," *Journal of Land and Public Utility Economics* 2, no. 1 (January 1926): 22. By concentrating on one location and using leasing policy to determine store "mix," "Nichols created the idea of the planned regional shopping center," Kenneth T. Jackson, *Crabgrass Frontier: The Suburbanization of the United States* (New York: Oxford University Press, 1985), p. 258.

16 Gwendolyn Wright, *Building the Dream: A Social History of Housing in America* (Cambridge, MA: MIT Press, 1981), p. 202.

17 Mark H. Rose, "'There Is Less Smoke in the District,' J. C. Nichols, Urban Change and Technological Systems," *Journal of the West* 25, no. 1 (January 1986): 48. Rose adds, "As late as 1917, no more than five Jewish families resided in the district, the result of resales."

18 "Up from the Potato Fields," *Time* (July 3, 1950), p. 70.

19 Ibid.

20 "The Most House for the Money," *Fortune* (October 1952): 156.

21 Jackson, *Crabgrass Frontier,* p. 234.

22 Wright, *Building the Dream,* p. 252.

23 "Up from the Potato Fields," p. 68.

24 Jackson, *Crabgrass Frontier,* p. 234.

25 "Up from the Potato Fields," p. 68.

26 Bruce Lambert, "Levittown Anniversary Stirs Memories of Bias," *New York Times* (December 28, 1997), p. 14.

27 Quoted in Herbert Gans, *The Levittowners: Ways of Life and Politics in a Suburban Community* (New York: Pantheon Books, 1967), p. 372.

28 Lambert, "Levittown Anniversary," p. 14.

29 Jackson, *Crabgrass Frontier,* p. 241.

30 Lambert, "Levittown Anniversary," p. 14.

31 Gans, *The Levittowners,* pp. 8–9.

32 Joe R. Feagin and Robert Parker, *Building American Cities: The Urban Real Estate Game,* 2nd ed. (Upper Saddle River, NJ: Prentice Hall, 1990), p. 211.

33 Robert Goldston, *Suburbia: Civic Denial* (New York: Macmillan, 1970), p. 68.

34 Kevin Fox Gotham, *Race, Real Estate, and Uneven Development: The Kansas City Experience, 1900–2000* (Albany, NY: State University of New York Press, 2002), p. 38.

35 Ibid.

36 Justin Wm. Moyer, "Racist Housing Covenants Haunt Property Records across the Country. New Laws Make Them Easier to Remove," *The Washington Post* (October 22, 2020), https://www.washingtonpost.com/local/racist-housing-covenants/2020/10/21/9d262738-0261-11eb-8879-7663b816bfa5_story.html.

37 Ibid.

38 Gotham, *Race, Real Estate, and Uneven Development: The Kansas City Experience, 1900–2000,* pp. 34–37.

39 National Association of Real Estate Boards, *Code of Ethics* (1924), art. 34 (Washington, D.C.: Author).

40 Harry Grant Atkinson and L. E. Frailey, *Fundamentals of Real Estate Practice* (Upper Saddle River, NJ: Prentice Hall, 1946), p. 34, quoted in Evan McKenzie, *Privatopia: Homeowner Associations and the Rise of Residential Private Government* (New Haven, CT: Yale University Press, 1994), pp. 61–62.

41 *Shelly v. Kraemer,* 334 U.S. 1 (1948). The Court had struck down racial zoning some 30 years earlier in *Buchanan v. Warley,* 245 U.S. 60 (1917).

42 McKenzie, *Privatopia,* p. 11.

43 Community Associations Institute, Association Information Services, CtreeseAIS@aol.com (2006).

44 Ibid.
45 McKenzie, *Privatopia,* pp. 158–164.
46 Ibid., p. 158.
47 Ibid., pp. 163–164.
48 Dennis R. Judd, "The Rise of the New Walled Cities," in *Spatial Practices,* ed. Helen Liggett and David C. Perry (Thousand Oaks, CA: Sage, 1995), pp. 144–166.
49 David Guterson, "No Place Like Home: On the Manicured Streets of a Master-planned Community," *Harper's Magazine* 285, no. 1710 (November 1992): 55–64.
50 Ibid., pp. 60–61.
51 Valerie Wilson, "Racial Disparities in Income and Poverty Remain Largely Unchanged Amid Strong Income Growth in 2019," *Economic Policy Institute Working Blog* (September 16, 2020), https://www.epi.org/blog/racial-disparities-in-income-and-poverty-remain-largely-unchanged-amid-strong-income-growth-in-2019/.
52 Gary J. Miller, *Cities by Contract: The Politics of Municipal Incorporation* (Cambridge, MA: MIT Press, 1981), p. 12.
53 Ibid.
54 C.B. Glasscock, *Lucky Baldwin: The Story of an Unconventional Success* (Indianapolis, IN: Bobbs-Merrill, 1933), p. 140.
55 Jon C. Teaford, *City and Suburb: The Political Fragmentation of Metropolitan America, 1850–1970* (Baltimore, MD: Johns Hopkins University Press, 1979), pp. 18–19.
56 Charles Hoch, "City Limits: Municipal Boundary Formation and Class Segregation," in *Marxism and the Metropolis: New Perspectives in Urban Political Economy,* 2nd ed., ed. William K. Tabb and Larry Sawers (New York: Oxford University Press, 1984), pp. 101–119.
57 Miller, *Cities by Contract,* pp. 49–50. Another good example of an industrial suburb is Teterboro, New Jersey, which in 1977 had only 24 residents but employed 24,000 nonresidents. Michael N. Danielson and Jameson W. Doig, *New York: The Politics of Urban Regional Development* (Berkeley: University of California Press, 1982), p. 92.
58 Teaford, *City and Suburb,* p. 18.
59 Data cited in Wood, *Suburbia,* p. 69; and in National Municipal League, Committee on Metropolitan Government, *The Government of Metropolitan Areas in the United States,* prepared by Paul Studenski with the assistance of the Committee on Metropolitan Government (New York: National Municipal League, 1930), p. 26.
60 See Anwar Syed, *The Political Theory of American Local Government* (Clinton, MA: Random House, 1966).
61 Teaford, *City and Suburb,* p. 6.
62 Ibid., p. 31.
63 U.S. Bureau of the Census, *Census 2000.*
64 Jon C. Teaford, *The American Suburb: The Basics* (New York: Routledge, 2008).
65 Quoted in ibid., p. 132.
66 Dolores Hayden, *Building Suburbia: Green Fields and Urban Growth, 1820–2000* (New York: Pantheon Books), p. 168.
67 Quoted in Teaford, *City and Suburb,* p. 115.
68 Quoted in ibid., p. 112.
69 Seymour I. Toll, *Zoned America* (New York: Grossman, 1969), p. 193.

70   Ibid., p. 197.

71   Ibid., p. 159.

72   Quoted in Michael N. Danielson, *The Politics of Exclusion* (New York: Columbia University Press, 1976), p. 54.

73   Toll, *Zoned America,* p. 183.

74   Ibid., pp. 182–183.

75   Ibid., p. 187.

76   *Police power* refers to the implied powers of government to adopt and enforce laws necessary for preserving and protecting the immediate health and welfare of citizens. The meaning of this, of course, is subject to a wide variety of interpretations.

77   *Village of Euclid v. Ambler Realty Co.,* 272 U.S. 365, 47 S.Ct. 114, 71 L. Ed. 303 (1926).

78   Danielson, *The Politics of Exclusion,* pp. 53–54.

79   "The End of the Exurban Dream," *The New York Times* (December 13, 1976).

80   Danielson, *The Politics of Exclusion,* p. 53.

81   Because of the fears concerning apartment developments, the planning process involving their construction was complicated, requiring petitions for zoning variances, public hearings, and lengthy review proceedings. For an excellent account of these complexities, see Daniel R. Mandelker, *The Zoning Dilemma: A Legal Strategy for Urban Change* (Indianapolis, IN: Bobbs-Merrill, 1971).

82   Quoted in Danielson, *The Politics of Exclusion,* p. 60.

83   Quoted in Merrill Folsom, "Westchester Finds Influx of Business a Worry," *The New York Times* (April 18, 1967); cited in Danielson and Doig, *New York,* p. 90.

84   A detailed discussion of the legal status of zoning is not included in this section. For further information, the following sources are especially useful: Danielson, *The Politics of Exclusion*; Richard F. Babcock, *The Zoning Game* (Madison, WI: University of Wisconsin Press, 1969); Richard F. Babcock and Fred P. Bosselman, *Exclusionary Zoning: Land Use Regulation and Housing in the 1970s* (New York: Praeger, 1973); Daniel R. Mandelker, *Managing Our Urban Environment* (Indianapolis, IN: Bobbs-Merrill, 1971); Randall W. Scott, ed., *Management and Control of Growth,* vol. 1 (New York: Urban Land Institute, 1975); and David Listokin, ed., *Land Use Controls Present Problems and Future Reform* (New Brunswick, NJ: Center for Urban Policy Research, Rutgers University, 1975).

85   *Dailey v. City of Lawton,* 425 F.2d 1037 (1970).

86   *Kennedy Park Homes v. City of Lackawanna,* 436 F.2d 108 (1971).

87   Quoted in *St. Louis Globe-Democrat* (January 11, 1977).

88   In 1975 the Supreme Court made it more difficult to challenge exclusionary zoning in federal courts by "refusing standing"—dismissing a case on the grounds that the plaintiffs had no right to sue. Those who want to challenge an exclusionary ordinance must prove "distinct and palpable injury"; a suit cannot be based on general injury to those who do not live in the town but want to live there; see *Warth v. Seldin,* 442 U.S. 490 (1975).

89   See *James v. Valtierra,* 91 S.Ct. 133 (1971), and *Shaffer v. Valtierra,* 402 U.S. 137 (1971).

90   Joseph F. Sullivan, "Restless Seeker for Justice," *The New York Times* (January 22, 1983); Robert Hanley, "After 7 Years, Town Remains under Fire for Its Zoning Code," *The New York Times* (January 22, 1983); Anthony DePalma, "N.J. Housing Woes Are All over the Map," *The New York Times* (April 17, 1983).

91 Robert Hanley, "Some Jersey Towns, Yielding to Courts, Let in Modest Homes," *The New York Times* (February 29, 1984).

92 1985 J.J. Sess. Law Serv. 222 (West).

93 Anthony DePalma, "Subsidized Housing Hurt in Ailing Market," *The New York Times* (May 15, 1990).

94 Ibid., pp. 42–43.

95 Ibid.

96 Rosalyn Baxandall and Elizabeth Ewen, *Picture Windows: How the Suburbs Happened* (New York: Perseus Books, 2000), p. 239.

97 Ibid., p. 250.

98 Alana Semuels, "Suburbs and the New American Poverty," *The Atlantic* (January 7, 2015). Accessed online: https://www.theatlantic.com/business/archive/2015/01/suburbs-and-the-new-american-poverty/384259/.

99 Peter O. Muller, *Contemporary Suburban America* (Upper Saddle River, NJ: Prentice Hall, 1981), p. 180.

100 Trevor Boddy, "Underground and Overhead: Building the Analogous City," in *Variations on a Theme Park: The New American City and the End of Public Space,* ed. Michael Sorkin (New York: Noonday Press, 1992), p. 139.

101 Betsy Blaney, "Texas Developers to Build Sex Offender-Free Subdivision," *Chicago Tribune* (June 15, 2005), p. 34.

102 Mike Davis, "Fortress Los Angeles: The Militarization of Urban Space," in *Variations on a Theme Park,* ed. Sorkin, p. 173.

103 For a comparative analysis of suburban development in advanced industrial countries, see Donald N. Rothblatt and Daniel J. Garr, *Suburbia: An International Assessment* (New York: St. Martin's Press, 1986), and Christopher M. Law, *The Uncertain Future of the Urban Core* (London: Routledge, 1988).

104 *United States Census Bureau,* "2017 Census of Governments," https://www.census.gov/data/tables/2017/econ/gus/2017-governments.html.

105 Kenneth Newton, "American Urban Politics: Social Class, Political Structure, and Public Goods," in *Readings in Urban Politics: Past, Present and Future,* 2nd ed., ed. Harlan Hahn and Charles H. Levine (New York: Longman, 1984).

106 NYSERDA, "Latest Surveyed Regular Grade Motor Gasoline Prices," Week of 8/23/2021.

107 "Gasoline prices in Europe, US Gallon, 23-Aug-2021, GlobalPetrolPrices.com, https://www.globalpetrolprices.com/gasoline_prices/Europe/.

108 Jon C. Teaford, *Post-Suburbia: Government and Politics in the Edge Cities* (Baltimore, MD: Johns Hopkins University Press, 1997), p. 1.

109 James Heilbrun, *Urban Economics and Public Policy,* 2nd ed. (New York: St. Martin's Press, 1981), p. 48.

110 Peter O. Muller, *Contemporary Suburban America* (Upper Saddle River, NJ: Prentice Hall, 1981), p. 123.

111 George E. Peterson, "Federal Tax Policy and Urban Development," in *Central City Economic Development,* ed. Benjamin Chinitz (Cambridge, MA: Abt Books, 1979), pp. 67–78.

112 David M. Gordon, "Capitalist Development and the History of American Cities," in *Marxism and the Metropolis: New Perspectives in Urban Political Economy,* 2nd ed., ed. William K. Tabb and Larry Sawers (New York: Oxford University Press, 1984), p. 41.

113 Robert Cervero, "Unlocking Suburban Gridlock," *Journal of the American Planning Association* 52, no. 4 (Autumn 1986): 389.

114 Brian J.L. Berry, *The Open Housing Question: Race and Housing in Chicago, 1966–1976* (Cambridge, MA: Ballinger, 1979).

115 Joel Garreau, *Edge City: Life on the New Frontier* (Garden City, NY: Doubleday, 1991), p. 6.

116 Robert E. Lang and Jennifer B. LeFurgy, *Boomburbs: The Rise of America's Accidental Cities* (Washington, D.C.: Brookings Institution Press, 2007).

117 Ibid.

118 R.E. Lang, Arthur C. Nelson, and Rebecca R. Sohmer: "Boomburb Downtowns: The Next Generation of Urban Centers," *Journal of Urbanism: International Research on Placemaking and Urban Sustainability* 1, no. 1 (2008). Accessed online: http://rsa.tandfonline.com/doi/full/10.1080/17549170801903694?scroll=top&needAccess=true.

119 Robert E. Lang and Jennifer B. LeFurgy, *Boomburbs: The Rise of America's Accidental Cities* (Washington, D.C.: Brookings Institution Press, 2007), pp. 56–57.

120 Office of Technology Assessment, Congress of the United States, *The Technological Reshaping of Metropolitan America*, OTA-ETI-643 (Washington, D.C.: U.S. Government Printing Office, 1995).

121 Anthony Downs, *The Costs of Sprawl: Environmental and Economic Costs of Alternative Development Patterns of Metropolitan America* (Washington, D.C.: Real Estate Research Corporation, 1974), p. 2.

122 Neal Peirce and Curtis Johnson, "St. Louis: Exploded Galaxy?" *St. Louis Post-Dispatch* (March 16, 1997), p. 6B.

123 Martha T. Moore, "Cool Climates, Hot Suburbs, Mixed Blessings," *USA Today* (November 11, 2003), p. 18A.

124 Russ Lopez and H. Patricia Hynes, "Sprawl in the 1990s: Measurement, Distribution, and Trends," *Urban Affairs Review* 38, no. 3 (January 2003): 325–352.

125 Derek Hyra, "The Back-to-the-City Movement: Neighborhood Redevelopment and Processes of Political and Cultural Displacement," *Urban Studies* 52, no. 10 (2015): 1753–1773.

126 Ibid.

127 Ibid.

128 Scott Bowles, "National Gridlock," *USA Today* (November 23, 1999), p. 2A.

129 Texas Transportation Institute, Texas A&M University, *The Urban Mobility Annual Report* (Lubbock, TX, 2006).

130 Mark Bowerman: "And the City with the Worst Traffic in the U.S. Is ..." *USA Today Network* (March 22, 2016). Accessed online: http://www.usatoday.com/story/news/nation-now/2016/03/22/worst-cities-traffic-united-states-tom-tom-traffic-index/82108390/.

131 Ibid.

132 Ibid.

133 Ibid.

134 James W. Hughes, Joseph J. Seneca: "The Beginning of the End of Sprawl?" *Rutgers Regional Report*, No. 21, March 2004.

135 Ibid.

136 Ibid.

137 James Howard Kunstler, *The Geography of Nowhere* (New York: Touchstone, 1993), p. 10.

138 Ibid., p. 118.
139 John A. Jakle and David Wilson, *Derelict Landscapes: The Wasting of America's Built Environment* (Savage, MD: Rowman and Littlefield, 1992), p. 182.
140 Ibid., p. 40.
141 Green Day, "Jesus of Suburbia," released 2004 on the Album *American Idiot.*
142 Iver Peterson, "In New Jersey, Sprawl Keeps Outflanking Its Foes," *The New York Times* (March 17, 2000), pp. A1, A19.
143 Jon C. Teaford, *The American Suburb: The Basics* (New York: Routledge, 2008).

CHAPTER 11

Economic and Fiscal Realities of the Metropolitan Mosaic

The Competition for Fiscal Resources

To the average citizen, local debates about taxes and spending may seem to be mostly routine and even boring. For urban officials, however, nothing could be more consequential. Without adequate resources, a city simply cannot offer the level of services and amenities that most people demand. This, basically, is the bottom line, and local officials may find themselves thrown out of office if they do not meet it. In finding revenues to finance these activities, though, municipal officials generally find that the choices available to them are extremely limited. One limitation is legal: State laws dictate the kinds of taxes and fees that cities are allowed to impose. The other limitation is political: Citizens and businesses do not like taxes. Local officials must be mindful that raising taxes past a certain point might tempt residents and businesses to other jurisdictions in search of a better deal. Because these considerations are always present, local fiscal policy is determined within a battleground in which cities are always trying to outbid one another, and there will be winners and losers.

Local officials devote a lot of attention to policies crafted to improve their competitive position. The stimulus package passed by Congress in 2009 revealed just how the competition among governmental jurisdictions works, whether for private or public dollars. When Congress authorized $144 billion for infrastructure projects, it set off a race that pitted states against states, states against cities, and cities against one another. Like every other public official in the country, Frank C. Ortis, the mayor of Pembroke Pines, Florida, declared, "We have a wish list."[1] In his case, the wish was to repair sewer lines. But it was clear that the federal money would not stretch far enough to fund all the wish lists across the country. States and cities scrambled to make the case that

DOI: 10.4324/9781003175315-14

their projects were especially urgent and that they fit the "shovel ready" criteria laid down by the Obama administration.

The stimulus package established a battleground among jurisdictions. The sudden availability of federal dollars made it newsworthy, but in fact, this kind of interjurisdictional competition for sources of the revenue goes on all the time. What cities compete for is virtually endless, ranging from federal and state dollars to malls, big-box stores, office parks, sports stadiums, tourism facilities, and on and on. Depending upon one's point of view, this competition is a positive and dynamic feature of the U.S. system, or it is a waste of public dollars when governments offer subsidies just to influence the location of activities that would occur anyway. The reality, though, is that the system is sustained by the fiscal needs of the governments that make it up, and this is one of the reasons why city budgets are intensely political and why they matter.

The gigantic bipartisan infrastructure bill passed by the United States Senate on August 10, 2021, the Infrastructure Investment and Jobs Act (IIJA), would mean a huge opportunity for local governments if passed by the House. The Act would provide important funding opportunities in terms of transportation infrastructure, water and climate resilience, broadband internet access and digital equity, and an expansion in usage of both private activity bonds and highway or surface freight transfer facility bonds.[2] Among these, funding opportunities for transit infrastructure and water and climate resilience projects would likely benefit cities much more than the latter two, which are more targeted at rural areas. What is clear, however, is that, if passed by the House (likely with some modifications), the IIJA would not only provide an impressive amount of funding opportunities for local jurisdictions. It would also drastically increase local competition for funding.

OUTTAKE

Hundreds of Little Hoovers Make the Economic Crisis Worse

Many historians and economists have commented on the blunder by President Herbert Hoover and the Republican Congress in 1932 when they increased taxes and cut spending in an attempt to balance the federal budget. The nation had already slid into a serious economic downturn, and their actions took money out of the economy at a time when it was desperately needed. In a similar fashion, during the economic crisis that began in the late summer of 2008, states and cities took money out of the economy by raising taxes and cutting services. In this way, states and cities made the recession worse and, in effect, canceled out much of the economic stimulus provided by the federal government.

The American Recovery and Reinvestment Act, as passed by Congress on February 13, 2009, sent $79 billion of fiscal assistance directly to the states and authorized $144 billion for infrastructure projects undertaken by state and local governments and $41 billion for school districts. The stimulus package provided a greater influx of federal money than at any time since the 1930s, but it did not do much to spare local governments from making deep cuts in their budgets. The federal dollars were designated for building and repairing infrastructure; cities were not allowed to use them to solve current budgetary problems. As a result, cities slashed their budgets deeper in 2010 than they had the year before.

To make ends meet, states and local governments took increasingly desperate measures. By February 2009, 83 percent of cities had cut expenditures and services. By December, Philadelphia had closed 11 of its 54 libraries and announced that 67 of its 81 pools would not open in the summer. Beginning January 1, San Diego eliminated all six of the centers it had established to help citizens with city services and cut the number of new police recruits by half. Seattle reduced spending on youth violence and homeless services. The hardest-hit cities began cutting even essential services; for example, Pontiac, Michigan, closed 8 public schools and reduced the number of police officers from 200 to only 73. Baltimore decided to consider allowing advertisements on their fire trucks to raise funds after closing several firehouses. Local governments even struggled to bury the indigent. The impact of such measures was magnified by budget cuts being imposed by state governments, which were feeling the same pressures. In March, 2009, 34 states were cutting a wide range of social-services programs.

A fundamental characteristic of the American intergovernmental system requires states and cities to balance their budgets despite the fact that they provide services that are essential to the immediate health and welfare of their citizens. The economist Paul Krugman wants to change the system so that it stops asking so much from the governments least equipped to adjust during times of economic hardship. He has proposed that the costs of most forms of medical care, education, and infrastructure be assumed by the federal government rather than by states and local governments. Most people, however, see strengths as well as weaknesses in America's intergovernmental system, and in any case, the political mood of the last few years favors an even lesser federal role. For these reasons, fundamental changes like those suggested by Krugman are not likely to come any time soon, but he is right when he says that economic crises raise issues about the way that the United States finances its governmental activities.

Sources: Paul Krugman, "Fifty Herbert Hoovers," *The New York Times* (December 28, 2008), http://www.nytimes.com/2008/12/29/opinion/29krugman.html; also Mary Williams Walsh, "Under Strain, Cities Are Cutting Back Projects," *The New York Times* (September 30, 2008), www.nytimes.com/2008/10/01business/01muni.html; Chris Hoene, "Fiscal Outlook for Cities Worsens in 2009," *Research Brief on America's Cities,* by National League of Cities, Issue 2009-1 (Washington, D.C.: National League of Cities, 2009), www.nlc.org; Legislative News, *Governing* (April 9, 2009); News, *Governing* (April 9, 2009).

Cities in the U.S. Federal System

Cities in the United States operate within a very peculiar system of governments, at least when compared with the practices in most of the world: "By not providing capital resources to subnational governments from the central government, the United States stands apart from almost every other advanced capitalist state, even other federal states."[3] In many Western nations, much of the basic infrastructure and many of the services provided to citizens are financed by the central governments even when they are administered by local governmental units. By contrast, cities in the United States derived only about 4 percent of their revenues from the national government in 2007, compared to 14 percent in Japan (in 2003) and one-half or much more in western European countries.[4] In addition, most cities outside the United States do not have to rely on private lenders to raise money for capital projects; those are generally financed by national governments. Such a system means that, unlike in the United States, local economic conditions only partly influence the ability of a city to find the revenues necessary to provide critical services and build infrastructure.

Municipal governments in the United States are located at the bottom of a three-tiered federal system of governance. At the top, the federal government enjoys the greatest freedom to impose taxes and go into debt. At its discretion, it may make states and cities implement policies that are costly (such as drunk driving, education testing, and antipollution laws), but it does not necessarily provide the money for such "unfunded mandates." The federal government has access to the best, most flexible sources of revenue: the personal income tax, payroll taxes (for Social Security), and corporate income taxes. States are next in line, collecting personal income taxes (but at a lower rate) and impose sales and receipts taxes. The states are not allowed to run deficits year to year, and neither are their cities. Ninety-nine of the 100 largest cities in the nation are, by law, required to balance their budgets.[5] State and county governments spend money within cities for such things as education, pollution control, and infrastructure such as roads, bridges, water and sewer lines, health clinics, and the like, but the cities finance nearly all of the basic municipal services and a great many infrastructure projects with their own revenues. A consequence of being at the bottom of the federal system is that cities have fewer sources of revenue and operate under more stringent budget rules than governments at any other level.

Local governments may be at the bottom in powers but not in responsibilities. As shown in Table 11.1, in 2007, local governments employed 13.2 million workers, with the largest employers being school districts, municipalities, and counties. This was more than four times the 2.7 million people who worked for the federal government and more than six times as many federal workers when postal workers and civilian military personnel are excluded. Local governments also employed more than twice as many workers as the states.[6]

TABLE 11.1 Federal, State, and Local Government Employment and Revenues, 2017/18

Employment (in Thousands) 2017

Federal civilian	3,050
Federal less U.S. Postal Service and Department of Defense	1,870
State	3,839
Local	10,953
School districts	6,209

Revenues (Own Source; in Trillions of Dollars), 2018

Federal	$3.33
State	2.1
Local	1.8

Note: The revenue figures do not include intergovernmental transfers or borrowing.

Sources: United States Bureau of the Census, "State Government Employment & Payroll Data," "Local Government Employment & Payroll Data," 2017 ASPEP Datasets & Tables, https://www.census.gov/data/datasets/2017/econ/apes/annual-apes.html.

United States Office of Personnel Management, "Federal Civilian Employment," Policy, Data Oversight, Data, Analysis & Documentation (September 2017), https://www.opm.gov/policy-data-oversight/data-analysis-documentation/federal-employment-reports/reports-publications/federal-civilian-employment/.

Statista, "Number of United States Postal Service Employees from 2004 to 2020," https://www.statista.com/statistics/320262/number-of-usps-employees/.

The Urban Institute, "State and Local Revenues," State and Local Finance Initiative (2011–Present), https://www.urban.org/policy-centers/cross-center-initiatives/state-and-local-finance-initiative/state-and-local-backgrounders/state-and-local-revenues.

Congressional Budget Office (CBO), "Revenues in 2018: An Infographic" (June 18, 2019), https://www.cbo.gov/publication/55345.

Even so, the federal government collected $1.8 trillion in revenue in the fiscal year 2002, three times as much as the $597 billion in own-source revenue collected by cities. One notable fact is that although local governments collect less revenue and spend less money, they hire far more workers than any other level of government because the services that local governments provide are extremely labor intensive, such as education, police, fire, and sanitation.

The budgetary policies of the federal or state government filter down to local governments. In December 2002, in the midst of a recession, state budget deficits reached levels not seen since World War II or, in some cases, since the Great Depression of the 1930s. Because the deficits had reached 13–18 percent of state expenditures, states took steps to slash spending. Because a substantial portion of state spending goes for functions that are extremely important to local residents, the impact of budgetary cuts made by the cities was magnified. When Congress passed the economic stimulus package in February 2009, it was the first time in many years that the national government provided substantial new resources to help cities, but the assistance was temporary.

Where the Money Goes

Only occasionally do the everyday operations of urban governments hit a nerve because most of what they do seems pretty routine. Because of this, it is difficult to appreciate the critical role that cities play in providing basic services. In a nation where nearly 40 percent of citizens lack health insurance, cities are frontline providers of health services provided through public hospitals and clinics, not only for the poor but also for families of the underinsured middle class. They provide essential housing services, even if most of this takes the form of contributing to or maintaining homeless shelters. During cold and heat emergencies, cities are expected to assist in providing immediate help.

Collectively, local governments in the United States spend huge sums of money. In fiscal 2018, for example, they spent $1.7 trillion.[7] In terms of expenses, the leading municipal budget by far is New York City, with $92.5 billion[8] in expenditures and appropriations for the 2020 fiscal year, compared to Chicago at $11.65 billion[9] and Los Angeles at $10.5 billion.[10] These huge volumes of money finance everything from everyday services such as police and fire protection, maintenance of water and sewer pipes, and 911 emergency phone services. These tend to virtually hidden from view because they are ubiquitous and expected aspects of our daily lives.

City spending is driven by powerful forces that are largely beyond the control of local officials and voters. City governments are not sovereign entities. Higher levels of government (state and federal) allocate responsibilities—generally called *mandates*—to city governments within the intergovernmental system. Equally important, no matter how dire their budgetary situation may be, cities must provide a minimum level of services and infrastructure maintenance necessary for preserving the physical well-being of city residents and the viability of a city: public health, police and fire protection, education, water distribution, sewage collection, parks, highways, museums, and libraries.

The relative distribution of municipal expenditures among various services and responsibilities for 2018 is shown in Table 11.2. Most cities spend their money on a variety of services that most citizens take for granted, such as education, highways, parks and recreation, sewage and waste disposal, and police and fire protection. However, the biggest cities tend to devote a larger proportion of their budgets to social programs such as housing and community development, health and hospitals, and public welfare. It should be noted that most cities, even most big cities, do not run the schools within their boundaries; normally, education is financed through independent school districts. The

TABLE 11.2 Direct Expenditures for Selected Services by Local Governments in the U.S. (Based on 2018 Population)	
Expenditure	**Percentage of Total Direct Expenditures**
Elementary and Secondary Education	40
Higher Education	3
Public Welfare	4
Health and Hospitals	10
Highways and Roads	4
Police	6

Source: *Urban Institute*, "State and Local Expenditures," State and Local Finance Initiative, (2011–Present), https://www.urban.org/policy-centers/cross-center-initiatives/state-and-local-finance-initiative/state-and-local-backgrounders/state-and-local-expenditures.

exceptions include some older cities, such as New York, Boston, San Francisco, and Baltimore, which built schools before it had become the usual practice to finance education through special districts, and Chicago, where the mayor took over the schools in 1995.

Except for education, many of the social services the cities provide would be considered by most people as redistributive in nature, in the sense that they disproportionately benefit less affluent residents. However, failure to treat the problems of the poor can reverberate through the urban community and affect everyone. Public hospitals and health clinics, for example, are used mostly by people without health insurance. In the absence of public health facilities, many families would quickly become reduced to desperation and penury in an attempt to find health services. Considered on its own merits, this would be a social disaster, but in addition, rates of communicable and contagious diseases such as tuberculosis and AIDS would spread more quickly.

Homelessness is another social problem that most big cities attempt to treat in a somewhat compassionate manner. Virtually all large cities have a population of homeless people wandering downtown streets. Law enforcement can manage but cannot solve the problem. In January 2003, Chicago's former mayor, Richard M. Daley, announced an effort to end homelessness in the city by 2013 by closing homeless shelters and using the money to fund permanent housing and social services. The mayor's proposal, which was drafted by non-profit organizations working with city administrators, was motivated, in part, by the expense and intractability of the problem. It cost $1,200 a month to provide temporary shelter for a family of three—money that could, instead, be devoted to rental of permanent housing and social services.[11] Alas, homelessness in Chicago did not end in 2013. In 2011, the state of Illinois had cut $2.3 million in funding for a city program providing rides to shelters for the homeless. As a consequence, the newly elected mayor at the time, Rahm Emanuel, cut the program altogether. When this sparked vigorous criticism among the aldermen, Emanuel reinstated the program (and its workers) on city money. The State of Illinois eventually refunded the program.[12]

Emanuel, Chicago's millionaire mayor, came up with myriad ways to cut city costs in dealing with homelessness since, many of which have earned a lot of criticism. In January 2016, the mayor announced his support of a new 4 percent tax on Airbnb rentals aimed at subsidizing the city's efforts to get homeless people into permanent housing. Many of his critics claimed that the mayor was less interested in permanently solving issues of homelessness in Chicago, rather than getting homeless "tent cities" away from the city beaches in time for the summer (and tourist season).[13]

Public health services account for a large chunk of the budgets of large cities, and they are too important to abandon. Cities and counties engage in restaurant inspections and move quickly when cases of food poisoning break out. Health clinics offer free flu shots and screening for diseases. There are constant reminders of the importance of such services. In the summer of 2002, an epidemic of the West Nile virus, which is carried by birds, spread throughout the Midwest, with a heavy outbreak in Illinois. The state of Illinois and city officials in Chicago moved fast in an attempt to track the disease. Local governments throughout the Chicago area sprayed ponds and rivers where mosquitoes might breed and launched an aggressive campaign of eradication at the start of the mosquito-breeding season in the spring of 2003. But such measures do not reveal how critical public health services are to the urban population. New York City, at the beginning of the COVID-19 pandemic, experienced how quickly a global pandemic can overwhelm a city's public health and service infrastructure.

Although smaller cities spend about the same proportion on health and hospitals, they spend less on other social services. Big cities take on more responsibilities for a variety of reasons: Their citizens demand more and better services (for example, well-trained police officers and firefighters), they pay higher salaries to their public employees, and they experience the high service costs made necessary by high-density populations, aging buildings and infrastructure, and high rates of poverty and unemployment. Because they do more, they spend more; on average, the cities with populations exceeding a million people spend about twice as much for each citizen as the average U.S. city and many times more than most small cities.

City expenditures rose sharply in the second half of the twentieth century, not only in total amount but also relative to the economy as a whole, increasing from 5 percent of the gross national product (GNP) in 1949–1950 to a high of 9 percent in 1975–1976. But after the recession of 1974–1975, the brakes were applied to municipal budgets. The six biggest cities experienced a 10 percent drop in their budgets from 1975 to 1980, when inflation is taken into account. After adjusting for inflation, cities of all sizes, on the average, did not increase spending at all over the same years. Since 1980, spending has declined slightly (after adjustment for inflation) for cities of all sizes.

Because they rely so much on their own sources of revenue, there is a close relationship between expenditure levels and local economic vitality. As shown in Table 11.3, some cities in the Frostbelt were forced to make deep cuts in their budgets in the 30-year period from 1975 to 2006. Measured in constant 2006 dollars (to account for inflation), Baltimore's budget shrank by 36 percent, Cleveland's by 16 percent, and St. Louis's by 28 percent. Of the Frostbelt cities shown in Table 11.3, only New York and Chicago were able to increase their budgets. The contrast with Sunbelt cities is striking. Of the five shown, four increased their budgets substantially; indeed, Phoenix more than doubled its spending. It is true that the populations of several Frostbelt cities fell during this period at the same time that Sunbelt cities grew rapidly. However, city expenditures are not related one to one with population; if anything, older cities bear a bigger burden because of old infrastructure and serious social problems.

Almost all the older industrial cities experienced significant population losses due to the flight of the middle class to the suburbs. As the population of the central cities fell, the cost of providing infrastructure and basic services, such as police and fire, did not decline correspondingly.[14] Even if they have fewer people than in the past, cities still have the same sewer and water lines—often old and in need of frequent repair—and the same miles of streets to plow and patrol. Once the middle class has fled, there are fewer taxpayers to pay for these services, and the taxpayers who are left make less taxable income and own less valuable property than those in surrounding jurisdictions.

By 2006, many Frostbelt cities have recovered from their post-war declines in terms of their budgets and expenditures. As shown in Table 11.3, the growth rates in spending seem to have somewhat leveled out between Sunbelt and Frostbelt cities, even though Phoenix and San Jose are still growing explosively. Industrial cities, which had been struggling economically and losing tremendous amounts of population during the second half of the twentieth century, have once again become attractive places to live. Where the middle class was once "escaping" the old industrial cities, it is now, at least to a certain extent, returning. Urban rents and real estate values are on the rise, and gentrification has become a buzzword in reference to urban neighborhoods. As cities are starting to catch up with their suburbs in terms of wealth, many suburbs are starting to see increases in poverty rates. In other words: Cities and suburbs are becoming more alike. By 2015, poverty rates in the suburbs had started to climb at slightly higher rates than in the cities: While cities saw their poverty rates increase at about 2 percent, suburbs saw a 3 percent increase.[15] The 2015 poverty rate was still lower in the suburbs, at 11.2 percent, as compared to the cities at 19.6 percent, but in absolute numbers, suburbs had started to surpass cities by the year 2000[16]: By 2015, roughly 3 million more poor people lived in the suburbs (16 million) as compared to the cities.[17] Yet suburbs are far worse equipped in terms of social infrastructure that can help support those in need.

TABLE 11.3 Total Expenditures for Selected Frostbelt and Sunbelt Cities, 1975–2006 (in Millions of 2005 Dollars[a])

	Fiscal Year 1975 Expenditures	Fiscal Year 1996 Expenditures	Fiscal Year 2006 Expenditures	Percent Change 1975–1996	Percent Change 1991–1996	Percent Change 1996–2006
Frostbelt Cities						
Baltimore	$3,842	$2,442	$2,783	−36	0	14
Chicago	3,932	5,271	5,731	34	12	9
Cleveland	1,043	873	–	−16	2	–
New York	46,855	52,507	62,917	12	2	20
St. Louis	916	660	–	−28	−14	–
Sunbelt Cities						
Dallas	$839	$1,622	$2,084	93	32	29
Denver	1,277	2,325	2,004	82	48	−14
New Orleans	901	883	–	−2	−15	–
Phoenix	773	1,654	2,462	114	6	49
San Jose	514	1070	1,618	108	5	51

Note: [a] Adjustments for inflation are calculated using the GNP Price Index for state and local government purchases, U.S. Bureau of Economic Analysis, *Survey of Current Business, Aug. 2012*, p. 199, Table 3. Accessed online: https://www.bea.gov/scb/pdf/2012/08%20August/0812%20gdp-other%20nipa_series.pdf.

Sources: U.S. Bureau of the Census, *City Government Finances: 1975–76*, GF 76, no. 4 (Washington, D.C.: U.S. Government Printing Office, 1977), Table 5; U.S. Bureau of the Census, *Statistical Abstract of the United States, 1995* (Washington, D.C.: U.S. Government Printing Office, 1995), Table 493; U.S. Bureau of the Census, *Statistical Abstract of the United States, 1999* (Washington, D.C.: U.S. Government Printing Office, 1999), p. 335, Table 531; and U.S. Bureau of the Census, *Statistical Abstract of the United States, 2012*, p. 297, Table 458.

Poverty boosts public spending not only for welfare and social services but also for a broad range of other services. Central-city governments spend money on lead paint poisoning prevention (a problem prevalent in older homes), rat control, and housing demolition. Courts have ordered cities to provide shelter for the homeless at a significant expense to local governments. In 1987, for example, a court order required New York City to provide emergency shelter to its homeless population, which cost the city $274 million.[18] Poverty also drives up the cost of everyday services. Fire protection, for instance, costs more in high-density areas where deteriorated and aging structures pose a high fire risk, and police protection is also more difficult in such environments.

Another factor that drives up the cost of city services is the panoply of expensive mandates forced on cities by higher levels of government. Cities are not mentioned in the U.S. Constitution; legally, city governments are the creatures of the states. Although many cities have home rule charters that allow them to govern themselves internally within broad guidelines, municipal corporations are not fully sovereign. The scope of a city's service responsibilities is beyond its control. State and federal governments can, and frequently do, order cities to provide particular services or meet minimum standards of service provision, and cities only rarely receive more money to cover the costs of the mandated standards and services.

Since the mid-1960s, the number of unfunded federal mandates imposed on cities has proliferated. In the case of concurrent powers shared by the federal and state governments, Congress has the power to preempt (override) state and local laws. According to the supremacy clause (Article VI) of the Constitution, when there is a conflict between a national law and a state (or local) law, the national law prevails. The Supreme Court upheld federal preemption in the 1985 *Garcia* decision.[19] In *Garcia*, the Court upheld the constitutionality of the 1974 amendments to the Fair Labor Standards Act, which applied minimum wage and overtime pay provisions to public transit workers in San Antonio. This decision made it clear that state and local governments are not protected from federal preemption statutes by the Tenth Amendment (which reserves powers not granted to the federal government to the states). Their only protection comes from political pressures they can put on Congress. In 1986, the U.S. Department of Labor estimated that the cost to state and local governments of complying with the new labor standards exceeded $1.1 billion.[20]

Various economic and political forces beyond the control of local officials impact local government expenditures. Economic downturns, concentrated poverty, unfunded mandates, and terrorist threats impose unpredictable costs. As one fiscal expert observed,

> A city's fiscal health ... depends on economic, social, and institutional factors that are largely outside the city's control. Poor fiscal health is not caused by poor management, corruption, or profligate spending, and a city government's ability to alter the city's fiscal health is severely limited.[21]

Over the last three quarters of a century, older cities became accustomed to dealing with chronic economic problems and a high level of poverty. Unfunded mandates added to the burden, and terrorist threats added still more responsibilities. The Great Recession dealt a blow to cities of all sorts, new and old, urban and suburban. For the first time in many years, they are all in the same boat.

Where the Money Comes from

The sources for the revenues that cities collect are dictated by two basic considerations: What state laws allow and what the local officials feel they can impose without harming their ability to compete for investors and middle-class residents.[22] There are many different ways to solve the problem; the challenge is to find a way to raise revenue without inciting too much resentment and opposition. Over time, local officials have learned that property taxes are not popular, and as a result, these have become less important to city budgets than in the past. A few states allow their cities to impose earnings or corporate income taxes, but these tend to be modest because they may drive away workers and their employers. In recent years, for obvious reasons, "stealth" taxes have become more and more common. These are charges imposed on citizens that amount to a tax but go under some other name: a fee for entering a museum, for example, or higher parking charges or fines. It is, in effect, a shell game that everyone agrees to play.

Almost all cities are allowed by their states to impose property taxes, probably because this tax has such a long history. Twenty-eight states allow their cities to impose taxes on retail sales, but only 8 percent of cities (most of them in Ohio and Pennsylvania) are able to impose income taxes.[23] Most of them are also allowed to charge user fees for such facilities as public parking, museums and zoos, ice rinks, and swimming pools, and in the same spirit, most cities are permitted to collect taxes that target visitors, such as hotel/motel and entertainment taxes. Cities also rely on a continuous flow of intergovernmental revenues, and a small amount from the federal government (e.g., for pollution control and law enforcement), but most of this is passed through the states or allocated by the states for particular functions; especially important are road construction and maintenance, corrections, and public safety. It is difficult to find a pattern that fits all cities.

The revenue source that saved the cities from the worst fiscal effects of the urban crisis in the years following World War II came in the form of federal aid in the 1960s and beyond. Between 1965 and 1974, intergovernmental transfers to all cities rose 370 percent, more than twice the 153 percent increase in municipal expenditures.[24] Figure 11.1 shows that federal aid to municipalities peaked at 10 percent of cities' own-source revenue in 1979 and then dropped like a stone. President Reagan ended the special relationship that had been forged between the federal government and cities under previous Democratic

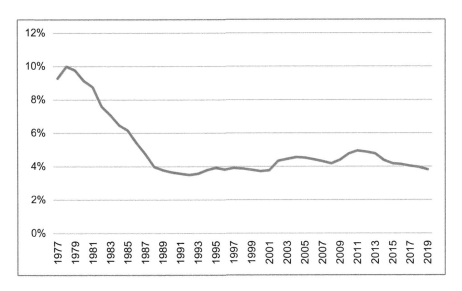

FIGURE 11.1 Share of Local Revenue from Federal Transfers, 1977–2019

Sources: U.S. Census Bureau Annual Survey of State and Local Government Finances, 1977–2019 (compiled by the Urban Institute via State and Local Finance Data: Exploring the Census of Governments; accessed 02-Dec-2021 01:20), https://state-local-finance-data.taxpolicycenter.org.

administrations. By 1992, federal aid bottomed out just below 4 percent of city revenues, climbed slightly to 5 percent by 2012 and fell again below 4 percent after 2017.[25]

Since the era of significant federal aid ended, cities have been very resourceful in finding ways to raise revenue. The creativity of local officials has been checked mainly by two considerations. First, when taxes reach a high enough level, taxpayers are prone to rebel, as evidenced by the taxpayer revolts against property taxes that swept the nation in the 1970s. Second, local officials are always aware that an excessive level of taxation may chase businesses and middle-class taxpayers away. This checks and balances system does not work perfectly, of course, but it does impose some general rules of the game.

The property tax was once the principal source of revenue for local governments. The most important and widely used form of property tax is the ad valorem real property tax, a levy imposed as a percentage of the value of land and its improvements. From colonial times through the early years of the republic, real property was taken to be the best indicator of both wealth and the ability to pay taxes. At the time, this assumption was accurate. Most of the wealth of the era was tied to the land, and fortunes were made in land speculation. Therefore, a tax on real property seemed to be the fairest and most reliable way to finance state and local governmental services.[26]

Taxation of personal (or non-real) property—that is, assets other than real estate and improvements—evolved as the cities became more complex. As trade and manufacturing grew in importance, more and more wealth became represented in bank accounts, merchandise, patent rights, machinery, capital stock, and corporate assets. Cities (and states) began to levy taxes on such sources of wealth in order to maintain a reliable relationship between individual tax burdens and personal wealth. Such assets were often hard to find and assess, however, and in any case, wealthy people used their considerable influence to discourage this kind of taxation. For these reasons, although the numbers of people with significant personal assets mushroomed after the Civil War, the proportion of the property tax attributable to personal property actually fell.[27]

Because they stir resentment among residents and businesses, in recent years, property taxes have steadily fallen as a proportion of the revenues collected by cities. In 1902, personal and real property taxes accounted for 73 percent of all municipal revenues, with license and franchise fees accounting for most of the rest. These taxes continued to provide approximately three-fourths of the tax receipts until the late 1930s and early 1940s, but after World War II the cities began finding new revenue sources.[28] By 1962, property taxes yielded barely 50 percent of municipal revenues in the 72 largest metropolitan areas (even though the property tax continued to generate almost all the revenue for school districts). Only a few years later, in the fiscal year 1975, property taxes accounted for little more than a third (35 percent) of the revenues in the largest metropolitan areas, despite a 130 percent increase in the average per capita levy since the early 1960s.[29] Clearly, other tax sources had gone up much faster, and they have continued to do so. The hot new revenue sources have been sales taxes, user fees, and charges for such entertainment costs as hotels, motels, and rental cars. Because of this trend, by 1996, reliance on the property tax had dropped to 19 percent for cities over 400,000 in population to 15 percent by 2002, when in some big cities, property taxes accounted for less than 10 percent of the budget.[30]

Over the past half-century, the property tax was an increasingly significant source of revenue growth only in the rapidly growing cities of the Sunbelt. This was possible because of rising property values. In Phoenix, the value of taxable property rose 251 percent from 1965 to 1973; by contrast, in Newark, it increased only 2 percent and in Detroit 14 percent during the same period.[31] However, the decades-long march upward disappeared during the recession of 2008–2009, when property values fell even faster in the Sunbelt than elsewhere, with real estate values falling by more than 40 percent in Florida, Arizona, and California. Property tax revenues were predicted to fall by 10 percent in California over a three-year period, but it would be even worse if property tax assessments actually kept up with changes in the value of real estate. Santa Clara County, which had experienced a 7 percent increase in property tax revenues the year before, was bracing for a 2 percent reduction by June 2009, and the assessor expected to review almost half the properties in the county before the next year.[32] These delays buy cities time to reconcile shrinking budgets; however, some cities have faced five consecutive years of shrinking budgets due to property assessment delays. Across the nation, a tax revolt began brewing because homeowners who saw their property values fall expected their tax bills to fall as well, but this often did not happen. Tax assessors' offices were inundated with appeals.[33]

Another disadvantage of the property tax is that a high proportion of property is tax exempt. According to one study, almost one-third of all real property in the United States is subject to some kind of exemption.[34] In 1982, in just 23 states and the District of Columbia, there was $15 billion in exempt property for religious institutions, $22 billion for educational institutions, $15 billion for charitable institutions, and $128 billion for government property.[35] In recent decades, the proportion of tax-exempt property has increased. Many cities have provided tax relief for the homes owned by elderly or poor people ("circuit breaker" laws). States and cities have tried to attract or retain businesses and investors by forgiving or reducing their property taxes. Many states have exempted various forms of business property, such as machines and inventory, from taxation without consulting local governments.[36]

The rationale behind the decisions regarding tax-exempt status for non-profits is not always entirely transparent. As scholar Michael Pagano pointed out in a piece in *The Atlantic*'s City Lab in 2012, the extent of public services that non-profits are assumed to provide as a basis for their tax-exempt status is not always reasonably adequate. Furthermore, a substitute tax, which is sometimes paid by non-profits to local governments on a voluntary basis (Payments in Lieu of Taxes, or PILOT), seem to be determined in a non-transparent and often seemingly random way.[37] Pagano concludes:

> Taxpayers should engage in a [...] dialogue about which entities should be provided services without charging them for the cost of service delivery and which entities should pay the full freight. [...] so that a deliberative dialogue on "who benefits" can be honestly and openly debated.[38]

The burden of tax-exempt property falls most heavily on those cities that are least able to afford it because central cities have twice as much exempt property located in them as their surrounding suburbs.[39] In 1985, more than 51 percent of the real property in Boston was tax exempt, up from 41 percent in 1972.[40] A 1983 article traced a 3.2-mile route through Boston where a walker would not set foot on a single parcel of taxable property.[41] Cities must provide services for these properties, including police and fire protection, but the owners pay no taxes. The situation in New York so incensed one taxpayer that he sued the city tax commission over the "subsidy of religion," going all the way to the U.S. Supreme Court before finally losing the case.[42]

Taxpayers' revolts that started in the 1970s forced governments to reduce their reliance on property taxes. During that period, at least 14 state legislatures enacted laws that limited property tax rates or spending by local governments.[43] Citizen initiatives went even further. The first widely publicized of these was

Proposition 13 in California, which was passed by popular referendum in June 1978. From March to November 1978, 16 states held initiatives or referenda to limit taxes or spending, although not all were binding on public officials.[44] Thirteen of the citizen initiatives passed. More such proposals were approved after 1978. Since that time, public officials have tended to regard any proposal to raise property taxes as the third rail of politics that they dare not touch. This, as much as any other consideration, explains why local officials have searched hard for alternatives.

More cities might use earnings taxes if their states allowed them to, but few do. Only about 8 percent of municipalities of 50,000 or more levy income taxes.[45] State law limits its use to Ohio, Pennsylvania, and Kentucky, although some of the larger cities in some other states, such as New York City, Kansas City, and St. Louis, collect such taxes as well. Nevertheless, 90 percent of the cities that collect income taxes are in Pennsylvania and Ohio.[46] Figure 11.2 displays on what types of taxes cities rely by state. Cities in some states rely on property taxes, others on sales taxes, and even more on combinations of taxes.

Sales taxes, user fees, and fees for permits and special services have been the taxes of choice since the 1970s. Currently, there are 35 states that allow their local governments to impose retail sales taxes.[47] Sales taxes have been useful because they are highly flexible. Taxes on retail sales can yield big revenues even

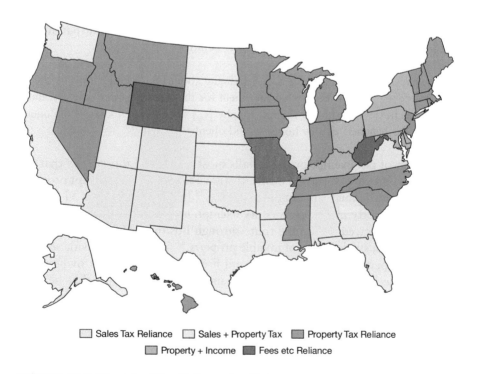

□ Sales Tax Reliance   □ Sales + Property Tax   ▨ Property Tax Reliance
▨ Property + Income   ■ Fees etc Reliance

FIGURE 11.2 Municipal Tax Reliance by State

when they are adjusted by tiny increments, and a substantial portion of the tax is paid by people not living within the city's boundaries. This is especially valuable for cities with large retailing centers serving a regional market, such as malls and big-box stores. Cities will go to great lengths to land big retailers, as revealed at the April 2009 meeting of the International Council of Shopping Centers held in Las Vegas. Economic development specialists and city officials from across the nation flocked to the convention to schmooze with developers and representatives of chain store retail outlets. For local officials, the stakes were both economic and symbolic: "Mom-and-pop stores may provide local flavor, but chain stores are societal benchmarks. Mayors hear it from their constituents all the time: 'Why don't we have a Trader Joe's? Why don't we have a Bass Pro Shops? What are we, some kind of backwater?'"[48] Changes in economic conditions question the long-term viability of sales taxes. While sales taxes cover the purchase of many goods, few cities extend their taxes to services. The expanding service sector promises an upside of economic growth and downtown renaissance but provides few added resources to the city's tax coffers.

With the fiscal bottom line and the reputation of local public officials riding on the outcome, the competition among jurisdictions for retail is extremely intense. Accordingly, governments try to outbid one another by offering subsidies to developers and retaining consultants to help them make deals. Businesses are skilled at shopping around, and they reap the rewards for their efforts: In 1995 and 1996, state and local corporate subsidies added up to almost $49 billion.[49] To put such numbers in perspective, it may be helpful to consider a 1998 study, which reported that the combination of federal, state, and local incentives offered to influence the location of business cost "every working man and woman in America the equivalent of two weekly paychecks" a year.[50]

However attractive they may be, reliance on sales taxes can be hazardous. Stores that move in can move out just as easily, and if this happens, subsidies appear to be a poor deal for local governments. During the 2008–2009 recession, the take from retail taxes dropped sharply because of declining sales and store closings. Officials in cities that relied heavily on sales taxes reported greater declines in revenues than those cities that had a more diverse mix of tax sources.[51]

In response to taxpayers' revolts and economic downturns, city officials have found ingenious ways to extract money from taxpayers without admitting that they are actually imposing new taxes. Since 2000, two episodes have prompted bursts of remarkable creativity. The terrorist attacks of September 11, 2001, changed the cities' economic fortunes very quickly. Travel and tourism plummeted, along with the stock market and retail sales. By March 2002, sales taxes had declined to 97 percent of earlier estimates, and income and tourist taxes had fallen to 90 percent.[52] Cities were squeezed between falling revenues and increases in costs for law enforcement and security. As a result, they began making deep cuts in expenditures. They had barely recovered from those budgetary problems when the economy plunged into recession in 2008.

Once they had recovered from the Great Recession, the nation's big cities were hit with the fallout from the COVID-19 pandemic. All of these events have posed extreme challenges to the fiscal health of cities and New York City in particular.

To create an illusion that they are not raising taxes at all, cities have imposed an astonishing variety of user and special-services fees. The trend began in earnest in the early 1990s. In 1991, 73 percent of cities increased user fees, and 40 percent adopted new charges for at least one city service.[53] Fees for parking, museums, botanical gardens, zoos, aquariums, planetariums, ice rinks, and swimming pools were increased, and many of the institutions and programs supporting these services were expected to be self-supporting. In many cities, garbage collection became a private service for which each household pays instead of being a public service paid for out of general tax revenues.

In response to mounting budget deficits in 2003, states and cities all over the nation redoubled their efforts to raise revenues by imposing new fees or hiking those already on the books. New York's former mayor, Michael Bloomberg, a Democrat turned Republican turned Independent, increased fees by $139 million while also proposing that the city's income tax rate be reduced. Literally, dozens of fees were involved, including a 33 percent increase in subway and bus fares, a 7 percent jump in tuition for public colleges, increases in parking fines, and higher fees to obtain a marriage license and birth certificate or to place a cell phone call from within the city. Fees had already been hiked for the use of public tennis courts and baseball diamonds. In California, a long list of new fees increased the costs of college tuition, car licenses, hunting and fishing licenses, admission to museums and parks, and even tuberculosis (a proposed $50 charge for anyone testing negative and $400 for positive).

The Great Recession prompted city officials to become more inventive than ever. Winter Haven, Florida, now levies a fee to cover the services provided by police and firefighters when they respond to auto accidents. Londonderry, New Hampshire, decided to charge a $25 fine for any dog owner who failed to renew a dog license on time. Cities learned that they could reap a steady revenue stream by hiring private companies to install and monitor cameras at intersections to record traffic violations. One mayor floated the idea of a "streetlight user fee" of $4.25 to pay for the city's cost of operating streetlights. Honolulu, Hawaii, considered raising its fees for zoo parking by 500 percent.[54] The real problem that arises from raising money through fees rather than taxes is that it is extremely regressive in nature: the fee costs the same regardless of the income of the person paying it. Over the last few years, less regressive forms of taxation (which is what fees are, in reality) have remained steady or even dropped.[55]

However creative local officials may be, there are times when even the most extraordinary efforts may fall short. In 2013, Michigan Governor Rick Snyder put the city of Detroit into receivership and appointed an emergency manager, Kevyn Orr, to oversee its fiscal affairs. The task he inherited was challenging in the extreme. The city was within months of becoming the largest city in the United States history to go bankrupt; against a $15–$17 billion debt and pension obligation, its total revenues added up to only $14.7 billion. In June 2013, Orr announced that the city would have to sell off assets to meet its obligations to creditors. Everything might be on the auction block: Detroit's half of the Detroit–Windsor Tunnel (worth more than $65 million), Belle Isle Park, with its miles of waterfront; the contents of the Detroit Historical Museum (which has, for example, a collection of 60 classic cars), even artwork from the Detroit Institute of Art. It was possible that almost anything might be considered distressed property—even animals at the zoo.[56]

Detroit's situation is extreme; indeed, bizarre. The measures taken to save the city will affect the economy and quality of life for citizens of the region for years to come. Other questions arise: "the possibility of selling off city assets also leads directly to questions such as, how much does a giraffe cost? And how does a citizenry cope with no-win scenarios pitting one indispensable gem against another?"[57] The questions facing other cities may not rise to the same level, but the issues are similar. When cities make normal services and amenities more expensive and its revenues sources more regressive, working-class families and poor are deeply affected. In this way, the fiscal policies of local governments go a long way toward canceling efforts by the federal government to erect a social safety net for people in need.

The Municipal Bond Market

If cities relied on taxation alone, they would never have been able to build the physical infrastructure on which all city life depends. Cities are authorized by state legislation to issue long-term bonds to pay for capital improvements, such as schools, highways, bridges, and hospitals, which will benefit city residents over a long period. To successfully compete in the market for municipal bonds, they must keep their credit rating as high as possible, and this requires them to please the rating services that advise investors about the soundness of the investment.[58] In the process, cities compete in a marketplace that is vastly larger than the metropolis. By competing for capital in this way, cities are subject to the same logic that drives the competition within urban regions: They must pursue policies that promote local economic growth. For private corporations, profits are a key indicator of health; for cities, it is the ability to generate enough revenues to provide adequate services and make the payments on long-term bonded debt.[59]

The continuing need to build and maintain public infrastructure makes access to the municipal bond market essential for the well-being of cities. Borrowing typically represents 20–25 percent of all state and local spending, making the municipal bond market a significant sector of the national economy. In 2007, the total long-term debt amortized by bond issues for all local governments amounted to $561 billion.[60] The reason municipal bonds are attractive to investors is that they are tax exempt, and for this reason, investors are willing to buy municipal bonds at a lower interest rate than they would pay for corporate bonds. In effect, the federal government provides cities with a subsidy by exempting municipal bonds from taxation. Although the U.S. Supreme Court has ruled that state and local governments have no constitutional right to borrow at tax-exempt rates, it is very unlikely that Congress would ever take away this subsidy to state and local governments.[61]

Municipal bonds are purchased by commercial banks, casualty insurance companies, pension funds, and, increasingly, wealthy individual investors, who find the federal tax exemption especially attractive.[62] The federal subsidy to cities through the bond market is inefficient because only part of it, in the form of lower interest rates paid to investors, goes to cities. The rest of the federal subsidy is siphoned off to investors who avoid paying federal taxes by buying the tax-exempt municipal bonds. Legislation was proposed but never passed that would allow municipalities to float bonds at normal interest rates in exchange for a direct subsidy by the federal government.[63] In this way, the subsidy would go entirely to cities and not, indirectly, to investors.

Cities issue two types of long-term bonds: general obligation bonds and revenue bonds. General obligation bonds pledge the "full faith and credit" of the city's taxing powers to pay off the bonds, generally require approval by voters or a representative body, and are used to build public infrastructures such as bridges and parks. Revenue bonds are paid off by anticipated future revenues from the facilities that are constructed. They are usually issued by public authorities established by state-enabling legislation.[64] When revenues are not sufficient to pay bond premiums (and they sometimes are not), local governments generally must make up the difference. Convention centers typically fail to generate enough revenue to fully cover bond payments, and sports stadiums sometimes fail to do so as well. In such cases, a general-purpose government (such as a municipality) must step in to cover the difference. Even so, because the debt will, in theory, be paid entirely through revenues, revenue bonds do not require a public referendum. This feature makes them especially popular with local officials.

Almost any facility that can charge user fees—sports stadiums, convention centers, museums, aquariums—is financed through revenue bonds. Local government borrowing through revenue bonds has risen sharply since the 1970s. Until the 1970s, general obligation bonds represented about 60 percent of outstanding local long-term debt.[65] By 2002, however, non-guaranteed revenue-bond debt represented 60 percent of all outstanding debt issued by city governments and special authorities.[66]

Revenue bonds permit cities to use their tax-exempt borrowing privileges to support private programs and activities. In the late 1970s, cities began issuing mortgage revenue bonds to subsidize interest rates for middle-income homebuyers, although in 1980, Congress restricted this practice with the passage of the Mortgage Subsidy Act. In an attempt to stimulate economic growth, in the 1970s and 1980s, cities increasingly issued industrial revenue bonds to subsidize a broad assortment of businesses, including big-box retailers such as

Walmart or Kmart, fast-food franchises such as McDonald's, and a mix of other businesses ranging from liquor stores to law offices. Critics charged that the tax-exempt borrowing was being used for private purposes that did not serve any public interest. Examples of flagrant abuses abounded. Chester County, Pennsylvania, for example, issued revenue bonds for an adult bookstore and topless go-go bar in downtown Philadelphia. Congress, noting the hemorrhage of federal tax revenues, restricted the use of revenue bonds by passing the Tax Equity and Fiscal Responsibility Act of 1982 and the Deficit Reduction Act of 1984.[67] The Tax Reform Act of 1986 placed state-by-state limits on what it termed governmentally subsidized "private-activity bonds."[68]

Besides being used for questionable private purposes, municipal bonds have been subject to a number of other abuses. Even before the economic crisis of 2008–2009, some local governments got into trouble by borrowing money and putting it into high-risk investments, hoping to make substantial profits. Unwilling to raise taxes, in 1993, Orange County, California, attempted to maintain services by putting the proceeds of bond sales into risky investments called *derivatives* that were essentially gambling on the direction of interest rates. When interest rates plunged, Orange County lost $1.6 billion. In April 1994, Orange County became the largest local government in history to file for federal bankruptcy protection under Chapter 9. More than 180 other governments lost money in similar high-risk investment pools in the same period.

Until the recent recession, however, such episodes were the exception rather than the rule. But the 2008–2009 downturn exposed serious deficiencies in the way the municipal bond market was run. In fact, the tip of the iceberg had been sighted years before. In the early 1990s, the municipal bond market had been rocked by charges that underwriters, in order to obtain lucrative government bond business, kicked back profits to public officials in the form of campaign contributions.[69] In April 1994, the Securities and Exchange Commission (SEC) enacted Rule G–37, which barred campaign contributions by municipal bond bankers. To get around this ban, municipal finance companies provided funding for lavish receptions at the 1996 Democratic and Republican conventions where bond underwriters could mingle with top state and local officials. At the Republican convention in San Diego, this included golf and tennis parties, a fishing expedition, and a luncheon honoring House Speaker Newt Gingrich.[70] A 1996 lawsuit alleged that underwriters overcharged municipalities for escrow accounts by as much as $1 billion.[71] Such abuses have led to repeated demands that the municipal bond industry be more closely regulated.[72]

As soon as the Great Recession began unfolding in the fall of 2008, hundreds of municipalities encountered problems with their bond investments. Like individuals, local government officials usually rely on experts in the financial industry to advise them on investments. One such advisor was David Rubin, who founded one of the leading consulting firms for municipal bonds, CDR Financial Products, in Beverly Hills, California. Beginning in the early 1990s, Rubin toured the country drumming up business, advising local government officials to refinance debt with risky interest-rate provisions (much like the adjustable-rate mortgages [ARMs] offered to homeowners) and invest in high-yielding but risky derivatives of the same kind that brought about the 2008 economic crisis. Rubin made campaign contributions even when these appeared to violate a ban imposed by the SEC. Some of his bonds ran up unusually high fees.[73] In Tennessee, Morgan Keegan was one of several firms invited by the state to run a seminar for local officials in 2008. By then, the company had already cornered the market in municipal bonds within the state; since 2001, it had sold $2 billion in bonds to 38 towns and counties. Because Morgan Keegan, like other financial firms, made higher commissions on derivative bonds rather than fixed-rate bonds, it took care to steer the clients into them. Right at the time that cities and towns in Tennessee began to see their municipal revenues fall, the interest rates they paid on the bonds soared because they were now considered risky.[74]

News broke in January 2009 that three federal agencies and several state attorneys general had been gathering evidence on price-fixing and collusion among municipal bond brokers. The sums involved were vast: States and cities bought $400 billion in bonds each year. Brokers, banks, and other firms divided up the spoils by secretly parceling out the business by fixing bids, which allowed them to reap higher fees. A system of campaign contributions and suspicious payments to governmental officials helped keep the system in place. An anti-trust lawyer representing state and local governments referred to it as "one of the longest-running, most economically pervasive antitrust conspiracies ever to be uncovered in the U.S."[75] Federal officials suggested that Congress adopt new regulations, but as late as February 2014, Congress had not taken up the matter. However, it is certain that federal and state agencies will continue their investigations, and more is bound to come to light.

In early 2015 and 2016, the SEC and the Justice Department launched respective investigations after a whistleblower complaint accused several big financial institutions, among them Bank of America, Citibank, JPMorgan Chase, Morgan Stanley, Goldman Sachs, Barclays, the Royal Bank of Canada, and Wells Fargo, of collusion on municipal bonds. The eight big banks allegedly colluded with one another in an attempt to get higher rates of return on variable rate demand obligation (VRDO) municipal bonds than they had originally agreed on in their remarketing agreements.[76] The consolidated lawsuit, *City of Philadelphia v. Bank of America Corporation*, is being led by the cities of Philadelphia and Baltimore, both of whom issued VRDOs worth $1.67 billion and $261 million, respectively, and alleged that the seven big banks shared proprietary information about their bond inventories, as well as rate changes.[77] In a 2020 opinion, U.S. District Judge Jesse Furman of the Southern District of New York argued that the two cities were within their rights in pursuing antitrust claims in a class-action lawsuit over how these banks marketed their VRDO municipal bonds between 2008 and 2016.[78] Both cities had argued that the banks' marketing scheme had had a significant negative impact on the availability of essential municipal funding for hospitals, power and sewage infrastructure, education and transportation, and other key social infrastructure funds. While Furman dismissed claims of unjust enrichment, he upheld the cities' key accusations of breach of contract and collusion against the banks.[79] How the final outcome of the case, which is yet to be decided, will impact the general regulations on municipal bonds remains to be seen.

Cities are at the mercy of the bond market because the cost of borrowing is basically determined by their bond ratings. A bond rating purports to represent the relative credit quality of the issuing municipality and thus determines the rate of interest a city must pay. A high rating means a lower interest rate, on the theory that there is less risk for the investor. When a city's bond rating is lowered due to fiscal problems, a bond may be more difficult to sell, and the additional interest paid over the amortized life of the bond can amount to millions of dollars.

Bond ratings are published by several national rating firms, but the big three include Moody's Investors Service, Standard and Poor's Corporation, and Fitch's Investor Service. Cities pay to have their bonds rated, but they have no choice but to seek a rating if they want to be able to market their bonds. Although the purpose of the rating is to assess risk, in fact, municipal bond ratings are totally unrelated to the likelihood of default. (Default may not mean the loan was not repaid; a payment may simply have missed a deadline.) The discrepancy in the interest rates between the highest and lowest investment grade bonds is inexplicable on the basis of relative risk.[80] From 1929 to 1933, when 77 percent of all municipal defaults of the twentieth century occurred, the highest-rated bonds recorded the highest incidence of default.[81] These statistics seems to indicate that ratings are almost worthless as a guide to investment, even though they give the ratings agencies a powerful voice in municipal fiscal policies.

It would be more or less impossible for the ratings to accurately reflect risk because cities so rarely fail to pay their debts. True, from the first recorded default in 1838 (Mobile, Alabama) through 1969, more than 6,000 bond defaults were recorded by local governments. Less than a third of these, however, involved incorporated municipalities (cities); most of the rest were small special districts that provided particular services such as irrigation. Seventy-five percent of all such failures occurred between 1930 and 1939, and less than 10 percent after the Great Depression.[82] During the worst period for municipal bonds, 1929 through 1937, only 8 percent of all cities and 20 percent of their bonded debt were ever in default, and almost all of the debts were eventually paid.[83]

From World War II through early 1970, a total of 431 state and local units defaulted on their obligations. The total principal involved was $450 million, approximately 0.4 percent of the outstanding state and local debt. Three special authorities, the West Virginia Turnpike Commission, the Calumet Skyway Toll Bridge, and the Chesapeake Bay Bridge and Tunnel Commission, accounted for over 74 percent of this amount (virtually all local governments are considered municipal in the bond market). Only 2 of 24 major default situations ($1 million or more) were related to general obligation bonds.[84] Of 114 defaults of less than $1 million, almost all were temporary or technical defaults. Of these, only 34 involved general obligation bonds and all of these involved cities with populations under 5,000 people.[85]

An analysis of cases filed in federal district courts between 1938 and 1971 reveals that nine cities took advantage of federal municipal bankruptcy legislation. With one exception (Saluda, North Carolina), all the cases came from rather obscure cities in Texas (Ranger, Talco, Benevides) or Florida (Manatee, Medley, Center Hill, Webster, Wanchula). Only in the case of Benevides (population 2,500) were general obligation bonds of post–World War II origin involved. In all other cases, the defaulted debt was of prewar origin, related to revenue bonds, or unrelated to bonds altogether.[86]

Before the state of Michigan put Detroit into receivership in 2013, no city had ever defaulted on its obligations, though in a very few cases, there were brief delays in paying bondholders. On December 15, 1978, Cleveland became the first major city to default, even in a technical sense, since 1933. On that day, the city failed to make payments on $14 million in short-term notes; the city renewed payments a few months later and officially ended default in 1980.[87] For the first time in decades, several cities defaulted on their loan payments during the Great Recession. Stockton, California, Jefferson County (Birmingham), Alabama, and Detroit declared bankruptcy. In these notable cases, investors may have to settle for less than full payment. Although we now know that in rare and extreme circumstances, cities may default, it would be virtually unthinkable that a state ever would, no matter how dire its budgetary situation might be.

The overwhelming weight of evidence indicates that except in unusual circumstances when it is clear that city is in trouble (one does not need a bond rater to determine such cases), there is little justification for the differential rating of city bonds except to make money for rating services, brokers, and investors. Nevertheless, the market in municipal bonds exerts a powerful influence on public officials by imposing a tight fiscal discipline and by reinforcing the dynamic of the metropolitan chase for business investment and affluent residents. The fact that local governments must finance nearly all their own activities without a regular source of aid from the national government forces them to place a high priority on promoting local economic development.

The Rise of Special Authorities

The terms "municipal debt" and the "municipal bond market" are convenient language devices used by just about everyone, but they are misleading in a very important respect: In fact, the biggest development and infrastructure projects are not financed directly by municipalities, but by independent special-purpose authorities that issue revenue bonds. If cities had been forced to rely on their own resources, they could not possibly have sustained the incredible level of public investment that has been poured into new urban infrastructure in recent decades. More than $2 billion was spent annually in the first half of the 1990s on sports facilities and convention centers alone.[88] By 2007, there were more than 35,000 special authorities in the United States, and they had issued $288 billion in new long-term debt.[89] In addition, billions of public dollars have been spent on urban entertainment and cultural districts, renovated waterfronts, aquariums, marketplaces, festival malls, and the other elements of urban lifestyle and the tourism/entertainment complex. Local officials have been resourceful in finding ways to finance public investment on this scale. The main instrument they have relied upon is the special-purpose authority.

Beginning in the 1980s, a generation of visionary mayors accepted the fact that they would have to find ways to regenerate their own economies. These "messiah mayors" preached a gospel of self-help for cities in desperate need of new ideas and directions. As noted by the historian Jon Teaford, "if nothing else the messiah mayors ... boosted the spirits of many urban dwellers and made them proud of their cities."[90] But much more was involved than cheerleading. These mayors also pioneered in the creation of institutions capable of financing and administering projects considered important for promoting the economic viability of the city. Thus, sports authorities were created for the purpose of building sports stadiums, mall authorities were incorporated to build and administer mall and entertainment complexes, and development corporations came into being to implement local development projects. These special-purpose authorities—institutions created to accomplish a specific public purpose—were essentially public development institutions run like a private corporation, established specifically to receive a combination of public subsidies and private investment funds.[91] They were empowered to earmark taxes, charge user fees, issue bonds, establish trust funds, and use other mechanisms for bringing public and private money together to finance big undertakings.[92]

This institutional device gave municipal officials a way out of the straitjacket of debt limitations imposed on municipal governments because they were now able to offload the costs of development onto institutions that were capable of generating their own resources; in this way, general obligation bonds backed by the municipal government could be replaced by revenue bonds issued by a separate entity. These public/private institutions were generally established through enabling legislation passed by state legislatures, and they were run by boards appointed by a governor and mayor, the mayor alone, or some combination of public officials. They were not bound by the rules that frustrated public initiatives by general-purpose governments. They could make decisions without worrying about what voters thought. Because they were run much like private corporations, they were able to protect their information and books from public scrutiny, but at the same time, because they pursued public objectives, they could act just like governments and generate revenue, receive funds from other governments, and borrow money and sell tax-free bonds.

The sprawling McCormick Place convention center and the renovated Navy Pier entertainment complex in Chicago provide good examples of how this works. Both are administered by the Metropolitan Pier and Exposition Authority (MPEA), which is governed by a board appointed by the mayor of Chicago and the governor of Illinois. The state of Illinois designates $98 million annually, derived from revenues from taxes (mainly a tax on cigarette sales) to pay off previous bonds for construction and remodeling.[93] In addition to this subsidy, in 2000, the MPEA floated a $108 million tax-exempt bond issue to build and own the Hyatt Regency McCormick Place Hotel[94] and completed a massive $750 million expansion in 2008. A combination of state subsidies and income from exhibitors and ticket sales for such events as the Chicago Auto Show, as well as rental fees for office space and other services, provide the center with the revenues to retire bonds and pay current operating expenses. In 2011, the MPEA outsourced the operation of Navy Pier to the newly formed, not-for-profit Navy Pier Inc. This effectively started shielding Navy Pier's previously public records from public scrutiny. MPEA also contracted the operations of McCormick Place out to be run by SMG, a global management company that same year. In 2017, the MPEA completed the construction of Wintrust Arena, a 10,000 seat arena, and an additional hotel tower, which, together, would add another component to the gigantic complex. But McPier has also come under scrutiny: Since the mid-2010s, the Better Government Association has attempted to acquire access to Navy Pier Inc.'s financial records, with Navy Pier Inc. fighting hard to maintain them sealed.[95] The BGA may have finally succeeded in 2021, when the Illinois Supreme Court sent the case back to the Illinois Appellate Court, which had previously, in 2020, ordered Navy Pier Inc to open its financial records.[96] The irony of a taxpayer-funded entity that has basically no accountability toward the public should not be lost on anyone. The *Chicago Tribune*'s editorial board said the following on the nature of public-private entities in 2021:

> Public-private partnerships are double edged. Mayor Lori Lightfoots's Investment South/West initiative is a public-private venture that enlists the private sector to help revitalize challenged neighborhoods on the South and West sides – an endeavor that shows promise. On the other hand, as with World Business Chicago and Navy Pier Inc., public-private entities can more easily shade their activities.[97]

Lightfoot's investment initiative has never held public meetings and therefore offers little to no public transparency and accountability.

It is a mistake to describe special authorities as mere mechanisms for financing and administrating large undertakings. They are also political in nature, in the sense that they are always on the lookout for ways to promote their own projects and enhance their fiscal and administrative capacity. In the case of the professional football and baseball stadiums in Baltimore, for example, an agency of the state government, the Maryland Stadium Authority, financed the two stadiums through proceeds from a sports lottery offered through the Maryland State Lottery.[98] The campaign to build the sports stadium was guided by this new agency, which commissioned studies to show a powerfully positive impact on Baltimore's economy. However, another study by a state agency estimated that the economic impact would be much lower, and independent studies sharply contested even the lower estimate as unrealistic, concluding that stadium development brought virtually no measurable economic benefit.[99]

The political nature of special authorities is illustrated in the case of the Denver Metropolitan Stadium District, which the Colorado legislature created in 1990 as a means of pushing forward plans for a new baseball stadium. The bill establishing the district did not contain financing mechanisms because any that would have been proposed would have ignited controversy. Instead, the task of lining up political support for a new stadium was left to the seven-member stadium district board. Securing financing was more a political than a fiscal exercise. In close collaboration with the city of Denver, the board ran an astute campaign that kept voters in the metropolitan counties outside Denver in the dark about whether the stadium might be built close to or within their own jurisdictions. The uncertainties about location carried the day. In August 1990, voters in the six-county district passed a sales tax levy to build the stadium; large majorities in the city and an adjacent county overcame a losing margin elsewhere.[100] Just as many voters had suspected, the fix had been in all along, and the stadium was built in downtown Denver. As all these examples illustrate, special purpose authorities are key players in the decision-making process about urban development, but they suffer from a serious lack of political transparency. In addition, their board members are appointed, not elected, which means that they do not face any electoral repercussions from disappointed voters.

Special-purpose authorities have sprung up to administer the many components that make up the tourism/entertainment complex in cities. In addition to the authorities established to finance and administer particular facilities such as convention centers, festival malls, and sports stadiums, redevelopment corporations have proliferated to refurbish business districts, revitalize neighborhoods, and provide amenities desired by local residents and visitors. In addition, since the 1980s, the number of tax increment finance (TIF) districts have multiplied. TIFs generate their revenues by marketing bonds to investors based on the taxes that are expected to be collected when a parcel of land is redeveloped. A TIF board, for example, might condemn homes in a residential neighborhood in order to take it for a new mall, which would be expected to generate sales tax revenue. These revenue projects would be used as the basis for a bond issue, which would provide the TIF district with the funds to make public improvements required by the mall developer. TIFs have become one of the main mechanisms for development in today's cities. For example, in 2002, there were more than 130 TIFs in the city of Chicago and 217 in suburban Cook County.[101]

The proliferation of special-purpose authorities throughout metropolitan areas has removed more and more of the most important public policies from general-purpose municipalities. Although municipalities are run democratically—with mayors, city councils, and other elected officials—special-purpose authorities operate out of the public eye. Some of the most expensive and sometimes controversial undertakings have been assigned to special-purpose authorities. Convention centers and stadiums are built with public money but with little or no public input. An absence of public accountability always raises troubling questions. In the 1950s, urban renewal authorities regularly abused their powers. Transportation authorities rammed highways through urban neighborhoods. Then, as now, the application of governmental authority without adequate public accountability led to abuses. The fiscal politics of metropolitan competition tempts governments to build now and ask questions later. In the competitive environment of today's metropolitan areas, it is a lesson worth remembering.

Fiscal Gamesmanship

Countless activities financed by cities are essential to the health and well-being of citizens. In a nation in which nearly 40 percent of citizens lack health insurance, they are frontline providers of health services provided through public hospitals and clinics, not only for the poor but also for families of the underinsured middle class. They provide essential housing services, even if most of this takes the form of contributing to or maintaining homeless shelters. These are only the normal, day-to-day activities. And in time of emergency, they are expected to do much more.

Between July 17 and 20, 1995, the city of Chicago was hit by a heat wave in which temperatures reached 106 degrees. City officials were not only unprepared, but they also did not feel it was in their purview to respond except through normal emergency services. By the time the heat wave had run its course, the number of excess deaths attributed to the heat wave reached 739. Realizing a repeat of such a disaster would become a public relations nightmare as well as a social catastrophe; the city subsequently (but quietly) put into place an emergency plan to mobilize its personnel and resources if a similar disaster struck.[102] The tragic events of that summer revealed a simple truth: Cities simply cannot opt out of their responsibilities without endangering the welfare of their citizens.

The ability of city officials to respond when needed is determined by the resources at hand, and these are always subject to change. Economic downturns play havoc with local budgets, but there is little or nothing that cities can do to avoid them. They try to control what they can, and this leads them to a developmental politics that promotes growth, sometimes at the expense of other objectives. Paul Peterson, a leading scholar of urban politics, has taken the position that because economic or market standing is fundamentally important to cities and their citizens, they should do nothing that might compromise the possibility of achieving economic success.[103] This logic leads him to conclude that cities should avoid policies that redistribute resources from wealthier to poorer residents; obviously, health clinics and homeless shelters (for example) would fit into this category. This position may provoke disagreement, but urban leaders often act as if they believe it is true. This makes them play a delicate game in which they try to balance the needs of their most vulnerable citizens against the goal of preserving a climate that lures new investment and keeps middle-class residents and businesses from moving elsewhere. It is a game made all the more dicey because most of the rules are set by other governments and by the institutions of the private economy.

Endnotes

1 Monica Davey, "States and Localities Angle for Stimulus Cash," *The New York Times* (February 15, 2009), www.nytimes.com/2009/02/16/us/politics/16stimulus.html.

2 Irma Esparza Diggs, "What the Senate Infrastructure Bill Means for Local Governments," *National League of Cities*, (August 10, 2021), https://www.nlc.org/article/2021/08/10/what-the-senate-infrastructure-bill-means-for-local-governments/.

3 Thomas H. Boast, "A Political Economy of Urban Capital Finance in the United States" (Ph.D. dissertation, Cornell University, 1977), p. 114.

4 U.S. Bureau of the Census, *2007 Census of Governments* (2007), Table 2, http://www2.census.gov/govs/estimate/07slsstab2a.xls. For national government transfers as a proportion of local revenue in Japan, see Japanese Ministry of Internal Affairs and Communications, White Paper on Local Public Finance (2005), www.soumu.go.jp/iken/zaisei/17data/jyoukyou_e.pdf.

5 Carol W. Lewis, "Budgetary Balance: The Norm, Concept, and Practice in Large U.S. Cities," *Public Administration Review* 54, no. 6 (November/December 1994): 517–518.

6 U.S. Bureau of the Census, *2002 Census of Governments*, vol. 3, *Public Employment* (2002), Tables 1 and 3, www.census.gov/prod/2004pubs/gc023x2.pdf; *2002 Census of Governments*, vol. 4, no. 5, *Compendium of Government Finances* (2002), Table 4; U.S. Bureau of the Census, *Statistical Abstract of the United States, 2003* (Washington, D.C.: U.S. Government Printing Office), p. 322, Table 475.

7 *Urban Institute*, "State and Local Expenditures," State and Local Financial Initiative (2011–Present), https://www.urban.org/policy-centers/cross-center-initiatives/state-and-local-finance-initiative/state-and-local-backgrounders/state-and-local-expenditures.

8 *The Council of the City of New York*, Corey Johnson, Daniel Dromm, Vanessa Gibson, Latonia R. McKinney, "Report of the Finance Division on the Fiscal 2020 Executive Budget" (May 6, 2019), p. 1, https://council.nyc.gov/budget/wp-content/uploads/sites/54/2019/06/FY20-Expense-Revenue-and-Capital-Report.pdf.

9 Mayor Lori E. Lightfoot, "2020 Budget Overview," *The City of Chicago*, p. 5, https://www.chicago.gov/content/dam/city/depts/obm/supp_info/2020Budget/2020BudgetOverview.pdf.

10 *Central City Association of Los Angeles*, "CCA Reflections: LA City Budget 101" (June 24, 2020), https://www.ccala.org/news/2020/06/24/cca-reflects/cca-reflects-la-city-budget-101/.

11 Gary Washburn, "City Maps Long-Term Homeless Program," *Chicago Tribune* (January 22, 2003), p. 3.

12 John Byrne, "Emanuel Turns over Homeless Services to Catholic Charities," *Chicago Tribune* (August 23, 2012). Accessed online: http://articles.chicagotribune.com/2012-08-23/news/chi-emanuel-turns-over-homeless-services-to-catholic-charities-20120823_1_homeless-shelters-homeless-youth-homeless-services.

13 John Byrne, "Emanuel Makes Moves on Homelessness; Critics Still Boo," *Chicago Tribune* (May 2, 2016). Accessed online: www.chicagotribune.com/news/politics/ct-rahm-emanuel-homeless-airbnb-tax-20160503-story.html.

14 Roy Bahl, Jorge Martinez, and Loren Williams, "The Fiscal Conditions of U.S. Cities at the Beginning of the 1990s," Urban Institute Conference on Big City Governance and Fiscal Choices, Los Angeles (June 1991), pp. 5–6.

15 Elizabeth Kneebone, "The Changing Geography of US Poverty," *Brookings* (February 15, 2017), https://www.brookings.edu/testimonies/the-changing-geography-of-us-poverty/.

16 Ibid.

17 Ibid.

18 Jonathan Kozol, *Rachel and Her Children: Homeless Families in America* (New York: Crown, 1988), p. 14.

19 *Garcia v. San Antonio Metropolitan Transit Authority*, 469 U.S. 528 (1985).

20 Employment Standards Administration, *Minimum Wage and Maximum Hours Standards Under the Fair Labor Standards Act* (Washington, D.C.: U.S. Environmental Protection Agency, 1986), pp. 110–111; U.S. Congress, House Committee on Education and Labor, *Report to Accompany H.R. 3530*, 99th Cong., 1st sess., 1985. H. Rept. 99–331, p. 30; both cited in Joseph F. Zimmerman, "Federally Induced State and Local Governmental Costs," paper delivered at the annual meeting of the American Political Science Association (Washington, D.C., August 29–September 1, 1991), p. 14.

21 Helen F. Ladd and John Yinger, *America's Ailing Cities: Fiscal Health and the Design of Urban Policy*, updated ed. (Baltimore, MD: Johns Hopkins University Press, 1989), p. 291.

22 Any summary of revenue sources for all cities is misleading and therefore not presented in this chapter. Cities simply vary too much for such summaries to be meaningful; earnings taxes can be collected by a few cities, but not most, sales taxes are allowed by 28 states, and so forth.

23 Michael A. Pagano, *City Fiscal Conditions in 2002: A Research Report on America's Cities* (Washington, D.C.: National League of Cities, 2002), p. 3.

24 Eric A. Anderson, "Changing Municipal Finances," *Urban Data Services Reports* 7, no. 12 (Washington, D.C.: International City Manager Association, December 1975), p. 2.

25 Megan Randall, "Census of Governments Illustrates Declining Aid to Localities, Other Trends in State and Local Finance," Figure: "Direct Federal Transfers to Local Governments," *Tax Policy Center, TaxVox: State and Local Issues,* https://www.taxpolicycenter.org/taxvox/census-governments-illustrates-declining-aid-localities-other-trends-state-and-local-finance.

26 Refer to Richard T. Ely, *Taxation in American States and Cities* (New York: Crowell, 1888), pp. 109–113; and Sumner Benson, "A History of the General Property Tax," in *The American Property Tax: Its History, Administration, and Economic Impact,* ed. C.G. Benson, S. Benson, H. McClelland, and P. Thompson (Claremont, CA: College Press, 1965), p. 24.

27 E.R.A. Seligman, *Essays in Taxation,* 9th ed. (New York: Macmillan, 1923), p. 24.

28 U.S. Bureau of the Census, *Historical Statistics of the United States: Colonial Times to 1970,* Bicentennial ed., pt. 2 (Washington, D.C.: U.S. Government Printing Office, 1975), p. 1133.

29 Calculated from the data in U.S. Bureau of the Census, *Local Government Finances in Selected Metropolitan Areas and Large Counties: 1969–70,* GF 70, no. 6 (Washington, D.C.: U.S. Government Printing Office, 1970), p. 7; U.S. Bureau of the Census, *Local Government Finances in Selected Metropolitan Areas and Large Counties: 1974–75,* GF 75, no. 6 (Washington, D.C.: U.S. Government Printing Office, 1976), p. 7.

30 U.S. Bureau of the Census, *2002 Census of Governments,* vol. 4, no. 4, *Finances of Municipal and Township Governments* (2002), Table 1, www.census.gov/prod/2005pubs/gc024x4.pdf.

31 George Peterson, "Finance," in *The Urban Predicament,* ed. William Gorham and Nathan Glazer (Washington, D.C.: The Urban Institute, 1976), p. 52.

32 Karen de Sa, "Santa Clara County Assessor Warns of Dramatic Plunge in Home Values, Lowered Taxes to Result," MercuryNews.com, www.mercurynews.com/ci_12068004?source.

33 Patrik Jonsson, "As Home Values Fall, Property Tax Revolt Brews," *The Christian Science Monitor* (April 2, 2009), features.csmonitor.com/economyrebuild/2009/04/02.

34 Alfred Balk, *The Free List—Property Without Taxes* (New York: Russell Sage Foundation, 1971), pp. 10–12.

35 J. Richard Aronson and John L. Hilley, *Financing State and Local Governments,* 4th ed. (Washington, D.C.: Brookings Institution Press, 1986), p. 136.

36 Ladd and Yinger, *America's Ailing Cities,* pp. 129–130, 180. See also Michael Wolkoff, "Municipal Tax Abatement: A Two-Edged Sword," *New York Case Studies in Public Management,* no. 4 (Albany, NY: Rockefeller Institute of Government, 1984).

37 Daphne A. Kenyon and Adam H. Langley, "Payments in Lieu of Taxes: Balancing Municipal and Nonprofit Interests." Policy Focus Report, *The Lincoln Institute of Land Policy,* 2010. Accessed online: https://www.lincolninst.edu/pubs/dl/1853_1174_PILOTs%20PFR%20final.pdf.

38 Michael A. Pagano, "How Nonprofits Can End Up Becoming a Drain on City Budgets," *City Lab, The Atlantic* (November 12, 2012). Accessed online: http://www.citylab.com/work/2012/11/how-nonprofits-can-end-becoming-drain-city-budgets/3798/.

39 Gregory H. Wassall, *Tax-Exempt Property: A Case Study of Hartford, Connecticut* (Hartford, CT: John C. Lincoln Institute, 1974), p. 27.

40 Todd Swanstrom, *Capital Cities: Challenges and Opportunities* (Albany, NY: Rockefeller Institute of Government), p. 17.

41 Michael J. Barrett, "The Out-of-Towners," *Boston Globe Magazine* (August 7, 1983).

42 *Walz v. Tax Commission of the City of New York,* 397 U.S. 664 (1970). See also Boris I. Bittker, "Churches, Taxes and the Constitution," *Yale Law Review* 78 (July 1969): 1285–1310.

43 John L. Mikesell, "The Season of Tax Revolt," in *Fiscal Retrenchment and Urban Policy,* ed. John P. Blair and David Nachmias (Beverly Hills, CA: Sage, 1979), p. 109.

44 Ibid.

45 Pagano, *City Fiscal Conditions in 2002*, p. 3.

46 Ibid.

47 Douglas F. Morgan, Kent S. Robinson, Dennis Strachota, and James A. Hough, *Budgeting for Local Governments and Communities* (New York, NY: Routledge, 2015).

48 Christopher Swope, "The Retail Chase: Cities Will Do Almost Anything to Land the Store of Their Dreams," *Governing* (April 2007), p. 28.

49 Kenneth Thomas, *Competing for Capital: Europe and North America in a Global Era* (Washington, D.C.: Georgetown University Press, 2000), as cited in Rachel Weber, "What Makes a Good Economic Development Deal?" in *Retooling for Growth: Rebuilding a 21st Century Economy in America's Older Industrial Areas*, ed. Richard M. McGahey and Jennifer S. Vey (Washington, D.C.: Brookings Institution Press, 2008), p. 284.

50 Donald Bartlett and James Steele, "Corporate Welfare," *Time* (November 9, 1998), as quoted in Rachel Weber, "What Makes a Good Economic Development Deal?" in *Retooling for Growth: Rebuilding a 21st Century Economy in America's Older Industrial Areas*, ed. Richard M. McGahey and Jennifer S. Vey (Washington, D.C.: Brookings Institution Press, 2008), p. 284.

51 Christiana McFarland, "State of America's Cities Survey: Local Retail Slowdown," Research Brief on America's Cities, by National League of Cities, Issue 2009-2, www.nlc.org.

52 Ibid., p. 20.

53 Michael Pagano, *City Fiscal Conditions in 199,* (Washington, D.C.: National League of Cities, Center for City Solutions, 1991), p. 24.

54 David Segal, "Cities Turn to Fees to Fill Budget Gaps," *The New York Times* (April 10, 2009), www.nytimes.com/2009/04/11/busines/11fees.html.

55 Michael Powell and Christine Haughney, "Wary of Taxes, Officials Boost Fees; Tactic Hurts Poor and Working Class, Critics Say," *Washington Post* (April 7, 2003), p. A3.

56 Mark Stryker and John Gallagher, "Detroit Zoo Giraffe? Belle Isle? Detroit's Treasure Trove Could Be Vulnerable to Sale to Settle Debt," *Detroit Free Press* (June 2, 2013), http://www.freep.com/article/20130602/NEWS01/306020080/Detroit-bankruptcy-assets-sale-DIA.

57 Ibid.

58 Bonds issued not only by cities but also by states and all local governments are referred to as municipal bonds, a cause of endless confusion.

59 Cities in most states can also borrow short term, using tax anticipation notes (TANs) repaid in 30–120 days to cover temporary budget shortages or to time their entry into the long-term bond market. Unlike the federal government, cities cannot use bond funds to cover long-term operating deficits.

60 U.S. Bureau of the Census, *2007 Census of Governments*, vol. 4, no. 5, *Local Government Finances by Type of Government and State* (2007), Table 2. http://www2.census.gov/govs/estimate/07slsstab2a.xls.

61 *South Carolina v. Baker*, 108 S.Ct. 1935 (1988).

62 Alberta Sbragia, "Finance Capital and the City," in *Cities in Stress: A New Look at the Urban Crisis*, ed. Mark Gottdiener (Beverly Hills, CA: Sage, 1986), p. 210.

63 See Robert Huefner, *Taxable Alternatives to Municipal Bonds, Research Report No. 53* (Boston, MA: Federal Reserve Bank of Boston, 1972); and *Building a Broader*

Market: Report of the Twentieth Century Fund Task Force on the Municipal Bond Market, with a background paper by Ronald W. Forbes and John E. Peterson (New York: McGraw-Hill, 1976).

64 For insightful discussions of the powerful role of local authorities, see Ann Marie Hauck Walsh, *The Public's Business: The Politics and Practices of Government Corporations* (Cambridge, MA: MIT Press, 1978); and Alberta M. Sbragia, *Debt Wish: Entrepreneurial Cities, U.S. Federalism, and Economic Development* (Pittsburgh, PA: University of Pittsburgh Press, 1996).

65 Elaine B. Sharp, "The Politics and Economics of the New City Debt," *American Political Science Review* 80, no. 4 (December 1986): 1271–1288.

66 U.S. Bureau of the Census, *Statistical Abstract of the United States* (Washington, D.C.: U.S. Government Printing Office, 1992), p. 285.

67 Thomas A. Pascarella and Richard D. Raymond, "Buying Bonds for Business: An Evaluation of the Industrial Revenue Bond Program," *Urban Affairs Quarterly* 18, no. 1 (September 1982): 73–89.

68 Daphne A. Kenyon and Dennis Zimmerman, "Private-Activity Bonds and the Volume Cap in 1990," *Intergovernmental Perspective* 17, no. 3 (Summer 1991): 35–37.

69 For citations on municipal bond corruption, see Sbragia, *Debt Wish,* pp. 224–225.

70 Leslie Wayne, "Ban on Political Contributions Considered for Bond Lawyers," *The New York Times* (August 5, 1996), p. D2.

71 Peter Truell, "Municipal Bond Dealers Face Scrutiny," *The New York Times* (December 17, 1996), p. D1; Michael R. Lissack, "A Giant Shell Game Snares Taxpayers," *Albany Times Union* (August 1, 1996), p. A11.

72 "Shine the Light on Muni Deals," *BusinessWeek* (August 26, 1996).

73 Mary Williams, "Bond Advice Leaves Pain in Its Wake," *The New York Times* (February 16, 2009), www.nytimes.com/2009/02/17/business/17muni.html.

74 Don Van Natta Jr., "Firm Acted as Tutor in Selling Towns Risky Deals," *The New York Times* (April 7, 2009), www.nytimes.com/2009/04/08/us/08bond.html.

75 Mary Williams Walsh, "Nationwide Inquiry on Bids for Municipal Bonds," *The New York Times* (January 8, 2009), www.nytimes.com/2009/01/09/business/09insure.html.

76 Mike Leonard, "Goldman, Citi, BofA, Others to Face Muni Bond Price-Fixing Suit," *Bloomberg Law* (November 2, 2020), https://news.bloomberglaw.com/antitrust/goldman-citi-bofa-others-to-face-muni-bond-price-fixing-suit.

77 Jonathan Stempel, "Eight Big Banks Must Face U.S. Cities' Allegations of Municipal Bond Collusion," *Metro* (November 2, 2020), https://www.metro.us/eight-big-banks-must/.

78 Ibid.

79 Ibid.

80 Thomas Geis, "Municipal Credit and Bond Rating System," paper delivered at the Municipal Officers Association Meeting (Denver, May 31, 1972), pp. 5–6.

81 Ibid.

82 U.S. Advisory Commission on Intergovernmental Relations, *City Financial Emergencies* (Washington, D.C.: U.S. Government Printing Office, 1971), p. 10.

83 Ibid., p. 12.

84 Ibid., p. 16.

85 Ibid., p. 17.

86 Ibid., pp. 81–82.

87 Todd Swanstrom, *The Crisis of Growth Politics: Cleveland, Kucinich, and the Challenge of Urban Populism* (Philadelphia, PA: Temple University Press, 1985), Chapter 7.

88 Peter Eisenger, "The Politics of Bread and Circuses," *Urban Affairs Review* 35, no. 3 (January 2000): 316–333.

89 U.S. Bureau of the Census, *2007 Census of Governments, Local Government Finances by Type of Government* (2002), Table 2, http://www2.census.gov/govs/estimate/07slsstab2a.xls.

90 Jon Teaford, *The Rough Road to Renaissance: Urban Revitalization in America, 1940–1985* (Baltimore, MD: Johns Hopkins University Press, 1990), p. 307.

91 These arrangements are described in Peter K. Eisenger, *The Rise of the Entrepreneurial State: State and Local Economic Development Policy in the United States* (Madison: University of Wisconsin Press, 1988).

92 James Leigland, "Public Infrastructure and Special Purposed Governments: Who Pays and How?" in *Building the Public City: The Politics, Governance, and Finance of Public Infrastructure*, ed. David C. Perry (Thousand Oaks, CA: Sage, 1995), p. 139.

93 State of Illinois, Compliance Audit Report (1998 and 1999), www.state.il.us/auditor.

94 William Fulton, "Paying the Bill," *Governing* 15, no. 11 (August 2002): 60.

95 The Editorial Board, "Shine the Light on McCormick Place, Navy Pier Financial Secrets," *The Chicago Tribune* (April 2, 2021), https://www.chicagotribune.com/opinion/editorials/ct-prem-editorial-navy-pier-bga-transparency-mcpier-20210402-2u4dj55ygbhxron33x54cycdf4-story.html.

96 Ibid.

97 Ibid.

98 Donald F. Norris, "If We Build It, They Will Come! Tourism-Based Economic Development in Baltimore," in *The Infrastructure of Play: Building the Tourist City*, ed. Dennis R. Judd (Armonk, NY: M. E. Sharpe, 2003), p. 162.

99 Ibid., p. 151.

100 Susan E. Clarke and Martin Saiz, "From Waterhole to World City: Place Luck and Public Agendas in Denver," in *The Infrastructure of Play*, ed. Dennis R. Judd (Armonk, NY: M. E. Sharpe, 2003), pp. 183–184.

101 Rachel Weber, "Equity and Entrepreneurialism: The Impact of Tax Increment Financing on School Finance," *Urban Affairs Review* 38, no. 5 (2003): 619–644.

102 Eric Klinenberg, *Heat Wave: A Social Autopsy of Disaster in Chicago* (Chicago, IL: University of Chicago Press, 2002), p. 9.

103 Paul Peterson, *City Limits* (Chicago, IL: University of Chicago Press, 1981), p. 22.

CHAPTER 12

Cities and the Challenges of Climate Change

The Threat of Water

By 2021, the human impact on the world's climate has become an undisputed scientific fact. A study published in October of that year found that at least 85 percent of the world's population have experienced weather events exacerbated by climate change.[1] Our climate is changing, often violently, and places where many people live in close proximity to one another, are exceptionally vulnerable to devastating disasters.

Hurricane Katrina, which struck the city of New Orleans in September 2005, was one of the deadliest hurricanes in the history of the United States. It claimed over 1,800 lives—1,170 of those in the State of Louisiana alone.[2] The flooding in the aftermath of the hurricane submerged 80 percent of the City of New Orleans and surrounding parishes under up to 20 feet of water.[3]

Hurricane Sandy, which struck the New York City tri-state area in October 2012, wrought disaster to the Island of Manhattan, as well as to the New Jersey and Long Island coast lines. Approximately 300 homes were completely destroyed, 69,000 residential units damaged, and 44 lives lost in New York City alone.[4] The financial fallout for New York City from the storm's destructive force, as well as from lost economic activity, was $19 billion.[5]

Hurricane Harvey made landfall in Texas in late August of 2017 as a category 4 hurricane, killing at least 68 people in the State of Texas alone, more than half of those in Harris County, which includes Houston.[6] Its biggest impact was on the city of Houston, where it caused catastrophic flooding, as the city recorded all-time high flood stages.[7] The damage from the fallout of the storm is estimated to be around $125 billion.[8]

Undoubtedly, hurricanes have gained in intensity over recent decades. According to a 2013 study, which found a significant increase in the proportion of category 4 and 5 storms, the strongest hurricanes on record, in recent decades, this change is likely caused by rising ocean temperatures.[9] At the same time, there appears to be a decrease in lower-intensity storms, such as category 1 and 2 hurricanes. Hurricanes also appear to be intensifying more rapidly, with winds gaining high speeds over a shorter period of time. Most prominently, hurricanes tend to produce more rain, as climate change is causing our air to continuously get warmer and, therefore, to hold moisture more efficiently. Therefore, storms like Hurricane Harvey, which produced an unprecedented amount of rainfall, are going to become much more commonplace. A researcher at MIT calculated an increase in likelihood by six times for such a record rainfall to occur.[10]

Rising water levels from melting polar ice caps, in combination with bigger storm surges from increased intensity hurricanes, and significantly more rainfall, means a significant threat for cities along the eastern seaboard of the United States, where hurricanes form during the late summer and early fall. New York City, in particular, has had to grapple with a growing threat of storm-surge related flooding. Some researchers found that, due to rising sea levels, the return period for a 500-year flood during the pre-industrial period has fallen to only 25 years in the early twenty-first century and is projected to fall to a mere five years by mid-century.[11] Many neighborhoods of the city that are built on landfill are expected to return to the sea within the next century. New York City is by far not the only city that is threatened by climate change: Charleston, South Carolina, Miami, New Orleans, and Houston are other cities that are severely threatened by the rising sea levels and strengthening storm intensity that climate change will inevitably bring.

Some cities have started to seriously consider implementing measures to limit the impact of flooding and storm surges for their most vulnerable areas: In New York City, strategies for flood mitigation range from nature-based initiatives to downright fortification.[12] Nature-based flood protection systems include beaches and dune creation, as well as the protection and expansion of coastal wetlands, which can serve as a buffer against flooding. Maritime forests and living shorelines similarly tolerate high amounts of salt water while stabilizing shorelines by adding structure and organic materials as a buffer. On the other hand, hard structures, such as seawalls, floodgates, levees, and other physical barriers, can protect the urban floodplain from heavy flooding by simply blocking the water. The most reasonable and likely-to-be-successful approach for most cities, like New York City, will be a combination of such measures, also called Integrated Flood Protection Systems. In trying to come up with the most appropriate response to the threat of storm surges and flooding, New York City is looking to cities like New Orleans, or Rotterdam in the Netherlands, for their integrated approaches to protect their extremely vulnerable coastlines.[13]

Still, flood resiliency planning and implementation, as anything else, appear to be a question of privilege. In New York City, resiliency planning has focused mainly on Lower Manhattan, which, admittedly, is extremely vulnerable to storm surges and flooding but also contains an agglomeration of concentrated wealth. Other, less wealthy areas, which may be similarly threatened, have seen little to no initiative for planning ahead.

In New Orleans, after Hurricane Katrina in 2005, high-stakes investments were made in protective infrastructure in order to prevent similar disasters in the future. The big test came on August 29, 2021, when Hurricane Ida, a category 4 storm, made landfall in New Orleans on the 16th anniversary of Hurricane Katrina. The walls, floodgates, levees, and pumps worked well, and New Orleans experienced minimal flooding and a death toll of 13, which, while still devastating, accounted for a fraction of the more than 1,000 people who died in the aftermath of Hurricane Katrina. Other, smaller and considerably poorer, towns were not so lucky. Just a few miles away, smaller, working-class towns on the bayou have been vying for funding for a similarly sophisticated system of protective measures as the ones that New Orleans currently has—with little to no success.[14] The New York Times reports that, as storm severity and threats increase, so does the cost—putting state legislatures in the impossible situation of having to decide which places will be saved and which will be left to their own devices amid ever more threatening weather events.[15] Questions about disaster-related funding have grown increasingly Darwinist and tend to revolve around questions of head counts and viability. Put another way, federal and state officials, when allocating disaster preparedness funding, have to ask themselves which sorts of investments could be considered a good use of taxpayer money: Small towns on a disappearing coastline tend to not make the federal viability cut. State officials in Louisiana have been arguing to the contrary: They have noted that implementing a system of protective levees along the Louisiana coastline now could, in fact, save federal dollars by preemptively reducing the cost of cleanups, as well as the amount of individual and business relief claims in the aftermath of storms.[16] A program to help shore up the Louisiana coastline along the Gulf was devised decades ago and approved by Congress in 1992 but has not yet received any federal funding. Morganza, as it is called, is intended to protect about a quarter of a million people from flooding. Localities have so far provided about $1 billion in funding and are hoping for another $2 billion from the federal government.[17] Morganza's levee system received $12.5 million in federal funding during the first nine months of 2021, but hopes are high for much more federal funding to arrive.[18] Local officials have argued that about one-fifth of the nation's oil comes from Louisiana and that much of it is being refined along the endangered coastline.[19] The federal focus, however, in determining where the funding for water resiliency gets allocated has been on population density, causing the working-class towns on the bayou to lose out on funding year after year. The federal approach seems questionable, at best: Determining aid for citizens purely based on a cost-benefit analysis comes across as a rather strange approach in a democracy.

Flood resilience has been taking place on a more micro-level scale as well: Besides cities and neighborhoods, buildings, too, are trying to become more resilient to flooding. The American Copper Buildings in New York City represent one example of such resiliency: Inspired by the havoc wrought on Manhattan by Superstorm Sandy in 2012, which turned the footprint in Murray Hill, in which the buildings now stand, into a pond, the buildings were constructed to be resilient to environmental impacts, such as flooding and storm surges, brought about by climate change. Emergency generators throughout the building are able to provide power for an indefinite amount of time in the event of widespread power loss.[20] Common spaces are outfitted with stone and copper instead of wood, both of which are able to withstand flooding without incurring damage. Giant drainage tubes are intended to transport water away from the building into the city's water reservoirs. Such resiliency planning has become more commonplace in luxury buildings all across the city, but it comes at a price: According to the building's (probably COVID-inflated) 2021 listings, a studio apartment rents at $3,790 per month, and a three-bedroom apartment is available for $17,170 a month.[21] While American Copper has 160 subsidized affordable units available (starting at $900 for a one-bedroom apartment), it has received more than 79,000 applications for those units.[22] Once again, the wealthy will be well-equipped to withstand the next flood, but for the less fortunate, climate change remains a fundamental threat to their very existence.

Money, however, is not an impenetrable shield against the threat of climate change. In October 2021, *The New York Times* ran a story on the effects of climate change on two towns in North Carolina, Avon and Fair Bluff, that experience flooding on a regular basis, one wealthy and one less so, and the question of whether they could be saved.[23] Avon, a wealthy, majority-white town in the Outer Banks, has been dealing with significant coastal erosion and storm-surge flooding. Because it benefits from the tourist industry and has a good number of wealthy residents, it for now has the resources to at least buy time to consider how and whether to adapt to climate change. Fair Bluff, a majority-Black, working-class community with a good number of retirees, is less well-positioned to defend against and recover from climate change. A significant number of blocks in the city still look like the last hurricane (Florence) hit yesterday, instead of years ago, in 2018. Yet, many residents are attached to the city and hesitant to abandon it completely. FEMA has offered local residents additional resources if they decide to leave Fair Bluff and relocate. Yet, while Avon, due to its significant financial resources, is better able to recover from flooding and storm damage than Fair Bluff, Avon, too, has started to face questions as to whether its residents may abandon it altogether. Money, Avon's city officials have started to suspect, will only keep the city afloat for so long. Even financial resources to increase preparedness may not be enough to ward off the catastrophic effects of climate change over time, as cities on the Eastern Seaboard face more and more extreme flooding and coastal erosion.

The Unpredictability of Climate Change

Flooding and storm surges are only one of the myriad issues that climate change has wrought. For the east coast, at least, as some local officials across the country have observed, the challenges of climate change are somewhat predictable: Cities can plan and fortify against the water, knowing that it will come eventually, but the onslaught will still happen relatively incrementally. Such relative predictability is absent in other parts of the country. Far away from the treacherous storms along the eastern seaboard of the United States and equally far removed from the ever-growing wildfires threatening the west coast, the City of Chicago is experiencing its own reckoning with climate change.

The City on the Lake has been thriving on and coexisting with the water since its founding. In part because of its ideal location at the heart of the country and near one of the nation's Great Lakes, Chicago grew into the country's third-largest city and a global powerhouse, as far as cities go. For over a century, Chicago has not only been able to benefit from its close proximity to Lake Michigan, but it has been able to control the lake and exploit it to its own benefit. The construction of the Illinois and Michigan Canal, which connected the Great Lakes to the Mississippi River in 1836, had propelled Chicago from a small, swampy outpost into a thriving metropolis by the end of the nineteenth century. The city had become a major shipping port for raw materials that moved from the American heartland to other ports around the country and beyond. However, with its explosive growth came water pollution so intense that it threatened—over time—the city's freshwater reservoir, Lake Michigan, into which the Chicago River sloshed animal carcasses and factory wastewater. The Chicago River is said to have been so polluted at one point toward the end of the nineteenth century that it would randomly catch on fire.

Chicago being Chicago—a city that built skyscrapers on swampy ground and connected the Great Lakes to the Great River—once again outplayed the basic physics of nature: To solve the problem, it simply reversed the flow of the Chicago River, away from Lake Michigan. This audacious move, according to folk tales, is to have famously fueled the already existing rivalry between Chicago and St. Louis, as Chicago was now sending its sewage and garbage down the Mississippi River in the direction of its smaller rival. The Chicago Sanitary District, founded in 1889, replaced the Illinois and Michigan Canal with the Chicago Sanitary and Ship Canal, reversing the Chicago River to flow southward through an intricate system of locks. This remarkable work of engineering was named Civil Engineering Monument of the Millennium by the American Society of Civil Engineers in 1999, and it worked, for the most part, flawlessly for more than 100 years—until it didn't.

Climate change has, in recent years, caused Chicago's bodies of water—the lake and the river—to become increasingly unpredictable. Storm surges from Lake Michigan have become more extreme over the past half-century, causing the city to dramatically expand its system of water reservoirs and underground drainage tunnels in recent years. Draining the waiter, however, seems no longer sufficient. Chicago, as of late, seems to be oscillating between extremes: Whereas the water level of Lake Michigan has fluctuated by only a few inches in the past, the rise and fall of its water level have recently reached unprecedented extremes: In 2013, the lake plummeted to its lowest point ever recorded, only to climb back to record heights the following summer.[24]

The New York Times commented foreshadowingly: "In just seven years, Lake Michigan had swung more than six feet. It was an ominous sign that the inland sea, yoked for centuries to its historic shoreline, is starting to buck."[25]

Climate change has caused the evaporation and precipitation of water to become more extreme, which is particularly significant for a lake as big as Lake Michigan. Rising temperatures around the Great Lakes region have caused the air to grow more humid, which has translated into much higher amounts of precipitation over the past 30 years. But those rising temperatures have also caused higher-than-average evaporation of water within the same region.[26] In addition, the destabilization of the polar vortex has also been the source of much colder-than-normal winters in Chicago, which, in turn, results in lower water temperatures and less evaporation.[27] In combination, all these phenomena have caused the lake to act in greater extremes and jump from extreme drought to extreme flooding within a matter of a year.[28]

After the 2013 record drought, in May 2020, Chicago experienced an unprecedented storm. Usually, when the water rises dramatically, the city's "river managers" open the lock gates within the Chicago River and temporarily reverse its flow into Lake Michigan in order to save the city from disastrous flooding. The trigger point, which is intended to reverse the flow of the river, is 3.5 feet above the city's ground level.[29] But the unprecedented amount of precipitation across the city had caused both the lake and the river to rise to unprecedented levels, threatening the city's very existence. In a breathtaking report of that night, *The New York Times* documented the utter helplessness of one of Chicago's river managers amid the overwhelming amount of water and the utter lack of options:

> There was nothing in the playbook for this scenario. Mr. Valley and the lock operators had to wing it, pinching the gates closed to let the river rise again above the lake, then swinging them open again to let the swollen river drain into the lake. (…) Still, it was not enough. The river kept climbing, eventually peaking at +5.12 feet a little after 7pm.

The commendable efforts of the river managers most certainly prevented a larger disaster in Chicago that night. However, they could not prevent the river from eventually flooding Lower Wacker Drive, one of the Loop's central thoroughfares, and causing a power outage in the entire Willis Tower (previously Sears Tower), the city's tallest skyscraper. More than 1,500 residential basements were reported to have been flooded.

A storm surge of two feet, which is not unusual in the Windy City, added onto an overflowing river and lake, could spell complete disaster for the city: The lake would simply flow overtop of the heavy lock gates shielding the river, submerge the city, and even threaten towns downstream on the Mississippi River. Uncertain times lay ahead for the Great Lakes region as it has to prepare for both extremes: the flood and the drought.

The West's Severe Drought Problems

If water is a threat on the east coast, the west coast is seeing new heat records every summer, which, in the long run, lead to record water evaporation and even more severe droughts, which, in turn, lead to an ever-growing risk of wildfires.

In recent decades, water shortages have become a common problem in western states with arid climates, such as California. Normally, during the summer, when the rains cease for months, especially in Southern California, the state's water supply comes from gradually melting snow in the sierras, which ensures water reservoirs to hold even during the dry season. However, record heat is fueling water evaporation, which diminishes the runoff, leading to water shortages in 41 California counties, or 30 percent of the state's population, by late June of 2021.[30] Combined with extreme heat waves, which have drastically increased in frequency and intensity even just in the past few years, the state's groundwater supply is in serious jeopardy—as is the local flora and fauna. Local rivers have heated up so drastically that fish needed to be removed from them as they had become uninhabitable.

Fire has become one of the greatest threats to humans and wildlife in California and other western states. In 2021, the drought conditions in May and June resembled those not typically observed until later in the year due to hotter- and drier-than-normal weather in the early summer months. Fires in California have been of record size, record heat, and largely uncontrollable in the past five years, and, according to scientists' predictions, things are only going to get worse. Fire-preparedness in terms of infrastructure, such as added firetrucks, but also larger-scale equipment, like planes, and readily available personnel, is one of the key measures that local officials are taking.

Cities in other western states also experienced an extreme year in 2021. In Phoenix, AZ, in early June 2021, a 115 degree Fahrenheit (or 46.1 degrees Celsius) heat wave was melting the asphalt, with doctors warning people about third-degree burns from hot surfaces.[31] Outdoor workers and people without access to shelter from the heat find themselves, particularly at risk of dying from heat exposure. In addition, increased use of air conditioning is stretching the electrical grid in some parts of the country, especially Texas. In California, droughts have affected the efficiency of its hydroelectric power, a major power source for the state.[32] In addition, scientists are finding that severe heat waves can negatively affect the efficiency and output of generators and power lines, and even of solar panels.[33] The COVID-19 pandemic has posed additional challenges: In some western cities, a number of cooling centers were shuttered amid the pandemic summer of 2020, and some of them have yet to reopen in 2021.

The challenges of climate change have forced many cities and municipalities to move beyond the mitigation of the immediate effects of climate change and engage in longer-term preventative measures, in combination with mitigation: The city of Tucson has become a forerunner in recycling its wastewater, so it can be used for irrigation, as well as for fighting wildfires. California cities have started to spend huge sums on water storage facilities, so they can save water from wet years during dry ones. One of the big controversies of climate change has become a financial one as well: Many cities, states, as well as the federal government have been discussing whether climate change prevention or climate change mitigation will be more costly in the long run. Scientists argue that climate change prevention strategies are still in their infancy, but governments at every level are hesitant to invest the stunning sums necessary to make the drastic changes necessary to prevent climate change from getting even worse. Waiting, on the other hand, may prove to be even more costly, and eventually, it may simply be too late for preventative measures.

Cities and Climate Change Mitigation

Too many cities and municipalities remain hesitant to make high-impact changes to prevent climate change from becoming even more threatening due to financial considerations: Sustainability initiatives, especially at their outset, are expensive. In many cities, the main focus of climate change policy still is mostly on mitigation of its immediate consequences. Some cities, on the other hand, have been starting to make some longer-term plans for addressing climate change. One such way of planning is the design and implementation of so-called CAPs (Climate Action Plans). According to a recent report on urban efforts at climate change mitigation by the *Brookings Institution*, more than 600 jurisdictions across the United States have now developed and adopted CAPs, which mostly target the reduction of greenhouse gas emissions.[34] The *Brookings* researchers found that about half (45) of the 100 most populous cities across the United States have adopted targets for reducing their greenhouse gas emissions. Most of them tend to follow the Paris Climate Accords, which call for an 80 percent reduction in greenhouse gas emissions by 2050. But many of these plans fail to implement broader strategies that would attempt to limit global warming to 1.5 degrees Celsius, as suggested by the Intergovernmental Panel on Climate Change (IPCC). If all 45 cities reached their respective goals, the United States would save 365 million metric tons of CO_2, which would be equal to taking about 79 million passenger cars off American roads.[35] While this is an impressive number, it only amounts to about 7 percent of the greenhouse gas emissions reductions the United States had committed to in the Paris Accords, and all cities would fall far short of the 1.5 degrees Celsius goal of the IPCC. Many U.S. cities are already lagging behind their goals, and yet other ones have actually drastically increased their emissions, mostly due to unmitigated and unplanned rapid growth in the shape of urban sprawl.[36] The top three cities to drastically reduce their greenhouse gas emissions are Los Angeles, San Francisco, and Washington, D.C., whereas the top three cities to drastically increase emissions are Tucson, AZ, Madison, WI, and Pittsburgh, PA.[37] Overall, the *Brookings* report found that bigger cities are more likely to have ambitious climate change mitigation strategies in place than smaller cities. The general tenor, however, suggests that the current strategies to mitigate climate change, even the more ambitious ones, are just not ambitious enough to prevent long-term disastrous effects of climate change.

Yet, since former president Trump announced in 2017 that he would withdraw the United States from the Paris Climate Accords, cities have been at the forefront of the battle against climate change. Many initiatives to significantly reduce carbon emissions have been urban initiatives, and, since the 2017 announcement, there has been a flurry of firm commitments by mayors of major U.S. cities to the goals of the Paris Climate Accords. It is generally questionable, however, how much cities can achieve by themselves, without national leadership, and a firm federal commitment to mitigate climate change.

The year 2021 was one that broke many weather records: Record heat waves on the west coast killed approximately 150 people. Because of the tremendous heat, the wildfire season on the west coast started early and is expected to be one of the more severe ones on record. The hurricane season on the east coast and in the southeast was equally severe, with hurricanes battering New Orleans, the Florida panhandle, and New York City. Record rain is in the forecast in the early fall for the Gulf coast.

The Inconsistency of Federal Policy in Mitigating Climate Change

After the Trump administration, during its four years in office, had rolled back almost every environmental protection it could get its hands on and withdrawn the United States from the Paris Climate Accords, the newly inaugurated Biden administration, who took office in January 2021, campaigned on the promise of implementing a serious climate change agenda. During his presidential campaign, Biden had outlined a climate plan that would cost almost $2 trillion and includes a zero-emissions goal for the United States power sector by 2035 and net-zero greenhouse gas emissions by 2050.[38]

On his first day in office, the newly elected president Biden re-joined the Paris Climate Accords. He also signed a collection of executive orders, reversing many of the Trump-era rollbacks on climate policy, among them the Keystone XL pipeline, which was intended to transport oil from the tar sands in northern Alberta, Canada. The production of oil from the tar sands is highly controversial, as it requires a high amount of energy, the pollution of large amounts of water, and open-pit mining, which is a highly destructive process that requires the deforestation and destruction of 740,000 acres of forests and wetlands.[39] Biden tasked his administration with reinstating all the Obama-era climate policies that the Trump administration had previously rolled back. In addition, the Biden administration has taken steps to replace fossil fuel production and development with renewable energy, including the suspension of drilling leases for oil and gas on public lands while opening the country's coastlines on the eastern and western seaboards to offshore wind farms.[40] The Biden infrastructure bill, which passed the Senate in August 2021, also includes a push for more sustainable infrastructure, such as $15 billion earmarked for electric vehicle charging stations and electric buses. The administration has also announced plans to push Congress to set aside hundreds of billions of dollars to help push for the transition to electric vehicles, which is only possible with the support of all Democrats in the Senate—a difficult feat: It is far from guaranteed that Democrats in Congress will agree to unanimously push automakers toward a transition toward electric vehicles much sooner than many automakers would like. Politics is, as always, at the center of the issue: Strictly regulating and even limiting oil and gas development or forcefully pushing the auto industry toward electric vehicles tend to be measures that policy makers are reluctant to take. Inaction on climate change, on the other hand, or even the sluggish implementation of environmental measures, will most certainly lead to devastating and perhaps irreversible consequences for the inhabitability of our planet, not to even mention the cost.

Environmental activists have been pleased with the Biden administration's ambitious plans but are concerned about the implementation of an actual climate policy. In order to make its case for climate policy, the administration has been attempting to utilize the flurry of extreme weather events of 2021 in order to drum up support in Washington and advocate for a swift implementation.

State-Level Initiatives to Address Climate Change

In a recent report, the Center for American Progress argued that states may be particularly well-positioned to take on climate change by passing legislation that could implement lasting climate goals. By 2020, 15 states, in addition to Washington, D.C. and Puerto Rico had binding plans to take legislative action to become 100 percent renewable and 0 percent carbon-based electricity-dependent by 2045. Among those states are California, Colorado, Connecticut, Illinois, Maine, Nevada, New Mexico, New Jersey, New York, Oregon, Rhode Island, and Virginia. Ten of these states, along with the District of Columbia and Puerto Rico, have already passed the 100 percent renewable goal through their legislatures.

One of the most ambitious state legislative actions on climate change is New York's plan, which passed through the state legislature in June of 2019. It requires the state to get to 100 percent carbon-free electricity by 2040 and to 0 percent carbon emissions statewide by 2050. The Climate Leadership and Community Protection Act represents an additional New York State measure, which mandates a minimum of 35 percent of clean energy investments to be made in marginalized communities, which tend to experience higher levels of pollution, and a more frequent presence of power plants and other pollutants in their neighborhoods and communities. A special working group, which includes representatives from the Departments of Health and Labor, as well as advocates and activists for environmental justice, is to ensure that those marginalized communities have adequate access to solar panels or sustainable energy upgrades.[41]

California has taken on leadership roles on climate change in multiple areas, among them low-carbon buildings. The United States ranks second only to China in terms of the production of carbon emissions through buildings.[42] Lights, as well as central heating and cooling systems, and other energy-intensive appliances contribute significantly to this. Gas, for instance, as a heating and warm water source, tends to be particularly damaging on the spectrum of carbon emissions.[43] In addition, better building insulation and high-efficiency appliances can lower a building's carbon footprint.

California amended its building code in 2018, which applies to any new construction projects built starting in 2020.[44] The new code requires each new building project to be net-zero energy efficient, which means that it must produce as much energy as it consumes. More specifically, buildings need to have solar panels as well as windows with high insulation standards.

In addition, California is trying to tackle its biggest carbon issue: transportation, which makes up 40 percent of the state's carbon emissions.[45] Marginalized communities represent an important group in this context: They tend to be highly transit-dependent but have less resources for less carbon emitting transportation, such as electric vehicles. In addition, the public transit infrastructure in the southern and western parts of the country leaves much to be desired: They rank from non-existent to severely underfunded and underdeveloped. California's Clean Mobility Options program targets specifically marginalized communities. Several pilot projects have been launched, which aim at providing marginalized communities better access to electric vehicles but also make accessible bike share programs and vanpools.[46]

The state of New Mexico has pioneered Wildlife Corridors, which are intended to help animals displaced from their natural habitat by the effects of climate change. Human infrastructure complicates relocation to a different, more habitable areas for many affected animals, and several species in the United States are in danger of going extinct. A 2016 study found that only 41 percent of the country's existing natural habitat is connected to allow for the migration of endangered or climate change impacted species. This includes the erection of highway crossings for wildlife, but also a different, more environmentally conscious way of infrastructure planning, which takes into consideration the migratory routes of animal wildlife.

Finally, carbon farming has become a way of sequestering carbon in the soil, where microorganisms eventually consume it. Decomposing plants engage in this process naturally, and it is estimated that such farming could help repossess 1.5 tons of CO_2 per acre per year.[47] This technique could also help fertilize the soil, which, in turn, could lead to a dramatic reduction in the usage of synthetic fertilizers, many of which cause their own separate problems for the environment.[48] In terms of implementing such a technique on a larger scale, Hawaii has been a recent frontrunner.[49] In 2018, the state introduced the Greenhouse Gas Sequestration Task Force, which is intended to figure out means of carbon storage in the soil. The state has provided a number of different financial incentives, which are intended to create initiatives for more composting and a wider distribution of composted soil.

Cities Are Trailblazers in Waste Management—But Is It Enough?

When considering the emissions from food production to waste processing, food waste generates an amount of greenhouse gases equivalent to that of 37 million cars, according to a 2017 report by the Natural Resources Defense Council,[50] making organic food waste composting an important aspect of carbon farming. Food and agriculture are also huge consumers of energy—they make up about 16 percent of the country's total energy usage and 67 percent of its freshwater use.[51] Since currently no initiatives for carbon farming in the form of composting exist at the federal level, the state and local levels have stepped in with their own programs. New York City became an early adopter of city-wide composting. Created in 1993, the NYC Compost Project represented an initiative by the local government to increase public understanding of the benefits of composting, as well as gear up grassroots support for a program. The program stalled after the September 11, 2001, terrorist attacks, and it took about three years for it to return to its pre-9/11 participation levels.[52] By 2013, the program had expanded to include over 200 community composting sites in all five boroughs.[53] The New York City Bureau of Waste Prevention, Reuse, and Recycling (BWPRR) started to partner with the city's four botanical gardens in order to foster awareness about and interest in recycling, and also to offer a Master Composter Certificate Course in order to help create a new generation of community leaders in composting. Over the years, the program has started to evolve from providing education and fostering awareness to an actively organized composting program, which reaches wide swaths of the city.

In 2011, GrowNYC was established as a composting program which runs active drop-off sites for food scraps throughout the city. In doing so, GrowNYC partners with the city's local community composting sites. The program has composting of household food scraps more readily available to a larger group of New Yorkers not directly involved in the composting process by giving them the opportunity to collect their own food scraps for composting.

By 2013, the city's mayor at the time, Michael Bloomberg, made a political attempt to require food scrap composting for all New Yorkers. His administration, surprised at the high level of participation in several composting pilot programs across the city, announced plans to hire a composting plant in order to start industrially composting about 100,000 tons of food scraps a year, or 10 percent of the city's food waste from residential homes.[54] The Bloomberg administration had plans to initially phase in the curbside composting program as a voluntary effort and then expanding it to all five boroughs by 2015 or 2016. Under Bloomberg's successor, Bill DeBlasio, the program was to have become mandatory by 2018. The new mayor also introduced a Zero Waste initiative for the city, which would reduce the city's landfill by 90 percent by 2030. DeBlasio, however, by his second term, ended up shelving the mandatory aspect of the curbside composting program due to the relatively high costs and abandoned the program altogether in May 2020, in the midst of severe budget cuts due to the impact of the COVID-19 pandemic, which had hit New York City, an early epicenter, particularly hard. Kathryn Garcia, the city's sanitation commissioner at the time, who has since acted as the city's food czar during the COVID-19 pandemic, and ran in the 2021 Democratic primary for mayor, told *The New York Times* that before the pandemic, the city sent an estimated 4,000 tons of organic waste, which could have been composted, to landfills and waste disposal locations around the city.[55] The impact of the city's composting initiatives is mixed at best: By 2020, curbside composting programs still remained exclusive to certain neighborhoods and were only available to about 50 percent of the city's households. Even in those neighborhoods where the brown composting bins were available to residents, only 5–30 percent of residents used them, according to a *The New York Times* report in 2020.[56]

Critics have argued that many of the city's communities of color remain completely excluded from access to the curbside program. In addition, the cost of the program does matter, especially in a city as big as New York City, where fiscal resources are scarce and have to accommodate a considerable number of social programs. Since the beginning of the COVID-19 pandemic, the city's budget has come under considerable additional strain, imposing additional fiscal restrictions. The Citizens Budget Commission, a non-partisan, non-profit watchdog organization, estimated in 2016 that a separate food curbside collection program for organic waste would impact the city's budget between $177 million and $251 million per year.[57] Other critics have argued that unless composting happens locally, transporting organic waste over long distances to processing facilities may cancel out any benefits on carbon emissions.[58] New York City still hopes to phase in local processing of organic waste in the future.

In March 2021, Mayor DeBlasio announced that the city would bring back curbside composting by October of that year. Critics noted that the program would not come back with the same force that it previously had: Buildings will need to sign up for curbside composting when they were automatically enrolled before, and the program will remain exclusive to certain neighborhoods around the city and not be available to all residents. Some strong proponents of the program also worry about the potentially negative effects that the lost COVID year may have on the program. Kathryn Garcia criticized the mayor for bringing back a lesser version of curbside composting, arguing that the program should become universal and mandatory.[59] It remains to be seen whether the city can find resources and ways to expand the program in a sustainable way and, eventually, make it mandatory for the more than 8 million New Yorkers.

Waste treatment in New York City, the largest city in the nation, can make a significant difference in terms of climate outcomes and CO_2 pollution for the entire country. Its current composting initiatives still have a long way to go in terms of accessibility and comprehensiveness. Other cities have made more significant inroads.

In 1996, San Francisco became the first city in the United States to introduce a sweeping program for composting organic waste. By the year 2000, San Francisco had achieved its ambitious goal of reaching 50 percent landfill diversion.[60] In 2002, the city announced that it wanted to push further toward waste reduction by reaching 75 percent landfill diversion by 2010 and zero waste by 2020,[61] which means that the city would send zero waste to landfills, garbage incineration, or high-temperature processing facilities. The city exceeded its first goal by reaching 78 percent landfill diversion in 2011. However, the city's zero waste goal turned out to be elusive. In 2018, San Francisco's mayor, London Breed, acknowledged as much and instead committed the city to the somewhat revised goals of (1) reducing municipal waste generation by 15 percent by 2030 and (2) reducing the city's shipment of waste to landfills or incineration facilities by 50 percent by 2030.[62]

In part, the city's failure to meet its ambitious waste reduction goals is related to developments outside of its own control: In 2018, China announced that it would no longer accept much of the world's recyclables, which it had bought from developed countries in large quantity since the 1980s, including around 40 percent of the U.S.' recyclable waste. Many cities were plunged into a significant crisis at the announcement, which also meant that they would have to suddenly pay for recyclables to be disposed of instead of earning a profit by selling them to China.[63] San Francisco's recycling program and zero waste initiative suffered likewise, but not quite as much. The city had long been working with a private waste collection company, which collects around 85 percent of the city's residential and commercial recyclables from the city's blue bin program.[64] Around 81 percent of those recyclables collected get recycled, which amounts to the highest recycling rate in the nation.[65] On the other hand, just less than half of the city's total garbage is still incinerated or ends up in landfills,[66] which is less than in other cities, but far from insignificant. In any case, this signals that San Francisco is still far from reaching its zero waste goal.

The example of San Francisco illustrates just how complex and globally interconnected the recycling system as such really is: According to a 2020 grand jury investigation into the city's recycling and waste disposal programs, the city's waste is processed in a variety of different locales:

> [...] paper and cardboard, which account for 75 percent of San Francisco's recyclables, are sent to [...] Southeast Asia. Glass is processed in the Bay Area, while steel and aluminum are shipped to domestic foundries. [...]

High-value plastics are recycled domestically, while low-grade plastics go to Southeast Asia.[67]

About 19 percent of the city's recyclables still end up in landfills.

San Francisco recently announced a revision of its zero waste goal. Its mayor has now pledged instead to reduce the production of waste by 15 percent and waste-to-landfill disposal by 50 percent by the year 2030.

Cities are still relatively alone in their efforts to address waste generation and CO_2 production. The City of San Francisco recently called on the private sector, and especially manufacturers, to help reduce waste by producing more sustainable products, less packaging, and more compostable components.[68] Many cities have also implemented bans on plastic bags and other plastic packaging. While this is a good first step, the trend to replace most plastic packaging with paper and cardboard is not a good long-term solution. While paper is recyclable and biodegrades much more quickly than plastic, many researchers and environmental activists have argued that paper is resource-heavy in terms of its production and that paper bags include chemicals and fertilizers that are harmful to the environment.[69] A *National Geographic* article explains that studies demonstrate that every single paper bag would have to be used between 3 and 43 times in order to neutralize its environmental impact in comparison to plastic. Anyone who has used paper grocery bags knows that they are not very durable and that using them up to 43 times seems rather unrealistic. Instead, consumers should be incentivized to bring their own grocery bags to the store, but most cities are unlikely to mandate this and give shoppers no options to purchase cheap grocery bags at the store, which goes to show that even progressive initiatives at reducing waste often do not go far enough and that cities need broader support in implementing and expanding such initiatives.

Congestion Pricing

Congestion pricing is one initiative to reduce car traffic and traffic jams that directly pertains to cities. The idea behind it is to surcharge users of public goods, such as roads and bridges, based on the excess demand they encounter during peak hours of usage. Such surcharges can also help build awareness of users about the impact their usage has on public goods in terms of fatigue, decay, as well as the mutual impacts users have on one another. Since cities are population centers that tend to experience the heaviest traffic congestion, it appears logical that cities would be at the frontlines of implementing such pricing models.

To say that the United States is woefully behind in terms of implementing congestion pricing, which can significantly reduce not just traffic congestion but also CO_2 pollution over the short- and long term is a serious understatement. A study conducted by Cornell University and City College of New York found that, in the case of New York City, imposing a $20 toll on cars and cabs entering midtown or downtown Manhattan could reduce traffic congestion by 40 percent, increase public transit ridership by 6 percent, and reduce carbon emissions by 15 percent.[70] The same study also discovered that 1 million tons of greenhouse gasses are produced by car and truck traffic in lower Manhattan alone every single year.

In 2019, then-New York State Governor Andrew Cuomo announced a congestion pricing system for New York City, which would charge passenger cars venturing below 60th Street in Manhattan. The announcement immediately sparked concerns of equity and that the congestion pricing could disadvantage low-income commuters. However, the Brookings Institution, in one of its reports about congestion pricing, noted that there are only approximately 4 percent of outer-borough commuters who come to Manhattan for work and that the vast majority of them are wealthy and would not be impacted significantly by such a toll.[71] In addition, the program is expected to generate about $1.1 billion every year,[72] which would, in turn, be invested in public transit improvement and expansions (both of with New York City needs badly) and thus help support lower-income commuters.

Unfortunately, the program's future and implementation are uncertain. Former governor Cuomo resigned in August 2021 amid numerous serious sexual assault and harassment allegations, and it is unclear as of the writing of this chapter what the new governor, Kathy Hochul, intends to do about congestion pricing and whether she intends to go ahead with her predecessor's ambitious plan.[73] As of October 2021, Hochul has signaled support for the idea, but only time will tell whether it can be effectively implemented or even expanded.

In other parts of the world, congestion pricing has seen solid successes, with London's "Ring of Steel" being the perhaps most well-known congestion pricing system, which has successfully managed to significantly reduce traffic in London's downtown. Similar to other such successful systems, like Singapore or Stockholm, London drivers are charged a fee upon entering the Central Business District. American cities would be well-advised to combine congestion-pricing with an expansion of their public transit system, which would provide drivers with efficient alternative options to driving. This would not only reduce traffic but also help get more cars off the roads and significantly reduce CO_2 pollution.

Cities Cannot Stand Alone

Cities can serve as powerful examples of how environmental initiatives can work. With their densely packed populations, cities are simultaneously examples for efficient resource-sharing, in terms of housing, transportation infrastructure, waste and water management, and the electric grid, as well as huge pollutants in and of themselves: Single-family homes are much more resource-intensive, in that fewer people need more heat, water, and large stretches of the power grid. Cities, on the other hand, concentrate human pollution so intensely that they are hotter and dirtier than any suburban and rural area could possibly be. For instance, the growing season for urban gardeners tends to be at least a month longer than that for their suburban counterparts because cities pack so much heat in their concrete surfaces and due to the exhaust from air-conditioned buildings and vehicles. But cities also hold much opportunity: If they find ways to make tight human coexistence more efficient, clean, and sustainable, they can serve as powerful incubators for climate innovation and sustainable coexistence. They need help, however. Without financial support and policy-backup from the state and federal levels, American cities will have a hard time standing alone as innovators and implementers of climate friendly initiatives. No political unit, no policy exists in a vacuum. Urban sustainability initiatives need all the support we can muster.

Endnotes

1   Annabelle Timsit and Sarah Kaplan, "At least 85 percent of the world's population has been affected by human-induced climate change, new study shows," *The Washington Post* (October 11, 2021), https://www.washingtonpost.com/climate-environment/2021/10/11/85-percent-population-climate-impacts/.

2   Poppy Markwell and Raoult Ratard, "Deaths Directly Caused by Hurricane Katrina," *Government of Louisiana* (2008), https://ldh.la.gov/assets/oph/Center-PHCH/Center-CH/stepi/specialstudies/2014PopwellRatard_KatrinaDeath_PostedOnline.pdf.

3   Ibid.

4   NYC Community Block Grant Disaster Recovery, "Impact of Hurricane Sandy," https://www1.nyc.gov/site/cdbgdr/about/About%20Hurricane%20Sandy.page.

5   Ibid.

6   Eric S. Blake and David A. Zelinsky, "National Hurricane Center Tropical Cyclone Report: Hurricane Harvey, 17 August–1 September, 2017," *National Oceanic and Atmospheric Administration (NOAA)/The National Weather Service* (May 9, 2018), p. 1, https://www.nhc.noaa.gov/data/tcr/AL092017_Harvey.pdf.

7   Ibid., p. 6.

8   Ibid., p. 9.

9   Jeff Berardelli, "How Climate Change Is Making Hurricanes More Dangerous," *Yale Climate Connections* (July 9, 2019), https://yaleclimateconnections.org/2019/07/how-climate-change-is-making-hurricanes-more-dangerous/.

10 Ibid.

11 Andra J. Garner et al., "Impact of Climate Change on New York City's Coastal Flood Hazard: Increasing Flood Heights from Preindustrial to 2300 CE," *PNAS—Proceedings of the National Academy of Sciences of the United States of America* 114, no. 45 (November 7, 2017): 11861–11866.

12 NYC Parks Department: "Planning for Flood Resiliency: Guidelines for NYC Parks," https://www.nycgovparks.org/pagefiles/128/NYCP-Design-and-Planning-Flood-Zone__5b0f0f5da8144.pdf.

13 Ibid.

14 Richard Fausset, Sophie Kasakove, and Christopher Flavelle, "Ida Reveals Two Louisianas: One With Storm Walls, Another Without," *The New York Times* (September 7, 2021), https://www.nytimes.com/live/2021/09/07/us/climate-change/hurricane-ida-louisiana-levees.

15 Ibid.

16 Ibid.

17 Ibid.

18 Ibid.

19 Ibid.

20 David W. Dunlap, "Building to the Sky, With a Plan for Rising Waters," *The New York Times* (January 26, 2017), https://www.nytimes.com/2017/01/26/nyregion/resilient-design-american-copper-buildings-weather-flooding.html.

21 *StreetEasy*, "American Copper Buildings, Rental Building in Murray Hill," retrieved on September 9, 2021: https://streeteasy.com/building/american-copper-buildings.

22 Dunlap, "Building to the Sky, With a Plan for Rising Waters."

23 Christopher Flavelle, "Which Towns Are Worth Saving?" *The Daily Podcast, The New York Times* (October 11, 2021), https://www.nytimes.com/2021/10/11/podcasts/the-daily/climate-crisis-resilience.html.

24 Lyndon French, "The Climate Crisis Haunts Chicago's Future: A Battle between a Great City and a Great Lake," *The New York Times* (July 7, 2021), https://www.nytimes.com/interactive/2021/07/07/climate/chicago-river-lake-michigan.html.

25 Ibid.

26 Ibid.

27 Ibid.

28 Ibid.

29 Ibid.

30 Faith E. Pinho and Alex Wigglesworth, "California's Drought and Wildfire Dangers Are Rising at a Stunning Pace," *The Los Angeles Times* (June 26, 2021), https://www.latimes.com/california/story/2021-06-26/drought-wildfire-conditions-evolving-at-unprecedented-pace.

31 Brad Plumer et al., "Climate Change Batters the West Before Summer Even Begins," *The New York Times* (June 17, 2021), https://www.nytimes.com/2021/06/17/climate/wildfires-drought-climate-change-west-coast.html.

32 Ibid.

33 Ibid.

34 Sam Markolf et al., "Pledges and Progress: Steps toward Greenhouse Gas Emissions Reductions in the 100 Largest Cities across the United States," *Brookings* Report (October 2020), https://www.brookings.edu/research/pledges-and-progress-steps-toward-greenhouse-gas-emissions-reductions-in-the-100-largest-cities-across-the-united-states/.

35 Ibid.

36 Ibid.

37 Ibid.

38 Katie Glueck and Lisa Friedman, "Biden Announces $2 Trillion Climate Plan," *The New York Times* (July 14, 2020), https://www.nytimes.com/2020/07/14/us/politics/biden-climate-plan.html.

39 Jeff Wells et al., "Danger in the Nursery: Impact on Birds of Tar Sands Oil Development in Canada's Boreal Forest," *Natural Resources Defense Council (NRDC), Boreal*

Songbird Initiative, and *The Pembina Institute for Sustainable Energy Solutions* Report (December 2008), https://www.pembina.org/reports/borealbirdsreport.pdf.

40   Maggie Astor, "A Crucial Test Is Coming for Biden's Climate Agenda," *The New York Times* (July 8, 2021), https://www.nytimes.com/2021/07/08/us/politics/biden-climate-agenda.html.

41   Hillary Rosner, "How State and Local Governments Are Leading the Way on Climate Policy," *The Audubon Magazine* (Fall 2019), https://www.audubon.org/magazine/fall-2019/how-state-and-local-governments-are-leading-way.

42   Ibid.

43   Ibid.

44   Ibid.

45   Ibid.

46   Ibid.

47   Ibid.

48   Ibid.

49   Ibid.

50   "Wasted: How America Is Losing Up To 40 Percent of Its Food from Farm to Fork to Landfill," *Natural Resources Defense Council* (August 2017), pp. 4–5, https://www.nrdc.org/sites/default/files/wasted-2017-report.pdf.

51   Ibid., p. 5.

52   Amelia Nierenberg, "Composting Has Been Scrapped. These New Yorkers Picked Up the Slack," *The New York Times* (August 9, 2020), https://www.nytimes.com/2020/08/09/nyregion/nyc-compost-recycling.html.

53   Nora Goldstein, "Community Composting in New York City," *BioCycle* (November 18, 2013), https://www.biocycle.net/community-composting-in-new-york-city/.

54   Mireya Navarro, "Bloomberg Plan Aims to Require Food Composting," *The New York Times* (June 16, 2013), https://www.nytimes.com/2013/06/17/nyregion/bloombergs-final-recycling-frontier-food-waste.html.

55   Nierenberg, "Composting Has Been Scrapped. These New Yorkers Picked Up the Slack."

56   Ibid.

57   "Can We Have Our Cake and Compost It Too? An Analysis of Organic Waste Diversion in New York City," *Citizens Budget Commission* (February 2, 2016), https://cbcny.org/research/can-we-have-our-cake-and-compost-it-too.

58   Nierenberg, "Composting Has Been Scrapped. These New Yorkers Picked Up the Slack."

59   Kevin Duggan, "New Yorkers Not Ready for Mandatory Compost Recycling: de Blasio," *AM New York* (April 23, 2021), https://www.amny.com/news/new-york-compost-not-ready-de-blasio/.

60   Yerina Mugica, Andrea Spacht Collins, and Alice Henly, "Food to the Rescue: San Francisco Composting," *NRDC* (October 24, 2017), https://www.nrdc.org/resources/san-francisco-composting.

61   Ibid.

62   *SF Environment,* "Mayor London Breed Challenges Cities, States and Regions Around the World to Join San Francisco in Setting Aggressive Sustainability Goals," Press Release (August 28, 2018), https://sfenvironment.org/press-release/mayor-london-breed-challenges-cities-states-and-regions-around-the-world-to-join-san-francisco-in-setting-aggressive-sustainability.

63   Amri Khafagy, "Other Cities Face Trash Crises, but NYC Is Navigating China's Recycling Import Ban," *City Limits* (September 17, 2019), https://citylimits.org/2019/09/17/other-cities-face-trash-crises-but-nyc-is-navigating-chinas-recycling-import-ban/.

64   Cori Brosnahan, "Despite Recycling Success, S.F.'s Zero Waste Goal Remains Elusive," *San Francisco Public Press* (November 6, 2020), https://www.sfpublicpress.org/despite-recycling-success-s-f-s-zero-waste-goal-remains-elusive/.

65   Ibid.

66   Ibid.

67   Ibid.

68   Ibid.

69   *National Geographic*, "Sustainable Shopping—Which Bag Is Best?" Resource Library, https://www.nationalgeographic.org/media/sustainable-shoppingwhich-bag-best/.

70   Blaine Friedlander, "Steep NYC Traffic Toll Would Reduce Gridlock, Pollution," *Cornell Chronicle* (June 22, 2020), https://news.cornell.edu/stories/2020/06/steep-nyc-traffic-toll-would-reduce-gridlock-pollution.

71   D.J. Gribbin, "Congestion Pricing Is All Around Us. Why Is It Taboo on Our Roads?" *Brookings* (October 16, 2019), https://www.brookings.edu/blog/the-avenue/2019/10/16/congestion-pricing-is-all-around-us-why-is-it-taboo-on-our-roads/.

72   Ibid.

73   Winnie Hu and Dana Rubinstein, "As Cuomo Exits, Will Congestion Pricing Still Come to New York City?" *The New York Times* (August 16, 2021), https://www.nytimes.com/2021/08/16/nyregion/new-york-congestion-pricing.html.

CHAPTER 13

Governing the Divided Metropolis

Though it was difficult to see at first, the dark clouds of deindustrialization had a silver lining. The loss of manufacturing was accompanied by a rapid rise in the number of service jobs. From 1975 to 1990, 30 million new jobs were created in service industries, so by the end of the 1980s, 84 million people were employed in services, as compared to 25 million in goods production.[1] Almost 80 percent of employment growth in the 1980s came in the form of service jobs.[2] At the same time that factory workers found their jobs disappearing, new opportunities opened up for educated white-collar workers. As shown in Table 13.1, in seven Northeastern and Midwestern metropolitan areas, the percentage of jobs in the manufacturing sector fell from 32 to 12 percent in the 40 years from 1960 to 2000. Over the same period, services grew from 15 to 36 percent of local employment. Wholesale/retail and finance, insurance, and real estate remained about the same, so it was clear that the increase in service jobs was driving economic growth. The new services economy pointed the way toward a strategy for reviving the inner cities and their downtowns.

Public subsidies made the downtown renaissance possible. By the mid-1980s, most big cities were beginning to sport a "trophy collection," that typically included at least one luxury hotel (preferably one with a multistory atrium), a new sports stadium (usually domed), a downtown shopping mall, a redeveloped waterfront, and a new convention center.[3] These facilities and the activities they generated helped to support corporate white-collar employment, entertainment, culture, and a burgeoning tourism and convention trade.

The data in Table 13.2 show that downtown populations increased in cities in all regions of the nation. Some cities (such as Atlanta, Baltimore, Boston, Chicago, Los Angeles, and Philadelphia) built on a downtown population base that was already substantial in 1990 (ranging from 19,763 in Atlanta to 75,823 in Boston). Other cities (such as Cleveland, Denver, Detroit, Houston,

DOI: 10.4324/9781003175315-16

TABLE 13.1 Change in Job Categories in Seven Northeastern and Midwestern Metropolitan Areas, 1960–2000					
	Percentage Employed in Each Category				
	1960	1970	1980	1990	2000
Manufacturing	32	26	21	14	12
Transportation, communications, and public utilities	8	7	6	5	5
Wholesale and retail trade	21	21	21	22	20
Finance, insurance, and real estate	7	7	8	9	8
Services	15	19	24	31	36
Government	13	16	17	16	14

Source: U.S. Department of Labor, Bureau of Labor Statistics, Earnings and Employment (Washington, D.C.: U.S. Government Printing Office, 1960, 1970, 1980, 1990, and 2000).

Memphis, and Norfolk) attracted new residents to downtown populations that were small in 1990 (in all cases about 7,500 or less). The total number of people who moved into the downtown areas of these cities was not large, but the new residents nevertheless catalyzed a dramatic change. Condominium and apartment towers sprung up alongside historic buildings renovated into lofts and condos; restaurants, bars, and personal service businesses quickly followed. The decades-long flight from downtown and the neighborhoods around it seemed about to come to an end.

The economic sectors that led the revitalization of downtown constituted the components of a new globalized economy revolving around high-level corporate and professional services, telecommunications, and technology. Globalization has been facilitated by technologies that make information exchange nearly instantaneous and by the ability of corporations to manage operations in many places at once. Since the 1980s, corporations have been growing larger through mergers and buyouts. Large firms are able to coordinate activities on a global scale—the movement of capital investment, the location of factories, and the distribution and marketing of products. The innovations required by modern corporations in product design, advertising, the adoption of new technologies, and corporate organization are made possible by frequent coordination among highly specialized professionals, most of whom do not work within a single organization. In the global age, corporations prefer to locate in close proximity to the highly skilled and eclectic mix of professionals on whom they rely.

The skyscrapers that sprout from the downtowns of American cities are the physical manifestation of this clustering of economic activities. Although

TABLE 13.2 Downtowns That Grew in the 1990s (18 Selected Cities)				
City	1990 Downtown	2000 Downtown	Population Change	Percentage Change
Atlanta	19,763	24,731	4,968	25
Baltimore	28,597	30,067	1,470	5
Boston	75,823	79,251	3,428	4.5
Chicago	27,760	42,039	14,279	51
Cleveland	7,261	9,599	2,338	32
Colorado Springs	13,412	14,377	965	7
Des Moines	4,190	4,204	14	0.03
Denver	2,794	4,230	1,436	51
Detroit	5,970	6,141	171	3
Houston	7,029	11,882	4,853	69
Los Angeles	34,655	36,630	1,975	6
Memphis	7,606	8,994	1,388	18
Milwaukee	10,973	11,243	270	2.5
Norfolk, VA	2,390	2,881	491	20.5
Philadelphia	74,655	78,349	3,694	5
Portland, OR	9,528	12,902	3,374	35
San Diego	15,417	17,894	2,477	16
Seattle	9,824	16,443	6,619	67

Sources: Adapted from Rebecca R. Sohmer and Robert E. Lang, *Downtown Rebound* (Washington, D.C.: Brookings Institution Press, Fannie Mae Foundation, 2001), pp. 2–3; also see Rebecca R. Sohmer and Robert E. Lang, "Downtown Rebound," in *Redefining Urban & Suburban America: Evidence from Census 2000*, ed. Bruce Katz and Robert E. Lang (Washington, D.C.: Brookings Institution Press, 2003), pp. 63–74.

large numbers of corporations are located in edge cities and in office parks in the suburbs, downtown areas have continued to attract the firms that benefit from being close to one another. Especially (but not exclusively) in larger cities, high-level professional offices and information industries have become clustered into "strategic nodes with a hyperconcentration of activities"[4] supporting layer upon layer of highly educated, technologically sophisticated professionals offering specialized services—corporate managers, management consultants, legal experts, accountants, computer specialists, financial analysts, media and public relations consultants, and the like.

Corporate headquarters cluster more densely than anywhere else in a few global cities, such as New York, Paris, London, Chicago, Los Angeles, Miami,

Hong Kong, Sydney, and Tokyo.[5] Sitting atop a new urban hierarchy created by globalization, these cities house corporations that manage production and distribution networks around the world. The largest firms, especially including international banks, stock and commodity exchanges, and media empires, are located in global cities. Second-tier cities, such as Montreal and Hamburg, normally host a few international companies, and further down the hierarchy, medium-sized cities such as Atlanta, Cleveland, and St. Louis serve as the hubs of regional corporate networks. Down the pyramid further still are cities that depend on quite specialized activities tied to the global economy, such as an auto plant (Smyrna, Tennessee), a cluster of electronics software firms (San Jose, California), or a meatpacking plant (Beardstown, Illinois). The places that cannot find a way to tap into sectors of the global economy are destined to slip into irreversible decline.[6]

The highly paid professionals who locate near or in downtown areas demand an exceptional level of urban amenities, and the expectation that cities should provide a high quality of life has filtered down to include almost everyone. By the end of the 1990s, successful downtowns and gentrified neighborhoods offered what they referred to as a "unique urban culture" based on a varying mix of amenities that are best provided in dense urban environments: restaurants, blues, and jazz clubs, art galleries, theaters and performance halls, bars, dance clubs, after-hours clubs, and coffee shops.[7] These cultural activities have a great economic consequence for cities; they are a major source of jobs, and they help keep young professionals from moving to more interesting places. In this way, economics and culture have become inseparable in the twenty-first-century American city.

OUTTAKE

City of Glass: The Condo Boom in Downtown Areas

A walk through the booming downtown construction sites in Vancouver, San Francisco, Miami, Toronto, or New York reveals a glassy building boom: Sleek, slender condominium towers are on the rise. But often, once nightfall sets in over the city, many of these towers will not brighten the skyline with homely lights but remain dark instead. The "dark towers" have become a recent characteristic of the urban skyline in many downtowns. In 2015, the New York Times reported that many of New York City's luxury condo buildings were sitting more than half empty because many of the units served either as investment properties or pieds-à-terres for the ultra-rich.[8] Citing the New York City budget office, the New York Times reported that 24 percent of the city's apartments did not serve as the primary residences of their owners.[9] This is quite remarkable, especially in a city whose rental apartment vacancy rate has consistently hovered below the 5 percent mark, leading the city to have maintained a continuous housing emergency since the 1960s.

Interestingly, the budget office's data also indicated that the majority of the pieds-à-terres are owned by local residents, many of them living primarily in the suburbs, who like to keep a foothold in the city.[10]

The city's luxury real estate, on the other hand, tells a very different story. An investigative report by the New York Times in 2015, entitled "Towers of Secrecy" revealed that 44 percent of all real estate over $5 million in the United States was purchased by shell companies—entities set up to funnel money into the country by purchasing real estate without revealing the identity of the investor.[11] In New York City, the percentage of foreign shell companies purchasing luxury real estate (worth $5 million or more) was 54 percent in 2014.[12] The corresponding percentage was 51 percent in L.A., percent in the Bay Area, and percent in the Miami area, all of which are urban areas that have seen a vibrant condo boom since the 1990s.[13] In May 2015, in response to the New York Times reports, the de Blasio administration imposed new disclosure requirements on shell companies involved in real estate transactions in the city.[14] The main purpose of these new regulations was for city administrators to be better able to identify real estate owners involved in tax evasion schemes by failing to declare residence in the city.[15]

The dramatic physical transformation of some of North America's urban areas from struggling downtowns into condo boomtowns is quite visually fascinating. The glassy landscapes of Miami, Toronto, San Francisco, or Vancouver are particularly striking. The condo as such does not merely promise shelter, but it promises a lifestyle. Not unlike the suburban mall, which once attracted suburban dwellers with its climate controlled, easily accessible "safe spaces" to shop, the modern condo tower offers a gated, controlled environment with luxury amenities, such as gyms, pools, gardens, and often even a supermarket, for a pre-selected group of people. Urban scholar Ute Lehrer points out that "[b]ecause condo owners have almost everything inside, they do no longer need to engage with the city below. Their everyday life is contained within controlled spaces, and any encounter with the 'other' is reduced to its bare minimum."[16]

A 33-story condo structure in New York City became a symbol of the contrast between the climate-controlled, glassy paradise of the condo tower and the reality of the downtown streets. A New York City tax incentive, called 421a, offers tax abatements for housing developers who provide affordable housing units on their properties, which many New York City developers take advantage of. The newly developed, 274-unit structure in Manhattan, 40 Riverside Blvd., planned to sell 219 of its units as condos and reserved the remaining 55 units to be rented to tenants at affordable rates in order to take advantage of the 421a incentive. However, the developer wanted to have the tenants of the 55 affordable units enter through a separate door— commonly referred to as a "poor door" in New York City. The controversy around the "poor doors" grew so intense that it led New York legislators to add provisions to the 421a program in June 2015, stipulating that market-rate and affordable unit occupants must share the same entrance.

Meanwhile, the "poor door" controversy has long moved beyond the confines of the five boroughs: London's former mayor-turned-prime-minister, Boris Johnson, noted in 2013 that he would not rule out allowing "poor doors" as they provided an opportunity for developers to offset costs:

> The difficulty is, and this is what the developers will say, is that the high charges, the concierge charges, the charges for all the services in the building, cannot always be met in a uniform way by all the tenants, and that's why they make this case for dual access.[17]

Opponents see the tax break developers receive from providing affordable housing as cost-offset enough: "Poor doors are just the latest in a trend that helps us haves not to have to see the have-nots!" Stephen Colbert quipped in the wake of the controversy He went on to say:

> There must be a simple way to get away from average people. I don't need a penthouse! I'd settle for something small and luxurious, maybe a tiny silk-lined apartment with a pillow to lay my head on – just room for one, a cart from a single piece of mahogany with beautiful brass handles for six of my servants to carry me up to my country place – it's not a big piece of land, but at least it's in a gated community![18]

Whether we like it or not, the downtown condo is here to stay for the time being. After all, cities have remaining vertical building space. The city of glass keeps growing upward, reaching for the sky.

The New Urban Culture

The recent population growth in America's downtowns has been driven by empty-nest retirees and by affluent young professionals known by a number of slang terms, such as *yuppies* (young urban professionals), *dinks* (dual-income, no kids), and *jingles* (singles with joint living arrangements). In only a few years' time, this movement fundamentally changed the spatial geography of cities because affluent professionals tended to crowd into downtowns and nearby neighborhoods, and they have often done so by displacing people who had previously lived there. Affluent people live in downtown areas with high property values; outside of the downtown, there is a patchwork of gentrifying neighborhoods, some of them located near or even within poverty-stricken areas. What makes this patchwork pattern possible is the nature of the new development. Members of the affluent middle class often live within condominium towers or gated communities, well "protected" from the surrounding city.[19]

The professionals who have flocked into downtown and gentrifying neighborhoods have driven up the cost of housing, sometimes to fantastic levels, and altered the local landscape. New condominium towers and townhouse developments have become signifiers of urban regeneration but also of displacement, as has the renovation of old factory and warehouse buildings (some of them long abandoned) for retail and housing. Lower-income neighborhoods have attracted an eclectic assortment of affluent yuppies, artists, and people with unconventional lifestyles who are attracted to the lower rents and/or the diverse urban environment. Two characteristics have made these neighborhoods attractive—the presence of historic and architecturally significant buildings such as old Victorians and row houses, and their location near the central business district and amenities such as waterfronts, museums, parks, performing arts venues, restaurants, bars, and nightlife.

The term *gentrification* is a complex and often loaded term that has become a shorthand way of referring to the process of displacement. The gentrification storyline goes something like this: affluent newcomers drive up demand, bringing sharp increases in land values; as a result, less affluent residents are forced to move. Property taxes escalate when land values rise; dilapidated property becomes subject to new standards of maintenance; and neighborhood institutions such as churches and schools close because families with children tend to be replaced by singles and childless couples. Some gentrified neighborhoods are mainly residential, but more frequently, they are composed of a mixture of housing, retail, and services establishments (especially hair salons, health clubs, cleaners, and coffeehouses). Within these neighborhoods, certain new amenities open up, among them restaurants, exclusive shopping districts, parks, and cultural facilities.

Some scholarly observers are highly critical of gentrification and point to one of the central harms associated with it: The displacement of low-income residents from urban neighborhoods through rising real estate prices. Others point to the fact that gentrification, the influx of new retailers, groceries, and mid- to high-income residents, can help turn downtown neighborhoods into safer and more comfortable places to live. Political scientist Peggy Kohn, who has written extensively on the issue of gentrification and neighborhood transformation, takes a very nuanced approach to gentrification, noting that it is merely a symptom of a larger problem:

> If the gentrification of downtown is harmful, should we view the
> establishment of dynamic new low-income, immigrant neighborhoods in
> the inner suburbs as a benefit? Not exactly. This question, however, helps us
> focus on the core harm of gentrification, which is not gentrification itself but
> rather inequality. Gentrification makes the increase in inequality and income
> polarization into something visible, vivid, and concrete. Moreover, it reminds
> us that the wealthy got to take what they want and leave everyone else with
> what they discard. Urban policy by itself cannot solve this problem.[20]

As Kohn points out, the harms associated with gentrification are not brought about by neighborhood change exactly. Neighborhood change is, in fact, often welcomed by the original neighborhood residents, who prefer to have access to better local amenities, such as schools, stores, parks, and public transit. The problem is that they often do not get to enjoy these amenities because, over time, they get priced out of the neighborhood. The root cause for this is income inequality rather than neighborhood change. The super wealthy maintain the highest level of residential mobility, whereas the poor have very few options. As Kohn argues, the urban policy itself cannot bring about solutions. Overcoming income polarization requires more systemic change.

Tourism and Entertainment

Tourism, entertainment, and culture are crucial to downtown revival. The reasons are not difficult to uncover. Travel and tourism make up the world's largest industry (measured by value added to investment).[21] Travelers and tourists spend huge amounts of money on lodging, food, entertainment and culture, transportation, souvenirs, and other services and products. Worldwide, about one-tenth of all jobs are generated by travel and tourism.[22] To remake themselves into places that tourists want to visit, cities have invested heavily in tourism facilities and the reconstruction of downtown environments. Indeed, the rebuilding of downtown areas to make them friendly for visitors has been so massive that the current period of city building may be compared to the building of the industrial city a century ago when cities invested in mass transit systems, paved streets, sewer and water systems, and parks. The only other city-building era that changed the urban landscape as dramatically occurred in the 1950s and 1960s, when federally funded urban renewal clearance leveled blocks of downtown real estate and entire neighborhoods.[23] The transformation that began in the late 1970s is still taking place, but already American cities have been changed almost beyond recognition.

In Chicago, as in many cities, the leading industry is now tourism and entertainment. The number of tourists increased from 32 million in 1993 to 43 million in 1997, a product of indefatigable promotion and a huge investment in the infrastructure of tourism.[24] Chicago has built the world's largest convention center, an entertainment district on a renovated pier (Navy Pier), and has one of the world's most extensive and beautiful park systems, which runs for miles along the Lake Michigan lakefront. The city is host to several extraordinary museums and other attractions (such as the John G. Shedd Aquarium and the Adler Planetarium), maintains elaborate floral and garden displays along Michigan Avenue and on many other streets, and hosts dozens of events each year in the parks. Grant Park, which stretches between the downtown Loop and Lake Michigan, is the most frequently visited park in the United States, attracting more visitors than even the Grand Canyon.[25] Chicago has a complex globalized economy, but it would be in trouble without tourism. Indeed, 2010 saw a decrease in tourism for Chicago, from 39.5 million visitors in 2009 to 38.11 million, a change which was felt as the local tourism industry battled the results of the struggling economy, high fuel prices, and competition from other cities. Chicago quickly unleashed a $1 million media campaign, aimed at both in and out of state residents, a campaign which has been said to have already boosted 2011 visitor statistics. Still, the Chicago Tribune predicted that regaining the peak numbers of 2007 would take several years.[26] Since then,

Chicago's tourism industry has experienced a significant boom. In 2014, the city set a new record by reaching 48.7 million domestic visitors (and totaling over 50 million visitors overall and outpacing New York City by more than 4 million[27]), a 3.7 percent increase from the record of 46.96 million domestic visitors, which the city had set in 2013.[28]

In older industrial cities, tourist and entertainment venues have often been constructed on sites that were once devoted to manufacturing, warehousing, retailing, or harbor activities. These developments often try to project a contrived, nostalgic, and idealized version of city life, and they do so by utilizing architectural features that call to mind an imagined city from the past. One example is South Street Seaport in New York, which strives to create an ambience evoked by "authentic reproductions" of a working harbor[29]—in effect, an urban mini-version of Disneyland (in Anaheim, California), with its Main Street U.S.A. and Frontier Village. Similar developments in other places include the Wharf and Ghirardelli Square in San Francisco and the several renovated Union Stations scattered from coast to coast (while the actual train stations are out of sight and sound).

Making older cities attractive to tourists was not an easy task. In the wake of the riots of the 1960s, downtowns became stigmatized as violent, dangerous places. Where crime, poverty, and urban decay made parts of a city inhospitable to visitors, specialized areas were built that were, in effect, tourist reservations. Such "tourist bubbles" made it possible for the tourist, who was unfamiliar with the local landscape, to move inside "secured, protected and normalized environments."[30] The aim was to create a secure and imaginary world within an otherwise alien or even hostile setting. Within a few years, falling crime rates allowed tourist venues to spill beyond the confines of these enclaves. Downtown office construction and neighborhood gentrification gained momentum, and street life and urban culture became the objects of fascination and consumption for locals and visitors alike. Where these processes have achieved critical mass, the central cities have once again become the true hubs of their metropolitan regions, the home of activities, culture, and a lifestyle not easily imitated in the suburbs.[31] In cities as different as Boston, San Francisco, Chicago, New York City, and Portland, Oregon, visitors wander and mingle freely with local residents. Indeed, except in and around convention centers, it is often hard to distinguish visitors from local residents. The "localization of leisure turned cities into entertainment destinations not only for out-of-town visitors but also for suburban commuters and the growing number of affluent downtown residents."[32] Increasingly, local residents have become "as if tourists," acting like tourists even when they stay home.[33] At the same time, tourists increasingly seek to integrate themselves and act like local residents. One of the latest trends that let tourists experience cities from outside the tourist bubble is Airbnb, a website where people can offer and rent local lodging space. The website invites tourists to rent rooms and apartments from the original owners or tenants for the duration of their trip, allowing them to experience hip or up-and-coming residential neighborhoods, such as Bed-Stuy in Brooklyn, NY, or Logan Square in Chicago.

The infrastructure that makes central-city tourism possible includes convention centers, sports stadiums, festival malls, urban entertainment districts, cultural venues such as performing arts centers and museums, and, in a few cities, gaming casinos.[34] Especially in the case of convention centers and sports stadiums, public funding has sometimes become a contentious issue, with proponents playing up the benefits associated with city marketing and economic growth and opponents countering with the argument that public support for such facilities is both a bad investment and a case of misplaced priorities. However, for mayors and other public officials, the economic benefits of city image-making, whether it involves expanding a convention center, building a new sports stadium, or improving a museum, are beyond dispute.

OUTTAKE

Money Out of Thin Air: The Blessing or Curse of Airbnb

"I don't know the draw, but they're coming from all over the world: Spain, Italy, Scotland, Paris. They love it here. We absolutely were not expecting so much demand. We work hard at it. But it's still kind of surreal," noted one Airbnb host in the recently gentrifying Brooklyn neighborhood of Bedford-Stuyvesant in a 2015 New York Magazine report on the changes on his block over the past 135 years.[35]

Airbnb, a San Francisco-based start-up, which provides an online platform for individuals to offer up and rent real estate for short-term intervals, has become an alternative to the conventional hotel for many urban travelers, especially those who are interested in experiencing the city outside the tourist bubble. Since its inception, Airbnb has expanded significantly with offices in several European cities, as well as in Russia, Australia, and Latin America.

The impact of Airbnb on cities and neighborhoods has received mixed

reviews. Some observers have praised Airbnb as a financial aid that helps urban residents with underwater mortgages, facing foreclosure, or those struggling to afford the high rents of San Francisco, Washington, D.C., or New York City, while others worry about the negative impact of Airbnb on rental vacancy rates, and the supply of affordable housing.[36] Yet others have expressed concerns about a loss of community, in this case in reference to the increase in short-term rentals in Ocean Beach, San Diego:

> [T]he even more drastic consequence of loss of community occurs when there are so many residential units within a neighborhood that have been turned into short-term units, that a goodly-sized chunk of the area has morphed into a resort candyland of beach, sure, and sand.[37]

The length of tenure, as well as the nature of it (referring to the difference between local residents following their daily routines with work and family versus tourists wanting to have a good time) mattered, according to many concerned community residents in Ocean Beach. They felt that their quiet residential routines would be disrupted by the increasing presence of partying tourists in their community, and the fabric of the community would be destroyed by the growing proportion of short-term visitors replacing permanent residents.[38]

Back in New York City, former Attorney General Eric Schneiderman initiated a large-scale investigation into Airbnb. The report found nearly three quarters of Airbnb hosts in violation of tax, zoning, and other laws.[39] Furthermore, Schneiderman's investigation revealed that more than one-third of Airbnb rental revenue was benefitting commercial operations rather than struggling New Yorkers.[40] Finally, the financial benefits from Airbnb hosting were found to be concentrated in popular neighborhoods in Manhattan and Brooklyn, leaving the remaining three boroughs behind.[41] This indicates that financially besieged New Yorkers may not reap as many benefits from Airbnb.

Kenneth Rosen, chair at the Fisher Center for Real Estate and Urban Economics at UC Berkeley, in a recent report for the Urban Land Institute, noted that the effect of short-term rentals on the prices of long-term rental housing in San Francisco was much too small to measure.[42] He further noted that

> Allowing residents to supplement their income by offering a spare bedroom helps households to remain in the city as the cost of living increases. The amount of income from a rental alone is not generally sufficient to live on, but it can go a long way in providing supplemental income for a family. To be sure, there are isolated cases of individuals who live on the income generated from renting out spare rooms, but the cost and effort involved in operating a full-time rental outweigh the benefit for the vast majority of households.[43]

One thing is fairly certain: The sharing economy is booming, and it is here to stay for the time being. Because it is such a recent phenomenon, however, it still remains fairly unregulated, its long-term impacts on the more regulated branches of the tourism industry still uncertain. Clashes and legal struggles should be expected. Much like private car services, such as Uber, in which drivers use their own personal vehicles to transport customers without having to acquire an expensive commercial taxi license, Airbnb ventures into legal territory that is under-regulated at best. The future will show whether lawmakers can catch up.

Convention Centers

Until the 1960s, few cities had built the huge convention centers that are so prevalent in and near downtown areas today. Only a few decades ago, town halls doubled as assembly facilities, if any were needed. In the 1920s, some cities built the first generation of meetings and exhibition halls; St. Louis, for example, built the St. Louis Arena in 1929 to accommodate an agricultural exhibit. During the Great Depression, the federal government, through the Public Works Administration, financed large public assembly and exhibition facilities in a number of cities. This generation of halls often contained one or more auditoriums as well as exhibition space under one roof, and in many cases, these structures were not replaced until the 1980s or 1990s. These facilities were expensive to operate and virtually always lost money, but they had the effect of attracting and even helping to create an array of traveling shows and exhibitions. The benefits to the local economy and to their own bottom line were soon comprehended by civic boosters, who then pushed for larger and better facilities.

In the 1950s, a few cities began constructing convention centers designed to attract professional meetings and trade shows. The proliferation of convention centers began in the 1960s and accelerated in the 1970s as air travel, growing affluence, and greater specialization in the job market gave rise to more meetings, exhibitions, and consumer shows (such as autos, boats, and electronics), and conventions. In the 1980s, cities began a virtual arms race for the convention trade, with even small towns joining the competition. More than 70 percent of the convention centers existing in 1998 had opened since 1970.[44] Actually, however, the race had just begun. In the ten years from 1993 to 2003, capital spending for convention centers doubled to $2.3 billion annually, and in the 13 years from 1990 to 2003, convention-center space increased by 51 percent. In the latter year, at least 40 cities were planning to build new facilities or expand the old ones. All of this activity meant that the size and cost of each facility escalated, but the available business had to be divided among an increasing number of contenders.[45]

All convention centers require annual subsidies for the payment of construction bonds and for operating costs, but rising construction, maintenance, and promotion costs have not deterred cities from investing in bigger and more elaborate facilities. Much is at stake. In 2002, there were nearly 23,000 associations and 6.5 million total private business establishments in the United States.[46] The 23,000-plus associations in the nation spent $32 billion for meetings in 1992, and corporations spent an additional $29 billion on off-premises meetings and conventions.[47] Tourism-related organizations alone had 1.4 million members in 1998, and the meetings industry produced $81 billion in economic output.[48] The average attendance at new exhibitions nearly quadrupled from 1990 to 1997.[49] Although only from 4 to 5 percent of meetings are held in convention centers (the rest are held in hotels, resorts, and other venues),[50] the size of the meetings and convention business has been large enough to prompt hundreds of cities to build or expand their existing facilities. Forty-one convention centers were being built or renovated in 2000, and 66 were slated for expansion or renovation.[51]

Sports Stadiums

Civic boosters believe that professional sports franchises are pivotal to the economic revitalization of central cities and often have used sports facilities as an anchor for development.[52] Cities compete vigorously for sports teams by helping to finance the construction of stadiums and by allowing owners to keep parking and concession fees and other revenues. Because teams sometimes threaten to move and occasionally do, sports cartels and team owners have been very successful in persuading cities to meet their demands. In the decade of the 1990s alone, approximately $10 billion in public funds were devoted to the building of sports facilities in urban areas for major league professional teams.[53] Although earlier studies seemed to make a convincing case that sports stadiums did not bring measurable benefits to local economies, recent research shows that in many contexts they do.[54] One study indicated that stadiums located in the downtown areas of six cities made a positive contribution to the regional economy, a study of the Gund Arena and Jacobs Field in Cleveland found that these facilities contributed to the economic redevelopment of downtown.[55]

It is important to add that economic impact is only one part of a complex picture. Sports teams have long been central to the civic and cultural life of American cities. Oddly, the assumption that a team expresses a city's essence, spirit, and sense of community has not been much eroded since teams and their players became highly mobile. Part of the reason for this is that local boosters regard professional sports teams as a signifier of "big league" status for a city. Sports teams carry a substantial emotional charge, so their worth is rarely if ever, calculated in simple economic terms. Through the national and international publicity accompanying network broadcasts of games and playoffs, professional sports teams are a powerful vehicle for conveying a city's image and fostering a sense of identity and community. When a team wins a World Series or the Super Bowl, a jolt of ecstatic happiness sweeps through the local population. For a moment, everyone is a fan.

Professional sports is a big business. Between 2010 and 2011, the value of Major League Baseball teams increased 7 percent and reached an all-time high of $523 million. The New York Yankees topped the list at $1.7 billion, while the Mets lost 13 percent of their worth for a total value of $747 million.[56] The National Basketball Association (NBA) and professional hockey franchises could be bought for smaller sums, making it possible, in some cases, for someone with $100–$200 million laying around to bid for a team.[57] Despite the claims of owners and the leagues, sports teams are profitable. In 2002, baseball commissioner Bud Selig testified to Congress that major league baseball generated an operating loss of $200 million that year, but *Forbes* magazine produced figures showing a $75 million profit.[58] The escalation of team values all through the previous decade made it a dubious claim that baseball owners lost money. The lucrative media contracts for most baseball teams made it even more suspect.[59]

For decades, professional sports teams were so closely identified with their cities of origin that moving would have been unthinkable. In baseball, this link was first broken in 1953, when the Boston Braves relocated to Milwaukee. The baseball franchise relocation game began in earnest in 1957, when owner Walter O'Malley moved the Brooklyn Dodgers to Los Angeles. O'Malley fought for years to find the land for a new stadium in Brooklyn to replace the decrepit Ebbets Field, which had opened in 1913. But he was repeatedly thwarted by Robert Moses, who, as head of New York's Bridge and Tunnel Authority, Park Commission, Construction Commission, and Slum Clearance Committee, controlled the land needed for a new park.[60] To lure the Dodgers out of New York, Los Angeles agreed to renovate its minor league stadium at Chavez Ravine and give the stadium to O'Malley. As the clincher, they offered him 300 acres of downtown Los Angeles real estate.[61] Considering the obstacles put in his way in Brooklyn, it would have been difficult for O'Malley to refuse the deal.

It did not take long for other owners to follow O'Malley's lead. Threats to move became potent weapons for prying more subsidies out of cities. Between 1953 and 1982, there were 78 franchise relocations in the four major professional sports: 11 in baseball, 40 in basketball, 14 in hockey, and 13 in football.[62] In only six years, from 1980 to 1986, more than half the cities with major league sports franchises were confronted with demands for increased subsidies, with relocation an implied if not always explicit threat hanging over negotiations.[63]

Except for baseball, where teams move less frequently, moves have become an ever-present possibility for many cities, in part because they pay off for the owners. In the 1990s, for example, the Quebec Nordiques (a hockey team) moved from a small market to Denver, Colorado, and renamed themselves the Avalanche. In 1995, in their first season, they won the Stanley Cup. Around the same time, the Winnipeg Jets moved from Winnipeg, Canada, a city of die-hard hockey fans, to the desert in Phoenix, AZ. The Jets had run into trouble in the early 1980s when the World Hockey Association (WHA) merged with the NHA, and the team started to lose. After the merger, salary regulations were liberalized, and salaries had to be paid in U.S. dollars. However, ticket sales, a central source of revenue source for NHL teams, were in Canadian dollars, and during the 1980s and 1990s, the exchange rate put Canadian teams at disadvantage. In this liberalized market, big, new arenas with luxury boxes could garner decidedly more revenue than the aging Winnipeg Arena, a small indoor arena built in 1955 without any luxury seats. Therefore, despite their loyal fan following, the Jets could not bring in a competitive amount of revenue.

The Winnipeg City government, in turn, was unwilling to pitch in any financial support for the team or build a new, modern arena with updated amenities and a higher proportion of luxury boxes. The team eventually was bought by several Phoenix businessmen and moved to Phoenix as the Coyotes in 1996, where, after initial problems with their arena, they received their own stadium during the 2003/04 season.

In the early 2000s, the local economy in Winnipeg improved considerably, and in 2001, the MTS Centre was built in the space of the iconic Eaton's building in downtown Winnipeg by a coalition of wealthy business leaders, led by True North Entertainment. Amid the construction of a new arena, rumors started flying regarding the return of an NHL hockey team to Winnipeg. In

2009, True North Entertainment made one of several unsuccessful bids to return the Coyotes to Winnipeg, but in 2011, True North was able to successfully move the Atlanta Thrashers to Winnipeg. Some small initial upgrades were made to the MTS Centre, but more profound upgrades have been implemented recently. In 2015, True North Entertainment invested $12 million for 278 premium lodge seats and a new scoreboard, and it plans to invest up to $30 million in the arena by 2020 via its TN 2020 Initiative.[64]

As teams became more and more footloose, cities found themselves at a disadvantage. In an attempt to improve their poor bargaining positions, some cities built stadiums even when they did not have teams. In the 1980s, Indianapolis built a football stadium and then set about persuading the owner of the Baltimore Colts, Robert Irsay, to move. After the Maryland legislature passed an eminent domain law to make it possible for Baltimore to seize the Colts for public use, Irsay packed up the team's equipment in moving vans and left in the middle of the night. But probably the most famous case is the $139 million domed stadium built by St. Petersburg, Florida, in 1988 in the hopes of attracting a major league baseball team. Called "heaven's waiting room," boosters justified the Florida Suncoast Dome as a way of changing the city's image as a conservative retirement community.[65] For years, the stadium remained the site of tractor pulls and concerts. In the 1990s, St. Petersburg tried to lure several major league baseball teams, including the Seattle Mariners, the San Francisco Giants, and a National League expansion team. When Florida won a baseball team in 1991, it was awarded to Miami. In October 1993, an expansion team of the NFL was awarded to Jacksonville; St. Petersburg's stadium was built expressly for baseball and would not have been suitable for football. St. Louis, which also put in a bid for one of the NFL expansion teams, lost out. St. Louis undertook the construction of a domed stadium anyway, many months before the negotiations that eventually brought the Los Angeles Rams to the city in 1995.

Stadiums require generous land, infrastructure, and direct public subsidies because almost all of them (but not usually the teams playing in them) lose money. Annual operating deficits are generally considerable; the New Orleans Superdome lost about $3 million a year during the 1980s, for example, compared to the annual $1 million loss for the Silverdome in Pontiac, Michigan. In its first year, the Florida Suncoast Dome lost $1.3 million, plus $7.7 million in debt payments.[66] Modern domed stadiums cost so much to build that they can rarely schedule enough events or charge enough for them to avoid operating deficits; the only one in the country without deficits in 2004 was the Metrodome in Minneapolis, which did not require a tax subsidy.[67] Toronto ended up paying $400 million for its domed stadium; St. Louis's domed stadium, completed in 1995, cost $301 million.[68] The costs have only escalated since. In September 2008, the Indianapolis Colts played their first football game in the Lucas Oil Stadium, built at the cost of $720 million. In the New York area, three teams were looking forward to playing in new stadiums. The New York Yankees opened their season in 2009 in a stadium built for $1.5 billion, while just a few miles away, the Jets and the Giants moved into one costing $1.6 billion.[69]

It is undoubtedly true, as civic boosters argue, that the most important benefits of a major sports franchise are intangible and therefore impossible to measure solely in economic terms. However, as teams became more mobile and owners asked for more, such arguments sometimes wear thin. In December 1996, the owners of the Seattle Mariners baseball team put the team up for sale, even though the city had earlier bought land and made plans to construct a new ballpark. Just a few months earlier, Seattle's football team, the Seahawks, had threatened to leave town, and it too demanded a new stadium. Together, the two stadiums were estimated to cost $760 million. A group called Citizens for More Important Things initiated a campaign opposing public subsidies behind this slogan: "Just say no to welfare for the wealthy."

From 2000 to 2006, public funds supplied 54 percent of the construction cost for new major league baseball stadiums and 55 percent of the costs for football stadiums.[70] These subsidies often provoked opposition, but there are other sources of dissatisfaction, too. Fans of the Mets, the Yankees, the Giants, and the Jets expressed outrage at the escalating price of tickets in the stadiums. At the three stadiums in New York, ticket prices in the new stadiums went up by two times or more. Season tickets for the best seats that had cost $1,000 each in the old Yankee stadium jumped to $2,500 when it opened in 2009.[71] In August 2008, the Giants announced that they would charge from $1,000 to $20,000 for personal seat licenses, which only entitled the holders to buy season tickets. "Here I am, buying a stadium for John Mara," a Giants ticket holder complained; "This is a greedy ploy with the only benefits going to them."[72]

Malls, Entertainment, and Lifestyle Complexes

Malls have become a weapon that cities use in the regional competition for recreational shopping and tourism. To ensure that they are in the game, cities typically have heavily subsidized the construction of downtown malls by allocating Community Development Block Grant and Urban Development Action Grant funds, floated bonds to finance site acquisition and loans to developers, offered property tax abatements, created tax increment districts, built utilities tunnels, constructed sewer lines and water mains, rerouted and repaved streets; the list goes on. Civic leaders are eager to support mall development because it promises to bring a special form of "entertainment" retailing downtown. Boston's early success set the tone for such expectations.

On August 26, 1976, Boston's mayor, Kevin White, presided over opening-day ceremonies for Quincy Market in downtown Boston. The brainchild of developer James Rouse, who made a fortune developing suburban shopping malls, Quincy Market was housed in three 150-year-old market buildings that were renovated, at a cost of more than $40 million, into a collection of boutiques, gourmet food shops, and restaurants.[73] Few expected Quincy Market—located as it was in the center of a declining central city with inadequate parking and no big-ticket items to sell—to succeed. Indeed, six weeks before the opening day, the retail complex was less than 50 percent leased. To hide the empty stores, Rouse came up with the idea of leasing pushcarts to artists and craftspeople for $50 a day, plus a percentage of the sales.

By 11 o'clock in the morning on the opening day, only a modest crowd had gathered for the ceremonies. When the speeches were over, Mayor White cut the ribbon, and developer Rouse and a company of kilted highland bagpipers led the crowd inside for a champagne reception. At lunchtime, the milling throng swelled as curious workers poured out of nearby office buildings, and by mid-afternoon, it was clear that opening day would be a huge success, with police estimating the crowd at 100,000.

People never stopped coming to Quincy Market. In its second year of operation, the market drew 12 million visitors—more than Disneyland that year. Newspapers reported the market's "instant acceptance" by the public, which delighted in the colorful sights, sounds, and smells of the food and imaginatively displayed merchandise and the festival air created by a liberal sprinkling of pushcarts, magicians, acrobats, and puppeteers. The banks that financed the project were originally skeptical; they calculated that Quincy Market would have to produce retail sales comparable to the most successful suburban shopping malls ($150 per square foot) to justify its unusually high development costs. Quincy Market shocked the experts by producing sales of $233 per square foot in its first year, with the pushcarts doing best of all. The opening of Quincy Market was hailed by the media as a sign of an urban renaissance in the making. It seemed to disprove the conventional wisdom that the downtowns of American cities were doomed to obsolescence and decline.

The first-generation downtown malls were important not only because they helped reverse the long-term decline of inner-city retailing but also because they provided a means of creating defended space in the midst of urban crime and decay. Malls built by the developers John Portman and James Rouse and their imitators became such common features of American downtowns that it was hard to recall how recently they had been constructed. The malls increasingly engulfed and centralized activities that were formerly spread through the urban community at large. Such complexes were easily criticized as "fortified cells of affluence,"[74] but there can be little doubt that as locations for tourism and entertainment, these spaces were extremely successful.

In the years after his Boston success, Rouse was invited to design festival malls for cities all across the country. What made Rouse's developments so distinctive and newsworthy was the artful combination of play and shopping. His formula was to create a carnival atmosphere, accomplished through a mixture of specialty shops, clothing stores, restaurants, and food stands, and with a changeable mix of musicians, jugglers, acrobats, and mimes to entertain shoppers. Rouse malls soon began to pop up all over the place: at the Gallery of Market Street East in Philadelphia, Grand Avenue in Milwaukee, Pike Street Market in Seattle, Horton Plaza in San Diego, Trolley Square in Salt Lake City, Union Station in St. Louis, Harborplace in Baltimore, South Street Seaport in New York, and on and on. Noticing the success of the formula, imitators began to appear, too. By the turn of the century, virtually every major city in the country had a Rouse mall or the equivalent.

Enclosed malls began opening in cities large and small, some modeled on Rouse's formula, some not. Many of them started modestly enough, but over time they accreted block by block, reaching over streets with a system of tubes and skyways. In Minneapolis, a sprawling mall complex grew almost invisibly by eating away the interiors of the downtown buildings but leaving their historic facades intact. In Kansas City, the Crown Center inexorably spread from its beginnings as a luxury hotel; by the mid-1990s, it occupied several city blocks. In Montreal and Dallas, sprawling underground malls were connected through a network of tunnels. The mall's assault on Atlanta has been much more direct; the huge Peachtree complex has been built on the rubble of the historic downtown.

Because they are an aspect of leisure and tourism, the kinds of malls built in downtown areas do not necessarily compete head-to-head with suburban malls. Rather, they rely on a style of shopping that combines entertainment with consumption. The malls' mix of gift and souvenir shops, specialty food stores, bars, and franchised fast-food restaurants sometimes calls to mind tourist villages such as Jackson Hole, Wyoming, and Estes Park, Colorado. In the West Edmonton Mall in Alberta, Canada, for example, leisure facilities take up about 10 percent of the total floor space, but their presence is essential to an ambience of leisure that permeates the entire mall.[75] The West Edmonton Mall copies Disney World in the theming of particular areas, such as an imitation Parisian street, Bourbon Street in New Orleans, Hollywood, and Polynesia. The combination of shopping and leisure in this way nurtures a "shop 'til you drop" consumer culture.

In these environments, consumers are prompted to act as if they are, in effect, moving in a dreamscape far removed from the outside world. The similarity between Disney theme parks and these mall environments is not accidental. Thirteen years before James Rouse opened Quincy Market in Boston, he asserted that Walt Disney was the most influential urban planner ever. And so he was. Malls and entertainment complexes establish the atmosphere and the context that potentially make every city, whatever its past function or present condition, a playground.

Sprawling indoor complexes connected by pedestrian bridges and tubes have proliferated in American cities.[76] For example, sprawling complexes have been built in Atlanta and Detroit, where large numbers of downtown office workers commute to the sealed realms of the Peachtree Center in Atlanta and the Renaissance Center in Detroit. In both of these structures, workers drive into parking garages and then enter a city-within-a-city where they can work, shop, eat lunch, and find a variety of diversions after work. They never have to set foot in the rest of the city or deal with its problems.

Architect John Portman pioneered the first "bubble city" when he opened the Peachtree Plaza in downtown Atlanta in 1967. The Peachtree complex was built outward from the cylindrical aluminum towers that distinguished Portman's first atrium hotel, which opened in downtown Atlanta in 1967. It was an instant hit with architectural critics, the media, and the public. The hotel lobbies and vaulted atriums that made up the complex were dazzling, filled with flowing water and pools, ascending ranks of balconies vanishing toward a skylight, corridors rigged with lights and mirrors, and glass elevators rising on the outside of the towers. Nobody had seen anything quite like it.

By the late 1980s, Peachtree Plaza had swallowed up Atlanta's historic downtown. Sixteen buildings clustered around the aluminum cylinder, which housed the Marriott Hotel. Shops, hotels and their lobbies, offices, food courts, and atriums were connected by a maze of escalators, skytubes, and arcades that isolated inhabitants from the streets below. The downtown streets of Atlanta were left almost deserted, especially at night. Pedestrians were able to gain access to the complex through a few grand porticos, usually the entrance to a hotel lobby. The effect was to create a separate city-within-a-city strictly segregated from the public streets on the outside.

Portman took his show on the road and built a series of stunning atriums, towers, and bubble environments. Although none of them approached the scale of Atlanta's, they were designed to provoke a sense of wonder and grandeur— the Renaissance Center in Detroit, the Hyatt at Embarcadero Center in San Francisco, the Bonaventure Hotel in Los Angeles, and the Marriott Marquis in Times Square, New York City. Unlike Atlanta, however, these indoor playgrounds do not swallow up an entire downtown, although they do enclose a large amount of space and house several related activities. Imitations of Portman's creations quickly spread. There were several advantages to building indoors: The developer is able to create a total experience of sights, sounds, and movement and also guarantee almost complete security. In this way, a space attractive to affluent people could rise even in the midst of a seemingly hostile environment, thus providing even the most dilapidated cities with a strategy for revitalizing the urban core.

New York City's Times Square and San Francisco's Yerba Buena Center both anchor urban entertainment centers, but such complexes have sprung up elsewhere as well, usually in historic areas and often in connection with revitalized waterfronts. Over time, a remarkably eclectic variety of activities have been brought together into a single venue. Contained within these districts are restaurants, coffeehouses, sports bars, jazz clubs, dinner theaters, and arcades, plus an array of corporate retail tenants offering an assortment of clothes, shoes, electronic goods, jewelry, and an endless array of other items.[77]

The degree to which space is segmented in cities varies significantly. In general, the activities in spaces fortified by walls and bubbles have spilled out into public streets and neighborhoods, a process that has brought a sense of street life and excitement that had long been absent. In recent years, Boston, San Francisco, Seattle, Portland (Oregon), and Chicago—in fact, most cities—have opened up and become more accessible to visitors and local residents. Cities have invested heavily in amenities such as street plantings, pedestrian malls, parks, and riverfronts. Local residents and visitors fill busy streets that only a couple of decades ago were quiet and forbidding. Tourists visit enclaves such as South Street Seaport in New York and Ghirardelli Square in San Francisco, but they also stream into nearby streets and neighborhoods. This trend will continue as long as crime rates remain relatively low.

The Politics of Tourism

Critics often note that many of the facilities of tourism and entertainment do not pay for themselves. Public officials and civic boosters do not, on the whole, much care if they do. This apparently cavalier attitude toward taxpayers' money can be explained by noting the general irrelevance—to city officials and civic boosters—of cost–benefit analyses of tourism infrastructure. The attitudes of public officials toward development projects have "little [to] do with the ... profitability ... of a project" and far more to do with the vision officials share about the overall direction a city is taking.[78] The intense interurban competition dictates that cities must compete; to do so, they must be as generous as their competitors in providing subsidies, and they must try to adopt every new variation that comes along. The competition imposes a logic of its own that is hard to resist.

Public officials may be proceeding on the basis of blind faith, but they feel they have little choice. It is true that abject, even humiliating failure is possible, as the attempt by Flint, Michigan, to become a tourist city makes clear. In the 1970s, after the closing of its General Motors plant devastated the local economy, public officials in Flint launched an effort at regeneration behind the motto "Our New Spark Will Surprise You." The city committed $13 million in subsidies to the construction of a luxury hotel, the Hyatt Regency. Within a year, it closed its doors. Approximately $100 million in public money was used to build AutoWorld, a museum that contained, among other items, the "world's largest car engine" and a scale model that portrayed downtown Flint in its more prosperous days. AutoWorld closed within six months. Still, more public subsidies were committed to the construction of the doomed Water Street Pavilion, a theme park/festival market built by the renowned mall developer James Rouse. But few, if any, mayors would be deterred by Flint's fiasco, which was wryly portrayed in Michael Moore's popular movie *Roger & Me*.[79]

Virtually all cities of consequential size must take steps to promote tourism, recreation, and culture. Now that the basic infrastructure is in place in so many cities, public support for the arts and culture has become common. Every one of the nation's 50 largest cities allocates public dollars to support the arts, and a lot of small cities do so as well. From the big cities (New York, with the Kennedy and Lincoln Centers and, more recently, the Ford Center on 42nd Street) to villages (Riverhead, a hamlet outside New York City on Long Island, which is building art and historic district), from the downtowns in need of a boost (Newark, with its $180 million New Jersey Center, opened in October 1997) to the already prosperous (San Francisco, with a newly renovated opera house and several other performance halls), the development of local culture has become a leading formula for urban revival.[80] The text for a major exhibit in 1998 sponsored by the National Building Museum in Washington, D.C., noted that culture has replaced both the urban renewal bulldozer and the preservation movements that followed in its destructive wake as the main focus for downtown revitalization.

Collectively, cities of all sizes support an almost unimaginable variety of events that carry the signature of local culture and community. Jazz and blues festivals, strawberry and garlic festivals, jumping frogs and gold rush days, rodeos, and fireworks—such activities help define and sometimes knit together local communities.[81] These activities usually take place in or near the new tourism/entertainment infrastructure (in smaller towns, this may mean at local parks, bandstands, waterfronts, or baseball diamonds). Every city must go through debates about how much of the public purse should be devoted to these activities, but few can afford to forgo public support altogether.

Old and New Downtowns

A host of writers have mourned the disappearance of the historic landscapes that once gave cities their identities and distinctive character. In 1961, when Jane Jacobs published her classic work *The Death and Life* of *Great American Cities*, she instantly became the best-known and most influential voice for preserving the everyday life of city streets. Writing in defense of her beloved Greenwich Village in the Lower East Side of New York, Jacobs attacked the master planning and large-scale development characteristic of the urban renewal era. Jacobs contrasted the virtues of small blocks, crowded streets, mixed uses, and what she called the "heart-of-the-day ballet" of street life with the "monotony and repetition of sameness" of planned environments.[82]

To Jacobs, a "marvelous order" was hidden beneath the surface of disorder on busy city streets, and both were necessary "for maintaining the safety of the streets and the freedom of the city."[83] Through their constant presence, people running the businesses fronting the sidewalk—storekeepers, barkeepers, shoe repairers, the owners of cleaners and barbershops, and their regular customers as well—kept their eyes on the comings and goings just outside the window. In this way, the sidewalk ballet made room for everyone, but at the same time, public safety and order were attended to, without anyone planning it or even thinking about it. Here is a description of the scene in front of her home on Hudson Street:

> When I get home from work, the ballet is reaching its crescendo. This is the time of roller skates and stilts and tricycles, and games in the lee of the stoop with bottletops and plastic cowboys; this is the time of bundles and packages, zigzagging from the drug store to the fruit stand back over to the butchers.[84]

More recently, Douglas Rae has decried the "end of urbanism," which he defines as the "patterns of private conduct and decision-making that by and large make the successful governance of cities possible."[85] Based on his study of New Haven, Connecticut, Rae concluded that in the past, the life of the city was focused on downtown streets and the densely settled residential areas surrounding them. Echoing Jacobs, Rae writes of the "dense fabric of tiny stores" that were "only partly in the business of selling groceries: they were also governing sidewalks and the people who walked them."[86] This "sidewalk republic" made it unnecessary for formal government to intervene in people's lives because informal social networks were adequate for preserving public order and supplying people's basic needs.

What brought about the demise of urbanism? In Rae's account, the main suspects include the automobile, suburbanization and the policies that encouraged it, the decline of industrial employment, racial strife, and globalization, which replaced locally oriented businesses with national corporations.[87] Taken together, these factors (and others) led to the decentering of residential and economic activities. Federally sponsored urban renewal and highway projects, though intended to save the core, only made things worse through the wholesale clearance of historic buildings, business streets, and residential areas.

The recent revival of downtowns and the gentrification of nearby neighborhoods should not be taken as evidence that the world that Jacobs, Rae, and others[88] write about is being resurrected. It is just as well to accept that the old downtowns have died for good and that they have been replaced by something else. Metropolitan regions continue to flow inexorably outward. Other nodes of activity—suburban business districts, malls, corporate campuses, edge cities—continue to grow. The downtowns of central cities will never be the singular focus of activity for their metropolitan regions that they were in the past.

In important respects, the new downtowns are also less diverse than those of the past. In central business districts, the dense collection of small shops has long been replaced by big buildings and, in the larger cities, by skyscrapers. Chain stores and outlets, such as Starbucks, the Gap, and Victoria's Secret, are outlets for national and international corporations. Cineplexes have replaced small theaters; chain supermarkets have replaced many of the specialized shops that separately sold meat, vegetables, candy, and ice cream.[89] Many business establishments, such as large appliance stores and automobile dealerships, have moved out of the downtowns entirely. Shopkeepers no longer keep their eyes on the street, if they can see it at all, and corporate minimum-wage employees do not have a vested interest in doing so.

Residential use is what drives the revival of downtowns today. In Manhattan, old commercial space has been in demand because the buildings are being turned into condominiums. In Philadelphia, office space has stayed about the same since 1990, but new residential towers poked into the skyline all over the downtown.[90] In St. Louis, many old warehouse and office buildings might have been torn down if not for condominium conversions; indeed, a downtown retail mall built as recently as the 1980s has been converted into a luxury condominium complex. By building inside the shells of historic structures, developers are able to give the new downtowns an ambiance of authenticity. According to the urban scholar Richard Florida, it mimics the kind of environment that young professionals prefer—places with "real buildings, real people, real history."[91] In fact, many gentrifiers seem to dream up versions of Jane Jacobs' West Village as the ideal place to live. Ironically, their arrival, over time, can contribute to the creeping homogenization of such a neighborhood. Another important question in this context concerns the sustainability of two-story neighborhoods in ever growing metropolises. Much like the sprawling suburban developments that have become an environmental nuisance, they stretch the electric grid, encourage the expansion of streets, and do not offer nearly enough housing to satisfy a big city's housing needs.

There is growing tension between historical preservationists, like Jane Jacobs' followers, and others, who say that the need for affordable housing can never be met by preserving or replicating the old eyes-on-the street neighborhoods of the nineteenth and early twentieth centuries. The economist Edward Glaeser addressed this tension in a lengthy article in the *Atlantic* in 2011:

> I grew up surrounded by white glazed towers built after World War II to provide affordable housing for middle-income people like my parents. The neighborhood [...] had plenty of fun restaurants, quirky stores, and even-quirkier pedestrians. [...] It was certainly a [...] vibrant urban space, albeit one with plenty of skyscrapers.[92]

There is some truth to Glaeser's argument. Conversely, however, it is important to recognize that neighborhood changes or urban renewal of downtown areas are quite different from those changes affecting the areas that have always been residential. Most of the residents who live downtown are exceptionally affluent, especially in global cities. In other parts of the city, the gentrified neighborhoods represent different stages of the gentrification process, from those made up of new condominium towers or old, architecturally significant factory buildings and townhouses that have been gutted and rehabbed, filled with affluent people to those still on edge, populated by a mélange of artists, musicians, and students, as well as affluent professionals.[93] This mix describes Logan Square in Chicago but does not apply to the Magnificent Mile on Michigan Avenue, with its rows of high-end chain stores and nearby condominium towers. Any generalizations about the character of "gentrified" areas must, to some degree, gloss over the fantastic differences in the urban environment from one neighborhood to the next, or even from block to block.

Are the new downtowns and the gentrified neighborhoods merely impoverished versions of what cities once had? It is hard to say. A century ago, the residential areas of New Haven that Rae studied contained people of all social classes, incomes, and ethnic backgrounds.[94] Similarly, diverse assortments of people live in some of the trendiest of today's urban neighborhoods. Superficially, these may bear a striking resemblance to another time, except that their historic buildings are occupied by restaurants, bars and taverns, music venues, art galleries, and shops, plus some sprinkling of chain stores. But the people walking the streets and the businesses they patronize are, in fact, completely unique to the twenty-first century. Those who live in such environments can put aside any anxiety about whether the city streets they walk on are authentic. They surely are, but that is because whatever exists in the present is fully as authentic as the lost world that many people pine for.

A Delicate Balancing Act

City governments are, in effect, mechanisms for managing the social and political differences among the contending groups that make up the city. The legitimacy of democratic governance rests on popular perceptions that the governmental institutions that represent them are responsive to their preferences and needs. When enough people feel aggrieved, they often demonstrate their disaffection by withholding their vote, refusing to participate in organizational or political life, and resorting to protest. Sometimes, if they are angry enough, they turn to violence. When conflict reaches this level, it becomes obvious that the governmental system has failed to mediate the social and political differences that divide people. Judged by this standard, urban governments in the United States have an uneven record.

The history of American cities is peppered with episodes of violent unrest and conflict. On many occasions in the nineteenth century, mobs attacked immigrants, sometimes in bloody riots that lasted for days, and in the twentieth century, Blacks became the frequent target of racial violence. White mobs attacked Blacks in New York City in 1863, East St. Louis in 1917, Chicago in 1919, and Tulsa in 1920. The harassment of Blacks became commonplace in the era of suburban white flight in the 1950s.

In the face of police harassment and racial discrimination, Blacks sometimes also vented their frustrations in the streets. Blacks protested in Detroit in 1944 and dozens of times over several hot summers in the 1960s. Incidents of police harassment of Blacks precipitated virtually all of the riots and protests in that turbulent decade and thereafter.[95] Riots erupted in African American areas in

Cuban-dominated Miami four times in the 1980s, beginning with the Liberty City disorders in May 1980. Each of the riots was associated with the killing of a Black man by Hispanic white police officers.[96] Police conduct still stokes frequent controversy, and from time to time, these have erupted into civil disorders. A quite typical incident occurred in early August 2006, in the Cabrini-Green public housing projects in Chicago, when police shot a 14-year-old boy who was brandishing a BB gun. In the wake of the shooting, demonstrators turned out to march around city hall.

The most serious riot of the twentieth century occurred in Los Angeles in 1992, following the acquittal of four police officers charged with the use of excessive force when they arrested and severely beat Rodney King. The acquittal came from a majority-white jury in suburban Ventura county, a good 80 miles away from L.A., where the beating had taken place. Incriminating video footage of the brutal arrest and subsequent beating showed several police officers standing by, watching the beating of Rodney King, which made their acquittal all the more unbelievable and led many observers to the conclusion that it represented a clear case of racial bias. The subsequent uprising left 53 people dead, 2,383 injured and resulted in 16,291 arrests, more than 5,500 fires, and over $700 million in property damage. Unlike previous uprisings, it was multiethnic, involving Blacks, Hispanics, and Asians.[97] In the course of the riots, 30 percent of the approximately 4,000 businesses destroyed were owned by Hispanics,[98] but Korean-owned businesses were especially singled out.[99] For a time, it seemed that racial and ethnic tensions had subsided, but in April 2000, renewed fears of violent protests ran rampant in Miami the day after federal agents seized Elian Gonzalez from relatives in Miami and returned him to his father in Cuba. Cuban American leaders called for calm, fearful that rioting might break out.

After the 2008 election of Barack Obama as President of the United States, the term "post-racial politics" surfaced in academia and beyond. The idea behind it was that the election of an African American president marked the endpoint to racial inequality and conflict in the United States. This, of course, was and is not the case. In fact, the entire premise behind the idea of "post-racial politics" was seriously flawed, as it wrongly assumed that race-based historical injustices do not have any enduring consequences. Not only does social inequality still correlate with race and ethnicity in the United States, but the Obama presidency also saw a resurgence of race-based violence in American cities and suburbs and culminated in the election of a president who ran his campaign and presidency explicitly on racist rhetoric.

Ferguson, MO, a suburb of St. Louis, which turned from a predominantly white suburb into a majority Black town over the past 30 years, became the center of renewed trauma for African Americans in the twenty-first century.[100] A 2014 Brookings report called Ferguson "emblematic of growing suburban poverty."[101] In August of that same year, an African American teenager named Michael Brown was fatally shot by police officer Darren Wilson. Brown had been suspected of having stolen a pack of cigarillos.[102] Wilson stopped the suspect and his friend in the street and a struggle ensued, during which Wilson shot Brown twice,[103] as, according to Wilson, Brown reached for his gun. As it turned out, Michael Brown was unarmed.[104] After Brown fled from Wilson's car, Wilson shot Brown several more times[105] for no apparent reason. After a grand jury in St. Louis decided not to indict Wilson, protests, which had been ongoing since the shooting, escalated in St. Louis, triggering a new wave of outrage at the killing of unarmed African Americans by police across the United States, a frequent phenomenon throughout the country's history.

The Ferguson protests were followed by protests in Baltimore after the death of Freddie Gray from spinal cord injuries in mid-April 2015 after being transported in a police van.[106] It was unclear why Gray had been arrested by police in the first place because he was not wanted at the time of his arrest.[107] A knife was found on Gray after his arrest.[108] Following Gray's death, Baltimore's State Attorney brought charges against six police officers. Two of them were acquitted, one ended in a mistrial, and the charges against the remaining three were dropped.[109] In addition, five of the six officers faced administrative charges for violating police department rules and neglect.[110] Two accepted the charges and minor disciplinary procedures, while two officers fought the charges in court and were acquitted.[111] The charges against the remaining officer were dropped.[112]

OUTTAKE

Black Lives Matter: Moving Beyond a Moment and Creating a Movement

By Christina M. Greer

#BlackLivesMatter was founded in 2012 after neighborhood vigilante George Zimmerman, the killer of then 17-year-old Trayvon Martin, was acquitted in the state of Florida for his crime. The three founders of Black Lives Matter—Alicia Garza, Opal Tometi, and Patrisse Cullors—witnessed what many Americans also saw, Trayvon Martin essentially being tried posthumously for his own murder. #BlackLivesMatter was founded as a response to anti-Black racism in America, more specifically, a seemingly historical and institutional disregard for Black lives and Black bodies. In addition, this chapter-based national organization serves as a call to action for those who support the resistance of the dehumanization of the Black experience in America. Garza, Tometi, and Cullors also contend that #BlackLivesMatter extends beyond the extrajudicial killings of Black people by the police and vigilantes. It is their mission to bring further awareness—locally, domestically, and internationally—to issues pertaining to gender, sexuality, disability, and economics, as well as violence.

Black Lives Matter is a movement, not just a hashtag. The use of social media has moved beyond the #BlackLivesMatter to activism in city streets across the country. It was Black Lives Matter activists who organized in Ferguson, MO so that people from all over the world would learn about the killing of 18-year-old Michael Brown by Officer Darren Wilson. It was also a cadre of Black Lives Matter activists who organized in cities across the country in May and June 2020 to protest the murders of George Floyd, Ahmaud Arbery, and far too many others. BLM's goal was also to make aware of the economic subjugation and racial segregation of Blacks in the twenty-first century. There are currently more than 40 chapters across the U.S. and Canada predicated on creating a network based on Black self-determination. Since her inception, the United States has systematically, substantively, and specifically targeted Black inclusion through inequities in education, housing, disproportionate incarceration rates, and various assaults on Black women and children. Black Lives Matter as an organization steadfastly affirms the resilience and humanity of Black lives, even in the midst of oppression and uses of deadly force by the police state and vigilantes.

Black Lives Matter has also challenged the historical notions of Black leadership and activism. By moving beyond the heteronormative promotion of straight cis Black male leadership (often religious in nature), BLM as a movement affirms Black queer and trans individuals, people with disabilities, Black undocumenteds, and those who have been in the criminal justice system. In addition, by affirming women, all Black lives along the gender spectrum, and those who have been marginalized or left out of Black liberation movements, BLM seeks to re(build) the Black liberation movement.

Indeed, not all Black Americans fully support the mission or activist strategies of the organization. However, diversity and dissent within the Black American freedom movements have existed as long as the desire to be treated equally under the law. In the 1960s, Dr. Martin Luther King, Jr., Malcolm X, the Black Panther Party, and the NAACP—to name just a few of the Black individuals and groups leading the movement for civil rights and civil liberties—all represented differing ideas as to how Black liberation should be attained. BLM is an extension of the complex debates surrounding race and racism in American politics, culture, and society.

The success of BLM has been the incorporation of protest politics to American democracy. In order to best understand racial politics and Black politics, in particular, it is imperative to understand the necessity and the intersection of electoral *and* protest politics. There are a myriad of Black political opinions and ideologies, and BLM represents just one of the many facets of twenty-first century Black politics. By recognizing and uplifting female, queer, and differently abled leadership, BLM has moved the struggle for Black equity one step closer to the intention of a just society.

Incidents of police violence against unarmed Black men, such as the ones in Baltimore or Ferguson, remain the norm rather than the exception. The killing of Eric Garner in a chokehold by New York City police officer, and the murders of Laquan McDonald in Chicago at the hands of police officer

Jason Van Dyke and of George Floyd, after Minneapolis police officer Derek Chauvin knelt on his neck for 9 minutes and 29 seconds, have become emblematic for a deep-seated bias in the policing of people of color by white police officers across the country. The 2020 Black Lives Matter protests following the murder of George Floyd, and the publicly available, excruciating video footage of his last minutes, represented another plea for systemic change amid the large proportion of Black Americans (many of them unarmed) killed each year by police. The Washington Post has kept track of police shooting related deaths since 2015 and found around 1,000 people die each year in fatal police shootings in the United States.[113] The proportion of Black Americans among those killed in such shootings is baffling: Blacks are killed at a rate of 37 per one million in police shootings, more than twice the rate of whites, where deaths in police shootings stand at 15 per one million.[114] This discrepancy stands in spite of the fact that Black Americans make up only 13 percent of the total U.S. population. Since these numbers have been steady for years, they are unlikely to change in the future, absent some more fundamental systemic change.

Local political systems began to open up in response to the civil rights movement of the 1960s, which produced a generation of activist African American leaders and a newly energized Black electorate. As late as the mid-1960s, it seemed unthinkable that an African American might become the mayor of a major American city, but within a few years, it had become commonplace. Before long, Latinos also entered the local political arena in increasing numbers. The presence of minorities in the public office made it possible for African American and Latino communities to turn from strategies of protest to incorporation into the politics of the city.

Incorporation into democratic processes provided an opportunity for historically disadvantaged groups to work for change from within. Despite these gains, however, urban governance continues to be a delicate balancing act because incorporation has not always brought the hoped-for rewards. Affirmative action programs changed the complexion of police forces, fire departments, school programs, and municipal offices to an extent. Nevertheless, racial and ethnic inequalities persist and continue to fuel conflict and resentment. African Americans and Hispanics continue to be disadvantaged in income, educational attainment, and participation in the workforce, and they have been disproportionately affected by increasing inequality and rising poverty levels. Since the turn of the twenty-first century, the number of people living in poverty has been steadily rising in the United States. According to the 2020 Census, 11.4 percent of the U.S. population was living in poverty, including 16.1 percent of children.[115] The 2020 increase by one percentage point from 2019 was the first increase in the national poverty rate after five consecutive years of steady decline.[116] Poverty rates also increased for married couple families and families with a female householder. For married couple families, the poverty rate increased by 0.7 percent (from 4 to 4.7 percent), but for families with a female householder, poverty rates increased by over a percentage point (from 22.2 to 23.4 percent), likely due to the particularly drastic impact of the COVID-19 pandemic on working women and mothers.[117] Among the major racial groups, the highest poverty rate persists among African Americans, at 19.5 percent (but with no significant increase from 2019), followed by Hispanics at 17 percent, non-Hispanic whites at 8.2 percent, and Asians at 8.1 percent. As long as systemic racial injustice persists, such inequalities will persist, and racial and ethnic tensions will remain a fact of life in America's metropolitan regions.

OUTTAKE

Multiethnic Coalitions Are Hard to Keep Together and Sometimes Based on Unrealistic Expectations

Since the civil rights struggles of the 1960s, a profound transformation has thoroughly altered the urban political landscape. Civil rights and community organizing activities helped mobilize the African American electorate, and within a few years, African American mayors and other public officials were taking the reins of city governments. Over time, the drive for representation in the political system embraced other groups as well. In addition to the symbolic benefits of incorporation, the material benefits were substantial; the gains in public employment contributed to economic gains for the middle-class, the integration of municipal workforces, the hiring of minority personnel in administrative posts in municipal governments and school systems, changes in police behavior, and improvements in the tone of racial and ethnic relations.

But the complex ethnic makeup of urban politics has revealed just how hard it is to build and maintain multiethnic coalitions. The expectation that Blacks and Latinos would find a common cause because both groups are systemically disadvantaged has rarely been realized because there are significant differences between and within each of these groups. Recently, doubt has been cast on whether we should even talk about a "Latinx community" when we are addressing people with different national origins, different racial and ethnic backgrounds, and, in many cases, different political preferences. The minority is a problematic term that papers over significant inter-group differences, and obscures the fact that certain ethnic and racial groups are often in the majority in metro areas; the challenge is to forge alliances over issues that attract support across ethnic groups.[118]

The problem of defining a singular "minority agenda" explains why it is hard to assemble interethnic coalitions and also why it is difficult to assess the actual gains from political incorporation. Perhaps an expectation that it could be any other way was always unrealistic for two reasons. First, many views tend to overestimate the ability of city governments to change the basic structures of the economy and society; in general, the conditions under which the majority of historically disadvantaged people live in society are outside of the control of city governments. To alter them would require more systemic changes at the national level that so far our country has not been able to make. Second, such an expectation amounted to a naïve assumption that there were few political differences among the groups lumped together under the "minority" label.

Sources: Albert K. Karnig and Susan Welch, Black Representatives and Urban Policy (Chicago: University of Chicago Press, 1980); Rufus P. Browning, Dale Rogers Marshall, and David H. Tabb, Racial Politics in American Cities, 3rd ed. (New York: Longman, 2002), pp. 374–377.

The Recent Revolution in Urban Governance

The civil rights struggles of the 1960s and community organizing activities of the same era precipitated a revolution in governance at all levels of the American political system. Until 1967, not a single African American had ever been elected mayor of a major American city. In that year, Richard Hatcher was elected mayor of Gary, Indiana, and Carl Stokes became the mayor of Cleveland. In the years since these watershed elections, Blacks and Latinos have been elected to office in cities of all sizes from coast to coast; by 1988, 28 African American mayors had been elected in cities of more than 50,000 in population, and the number reached 38 only five years later.[119] From 1970 to 2001, the number of African American elected officials in the United States increased from 1,469 to 9,101; 454 of them were mayors.[120] By 2014, the total number of African American elected officials in the United States had crossed the 10,000 thresholds.[121] Many of these officials were elected to positions in local governments, with large numbers in education, the judicial system, and law enforcement.

With the election of Kurt Schmoke as the first African American mayor of Baltimore in 1987, every city of more than 100,000 people that had a majority Black population had elected an African American mayor. At different points in the 1980s, African American candidates won the mayor's office in four of the five largest cities in the country, even though African American voters were in the minority in all of those cities (David Dinkins in New York, Tom Bradley in Los Angeles, Harold Washington in Chicago, and Wilson Goode in Philadelphia). Again in the 1990s, African Americans won in several cities where they constituted a minority of voters, including St. Louis, Denver, Kansas City, and Seattle.

City politics experienced another profound change in the 1980s when Latinos began entering political office in large numbers. The number of Latino elected officials at all government levels in the United States grew from 3,147 in 1985 to 5,459 in 1994 before dropping off slightly to 5,041 in 2005.[122] By 2014, the number of Latino elected officials at all levels of government had increased to 6,084.[123] Latino mayors won office in Denver, Miami, San Antonio, and numerous smaller cities. Federico Peña's election in Denver in 1983 was considered a breakthrough because he was the first Latino to be elected mayor of a large American city without a Latino majority. At the time, Latinos constituted just 18 percent of the city's population, with Blacks making up another 12 percent.[124] The gains realized in cities reverberated throughout the American political system. For instance, Peña and the former mayor of San Antonio, Henry Cisneros, were appointed to President Bill Clinton's cabinet in 1993.

African American and Latino mayors have faced a daunting challenge because, in most cities where they have won, white voters have commanded a clear majority. Because of this political reality, minority candidates have been forced to walk a fine line: If they campaign on issues of great importance to their racial and ethnic constituents, they risk alienating their white voters. Once in office, they have found that whatever the composition of their electoral coalition, they are unable to get much done unless they forge a good working relationship with the one group that can bring investment to the city—the business community. A politics of trade-offs and negotiation that fully satisfies no one at all is virtually guaranteed by this circumstance.

Political struggles in the nation's two largest cities, New York and Los Angeles, shed light on the difficulties of governance when complex interracial and interethnic coalitions must be assembled. By 1990, non-Latino whites made up less than half—43 percent—of the population of New York City. Blacks accounted for 25 percent, Latinos 24 percent, and Asians 8 percent.[125] With a large Jewish population that was historically sensitive to discrimination and supportive of the civil rights movement, New York City seemed to be an ideal setting within which a diverse racial and ethnic coalition might emerge. In fact, however, this context produced a fractious politics that resulted in the election of Ed Koch, a self-styled conservative white mayor. After serving three terms from 1977 to 1985, he was defeated in 1989 by an African American, David Dinkins, who was defeated after one term by a Republican conservative, Rudolph Giuliani, who served from 1993 to 2001.

By contrast, Los Angeles, which is also racially and ethnically diverse, elected an African American mayor, Tom Bradley, in 1973, and the voters kept him in office for five consecutive terms. Throughout this period, Blacks accounted for no more than 14 percent of the population of Los Angeles. Much can be learned about the delicate nature of coalition politics by an examination of the Bradley years.

Tom Bradley, the son of Texas sharecroppers, moved to Los Angeles with his family at the age of seven. An exceptional student and athlete, he attended the University of California, Los Angeles, and then took a job with the Los Angeles Police Department. After putting down roots in a mostly white neighborhood on the West Side, he organized a community relations group, and through this activity, he forged close personal contacts with Jewish merchants and civic leaders. By taking night courses, he earned a law degree, quit the police force, and opened his own legal practice. His entry into the politics of the local Democratic Party came at a perfect time, just when an alliance of upwardly mobile African Americans, Jews, and liberals began to challenge the regular Democratic Party, which had previously excluded them.

In 1969, the reform coalition pushed Bradley forward as a challenger to the Democratic incumbent, Sam Yorty. Bradley's chances were hurt by the racial tensions that continued to linger throughout the city. Yorty won the election by securing support from an overwhelming majority of white votes and received particularly strong support from upper-middle-class homeowners in the San Fernando Valley. When he ran against Yorty four years later, however, Bradley defused the issue of race by avoiding overt racial issues and emphasizing the importance of revitalizing the downtown and keeping taxes low. He defeated Yorty by assembling a diverse coalition composed of African Americans of all income levels, Latinos, higher-income, and especially Jewish white liberals. Bradley succeeded largely because he was able to symbolize different things to different people: "Whites saw Bradley as a symbol of racial harmony, while blacks saw him as a symbol of racial assertion."[126]

Bradley's success was predicated on a long history of collaboration between white liberals and the upwardly mobile Black middle class. Both groups had been systematically excluded from local politics prior to Bradley's victory, and therefore they viewed each other as allies in the cause of ousting the Yorty regime. As soon as he entered City Hall, Bradley assembled a formidable coalition that would allow him not only to win elections but also to govern. To accumulate the resources necessary for realizing his aspiration to remake the downtown, he forged an alliance with downtown banks and business corporations. In this way, he was always able to raise the massive amounts of money necessary for winning election in a city as diverse and sprawling as Los Angeles.

The conditions that allowed an African American to become the mayor of Los Angeles were absent in New York, despite the fact that Blacks were already well entrenched in New York City's government by the mid-1960s.[127] By the time Blacks entered New York City's political system, liberals and Jews had already established themselves by successfully electing a liberal Republican, John Lindsay, as mayor for two terms (1966–1973). Although New York's Blacks, Jews, and white liberals could clearly cooperate, their leaders viewed one another with suspicion. These tensions came to a head in 1968 when the African American community launched an experiment in community control in the Ocean Hill–Brownsville schools in Brooklyn. The school board's plan to transfer 19 teachers, some of them Jewish, out of the district resulted in a bitter citywide strike by the teachers' union, which drove a wedge between Blacks and Jews that endures in New York even to the present day. The same sorts of conflicts and suspicions have characterized the political relationships between African Americans and Latinos, who are themselves divided into many factions based on national origin and language.[128] Ed Koch was able to exploit these divisions, and he succeeded in assembling a coalition of Jews, Catholics, and ethnic whites. This alliance proved to be enduring enough to keep him in office through three elections.[129]

An African American, David Dinkins was able to beat him in 1989 because he had close ties to the regular Democratic Party, and he possessed a dignified, non-confrontational style that did not seem threatening to white voters. In the early stages of the 1989 mayoral contest, Koch miscalculated by criticizing Jesse Jackson, who had made a run for the presidency the year before, for expressing support for the Palestine Liberation Organization (PLO). Koch commented that Jews "would have to be crazy" to vote for Jackson. An African American newspaper, *Amsterdam News*, replied bitterly by reminding Koch that "he is mayor of the city; not just of New York Jewry."[130] Dinkins secured enough support from voters who had tired of Koch's racial rhetoric to carry the election.

As it turned out, Dinkins' election did not bring an end to racially charged politics in New York City. After serving one term, he was defeated by a self-styled political conservative, Rudolph Giuliani. Giuliani, a former prosecutor, broke the mold by winning as a Republican in a Democratic city. He quickly set out to terminate affirmative action programs, slash spending for welfare and housing, cut health services, and beef up the police forces.[131] Crime control became the central cause of his administration, and he became nationally known for championing the "broken windows" theory of crime control, which was based on the premise that a systematic punishment for small crimes would deter more serious ones (taken literally, this meant that if someone metaphorically "broke a window" by jaywalking or littering, he could be arrested). While in office, Giuliani went out of his way to snub African American leaders. In 2001, when he was forced to leave office because of term limits, he was succeeded by Republican Michael Bloomberg, who with his own money spent $99 per vote to narrowly defeat the Democratic candidate.[132]

New York's political coalitions remain interesting. In 2014, Bill De Blasio succeeded Michael Bloomberg, running on a progressive platform, which included tax increases for the super-rich, the promise of de-escalation of police violence and reduced sentencing for marihuana possession, as well as a universal pre-kindergarten program, and an expansion of the city's after-school programs. The real campaign-winner for De Blasio, who was lingering between the fourth and fifth places in New York City's 2013 mayoral race, was a campaign ad he shot with his son, Dante, that fall. The white candidate's African American teenage son, who identified himself in the ad only as 15-year-old Dante from Brooklyn, sat in a kitchen in the ad, outlining his father's campaign platform over images of the bi-racial de Blasio family and explaining clearly why his father represented a drastic break from Bloomberg's policies:

> I want to tell you a little bit about Bill de Blasio. He is the only Democrat with the guts to really break from the Bloomberg years. [...] Bill de Blasio will be a mayor for every New Yorker, no matter where they live or what they look like and I'd say that even if he weren't my Dad.[133]

The viral ad, some commentators noted, promised a sort of change many New Yorkers had been longing for. William Cunningham, formerly Michael Bloomberg's communications director, observed: "Everybody is talking about Dante's afro. After 20 years of Bloomberg and Giuliani, [New Yorkers] were ready for a change, and he gave them a very distinct picture of what his change would look like."[134] De Blasio was the only person within the leading group of mayoral candidates who had problematized the Bloomberg-era policy of stop-and-frisk, a policing tactic, which predominantly targeted people of color. Stop-and-frisk, also known as Terry stop (after the 1968 Supreme Court decision Terry v. Ohio), is a policing practice based on which civilians can be temporarily detained, questioned, and searched without a search warrant. The practice has come under significant scrutiny, as research has demonstrated that it opens the door for racial profiling. Research by the New York City Liberties Union shows that 9 out of 10 individuals who are stopped and frisked in New York City are completely innocent.[135] The research by the NYCLU also demonstrates the disproportionate impact the practice has on communities of color: In 2019, of the 13,459 stops recorded by the NYPD, 59 percent (or 7,981 people) were Black, 29 percent (or 3,869) were Latinx, and only 9 percent (or 1,215 people) were white.[136] In other words, De Blasio's platform, as well as his well-timed, soft-power campaign ad, convinced enough people from communities of color to vote for him, which, in the end, gave him the edge. Many progressives have since soured on De Blasio, especially during the summer of 2020, when during the wide-scale Black Lives Matter protests in the city, the NYPD drove an SUV into a crowd of protesters in Brooklyn and kettled another group of peaceful protesters.[137] There were also instances of police officers pulling down protestors' face masks to pepper spray them. The city's aggressive 8 p.m. curfew, which accompanied the protests, also did not sit well with New Yorkers. De Blasio acted defensive on the multiple occasions he was interviewed and questioned about the NYPD's aggressive tactics against the mostly peaceful civilian protesters, much to the anger and disappointment of progressives in the city. The NYPD's policing tactics were by no means the only issue that marked De Blasio's fall from grace with progressives and the city's communities of color during his second term. But they are somewhat symbolic of his complicated legacy, as well as of the ongoing struggle by progressive mayors to curb racialized policing tactics. It remains to be seen whether his apparent successor, the moderate Democrat Eric Adams, a Black Brooklynite, and former New York City police officer, who won the city's 2021 Democratic primary against a good number of more progressive candidates, can maintain a multi-racial and multi-ethnic coalition as mayor.

American cities contain a multitude of groups and interests, and urban officials have become skilled in the practical task of managing conflict within a complex political environment. They have learned how to do so because the politics of cities has become generally more accessible than in the past, making it hard to shut out anyone completely. A complex institutional structure provides numerous points of access into the political process. The result is a lively and often contentious struggle over the policy priorities of the city.

The Benefits of Incorporation

The incorporation of African Americans and Hispanics into local political structures has brought substantial benefits to both groups. The first generation of African American mayors successfully pushed for more spending for health, education, housing, and job training programs and for increases in federal grants.

Public employment provided an important avenue for minority employment. Research has consistently shown that when Blacks win the mayoralty and start to occupy important positions in city government, the employment of people of color in city government increased.[138] From 1973 to 1991, Mayor Bradley managed to increase the jobs held by Blacks, Latinos, and Asians in municipal government from 36 to 50 percent. People of color are often concentrated in lower-level jobs, but in Los Angeles during this period, their representation in top-level city jobs increased as well.[139]

Mayors of color also initiated preferential procurement programs requiring that a minimum percentage of city contracts be given to minority business enterprises (MBEs). In 1973, Blacks accounted for a majority of Atlanta's population, but firms owned by African Americans received only one-tenth of 1 percent of the city's contracts. By 1988, the preferential procurement program had raised the proportion to 35 percent. There were, though, two drawbacks. First, some MBEs acted as mere fronts for non-minority firms doing most of the work.[140] Second, preferential procurement generally benefited higher-income and better educated people within communities of color. Atlanta's first Black mayor, Maynard Jackson, boasted that the minority set-asides for Atlanta's airport expansion created 21 African American millionaires; however, benefits to the low-income community were more difficult to identify.[141]

Beginning in 1989, the U.S. Supreme Court made it harder for cities and states to use preferential procurement programs to increase minority employment. In *City of Richmond v. J. A. Croson Co.* (1989), the Court ruled that Richmond's program requiring that 30 percent of contracts be set aside for MBEs violated the equal protection clause of the Fourteenth Amendment.[142] To withstand the "strict scrutiny" standard of constitutionality, cities must document past discrimination by the city government and demonstrate that race-neutral alternatives will not solve the problem. This ruling makes preferential procurement difficult but not impossible to implement.[143]

Police reform was one of the most important policy benefits that flowed from political incorporation. Police brutality and inadequate police protection have long been two of the most frequently expressed grievances in communities of color around the country. For many years, the police department of Los Angeles was loathed among people of color. Under the city's governmental structure, the LAPD operated well beyond the influence of elected officials. Appointed by an independent police commission, the chief of police had a free hand in running the department. The LAPD had always prided itself on its tough, law-and-order approach to law enforcement, and the chief liked to brag about the department's state-of-the-art, high-tech weaponry. In Los Angeles, policing relied on helicopters equipped with infrared cameras for night vision and 30-million-candlepower spotlights, called Nightsuns, that could turn night into day. Street numbers painted on rooftops gave police helicopters a navigable street grid from the air (now replaced by satellite navigation). Synchronization with patrol cars was facilitated by a communications system conceptualized by Hughes Aircraft and refined by NASA's Jet Propulsion Laboratory.[144] In low-income areas, this strategy meant the LAPD acted more like an occupying army than as an instrument for preserving public safety.

From 1978 to 1992, Chief Daryl Gates ran the LAPD as his personal fiefdom. Under operation HAMMER, patrol officers and elite tactical squads descended on South Central Los Angeles, arresting thousands of youths of color in each sweep. Young men were brought in for a wide range of infractions, from selling drugs to suspected gang activity to charges of loitering and jaywalking. In the absence of other charges, resisting arrest became a favorite police option. By 1990 as many as 50,000 suspects had been arrested in these sweeps, which is astounding considering only about 100,000 African American youths lived in all of Los Angeles.[145] The LAPD had a practice of using a dangerous chokehold to control people in custody. In 1982, after frequent use of the chokehold resulted in a rash of deaths among young Black men, Chief Gates made the inflammatory statement that the problem could be traced to the anatomy of Blacks rather than to police practices: "We may be finding that in some Blacks when [the carotid chokehold] is applied the veins or arteries do not open up as fast as they do on normal people."[146] The beating of Rodney King, which set off the 1992 riots, came as no surprise to Blacks in Los Angeles.

Mayor Bradley, who had the advantage of being a former cop, succeeded in bringing the LAPD under some degree of civilian control, but only after 20 years of fierce political battles. The LAPD's share of the city's budget fell from 23 percent in 1972–1973 to 18 percent in 1987–1988. Between 1980 and 1988, minority representation in the LAPD increased from 20 to 32 percent, but the numbers of minorities in leadership positions still lagged. Most important, in June 1992, shortly after the riots, the voters approved Proposition F. Strongly supported by Bradley, Proposition F limited the terms of police chiefs and removed their civil service protection. Having campaigned vigorously against Proposition F, Chief Gates resigned and was succeeded by an African American, Willie Williams, who pledged to implement community-based policing.[147]

What the Los Angeles case shows is that even under adverse conditions, when minorities are incorporated into the political system, they are able to bring about important changes. In Los Angeles, the Black community considered it essential that more African American police officers are hired, and the police department be brought under greater civilian control.[148] Racism and police brutality still occur within integrated police forces but changing the composition of the force marked at least one big step toward reform.

It may be difficult to forge political coalitions across racial and ethnic groups, but the biggest problem facing these alliances has not been their fragility but their lack of success in persuading state legislatures and the federal government to increase funding for social programs. In the 1960s and 1970s, when federal grants were flowing into cities, the first generation of mayors of color successfully lobbied for programs that benefited the poor. Since the withdrawal of federal funds, mayors have found it difficult to generate the revenues necessary to fund housing, health, jobs, recreation, and other initiatives. Mayors of color emphasize economic development as much as they do, not because they have given up on the goal of providing benefits to their constituents, but because they see no other way to raise the resources necessary to deliver on their promises. In short, they pursue trickle-down policies based on the logic that "private economic development in the city produces jobs in the private sector and tax money that may be used for jobs and purchases in the public sector. Through the various affirmative action devices … a certain proportion of these jobs and purchases may be channeled to the black community."[149]

The problem is that public-sector jobs have been marginal to the goal of advancing the economic well-being of Blacks and Latinos.[150] At most, the public sector can supply employment to no more than 6–8 percent of the African American population of central cities—even assuming no jobs would go to other groups.[151] In any case, large proportions of public jobs, minority business contracts, and other benefits have gone to middle- and upper-income people and even to suburban residents.[152]

It is unrealistic to expect political participation to deliver a fundamental redistribution of economic resources. Only broad systemic change could achieve something like that, and even though such change is necessary in the interest of social justice, it seems tough to bring about. The political incorporation of a group cannot overturn the political, economic, and social arrangements that preserve inequality. As noted by one scholar, "There is no precedent for expecting political participation to produce revolutionary outcomes for any group in American urban politics specifically or American politics in general."[153] Still, considerable progress has been made. Regimes of color have been quite successful in altering hiring policies and curbing abuses by the police. These are important accomplishments.

Studies provide little evidence that the incorporation of Blacks and Latinos into local political systems has led to significantly different taxing, spending, and service delivery policies. For the most part, African American mayors have been enthusiastic advocates for policies that favor business investment and the downtown development. Even so, the incorporation of African Americans and Latinos has had the effect of making people feel better about local politics.

Survey research shows that Blacks living in cities with an African American mayor expressed more trust in and paid more attention to political affairs, and more of them participated in politics.[154] Participation by Latinos has increased when they have been brought into local power structures.[155] Regardless of its limitations, minority incorporation has enhanced the legitimacy of city governments among a substantial portion of the urban population.

The Sanctuary Movement

Besides their minority status, Hispanics face additional hurdles of incorporation. With a growing undocumented population, which hovers around 11 million in 2021, half of them Mexican, and a majority Hispanic,[156] a considerable part of the Hispanic minority also lacks legal immigration status. This makes political incorporation problematic, to say the least. Nevertheless, cities have been at the forefront of catering to the undocumented population in the United States and sometimes even protecting them from federal immigration enforcement.

The Sanctuary City movement has borrowed its name from the Sanctuary Movement of the 1980s when thousands of people from Central America were escaping civil war and political and civil unrest in their countries and coming to the United States.[157] The Reagan administration, on the other hand, saw itself in support of many of the military regimes in Latin America, as part of its anti-communist offensive, and therefore framed these immigrants as economic immigrants, rather than refugees with a well-founded fear of persecution in their home countries, and granted asylum to a tiny fraction.[158] Churches, synagogues, universities, and cities in over 30 states across the United States started providing sanctuary to around 2,000 refugees, risking felony charges.[159]

Based on this very movement, cities across the United States have declared themselves sanctuary cities. The exact significance of a Sanctuary City, however, can vary widely. Unlike the federal government, states and municipalities have no legal authority to implement of change immigration law. Therefore, sanctuary cities cannot introduce a separate immigration policy next to that of the federal government. They can, however, refuse to collaborate with federal law enforcement in terms of information-sharing, as well as offer certain services independent of one's immigration status. In 2015, there were more than 360 municipal jurisdictions across the United States that had officially limited the information they share with the Department of Homeland Security (DHS), which includes Immigration and Customs Enforcement (ICE).[160] New York City, for instance, has implemented the IDNYC program, which allows all New York City residents to obtain an NYC ID card, regardless of immigration status. New York City residence can be proven via a simple phone bill. This is particularly important for undocumented immigrants since proof of (legal) immigration status is required to obtain a New York State ID. The Migration Policy Institute (MPI) estimates that, together, American sanctuary cities host around 5.9 million undocumented immigrants, more than 50 percent of the total undocumented population in the United States.[161] In June 2019, New York State enacted the Green Light Law, which allows New York State residents to obtain a driver's license or permit (one that cannot be used as a federal ID) regardless of their immigration status. To date, a total of sixteen states, California, Colorado, Connecticut, Delaware, Hawaii, Illinois, Maryland, Nevada, New Jersey, New Mexico, New York, Oregon, Utah, Vermont, Virginia, and Washington, as well as the District of Columbia, allow undocumented immigrants to obtain a driver's license or permit in spite of their immigration status, if they can provide officials with certain documentation that confirms their identity, such as a foreign passport, birth certificate, and any proof of residency in the state.[162]

Federal authorities across party lines had long relied on the cooperation of state and local authorities in immigration enforcement. The Bush administration had aggressively extended the 287(g) program.[163] This program delegates special immigration control and enforcement functions to specially trained state and local officials.[164] In 2008, the Bush administration launched Secure Communities, which implemented an automatism that checked fingerprints sent to the FBI by local law enforcement against the DHS database in order to also check for immigration status.[165] The Obama administration continued this highly controversial program until 2014, which identified over 500,000 non-citizens in jails across the country and accounted for 75 percent of all non-border deportations, which more than tripled from around 75,000 in 2006 to 188,000 in 2011.[166] The Secure Communities program soon grew unpopular with many urban communities and municipalities because it increasingly eroded trust between local law enforcement and immigrant communities. As DHS refused to make changes to the program, states and municipalities either passed ordinances limiting their cooperation or dropped out of the program altogether.[167] On July 1, 2015, the Obama administration replaced Secure Communities with a new program, the Priority Enforcement Program (PEP), which still mandates the sharing of fingerprint data with immigration authorities, but limits enforcement to those individuals who have committed a serious crime and pose a threat to public safety.[168]

In 2017, there seemed no real perspective for mending the relationship between federal immigration authorities on the one hand and many state and local governments on the other. Immigration was one of the most salient issues during the 2016 presidential election campaign. During his campaign bid for the presidency, then-candidate Trump called Mexicans "rapists" and a threat to national security, and, after taking the White House, new president-elect Trump threatened sanctuary cities with serious cuts in federal funding should they continue on their course. On January 25, 2017, just days after his inauguration, the new president signed an executive order, blocking federal funding from sanctuary cities, claiming that by their refusal to fully cooperate with federal immigration enforcement, such municipalities "willfully violate federal law."[169] In April 2017, a federal court in California blocked the order, "calling it coercive and ruling that Trump's attempt to withhold all federal money for such cities violates constitutional principles."[170] Nevertheless, the Trump administration's relationship with sanctuary cities remains strained. In September, the administration launched "Operation Safe City," a federal immigration crackdown in those cities, which had voiced the most vocal opposition to the Trump administration's immigration policy, such as New York City, Los Angeles, Baltimore, and Washington, DC.[171] The four-day operation resulted in the rounding up of almost 500 undocumented immigrants and was largely interpreted to be a provocative move by the administration against sanctuary cities.[172] Sanctuary cities, on the other hand, in the wake of the operation confirmed their commitment to the sanctuary movement.[173]

When President Biden took office in January 2021, he announced plans for one of the most ambitious pieces of immigration reform legislation in American history. The Biden administration asked the Supreme Court in May 2021 to dismiss the still-pending cases against Sanctuary Cities, who had limited cooperation between the local law enforcement and federal immigration authorities, brought by the Department of Justice under the Trump administration. The new president also redirected the focus of ICE in identifying and deporting undocumented immigrants to violent criminal offenders and away from Trump's blanket policy of deporting anyone without documentation. While Biden's proposed U.S. Citizenship Act of 2021 is unlikely to pass a Congress strongly divided on the topic of immigration, the *Washington Post* reported in October 2021 that immigration arrests in the interior of the United States (so excluding border apprehensions) had fallen to a record low in over a decade[174]—a sign that undocumented immigrants—and Sanctuary Cities—may get a reprieve for now.

Striking a Balance

The institutional fabric that guarantees that neighborhoods and their residents will be able to exert some degree of influence in City Hall does not mean that they have become the most important powerbrokers in local political systems. This is not even the case in cities where they are relatively powerful. A mayor cannot afford to be captured in this way. Once a mayor takes office it becomes obvious that there are always more claimants than resources and that it is impossible to satisfy everyone. In American cities, authority is fragmented and dispersed.[175] The mayor has political authority, but many other centers of power also exist. Mayors need cooperation from institutions well beyond the neighborhoods. Typically this may include the city council, labor unions, the media, independent authorities (such as school boards), the courts, state and federal officials, and, perhaps most of all, the business community.

In most cities, there is a constant struggle that seems to pit downtown and economic development advocates against neighborhoods and their residents.

Neighborhood groups are often viewed as antibusiness, indifferent to the need to promote economic development. Big downtown projects pushed by mayors and business elites—convention centers, sports stadiums, subsidized malls, and entertainment districts—are questioned, if at all, mostly by neighborhood organizations and community activists. But no mayor can ignore the fact that little can be accomplished without the support of business. A few mayors manage to strike a balance, but the logic of economic development is so overwhelmingly strong that more often, they end up pursuing a pro-growth agenda. This seems to happen regardless of the racial or ethnic background of the incumbent. African American mayors, for example, have invariably ended up advocating pro-growth downtown development policies even if their electoral base might suggest they would not.[176]

The administration of Mayor Tom Bradley, who was elected the mayor of Los Angeles in 1973, illustrates the importance that mayors attach to economic growth. Early on, Bradley stressed the need to make Los Angeles a "world class" city. He courted Japanese investors, who poured more than $3 billion into Los Angeles real estate in 1988 alone. Before Bradley, there was almost no downtown in Los Angeles; in 1975, only five buildings were above 13 stories. By 1990, there were over 50 such buildings—many of them visible in the dramatic footage that opened the television series *L.A. Law*.[177]

To subsidize downtown development, Los Angeles created a huge 255-block tax increment finance (TIF) district. The TIF district allowed the city to float bonds to provide public improvements and services to stimulate private investment. But because the city was required to use all of the additional taxes from the downtown redevelopment to retire the bonds or to support further development, the new taxes could not be used for projects or services elsewhere in the city.[178] The downtown office complex experienced a boom, but the high-level professional jobs generated by corporate investment were taken either by suburban residents or by professionals who moved into gentrified neighborhoods close to the downtown. The overall effect was to displace lower-income residents, drive up the cost of housing, and segment urban space into enclaves. Finally recognizing the depth of the housing crisis, in 1991, Mayor Bradley began to push for "linkage" fees that would require developers to allocate funds for low-income housing in exchange for approval of downtown building projects. But it was too little, too late.

The 1992 protests showed how difficult it was for Bradley to satisfy all of the contending interests in the city's politics. His policies had mainly aided real estate developers and expanded opportunities for white-collar professionals, including some who were Black and Latino. The redevelopment did not benefit the poor. According to the 1990 census, the poverty rate in South Central Los Angeles, where the 1992 protests started, was 33 percent. The area was seething with tensions between newly arrived Central American immigrants and long-time African American residents. The protests exposed the depth of the racial and ethnic tensions in the city. They were also an outlet for the deep-seated frustration of African Americans at the lingering effects of a justice system strongly biased against them, as had once again been demonstrated with the beating of Rodney King and the subsequent acquittal of the perpetrators by a majority-white, suburban jury.

Bradley did not even succeed in satisfying affluent white voters. When development spread from downtown to the affluent West Side, Bradley began to encounter stiff opposition from environmentalists who objected to increased air pollution and traffic congestion. Unable to keep up with new development, the sewage system broke down in 1987, dumping millions of gallons of raw sewage into Santa Monica Bay. Bradley proposed a cap on new sewer construction to slow the pace of new development. The next year, however, Bradley infuriated environmentalists by reversing his long-standing opposition to oil drilling in the Pacific Palisades, an area on the ocean floor extending several miles out from Los Angeles. Under siege from residents in low- as well as high-income neighborhoods, Bradley chose not to run for a sixth term in 1993.

Despite the risks that such a strategy sometimes poses, the fact remains that the policy priorities of most cities continue to be focused on downtown development. In a large number of cities, especially in Sunbelt cities such as Phoenix, Las Vegas, and Houston, neighborhood groups have had little influence at all. Commenting on politics in Houston, one study called its neighborhood groups "largely invisible."

In cities with strong neighborhood organizations, mayors must somehow strike a balance between a downtown growth agenda and a program for neighborhood development. Ray Flynn of Boston was one of the nation's most successful mayors in bridging this gap. First elected in 1983, Flynn left office nine years later to become ambassador to the Vatican. Growing up in South Boston, Flynn's father was an immigrant longshore worker, and his mother cleaned downtown office buildings. After serving 15 years on the city council, Flynn mounted a surprisingly vigorous campaign in the 1983 mayoral race by building on his support from tenants' groups and neighborhood organizations. He stirred up his poor, largely Roman Catholic followers by pitting them against the Yankee blue-bloods and downtown Republicans and promised to implement linkage policies to force developers to help the neighborhoods.

Once in office, Flynn recognized the importance of forging a governing coalition. Abandoning the confrontational rhetoric that had gotten him elected, he forged an alliance with a business based on a program that would pursue downtown development and residential revitalization at the same time. Boston's booming downtown office market allowed developers to make profits even while paying linkage fees, which required them to help pay for public improvements in exchange for development permits. He strengthened the city's rent control laws and enacted regulations to limit the conversion of rental units into condominiums. Flynn persuaded the city council to enact a housing policy that required developers of projects with ten or more units to set aside 10 percent of the units for low- and moderate-income families and a "linked deposit" policy in which the city would deposit its funds only with banks that demonstrated a commitment to their surrounding areas. The city contributed funds to Boston's non-profit housing developers and also gave crucial support to one of the most successful comprehensive neighborhood revitalization projects in the country, the so-called Dudley Street Neighborhood Initiative (DSNI). With one-third of the land vacant, DSNI was blocked from assembling desirable parcels by an impossibly complex jigsaw puzzle of private ownership. In an unprecedented move, the city gave DSNI, a community-based organization, the power of eminent domain so that it could force owners to sell their properties.[179]

How successful was Flynn in improving the lives of neighborhood residents? By 1993, linkage fees had raised about $70 million and helped build 10,000 affordable housing units, and by the end of Flynn's second term, community-based housing corporations had built or rehabilitated another 5,000 units. The banks agreed to commit $400 million to a community reinvestment plan for low- and moderate-income areas. The Flynn administration even gave a few neighborhood councils authority over land use decisions. But only so much could be accomplished purely through local efforts.[180] Innovative local housing policies could not compensate for cuts in federal housing assistance imposed by the Reagan administration. And there was relatively little the Flynn administration could do about the income inequality arising in Boston from the combination of a booming corporate services sector and a rapidly declining industrial base.

The Decisive Turning Point

For as long as most people can remember, the central cities had been the special preserve for Democratic, liberal politicians. But beginning in the 1980s, white working-class and middle-class voters began supporting a new generation of mayors who promised to cut taxes by holding down spending, and in the 1990s, the national conservative movement began to put down roots in local politics, energized in considerable measure by racial, ethnic, and class divisions within the cities. To bring order to the streets, the new breed of urban leaders promised to get tough with criminals, panhandlers, and homeless people. Within a few years, self-styled conservative white mayors replaced prominent African American mayors in several cities. In 1993 Rudolph Giuliani, a former district attorney, defeated New York's first Black mayor, David Dinkins; that same year in Los Angeles, millionaire financier Richard Riordan defeated Mike Woo, an Asian American who tried unsuccessfully to reconstruct Tom Bradley's coalition. A year earlier, Bret Schundler had become the first Republican in 75 years to be elected mayor of Jersey City, New Jersey, and Republican Stephen Goldsmith became mayor of Indianapolis.

Elsewhere, African American mayors were defeated by Democrats who advocated distinctly downtown-oriented agendas. Richard M. Daley, the son of Democratic machine boss Richard J. Daley, twice defeated African American opponents, and Edward Rendell replaced Philadelphia's first Black mayor, Wilson Goode. Although it would not be accurate to call all of these mayors conservative if we are using the ideological yardstick employed in national political discourse, their rise to power signaled a distinct turn toward new policy priorities.

The change in direction was provoked by resentments about political demands by people of color, especially in the areas of affirmative action and busing; opposition by downtown business elites to higher taxes and programs with a social welfare dimension; and widespread anxiety about crime and disorder. The first generation of conservative mayors came into office during a period of high tension. In the wake of the Los Angeles protests of 1992, issues connected to social disorder, drugs, and crime reverberated all through the American political system. By playing on such themes, Republican Rudolph Giuliani was able to overcome a six-to-one Democratic advantage in party registration in the 1993 mayoral race in New York City. Giuliani received 78 percent of the white vote; by contrast, the African American incumbent, David Dinkins, carried 95 percent of the African American vote. Giuliani's campaign slogan, "Taking Back the City," played on a law-and-order theme and racial antagonisms. Hispanics played a crucial role in the election. Giuliani had lost by a narrow margin in 1989 when he received 34 percent of the Hispanic vote. In the 1993 election, Giuliani put a prominent Latinx politician, Herman Badillo, on his ticket for the office of city comptroller. This time, Giuliani got 39 percent of the Latinx vote. He also benefited from an unusually high voter turnout in the borough of Staten Island, a turnout stimulated by a ballot initiative calling for secession from New York City. Racial tensions provided the main motivation for the controversial proposal to secede.[181]

The conservative mayors fought hard to reverse policies perceived as unfairly benefiting Blacks. On taking office, Giuliani repealed the city's affirmative action policies in hiring and contracting, and he began to reduce city payrolls. Within two years, the city's workforce had been trimmed by 17,000 workers.

Concerns about law and order also contributed to the new turn in city politics. Crime became a highly charged symbolic issue, "a shorthand signal, to crucial numbers of white voters, of broader issues of social disorder, tapping powerful ideas about authority, status, morality, self-control, and race."[182] Some voters perceived Black mayors as being soft on crime because they tended to advocate more spending on social services and supported civilian review boards to monitor police conduct.[183] Conservatives vowed to "get tough" with criminals. As a former federal prosecutor, Giuliani was ideally situated to portray himself as a law-and-order candidate.

Giuliani delivered on his promises by cutting budgets for almost every city agency except the police and fire departments. He hired William Bratton as his police commissioner. Bratton instituted three controversial policing strategies. First, officers were allocated to hotspots identified from daily computer mappings of shootings and drug sales. Second, police began to crack down on minor offenses such as drinking in public, urinating on the street, and hassling motorists by demanding money for cleaning their windshields. This strategy was derived from the so-called broken windows theory of urban decline. Stated broadly, the theory suggested that small signs of decay, such as broken windows and trash on empty lots, serve as signs that an area is dangerous and in decline. As applied to crime control, it meant that even small offenses would be punished. Third, officers were encouraged to frisk people who were stopped for minor violations, such as playing loud music or drinking in public, in order to get guns off the street.

The new policing strategies appeared to work when New York's crime rate dropped dramatically. The number of murders fell nearly 60 percent, from a high of 2,262 in 1990 to 983 by 1996. Formerly regarded as one of the most dangerous cities in the nation, for the first six months of 1996, New York City ranked 144th out of the largest 189 cities in per capita total crime.[184] Although the media attributed the decline to the new policing strategies, in fact, the crime rate had begun to drop in the last year of the Dinkins administration, and the fall in the city's crime rate followed a national trend that has continued to unfold. Nevertheless, Giuliani made the improved crime statistics a major plank in his successful 1997 reelection campaign. In Giuliani's second term, crime continued to fall (again, in parallel with a national trend). There were 672 murders committed in the city in 2000.[185]

In addition to exploiting racially charged issues, the new generation of mayors also claimed to possess the magic formula for bringing prosperity to the local economy. The formula was made up of a combination of cuts in spending and aggressive policies to stimulate investment. Conservatives had initially developed their analysis of the urban condition in response to New York City's fiscal crisis of 1975. When the banks refused to underwrite any more of its loans in April of that year, the city suddenly found it impossible to borrow the money it needed to meet payroll obligations and redeem outstanding notes. Conservatives blamed the crisis on a habit of profligate spending. The writer Ken Auletta said the prominent conservative William F. Buckley had been right when he ran for mayor in 1965. As Auletta put it: "We [in New York City] have conducted a noble experiment in local socialism and income redistribution, one clear result of which has been to redistribute much of our tax base and many jobs right out of the city."[186]

Ed Koch won the mayoral race in 1977 by emphasizing just such an analysis of the causes of New York's fiscal crisis. Soon after entering city hall, Koch asserted that "the main job of municipal government is to create a climate in which private business can expand in the city to provide jobs and profit. It's not the function of government to create jobs on the public payroll."[187] As mayor Koch provided billions of dollars of incentives for businesses at the same time that he laid off 60,000 city workers. His policies appealed to homeowners in Brooklyn and Queens, who were sick of high taxes, and to real estate developers and to Wall Street firms, who expressed their gratitude in the form of generous campaign contributions.

Privatization, which was often identified as part of the conservative agenda of the 1980s, quickly became popular with mayors across the political spectrum. The term meant that to reduce costs, city governments should contract out such services as garbage collection and even education (in the form of charter schools). As a way of cutting costs and improving quality, privatization is long standing and non-controversial. In the city-building era at the beginning of the twentieth century, cities contracted for streetcar, telephone, and utility services, and many also contracted with private firms for water supply. The city of San Francisco contracted out garbage collection to private companies as early as 1932.[188] Partial privatization, which involves contracting out publicly funded services, often saves city governments money. One of the earliest scholarly evaluations concluded that Scottsdale, Arizona, by contracting for fire protection from a private firm, paid about half of what it would have had to pay if it had provided the service itself.[189] A 1982 survey of 1,780 cities found that the average city contracts approximately 26 percent of its services, in whole or part, to private firms.[190]

In the 1980s, however, privatization had become a strategy not only to make government more efficient but also to reduce its size and scope. E.S. Savas, called the "the godfather of privatization," served as assistant secretary of Housing and Urban Development (HUD) during the Reagan administration. In his several books, Savas stressed that privatization was a tool not only to make a better government but to make a more limited government—"limited in its size, scope, and power relative to society's other institutions."[191] Savas later became an adviser to the Giuliani administration, which used privatization mainly as a threat to squeeze concessions out of municipal unions.

It is difficult to assess the political significance of the conservative mayors and their peers, in part because policies at the urban level rarely can be neatly put into an ideological box. Mayors respond to the constituencies that elect them and to the overall demographic profiles of their cities. All mayors realize that they must appeal to a diverse array of racial and ethnic groups. For this reason, conservative mayors have not tended to toe the line in observing the national Republican platform. For example, in the 1990s and beyond, both Giuliani and Riordan bucked the national Republican agenda and opposed legislation that would deny government benefits to immigrants who had not yet become citizens. Giuliani's stance cost him dearly in his bid for the presidency in 2008.

In the 2010s, it appears that cities have "bounced back" a bit from the "neoliberal turn" in urban politics.[192] Michael Bloomberg, who succeeded

Rudi Giuliani, spurred urban investment and development. His social legacy, if there ever was one, would be mixed at best, as he cut down on public housing programs, and the homeless population in the city increased considerably during his time in office.[193] Bloomberg's 12 years of tenure as mayor of New York City ended in early 2014. His successor, Bill de Blasio, was the first Democratic mayor of the city since Ed Koch to be re-elected to a second term in 2017.[194] The progressive mayor, who has been building his agenda around (re-)introducing broader social programs (among them his signature program, universal [free] pre-kindergarten for all New York City residents), may encountered serious difficulties in implementing this agenda under the Trump administration.[195] Yet, residents of the five boroughs initially showed a strong interest in the mayor's agenda, and, during his first term, he enjoyed broad support. De Blasio's legacy as the outgoing mayor in 2022 is rather mixed. The mayor's second term was no easy feat, as his city became the early epicenter of a global pandemic that killed millions worldwide and temporarily shuttered the economy of the city, the nation, and the world. Home to the country's largest public school system, New York City became an early experiment of pandemic schooling and hybrid instruction throughout the 2020/21 academic year. As vaccination rates ticked up in early May, and his archenemy, former New York Governor Andrew Cuomo, became embroiled in a sexual assault scandal, with several women accusing him of inappropriate and unethical behavior over decades, things started to look up for the embattled mayor. At the same time, new conflicts and promises unkept, such as the unfolding humanitarian crisis on Rikers Island, where prison infrastructure is crumbling and inmates live under unsafe conditions, his growing conflict with the city's unions over vaccine mandates for public employees, his fizzling Vision Zero initiative, and the death of 13 New Yorkers during the onslaught of Hurricane Ida, which pummeled the city in early September of 2021, threaten the progressive mayor's legacy. It remains to be seen what will change under De Blasio's almost-guaranteed successor, Eric Adams.

The Racial and Ethnic Future

The nature of a city's economy and its political culture powerfully shapes a mayor's municipal agenda. Urban leaders, even when they identify as conservatives, reflecting the complex makeup of their constituencies. They generally take moderate positions on such explosive social issues as affirmative action hiring and multicultural curriculums in the schools. Likewise, self-styled progressive mayors who emphasize issues of social justice tend to move to the political center and join their more conservative counterparts in pursuing policies that promote economic growth and downtown development. At the local level, partisan and ideological differences break down and often do not matter at all.

Nevertheless, it is important to emphasize that racial and ethnic conflict remains as a powerful force shaping city politics. Examples are not hard to find. In 2012, for instance, the District of Columbia's District Ward 5 faced an election after its former councilman was forced from office by a criminal conviction. A crowded ballot, with 10 Democrats, an Independent and a Republican, assured that the campaign would be hotly contested, and the makeup of the district virtually guaranteed that it would have a racial dimension. An Advisory Neighborhood commissioner stated that the election's outcome could well be determined along racial lines: "I am very concerned that rigor mortis will set in and white folks will get mad and vote, and black folks will get mad and stay home."[196] The African American population is decreasing, from 90 percent in 2000 to 77 percent in 2010.[197] Despite the commissioner's worries, Harry Thomas, Jr., an African American Democrat, won the election.

In an April 2013 column, *Washington Post* columnist Colbert I. King, in a column about the April 23rd council elections, wrote that "race doesn't belong in D.C. Council election."[198] It was a forlorn hope. When one of the candidates pulled out of the race, Anita Bonds, a Democrat, remained the only African American candidate in the race, and she quickly sought to garner the support of Black voters on the basis of a shared racial identity. Candidate Patrick Mara, the only Republican candidate, responded in kind by appealing to the white residents of Chevy Chase, urging them to vote as a "bloc" and keep the only possible Black candidate out of office.

Racial and ethnic issues are certain to remain as a pivotal feature of politics at all levels of governance into the foreseeable future. It has been estimated that around the year 2050, white people in the United States will become a minority, but such a statistic does not mean that people of color, as a group, will be able to wield decisive power. The relationship between African Americans and Latinos is complex, and it is constantly evolving. A 2008 survey by Pew Research found that "overwhelming majorities of both blacks and Hispanics have favorable views of each other,"[199] and a majority from both "sides" agrees that the two groups get along well or fairly well. Hispanics and Blacks living in counties with high concentrations of African Americans are more likely to say that the two groups get along well than Hispanics and Blacks living in low-density Black counties, indicating perhaps that proximity is associated with an increased tolerance or acceptance.

But the harmony that is sometimes achieved between different minority groups is a fragile thing. Recently, disagreements on issues of immigration threaten to increase, rather than bridge, the divide between the two groups. The growing Hispanic population, which is projected to surpass the African American population by 2050, is causing concern among some Blacks, with many hoping that "… Latinos understand they're not White and that they will stay connected to African Americans … Black folks hear Latinos say 'We get it, and we're also discriminated against' … and have a hard time accepting that Latinos face any kind of discrimination that is similar or as extreme as what they experience."[200] The possibility for both cooperation and conflict is an ever-present reality in American urban politics, and it will not soon go away.

Endnotes

1 U.S. Bureau of the Census, *Statistical Abstract of the United States, 1992,* 112th ed. (Washington, D.C.: U.S. Government Printing Office, 1992), p. 397.

2 Robert B. Reich, *The Work of Nations* (New York: Random House, Vintage Books, 1991), p. 86.

3 Bernard J. Frieden and Lynn B. Sagalyn, *Downtown, Inc.: How America Builds Cities* (Cambridge, MA: MIT Press, 1989), p. 43.

4 Saskia Sassen, *Cities in a World Economy* (Thousand Oaks, CA: Pine Forge Press, 2001).

5 The concept of the global city is somewhat imprecise. Some scholars would question whether Chicago, Miami, and Los Angeles are global cities in the same sense as New York, London, and Tokyo, which clearly contain a much denser concentration of financial and media firms and corporations with true international reach. The two books to consult regarding this debate are Saskia Sassen, *The Global City: New York, London, Tokyo,* 2nd ed. (Princeton, NJ: Princeton University Press, 2001); and Janet L. Abu-Lughod, *New York, Los Angeles, Chicago: America's Global Cities* (Minneapolis: University of Minnesota Press, 1999).

6 Norman J. Glickman, "Cities and the International Division of Labor," in *The Capitalist City,* ed. Michael Peter Smith and Joe R. Feagin (Cambridge, MA: Basil Blackwell, 1987), pp. 66–86.

7 Richard Florida, *The Rise of the Creative Class and How It's Transforming Work, Leisure, Community and Everyday Life* (New York: Basic Books, 2002), p. 225.

8 Julie Satow: "Why the Doorman Is Lonely: New York City's Emptiest Co-ops and Condos," *The New York Times* (January 9, 2015).

9 Ibid.

10 Ibid.

11 Louise Story and Stephanie Saul, "Towers of Secrecy: Stream of Foreign Wealth Flows to Elite New York Real Estate," *The New York Times* (February 7, 2015).

12 Ibid.

13 Ibid.

14 Stephanie Saul, "New Disclosure Rules for Shell Companies in New York Luxury Real Estate Sales," *The New York Times* (July 20, 2015).

15 Ibid.

16 Ute Lehrer, "'If You Lived Here …': Lifestyle, Marketing, and the Development of Condominiums in Toronto," *Scapegoat: Architecture/Landscape/Political Economy* no. 03 (2009): 23.

17 Quoted in Justin Wm. Moyer, "NYC Bans 'Poor Doors—Separate Entrances for Low-Income Tenants," *The Washington Post* (June 30, 2015).

18 Stephen Colbert, "The Word" *The Colbert Report,* aired July 28, 2014.

19 Mark Abrahamson, *Global Cities* (Oxford & London: Oxford University Press, 2004), p. 33.

20 Margaret Kohn, "What Is Wrong with Gentrification?" *Urban Research and Practice* 6, no. 3 (2013): 309.

21 World Travel & Tourism Council (WTTC) website, www.wttc.org.

22 Ibid.

23 Norman Fainstein, Susan S. Fainstein, Richard Child Hill, Dennis Judd, and Michael Peter Smith, *Restructuring the City: The Political Economy of Urban Redevelopment* (New York: Longman, 1983).

24 Terry Nichols Clark, Richard Lloyd, Kenneth K. Wong, and Pushpam Jain, "Amenities Drive Urban Growth," *Journal of Urban Affairs* 24, no. 5 (2002), p. 504.

25 Ibid., p. 505.

26 Wangui Maina, "Chicago Visitor Numbers Down for 2010," *Chicago Tribune* (June 20, 2011).

27 Bill Kissinger and Julian Crews, "Chicago Tourism Hits Record with More Than 50M Visitors in 2014," *WGN* website (February 5, 2015). http://wgntv.com/2015/02/05/chicago-launches-new-tourism-campaign-amid-record-visitor-numbers/.

28 Choose Chicago Research & Analysis website. "2014 Chicago Visitation," http://www.choosechicago.com/includes/content/docs/media/Chicago-Visitation-Annual-2014-6.20.15-.pdf.

29 Christine Boyer, "Cities for Sale: Merchandising History at South Street Seaport," in *Variations on a Theme Park: The New American City and the End of Public Space*, ed. Michael Sorkin (New York: Hill and Wang, 1992), pp. 189–190.

30 G.J. Ashworth and J.E. Tunbridge, *The Tourist-Historic City* (London and New York: Belhaven Press, 1990), p. 153.

31 For an expanded discussion, see Dennis R. Judd, "Visitors and the Spatial Ecology of the City," in *Cities and Visitors*, ed. Lily M. Hoffman, Susan S. Fainstein, and Dennis R. Judd (New York: Blackwell, 2003), pp. 22–38.

32 John Hannigan, *Fantasy City: Pleasure and Profit in the Postmodern Metropolis* (New York: Routledge, 1998).

33 Richard Lloyd, *Neo-Bohemia: Art and Commerce in the Postindustrial City* (New York: Routledge, 2006), p. 126; also "Neo-Bohemia: Art and Neighborhood Redevelopment in Chicago," *Journal of Urban Affairs* 24, no. 5 (2002): 517–532.

34 See also Dennis R. Judd, "Constructing the Tourist Bubble," in *The Tourist City*, ed. Dennis R. Judd and Susan S. Fainstein (New Haven, CT: Yale University Press, 1999).

35 Ronn Koontz, interviewed in "1 Block, 135 Years," *New York Magazine* (November 16–22, 2015), p. 51.

36 Richy Rosario, "Is Airbnb Friend or Foe to Cash-Strapped New Yorkers?" *The Observer* (March 28, 2014).

37 Frank Gormlie, "Loss of Community Is Greatest Threat From Airbnb and Other Short-Term Vacation Rentals," *San Diego Free Press* (September 3, 2015). Accessed online: https://sandiegofreepress.org/2015/09/loss-of-community-is-greatest-threat-from-airbnb-and-short-term-vacation-rentals/#.YiEfuN9Ok6g.

38 Ibid.

39 Streitfeld, David, "Airbnb Listings Mostly Illegal, New York State Contends," *The New York Times* (October 15, 2014).

40 Ibid.

41 Ibid.

42 Kenneth Rosen, "Short-Term Rentals and the Housing Market," *Urbanland: The Magazine of the Urban Land Institute.* (November 22, 2013). Accessed online: https://urbanland.uli.org/news/short-term-rentals-and-the-housing-market/.

43 Ibid.

44 David H. Laslo, "Proliferating Convention Centers: The Political Economy of Regenerating Cities and the St. Louis Convention Center Expansion" (Ph.D. dissertation, University of Missouri–St. Louis, May 1999).

45 All data from Heywood Sanders, *Space Available: The Realities of Convention Centers as Economic Development Strategy* (Washington, D.C.: Brookings Institution Press, January 2005), p. 1.

46 *Encyclopedia of Associations*, 38th ed., *National Organizations of the United States*, vol. 1–3 (New York: Author, 2002).

47 George G. Fenich, "The Dollars and Sense of Convention Centers" (Ph.D. dissertation, Rutgers University, 1992), p. 34.

48 Laslo, "Proliferating Convention Centers," p. 67.

49 *Tradeshow Week Data Book, 1998* (New York: Bill Communications, 1998), p. 6.

50 "State of the Industry 1993," *Successful Meetings* (July 1993): 32–33.

51 *Convene Magazine* website, www.pcma.org/convene.

52 Robyne S. Turner and Mark S. Rosentraub, "Tourism, Sports and the Centrality of Cities," *Journal of Urban Affairs* 24, no. 5 (2003): 489.

53 Charles Santo, "The Economic Impact of Sports Stadiums: Recasting the Analysis in Context," *Journal of Urban Affairs* 27, no. 2 (2005): 177.

54 Ibid., pp. 177–191. Some leading studies are Robert A. Baade, "Professional Sports as Catalysts for Metropolitan Economic Development," *Journal of Urban Affairs* 18 (1996): 1–17; Mark Rosentraub, David Swinderll, M. Przybylski, and D.R. Mullins, "Sports and Downtown Development Strategy: If You Build It, Will Jobs Come?" *Journal of Urban Affairs* 16, no. 3 (1994): 211–239; John Zipp, "The Economic Impact of the Baseball Strike of 1994," *Urban Affairs Review* 32, no. 2 (November 1996): 157–185; Dan Coates and B. Humphries, "The Growth Effects of Sports Franchises, Stadia, and Arenas," *Journal of Policy Analysis and Management* 18, no. 4 (1999): 601–624; Robert Noll and A. Zimbalist, eds., *Sports, Jobs, and Taxes: The Economic Impact of Sports Teams and Stadiums* (Washington, D.C.: Brookings Institution Press, 1997); and Phillip A. Miller, "The Economic Impact of Sports Stadium Construction: The Case of the Construction Industry in St. Louis, MO," *Journal of Urban Affairs* 24, no. 2 (2002): 159–173. Some smaller teams have been able to turn minor league teams into profitable investments for the public by resorting to public ownership—see Joseph W. Meder and J. Wesley Leckrone, "Hardball; Local Government's Foray into Sports Franchise Ownership," *Journal of Urban Affairs* 24, no. 3 (2002): 353–368. This option is not open with the major sports because the sports cartels are able to exclude all teams that do not meet their regulations, which include private ownership.

55 Z. Austrian and Mark S. Rosentraub, "Cleveland's Gateway to the Future," in *Sports, Jobs, and Taxes*, ed. R. Noll and A. Zimbalist (Washington, D.C.: Brookings, 1997), pp. 355–384.

56 "Forbes: Mets' Value Drops 13 Percent; Yankees Top List," *CBS New York* (March 24, 2011).

57 Kurt Badenhausen, Cecily Fluke, Lesley Kump, and Michael K. Ozanian, "Double Play," *Forbes* (April 15, 2002), www.forbes.com.

58 Michael Ozanian, "Is Baseball Really Broke?" *Forbes* (April 3, 2002), www.forbes.com.

59 Infoplease.com; keywords Sports—Business/Ballparks/Arenas. Comparisons among the professional sports are difficult to make. The National Football League has a fully nationalized media arrangement, with teams sharing in revenues (which has promoted equity among the teams). By contrast, major league baseball teams sign

their own contracts with mostly local or regional media outlets, with limited revenue sharing among the teams. Thus, in 2002, major league baseball's four-year media contract was estimated at almost $1.8 million, but this figure is a tiny proportion of all media revenues collected by the individual teams.

60 For a closely textured and entertaining account of the battle between O'Malley and Moses, see Michael Shapiro, *The Last Good Season: Brooklyn, The Dodgers, and Their Final Pennant Race Together* (New York: Doubleday, 2003).

61 Neil J. Sullivan, *The Dodgers Move West* (New York: Oxford University Press, 1987).

62 Arthur T. Johnson, "The Sports Franchise Relocation Issue and Public Policy Responses," in *Government and Sport: The Public Policy Issues*, ed. Arthur T. Johnson and James H. Frey (Totowa, NJ: Rowman and Allanheld, 1985), p. 232.

63 Arthur T. Johnson, "Economic and Policy Implications of Hosting Sports Franchises: Some Lessons from Baltimore," *Urban Affairs Quarterly* 21, no. 3 (March 1986): 411.

64 "MTS Centre Makeover: Spiffy New Scoreboard; New 'Loge' Seating Unveiled," *Winnipeg Sun* (September 16, 2015).

65 Ronald Smothers, "No Hits, No Runs, One Error: The Dome," *The New York Times* (June 15, 1991).

66 Charles C. Eichner, *Playing the Field: Why Sports Teams Move and Cities Fight to Keep Them* (Baltimore, MD: Johns Hopkins University Press, 1993), p. 67.

67 See the websites www.gophersports.com and www.msfc.com.

68 Donald Phares and Mark S. Rosentraub, "Reviving the Glory of Days Past: St. Louis's Blitz to Save Its Image, Identity, and Teams," in *Major League Losers: The Real Cost of Sports and Who's Paying for It*, ed. Mark S. Rosentraub (New York: Basic Books, 1997).

69 Richard Sandomir, "New Stadiums: Prices, and Outrage, Escalate," *The New York Times* (August 28, 2008), www.nytimes.com/2008/08/26/sports/26tickets.html.

70 Josh Goodman, "Skybox Skeptics," *Governing* 19, no. 6 (March 2006): 41–42.

71 Sandomir, "New Stadiums."

72 Ibid.

73 This account of Quincy Market is based on Frieden and Sagalyn, *Downtown, Inc.*, pp. 1–7, 175.

74 Mike Davis, "Fortress Los Angeles: The Militarization of Urban Space," in *Variations on a Theme Park*, ed. Michael Sorkin (New York: Noonday Press, 1992), p. 155.

75 Myriam Jansen-Verbeke, "Leisure + Shopping = Tourism Product Mix," in *Marketing Tourism Places*, ed. Gregory Ashworth and Brian Goodall (London and New York: Routledge, 1990), p. 132.

76 Sharon Zukin, *Landscapes of Power: From Detroit to Disney World* (Berkeley: University of California Press, 1991).

77 The Urban Land Institute, *Developing Urban Entertainment Centers* (Washington, D.C.: Urban Land Institute, 1998).

78 Michael A. Pagano and Ann Bowman, *Cityscapes and Capital: The Politics of Urban Development* (Baltimore, MD: Johns Hopkins University Press, 1995), p. 74.

79 Michael Moore, *Roger and Me*, A Dog Eat Dog Films Production (Warner Bros. Pictures, 1989).

80 Bruce Weber, "Cities Are Fostering the Arts as a Way to Save Downtown," *The New York Times* (November 18, 1997), p. A1.

81 Dennis R. Judd, William Winter, William Barnes, and Emily Stern, *Tourism and Entertainment as a Local Economic Development Strategy: The Report of a NLC Survey* (Washington, D.C.: National League of Cities: A Research Report, 2000), p. 8.

82 Jane Jacobs, *The Death and Life of Great American Cities* (New York: Vintage, 1961), pp. 51, 223.

83 Ibid., p. 50.

84 Ibid., p. 52.

85 Douglas Rae, *City: Urbanism and Its End* (New Haven, CT: Yale University Press, 2003), p. xiii.

86 Ibid.

87 Ibid., p. xiv.

88 Two other excellent books dealing with these themes are Ray Suarez, *The Old Neighborhood: What We Lost in the Great Suburban Migration: 1966–1999* (New York: Free Press, 1999); and Shapiro, *The Last Good Season.*

89 For details on New Haven's experience, see Rae, *City: Urbanism and Its End,* pp. 234–243.

90 Alan Ehrenhalt, "Extreme Makeover," *Governing* 20, no. 7 (July 2006): 29.

91 Florida, *The Rise of the Creative Class,* pp. 227–229.

92 Edward Glaeser, "How Skyscrapers Can Save the City," *The Atlantic* (March 2011 Issue) https://www.theatlantic.com/magazine/archive/2011/03/how-skyscrapers-can-save-the-city/308387/.

93 Lloyd, *Neo-Bohemia.*

94 Rae, *City: Urbanism and Its End.*

95 Anonymous, *Report of the National Advisory Commission on Civil Disorders* (New York: Bantam Books, 1968).

96 Christopher L. Warren, John G. Corbett, and John F. Stack Jr., "Hispanic Ascendancy and Tripartite Politics in Miami," in *Racial Politics in American Cities,* ed. Rufus P. Browning, Dale Rogers Marshall, and David H. Tabb (New York: Longman, 1990), p. 166.

97 James H. Johnson Jr., Cloyzelle K. Jones, Walter C. Farrell Jr., and Melvin L. Oliver, "The Los Angeles Rebellion: A Retrospective View," *Economic Development Quarterly* 6, no. 4 (November 1992): 356–372.

98 Jack Miles, "Blacks vs. Brown," *Atlantic* (October 1992), pp. 41–68; see also Mike Davis, "In L.A., Burning All Illusions," *Nation* (June 1, 1992), pp. 743–746.

99 Tim Rutten, "A New Kind of Riot," *New York Review of Books* (June 11, 1992), pp. 52–54.

100 Elizabeth Kneebone, "Ferguson, Mo. Emblematic of Growing Suburban Poverty," *The Brookings Institution* (August 15, 2014). Accessed online: https://www.brookings.edu/blog/the-avenue/2014/08/15/ferguson-mo-emblematic-of-growing-suburban-poverty/.

101 Ibid.

102 Q&A: What Happened in Ferguson?" *The New York Times* (Last updated August 10, 2015). Accessed online: https://www.nytimes.com/interactive/2014/08/13/us/ferguson-missouri-town-under-siege-after-police-shooting.html.

103 Michael S. Schmidt, Matt Apuzzo, and Julie Bosman, "Police Officer in Ferguson Is Said to Recount a Struggle," *The New York Times* (October 17, 2014). Accessed online: https://www.nytimes.com/2014/10/18/us/ferguson-case-officer-is-said-to-cite-struggle.html?smid=pl-share.

104 Monica Davey and Julie Bosman, "Protests Flare After Ferguson Police Officer Is Not Indicted," *The New York Times* (November 24, 2014). Accessed online: https://www.nytimes.com/2014/11/25/us/ferguson-darren-wilson-shooting-michael-brown-grand-jury.html.

105 Schmidt, Apuzzo, and Bosman, "Police Officer in Ferguson is Said to Recount a Struggle."

106 Tim Prudente, "With Prosecutions over, Six Baltimore Officers Back at Work After Death of Freddie Gray," *The Baltimore Sun* (November 30, 2017). Accessed online: http://www.baltimoresun.com/news/maryland/crime/bs-md-ci-officers-back-to-work-20171128-story.html.

107 David A. Graham, "The Mysterious Death of Freddie Gray," *The Atlantic* (April 22, 2015). Accessed online: https://www.theatlantic.com/politics/archive/2015/04/the-mysterious-death-of-freddie-gray/391119/.

108 Ibid.

109 Prudente, "With Prosecutions over, Six Baltimore Officers Back at Work After Death of Freddie Gray."

110 Ibid.

111 Ibid.

112 Ibid.

113 *Fatal Force:* "937 people have been shot and killed by police in the past year," *The Washington Post* (updated September 30, 2021), https://www.washingtonpost.com/graphics/investigations/police-shootings-database/.

114 Ibid.

115 U.S. Bureau of the Census, Income and Poverty in the United States: 2020, https://www.census.gov/library/publications/2021/demo/p60-273.html.

116 Ibid.

117 Ibid.

118 Raphael Sonenshein, "The Prospects for Multiracial Coalitions: Lessons from America's Three Largest Cities," in *Racial Politics in American Cities,* 3rd ed., Rufus Browning, Dale Rogers Marshall, and David H. Tabb (New York: Longman, 2003), pp. 333–356.

119 U.S. Bureau of the Census, *Statistical Abstract of the United States: 1995* (Washington, D.C.: U.S. Government Printing Office, 1995), p. 287.

120 Joint Center for Political and Economic Studies, *Black Elected Officials: A Statistical Summary, 2001* (Washington, D.C.: Author, 2001), p. 8.

121 The Joint Center for Political and Economic Studies, "History of the Joint Center for Political and Economic Studies" (March 3, 2014). Accessed online: http://jointcenter.org/about/history-joint-center-political-and-economic-studies.

122 National Association of Latino Elected and Appointed Officials (Washington, D.C.: Author, *National Roster of Hispanic Elected Officials,* annual).

123 NALEO Educational Fund, 2014 National Directory of Latino Elected Officials, p. 334.

124 Rodney E. Hero and Susan E. Clarke, "Latinos, Blacks, and Multiethnic Politics in Denver," in *Racial Politics in American Cities,* 3rd ed., Rufus Browning, Dale Rogers Marshall, and David H. Tabb (New York: Longman, 2003), p. 316.

125 John Mollenkopf, *A Phoenix in the Ashes: The Rise and the Fall of the Koch Coalition in New York City Politics* (Princeton, NJ: Princeton University Press, 1992), p. 12.

126 Raphael J. Sonenshein, *Politics in Black and White: Race and Power in Los Angeles* (Princeton, NJ: Princeton University Press, 1993), p. 63.

127 Patrick D. Joyce, "A Reversal of Fortunes: Black Empowerment, Political Machines, and City Jobs in New York City and Chicago," *Urban Affairs Review* 32, no. 3 (1997): 291–318.

128 Charles P. Henry, "Urban Politics and Incorporation: The Case of Blacks, Latinos, and Asians in Three Cities," in *Blacks, Latinos, and Asians in Urban America: Status and Prospects for Politics and Activism,* ed. James Jennings (Westport, CT: Praeger, 1994), p. 18.

129 Our account of Koch is based on Mollenkopf, *A Phoenix in the Ashes.*

130 Quotes in ibid., pp. 171–172.

131 John Mollenkopf, "New York: Still the Great Anomaly," in *Racial Politics in American Cities,* 3rd ed., Rufus Browning, Dale Rogers Marshall, and David H. Tabb (New York: Longman, 2003), p. 120.

132 Ibid.

133 Quoted in Eliza Gray, "The Ad That Won the New York Mayor's Race" (September 11, 2013), *TIME,* https://nation.time.com/2013/09/11/the-ad-that-won-the-new-york-mayors-race/.

134 Quoted in Ibid.

135 NYCLU, "Stop-And-Frisk Data" (2019), https://www.nyclu.org/en/stop-and-frisk-data.

136 Ibid.

137 Ali Watkins, "'Kettling' of Peaceful Protesters Shows Aggressive Shift by N.Y. Police," *The New York Times* (June 5, 2020).

138 Rufus P. Browning, Dale Rogers Marshall, and David H. Tabb, *Protest Is Not Enough: The Struggle of Blacks and Hispanics for Equality in Urban Politics* (Berkeley: University of California Press, 1984), pp. 171–174; Peter K. Eisinger, "Black Mayors and the Politics of Racial Economic Advancement," in *Urban Politics: Past, Present, and Future,* 2nd ed., ed. Harlan Hahn and Charles H. Levine (New York: Longman, 1984), pp. 249–260; Kenneth R. Mladenka, "Blacks and Hispanics in Urban Politics," *American Political Science Review* 83, no. 1 (March 1989): 165–191. Mladenka concludes that minority mayors have little impact on policy outcomes, but minority council majorities do.

139 Sonenshein, *Politics in Black and White,* p. 152.

140 Timothy Bates and Darrell Williams, "Preferential Procurement Programs and Minority-Owned Businesses," *Journal of Urban Affairs* 17, no. 1 (1995): 1.

141 Clarence N. Stone, *Regime Politics: Governing Atlanta 1946–1988* (Lawrence: University Press of Kansas, 1989), p. 145, Chapter 1.

142 *City of Richmond v. J. A. Croson Co.,* 109 S.Ct. 706 (1989).

143 Mitchell F. Rice, "State and Local Government Set-Aside Programs, Disparity Studies, and Minority Business Development in the Post-*Croson* Era," *Journal of Urban Affairs* 15, no. 6 (1993): 529–553.

144 Mike Davis, *City of Quartz: Excavating the Future in Los Angeles* (London: Verso, 1990), pp. 251–253.

145 Ibid., p. 277.

146 Ibid., p. 272.

147 Sonenshein, *Politics in Black and White,* pp. 155–161.

148 Albert Karnig and Susan Welch, *Black Representation and Urban Policy* (Chicago, IL: University of Chicago Press, 1980); Eisinger, "Black Mayors"; Browning, Marshall,

and Tabb, *Protest Is Not Enough;* Mladenka, "Blacks and Hispanics in Urban Politics"; Grace Hall Saltzstein, "Black Mayors and Police Policies," *Journal of Politics* 51, no. 3 (August 1989): 525–544.

149 Eisinger, "Black Mayors," p. 257.

150 See the detailed case studies of 12 cities in Browning, Marshall, and Tabb, *Racial Politics in American Cities.*

151 Eisinger, "Black Mayors," p. 258.

152 William Julius Wilson, *The Truly Disadvantaged: The Inner City, the Underclass, and Public Policy* (Chicago, IL: University of Chicago Press, 1987), p. 115.

153 Perry, in Browning, Marshall, and Tabb, *Racial Politics in America*, 3rd ed., p. 251.

154 Lawrence Bobo and Franklin D. Gilliam Jr., "Race, Sociopolitical Participation, and Black Empowerment," *American Political Science Review* 84, no. 2 (June 1990): 377–393.

155 See Browning, Marshall, and Tabb, *Racial Politics in American Cities.*

156 "Profile of the Unauthorized Population: United States," *The Migration Policy Institute* (2014). Accessed online. https://www.migrationpolicy.org/data/unauthorized-immigrant-population/state/US.

157 Clyde Haberman, "Trump and the Battle Over Sanctuary in America," *The New York Times* (March 5, 2017).

158 Ibid.

159 Ibid.

160 Marc R. Rosenblum, "Federal-Local Cooperation on Immigration Enforcement Frayed; Chance for Improvement Exists," *The Migration Policy Institute* (July 2015). Accessed online: https://www.migrationpolicy.org/news/federal-local-cooperation-immigration-enforcement-frayed-chance-improvement-exists.

161 Ibid.

162 National Conference of State Legislatures, "States Offering Driver's Licenses to Immigrants' (August 9, 2021), https://www.ncsl.org/research/immigration/states-offering-driver-s-licenses-to-immigrants.aspx.

163 Marc R. Rosenblum, "Federal-Local Cooperation on Immigration Enforcement Frayed; Chance for Improvement Exists," *The Migration Policy Institute* (July 2015). Accessed online: https://www.migrationpolicy.org/news/federal-local-cooperation-immigration-enforcement-frayed-chance-improvement-exists.

164 Ibid.

165 Ibid.

166 Ibid.

167 Ibid.

168 Ibid.

169 Jon Campbell, "Attorneys General Fight Trump's 'Sanctuary City' Threats," *USA Today* (May 17, 2017). Accessed online: https://www.usatoday.com/story/news/politics/2017/05/17/donald-trumps-sanctuary-city-executive-order-under-fire-attorneys-general/327670001/.

170 Ibid.

171 Maria Sacchetti, "Trump Administration Targets 'Sanctuary' Cities in Latest Wave of Immigration Arrests," *The Washington Post* (September 28, 2017). Accessed online: https://www.washingtonpost.com/local/immigration/trump-administration-targets-sanctuary-cities-in-latest-wave-of-immigration-arrests/2017/09/28/9b5e7de2-a477-11e7-ade1-76d061d56efa_story.html?utm_term=.e2cf8479adb6.

172 Ibid.

173 Ibid.

174 Nick Miroff and Maria Sacchetti, "Immigration Arrests Fell to Lowest Level in More Than a Decade during Fiscal 2021, ICE Data Shows," *The Washington Post* (October 26, 2021), https://www.washingtonpost.com/national/ice-arrests-biden-trump/2021/10/25/f33130b8-35b5-11ec-9a5d-93a89c74e76d_story.html.

175 Barbara Ferman, *Governing the Ungovernable City: Political Skill, Leadership, and the Modern Mayor* (Philadelphia, PA: Temple University Press, 1985), Chapter 1; Stone, *Regime Politics*, Chapter 1. Urban regime theory stresses that cities are not governed by elected officials but by "informal arrangements by which public bodies and private interests function together in order to be able to make and carry out governing decisions." Ibid., p. 6.

176 See Adolph Reed, "The Black Urban Regime: Structural Origins and Constraints," *Comparative Urban and Community Research* 1, no. 1 (1987): 138–189; and "Demobilization in the New Black Political Regime: Ideological Capitulation and Radical Failure in the Postsegregation Era," in *The Bubbling Cauldron: Race, Ethnicity, and the Urban Crisis*, ed. Michael Peter Smith and Joe R. Feagin (Minneapolis: University of Minnesota Press, 1995), pp. 182–208.

177 Wilson, *The Truly Disadvantaged*, p. 135.

178 Sonenshein, *Politics in Black and White*, p. 168.

179 Peter Medoff and Holly Sklar, *Streets of Hope: The Fall and Rise of an Urban Neighborhood* (Boston, MA: South End Press, 1994).

180 Peter Dreier and W. Dennis Keating, "The Limits of Localism: Progressive Housing Policies in Boston, 1984–1989," *Urban Affairs Quarterly* 26, no. 2 (December 1990): 191–216.

181 Karen M. Kaufmann, "A Tale of Two Cities: The Impact of Intergroup Conflict on Mayoral Voting Behavior in Los Angeles and New York," paper delivered at the American Political Science Association Meeting (San Francisco, August 29–September 1, 1996), p. 18. Giuliani was reelected by a wide margin in 1997.

182 Thomas Byrne Edsall and Mary D. Edsall, *Chain Reaction: The Impact of Race, Rights, and Taxes on American Politics* (New York: Norton, 1991), p. 224. Emphasis on the word *signal* removed from the original.

183 Saltzstein, "Black Mayors and Police Policies," pp. 525–544.

184 Randy Kennedy, "FBI Reports New York Safer Than Most Cities," *The New York Times* (January 6, 1997), p. B5.

185 University of Virginia Library, Geospatial and Statistical Data Center, http://cba.unomaha.edu/faculty/cdecker/WEB/Geospatial%20and%20Statistical%20Data%20Center.htm.

186 Quoted in William E. Simon, *A Time for Truth* (New York: Berkeley Books, 1978), p. 155.

187 Quoted in Martin Shefter, *Political Crisis/Fiscal Crisis: The Collapse and Revival of New York City* (New York: Basic Books, 1985), p. 175.

188 David F. Linowes, *Privatization: Toward More Effective Government. Report of the President's Commission on Privatization* (Urbana, IL: University of Illinois Press, 1988), p. 2.

189 Roger S. Ahlbrandt Jr., *Municipal Fire Protection Services: Comparison of Alternative Organizational Forms* (Beverly Hills, CA: Sage, 1973).

190 Derived from *Rethinking Local Services: Examining Alternative Service Delivery Approaches* (Washington, D.C.: International City Management Association, 1984),

Table B; as reported in E. S. Savas, *Privatization: The Key to Better Government* (Chatham, NJ: Chatham House, 1987), p. 72.

191 Ibid., p. 288.

192 Jamie Peck, Nik Theodore, and Neil Brenner, "Neoliberal Urbanism: Models, Moments, Mutations," *SAIS Review* 29, no. 1 (Winter/Spring 2009): 50.

193 The Editorial Board, "12 Years of Mayor Bloomberg," *The New York Times* (December 28, 2013). Accessed online: http://www.nytimes.com/2013/12/29/opinion/sunday/12-years-of-mayor-bloomberg.html.

194 William Neuman and J. David Goodman, "De Blasio Coasts To Re-election, as Second-Term Challenges Await," *The New York Times* (November 7, 2017).

195 Ibid.

196 Liz Farmer, "Anti-Thomas Sentiment Expected to be Factor in Ward 5 Election," *The Examiner* (May 7, 2012).

197 Ibid.

198 John V. LaBaume, "Op-Ed: No Room for 'Race' in D.C. Council Election but There is Lots for 'Reform'," *The Examiner: Opinion* (April 16, 2013).

199 "Do Blacks and Hispanics Get Along?" *Pew Research: Social and Demographic* (January 31, 2008).

200 Wendy Conklin, "Latinos and Blacks: What Unites and Divides Us?" *The Diversity Factor* 16, no.1 (Winter 2008): 25.

CHAPTER 14

Epilogue: Cities After the Year 2020: A Year of Upheaval, Reckoning, and Change

The Cities and the Pandemic

The year 2020 was not what the world had bargained for, yet it will be one of those years that movies will be made about and history books will refer to in bold print. For American cities, it was a year of terrifying challenges, a year of anger, frustration, and violence. In 2021, a year on, with the global pandemic still lingering and profound political change uncertain, it is difficult to predict the long-term impact of the events of 2020. Yet, the debates and questions these events have laid bare are critical to discuss, even in the short term.

In March 2020, life in the nation's big cities ground to a sudden and traumatic halt amid the impact of the global COVID-19 pandemic. New York City, the country's largest city, became an early epicenter of this pandemic, which had originated in a market in Wuhan, China, at the end of 2019, and which we knew little about, except that it appeared to cause anything from asymptomatic infection to life-threatening respiratory disease. At the time of the writing of this final chapter, the United States has passed 750,000 casualties linked to the Novel Coronavirus, which causes COVID-19—an unimaginable human toll. For comparison, the 1918 Spanish flu pandemic caused approximately 675,000 deaths in the United States.[1] Seemingly post-apocalyptic images of eerily empty Times Square, of shuttered stores, restaurants, and businesses swept the nation and the world. News sites and social media shared images of animal life taking back once busy downtown areas. Anything from deer to bears and raccoons was spotted on once-busy streets and sidewalks in American cities under COVID-lockdown. By early April of 2020, when everyone was still counting COVID cases, New York State accounted for more than a quarter of the total Coronavirus cases in the United States. New York State alone had more cases than Spain, Italy, France, or Germany, which also all suffered early COVID outbreaks. On April 10, 2020, New York City alone had 87,725 confirmed cases of COVID-19, accounting for more than half of New York State's total of 159,937 cases and for more than one-fifth of the United States' 466,000 cases at the time.[2,3] Almost two years into the pandemic, we can say with confidence that COVID-19 has had a more devastating effect on New York City than the aftermath of the September 11 attacks, and the city is not expected to fully recover to pre-pandemic levels until at least after 2025.[4]

As one of the pandemic's early epicenters, the immediate effects of the pandemic and the lockdown on New York City were eerier, harsher, and more devastating than they were on any other city in the country. And they were the most dramatic for the most vulnerable New Yorkers: Those with limited means, who often live in dangerously unsafe and overcrowded conditions. *The New York Times* description of life in the epicenter of the epicenter, an immigrant neighborhood between the Queens neighborhoods of Jackson Heights, Elmhurst, and, fatefully, Corona, provides a poignant insight into the early days of the outbreak in New York City:

> In one building, an immigrant from Ecuador worries about the many relatives living in her cramped apartment, including her frail parents. A family member, her brother-in-law, has a persistent cough.
>
> [...]
>
> Is it here? The deadly coronavirus?[5]

To a New Yorker, writing this, remembering, invokes a certain amount of post-traumatic stress. By mid-March 2020, an eerie silence had settled over the entire city, only to be pierced, at any moment, day or night, by the deafening sound of sirens of the emergency vehicles racing through the empty streets. The nervous flicker of the blue-and-red ambulance lights down in the streets, reflecting on the ceiling of any New York City apartment began to signify yet another COVID case. This time maybe a neighbor. A friend. By the end of the month, the deaths had overwhelmed the city so much that hospitals had cooling trucks parked in their courtyards to store the bodies. The daily gatherings by open windows and on balconies with pots and pans to cheer on the first responders and frontline workers became a way of cheering on one's fellow New Yorkers as well. A daily signal of "we are still here, still alive, and not alone." Time somehow became meaningless, as there was no palpable end in sight to the silence, the sirens, the dying.

A 2020 early analysis conducted by the Furman Center on the impact of the COVID-19 in the New York City pandemic shows the disparate impact on historically disadvantaged groups in terms of the likelihood of infection, as well as mortality:[6] Mortality rates from COVID-19 have been found to be disproportionately higher among Black, Hispanic, and other populations of color. Other factors, such as a lack of ability to work from home and residing in overcrowded units were strongly correlated with higher rates of COVID-19 infections and death. Conversely, the city's most densely populated neighborhoods (coincidentally the same Manhattan neighborhoods that concentrate most of the city's wealth) were not experiencing higher rates of infection, which directly contradicts one of the most politicized narratives of the pandemic: that dense cities are unsustainable during a global pandemic.

A flurry of media reports proclaimed the end of cities as we know them, blamed public transit, and urban density for the disastrous early spread and the unimaginable death toll America's largest cities experienced. By the time the pandemic spring of 2020 was in full bloom, the suburban housing market had started to explode. Hip urban condos in happening neighborhoods started to suddenly feel very cramped with entire families being stuck working, schooling, and playing from home. If they were in a position to do so, many urban middle-aged parents, young parents, and prospective parents became adamant about trading in their two-bedroom condos in trendy urban neighborhoods for spacious single-family homes in the suburbs. By the end of the fourth quarter of the 2020 calendar year, real estate sales in suburban Westchester County, just north of New York City, had surpassed those from the previous year by 13 percent, whereas real estate sales in Manhattan were down by 21 percent from 2019.[7] A real estate agent in Connecticut explained to *The New York Times* that the dramatic increase in demand for suburban single-family homes had resulted in what she called "the strongest market I have seen in two decades."[8] The suburban housing inventory, by late 2020, was unable to meet the vigorous demand, resulting in many houses "in contract" even before they were officially listed for sale. The sales brackets that were booming the most in 2020, however, also indicate that the pandemic-related suburban boom was highly exclusive: The price brackets with the highest pandemic-infused demand were the ones between $1 and 2 million, with the $600,000–$800,000 bracket in second place.[9]

Crucially, the COVID-19 pandemic has revealed what students of urban life have known for decades: Social inequality is among the key determinants of the effects of severe crises, such as the global pandemic, on urban (and suburban) life. Housing mobility, for one, is a privilege, and one that is only open to a select group of urban residents that have a wide choice of neighborhoods, from the white-hot, busy downtown Manhattan block, to the hip Brooklyn neighborhood and its coffeeshop- and tree-lined streets, to the serenity of the suburbs. Many urban families never had a choice of moving to the suburbs (or temporarily relocating to their country homes) during the pandemic. They did not have a choice to work remotely or to live and work according to social distancing guidelines.

More than anything, the COVID-19 pandemic has shined a cruel light on the persisting social inequities among racial and ethnic groups in American cities. Communities of color have suffered and died from the Coronavirus in much higher proportions than whites. In New York City, infection rates among African Americans per 100,000 residents were more than 30 percent higher than those among white people, and death rates of Blacks and Hispanics per 100,000 were more than double those of whites, according to the NYC Department of Health and Mental Hygiene. Housing inequality, in particular, was one key aspect that determined one's vulnerability to the pandemic.

Unsafe and overcrowded housing, however, is not particular to urban environments. Research suggests that housing in urban areas only has a slightly higher likelihood of being overcrowded compared to rural areas. On the other hand, poverty rates tend to be higher in rural than in urban areas. Researchers found not only that poverty rates in rural areas consistently hover between 2 and 5 percent above those in urban areas over time, but also that rural residents on average spent longer amounts of time in poverty, which made them less likely to be able to exit over time.[10] Housing overcrowding, which should not be confused with population density (that is obviously more prevalent in cities), is strongly correlated with poverty. The percentage of overcrowded housing units, defined as more than one occupant per room, averages 2–4 percent in urban areas,[11] compared to a rural average of 2.4 percent.[12] However, that percentage is 3–4 times higher among American Indian and Hispanic populations living in rural or tribal areas,[13] suggesting that racial and ethnic inequalities persist beyond the rural-urban divide. In other words, poverty among historically disadvantaged groups was one of the biggest risk factors not only for contracting but also for developing complications from COVID-19, as such population groups tend to live in generally less healthy environments with greater exposure to environmental hazards and a subsequent higher likelihood for preexisting health conditions.[14] This fact made at least some headlines during the pandemic, but policy makers have yet to show any interest in addressing it.

In the current hyperpolarized political climate, the pandemic became highly politicized at every level of government, as the country's biggest cities, such as New York, Chicago, or Los Angeles, all severely hit in the early onslaught of COVID-19, are also its most diverse, and most politically liberal. Cities, however, defied early predictions of their demise, and New York City, in particular, emerged as a model metropolis in pandemic management, with the country's lowest case load over the 2020 summer months, in spite of its residential density. Yet, despite such facts, the pandemic, coupled with the country's divisive political climate increased geographic polarization in the United States. Conservatives were once again proclaiming the end of the city, or even using the pandemic as justification to demonize cities, and more diverse, coastal blue states, such as New York and California, both major economic engines of the nation that were severely hit early in the pandemic.

In March 2020, Florida Governor Ron DeSantis urged then-President Trump to implement a domestic travel ban so as to prevent Americans from states like California, New York, or Washington from traveling to Florida, claiming that they (as opposed to the lack of mask mandates and social distancing guidelines) were contributing to the spread of COVID-19 in Florida.[15] Former President Donald Trump, starting in late March, when COVID cases spiked in New York City, began blasting New York State for its "late" and "poor" response to the pandemic, neglecting the fact that his administration had time and time again denied the seriousness of the virus and refused to implement proper, nation-wide safety measures. By September 2020, Trump was threatening to withdraw federal funding from New York City and other cities around the nation for their "failure" in combatting the pandemic. This statement came despite the fact that those cities had actually been able to flatten the infection curve with mask mandates and social distancing measures. Many Republican governors were refusing to impose such measures in states like Texas and Florida, which had some of the highest COVID case counts by the fall of 2020.[16] In November 2020, the former president announced that the federal government would not be delivering the COVID-19 vaccine to New York State because the state's former governor, Andrew Cuomo, had announced in September 2020 that the state would have an independent task force of scientists, doctors, and health experts review the U.S. Food and Drug Administration's approval data for every COVID vaccine approved in the United States.[17] The states of California, Washington, Oregon, and Nevada quickly followed New York's example. This announcement came amid growing mistrust among Americans about the Trump administration's involvement in the vaccine approval process. In response, New York state's Attorney General Letitia James threatened to sue the administration if it were to exclude New York state from the vaccine distribution process, noting that "This is nothing more than vindictive behavior by a lame-duck president trying to extract vengeance on those who oppose his politics."[18]

Public health issues, such as social distancing, mask, and vaccine mandates, which generally are decided based on scientific facts publicized by medical experts, turned into matters of party identity and political beliefs during the pandemic year, thanks to a presidential administration that was making public health decisions against the advice of the nation's top health scientists—a dangerous development in the midst of a global pandemic that has already claimed hundreds of thousands of lives. The new Biden administration, inaugurated in January of 2021, after a harsh and jarring election season, and an attempt by Trump supporters and conspiracy theorists to overthrow a legitimate democratic election, has tried its best to follow a more science-based approach and take the politics out of the battle against the pandemic. But the damage done by the previous administration seems deep-seated with conservatives continuing rally against mask and vaccine mandates in schools and offices, leading to more preventable casualties.

A Renewed Debate on Race

U.S. cities again rose to the headlines in May 2020, after the murder of George Floyd, a 46-year-old Black man in Minneapolis. He was arrested by police after being accused of using counterfeit money. In the process of the arrest, a white police officer, Dereck Chauvin, knelt on Floyd's neck for almost nine minutes. Floyd was already handcuffed and complained several times that he was unable to breathe. He died of cardiopulmonary arrest, as a result of mechanical asphyxia, in the aftermath of this incident. Chauvin was later tried on counts of second-degree murder, third-degree murder, and second-degree manslaughter and convicted on all counts by six white, four Black, and two multi-racial jurors in Minneapolis, on April 20, 2021, after ten hours of deliberation. The murder of George Floyd sparked protests against police violence and the treatment of people of color across American cities. It did so primarily because it was not an isolated incident, but part of a pattern of violence against people of color across the country, which, in turn, is symptomatic for the historic injustices and unequal treatment that communities of color in general, and African Americans in particular, have experienced in the United States. As this book has tried to show, the long arch of this history spans from the institution of slavery as a key cornerstone of the American economy for centuries to state-sponsored and institutionalized segregation not only in the Jim Crow South but also in the industrialized North through housing and employment discrimination, to systematic racism, voter suppression, and violence against African Americans even after the implementation of the historic civil rights legislation in the 1960s. Many of these issues still remain unresolved today, and some, in fact, have experienced serious setbacks, such as the rolling back of key section of the Voting Rights Act by the Supreme Court in *Shelby County v. Holder* in 2013, and then again in *Brnovich v. Democratic National Committee* in 2021.

The incidents of the year 2020 have forced the country to refocus its attention on the inequities in this country. The continued violence against Black people, the resurgence of the BLM protests, which were bigger and more momentous than ever since the movement's inception seven years ago in response to the brutal killing of the Black Florida teenager, Trayvon Martin, by a white man, George Zimmerman, and Zimmerman's subsequent acquittal are testament to this.

In September 2020, in response to the Black Lives Matter protests, former President Trump's Department of Justice declared New York City, Portland, and Seattle "anarchist jurisdictions." In a statement, former United States Attorney General, William Barr, noted that these cities "have permitted violence and destruction of property to persist and have refused to undertake reasonable measures to counteract criminal activities," leading DOJ to designate them as "anarchist jurisdictions." If implemented, this would have made these cities ineligible for federal funding, especially federal grants. In the wake of the strains the COVID-19 pandemic has put on many cities' budgets, this would have been particularly devastating. If the Trump administration had won reelection and implemented this punitive agenda: For the fiscal year 2021, New York City would have had to rely on $7 billion in federal grant money, an anticipated 7.5 percent of its projected 2021 budget. On February 24, 2021, roughly one month after his inauguration, President Biden revoked Trump's orders that had designated several of the nation's largest cities "anarchist jurisdictions." Seattle's Mayor Jenny Durkan, who had been through several rounds of online arguments with the former president, tweeted in response that "Seattle no longer has to face the insanity of a President who governs by Twitter or political threats. Instead of attempting to withhold all federal funding from Seattle, [President] Biden has proposed support for cities to help our residents and small businesses."[19]

The Biden presidency may give cities a break from the hostility they experienced from the federal government during the four Trump administration, and especially the fourth and final one—the pandemic year of 2020—in the short term. What kind of fate they will encounter in the long run in a hyperpolarized country under ever-changing federal policy approaches, which are only bound to get more extreme as Republicans and Democrats drift further apart, is profoundly uncertain.

Cities in a Time of Change

Cities and urban regions have been utterly transformed by the globalization processes that have defined the twenty-first century. The rapid movement of capital around the globe has forced to cities into an intense inter-urban competition for investment. For many cities, the outcome was very much in doubt. Those that had prospered during the industrial era went through a painful period of economic restructuring when manufacturing jobs moved elsewhere, and service employment became the new engine of growth. Those that have made the transition have experienced a stunning revival. Downtown skylines and old neighborhoods have been transformed, and as a visitor to one of these cities can observe, an exciting street life and urban culture have emerged. Bicycle and walking paths snake by sparkling waterfront developments and urban parks. All of these amenities are part of a new economy that makes the modern city into "a dreamscape of visual consumption."[20]

Some people would regard these changes as positive developments, but there is also another side to the story. Even while cities were becoming more prosperous, they were also becoming more divided. Two streams of movement have transformed large and small cities alike in the space of a remarkably few years. One stream has been made up of highly educated white-collar professionals:

corporate managers, management consultants, legal experts, accountants, computer specialists, financial analysts, media and public relations specialists, and more. Another stream has been composed of service workers who fill jobs at the other end of the pyramid. The maintenance, clerical, and personal services jobs required in high-rise office buildings and the low-wage, often seasonal work available in restaurants, entertainment venues, tourism, and associated businesses have drawn large numbers of immigrants and people of color. These twin migrations have created an easily recognized patchwork geography. While affluent professionals have moved into downtown condominium towers, gentrified neighborhoods, and suburban gated communities, the less fortunate live in poorer neighborhoods sprinkled throughout the metropolitan region. And, contrary to the trends of the late 1990s and early 2000s, in the 2010s, the divisions between the poor and the wealthy have become more pronounced. According to recent census data, in the year 2000, around 50 million Americans lived in poverty areas, which means neighborhoods and/or census tracts where poverty is concentrated. Of those 50 million, 29 million lived in urban areas, 9.9 in suburban parts of larger metros, and 10.7 million in rural settings.[21] By 2010, the picture had become more dire, as well as more complex: The total number of Americans living in poverty areas was 77.4 million in 2010, a more than 50 percent increase from the year 2000.[22] Of those people, 39.5 million were located in central cities, 22.1 in metro area suburbs, and 15.8 million in rural areas.[23] In other words, suburban poverty had almost doubled over the course of ten years, and the amount of people living in poverty in cities had also grown, in spite of the positive demographic changes that cities have seen at the same time.

Therefore, the latest version of the revitalized city and of the fragmented metropolis is different from what came before. Urban regions are no longer divided between disadvantaged inner cities and affluent suburbs. The demographic movements associated with the global economy have made the city and its suburbs racially, ethnically, and socially diverse. But it is not easy to interpret what this means. Some observers find evidence of progress and improvement wherever they look; others believe it is the same old politics in a new guise. What is clearer than ever before after the traumatic year of 2020 is that social inequalities across the country are severe and must urgently be addressed. At the same time, the polarized political climate in our country will make exactly that an almost impossible feat.

The New (but Actually Old) Growth Politics

In recent decades, cities (as well as nations) have joined a fierce competition for a share of the global economy. Local efforts have had some effect, as evidenced by the groves of skyscrapers and clusters of entertainment facilities that have sprouted in recent years in the larger cities to house the new economic activities driving downtown development: finance, telecommunications, corporate and professional offices, tourism, and leisure. Cities of all sizes and circumstances try to get their share. Just two months before Hurricane Katrina hit the city, the state of Louisiana agreed to give the New Orleans Saints $12.4 million to keep the team from leaving,[24] and in 2010 the Saints won the Super Bowl. Meanwhile, devastated neighborhoods still lay in ruins and levees were still in bad repair. For some people, this policy trade-off might be interpreted as a metaphor for the policy priorities that exist almost everywhere.

Who reaps the benefits of the global economy? The advantages for a cosmopolitan class that holds the best jobs can be observed in the images conveyed in the urban lifestyle magazines. These colorful, advertisement-filled publications are similar from city to city because the target audience is unvarying: an affluent middle class. But what is that middle class? In the nation's big cities, it is, more than anything, shrinking rapidly. Urban income distributions have become increasingly bell-shaped since the 1970s, with a growing number of households on each extreme end of the curve: a growing class of the super-rich and, simultaneously, a stagnant number of people in poverty. In 2015, Manhattan's wealthiest neighborhoods had a median household income of more than $250,000, whereas 42 percent of the city's census tracts are considered low-income (compared to 43 percent in 1970).[25]

Each month, columns written by lifestyle writers and critics promote restaurants and entertainment spots, wine and cigar bars, shopping opportunities, and the other amenities and entertainments of an urbane lifestyle. One could get the impression that every downtown in America is unique and exciting, although they also seem to be little more than copies of one another.

It may be useful to consider whether affluent urban residents live, work, and play in "Potemkin cities,"[26] where a thriving downtown and a tourist bubble mask serious urban problems, or in "boutique cities" such as Seattle and Denver, where highly paid professionals are able to sustain a critical mass of expensive restaurants, international boutique and clothing stores, and neighborhoods with stratospheric housing prices.[27] In the 1950s and 1960s, African Americans in poor neighborhoods were often threatened by the urban renewal bulldozer. In the new century, ethnic minorities and new immigrants sometimes face a bulldozer with a friendlier face; after all, homeowners living in gentrifying neighborhoods can reap benefits from rising property values. But there is no use glossing over the fact that there are many who suffer from this kind of neighborhood transformation: Working-class residents and the poor are regularly shoved out by the gentrifying professional class. The politics of economic inequality plays out a little differently in the suburbs, but with equal force. The residents of older inner-ring suburbs often are displaced by gentrification similar to that encountered by their urban counterparts and end up living in suburbs where the tax base is too low to support adequate services.

What remedies are there for these problems? Judging by the policies they favor, local political leaders seem to believe that the most effective thing they can do is more of the same. Other issues may seem pressing, but none receive more care and feeding than businesses, investors, affluent homeowners, and others (such as tourists) who might help bring prosperity to the local economy. At the same time, urban leaders go to great pains to persuade the citizenry that everyone benefits from these policies. Such public relations work often enough but sometimes wear thin when ugly social problems become hard to ignore.

The Delicate Art of Urban Governance

Despite its manifest importance, the economic imperative sometimes must give way or is balanced by another imperative: The need to attend to the competing claims made by the complex mixture of groups making up the local polity. The wide array of needs and issues faced by cities' nationally, socially, ethnically, and racially diverse populations guarantees that urban governance will remain a delicate art. Though issues of race and ethnicity are constantly present and sometimes contentious, it must be emphasized that the various racial, ethnic, and national groups are rarely brought together around a single cause. If broad alliances within the urban environment are thus far uncommon, they are even rarer in the suburbs, where urban governance is complicated become it is divided up into a multitude of separate jurisdictions. A racial or ethnic group may exert influence in one community, but in the next suburb over the same group may be absent from the political scene altogether. The Black Lives Matter protests during the summer of 2020 were historical in their diversity and a break from this norm. Recent research shows that, unlike previous protests for racial equality, the 2020 protests included a record number of protestors that were not Black. The protests were also supported by majorities across ethnic and racial groups: According to the Pew Research Center, in addition to the 86 percent of Black Americans who expressed support for the protests, 60 percent of whites, 77 percent of Hispanics, and 75 percent of Asian Americans expressed at least some support.[28] In addition, *The New York Times* compiled polling data from several large polling organizations about the amount of people who said they participated in the 2020 Black Lives Matter movement. They found that between 15 and 26 million people participated in the protests, which would make BLM the largest movement in American history. They also found that, unlike in past civil rights protests, almost 95 percent of counties that had a BLM protest during the summer of 2020 were majority white, with three-quarters of them 75 percent white.[29] This, of course, says nothing about the racial composition of the actual protestors, but it provides a clue about how widespread the 2020 BLM movement actually was. None of this means that the United States has in any way moved to overcome its devastating past of racial injustice or that racial and ethnic differences mattered less in 2020 than before. But perhaps it can be interpreted as a small first step in the right direction: More people across racial and ethnic groups throughout the United

States seemed to have understood the prevailing injustices against people of color than before.

The gentrification of neighborhoods remains a chronic source of change and dislocation. For more than 40 years, the Humboldt Park neighborhood in Chicago has been home to the largest Puerto Rican population in the city and one of the largest in the United States. Two steel sculptures of the Puerto Rican flag serve as a reminder that the neighborhood has a distinctive culture. In the years before the housing boom went bust, white professionals and artists flooded into the neighborhood and housing prices rose, which drove out a longtime residents. In 2006, one store window displayed a "No Yuppies" sign, and verbal confrontations sometimes occurred. As if to pour gasoline onto the flames, one of the newcomers naively said, "I try to tell them before Puerto Ricans were there, there were European Jews. And before the Jews, the Polish community was here. Neighborhoods change."[30] Perhaps so, but not without resentment, resistance, and the myriad problems that displacement brings in its path.

Economic inequality is an issue shared in common by African Americans, Hispanics, and new immigrants. The number of people living in poverty had started to decline slightly in the United States to 11.8 percent in 2018 and 10.5 percent in 2019, but increased in 2020 in the wake of the global pandemic, to 11.4 percent. The poverty figures were much higher for children; by 2019, 14.4 percent of the population under the age of 18 was living in poverty households, which increased to 16.1 percent in 2020. Even though poverty rates fell across demographics in 2019, they increased across the board during the pandemic year of 2020 (except for among Blacks and Asian Americans, where the poverty rate remained stagnant, compared to 2019).[31] The fallout from the COVID-19 pandemic will likely impact the United States' most vulnerable populations for years to come.

The Politics of the Patchwork Metropolis

The falling crime rates of the 1990s were directly related to the revival of street life and nightlife in central cities. In most American cities, people representing all income, ethnic, and racial groups mingle freely on streets and in tourist and entertainment venues. But at the same time, the new downtowns and gentrified neighborhoods are as segregated as the suburbs, though on a smaller scale. Many affluent urban residents commute from subdivisions, gated communities, townhouse developments, or condominium complexes (or at the other end of the social scale, from struggling neighborhoods and food deserts) to high-rise downtown office buildings or suburban office parks, and they drive to enclosed malls or mall complexes for shopping and commute to tourist bubbles to enjoy themselves.[32] This lifestyle creates a situation in which some urban residents experience the urban environment as little more than a series of enclosures, each connected by a transportation corridor that is itself cut off from the rest of the city.

Evidence indicates that the construction of enclaves and some degree of residential integration are happening at the same time. In the 1990s, Asians and Hispanics settled in the suburbs in large numbers, but large proportions of both groups now live in ethnic enclaves that are more separated from whites than before.[33] Residential segregation levels for Latinos and Asians increased slightly in the 1990s,[34] but these groups were less segregated in the suburbs than in the central cities.[35] Some suburbs are highly segregated, whereas others provide housing opportunities for minorities and immigrants, especially if they earn middle-class incomes. Clearly, contradictory messages can be read in these trends. In a recent study, some scholars found that not only does socioeconomic disadvantage correlate with race, but also that residential segregation is still initiated by whites.[36] Those in the highest income brackets with the highest amount of economic (and thus physical) mobility are also in the position to make very active and conscious choices about the neighborhoods (and school districts) they want to reside in.[37] Individuals in lower-income brackets do not have this amount of choice and have to limit their choices to what is affordable to them. Clearly, income segregation is not new, but research links it specifically to race and shows that racial segregation is actively perpetuated by the lifestyle choices of the (predominantly white) high earners in any given metro area.

It is difficult to predict the spatial future of the suburbs from present patterns. There can be no doubt that suburbs have opened to minorities and to the poor. The immigration of Asians, Hispanics, and other groups has made most metropolitan areas, including their suburbs, multiethnic rather than biracial. During the 1990s, for example, two parallel streams moved to Orange County, California, just outside Los Angeles: highly educated professionals and foreign-born immigrants. The two streams could hardly have been more different; high-income families making more than $150,000 per year jumped by 184 percent in the county, but at the same time, the number of foreign-born immigrants increased by 48 percent.[38] Commenting on these trends, a noted demographer said the county could go into two directions, either a "mostly gated-community-type mentality" or "immigrants start integrating into middle-class areas, so you have a blended suburbia."[39]

To some degree, residential patterns may be a consequence of how recently minorities and immigrants have moved into the suburbs. Over time, they may become incorporated into the politics of suburbs in the same way they long ago became part of the political process in central cities. Suburbs are highly variable. The adjoining suburbs of Oak Park and Cicero, both on the border of Chicago, have changed quickly in the last few years. Oak Park is a middle-class to upper-income suburb that also has a stock of affordable housing. Cicero is very different: Long a white working-class bastion known for rough-and-tumble, often corrupt politics, in only a decade, it has become a majority-Hispanic city. Suburbs of all types are similarly changing in metropolitan areas across the United States. Cities and suburbs will continue to change, often in somewhat unpredictable ways. Only time will tell where the tumultuous 20s of the twenty-first century will lead us.

Endnotes

1   Centers for Disease Control and Prevention (CDC), "History of the 1918 Flu Pandemic," Pandemic Influenza (Flu), https://www.cdc.gov/flu/pandemic-resources/1918-commemoration/1918-pandemic-history.htm.

2   PIX11 Web Team, "Latest Coronavirus Updates in New York; Friday, April 10, 2020," *PIX11 New York* (April 10, 2020), https://pix11.com/news/coronavirus/latest-coronavirus-updates-in-new-york-friday-april-10-2020/.

3   Yelena Dzhanova, "New York State Now Has More Coronavirus Cases Than Any Country Outside the US," *CNBC* (April 10, 2020), https://www.cnbc.com/2020/04/10/new-york-state-now-has-more-coronavirus-cases-than-any-country-outside-the-us.html.

4   "Outlook for the City's Economy: A Slow and Fragile Recovery," *New York City Independent Budget Office* (March 2021), https://ibo.nyc.ny.us/iboreports/outlook-for-the-citys-cconomy-a-slow-and-fragile-recovery-march-2021.pdf.

5   Dan Barry and Annie Correal, "The Epicenter," *The New York Times* (December 3, 2020), https://www.nytimes.com/2020/12/03/nyregion/coronavirus-new-york.html.

6   "COVID-19 Cases in New York City, a Neighborhood-Level Analysis," *The Stoop, Furman Center Blog* (April 10, 2020), https://furmancenter.org/thestoop/entry/covid-19-cases-in-new-york-city-a-neighborhood-level-analysis.

7   Michael Kolomatsky, "Did the Suburbs Kill the City Real Estate Market? Maybe Not," *The New York Times* (May 6, 2021), https://www.nytimes.com/2021/05/06/realestate/did-the-suburbs-kill-the-city-real-estate-market-maybe-not.html.

8   Vivian Marino and C.J. Hughes, "Suburban Home Sales Soar in the New York Region," *The New York Times* (March 5, 2021), https://www.nytimes.com/2021/03/05/realestate/nyc-suburbs-housing-demand.html.

9   Ibid.

10 Iryna Kyzyma, "Rural-Urban Disparity in Poverty Persistence," *IRP focus* (December 2018), Vol. 34, No. 3 (pp. 13–19), https://www.irp.wisc.edu/wp/wp-content/uploads/2019/01/Focus-34-3c.pdf.

11 U.S. Department of Housing and Urban Development, "Measuring Overcrowding in Housing," *Office of Policy Development and Research* (September 2007).

12 *Shelterforce*—The Original Voice of Community Development, "Is Rental Housing a Rural Issue?" (October 21, 2019), https://shelterforce.org/2019/10/21/q-is-rental-housing-a-rural-issue/.

13 Ibid.

14 "Health Equity Considerations and Racial and Ethnic Minority Groups," *Centers for Disease Control and Prevention (CDC)* (April 19, 2021), https://www.cdc.gov/coronavirus/2019-ncov/community/health-equity/race-ethnicity.html.

15 Arek Sarkissian, "Florida Governor Urges Trump to Restrict Domestic Travel," *Politico* (March 14, 2020), https://www.politico.com/states/new-york/albany/story/2020/03/14/florida-governor-urges-trump-to-restrict-domestic-travel-1267088.

16 "Audio & Rush Transcript: Governor Cuomo Addresses President Trump's Threat to Defund New York City and The Federal Government's Failure in the Ongoing COVID-19 Crisis," *New York State Press Office of the Governor* (September 3, 2020), https://www.governor.ny.gov/news/audio-rush-transcript-governor-cuomo-addresses-president-trumps-threat-defund-new-york-city-and.

17 Berkeley Lovelace Jr. and Noah Higgins-Dunn, "Trump Says Coronavirus Vaccine Won't Be Delivered to New York Right Away," *CNBC* (November 13, 2020), https://www.cnbc.com/2020/11/13/trump-says-coronavirus-vaccine-wont-be-delivered-to-new-york.html.

18 Ibid.

19 "'Anarchist Jurisdictions' No More: Biden Revokes Trump's Order," *Al Jazeera* (February 25, 2021), https://www.aljazeera.com/news/2021/2/25/anarchist-jurisdictions-no-more-biden-revokes-trumps-order.

20 Sharon Zukin, *Landscapes of Power: From Detroit to Disney World* (Berkeley: University of California Press, 1991), p. 221.

21 Alemayehu Bishaw, "Changes in Areas with Concentrated Poverty: 2000 to 2010," *American Community Survey Reports,* Report No. ACS-27 (June 2014): 1–27.

22 Ibid.

23 Ibid.

24 "Louisiana Forks over $12.4M to Saints," *USA Today* (July 6, 2005), p. 15C.

25 Max Galka, "America's Geography of Wealth: The Shrinking Urban Middle Class Visualized," *The Guardian* (May 17, 2017), https://www.theguardian.com/cities/2017/may/17/america-geography-wealth-shrinking-urban-middle-class-visualised.

26 According to historical accounts, General Potemkin constructed fake villages in preparation for a tour by Catherine II of the Crimea in 1787. The purpose was to fool her into thinking his conquests were of great value to the Russian empire.

27 Neal R. Peirce, "Business Basic: Rx for All Cities," *Washington Post* (March 5, 1999).

28 Kim Parker, Juliana Menasce Horowitz, and Monica Anderson, "Amid Protests, Majorities Across Racial and Ethnic Groups Express Support for the Black Lives Matter Movement," *Pew Research Center* (June 12, 2020), https://www.pewresearch.org/social-trends/2020/06/12/amid-protests-majorities-across-racial-and-ethnic-groups-express-support-for-the-black-lives-matter-movement/.

29 Larry Buchanan, Quoctrung Bui, and Jugal K. Patel, "Black Lives Matter May Be the Largest Movement in U.S. History," *The New York Times* (July 3, 2020), https://www.nytimes.com/interactive/2020/07/03/us/george-floyd-protests-crowd-size.html.

30 Antonio Olivo, "Edge about 'Yuppies,'" *Chicago Tribune* (June 12, 2006), pp. 1, 20.

31 Emily A. Shrider, Melissa Kollar, Frances Chen, and Jessica Semega, "Income and Poverty in the United States: 2020," *United States Census Bureau* (September 14, 2021), https://www.census.gov/library/publications/2021/demo/p60-273.html.

32 Dennis R. Judd, "Enclosure, Community, and Public Life," in *Research in Community Sociology: New Communities in a Changing World*, ed. Dan A. Chekki (Greenwich, CT and London: JAI Press, 1996), pp. 217–238.

33 John R. Logan, "The New Ethnic Enclaves in America's Suburbs," a report by the Lewis Mumford Center for Comparative Urban and Regional Research (Albany, NY, 2002), pp. 1–2.

34 Ibid., p. 253.

35   William A.V. Clark and Sarah A. Blue, "Race, Class, and Segregation Patterns in U.S. Immigrant Gateway Cities," *Urban Affairs Review* 39, no. 6 (2004): 667–688.

36   Richard Florida and Charlotta Mellander, *Segregated City. The Geography of Economic Segregation in America's Metros* (Toronto, Canada: The Martin Prosperity Institute, Rotman School of Management, University of Toronto, 2015).

37   Ibid.

38   Jim Hinch and Ronald Campbell, "Gated Enclaves One Future for Orange County," *Orange County Register* (May 15, 2002), www.ocregister.com.

39   Ibid., quoting William Frey, a demographer in the Milken Institute of Los Angeles.

INDEX

Note: Page numbers in *italics* indicate figures, in **bold** tables, and with n "endnotes."

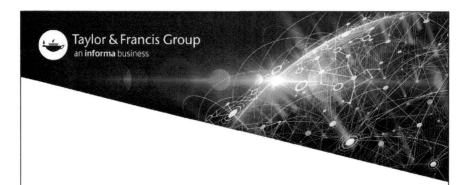